Professional
SQL Server® 2005
Performance Tuning

Professional
SQL Server® 2005
Performance Tuning

Steven Wort
Christian Bolton
Justin Langford
Michael Cape
Joshua J. Jin
Douglas Hinson
Haidong Ji
Paul A. Mestemaker
Arindam Sen

WILEY

Wiley Publishing, Inc.

Professional SQL Server® 2005 Performance Tuning

Published by
Wiley Publishing, Inc.
10475 Crosspoint Boulevard
Indianapolis, IN 46256
www.wiley.com

Copyright © 2008 by Wiley Publishing, Inc., Indianapolis, Indiana

Published simultaneously in Canada

ISBN: 978-0-470-17639-9

Manufactured in the United States of America

10 9 8 7 6 5 4 3 2 1

For general information on our other products and services or to obtain technical support, please contact our Customer Care Department within the U.S. at (800) 762-2974, outside the U.S. at (317) 572-3993 or fax (317) 572-4002.

Library of Congress Cataloging-in-Publication Data

Professional SQL server 2005 : performance tuning / Steven Wort ... [et al.].
       p. cm.
   Includes bibliographical references and index.
   ISBN 978-0-470-17639-9 (paper/website)
   1.   SQL server. 2.   Client/server computing.   I. Wort, Steven.
   QA76.9.C55P752 2008
   005.75′85--dc22

                                                    2007045707

About the Authors

Steven Wort has been working with SQL Server for the past 14 years. He is currently a developer in the Windows group at Microsoft where he works on performance and scalability issues on a large database system. Steven has been at Microsoft for nearly 7 years, working in the Windows group for the past 2 years. Prior to this, Steven spent 2 years in the SQL Server group working on performance and scalability. His first job at Microsoft was 3 years spent working in what is now CSS as an escalation engineer on the SIE team. During this time Steven was able to travel the world working with some of Microsoft's customers on their performance and scalability problems. Before coming to Microsoft, Steven spent 20 years working in the United Kingdom as a freelance consultant specializing in database application development. When Steven isn't busy working, he can be found spending time with his family and enjoying many fitness activities in the great outdoors of the Pacific Northwest.

Christian Bolton has been working with SQL Server since 1999 and in 2007 became a director and database architect for Coeo Ltd, a Microsoft Certified Partner focused on large-scale and complex SQL Server projects in the United Kingdom. Prior to this, Christian worked for 5 years as a senior premier field engineer for Microsoft UK, working with some of Microsoft's biggest customers across EMEA. His specialist areas are high availability, scalability, and performance tuning. Christian works out of London and lives in the south of England with his wife and daughter. He can be contacted at `http://coeo.com` or through his blog at `http://sqlblogcasts.com/blogs/christian`.

Justin Langford has worked as a premier field engineer for Microsoft specializing in SQL Server for the past 3 years. Much of this time has been focused on sharing best practices for operations and optimization with some of the United Kingdom's largest financial and government organizations. Justin previously worked as a consultant for a Microsoft Partner focusing on upgrade, migration, and software deployment projects for enterprise customers. Outside of work, Justin enjoys yacht racing, snowboarding, and has a keen interest in classic British sports cars.

Michael Cape is a database developer with experience in a variety of industries. Those industries are mortgage banking, pension administration, advertising, logistics, insurance, and labor management. Michael holds a BSCS degree and got his start with database development with SQLBase from Gupta. Michael also has 5 years experience with DB2, and has been working with SQL Server, starting with version 7, for the last 7 years. Outside work, Michael spends time with his wife and two children. He also enjoys golf, bicycling, fishing, and kite flying.

Joshua Jin works for the Intel Corporation. He is a certified SQL Server MCITP database administrator, MCITP database developer, and MCITP business intelligence developer. He specializes in the performance tuning of large-scale and high-volume SQL databases. Prior to working at Intel, he worked on the largest Internet banking implementation in the United States, using SQL server as its database engine. He can be reached at joshua_jin?@yahoo.com.

Douglas Hinson is an independent software and database consultant in the logistics and financial industries, with an extensive SQL Server background. He has co-authored several Wrox books, including *Professional SQL Server 2005 Integration Services*.

Haidong "Alex" Ji is a professional trainer and consultant specializing in SQL Server administration, performance tuning, high availability, and many other facets of SQL Server. In addition, he also excels at database interoperability issues, having worked extensively with Oracle and MySQL on Unix and Linux. Haidong enjoys learning and sharing his expertise through technical writing, speaking, consulting, training, and mentoring. He co-authored *Professional SQL Server 2005 Integration Services* (Wrox Press) and *Professional SQL Server 2005 Administration* (Wrox Press). Haidong maintains a blog at www.haidongji.com/category/technology/. He can be contacted at Haidong.Ji@gmail.com.

Paul Mestemaker is a program manager at Microsoft on the SQL Server product team. During the SQL Server 2005 product cycle, he worked closely with the new dynamic management views on the SQL Server Engine team. Following the launch, Paul moved to the SQL Server Manageability team to create tools on top of the new SQL platform technologies. He was influential in the release of SQL Server 2005 Best Practices Analyzer, Performance Dashboard Reports, and SQL Server 2005 Service Pack 2. He is now a member of the SQLCAT Best Practices team, where he works with subject matter experts across Microsoft and in the community to develop new rules for SQL BPA. Paul has been a speaker at TechEd, PASS, Connections, and other Microsoft conferences. He blogs occasionally; you can check it out here: http://blogs.msdn.com/sqlrem/.

Arindam Sen has worked with SQL Server for the past 8 years and has significant experience with Siebel deployments using SQL Server databases. His interests lie in the area of high availability and performance tuning. He is an MCSE, MCSA, MCAD, and MCDBA. He won the SQL Server innovator award (*SQL Server Magazine*) in 2003 and 2004. He holds an engineering degree in electronics and an MBA from Duke University.

Credits

Executive Editor
Robert Elliott

Development Editor
Kelly Talbot

Technical Editors
Sunil Agarwal
Uttam Parui
Alan Doby
Stephen Olson

Production Editor
Dassi Zeidel

Copy Editor
Jack Peters

Editorial Manager
Mary Beth Wakefield

Production Manager
Tim Tate

Vice President and Executive Group Publisher
Richard Swadley

Vice President and Executive Publisher
Joseph B. Wikert

Project Coordinator, Cover
Lynsey Osborn

Proofreader
Ian Golder

Indexer
Robert Swanson

Acknowledgments

We have to start by thanking our families. They have been infinitely patient and understanding while we have spent many long hours working on this book. Thanks to all the team at Wiley Publishing. Robert Elliot who got me started on this project, Kelly Talbot for his patience and guidance along the way, and everyone else in the team who took the writings of the authors and turned them into this great book. Thanks to all the technical editors. Thanks to everyone at Microsoft in the SQL Server group, on the many discussion lists, and in CSS who were so willing to share their knowledge.

Contents

Contents

Contents

Contents

Contents

Introduction

SQL Server is a tremendously successful database server that does an exceptional job of self-tuning. Out of the box SQL Server does a tremendous job of running well and delivering great performance with absolutely no user configuration. With the advent of cheaper hardware and the explosion of data, today's SQL Server systems are routinely operating in a space previously dominated by yesterday's enterprise class main frame system.

With the availability of cheap disks, disk controllers, and memory, almost anyone can now build a multi-terrabyte database on a reasonably modest system. This massive explosion of database size means that more SQL Server systems are pushing the frontiers of SQL Server's ability to self tune. Consequently, many more SQL Server users are experiencing performance problems.

This book provides a comprehensive resource for all the consultants, developers, database administrators, and anyone else who has to deal with SQL Server performance problems for the first time. It's also a great resource for anyone who already deals with SQL Server performance who needs a fresh look at how to do performance tuning.

This book approaches performance tuning from a new perspective. The book walks you through how to find performance problems, rather than assuming you already know what the problem is.

Who This Book Is For

If you are a consultant, developer, DBA, architect, or just someone with an interest in SQL performance, this is the book for you.

You will need a working knowledge of T-SQL, and know how to perform basic SQL Server and operating system administrative tasks. With this basic knowledge you're ready to get started on performance tuning SQL Server.

If you're a SQL Server developer and have been working with SQL Server for 1 to 2 years, and you're facing your first round of performance problems, then you're ready to get started with this book.

If you're a SQL Server consultant on your way to a customer with a performance problem, then this the one book you should have in your carry-on luggage and read on the flight to the customer's location.

If you're a SQL Server DBA and your systems are starting to slow down, then this is a great book to get started with.

What This Book Covers

This book covers performance tuning of SQL Server 2005.

The material is written using features available in SQL Server 2005. Some of the examples make use of new features in SQL Server 2005. In these cases the examples won't work with earlier versions. The concepts being discussed are usually relevant to any version of SQL Server. Some specific examples where examples won't work with earlier versions are where they are based on new features, such as any time we refer to the new dynamic management views.

How This Book Is Structured

The book is laid out in four parts:

❑ Part I is where you go when you need to find out what is causing your performance bottleneck.

❑ Part II shows how to remove bottlenecks.

❑ Part III discusses preventative measures, baselining, and a variety of useful tools.

❑ Part IV discusses topics around building in good performance from the start, rather than the traditional approach which is to create a functional design and then try to bolt on performance as an after-thought.

Part I — Finding Bottlenecks When Something's Wrong

Chapters 1 through 5 deal with how you find the current bottleneck. This part is where you go when the phone rings and it's one of your users who isn't happy with performance:

❑ Chapter 1 deals with the overall methodology of this approach to performance tuning.

❑ Chapter 2 looks at how you examine server resources to see whether there is a server resource bottleneck.

❑ Chapter 3 looks at how you monitor SQL Server resources to see whether there is a resource bottleneck.

❑ Chapter 4 shows you how to use the SQL Server wait types to find resource bottlenecks and the queries that are creating them.

❑ Chapter 5 shows you how to use SQL Profiler to look for long running queries.

By the end of this part you should be able to find a bottleneck. The next step is to find a way to remove that bottleneck. That's covered in Part II.

Part II — Removing Bottlenecks with Tuning

Chapters 6 through 9 cover the ways you can remove the various types of bottlenecks that may be causing the performance problem. Once you have identified a bottleneck, this is where you go next to find ways to remove the bottleneck.

❑ Chapter 6 covers tuning server configuration settings to remove bottlenecks found in Chapter 2.

❑ Chapter 7 covers tuning SQL Server settings to remove bottlenecks found in Chapter 3.

❑ Chapter 8 covers tuning the schema. This is where you remove bottlenecks found in the underlying schema.

❑   Chapter 9 covers tuning T-SQL. This is where you remove many of the bottlenecks found in Chapters 4 and 5.

By the end of this part you should be able to remove a bottleneck. But what can you do to help preven bottleneck from occurring in the first place? That's covered in Part III.

Part III — Preventative Measures and Baselining Performance with Tools

This part covers the things you should be doing *before* the users call you complaining of bad performance. These are the preventative measures you can take to try to make sure the phone doesn't ring. It covers using the different tools to capture metrics around the baseline performance of the system.

❑   Chapter 10 covers using SQL Profiler to replay workloads. This is very useful for creating standard workloads for use in performance testing.

❑   Chapter 11 covers missing indexes and the Database Tuning Advisor.

❑   Chapter 12 covers storage subsystem performance and robustness and shows how you can use SQLIO and SQLIOSim to great effect.

❑   Chapter 13 covers using SQL Server Performance Dashboard, which helps you find performance problems and is a great way to capture performance metrics.

By the end of this part, you should have a good idea of how to reduce the occurrence of a variety of bottlenecks.

Part IV — Roadmap to Server Performance

In this part we discuss topics to help you achieve better performance, as well as some of the challenges facing performance tuning at the later stages of a product's life cycle.

❑   Chapter 14 covers best practices for designing in performance from the start.

❑   Chapter 15 covers best practices for a successful deployment.

What You Need to Use This Book

To follow along with the examples in this book, you will need to have SQL Server 2005 installed. You should always have the latest Service Pack installed. At the time of writing, the latest service pack was Service Pack 2.

Because the book is targeted at small- and medium-sized business users, you will be able to use SQL Server Standard edition, Workgroup edition, or Developer edition for most of the examples. SQL Server Workgroup edition will not work for the examples on Database Tuning Advisor.

It is not recommended to use SQL Server Express or SQL Server Compact Edition. Although many of the examples will work, the behavior we are trying to illustrate will be different on these versions of SQL Server.

using SQL Server Enterprise edition, then you may find some differences in the exact details of the query plans you obtain in some examples, but the end result should remain the same.

machine you use needs to meet the minimum hardware requirements for the version of SQL Server using. In many cases the examples in the book were created and tested on laptop systems mostly ng Windows Vista (RTM build 6.0.6000.2.0.0)

will also need a working knowledge of T-SQL, and know how to perform basic SQL Server and erating system administrative tasks.

onventions

To help you get the most from the text and keep track of what's happening, we've used a number of conventions throughout the book.

- ❑ We show keyboard strokes like this: Ctrl + A.
- ❑ We show URLs and code within the text like so: `persistence.properties`.
- ❑ We present code in two different ways:

  ```
  We use a monofont type with no highlighting for most code examples.
  ```

  ```
  We use gray highlighting to emphasize code that's particularly important in the
  present context.
  ```

- ❑ We point out best practices like this:

> ### Best Practice
> Individual best practices are presented as sidebars that have a "Best Practice" heading. However, there are some places in the book where the discussion of best practices becomes complex enough that they have their own section, or even an entire chapter.

Source Code

As you work through the examples in this book, you may choose either to type in all the code manually or to use the source code files that accompany the book. All of the source code used in this book is available for download at www.wrox.com. Once at the site, simply locate the book's title (either by using the Search box or by using one of the title lists) and click the Download Code link on the book's detail page to obtain all the source code for the book.

Because many books have similar titles, you may find it easiest to search by ISBN; this book's ISBN is 978-0-470-17639-9.

Once you download the code, just decompress it with your favorite compression tool. Alternately, you can go to the main Wrox code download page at www.wrox.com/dynamic/books/download.aspx to see the code available for this book and all other Wrox books.

Errata

We make every effort to ensure that there are no errors in the text or in the code. However, no one is perfect, and mistakes do occur. If you find an error in one of our books, like a spelling mistake or faulty piece of code, we would be very grateful for your feedback. By sending in errata you may save another reader hours of frustration and at the same time you will be helping us provide even higher quality information.

To find the errata page for this book, go to `www.wrox.com` and locate the title using the Search box or one of the title lists. Then, on the book details page, click the Book Errata link. On this page you can view all errata that has been submitted for this book and posted by Wrox editors. A complete book list including links to each book's errata is also available at `www.wrox.com/misc-pages/booklist.shtml`.

If you don't spot "your" error on the Book Errata page, go to `www.wrox.com/contact/techsupport.shtml` and complete the form there to send us the error you have found. We'll check the information and, if appropriate, post a message to the book's errata page and fix the problem in subsequent editions of the book.

p2p.wrox.com

For author and peer discussion, join the P2P forums at `p2p.wrox.com`. The forums are a Web-based system for you to post messages relating to Wrox books and related technologies and interact with other readers and technology users. The forums offer a subscription feature to e-mail you topics of interest of your choosing when new posts are made to the forums. Wrox authors, editors, other industry experts, and your fellow readers are present on these forums.

At `http://p2p.wrox.com` you will find a number of different forums that will help you not only as you read this book, but also as you develop your own applications. To join the forums, just follow these steps:

1. Go to `p2p.wrox.com` and click the Register link.
2. Read the terms of use and click Agree.
3. Complete the required information to join as well as any optional information you wish to provide and click Submit.
4. You will receive an e-mail with information describing how to verify your account and complete the joining process.

You can read messages in the forums without joining P2P but in order to post your own messages, you must join.

Once you join, you can post new messages and respond to messages other users post. You can read messages at any time on the Web. If you would like to have new messages from a particular forum e-mailed to you, click the Subscribe to this Forum icon by the forum name in the forum listing.

For more information about how to use the Wrox P2P, be sure to read the P2P FAQs for answers to questions about how the forum software works as well as many common questions specific to P2P and Wrox books. To read the FAQs, click the FAQ link on any P2P page.

Part I

Finding Bottlenecks when Something's Wrong

1

Performance Tuning

SQL Server 2005 works great right out of the box. For most SQL Server users, performance is never an issue. They install SQL Server, load up their data, and the system works just great. Over the past few years, however, there has been an explosion in database size and in the hardware performance that is available to small and medium-sized businesses. This has allowed many more users to build larger and larger systems. Many of today's systems are now larger than yesterday's enterprise class systems that required mainframe class hardware. This explosion in size and performance is pushing more users against the limits of the out-of-the-box performance of SQL Server. This means that more and more SQL Server users are having to start learning about a side of SQL Server that they never needed to know about — performance tuning.

The good news is that as with the out-of-the-box experience, the SQL Server team has spent a lot of time working on making SQL Server an easy database system to performance tune. Unlike many of SQL Server's competitors, where you need many highly trained and very expensive consultants to diagnose and finetune performance problems, SQL Server has the tools and information available so that just about anyone can jump in and start tuning their databases.

Art or Science?

Performance tuning has always had a certain aura of mystique around it. The few masters of the art are regarded with awe and suspicion by those who haven't mastered the skills. For those outside the inner circle of those masters, the perception is that it takes many years to acquire the skills necessary to become a performance tuner.

The reality is that with a methodical approach, the right tools, and the right knowledge, anyone with a basic knowledge of T-SQL can start taking steps to improve the performance of their database system. As you start to master these skills, performance tuning begins to look less like an esoteric art and more like a focused science.

This book is about providing you with the knowledge you need to start taking a methodical approach to performance tuning, to show you which tools to use and when, and to give you the knowledge you need to be a successful SQL Server performance tuner.

The Science of Performance Tuning

Performance tuning SQL Server is a science. In this chapter I will show you how to get started, and I will walk you through the steps necessary to approach any performance problem — in fact, more than just any performance problem. The approach used here is one that works with just about any problem that needs troubleshooting.

This approach is nothing new or revolutionary. It is just a methodical scientific approach to problem solving using data collection and analysis to determine the root cause of any problem. This is the approach I learned during the three years I spent working in support at Microsoft. It is an approach that enabled me to solve problems for many Microsoft customers on a wide variety of different products and technologies:

1.   You start with a problem statement that helps you describe what you are addressing, and what an acceptable outcome might be. This helps frame the rest of the process.

2.   From the problem statement you can form some ideas as to what the problem might be. From these early ideas comes a plan of attack. The plan of attack includes details of the data you want to collect to support (or, unfortunately sometimes, refute) those ideas.

3.   Once you have some data, you analyze it to confirm or reject the original idea, and use this to refine the problem statement as needed.

4.   If the analysis produced a clear culprit as the root cause of the problem (in the case of performance tuning this would be that you have identified a bottleneck), then you proceed to find ways to remove the bottleneck.

5.   When you think you have removed the bottleneck, you collect more data, re-analyze, and confirm that the issue is resolved.

Performance tuning is an iterative process. You may need to repeat the above steps many times before the system as a whole arrives at an acceptable level of performance. This doesn't change the basic process that needs to be followed. You simply repeat the steps until you have removed enough bottlenecks that the system has acceptable performance.

Unfortunately in some cases you may reach the limits of your budget in terms of time, money, or resources before you have acceptable performance. It is always important to understand what your time, financial, and resource constraints are as you start a project. If these matters haven't already been defined by your client or employer, make sure that you ask them to define these matters for you. Understanding the scope of these expectations is every bit as important to your success as your actual performance-tuning skills.

The Problem Statement

The first step in this approach is to develop a problem statement. The problem statement doesn't need to be more than a simple sentence or two that briefly describes the issue you are dealing with. This is a very valuable first step as it starts to help you determine the true nature of the problem, and will help you determine a starting point for the following steps.

If you already have a problem query isolated, then the problem statement is pretty simple, and it will read something like, "Stored procedure X takes too long to run. It is currently taking x seconds and needs to take less than y milliseconds."

Many times a customer will call for assistance with a problem that they will describe simply as: "Our SQL Server is running slow." Although that may well seem like a good description of the symptom to their end users, it's not really of much use in starting to performance tune a complex database system. Sometimes it may be all you have to go on. However, I would hope that after asking yourself a few questions you can come up with something a bit more descriptive.

Whenever you take a call like that, your immediate response should be to start asking questions. You should ask the customer to describe what it is that's slow. Are there multiple users on the system? Is it slow for all of them? Do they all do the same kind of work? What kind of workloads run on the system, and are there any batch jobs running at any time? These questions are all aimed at digging more information from the customer, partly for your benefit so you can better understand what the problem might be, but they are also aimed at getting the customer to think more about their system and to help them try and arrive at their own problem statement.

A much more focused problem statement would be something like

> "User X has a slow running query. He uses the Y system, which calls A, B, and C stored procedures in the Foo database. This happens all the time."

The key elements to a good problem statement are:

- ❑   Who
- ❑   What
- ❑   When

And one final element that's not essential but can be useful would be to outline a successful resolution to the problem.

Who Is Having the Problem?

Is it just one user reporting the problem? What type of user is it? Does it affect multiple users? Are these users all of one type (for example, do they only access one set of features of the system), or are they spread out across many different features? Where are these users? Are they all in the same department, location, or region? Is their anything else unique about the users reporting the problem?

What Is the Problem?

How did the user report the problem? Is it a slowdown that's impacting them, or are they getting timeouts or deadlocks that are causing loss of functionality? What were they doing when the problem occurred? What else was going on when the problem occurred?

When Did the Problem Occur?

When did the problem occur? Did this just occur? Has it happened before? Is it consistent or intermittent? Is it happening now?

What Is the Resolution?

It is important to know from the beginning what a successful resolution might look like. In many cases with performance tuning, the goal is very poorly described simply as "make it go faster". How much faster do you want it to go? What is a reasonable amount of time for the query to take? What is an acceptable amount of time for the user to experience?

These are all vital bits of information that help you arrive at a problem statement that starts to describe the issue you need to investigate.

The Plan of Attack

Once you have a problem statement, you can formulate a plan of attack. This should simply state what you think the underlying problem is, what the data is that you want to collect, and what analysis of that data should show.

This step is short and easy, but it is also very important. It makes sure you start on the next step correctly and have thought about what you are going to do with any data you collect.

An example of a problem statement and plan of attack is shown below.

Problem statement:

Several users of system X have reported poor performance. They are reporting this problem during peak hours, which for them are from 1 pm through 3:30 pm on Mondays, Wednesdays, and Fridays. They are connecting to database Y on Server Z. This application is the only application using this database and server. The server has dedicated local storage.

Plan of attack:

Capture Perfmon counters for server resources from Server Z. Review for system bottlenecks. Capture SQL Server wait types from database Y on Server Z. Review for long wait types. Data will be captured during three periods when the system exhibits the performance problem.

Capture server level performance counters at 1-second intervals over three 5-minute sampling periods between 1 and 3:30 pm on days when the problem is reported. Capture counters at 5-second intervals between 1 and 3:30 pm on days when the problem is reported. If no baseline is available, capture server performance counters at 15-second intervals over a 24-hour period on days when the problem occurs, and also on at least one day when it doesn't occur.

Capture SQL Server Wait stats. Sample at 30-second intervals over a 5-minute period. Repeat three times over the period when the user reports the problem. Review for long wait times.

The plan of attack should detail what data you intend to collect, what you intend to do with it, and maybe even mention some follow-up actions depending on the analysis of the data collected. Another important aspect of the plan of attack regarding data collection is when you want to collect the data and for how long. This information may come from the problem statement (as in the above example), but in a case where the problem is either continuous or intermittent, you will need to be creative about when and for how long to sample.

Data Collection

The plan of attack has defined what data you want to collect and what you intend to do with it. Now you can go ahead and start collecting the data.

This step will involve setting up the data collection, then sitting back and letting the data roll in for some period of time. This could include collecting hundreds of GB of Performance Monitor logs, running a

SQL Trace for hours or days, or other data collection activity that may have a serious impact on the performance of the system from which you need to capture data.

Carefully consider what data to collect so that you can confirm any theory about the root cause of the problem while minimizing the impact on the system you need to tune.

Data Analysis

After you have collected the data you think you need, the next step is to analyze the data to confirm the original theory.

If after careful analysis of the data collected, it appears to confirm your theory, then you have just identified your bottleneck and can move onto removing it.

In some cases the data analysis may not be conclusive. In this case you may need to make a minor modification to the data collection policy and re-collect data.

The analysis may also provide results that point toward a different problem. When this occurs it is time to go back and revisit the problem statement again and to refine it with this new information.

In some cases the data analysis will show no problem at all. In fact, from the data everything looks just great. This is often the hardest option as you now have to go back to the problem statement with what at first seems like no additional data. You have, however, ruled out one potential cause, so you can start again with a few less places to go looking for the bottleneck.

Performance Tuning Applied

Now that we have introduced the scientific approach based on data collection and analysis, we will walk you through two different scenarios to help illustrate how this process might work in practice. The first scenario is one where your users start reporting apparently random performance problems. In the second scenario, you know exactly where the problem is, but you don't know what the exact bottleneck is.

Example 1 — Your Application Is Slow

This is the typical problem where the phone rings, and it's one of your users calling to report poor performance. This comes out of the blue and is soon followed by many more users all calling to report the same kind of problem with poor performance.

Problem Statement

Writing a problem statement for these general performance problems can be quite hard, but it's okay for it to be very general. As you start collecting data, you can refine the problem statement, making it more specific with each iteration. Here is a first draft of a problem statement for this problem.

Problem Statement:

Users of application X on Server Y are reporting performance problems when accessing features Z1, Z2, and Z3.

Plan of Attack

When you don't have a clear target for data collection, it is necessary to start at the top (the server resources) and work down until you find a bottleneck that is the root cause of the problem. In this case, on the first iteration you can collect multiple sets of data. A good place to start is with collecting performance counters of the server and SQL resources, maybe also collecting wait stats, and capturing a Profiler trace looking for long-running queries. This can be a lot of data to collect and analyze. Although it's a nice idea to cast a broad net like this, in practice it's better to start with just a few data sets and zoom in on the problem from there.

> *Plan of Attack:*
>
> *Collect Perfmon counters of the top level server and SQL resource counters at 5-second intervals for 20 minutes at some point between 09:00 and 11:00.*

There are a couple of things to note about this plan of attack. It's gone into quite a lot of detail about the frequency of counter sampling, how long the counters need to be collected for, and over what time the counters should be collected. This is all important information to have thought about and to define at this stage. In a larger organization or anywhere where you are dealing with a team of people who are responsible for the servers, this is very important as it may often be that this information has to be passed from the DBA team to the Ops team that will actually run the data collection.

Even if you don't have an environment with a separate team, it's still very useful to go into this amount of detail as it forces you to think about how much data you really need to collect.

Data Collection

With the plan of attack defined, you can proceed with data collection. In this case it's a pretty simple set of data to collect. This can be made even easier if you have a set of Logman scripts around that set up counter logs. An example of using Logman to set up a counter log is given in Chapter 12.

In the case where a separate Operations team manages the server, this is where you sit back and wait for the files to be dropped onto a shared server somewhere. If your environment is smaller and you are responsible for all activities on the server, then you will be busy setting up and running the relevant data collection tools.

Chapters 2 and 3 cover using Performance Monitor to capture Server and SQL resource counters.

Data Analysis

Once the data collection is complete, the task of analyzing the data starts. In this example there will be a single Performance Monitor log file to be analyzed. Chapters 2 and 3 cover interpreting the contents of the Log File.

Once the analysis is complete, it will hopefully point to a resource bottleneck with a server resource like CPU, Memory, or disk I/O. Alternatively, it might point to a SQL Server resource bottleneck.

The third option is that it doesn't indicate any resource bottleneck. In this case you will need to refine the problem statement and plan of attack and collect more data. The next iteration should focus on looking either at SQL Server waits or a Profiler Trace looking for long-running queries.

Example 2 — Stored Procedure X Is Slow

This example is a very different kind of problem. In this example, the problem is very well-defined. Rather than the whole application slowing down as in the previous example, in this case, a single function is reported with the problem. In this case you can trace the feature to a single stored procedure, or a small set of stored procedures. In this example we will deal with a single stored procedure.

Problem Statement

Unlike the previous example, in this example you know where the problem is, but you don't yet know what is causing it. There could be many reasons for a stored procedure slowing down. The goal of this performance tuning operation will be to determine why the stored procedure is slow. In essence, this means finding the bottleneck to be able to remove that bottleneck.

In this case, you can write a much more focused problem statement.

Problem Statement:

Stored procedure X is running slowly. In previous executions it takes on average 10 msec, with a min of 2 msec and a max of 15 msec. Since this morning it has been taking on average 600 msec. The goal is to identify the root cause of this slow-down and tune the stored procedure to improve performance back to the original execution speeds.

Plan of Attack

With a much more focused problem statement, the plan of attack will be correspondingly more focused. You shouldn't need to look at the server as a whole, and you don't need to find one particular long running query. A lot of the work you had to do in the previous example isn't needed here. A good plan of attack for this example is listed below.

Plan of Attack:

Review the execution of Stored Procedure X. Capture an execution plan of the stored procedure. Review the plan and tune the stored procedure to optimize execution time.

Data Collection

The data collection in this example is much easier, although there can be challenges with capturing a plan for the stored procedure. In some cases this might be as easy as running the query in SQL Server Management Studio with the relevant options enabled to show a graphical plan or to return a text plan. In other cases the data passed to the stored procedure is critical. In these cases you might need to capture real parameters using a Profiler Trace so that you can execute using the real data in Management Studio. In other cases you might need to use SQL Server profiler to capture the actual execution plan of a live running instance of the stored procedure being called by the application.

Data Analysis

The data analysis stage in this example is all about interpreting the execution plan and tuning it. This is covered in Chapter 9.

The iterations here are around the data collection and analysis pieces. As the problem has already been narrowed down to a particular stored procedure and the goal is to improve the performance of this one stored procedure, there isn't usually a need to revisit the problem statement or the plan of attack. However, in some cases the reason for the stored procedure running slowly might be due to a server resource bottleneck. It might be that the data has grown to the point where processing it now takes more CPU than is available, that it needs more memory than is available, or that it now needs more I/O capacity than is available. In these cases then the problem statement remains the same, but the plan of attack might change to alter the data collection to review the server or SQL Server resources.

Tools

There is a wide variety of tools available to help you in your data collection and analysis, and to help with preventive measures such as monitoring activity, and capturing a baseline of your system's performance.

System Monitor

Also known as Perfmon or Performance Monitor on Windows Vista, this is the first tool you should think of when looking at performance tuning. There is a massive number of counters available to show you all aspects of performance from many different applications. Chapters 2 and 3 cover using System Monitor and discuss in detail which counters to look at.

SQL Server Profiler

SQL Profiler is the tool of choice when you need to find long-running queries in a highly variable work-load. Profiler lets you capture a record of every query executed by SQL over a period of time. This is extremely useful when either there is a wide variety of queries run infrequently in the server or there are ad hoc user queries running as well. Under those conditions other tools don't help you find the long running query, and that's where Profiler comes in.

Using Profiler you can also capture a workload over a given period of time and then use this later to replay against a restore's database system. This is a great way of running a stress or performance test, and for repeatedly reproducing a database workload.

Chapters 5 and 10 discuss using SQL Server Profiler.

SQL Server Management Studio (Query Analyzer)

For many SQL Server users, SQL Server Management Studio will be the application they spend their work lives inside. It is now a Visual Studio compatible integrated development environment (IDE) and provides a single place to perform all your SQL-related work. Starting with a new Visual Studio solution/project-based approach, it includes:

- ❑   A server/database object explorer
- ❑   The template explorer, which is an invaluable aid for writing T-SQL scripts
- ❑   The Query Analyzer interface
- ❑   SQL Server profiler
- ❑   Database Tuning Advisor (DTA)
- ❑   A shell to launch third-party tools

SQL Server Performance Dashboard

SQL Server Management Studio comes with many performance-related reports already built. The SQL Server Performance Dashboard reports are a suite of reports that can be downloaded and installed.

These reports are a new feature that shipped after SQL Server 2005. The reports provide a wealth of performance information with no work required other than installing them. All you need to know is that they are there, where to find them, and how to read them. Chapter 13 covers the SQL Server Performance Dashboard.

Dynamic Management Views

The Dynamic Management Views (DMVs) in SQL Server 2005 are the source of a wealth of information about what is going on inside SQL Server. In earlier versions of SQL Server, some of this information was made available in system tables. In SQL Server 2005, the amount of information about what SQL Server is doing internally has increased dramatically.

Anyone looking at SQL Server performance should have a good understanding of the key DMVs.

Many of the chapters in this book discuss in detail the DMVs relevant for each chapter's topic. Another great source of information on using these DMVs is the SQL Server Best Practices website at:

`http://technet.microsoft.com/en-gb/sqlserver/bb331794.aspx`

This page includes a link to the SQL Server Best practices toolbox, which contains yet more extremely useful Scripts for querying the DMVs:

`http://www.microsoft.com/technet/scriptcenter/scripts/sql/sql2005/default.mspx?mfr = true`

Direct Administrators Connection — DAC

Sometimes a DBA trying to diagnose a busy server needs to find who is using all the resources. Other times a DBA needs to kill a long-running query. One of the challenges is that it is not always possible to get a new connection to SQL to start looking at what is going on. This is because the server no longer has any resources available to create a new connection.

SQL Server 2005 resolves this problem with the Direct Administrators Connection. This is a special connection that uses considerably fewer resources and is quite strongly restricted in what it can do, but it does allow a DBA to connect to a system that wouldn't be available otherwise. This is a tremendously useful feature and one that every SQL Server performance tuner should be aware of.

If your server is in a state where you need to use the DAC to connect, you want to make sure you use as few resources as possible. Connecting using SQL Server Management Studio can be very resource intensive as the simple task of clicking different nodes in the server explorer can cause resource intensive queries to run on the server.

The better option for using the DAC is to connect through SQLCMD, the command line interface to SQL Server. Using SQLCMD will use much fewer server resources than using SSMS, but it does challenge the user to know the many useful DMVs needed to identify any resource-hogging queries. Alternatively, you can keep a suite of useful SQL Scripts accessible and run these through SQLCMD across the DAC to find and kill the resource hog. The question is where to keep these valuable scripts so they are accessible. Some useful places include:

❑   A USB thumb drive

❑   A team website

❑   A well-known file share

Each has its advantages and disadvantages. You can try and keep your most useful scripts in all three locations. The challenge then is keeping them all synched with the latest version. Robocopy and a good source code control system can really help.

PSSDiag

PSSDiag is a general-purpose data collection tool used by CSS to collect data from a customer's server. If you are familiar with this, it is most likely because you called CSS with a server performance issue and they asked you to use it to collect data. PSSDiag can be found by searching the web for the latest download.

SQLDiag

SQLDiag is another CSS data collection tool, but this one is focused on collecting SQL Server statistics to help a support engineer diagnose your SQL Server performance problem. SQLDiag can also be found by searching the web for the latest download location.

Blocking Scripts

This CSS tool is a set of scripts to help identify blocking issues. Check out the PSS SQL Server Engineers Blog for the latest information on the new version called *Perf Stats Script*. A web search for SQL Blocking Script should reveal the latest download location.

Network Monitor and Netcap

Network Monitor (Netmon) and the network monitor capture utility (Netcap) are tools for capturing network traffic. Netmon includes both capture and analysis tools. Netcap is just a capture utility. Capturing a network trace can be helpful when the issue might be a connection problem or an authentication problem and it is not possible to see what is going on with the other SQL Server tools. The ability to capture a trace of every packet sent to and from the server over the network is an invaluable aid, although interpreting the results can require a lot of time and a deep knowledge of network protocols. In many cases there are protocol wizards built into Netmon that will help with interpreting network packets by breaking down the raw data into the relevant data structures.

Windbg, ntsd, and cdb

Windbg, ntsd, and cdb are the Windows debuggers. These are hardcore code development debuggers, and you wouldn't normally expect to hear anyone mention them in a discussion on SQL Server. However, they can be extremely useful for diagnosing client-side performance issues where there is no low-level tracing.

Visual Studio 2005 Team Edition for Database Professionals

Sometimes also referred to as Data Dude, this is a new application life cycle tool to empower team development of SQL Server. Anyone working on a production database should be using this, even if they are not on a team. The basic product has enough cool features to make it a great addition for any DBA. The team also recently released a cool suite of Power Tools that add some additional features. Keep an eye on Gert Draper's blog (listed in the next section) for the latest breaking news on this tool.

Knowledge

Another invaluable tool in performance tuning is knowledge, and there is no better source on internal knowledge on SQL Server than the blogs of the people who work on the product themselves. Some of the many useful blogs include:

- ❑ **SQL Server storage team blog:** `http://blogs.msdn.com/sqlserverstorageengine/default.aspx`
- ❑ **Gert Draper:** `http://blogs.msdn.com/gertd/`
- ❑ **Euan Garden:** `http://blogs.msdn.com/euanga/default.aspx`
- ❑ **Slava Ok:** `http://blogs.msdn.com/slavao/`
- ❑ **SQL Engine Tips:** `http://blogs.msdn.com/sqltips/default.aspx`
- ❑ **Ian Jose:** `http://blogs.msdn.com/ianjo/`
- ❑ **Wei Xaio:** `http://blogs.msdn.com/weix/`
- ❑ **SQL Manageability:** `http://blogs.msdn.com/sqlrem/default.aspx`
- ❑ **Query Opt team:** `http://blogs.msdn.com/queryoptteam/`
- ❑ **Craig Freedman:** `http://blogs.msdn.com/craigfr/`
- ❑ **SQL CAT Blog:** `http://blogs.msdn.com/sqlcat`
- ❑ **SQL BP website:** `http://www.microsoft.com/technet/prodtechnol/sql/bestpractice/default.mspx`

Preventative Measures

Routine monitoring of SQL Server systems will help show performance problems as they start to arise, and not as they erupt into crisis. Addressing a small issue as it starts is often a lot easier than dealing with an erupting volcano of an issue when it occurs unexpectedly.

Capturing baseline performance numbers and understanding workload characteristics are another important part of monitoring system performance. A customer question might be about the value for a specific performance counter. This might take the form of a question something like this:

> *"Our system is getting 50 transactions per second. Is that OK?"*

Without any idea what the hardware is, what the database looks like, and how much work is there in each transaction, the numbers are meaningless.

On the other hand, what if the customer had a performance baseline that showed that for a specific workload they could achieve 75 transactions per second with 100 users at 50 percent CPU load with an I/O throughput of 1.5 MB/Sec at a latency of 2 msec? From that baseline they can now see that only getting 50 transactions per second is only about two-thirds of what their system is capable of.

If they also noticed that those 50 transactions per second are consuming 95 percent CPU and the I/O throughput is now at 4 MB/Sec with a latency of 25 msec, that's a good indication that there are some serious problems. First of all you are getting 60 percent of the transactions with almost double the CPU load. That's a great indication you either changed a query somewhere, you are getting a sub-optimal execution plan, your indexes are shot, you reached some size threshold on one of the tables, or some other bottleneck is occurring.

Without the baseline, 50 transactions per second is just a talking point with no point of reference to compare to. With the baseline, 50 transactions per second is the start of a meaningful investigation into a performance issue.

Part III of the book covers some of the basic techniques for monitoring and baselining system performance.

Summary

Performance tuning isn't an art, it's a science. In this chapter you learned about the science of performance tuning. You started with the steps in the methodical approach to performance tuning: starting from the problem statement, moving onto the plan of attack, data collection, followed by data analysis, and then repeating until you achieve your goal. You were introduced to some of the many tools available to assist with performance tuning. Some of these are covered in more detail throughout the remainder of this book. In the next chapter you will learn about using Performance Monitor to look at server resources.

2

Monitoring Server Resources with System Monitor

Understanding how your server is performing can be invaluable when troubleshooting problems and is useful in effective management of your systems such as capacity planning. This chapter covers when to use System Monitor and how to get the most from monitoring to determine how your server is performing. Deciding what data to gather is the first step; interpreting the data is the next step in resolving an issue before putting a fix in place. At the end of this chapter, you should expect to better understand how to:

- ❏   Analyze a performance problem
- ❏   Proactively monitor server resource usage
- ❏   Apply best practices when using System Monitor

Familiarizing yourself with the tools and your system's regular workload means that you're able to differentiate between the usual creaks and groans of your server and an actual performance problem. Performance tuning is a science. Getting to the root cause is a journey that can be long and arduous, but if you're comfortable with the tools and familiar with your environment, it should be an enjoyable and interesting challenge.

Why Might I Need System Monitor?

In almost all application performance–related problems, a decent problem description, the Windows event logs, and System Monitor will provide sufficient data to allow you to eliminate or incriminate many components of the overall software and hardware solution. Usually, when we receive a problem report by phone, e-mail, or a trouble-ticketing tool, the scope of the problem is wide. The problem may be client side, network-related, or server-related. It also could be hardware- or software-related. Or it could have to do with the operating system, infrastructure (SQL Server, IIS, and so on), or application.

Much like a doctor arriving at the scene of an accident, your first step should be an initial assessment of the situation to get a feel for the scale of the problem, severity, and priorities. Some aspects will be implicit in the problem statement; other aspects will need more data before a proper diagnosis can be made. Essentially, in the early stages of fault-finding you should be looking to rule out software or hardware components that could have caused or contributed to the performance problem.

System Monitor can equip you with some powerful information on which you can base decisions about how and whether to proceed with troubleshooting. Accurate identification of the likely area of the problem at this stage can drastically reduce the time to resolution for your users. Naturally, there are many situations where System Monitor can't provide sufficient granularity of information or can't reveal particulars of application behavior. However, there are many other tools (especially for SQL Server) that do this job really well.

When Should I Use System Monitor?

Any time you deploy a new server or service or make a significant configuration or application change, you should use System Monitor. Although this may sound time consuming, cumbersome, and unrealistic, it need not be this way and having some form of relevant performance baseline to which you refer during problem investigation could save hours, days, or weeks in terms of root cause analysis. Organizations in possession of up-to-date performance benchmark data for their key systems typically experience a lower meantime to resolution for performance-related faults in their environments.

Additionally, how do you know what sort of utilization your servers have? How can you tell whether they have spare CPU cycles or if they may require additional processors next month? System Monitor can be used to create a lightweight trace to provide powerful data for capacity planning, usage monitoring, and trend analysis.

Performance Monitor Overview

Within System Monitor in Windows Server 2000 and 2003, one of the most useful components is known as *Performance Monitor*, which exposes around 50 performance objects and 350 performance counters. Each performance object provides access to a number of performance counters which give real time access to system resources. The performance counters and objects are populated from the Windows registry and using Performance Library DLLs. Additionally, each application installed on a server may add its own performance objects. For example, a single instance of SQL Server will add more than 30 of its own performance objects, each object with numerous counters.

Common tasks you can use Performance Monitor for include:

- ❑ Collect real-time performance data from your server
- ❑ Log performance data over an extended timeframe

❏   Collect and compare performance data from different servers

❏   View a graphic representation of server performance

❏   Save and export performance data

❏   Measure the performance impact of system and/or software changes

❏   Send performance alerts based on performance thresholds

In situations where you're experiencing performance or reliability issues, Performance Monitor can reveal the source of the problem very quickly, if the problem is simple. On many occasions, however, Performance Monitor will provide you with a better understanding of the scope and nature of a problem, but you'll likely have to use other specific tools to proceed with troubleshooting. It's quite likely that your initial troubleshooting Performance Monitor will lead you to require more detailed diagnosis and frequently this will require tools such as SQL Server Profiler or a network monitoring application, such as Windows Network Monitor or Ethereal.

Performance troubleshooting typically requires an iterative approach, starting by qualifying the initial problem statement and continuing by performing a detailed fault diagnosis and analysis until you reach a conclusion. As a first step, your objective should be to determine whether a problem exists at all, and you want to be sure that what you're monitoring is relevant to the symptoms expressed in the problem statement. This qualification process will often begin with the error message and the attempt to identify a corresponding error on the server at the time the user/service experienced the reported error. In the case of web servers, this can be as straightforward as locating a matching GET request in a log file from the client IP address. Other times, depending on the nature of the problem, it can be difficult to find anything that matches on the server. It can be very useful to initially familiarize yourself with the Windows Application and System event logs. Assuming these are adequately sized, they should contain sufficient history to give you some level of confidence of the server's availability (uptime of services and so on) and will provide you with a feel for the health of the server. When examining the Application and System event logs, it's a good idea to isolate any entries flagged with Warning or Error types and try to eliminate them as potential causes (unless they're clearly unrelated). It's always surprising the number of server engineers who overlook clues to the root cause of their issues by overlooking the Application and System logs or by dismissing entries that are subsequently proven to be important.

Once any warning and errors in the Windows Application and System logs have been resolved or dismissed as unrelated to the problem being investigated, it would be useful to begin performance monitoring to determine the state and current workload of the server to identify any bottlenecks. When considering likely candidates for performance issues, you should consider the following four areas for initial monitoring:

❏   Memory

❏   Disk

❏   Processor

❏   Network

The objective of using Performance Monitor is to provide you with a feel for the health and workload of the server. By selecting between 5 and 10 counters that cover the fundamental areas for initial monitoring as listed above, you'll gain a quick and meaningful insight into the real-time state of the server.

Why are these areas so important? They're the major hardware components of a server, and each component is involved in servicing user requests. The timely performance of these components is directly related to overall perceived application performance. Therefore, a problem with one or more of these four areas is likely to result in user complaints. SQL Server relies heavily on CPU performance, available memory, and disk throughput, whereas the client performance depends heavily on network performance. Any processor which is consistently busy for 90 percent of the time or more will result in the buildup of a queue of work requests, and performance will likely suffer. Additionally, SQL Server can be very demanding of memory and performance can really suffer if physical memory becomes exhausted, when typically Windows is forced to use the page file. Disk is almost certainly the slowest component, inherently because it's mechanical. SQL Server's necessity to retrieve data from disk often means any delays at the disk Input/Output (I/O) will impact overall performance. Finally, your database could be performing perfectly well, but if there's latency in the network or if packet loss is high, forcing retransmissions, all the good work done until this point is negated by poor performance when talking to the requestor.

Getting Started with System Monitor

System Monitor is provided as part of the operating system to allow system administrators to get visibility of server workload and resource utilization. The tool can be useful for providing data helpful in troubleshooting problems, trend analysis, and system capacity planning.

This section is intended to help familiarize you with the tool, the information it can provide, and how you can present this information natively within System Monitor. The Performance Console Microsoft Management Console (MMC) snap-in includes two key tools for monitoring server performance:

❑   System Monitor

❑   Performance Logs and Alerts

The first component, System Monitor (commonly known by the name of the executable perfmon.exe, and generally what is known as Perfmon), is the realtime monitoring tool. Performance Logs and Alerts contains three sub-components: Counter Logs, Trace Logs, and Alerts.

> *Throughout this chapter Performance Monitor and System Monitor are used interchangeably as terms referring to System Monitor (rather than Performance Console), since these names are more commonly used.*

Begin by launching the Performance Console from Administrative Tools (the same tool is known as *Reliability and Performance Monitor* in Windows Vista), or add the Performance snap-in to MMC. The figures shown in this chapter were created using Reliability and Performance Monitor in Windows Vista, so the interface may differ slightly in appearance, although functionally they're the same. Note that some counters are present by default; you'll see a graph beginning to form as values are sampled for the default counters (see Figure 2-1).

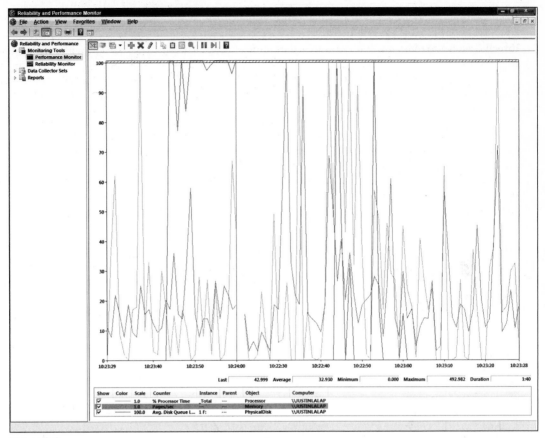

Figure 2-1

Even with a relatively small number of counters it can be difficult to distinguish between counter values. In Windows Server 2003 there's a toolbar icon showing a lightbulb (which is represented by a pen-shaped highlighter in Windows Vista). The highlight tool can be used to match counters on the line graph with the counter selected in the counter list. This can be really useful when handling more than a few counters. It can also be enabled by pressing Ctrl+H.

The form in which the data is displayed can be changed either using right-click properties or through the toolbar icon symbolizing a line graph. A bar graph display is available, although this tends to be less useful than the line graph. Additionally a report view is available that presents data in a numeric form (see Figure 2-2). This can be useful when monitoring a large number of counters, and can also help ensure that your interpretation of the data isn't skewed by scale.

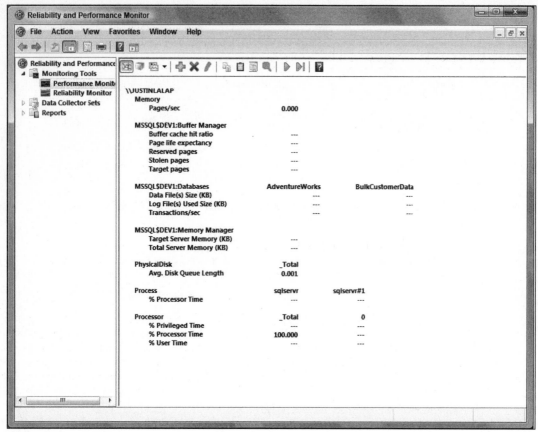

Figure 2-2

Additional counters can be added using the toolbar icon with the plus symbol or by right-clicking anywhere in the graph area and choosing Add Counters. When the Add Counters dialog box is displayed, you'll first have to select the counter you're interested in adding. Then, depending on the specific counter, you may also need to select a specific instance of an object.

Many counters contain an object called _TOTAL and another called <ALL INSTANCES>, and often other objects as well. It's important that you take note of which instance you're adding to a log, because choosing the object that meets your monitoring needs is essential to getting meaningful data and making the right decisions subsequently in your investigation. As an example consider the counter Physical Disk. This counter contains more than 20 objects, and each object can be monitored as a total or on a per-disk basis. Often you'll be working with servers that contain local disks and could also be attached to SAN or NAS disk arrays. One of the counters used most commonly when attempting to identify whether disk performance is acceptable is Average Disk Queue length. In the event that a disk subsystem becomes slow or unresponsive, a queue of work items (typically disk read or write requests) will begin to form.

The length on this queue is exposed as Average Disk Queue Length. Take, for example, the sample server disk configuration in Table 2-1.

Table 2-1: Sample Database Server Disk Configuration

Drive	Purpose	Storage	RAID Level
C	Operating system	Internal disks	5 - Striping with parity
D	Application	Internal disks	5 - Striping with parity
E	Database data files	SAN storage	10 - Striping with parity, mirrored
F	Database transaction log files	SAN storage	2 - Disk mirroring

If you were working on a performance issue on the server with the hardware configuration in Table 2-1, you'd be keen to eliminate any disk input/output (I/O) as the cause of poor performance. If you were to use Performance Monitor and add the counter for Physical Disk — Average Disk Queue Length, this would provide a reasonable basis on which to make a decision around whether there was a likely disk performance issue. However, the server is provided with varying disk sub-systems and structures, and in order for you to make an informed decision about whether there is a disk performance issue, you'll need to make sure that your decision is based on valid data. If you were to launch System Monitor, add the Physical Disk — Average Disk Queue Length, and select the default object. This would provide you with _TOTAL object. You would almost certainly be considerably better served by selecting the specific drives that you're monitoring (which might be all of them), but you'll expose individual drive performance, instead of it potentially being masked in a total of average values (see Figure 2-3).

When using the graph view (as shown previously in Figure 2-1), the scale values on the Y (vertical) axis can be changed on a per-counter basis, allowing counters with dissimilar scales to be displayed together. The scale is displayed in the selected counters grid at the bottom of System Monitor, and don't make the mistake of comparing two similar-looking values that are displaying on different scales!

The general tab of the System Monitor properties allows you to control the sampling (polling) interval. Don't underestimate the effect of adjusting the sampling interval, both in terms of the impact on the target server and with respect to the impact on the shape of the data produced. The default sampling interval is 1 second, and this is usually suitable for short-term real-time monitoring, although you might like to reduce this on systems where resources are particularly low. Additionally, if system resources are very low, you should monitor from a remote server instead of locally as this will require fewer system resources (inevitably there will be some overhead, such as network traffic). As with any kind of monitoring, you should try to reach a balance between the overhead placed on the server and perfor-mance data generated. Your objective should always be to monitor the fewest counters possible while still revealing enough information about the performance problem to allow diagnosis — or at least a better understanding!

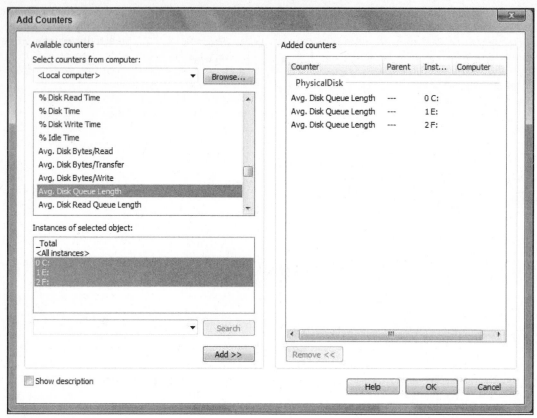

Figure 2-3

Performance Logs and Alerts

There may also be occasion when you need to start and stop system logging automatically. You may need to capture system utilization during a specific timeframe or while a certain activity is being completed, perhaps outside normal working hours. You may also want to start a log and have the computer stop the log capturing at a certain time. Performance Monitor allows all of these tasks to be carried out natively.

If you're operating in an environment without a system management tool (such as Microsoft Operations Manager or Microsoft System Center) you can also configure Performance Monitor to trigger alerts when performance thresholds are breached.

What's the Impact of Running System Monitor?

Typically managers want problems fixed fast — with as little risk to further degrading service as possible. Often they'll seek reassurances that any monitoring or troubleshooting steps you take won't impact system performance or affect perceived user experience any further. Unfortunately, without having been in this exact same situation previously and using monitoring tools — the outcome/impact can be difficult to predict. Every type of monitoring, whether System Monitor, PSSDiag, SQL Server Profiler, or third-party tools, creates an overhead on the server. Essentially you're asking the server to record all activity or a subset of activity to a performance tool. This activity record will reside either on disk or in memory, and the performance of this media will itself affect the impact of monitoring. Additionally, the target disk or memory could reside on a different server from the one you are monitoring, which will introduce its own characteristics that you should also be aware of.

Creating a System Monitor log file on the same disk volume that hosts a database file or the operating system paging file will exaggerate any existing memory problems. This is because the monitoring process competes for server resources with genuine user activity on a server, increasing contention, disk queue lengths, and wait times.

Managing Monitoring Impact

You should be prudent in the number of counters logged and the sampling frequency. Start lightweight and broad to provide a holistic system overview, and as you zoom in to the problem area, remember to remove counters that are no longer relevant as you add more detailed and specific counters based on your findings. Changing the polling interval from the default 15 seconds to 30 seconds reduces the load of monitoring by 50 percent.

Performance tuning is often an iterative process. Based on results of monitoring, you can further refine what and how you monitor, and perhaps change between tools that are more appropriate for the job.

Capturing at the Right Time, for the Right Duration

Customers who lack troubleshooting experience or lack confidence in the impact of monitoring tools or the durability and robustness of their applications tend to be cautious around the time and duration of monitoring. Frequently engineers will select periods of low activity and limit monitoring duration to 15 minutes or less, but this can often prove inefficient in terms of getting the problem resolved. A concise problem description along with the System Monitor log and SQL Profiler trace in many cases will provide all the data you need to identify and resolve a performance problem. However, you're entirely reliant on the problem showing itself during your data capture window and as such, the longer you monitor, the more likely you are to capture an occurrence of the problem.

When handling performance problems, troubleshooting servers with mediocre performance (such as "somewhat slower than usual" problem statements) can be much harder than troubleshooting servers with acute performance issues. Similarly, during your data capture (monitoring) window, you should look to gain an insight into the server at its worst. This will provide you with the most meaningful data and give you the very best chance of identifying the cause as early as possible!

How Much Data Will System Monitor Generate?

Ideally, your performance log contains just enough information to allow you to identify the problem — no more. Getting to the point that you only record meaningful data (data that will be used in diagnosing an issue) is not trivial. To do this it will be necessary to undertake a number of iterations of performance logging using System Monitor. Once the scope of the problem has been more closely defined (through system-wide troubleshooting early in the process), you can refine the number of counters you're monitoring by removing less relevant or superfluous counters and drilling down in the areas of specific interest or relevance.

The two factors that significantly influence the amount of data generated by System Monitor are as follows:

❑   Number of counters

❑   Sampling interval

Managing the overhead of monitoring system performance and the volume of data generated is a delicate balance that can be achieved by carefully observing the output and continuously refining counters.

As a best practice it's a good idea with any kind of monitoring (System Monitor, SQL Profiler, and so on) to avoid logging to a system partition. In the event that you have selected too many counters or objects or if the server is significantly busier than you expected, the impact of filling a non-system drive may still be problematic, but it shouldn't be disastrous. If you fill a disk partition that contains a database log file, the log file will be unable to grow, and without the ability to log operations to the transaction log, SQL Server will stop servicing the database. This may be disastrous in terms of providing service to your users, as they will no longer be able to go about their work in the database, but this is a relatively straightforward position to recover from (simply free some disk space and SQL will resume fairly promptly). However, if you were in a position where the system partition became full, this could cause some real problems for Windows that might be much harder to recover from. Therefore, it's generally a good idea to avoid any risk of getting into this situation by always logging to a target drive that is non-system.

The actual amount of data generated by System Monitor can be predicted fairly reliably — when compared with a load-dependent tool like SQL Server Profiler, where the volume of trace data is highly variable and as such can be difficult to predict. System monitor data capture is essentially linear. For example, if you're capturing 30 counters with a 15-second sampling interval (polling interval), this might produce 1 MB of data in the first 15 minutes of data capture. It would be fairly safe to assume that log growth will continue at 4 MB per hour, regardless of whether the server is being thrashed by thousands of concurrent users or sitting idle. Predictable log growth will allow you to run medium- to long-term system monitoring with some confidence around the size and nature of the data being produced.

Resource Utilization

Ideally, you'll estimate your workload accurately, buy commodity hardware, and distribute application roles or functions to ensure an even spread of work and effective use of all resources while not over-burdening any single server or resource. The practicalities of the testing and measurement required to estimate workload often mean that you'll be in a situation where you have to go live with a service or application with less testing than you'd have liked (indeed occasionally with none), and you have to deal with the problems there and then.

On many occasions, making sensible assumptions and realistically quantifying risks along with a mitigation plan is the only way to get projects off the ground. In these situations the tendency is usually to conservatively over-specify hardware in an effort to avoid upgrading at a later date. One of the characteristics of working with SQL Server that makes it so interesting is that frequently no amount of hardware can compensate for a bad database design or poorly thought-through disk subsystem.

A resource bottleneck is the highest cost component in terms of time, on the critical path when performing user-requested activity. In terms of overall perceived application performance, you could consider the network, user authentication, or a database as a bottleneck. More relevant, within the database server, you could consider memory, CPU, or disk throughput as a bottleneck if performing an operation is impaired significantly by any one of these.

Successfully identifying a bottleneck involves using System Monitor to understand individual performance counters, in the context of overall system performance. Abstracted, there is little useful performance data as this is all relative to the hardware and use profile of the server. Jumping to conclusions and making assumptions are quick ways to prolong a poor performance condition. Always consider the key components together when making your assessment.

Kernel Mode versus Application Mode

When considering server performance, you should be familiar with the difference between Kernel mode and Application mode operations. Once you understand this concept, this knowledge can be applied to both CPU and memory resources or bottlenecks. Most performance-related discussions will seek to identify kernel mode or application mode pressure or contention early in the trouble-shooting cycle in order to further narrow down likely causes and to determine potential routes to seek resolution.

Kernel mode refers to core windows internal operations where the kernel has unrestricted access to system memory, external devices, and so on. For example, processes or threads are managed, and the I/O manager takes care of device drivers. Also the virtual memory manager controls all virtual memory and the hard disk.

Application mode (also known as *user mode*) is responsible for everything else, such as servicing all requests from user applications including IIS and SQL Server. All user mode applications access resources through the executive, which runs in Kernel mode. An application requesting disk I/O submits the request through the kernel mode executive, which will carry out the request and return the results to the requesting user mode process.

Identifying Bottlenecks

When investigating performance issues, you should seek first to identify a bottleneck and second to resolve the bottleneck! Bottlenecks are typically caused through misconfiguration or by reaching performance or scalability limitations within software or hardware. Identifying a bottleneck is a major aspect of performance troubleshooting. Doing so in a timely and efficient fashion is a skill that requires understanding of system and software architecture and a methodical approach.

Locating Memory Bottlenecks

SQL Server just loves memory — it can't get enough of it! If ever there was an application that can use all the memory in a server, it is SQL Server. However, this is for the benefit of users. Disks are slow and therefore SQL Server will do all it can to pre-empt user requests by reading ahead and loading data pages into memory so they're provided to users as quickly as possible when requested.

When designing a platform to deliver a new service, or definitely when reviewing capacity on existing infrastructure, it's necessary to determine how much free memory is available. This can also be useful in determining whether a memory shortage is contributing to or even causing a performance issue.

Identifying memory pressure can be further categorized as identifying either internal or external memory pressure. If SQL Server is unable to acquire sufficient memory, it is external memory pressure, or if there's contention within memory allocated to SQL Server, it is internal memory pressure. Internal Memory pressure can occur when the SQL Server Buffer Pool (the memory location that holds data pages) is reduced in response to other processes (linked server, extended stored procedures, COM+and so on) consuming memory in the same memory address space as SQL Server. System Monitor can help in identifying and eliminating external memory pressure, and with some of the SQL Server–specific counters (such as Buffer Manager) you're able to get good visibility of internal memory pressure too. There are also some great Dynamic Management Views (DMVs) and Database Consistency Checks (DBCCs) that you can use to investigate memory pressure.

An initial high-level indicator of the status of user mode memory availability is the Memory counter Available Bytes (also available as Available KBytes and Available MBytes). On most healthy servers you should expect to see at least some available memory at all times. Typically you should be concerned if available memory drops below around 4 MB.

Windows creates a Virtual Address Space (VAS) for every application. The VAS may be made up from physical memory and memory provided in the page file. The page file will reside on the system drive (unless it's been moved elsewhere), and accessing data from the page file is considerably slower than accessing pages that are held in memory. Notably, in the case of SQL Server you can sometimes see SQL making great efforts to pre-empt user requests and load data pages from disk into memory, only to see the operating system serve this requirement from the page file. Obviously this is counter-intuitive, increases disk I/O, and defeats the purpose of SQL Server reading the data pages ahead. Unfortunately, SQL Server doesn't know whether Windows will offer memory from physical RAM or the page file, as it's only aware of the VAS. There is a way to request the operating system only serve requests from SQL Server from RAM, not from the page file. This is controlled by the Lock Pages in Memory privilege, which must be granted to the SQL Server service account, which is covered in more detail in Chapter 6.

Monitoring page file activity will also give you some idea of whether you're experiencing a memory shortage. There's a counter within System Monitor that you can use for this very purpose. It's called *memory pages/second*. This will tell you the total number of data pages that have to be read into memory from the page file or written to the page file, per second. If a system is running low on memory, you should expect to see a ramp-up in memory pages/second as the operating system is forced to use the paging file for temporary data storage. The reason the memory pages/second counter increases is that as a system runs low on memory, Windows becomes more reliant on the page file to service user requests. Hence more data pages are read and written. You should expect this counter to sit at or around zero. If it's any different (especially on a SQL Server), you should continue investigating memory pressure.

If you suspect a system is experiencing poor performance because memory pressure is causing increased page file activity, you can confirm this. Take a look at the Paging File counters. Here you'll see two objects: % Usage and % Usage Peak. If you're not familiar with the server or haven't checked already, it might now be worth checking how much physical memory the system has and the size and location of the Page File. Once you've added % Usage and % Usage Peak, you should look for some correlation between an increase in memory pages/second and an increase in % Usage of the paging file. If you see a relationship between high memory pages/second and increased paging file % Usage, you can be confident that you're seeing external memory pressure.

It's worth mentioning at this point that an increase in memory pages/second alone isn't necessarily indicative of a low memory condition. This counter also includes a count of sequential reads for memory mapped files. So you'll need to qualify memory pressure by considering available memory and page file activity too.

Discovering Disk Bottlenecks

Whether you have an enterprise SAN or a local SATA array, retrieving data from disk is without a doubt the slowest step in returning query results to a user. There are many ways you can identify and isolate disk performance issues, and there are a number of alternatives to resolving disk issues.

The marketing teams at SAN manufacturers do a great job of persuading customers that they have the fastest, most responsive, lowest latency, cheapest SAN available today. The reality is often that no matter how fast the disks are, how short the seek time is, or how large the cache is, application workload can cause SQL Server to request or write data faster than most SANs can read or commit data.

At a high level, keeping an eye on % Disk Time will help you understand the amount of time an individual thread spent waiting on disk I/O. You should begin to be concerned about disk performance if either of these values are 20 milliseconds (ms) or higher. If either of these is high, there are a number of additional counters you can use to get a better picture of disk activity.

One of the most useful counters in the system monitor is Average Disk Queue length. Traditionally it really did give an indication of queue depth (by dividing queue length by the number of spindles in a disk array). However, in times of SANs, which dynamically and intelligently manage the mapping of LUNS to spindles within a disk group, it has becoming increasingly difficult to determine exactly how many spindles host a particular LUN, and if these spindles are shared with another LUN. This abstraction by SAN vendors has in many instances drastically improved performance, reliability, and scalability of disk subsystems while reducing the cost of ownership.

With this in mind, you can still make use of Average Disk Queue length. It's just more arbitrary now than it used to be. It's still a great counter to include in your baseline and to reference in the event of a performance issue because it's usually fairly representative of disk performance. Don't forget to add the counters for specific drives; don't add the _TOTAL counter, as this can generalize the result and mask problems which could lead to you making false assumptions about disk performance.

In order to approximate disk array response time, you should look to monitor Average Disk Seconds/Read and Average Disk Seconds/Write. As the names would suggest, these two counters will provide an indication of the average time taken to read or write to disk. The ceiling value you should have in mind is 20 ms. This means that if your disk sub-system takes longer than 20 ms to respond to either a read or write request, you can expect degraded SQL Server performance.

The good news is that there's a whole bunch of options to remedy poor disk performance. Once you've established that you have a disk performance issue, often you'll have multiple remedial options.

Best Practice

There are a few fundamental best practices to mention first, including separation of SQL Server data and log files. These files have distinctly different I/O patterns. In an Online Transaction Processing (OLTP) environment, you should expect to see random reads and writes to the data file, whereas you'll see sequential writes and very low read activity to the transaction log file. For these reasons you should plan to place these two files on separate drives. If you're using a SAN with an intelligent controller, this will allow the controller to manage the physical disk-to-drive mapping better.

> **Best Practice**
>
> Secondly, as a best practice you should always look to separate system databases from user databases. This will minimize disk contention between these databases. There's one specific database, tempdb, which is responsible for instance-wide temporary storage. The demand on tempdb varies enormously depending on the type of activity on the server and the features used within SQL Server. For example, certain DBCC commands will use database snapshots, and online index rebuilds can also consume space within tempdb in addition to the normal sorts and joins that might take place.

Identifying CPU Bottlenecks

CPU time is one of the most expensive and precious server resources, and overall system performance is often very sensitive to CPU utilization. For example, a high CPU condition (even for a short period) can often be felt by users. SQL Server itself can often create high CPU conditions through execution of unqualified queries, hash or merge joins, or during query plan compilation/recompilation. Typically these require SQL Profiler traces or use of DMVs to identify/resolve. System Monitor can be useful in the initial identification.

It's worth clarifying that everything discussed in this section refers to logical processors, which are processors as exposed to Windows. These may exist physically as Hyper Threaded (HT) or multi-core processors, and both will expose themselves to Windows (and therefore to SQL Server) as logical processors. In this way a four-CPU, dual-core system with hyper threading enabled will appear as 16 logical processors. It's not actually terribly easy for SQL Server or Windows to differentiate between logical and physical processors.

There are two performance monitoring objects that are quite distinct but often confused: process and processor. The process object refers to windows processes; there is an instance of this counter for every Windows process, such as `sqlservr.exe` and `notepad.exe`. The processor object has an instance for each logical processor — the actual CPUs themselves.

Similar to the counters you've seen in the disk section, you'll be able to get a fairly good understanding of the state of health of the processors by adding the % Total Processor time from the Processor object. This counter measures percent time the processor is busy servicing requests, which includes kernel mode and application mode requests across all processors. If this is consistently above 80 percent, you know you're seeing some CPU pressure, and you'll need to add some further counters to identify what the source is and how the pressure is occurring.

The next step is to break down the Total Processor time to understand the composition of the CPU time. (For example, is the CPU being heavily loaded by a kernel mode or a user mode process?) You should examine the % Privileged Time and % User Time within the Processor object to determine where the CPU demand originates. On a healthy server you should expect to see fairly minimal privilege time. One of the side-effects of low memory conditions can be high kernel mode CPU, and the processors are involved in handling paging.

You can confirm an application problem if you see the User Time line on the line graph in System Monitor almost shadow Total Processor Time. This indicates that there is a user mode process consuming almost all CPU cycles. Should this happen, you'll need to work through the processes to determine which is consuming the CPU time. You should add instances of the % Processor Time counter in the Process object for each process, for example, `sqlservr.exe`. Once you've identified the culprit, it will be a case of trying to determine why demand is so high. There are a number of DMVs which expose this information very readily. A lot of useful DMV information can be found in Chapters 4, 12, 13, and 14.

Using System Monitor Proactively

A baseline is invaluable. Understanding how your systems behave while under normal load will assist when troubleshooting and while making decisions around capacity planning and resource utilization. It can be really useful to authoritatively answer questions around typical CPU utilization, normal memory consumption, and average disk performance. Using System Monitor proactively can help with each of these.

Regularly running System Monitor to obtain system baseline data can be readily used for trend analysis and capacity planning. Server overhead can be minimized by running System Monitor remotely, and reducing sample frequency to between 15 and 30 minutes. Allowing the log to run continuously over 24 hours (or longer) will provide a useful system overview which should be retained for future reference.

Once you've done this, the next time you receive a problem report from a user that indicates a potential performance issue, you'll be in a really strong position to run System Monitor on your production server and alongside display your most recently saved baseline. A comparison will be easy, and while server load won't necessarily be identical, you'll be able to compare averages and very quickly get a feel for general server performance and any likely problem areas.

Running System Monitor on 64-bit Systems

If you're using x64 Windows and x64 SQL Server you shouldn't have any issues. System Monitor will by default have the correct counters loaded and available for you to view and the same applies to IA64 Windows and IA64 SQL Server deployments. However, if you're using SQL Server in a Windows-On-Windows (WOW) mode on x64 (which is to say that x64 Windows is emulating a 32-bit environment to facilitate you running an x86 instance of SQL Server), then this section will definitely be relevant.

This situation (x86 SQL running on x64 Windows) can be particularly useful for multi-instance test environments or at times when applications specifically require 32-bit SQL Server. When you start System Monitor on the x64 host, you'll find that none of the counters relating to the 32-bit SQL Server instance are available. This is because on an x64 host you'll be running an x64 version of System Monitor by default. Monitoring the 32-bit SQL Server instance in the scenario will require running a 32-bit instance of System Monitor, and this can be achieved by running the following from the Start⇨ Run box:

```
mmc /32 perfmon.msc
```

Once the 32-bit MMC console has started with the Perfmon snap-in, the 32-bit SQL Server counters should be available for addition to your log.

Combining System Monitor Logs and SQL Profiler Traces

Analysis of performance data has been significantly improved in SQL Server 2005 with a feature allowing the import of Performance Monitor log files into a SQL Profiler trace. The process is quite straightforward, and necessitates both Perfmon and Profiler traces being captured to the file. There are more details in the next chapter about how to achieve this (and there is more information about Perfmon in general in Chapter 12). For now, suffice it to say it can make log and trace analysis significantly less cumbersome as all data is presented in one application, mapped against a combined timeline. Figure 2-4 illustrates the result of combining a SQL Profiler trace with a Perfmon log.

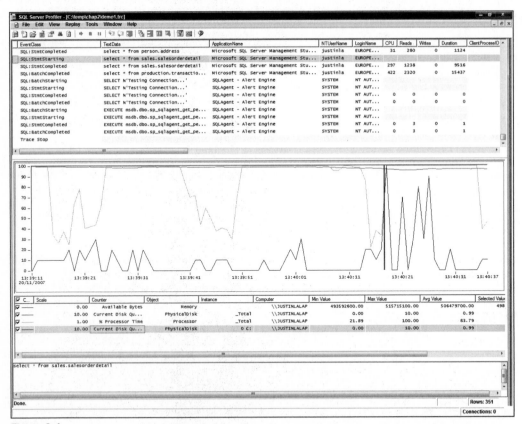

Figure 2-4

This level of data analysis and integration of performance data has never been seen before and sets new standards for Microsoft applications integrating with Operating System performance tools. This performance data integration means SQL Server DBAs will save many man-hours. You're much more likely to be able to identify and resolve performance problems without requiring specialist tools and deep internals knowledge that would normally be accessed via Microsoft Product Support Services.

Monitoring Remote Servers

When monitoring any service on any server there's always a trade-off between running the monitoring tool locally versus remotely. There's no right answer that works for every situation, since there are benefits and disadvantages of every monitoring configuration. Importantly, performance data should always be analyzed with awareness of the environment and configuration with which the data was gathered (specifically network configuration/limitations when using remote monitoring). As discussed earlier, running any kind of monitoring tool creates a performance overhead on the computer being monitored. When troubleshooting a specific issue, the use of Performance Monitor is usually confined to a relatively short timeframe before logging is stopped and often the output is copied to another computer for analysis. On most such occasions it would be suitable to run System Monitor on the server being monitored. However, if the purpose of monitoring is capacity planning or trend analysis, a remote server is preferred. This limits the impact of monitoring on the target server to creating some additional network input/output (I/O).

When monitoring SQL Server remotely, it's worth mentioning that Performance Monitor relies on NetBIOS. If there are any firewalls or port filters between the source and target for monitoring, it's possible that monitoring will be problematic. Once the target server has been specified within Performance Monitor, the performance objects and counters should automatically populate to reveal those available on the target system. If they don't appear, review the Application Event log on the source system (because any errors will appear on the source system, not the monitoring system), and ensure that there are no other instances of Performance Monitor running.

If you're still experiencing problems registering counters from a remote server, it may be worth looking at the Remote Registry service. Often restarting this service will reset any connections. Once this service is restarted, attempt to add the performance counters again and you should find that this works.

Best Practices for System Monitor

There are a number of best practices that you should consider when running System Monitor that will help you get the most from System Monitor and avoid some of the common pitfalls.

Taking a Baseline

It's probably the last thing on your mind. The phone has finally stopped ringing, and you finally have a chance to make sure the backups ran last night and grab a coffee. However, you may be grateful at some point soon that you did actually make time to take a baseline. All that's needed is to run System Monitor for 24 hours with a 15-minute sample interval, covering the main system components. This alone could be instrumental in prompt fault resolution. Try to invest a few minutes to set up a trace, and you'll see the benefits if you ever have a performance problem.

Each time you make a significant change to a software or hardware configuration, re-run your System Monitor baseline for 24 hours. Very quickly, you and the Change Managers should become comfortable with the likely (low) performance impact and associated risk of running System Monitor. Don't forget, each time you apply an operating system or application patch, upgrade the SAN fabric firmware, or change the networking routing table, take a new baseline.

Retaining Performance Logs

Anytime you take performance logs, keep them for future reference. You never know when the next problem may occur, and having historic log data available will enable you to make comparisons around factors that have changed, either since the last problem or since the last baseline was acquired while the server was operating normally.

Additionally, you could load the data from System Monitor logs into a database that will allow you to query and report on the data for capacity planning. System Monitor provides the ability to log directly to a database. However, the overhead associated with this is dependent on the target database server being available and responsive. Often, recording performance data to a flat file and then importing into a database is a more reliable approach that requires less overhead.

Patterns and Trends

Look to the future. Analyze the data you're collecting to establish any patterns or trends, and establish a high-water mark and normal operations mark for each service on your servers with respect to the key components. Once you know roughly what performance on your servers looks like, you can see how performance is changing and attempt to estimate when you might need to upgrade.

Servers Suffering Very Poor Performance

If you're working on a server which is really suffering seriously poor performance, don't attempt to run System Monitor locally. In this situation, run System Monitor from a remote server to reduce the overhead on the target server. Additionally, reduce the sampling interval to every 10 seconds; even every 30 seconds wouldn't be unreasonable in some situations.

If you can't monitor remotely (there could be security or network constraints), try to keep the number of counters monitored to a minimum; this will restrict the impact of monitoring. You should also log data to a file, instead of monitoring in graph or report view, as this can help reduce overhead. Remember when you log to a file, this will likely increase disk activity. If you do decide to log to a file, try to find an appropriate drive to log to. Try to avoid disks hosting the page file or the database or transaction log files.

Tuning Performance

Take action based on your findings. Evaluate the server workload, tune your applications, and review your hardware configuration and design to get the most from your investment. Once you've made changes, re-run System Monitor to review the impact of the changes. Always retain your log files, and keep a record of the date and environment setup (hardware configuration, relevant software levels, and so on) when the logs were taken.

Being Proactive

Don't wait for users to call you. Configure Alerts to have servers notify you when they're running low on resources. You'll need to define meaningful alert thresholds. For example, how busy does the CPU have to be before it impacts user experience? Or how low on memory does the server become before your web servers start experiencing timeouts? Only you can determine these answers — by collecting the data. Once you have access to this data, be proactive and configure some performance alerts based on typical thresholds.

My System Monitor Counters Are Missing — What Should I Do?

There could be a number of causes of missing performance counters. This is a common situation. Specifically on clustered servers, many counters are shared and can be problematic if counters have been updated by a hotfix or service pack, and the instance hasn't subsequently failed-over or has experienced errors during a fail-over.

There's a Windows Resource Kit command line utility called CTRLIST.EXE that reports on all objects and counters loaded on a system. The Windows Resource Kit can be downloaded from the Microsoft website. Once you've installed the Resource Kit, the most useful method is usually to pipe the output to a text file (rather than reading in a command prompt window). You can use the following command to pipe the counter list to a text file:

```
CTRLIST >c:\temp\counters.txt
```

A second alternative to the command line Resource Kit utility is a newer, GUI version. The GUI version is very similar, and allows you to enumerate loaded counters from remote servers too (assuming security criteria have been satisfied). The GUI version looks like Figure 2-5.

The main purpose for using either the command line utility or the GUI tool to expose the loaded counters is to determine the specifics of the DLLs related to each counter. In a situation where you experience a problem with a counter that is either missing or misbehaving, you'll need to know the DLL name and location.

Once you've identified an object or counter that is missing or malfunctioning, check the Windows application and system log to see if there are any warnings or errors relating to loading the performance library. If there are no apparent issues recorded in the log, it may be a good idea to attempt to unload and reload the counter. It's worth mentioning that even if a counter is completely missing, it's probably still worth executing the unload prior to trying to load the counter again. This is a relatively painless process that can be undertaken with a couple of commands. The following example refers to the SQL Server counter for a default SQL instance:

1.   Note the path to the .ini or .dll file in the counter list output obtained either through the command line utility or GUI as discussed above.

2.   To unload SQL Server counters, execute the following command:

```
Unlodctr mssqlserver
```

3.   Next, reload the counters using the following command:

```
Lodctr D:\Program Files\SQL\MSSQL.1\MSSQL\Binn\sqlctr.ini
```

The procedure is very similar for a named instance or a clustered server. In these cases the instance name or Virtual Server name is included in the unload and load commands. Feel free to execute this procedure on a non-production server that is healthy prior to production changes. You should see that on a normal server you can successfully unload and reload counters on demand.

If after carrying out these steps the counters still don't appear, there is a Microsoft Knowledge Base article that details a procedure to rebuild the entire Performance Counter library. It might be worth looking up this article if you're still not seeing the counters you expect.

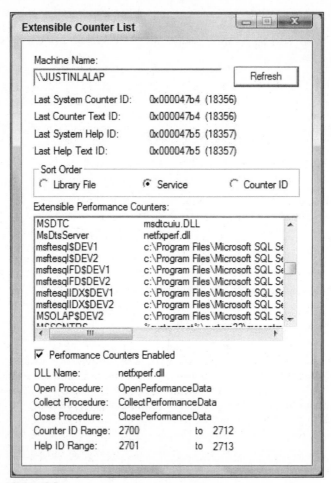

Figure 2-5

Built-in Log Management Tools

There are two tools of choice provided within Windows to assist with log automation, log handling, and interpreting log data. This section provides an overview and in some cases samples of these tools and utilities.

LogMan

You can use LogMan to schedule the start and stop of logging. This is a useful alternative to using the Windows AT scheduler or the Performance Monitor features to achieve similar results. The benefits of LogMan over configuring scheduling within individual Performance Monitor instances is that LogMan enables you to configure a data collection and to copy that collection to multiple computers from a single location. A data collection is essentially a System Monitor log definition.

Once you've defined a data collection, you're able to copy this to all target servers and then centrally control the start and stop of logging. The following command can be used to create a data collection that will run for two hours from 11 p.m. (23:00:00) and sample % Processor Time, Average Disk Queue Length, and Available Bytes every 30 seconds:

```
Logman create counter nightly_log -b 7/27/2007 23:00:00 -e 7/28/2008 01:00:00
-r -o "D:\logs\nightlylog" -c "\Processor(_Total)\% Processor Time"
"Physical Disk\Average Disk Queue Length" "\Memory\Available bytes" -si 00:30
```

You may also use the following command to query a data collection or currently running log:

```
Logman query
Logman query nightly_log
```

Relog

Provided with Windows, Relog is a command line tool that enables administrators to extract and manipulate performance counter data from System Monitor logs. For example, Relog allows users to resample from a performance log, changing characteristics such as the sample interval and output format. Additionally, you may also use relog to insert an entire log file into a database. Relog simply requires an ODBC DSN name, and it will load the performance data directly into a database for analysis and reporting purposes. The following command resamples an existing log file with a sample time of 30 seconds and provides a list of the counters recorded:

```
Relog D:\logs\11am.blg -cf ctr_list.txt -o D:\Logs\smallerint.csv -t 30 -f csv
```

Another helpful function of Relog is to combine log files. This can be useful if you're running continuous performance monitoring, but a service restart or reboot interrupts monitoring, causing log files to be split but covering consecutive timeframes. Relog allows these log files to be concatenated to produce a new log file with the following command:

```
Relog logA.blg logB.blg logC.blg -o logALL.blg
```

Beware when running this: As you append more and more files to the end, the target log file can become somewhat large (and thus harder to manage in itself). Once the logs have been combined, you can make use of the −b and −e switches to extract performance data relating to a specific timeframe.

Analyzing Log Data

Much of the discussion to this point has been concerned with the collection of data, how you can minimize the impact of monitoring, and acquire meaningful data. The ability to import System Monitor performance data into SQL Profiler has been discussed, and this significantly reduces the time and effort required to correlate specific user activity with server performance characteristics.

This section looks at two other tools available out of the box or provided freely for performance data analysis of Windows and SQL Server. The availability and scope of these tools has improved greatly recently, and future releases promise to hold further improvements to make log data analysis more accessible and more convenient.

LogParser

Well-known and well-loved by web server administrators for analyzing IIS log files, LogParser can be used for examining a range of log file types, and the output can be manipulated to various forms. Once installed on a server, LogParser allows SQL-like querying of log files. This can be really useful when searching all manners of Windows event logs, IIS Logs, or performance logs. LogParser is part of the Windows Resource Kit, and is available as a standalone download from the Microsoft web site. Figure 2-6 gives some idea of the multitude of formats accepted as inputs, and output options from LogParser.

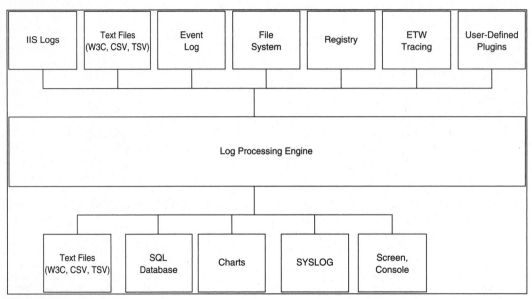

Figure 2-6

When analyzing raw Performance Log data, you'll first need to execute relog to convert the raw .BLG files into a format that can be directly read by LogParser, such as .CSV.

Performance Analysis of Logs

Performance Analysis of Logs (PAL) is a great new tool for interpreting Performance logs that is available from an Open Source Project Hosting location at www.codeplex.com/pal. Developed by Clint Huffman from the Microsoft Product Support team for Microsoft Biztalk, this tool includes XML templates for performance thresholds that can be configured to suit your environment. The concept behind the tool being open source is that users will contribute their own XML templates for various reusable scenarios. A number of XML templates are available that have been put together with the Microsoft Product Support teams with recommended threshold values (while still being completely configurable to your environment).

PAL simplifies analysis of large volumes of data or can be useful for comparing performance data from different systems. The development cycle is short; consequently new and better versions are regularly available. A GUI version has been recently released that builds the command line instead of the user having to construct this. PAL uses LogParser, which must be installed on the system, and it currently supports Windows XP, Vista, and Windows Server 2003 all with Office Web Components installed.

PAL uses a traffic light system to flag areas for attention within the performance logs, and summarizes these really nicely in an HTML page. Clearly the relevance of the traffic light system is dependent on you customizing the suggested thresholds to those that will be meaningful within your environment. Figure 2-7 provides an illustration of the type of output you can expect.

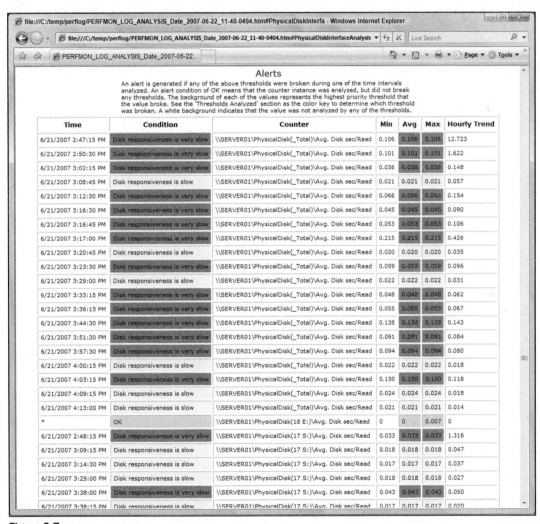

Figure 2-7

With the recently released GUI and much momentum behind the project, future releases promise to make this tool even more powerful and easier to use. Combined with contributions from the open source community, as more performance templates are developed and made available, the relevance and ease of adoption will improve too.

Summary

System Monitor is a powerful tool. While it doesn't yield all the answers, it's certainly key to gaining a holistic understanding of server performance. When used in combination with SQL Profiler and Dynamic Management Views (DMVs), most System Administrators should be able to quickly qualify the scope of a problem and drill down to the root cause.

While System Monitor itself has remained largely unchanged for a number of versions of Windows, tools which facilitate automation of performance data collection have eased the administration burden. This is especially true of groups of remote servers where scripted proactive monitoring has become very accessible. Additionally, log analysis continues to progress, distilling the "black art" myth that exists within many organizations around deep performance analysis. The availability of PAL is exciting. Although this simplifies log file interpretation, undoubtedly there's still skill and experience required to ensure results are not misread and appropriate corrective action is taken.

Following the best practices described in this chapter should improve your experience using System Monitor. Make sure you don't add too many counters to begin with; instead, get comfortable with a small set under differing workloads and build from there. Ensure you have a baseline of each of your key servers so that you can build your experience and confidence in proactive monitoring. Maintaining regular system baselines will place you in a position of authority should a performance issue arise; you'll be able to run System Monitor and immediately diagnose what's changed, which can be very powerful.

3

Monitoring SQL Server Resources with System Monitor

When you've established SQL Server as the likely cause of your performance problem, the next step is to drill down to identify the specific SQL Server resource bottleneck causing the issue. When you've located the cause, the next step (and the purpose of this whole activity) is to resolve the problem. System Monitor is able to help with preliminary steps in identifying and resolving SQL Server bottlenecks. Additionally there are a number of tools to allow excellent visibility of SQL Server internals.

Understanding how and when to use System Monitor are both important as this determines the quality of the data collected. You may have had poor experiences with System Monitor in the past. Perhaps this was because you were collecting too much, or not the right kind of data — meaning that you don't see the value this tool can provide. The challenge is multi-layered: collecting the right data, at the right time, and knowing what to do with it. At the end of this chapter, you should be familiar with:

❑ Identifying SQL Server resource issues with System Monitor

❑ Understanding configuration versus schema problems

❑ Knowing best practices for monitoring SQL Server with system monitor

One of the numerous significant improvements in SQL Server 2005 is improved supportability; this means better out-of-the box tools for administration and troubleshooting. SQL Server Profiler and the Database Tuning Advisor (DTA) have both been improved to enable easier monitoring and shorter time to identify and resolve issues. Positioning these tools, and familiarizing yourself with each of them will enable you to use the right tool the first time when working on a production performance problem. You should feel encouraged and interested in identifying a performance problem — these are typically challenging and may require computer architecture and software implementation experience and as a result are usually very satisfying once resolved. Almost every performance problem will offer you an opportunity to learn more about how Windows, SQL Server, and your specific applications communicate and respond to each other.

The Beginning

System Monitor is the beginning of performance troubleshooting. The tool does a great job of providing a real time overview and logging of system performance data. There are a number of other applications and functionality that you should consider part of your troubleshooting toolset. In fact, these tools are so good and enable you to harvest such a lot of useful information that the rest of this book is dedicated to their use!

In SQL Server 2000 some of this diagnosis information was exposed through system tables such as sysprocesses. However, there wasn't always sufficient detail to enable you to determine the root cause of a problem. As such, memory dumps were frequently required to enable detailed performance analysis — for most customers these were difficult to obtain; the process was time consuming and usually resulted in a support call to Microsoft for analysis. Microsoft has reviewed these cases, and in an attempt to reduce the cost to them of supporting SQL Server 2005 and improving customer satisfaction with the product they have provided extensive information on the SQL Server Operating System (SQLOS) and internal structures through Dynamic management views (DMVs).

There are few genuine performance problems that you'll be able to resolve with any one tool; most will require data from at least two and often three separate tools to be analyzed and interpreted to identify and resolve the bottleneck. The purpose of this chapter is for you to understand how and when to use System Monitor. Invariably, in many poor performance situations, you'll reach a point when you'll need a SQL Profiler trace or DMVs to reveal more information. By the end of this chapter you should be familiar with the point at which this switch should take place and by the end of the book, you should be comfortable with how to use these other tools too!

System Monitor should be considered largely un-intrusive, assuming sensible sample intervals and a realistic number of counters monitored. System Monitor has the advantage of availability on every Windows server — there are many other third-party applications specifically targeted at meeting similar need. However these usually require additional license purchases and most organizations will have some change control or acceptance process.

Types of Performance Problems

In its simplest form, performance problems have as many potential causes as the number of hardware and software components in a system. On this basis the scope of an individual problem can be quite huge, but it is possible to reduce this scope somewhat. Typically we can characterize SQL Server performance problems in one of two areas:

❑   Configuration-based performance problems

❑   Schema-based performance problems

That isn't to say that every single SQL Server performance problem you'll ever investigate will fall into one of these two areas, but it provides a useful logical grouping for most problems. The following section provides further detail on the classification of each problem area, with examples of the types of problems you can expect to see within each problem area.

Configuration-Based Performance Problems

SQL Server doesn't require any specialist knowledge to install and get started with databases, but this can be its downfall at times. There are often cases where server engineers are asked to install and configure SQL Server and make decisions based on assumptions or unfamiliarity with the product. Common examples include not separating data and log files onto separate disks (where performance gains can be made through Input/Output (I/O) optimization by the disk controllers reducing disk head movement. A similar example is an sp_configure option within SQL Server that calls Priority Boost, which sounds attractive, almost too good to be true — a hidden switch that makes SQL Server go faster! In fact Priority Boost can reduce SQL Server performance by prioritizing activity over that of the operating system (which is why it's disabled by default). There are some niche cases where there is a performance gain, but generally this would require detailed testing in a lab environment to qualify enabling this switch.

From this discussion, it becomes apparent that configuration-based performance problems generally fall into two further sub-areas:

❏ Hardware/operating system configuration
❏ SQL Server configuration

Microsoft invests a great deal of time and energy in determining the default values for each configuration setting within Windows and SQL Server itself. In most situations, the scenarios under which customers operate SQL Server fall within the use-case scenarios that map to the default configuration values.

However, there may be times when this one-size-fits-all approach might not meet your requirements and there are many good reasons to change a number of settings. It's important that you have undertaken an initial baseline and then performance test to measure the impact of any settings you change.

Schema-Based Performance Problems

SQL Server as a database platform allows customers to host an increasingly diverse array of applications, storing new data types and with new connectivity options. On this basis, performance of the SQL Server database engine is to a large extent dependent on good database design and implementation. Regardless of how fantastic the SQL Server query optimizer operates, there are relatively few design issues that the database engine can overcome entirely. While fast hardware and the latest version of SQL Server may compensate for some design flaws, this approach is fairly limited in terms of scalability and can restrict return on investment for the business.

In many cases the best opportunity to optimize the database schema is while designing the database. Understanding the type of the data stored and the method and frequency of retrieval will influence the design and overall approach. Changing the database schema when an application has already been written may require application changes, which can be time-consuming and therefore often expensive and risk-prone.

Achieving a fully normalized database can be an interesting challenge. Adhering to the structured procedure for normalization typically results in an academically correct database schema. It is important to consider the way users interact with the database to apply design adjustments based on data access patterns. Common design decisions that may negatively affect database performance include poor choice of keys, schema over-normalization, and missing or inappropriate indexes. Each of these can be addressed in turn. More detail is provided in Chapter 8.

Indexes are important because they can significantly reduce the cost of query execution. The query optimizer is responsible for evaluating execution plans and determining the lowest cost plan, which is then cached in memory (so that it may be re-used by subsequent executions of queries with the same structure). The cost of executing a query is an arbitrary value determined by cost for the resources required to deliver query results. Indexes are important to the query optimizer because they reduce the number of reads required to return a result set. Disk Input/Output (I/O) is almost always the slowest task when returning results to an application or user. As a result the purpose of indexes is to reduce the number of reads required to locate a particular row or set of rows.

Indexes are much like the contents page at the front of this book or the alphabetical index at the end of the book. These indexes need to be maintained. For example, if a new section is added to this book or if content is changed or removed when revising editions, the indexes should be updated to reflect these changes. In much the same way, indexes within a database should be maintained to ensure the data referenced is still present and valid. You've probably guessed by now that there is some overhead involved in maintaining indexes, particularly in environments where there is a high level of new data inserted or changes to current data.

Ultimately there's a balance to achieve where indexes are useful and improve query execution performance while maintenance overhead is manageable. Determining this balance up-front at design time can be achieved if detailed knowledge of patterns of user activity is known. (A typical situation is where an existing system is being replaced or upgraded.) However, in situations where you're working on a brand new implementation, these should be regularly reviewed to ensure relevance and accuracy. SQL Server 2005 has a great DMV, which allows you to evaluate index usefulness. This means that evaluating index usefulness is significantly improved compared with SQL Server 2000, where deep analysis of SQL Profiler traces was required to extract the same information!

SQL Server creates statistics automatically (if the default settings haven't been changed); these are used when the query optimizer is evaluating index usefulness. Statistics model the shape of data by sampling at pre-determined intervals throughout the entire data set. Statistics are then recorded with the data and used by the query optimizer to estimate how many rows will be returned by executing various components of a query. The query optimizer will iterate through different combinations of reading tables directly and using indexes, once the optimum execution plan is identified. This will be executed, and the execution plan will be held in cache in case it needs to be re-used by a query executing with the same structure in the future.

Types of Bottlenecks

A bottleneck is any resource restricting database performance. The purpose of performance troubleshooting is to identify any resource causing a bottleneck and resolve it. For example, with a server running with 100 percent CPU utilization, you could say there was a CPU bottleneck.

Bottlenecks are many and various. Often performance troubleshooting is an iterative process whereby a number of problems are identified and resolved before an optimal configuration is determined. You should be working toward a database server that provides acceptable performance and is balanced in terms of resource utilization (that is, there isn't one resource that is completely exhausted while others have spare capacity).

Bottlenecks are often grouped into three areas: Memory, Disk, and CPU. These are listed in order of likely occurrence with SQL Server implementations. SQL Server is dependent on all of these components to perform well. However, it is especially reliant on memory to hold data pages that have been read from or are waiting to be written to disk. A lack of memory can severely impact performance as SQL Server may be forced to read data pages from disk (instead of memory, which is much faster). In some low-memory situations, SQL Server may be paged to disk by Windows. Again, this will cause performance to suffer as disk access is much slower than memory access.

Almost as important as memory, a healthy disk subsystem is required to allow SQL Server to read and write data pages as quickly as possible. Poor disk throughput can cause delays in data being read or written and can have a direct impact on user experience.

There are times when SQL Server will be asked to calculate sums, re-order data, or join tables (plus many other operations provided by SQL Server) that may require CPU cycles to action. In these situations, availability and responsiveness of the CPUs will be important and may impact user experience if these aren't readily available. For this reason making sure there are sufficiently free CPU resources is key to ensuring good response times from SQL Server.

Memory Bottlenecks

In so many performance problem scenarios, it seems as though memory is an easy target, blamed by system administrators the world over. There are a small handful of performance counters that will allow you to correlate performance data to determine whether memory is a bottleneck in your environment.

SQL Server performance and stability are entirely dependent on sufficient available memory. A memory shortage often results in Windows serving the virtual address space (VAS) from the paging file, which will usually have an immediate and very apparent impact on performance. The first stage is to identify that you are actually seeing a memory bottleneck. After you've established a memory problem, you can then work to discover whether you have internal or external memory pressure.

Understanding the nature and characteristics of memory problems will help with early identification of these conditions and help you make a decision about the best route to resolution.

Types of Memory Bottlenecks

Memory problems experienced on SQL Server machines can typically be categorized in two ways: VAS or physical. If memory pressure is caused by the process itself, it's usually considered internal memory pressure. Physical memory pressure is usually caused by other Windows processes.

External Memory Pressure

External memory pressure can occur on servers running SQL Server alongside other applications that may be competing for memory. From a SQL Server perspective, you'll see Windows signal to the Resource Monitor within SQL Server Operating System (SQLOS) a request for SQL to reduce its committed memory. This will cause SQL to recalculate its target commit level and if required reduce its commit level (although this won't ever reduce to less than the sp_configure min server memory setting).

In order to determine if you're experiencing external physical memory pressure, take a look at the following counters:

❑ **Process — Working Set:** This shows the size of recently referenced pages in each process's virtual address space. Looking for the top memory consumers from this output will give you a good idea of any applications outside SQL Server which are consuming lots of memory! Take a look at the following counters to determine whether SQL Server has access to enough memory:

❑ **SQLServer:Buffer Manager — Total Pages:** This Buffer Manager/Total Pages counter will expose the total number of pages acquired by SQL Server.

❑ **SQLServer:Buffer Manager — Target Pages:** This Buffer Manager/Target Pages counter records the ideal number of pages required for the SQL Server Buffer Pool.

If the target and total pages values are the same, SQL Server has sufficient memory. If the target is greater than the total, it's likely that some external memory pressure (usually another Windows process) is preventing SQL Server acquiring as much memory as it would like to operate.

Internal Memory Pressure

Internal memory pressure is typically caused by shrinking the buffer pool. In this situation the buffer pool has reduced in size — perhaps as a result of a reduction in Max server memory sp_configure setting leaving SQL Server with a buffer pool that is too small.

A further cause of internal memory pressure could be tasks that consume memory within the SQL Server process space but outside the buffer pool. Extended stored procedures, COM objects, SQLCLR, and linked servers are all examples of components that may consume process space and could cause pressure on the buffer pool.

If you suspect internal memory pressure, you'll need to look at the sys.dm_os_memory_clerks DMV or take a look at the Buffer Counts section of DBCC MEMORYSTATUS output to confirm whether this is the case. The most useful values provided by the buffer count output section are the Committed and Target memory values. The committed memory is the amount of memory that SQL Server has been able to acquire. Target memory is the amount of memory SQL Server would like in order to operate effectively. On a *warm server* (a server which has SQL Server running for some time), with adequate virtual memory, you should expect to observe committed memory and target memory values that are approximately the same. If you're seeing a difference between committed and target memory on a warm server, you should investigate memory consumption further to see if there's a problem.

Confirming Memory Bottlenecks

In order that you satisfy yourself that you really do have a performance problem, there are a number of performance counters you should evaluate once you've checked the standard Available Bytes, Pages/second, and Paging File utilization counters. These counters will allow you to positively identify SQL Server as being short of memory or otherwise:

❑ **SQLServer:Buffer Manager — Page Life Expectancy:** The Page Life Expectancy counter within the Buffer Manager refers to the duration in seconds that a data page is likely to reside in the buffer pool. The longer the page life expectancy, the healthier the server looks from a memory perspective. A server suffering from memory pressure will typically see page life expectancy values of 300 seconds or below. If you find this, you'll have reasonable grounds to suspect a low memory condition. Similarly, if during monitoring you observe any significant drops in page life expectancy, this would be a cause for concern. If you're able to correlate any drops in performance with perceived application performance issues (assuming the poor performance isn't completely continuous), this could be very valuable in understanding the performance issue.

❑   **SQLServer:Buffer Manager — Buffer cache hit ratio:** The buffer cache hit ratio reports the number of pages requested by a query that were found in the SQL Server buffer pool (in physical memory). If data pages are not found in the buffer, SQL Server must read them into the buffer from disk. This is usually a slow process because of disk latency and seek times. Even on a responsive enterprise SAN, the time to read a page from disk compared with time to read a page from memory is many multiples greater.

❑   The size of the buffer pool is determined by the sp_configure min and max server memory options. It's worth noting that just because you've configured these options, that doesn't mean that SQL Server has been able to reserve this memory. This is especially true on a shared server where other applications may reserve that memory faster than SQL Server and the operating system is unable to release the memory addresses to SQL Server.

Best Practice

You should plan for a buffer pool of sufficient size to achieve at least a 98 percent buffer cache hit ratio. While monitoring, if you observe a buffer cache hit ratio of less than 98 percent, it's likely that the server doesn't have sufficient free memory.

❑   **SQLServer:Buffer Manager — Stolen pages:** Stolen pages are those pages in memory which are stolen by another process. Servers which are experiencing memory pressure will typically show high quantities of stolen pages relative to the total target pages. More detailed information on memory pressure can be obtained with the DBCC MEMORYSTATUS command from a query window.

❑   **SQLServer:Memory Manager — Memory Grants Pending:** Memory grants pending is effectively a queue of processes awaiting a memory grant. In general, if you have any processes queuing waiting for memory, you should expect degraded performance. The ideal situation for a healthy server is no outstanding memory grants.

❑   **SQLServer:Buffer Manager — Checkpoint pages/sec:** The SQL Server checkpoint operation requires all dirty pages to be written to disk. The checkpoint process is expensive in terms of disk input/output (I/O). When a server is running low on memory the checkpoint process will occur more frequently than usual as SQL Server attempts to create space in the buffer pool. If you observer sustained high checkpoint pages/second compared with normal rates for your server, it's a good indication of a low memory condition.

❑   **SQLServer:Buffer Manager — Lazy writes/sec:** This counter records the number of times per second that SQL Server relocates dirty pages from the buffer pool (in memory) to disk. Again, disk I/O is expensive and you should attempt to provide SQL Server with enough space for the buffer pool that lazy writes are as close to zero as possible. If you're seeing lazy writes of 20 per second or more, then you can be sure the buffer pool isn't big enough.

Configuration-Based Memory Bottlenecks

There are two groups of memory problems that you should be familiar with; these are internal memory pressure and external memory pressure. External memory pressure arises when SQL Server can't acquire enough memory. This might be because there isn't sufficient memory in the server or because of competition with another process or application running on the same server. Internal memory pressure generally refers to memory consumers within SQL Server, and these will typically require DMVs or DBCC commands to investigate.

Memory pressure itself isn't necessarily a problem and doesn't always result in poor performance or problems. Understanding the capacity of a server and how close it's running to maximum capacity is useful and will help you understand behaviors/characteristics of server behavior later on.

There's an important differentiator to make between virtual address space (VAS) and physical memory. Each Windows process has a VAS, and the size of the VAS varies with architecture (32bit or 64bit) and the operating system. The VAS is a fixed resource which could be exhausted (even on a 64bit server) while there could be physical memory available.

Memory within SQL Server is separated into two regions, the buffer pool and the MemToLeave area. The size of the buffer pool is controlled using the Min and Max server memory options in `sp_configure`. SQL Server uses the buffer pool to store data pages read from or waiting to be written to disk. The MemToLeave area is sized dynamically based on the number of worker threads (see the CPU section — this is determined by the processor architecture and number of processors). MemToLeave is a completely separate memory address range and can be used by linked servers, extended stored procedures, COM objects, or third-party DLLs.

A common misconception is that you can control the amount of memory consumed by SQL Server with the min and max server memory settings. This isn't accurate because this only controls the buffer pool and there may be many other consumers of SQL memory space outside the buffer pool (components such as linked servers, extended stored procedures, SQLCLR and COM objects, and so on) influencing the size of the memory space known as the MemToLeave area.

Schema-Based Memory Bottlenecks

Schema-based memory bottlenecks are a little harder to detect with System Monitor. If you were in a situation where you had identified internal memory pressure, it would be natural for you to evaluate activity on the server to determine if there are any schema changes which may reduce memory pressure. These may include inappropriate join syntax, or sub-optimal join or merge syntax involving excessive reads or sorts in order to complete joins.

In this scenario you'd probably be experiencing some form of memory pressure but you'd be unlikely to determine the specifics of what and where with System Monitor. SQL Server has several tools which are specifically designed to make this kind of information readily available; these are DMVs, DBCC commands, and SQL Profiler.

Specifics around which DMVs are best to use and how to take a SQL Profiler trace is covered in some detail in the chapters following this.

CPU Bottlenecks

If you find yourself in a situation where the process `sqlservr.exe` is consuming the lion's share of your CPU cycles, you'll already have a good idea that something has gone wrong within SQL Server.

Typically you'll hear problem reports from users who may be experiencing poor performance or connection timeouts. You might be in a position where you've run Task Manager and perhaps even System Monitor and you've observed excessive CPU utilization that is caused by SQL Server. Now you'll need to determine the cause of this CPU demand within SQL Server to try to get a better understanding of the cause of the CPU activity. As with most resource shortages, high CPU conditions could be triggered by mis-configuration of the hardware or operating system or could be related to problems with the database schema.

Confirming CPU Bottlenecks

In a situation where you suspect a CPU bottleneck, it can be fairly straightforward to confirm this with the following counters in System Monitor:

❑ **System — Processor Queue Length:** If your processors are constantly busy, you'll expect to see a queue building. Any queue for processors has the potential to impact user experience. Therefore, monitor queue length closely as any consistent queue will inevitably impact overall performance. If queue length is averaging more than three, then consider this a cause for concern.

❑ **Processor — %Privilege Time:** Privilege Time is time spent by the CPU servicing kernel mode activities — that is Windows internal operations. If CPUs spend too much time working on internal activities, performance will suffer significantly. For example, low memory conditions may cause excessive page faults which require CPU cycles for management. In this situation a low memory condition may present itself as a high-privilege time for CPUs.

❑ **Processor — %User Time:** User time is the time spent by the CPU working on requests for user mode applications, such as SQL Server. If there are configuration or schema problems, or excessive unqualified queries, these may lead to SQL Server consuming too much CPU time. Further investigation will be required to determine the specific process or batch within SQL Server causing the high CPU usage.

❑ **Processor — %User Time — sqlservr:** This counter shows the specific amount of CPU time consumed by the SQL Server process. It can be useful to conclude CPU consumption investigation by confirming whether high User Mode CPU activity is caused by SQL Server, and this counter will confirm this. Note that servers running multiple SQL instances will show sqlservr#2, sqlservr#3, and so on. It will be necessary to identify the instance you're monitoring by the Process ID (found in the SQL Server error log) and associate this with the running process list in Task Manager to determine which instance you should monitor.

❑ **SQLServer:SQL Statistics — SQL Compilations/sec and SQLServer:SQL Statistics — SQL Re-Compilations/sec:** A common cause of excessive CPU utilization, which could be caused by schema problems or low memory, conditions is query execution plan compilation and re-compilation. When compiled, plans should remain in memory — unless there is excessive memory pressure that may cause plans to be dropped from the cache. Additionally, if only ad hoc T-SQL is used or queries are not parameterized properly, SQL Server may not re-use any plans, or cause plan compilation for every query.

These counters should provide you with a good picture of CPU utilization and an understanding of whether the activity is generated by SQL Server. Based on these initial findings, you can investigate further to understand more about the origin of the CPU activity.

Configuration-Based CPU Bottlenecks

Typical configuration-based CPU bottlenecks could be related to incorrect configuration of Priority Boost, Maximum Degree of Parallelism, Max Worker Threads, Affinity Mask, and Hyper Threading. While handling processor issues, it's important to remember that SQL Server handles logical processors. This means SQL Server views all processors as equal, whether they're actual physical processors, multi-core, or hyper threaded. There is no way for SQL Server to differentiate between these types because to a large extent they appear as equal to Windows, too.

Throughout any performance investigation, it's important to keep in mind the sp_configure settings that relate to CPU configuration as these can significantly affect the workload shape and size on the processors. Unfortunately, there are no counters that provide direct recommendations for many of these settings, although Books Online and other whitepapers from Microsoft exist to assist in determining optimal configuration.

For example, when investigating a performance scenario involving uneven CPU load, it's imperative to understand the Affinity Mask and Maximum Degree of Parallelism settings as these should be considered when analyzing any performance logs.

Paging to Disk Can Cause High CPU

SQL Server should always run entirely in memory. Performance will suffer considerably if Windows uses the paging file to service SQL Server. There's a curious side effect of a server running low on memory, which is high CPU utilization. This is somewhat non-intuitive but is reasonably easy to identify, once you know what to look for! If you're monitoring a server which is seeing excessive CPU and you've identified this as privilege mode CPU activity, you should also monitor the Memory — Pages/sec counter.

This counter reveals the total number of pages that are input and output per second. On its own, this counter isn't sufficient to diagnose a low memory condition, but if you combined it with high privilege mode CPU and look at Memory — Available Bytes, a picture should start to form.

Best Practice

Ensure that the SQL Server buffer pool and memtoleave areas are sized to fit into application mode memory on your servers. This is especially important on multi-instance servers and failover clusters to ensure consistent performance and predictable failover times.

Schema-Based CPU Bottlenecks

There are a number of scenarios whereby issues with a database schema may result in excessive CPU utilization. To a certain extent, your ability to be able to proactively prevent some of these events is limited. However, recognizing the symptoms and being able to positively identify the problem will go a long way to understanding the problem and helping you investigate alternatives which may reduce the likelihood of a recurrence, if not eliminate it altogether.

Excessive Compilation/Recompilation

The rate of execution plan compilation and recompilation can be measured with the following system monitor counters:

- ❑   SQLServer:SQLStatistics — SQL Compilations/sec
- ❑   SQLServer:SQLStatistics — SQL Re-Compilations/sec

With a warm server (that is, a server that has been operating long enough to fill its buffers and charge its cache) you should expect to see at least 90 percent plan re-use. That is to say, no more than 10 percent of queries will require plan compilation during execution. More information can be gleaned from a SQL Profiler trace, which will often hold an insight into specific operations or stored procedures that are subject to recompiles.

Disk Bottlenecks

Moving data onto or off disk is almost always the most time-consuming (therefore expensive) operation SQL Server needs to undertake. SQL Server goes to great lengths to avoid the user having to wait while data is transferred between memory and disk because any slight delay in this process is likely to impact perceived server performance. To do this SQL Server has a buffer cache that it pre-loads with data and a plan cache that is loaded with optimal plans detailing the most efficient way to retrieve data.

There are a couple of factors which often mislead engineers working with SQL Server specifically when related to disk problems. The first is listening too much to the sales guy from the SAN manufacturers; the second is not having a baseline. Here's a summary of each of these:

SAN vendors have impressive marketing engines, and their representatives often penetrate deep into customer organizations — so much so that they'll come on-site and help you configure the SAN. Often these SAN engineers believe their own marketing pitch too. They can be heard making impressive claims about disk, controller, and cache performance on their particular SAN. However, few of them fully understand SQL Server and the patterns and I/O demands it places on the disk subsystem. No matter how fast the disk spindles rotate, how good the controllers operate, or how large the cache is, demanding OLTP applications running with SQL Server even on commodity hardware can nearly always request data be read from and written to disk at a rate much faster than any SAN can deliver.

Secondly, you should always have a baseline. Troubleshooting disk performance is one of those times when you'll nearly always wish that you took a baseline. When you're staring at disk queue lengths on various volumes and average latency, you'll usually be asking yourself these questions: Is this normal? Is there anything you should worry about here? In order to answer these questions, you'll need to know how the SAN was behaving yesterday, last week, or before the controller firmware was upgraded or a service pack was applied. In this position, if you have a baseline you'll be able to positively confirm the disk subsystem as behaving either within normal operating performance expectations or problematically.

Confirming Disk Bottlenecks

Once you're suspicious of a disk bottleneck, there are several key system monitor counters that you can use to confirm whether this is the case. If you have taken a baseline of system performance, you'll be in a strong position to compare data captured with these same counters against your baseline. If you don't have a baseline, you can use the guide values provided below to determine whether you should expect some sort of performance issue.

❑ **PhysicalDisk — Avg. Disk Queue Length:** Exactly as described in the counter name, this reports the queue length for each disk. Ensure you select the queue length on the drive letters, not for _TOTAL object. Although the average disk queue length can't usually be divided by the number of spindles participating in the array (as it used to be prior to SANs), it still provides a meaningful measure of disk activity. If the disk queue length is consistently above 2, it's likely to impact performance.

❑ **PhysicalDisk — Avg. Disk sec/Read and PhysicalDisk — Avg. Disk sec/Write:** This counter pair refers to the average disk time spent on each read or write. If there's a problem with the HBA queue depth, controller utilization, or disk performance, you should expect to see higher than usual times for each of these counters. The nature of your application (reads versus writes) will determine which or both counters are important to you. If either of these values is 20 ms or greater, you should expect perceived user experience to be affected — although ideally this should be 10 ms or less. You'll find further details on identifying and resolving storage performance problems in Chapter 13.

❑ **SQLServer:Access Methods — Full scans/sec:** This counter will provide visibility of the number of full index or base table scans requested per second. If you're seeing scan frequency greater than one per second, this could be indicative of poor or missing indexes.

❑ **SQLServer:Access Methods — Page Splits/sec:** Page splits are an I/O intensive operation that occur when there is insufficient space in an 8 KB data page to allow an insert or update operation to complete. In this circumstance a new page is added and the original data is shared between the two pages before the insert or update takes place. Too many page splits will harm performance. These can be avoided through proper index maintenance and good fill factor selection.

Identifying disk performance problems will lead you to review the design and implementation of the storage subsystem. Often this will involve some work to characterize the use of the storage and working with the storage administrators or vendor directly to eliminate performance bottlenecks or to redesign the storage with a better understanding of your workload.

Configuration-Based Disk Bottlenecks

After you've identified a disk-based bottleneck, potential resolutions are usually fairly readily available, although implementing these will depend on your hardware configuration and spare capacity. For example, if you identify a specific drive as having long read and write times, it's a relatively quick operation to examine what's on the drive and identify what can be moved elsewhere to spread the I/O load more evenly. If, however, this is a 2 TB database, it may require further planning to understand what spare capacity is available on the disk storage and logistics planning to evaluate the practicalities of moving a database of such size.

Data and Log File Placement

Separating data and log files has been a long-standing recommendation for SQL Server administrators. The typical OLTP platform will generally consist of fairly random read/write patterns across the data file, while the transaction log is usually written to sequentially and will see very little read traffic.

Best Practice

Consider grouping data files onto one LUN (Logical Unit Number, a unit of presentation from a SAN) and log files onto a separate LUN. This will allow the disk controller to better manage the two I/O patterns and service each type from the resources it has available.

Data and Log File Autogrowth

Data and log file autogrowth is enabled by default on all new databases. This operation will automatically grow these files in the background with no user intervention required. As you are aware, disk I/O activity is expensive in respect that it's often time consuming. The default growth increment for a data file is 1 MB increments with 10 percent growth rate for transaction log file. If these files aren't properly managed, imagine attempting to load data into a database that is inadequately sized, and the database is expanding in 1 MB increments. This will significantly impair performance.

Best Practice

Pro-actively manage data and log file growth. This means pre-empt any auto-grows by manually controlling them. This way you can be sure they happen in a controlled way during periods of low activity and at sensible growth increments. You should consider data and log file autogrowth very much as a safety net.

Tempdb Configuration

SQL Server uses tempdb as a holding area during join, sort, and calculation operations as well as by the version store. Depending on the type of applications and user activity within SQL Server, the performance of tempdb can directly affect user experience. Under workloads that make extensive use of tempdb, it's worth planning the placement and size of tempdb to ensure optimal performance.

Best Practice

Size tempdb sufficiently to ensure no autogrowth will be required. It's important that the initial file size is correctly specified as well, otherwise a service restart can result in tempdb being sized at the default size.

Tempdb is shared by all databases within an instance. At times it can itself become a resource bottleneck. It's therefore important that the configuration is optimized to make best use of the resources available. One of the ways to achieve this is to create a separate data file per CPU. This allows CPUs round-robin access to the tempdb files, often achieving better performance than with a single data file.

Best Practice

Create one tempdb data file per CPU or core. (Hyperthreaded processors aren't included.) This will help achieve better Tempdb performance, particularly where user activity is resource-intensive on Tempdb.

Contention Within Tempdb

Tempdb is transient — it only exists while the SQL Server service is running. Tempdb is a shared global resource. This means if one database or application is heavily dependent on tempdb, other databases within the same instance may suffer performance problems which are outside their control.

There are a number of features new to SQL Server 2005, such as online index rebuilds, where a version store can be held within tempdb to maintain data availability during index rebuild operations. System monitor counters are available to report free space in tempdb and the version store size, and the following counters can be useful to get an idea of the tempdb workload:

❑ **SQLServer:General Statistics — Temp Tables Creation Rate:** Reveals the number of temporary tables or variables created per second.

❑ **SQLServer:General Statistics — Temp Tables For Destruction:** Shows the number of temporary tables that are no longer required and are awaiting destruction by the system thread that carries out cleanup.

Additionally, there are a number of DMVs that may help you understand the nature of use of tempdb. One common concern is to understand the top consumers of space within tempdb. This can be ascertained by joining the sys.dm_db_task_ space_usage and sys.dm_exec_requests. Here's a sample query that maybe useful in determining tempdb space used by each server process:

```
select tsu.session_id
     , tsu.request_id
     , tsu.alloc_count
     , tsu.dealloc_count
     , er.sql_handle
     , er.statement_start_offset
     , er.statement_end_offset
     , er.plan_handle
from (
     select session_id
          , request_id
          ,sum (internal_objects_alloc_page_count) as alloc_count
          ,sum (internal_objects_dealloc_page_count) as dealloc_count
     from sys.dm_db_task_space_usage
     group by session_id, request_id
) as tsu
     , sys.dm_exec_requests as er
```

```
     where tsu.session_id = er.session_id
           and tsu.request_id = er.request_id
     order by tsu.alloc_count desc
```

Once you've identified the top consumers of tempdb space, you should look to see how you can optimize or modify the stored procedures or activity to reduce the reliance on tempdb.

Disks/ Controller Contention

System Monitor provides sufficient data to identify a problem area. However, it often lacks the access or visibility of controller and disk activity. Most SAN vendors provide tools to meet this specific requirement, and if you suspect a disk or controller performance problem, it will be worthwhile to investigate the tools provided by the SAN vendor to gain visibility of the disk group configuration, Logical Unit Number (LUN) allocation, and cache configuration. These tools can usually monitor each of these components and capture performance data that can be useful during troubleshooting.

Schema-Based Disk Bottlenecks

There are a number of ways you can look to make schema changes that can help reduce or distribute the load placed on the disk sub-system by SQL Server. These options should be considered carefully in the context of your application and hardware environment. Testing will often be required in order to determine the most effective approach.

Inappropriate or Missing Indexes

The Database Tuning Advisor (DTA) is often the most effective approach if you're unsure of the database schema or usage patterns. DTA replaced the Index Tuning Wizard of SQL 2000. It has been significantly improved to more accurately recommend additional indexes and changes or removal of existing indexes if they're ineffective. Additionally, DTA is able to script the recommendations, simplifying the process.

Additionally, there is a DMV called sys.dm_db_index_usage_stats that reports information on the data and frequency of use of indexes. This can be useful in identifying indexes that are not selected by the optimizer and as such are candidates to be dropped.

Files and File Groups

Files and file groups provide opportunity to relocate individual objects, such as tables or indexes in a separate file. This can be useful if you can identify specific objects which are in high demand and are causing disk I/O problems. If this is possible, moving these objects to a standalone drive may reduce the disk contention and improve overall performance. Typically these benefits can only be achieved if the new file is placed on its own drive or a separate LUN.

In the event that you are working with very large databases, or in an environment where the recovery window is short, file groups may assist in reducing the overall time to complete a backup or restore and will provide smaller units for these operations.

Partitioning

Table partitioning is a feature new to SQL 2005 that allows horizontal separation of data into separate tables. SQL Server will then manage the metadata to ensure this is transparent to the application. This can be advantageous in situations where different types of storage are available — typically short-term faster storage and longer-term slower storage. In situations where you're seeing performance degrade and you have one very large table, you could consider partitioning as a method to spread I/O across multiple partitions.

Index/Table Fragmentation

Index fragmentation occurs over time as data is added, changed, and deleted from a table. It's part of everyday life as a database and is unavoidable. When fragmentation is severe, it will impact performance because inserts require page splits which are I/O intensive and reads become ineffective because there is little valuable data held in each 8 KB data page retrieved from disk.

Fragmentation occurs in two forms; internal and external. Internal fragmentation refers to 8 KB data pages that have lots of free space (meaning they don't contain much data). External fragmentation refers to discontiguous data pages, which is to say that the data pages are not side by side on the disk. This results in increased movement in the disk head, which is slow. The DMV sys.dm_db_index_physical_stats will provide all the information you'll need about current fragmentation levels.

Indexes can only be rebuilt on tables with clustered indexes. Fragmentation can't be removed from heaps. Non-clustered indexes can be rebuilt at the same time or separately. The best way to remedy index fragmentation is with an ALTER INDEX command. This should be appended with the fully qualified index and schema names and then either REBUILD or REORGANIZE. The reorganize operation is more lightweight, but it can't resolve inter-leaved data and index pages (external fragmentation). An index rebuild is an I/O intensive operation that will resolve both internal and external fragmentation and can be carried out online with Enterprise or Developer editions of SQL Server 2005. Other editions allow the same result but require the table to be taken offline during the index maintenance operation.

Proactive and regular index reorganization will maintain indexes in a good state and should reduce the frequency with which index rebuilds are required. It's possible to put together a script which will interrogate the DMV mentioned previously and take the necessary corrective action — either a reorganize or a full index rebuild based on fragmentation levels identified by the DMV. This approach, together with some sort of audit trail for the activity history, is best practice and will mean you no longer have to worry about index or table fragmentation. Books Online for SQL Server 2006 contains a sample script to rebuild or reorganize indexes based on fragmentation levels. This may provide a useful starting point to customize for your environment.

> **Best Practice**
>
> Index maintenance is essential for continued SQL Server performance. Fragmentation occurs through everyday inserts, updates, and deletes. Use the DMVs and index maintenance operations mentioned above to ensure your indexes are properly maintained.

Monitoring Database Mirroring Performance

There are a number of counters which can be revealing when investigating performance problems with database mirroring. You can measure the performance of each database as well as mirroring within the entire server. When investigating performance problems with mirroring, you'll probably be interested in the latency between the principal and the mirror to determine how far behind the mirror is in applying changes made at the principal. The following counters will give you some idea as to the performance of database mirroring:

❑ **SQLServer:Database Mirroring — Log Bytes Sent/sec:** Shows the rate at which data is sent from the transaction log on the principal to the transaction log on the mirror.

❑ **SQLServer:Database Mirroring — Log Send Queue KB:** Shows the number of log bytes held in the transaction log buffer still to be sent to the mirror. Similarly, on the mirror server you can monitor the following counter to determine the rate at which the received transaction log is received:

❑ **SQLServer:Database Mirroring — Log Bytes Received/sec:** Following this, monitoring the size of the redo queue and redo bytes/ second will help you understand the rate at which the mirror is processing log data in order that it stays up to date with the principal.

Monitoring Wait Statistics

There is a new performance object for SQL Server 2005 that monitors wait types. This counter contains wait information for specific global resources that may experience contention and therefore cause performance problems.

Each counter object contains the same four instances that describe wait times (average and cumulative), waits in progress, or waits started per second.

❑ **SQLServer:Wait Statistics — Lock Waits:** This counter will give you an idea of whether processes are waiting too long to acquire locks. Measuring the ability of a process to acquire a lock is useful in terms of determining whether locking is an issue.

❑ **SQLServer:Wait Statistics — Memory Grant Queue Waits:** Shows the number of processes or length of time processes spend queuing waiting for memory grants to become available.

❑ **SQLServer:Wait Statistics — Page I/O Latches:** SQL Server requires latches to ensure data synchronization. The availability of latches directly affects SQL Server performance and as such, monitoring latches in the event of poor performance can be useful in identifying the root cause.

There are another nine performance counters within the Wait Statistics object, many of which can be useful in specific troubleshooting circumstances. Take a look through the description in SQL Server Books Online for a description of each of these, as you'll find it beneficial to be familiar with them.

Typical Performance Problems

When investigating any kind of performance problem, it's important to first identify the area of concern, and in many causes your first step should be to rule SQL Server in or out of suspicion.

The following section contains an overview of some typical SQL Server poor performance scenarios, using some of the counters discussed to gain visibility of the problem and a better understanding of the causes.

Typical Disk Problems

Disk problems are the most common type of performance problem since SQL Server is so dependent on disk I/O to serve the databases. Lack of proper housekeeping, poor initial disk design, or database architecture can all worsen over time. Figure 3-1 shows a disk with two volumes, where data was stored on T: and logs stored on drive S:

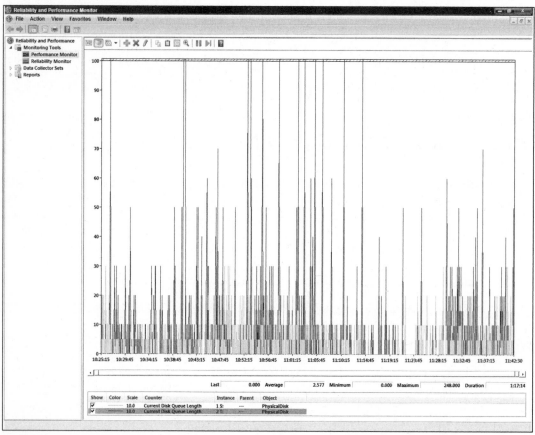

Figure 3-1

Here you'll see excessive disk queue lengths on the data partition, which caused SQL Server to appear unresponsive at times. Once identified, the problem was rectified by moving the busiest database to an isolated partition, which allowed normal response times to resume.

Memory

Figure 3-2 shows a memory problem with SQL Server operating normally until it receives notification from Windows to relinquish memory. In this case, an extended stored procedure, called within SQL

Server, caused the buffer pool to shrink. Here it would be relatively easy to identify SQL Server as being short of memory, and it's encouraging to see SQL Server respond positively to the request from the operating system for memory to be released.

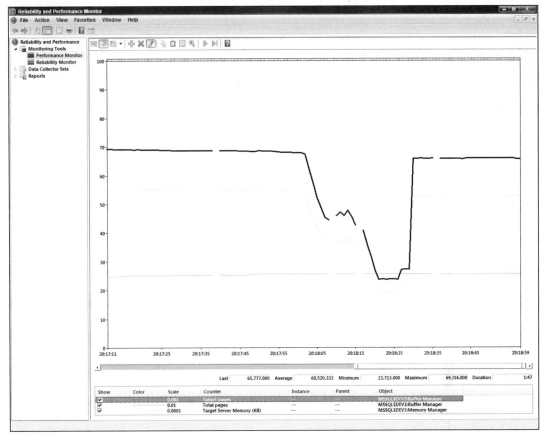

Figure 3-2

Typical CPU Problems

When looking into CPU problems, it's essential you identify early whether you have a kernel mode (internal windows operations) or application mode (SQL Server, or any other application) CPU consumption issue. You can determine this quite quickly with these three counters: % Processor Time, % Privilege Time, and % User Time. Figure 3-3 illustrates an isolated CPU problem (for example, when a specific CPU-intensive stored procedure is executed):

Remember that User Mode + Privilege Mode CPU activity will provide total CPU time. It's clear from this performance graph that while there is some Privilege mode activity, the majority of CPU work being carried out is User Mode activities. This can be identified because the User Mode activity line graph almost mirrors movements of the total CPU line on the graph.

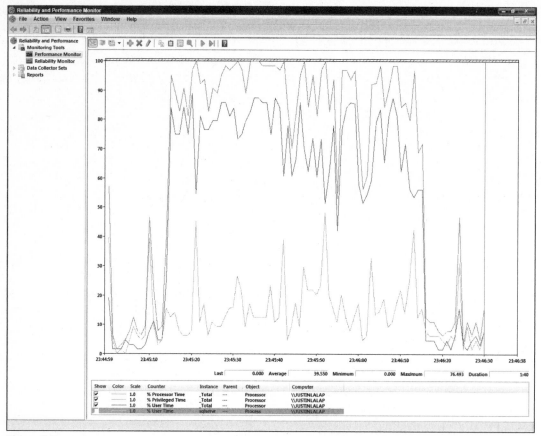

Figure 3-3

Now that you've confirmed a User Mode process is consuming the CPU time, you can drill down further by including details from the process object. Here you'll find a counter for each running process. In this case, adding the process % User Time for sqlservr.exe confirms that SQL Server is consuming the CPU cycles. See Figure 3-4.

Similar to the way % User Mode CPU mirrored the movement on the graph of Total CPU time, the movement of the sqlservr.exe process User Mode CPU time appears to be mirroring the Total User Mode CPU time, confirming SQL Server as the principal consumer of CPU cycles during this period! Once SQL Server has been identified as the culprit, SQL Profiler or the reports found in the Performance Dashboard (available on Service Pack 2 and greater machines) will allow you to identify the longest running queries/ stored procedures by CPU time. When you've found the resource intensive query, you can work to optimize through better query design or perhaps by adding an index.

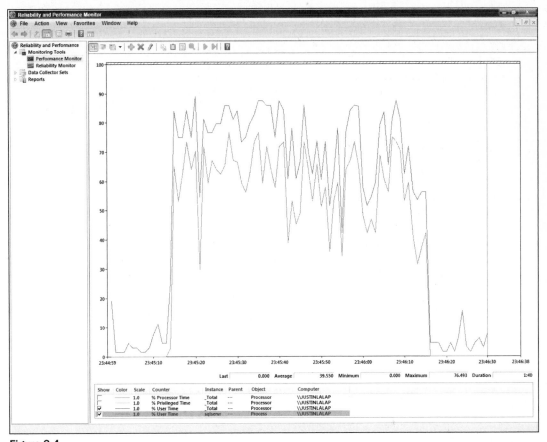

Figure 3-4

Using SQL Server to Analyze Performance Logs

As someone interested in SQL Server, you'll probably be comfortable with Transact-SQL and more interested in knowing how to analyze logs using TSQL than learning a specialist scripting tool for analyzing logs such as LogParser and so on. If this is true, then you'll be interested to learn there are a couple of ways to get performance data into SQL Server to enable you to manipulate and analyze the data in an environment you're already familiar with and making patterns or trends easier to identify.

If you think analyzing performance data in a SQL Server database sounds useful, there are two possible methods to achieve this:

❑   Configure System Monitor to log in live and direct to SQL Server

❑   Import performance data to SQL Server post data capture

Logging Directly to SQL Server

Using a regular ODBC DSN, you can configure System Monitor to log directly to a database. When monitoring is complete, performance data is immediately available for analysis directly within SQL Server. The CPU, memory, and disk resources required to administer monitoring and having a server logging directly to a SQL Server database will usually incur a fair amount of overhead. This could affect the server being monitored and thus the results of the monitoring. At the very least, monitoring overhead should be taken into account when recording performance baseline data and when making any recommendations to alter a configuration or schema.

As a second option, system monitor could be configured to populate a database on a remote server. This would reduce the monitoring overhead on the monitored server. However, it could affect the integrity of the results because these will include network time. Logging to a remote server, whether to the console, a flat file, or a SQL Server database, will include time for the data to travel across the network to the logging server. This isn't necessarily a problem if any network latency is consistent. However, due to the nature of networks, this can't usually be guaranteed.

Additionally, it is worth noting that Performance Monitor is supported when used with DSNs that use the MDAC SQLODBC driver. The SQL Native Client cannot be used as a data logging destination with Performance Monitor.

Importing Performance Log into SQL Server

The lowest monitoring overhead can usually be obtained by logging to a file saved locally (or perhaps remotely). Once the log has been created, it may be copied to a different computer for analysis or interrogation. SQL Server doesn't support directly reading or importing the .BLG (system monitor) file type, so one of the easiest ways is to re-save the data as a comma-separated values (CSV) file that can be readily imported into SQL Server. The import operation is driven by a wizard and will create the destination table ready for analysis with TSQL. The following procedure assumes you've already created and saved a .BLG file, and includes the operations required to import the data to SQL Server:

1.   Prepare the log file.

   a.   Open the saved .BLG file in System Monitor.

   b.   Add interesting counters (potentially all objects/counters, since they'll then be available within the database for inclusion/exclusion within queries).

2.   Save the log as a CSV file.

   a.   Right-click anywhere on the performance chart.

   b.   Click Save Data As.

   c.   Choose name and location for the file.

   d.   Select the Save as Type: Text File (comma delimited) (*.csv).

3. Create a new database.

    a. Launch SQL Server Management Studio.

    b. Create a new database to store the performance data.

4. Launch the Import Data Wizard.

    a. Right-click the database name.

    b. Highlight Tasks.

    c. Under the drop-down menu, select Import Data.

5. Configure the Data Source.

    a. Choose Flat File as the data source.

    b. Browse and select the CSV file created earlier in this procedure.

    c. Replace the text qualifier field with a double quote.

    d. Check Column names in the first data row (see Figure 3-5), and click Next.

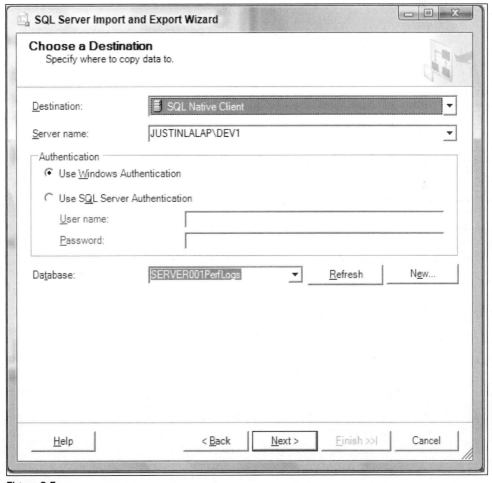

Figure 3-5

6. Configure the Destination. See Figure 3-6.

   a. Verify that the Destination database is correct and the connection credentials are valid.

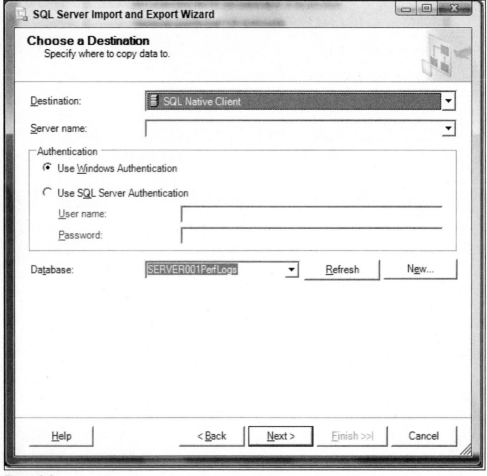

Figure 3-6

   b. Click Next when complete.
   c. Verify Source and Destination are correctly configured and click Next.
   d. Accept default Execute Immediately and click Next.
   e. Click Finish.
   f. Confirm the import execution was successful (see Figure 3-7).

You've now successfully imported the performance log into SQL Server, where a table has been automatically defined based on the source data. The column names will be configured with the full server and counter name, for example: [SERVER001 Memory Available Bytes]. Although this is meaningful, the name can be cumbersome to handle in a query. As such it's worth just spending a couple of minutes updating the column names with more manageable names.

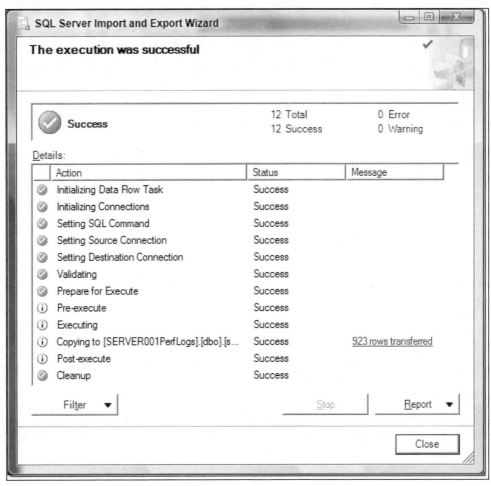

Figure 3-7

Now that the data is held within SQL Server, you should find it fairly trivial to make joins to determine the frequency of resource situations that you may find concerning. Consider a situation when you might like to find all instances where a server ran low on memory during a monitoring period. You'd first need to determine the characteristics (counters) and thresholds (values) that you'd consider representative of a low memory condition. Often these values will need to be tailored to your application and environment to be meaningful. As an example, you could consider the following scenario to represent a low memory situation:

- ❑ Available memory is less than 10 MB

- ❑ Page life expectancy less than 60 seconds

- ❑ Buffer cache hit ratio less than 90 percent

You'd be fairly confident that a server exhibiting all three of these symptoms was experiencing a low memory condition. You should be able to write a fairly simple query to determine whether the server you're monitoring has these symptoms. Although your columns may be defined with different names, a query such as this should provide this information:

```
SELECT *
FROM subset
WHERE Mem_Avail_Bytes < 100000
AND Buff_Mgr_Page_Life_Expect < 60
AND Buff_Cache_Hit_Ratio < 90
```

There are as many useful examples as there are counter combinations, and making the data available within a database means limiting searches by columns, date range, and pre-defined or template conditions is trivial. Additionally, with a little extra effort, Reporting Services could be used to present and deliver performance analysis findings.

Combining Performance Monitor Logs and SQL Profiler Trace

Troubleshooting performance related problems in SQL Server 2000 often required gathering Performance Monitor logs, SQL Profiler traces, and activity details from system tables such as sysprocesses. There was no capability provided to combine the log and trace data to provide any kind of unified view. Interpreting this data often required system administrators to undertake the arduous and pain-staking process of manually stepping through SQL Profiler traces and then switching to the same point in time of the Performance Monitor logs to gain an understanding of resource status while a specific query or stored procedure was executed. While laborious and time consuming, this method did allow system administrators to correlate SQL Server activity (Profiler) with resource utilization (Performance Monitor).

Fortunately, analysis of performance data has been significantly improved in SQL Server 2005 with a feature allowing importing of Performance Monitor log files into a SQL Profiler trace. The process is quite straight forward, and necessitates both Perfmon and Profiler traces be captured to file. Of course you'll need to configure each Profiler and Perfmon separately, although these should run simultaneously. Once the log and trace files have been created, you should open the trace file in SQL Profiler and from the file menu select Import Performance Data and select the Perfmon log file. Further details, including a screen capture of the end result (shown in Figure 2.4), can be found in Chapter 2, "Monitoring Server Resources with System Monitor."

Summary

System Monitor is an effective tool for gathering data about overall server and SQL Server performance. System Monitor can provide you with data to help identify and diagnose resource bottlenecks. SQL Server is provided with many System Monitor performance counters, SQL Profiler, dynamic management views, Database Tuning Advisor, and error logs to assist in troubleshooting. Knowing when to use each of these tools is important as they each perform a different role and provide access to performance data at different levels.

Once you're accustomed with using System Monitor to collect performance data, you'll be interested to know what tools are available to assist with analyzing the data in order to help you determine a performance baseline for capacity planning or future reference, as well as in troubleshooting scenarios. The longer monitoring continues, and the more servers or SQL instances that are monitored, the more important tools for managing the data become. SQL Profiler itself provides the powerful capability of combining system monitor data with profiler logs, which enables direct correlation between resources usage spikes and SQL execution on the server.

Taking a baseline of system performance during a period of normal activity will be invaluable when investigating any performance problems. Knowing CPU utilization, typical disk I/O, and memory consumption during a normal working day can significantly reduce the mean-time-to-resolution of performance-related issues, as this often takes the guess work out of decisions/recommendations.

Performance data can be logged directly or imported post-capture into a SQL Server database where TSQL and SQL Server Reporting Services make a powerful combination for managing and manipulating performance data, allowing fast access to the data required to make decisions and recommendations based on performance criteria.

4

SQL Server Wait Types

Now that you have a good idea of what's going on at the server level using System Monitor, you can start to look at what's going on within SQL Server. Think about what happens when you issue a query to update a row, for example:

1. The optimizer uses statistics to help decide on the best way to execute the query.
2. The query is executed.
3. The row will be read from disk into memory.
4. The update will be written to the transaction log.
5. The row will be changed in memory.
6. Confirmation will be sent back to the client.

Imagine if you could measure the amount of time that was spent waiting for things within each of these stages. It probably won't surprise you to read that this chapter doesn't end here and you can. Not only are monitoring waits possible, but they can actually form a very effective part of a performance troubleshooting strategy.

Wait time is effectively dead time, and if you can reduce the amount of time you spend waiting, you'll be able to achieve better overall performance. This chapter covers how SQL Server waits work, what types there are, and how to view and track them. It also covers common scenarios and their associated wait types. Because SQL Server waits represent just a single view of performance, you will also see when to correlate the results with the system monitor counters discussed in the previous chapter.

The chapter concludes with a closer look at a very common waiting scenario: locking and blocking.

SQL Server Waits

Whenever a task in SQL Server has to wait for something before it can continue, information on the reason for the wait is tracked by SQL Server and can be viewed through Dynamic Management Views (DMVs). Aggregating this data across all connections will give you a performance profile for SQL Server and tracking it for a particular connection will allow you to see what the bottleneck for a specific workload is.

All waits in SQL Server are categorized into wait types and can be grouped into three areas:

- ❑ **Resource waits:** Occur when the requested resource is unavailable.
- ❑ **Queue waits:** Occur when a worker is idle, waiting for work.
- ❑ **External waits:** Occur when waiting for an external event.

Resource waits, which include I/O, locking, and memory, tend to be the most common and provide the most actionable information and so receive the most attention in this chapter.

Architecture

The SQL Server Operating System (SQLOS) uses schedulers to manage the execution of user requests. The number of schedulers defaults to the number of logical CPUs in the server because only one scheduler at a time can be executing on a CPU. If you have a 4 CPU server, you'll have four schedulers, 8 if they are dual-core, and 16 if they are dual-core and hyper-threaded. See Chapter 6 for more details on CPU types and configuration.

Within a scheduler, a session (actually a task associated with a session) can be in one of three states: running, runnable, or suspended. (There are also three other states: pending, spinloop, and done; however, they're not important to the concept being discussed here.) Only one session can be *running* on a scheduler at any one time. All sessions waiting to run are in a *runnable* queue. Sessions that stopped executing to *wait* for something have a status of *suspended*. This is illustrated in Figure 4-1.

Windows uses a scheduling model called pre-emptive scheduling, which basically means that it decides when a thread running a task needs to make way for another task and switches it out. This works great for a server running lots of different services of equal importance, but for a server that is dedicated to running SQL Server it would be bad because a SQL Server task might get switched out unexpectedly to give a minor Windows task some CPU time. SQL Server instead has its own scheduler that uses a non-preemptive or cooperative model whereby it relies on all of its threads to yield processor time whenever that thread has to wait for something. It's a more efficient model for SQL Server because it knows that its threads will yield appropriately. For Windows, however, the threads could be running anything, so the pre-emptive model is better to guarantee performance.

In the diagram you can see that session_id 55 is currently executing, there are three sessions waiting on resources (which you'll see descriptions of later in this chapter), and there are four sessions in the runnable queue. The runnable queue contains sessions that are waiting to be scheduled some CPU time, so this represents a pure wait on the CPU, which we can translate into CPU pressure. Time in the runnable queue is measured as *signal wait* time.

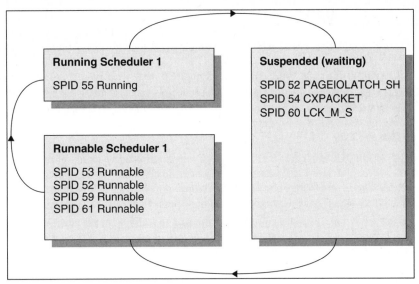

Figure 4-1

All this talk of waiting makes it sound like a horrendous thing to find on your system. In fact it's perfectly normal and expected to see waits. This is how SQL Server scales so efficiently. You're really looking for unexpected waits and large wait times when troubleshooting performance.

Common or Noteworthy Resource Wait Types

The following wait types are worthy of mention for their regularity in a system or because their meaning should be understood. For a description of all the wait types, search in SQL Server 2005 Books Online for `sys.dm_os_wait_stats`.

❑ **WAITFOR:** Is the resulting wait after issuing the WAITFOR T-SQL command. It is a manually instigated wait and shouldn't be considered a performance issue.

❑ **LAZYWRITER_SLEEP:** Signifies time that the lazywriter process is sleeping and waiting to run. It should not be considered in a performance profile.

❑ **SQLTRACE_BUFFER_FLUSH:** Occurs when the system is waiting for a SQL Trace buffer to be written to disk. You will see this on most servers in SQL Server 2005 because a rolling 100 MB trace runs permanently by default in the background and is used by the management reports in SQL Server Management Studio. You can normally discount this wait as an ever present feature.

❑ **SLEEP_BPOOL_FLUSH:** In SQL Server 2005 checkpoint operations are throttled to prevent them from overloading the disk subsystem and waiting for this operation is represented by SLEEP_BPOOL_FLUSH.

❑ **RESOURCE_SEMAPHORE:** All hash, sort, bulk copy, and index creation operations require space in what is called workspace memory, which is dynamically managed between 25 percent and 75 percent of non-AWE memory (see Chapter 16 for a description of AWE).

This wait represents time spent pending a memory grant in workspace memory and should be correlated with the Memory Grants Pending Performance Monitor counter. A consistent non-zero value will indicate memory pressure and the wait time will tell you how much time you are losing.

❑ **RESOURCE_SEMAPHORE_QUERY_COMPILE:** This wait type is set when SQL Server throttles the number of concurrent compiles in the system to limit the amount of memory being used by the optimizer in response to too many compilation requests. If you see this wait type, reduce the number of compilations by parameterizing queries so that the query plans can be re-used in cache.

❑ **SOS_SCHEDULER_YIELD:** Occurs when a task voluntarily yields processer time and waits to be scheduled again. This cooperative scheduling model was explained in the Architecture section. High waits here indicate CPU pressure and further evidence should be obtained by totaling the signal waits (using signal_wait_time_ms column in sys.dm_os_wait_stats).

❑ **CXPACKET:** This wait type means that the task is waiting on the synchronization of a parallel execution and is very often the reason for an "all processors running at 100 percent" scenario. On an OLTP system you shouldn't see this at all unless you're doing a large index rebuild. Setting Max Degree of Parallelism equal to the number of physical processors is a general Microsoft recommendation to avoid 100 percent CPU scenarios.

❑ **I/O_COMPLETION, ASYNC_I/O_COMPLETION:** These wait types occur when waiting for non-data page I/Os to complete and you may see them during a long running I/O bound operation such as BACKUP. These wait types can also indicate a disk bottleneck.

❑ **PAGEIOLATCH_*:** A PAGEIOLATCH is generally a measure of the time it takes to retrieve a data page from disk into memory and is one of the most likely waits you'll see on a system with a strained I/O subsystem.

❑ **WRITELOG:** This also indicates a disk problem as it's a wait on the transaction log file that occurs during checkpoints or transaction commits.

❑ **LCK_M_*:** This wait type indicates a wait to gain a lock on a resource and is covered in the "Locking and Blocking" section later in this chapter.

How to Track Waits

There are three DMVs available that allow you to view waits directly. You can use sys.dm_exec_requests to view session-level information. The sys.dm_os_waiting_tasks DMV allows you to see information at the task level. The sys.dm_os_wait_stats DMV shows you an aggregation of wait times.

sys.dm_exec_requests – Session Level Information Only

This DMV shows all the waiting and blocking information that you would have queried sysprocesses for in SQL Server 2000. However, both sysprocesses and sys.dm_exec_requests are based at the session level, and a better view of performance can be obtained by looking at the task level. System processes can run tasks without a session, so they wouldn't be represented here, and parallel queries are harder to troubleshoot when only a single wait is shown at the session level. Following is a sample script that shows wait information and the T-SQL currently running in each session where available:

```
SELECT    er.session_id,
          er.database_id,
          er.blocking_session_id,
          er.wait_type,
          er.wait_time,
          er.wait_resource,
          st.text
FROM sys.dm_exec_requests er
OUTER APPLY sys.dm_exec_sql_text(er.sql_handle) st
```

sys.dm_os_waiting_tasks – All Waiting Tasks

sys.dm_os_waiting_tasks lists all tasks that are currently waiting on something and is the most accurate for viewing current waits. It contains information to identify a task, an associated session, details of the wait, and blocking tasks as well. However, a task only has an entry for as long as it's waiting, so sys.dm_os_waiting_tasks tends to be used for interactive investigations rather than for monitoring purposes. You can use the columns that report on blocking tasks to identify blocking locks, which is discussed toward the end of the chapter. Here is a sample script that shows all the information for waiting tasks with the T-SQL currently running when a session_id is available:

```
SELECT    wt.*,
          st.text
FROM sys.dm_os_waiting_tasks wt LEFT JOIN sys.dm_exec_requests er
ON wt.waiting_task_address = er.task_address
OUTER APPLY sys.dm_exec_sql_text(er.sql_handle) st
ORDER BY wt.session_id
```

sys.dm_os_wait_stats – Aggregated Times by Wait Type

This DMV is an aggregation of all wait times from all queries since SQL Server started and is ideal for monitoring and server-wide tuning. You can reset the wait statistics by running DBCC sqlperf ('sys.dm_os_wait_stats', clear). The following sample script from Microsoft is a great way to check for CPU pressure by comparing signal wait times (CPU wait) with resource wait times:

```
Select signalWaitTimeMs=sum(signal_wait_time_ms)
    ,'%signal waits' = cast(100.0 * sum(signal_wait_time_ms) / sum
(wait_time_ms) as numeric(20,2))
    ,resourceWaitTimeMs=sum(wait_time_ms - signal_wait_time_ms)
    ,'%resource waits'= cast(100.0 * sum(wait_time_ms - signal_wait_time_ms) /
sum (wait_time_ms) as numeric(20,2))
from sys.dm_os_wait_stats
```

If you want to clear the historical data before you run the load to monitor, run this:

```
DBCC sqlperf ('sys.dm_os_wait_stats',clear)
```

It will clear out data that we're not interested in and give you a fairly clean measurement:

signalWaitTimeMs	%signal waits	resourceWaitTimeMs	%resource waits
445837	17.92	2042154	82.08

Signal waits should be tiny in comparison to resource waits, so these results indicate a very heavy demand for the CPU.

DMVStats

DMVStats is a great new performance tuning tool from the SQL Server Customer Advisory Team at Microsoft that enables you to set up an automated performance data warehouse for a SQL Server 2005 instance. It installs a number of data gathering scripts which are scheduled to pull data out of your instance and insert it into a database that can then be used to report on past performance. A number of SQL Server Reporting Services reports are included for you to view the data and even configure the data collection. It's surprisingly straightforward to set up and use and includes a couple of good reports focused on waits. You can see the list of available reports in Figure 4-2. Figure 4-3 shows the Wait Stats report, which groups all the wait types into a chart with the ability to drill-through. Figure 4-4 shows the Executing Requests and Waiting Tasks report, where I have drilled down into I/O waits to see the statement within a stored procedure that had a wait on WRITELOG.

Figure 4-2

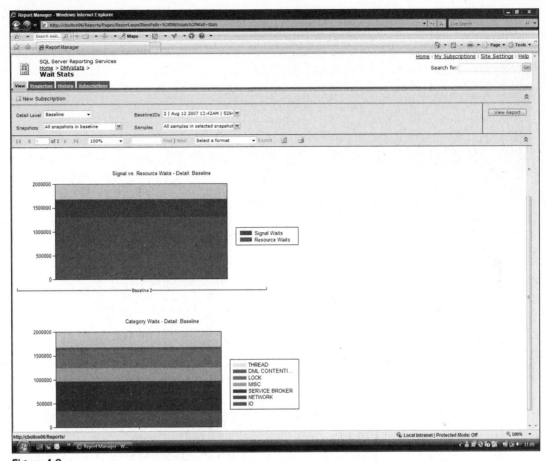

Figure 4-3

Performance Dashboard

The SQL Server Performance Dashboard is a set of SQL Server Reporting Services reports written by the SQL Server support team at Microsoft to take advantage of the Custom Reports feature available in Service Pack 2. Custom reports allow you to add your own Reporting Services reports to SQL Server Management Studio. The support team at Microsoft has provided a great set of performance reports including the one on wait stats seen in Figure 4-5. Chapter 3 looks at the Performance Dashboard in depth.

Wait Stats in Action

For demo purposes we've used the sample database described in Chapter 11. We've loaded the people table with 250,000 rows and we're going to run a stored procedure called usp_marriageUpdate which makes 10,000 "marriages" between these people by updating a girl's surname to match a chosen boy. There are no indexes.

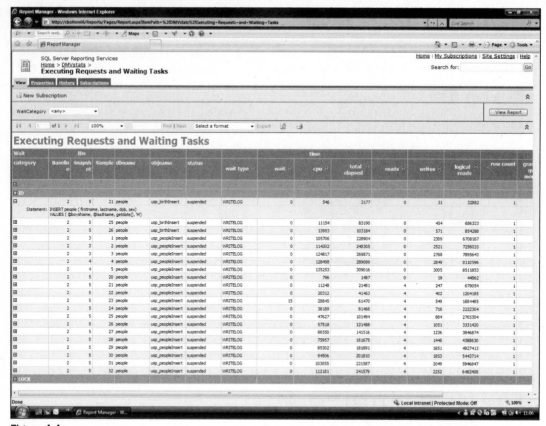

Figure 4-4

We're going to use `sys.dm_os_wait_stats` as our start point for troubleshooting and because it represents all waits since SQL Server started we're going to run:

```
DBCC sqlperf ('sys.dm_os_wait_stats',clear)
```

This will clear the statistics before the start of every run. In a production environment you might not want to lose this data, so alternatively you could take a view of the DMV before and after execution of your tests and measure the delta between the two. Our test machine is a dual-core 2 GHz laptop with 2 GB of RAM, with a maximum memory setting for SQL Server of 256 MB. Running the following workload script for the first time

```
DBCC sqlperf ('sys.dm_os_wait_stats',clear)
GO
exec usp_loopmarriageupdate
GO
SELECT * FROM sys.dm_os_wait_stats
ORDER BY wait_time_ms DESC
GO
```

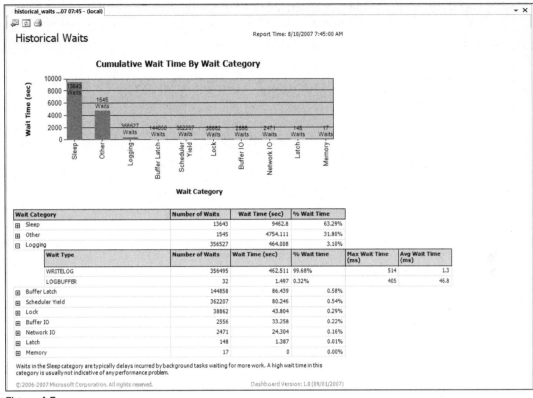

Figure 4-5

```
SELECT session_id,cpu_time,total_elapsed_time
FROM sys.dm_exec_sessions
WHERE session_id = @@SPID
```

yielded the following results (with zero-valued results removed; (the columns' names have been edited to make the results easier to read in print form):

waitType	waitingTasks	waitTimeMs	maxWaitTimeMs	signalWaitTimeMs
LAZYWRITER_SLEEP	2537	2538417	1232	1185
BROKER_TASK_STOP	508	2536779	5070	624
SQLTRACE_BUFFER_FLUSH	634	2533019	4056	46
CXPACKET	42045	605798	452	17362
WRITELOG	12883	68874	733	5694
PAGEIOLATCH_UP	2880	11419	156	312
SOS_SCHEDULER_YIELD	773663	11388	249	10904
LATCH_EX	35127	9516	109	5647
SLEEP_TASK	2948	2527	46	2527
SQLTRACE_LOCK	18	764	405	0
PAGELATCH_SH	79994	468	15	405

```
LOGBUFFER                 5         109           62              0
LATCH_SH                914          78           15             78
CMEMTHREAD               16          46           31             15


session_id cpu_time    total_elapsed_time
---------- -----------  ------------------
        52  2719393             3521547 (40:21)
```

You can remove the top three waits because they are just system threads waiting for events and the bottom six because they're negligible values or waiting system threads. This results in this shorter table:

waitType	waitingTasks	waitTimeMs	maxWaitTimeMs	signalWaitTimeMs
CXPACKET	42045	605798	452	17362
WRITELOG	12883	68874	733	5694
PAGEIOLATCH_UP	2880	11419	156	312
SOS_SCHEDULER_YIELD	773663	11388	249	10904
LATCH_EX	35127	9516	109	5647

```
session_id    cpu_time total_elapsed_time
----------  ----------- ------------------
        52    2719393          3521547 (40:21)
```

CXPACKET means parallelism is occurring, which will drive the CPUs hard. In an OLTP system this shouldn't be present or at least shouldn't be a significant wait type, so finding the source will be the top priority. SOS_SCHEDULER_YIELD backs up the evidence for a CPU bottleneck. It's a very common wait to see as it represents threads that are voluntarily yielding processor time, but to see it high on a list of waits suggest a CPU bottleneck. The final evidence is found in the signal wait times, which if you remember from the architecture description represent time in the runnable queue and therefore constitute a pure CPU wait. The total elapsed time represents the total time to run the workload. We've added the minutes:seconds measurement in brackets from Management Studio to save you from having tocalculate it from the results.

Investigation of the actual execution plan for usp_loopMarriageUpdate reveals that a table scan is being executed in parallel. Figure 4-6 shows part of the graphical execution plan. The circle with the two arrows pointing left on the Parallelism and Table Scan icons indicates a parallel activity. Figure 4-7 is the details screen from the parallel table scan.

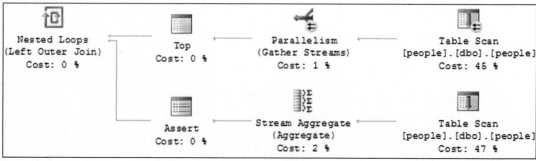

Figure 4-6

```
                          Table Scan
Scan rows from a table.

Physical Operation                     Table Scan
Logical Operation                      Table Scan
Estimated I/O Cost                        6.47802
Estimated CPU Cost                       0.275037
Estimated Operator Cost           6.75306 (45%)
Estimated Subtree Cost                    6.75306
Estimated Number of Rows                        1
Estimated Row Size                           31 B
Ordered                                      True
Node ID                                         6


Predicate
[people].[dbo].[people].[personId]=[@girlID]
Object
[people].[dbo].[people]
Output List
Bmk1000
```

Figure 4-7

First, try disabling parallelism by running:

```
sp_configure 'max degree of parallelism', 1
go
reconfigure
```

The query results (edited for relevance) are:

```
waitType            waitingTasks  waitTimeMs maxWaitTimeMs signalWaitTimeMs
----------------    ------------  ---------- ------------- ----------------
WRITELOG                  12416       71261           702             9032
PAGEIOLATCH_UP             2423       19812           327              124
SOS_SCHEDULER_YIELD      747994       19032           967            18595
PAGEIOLATCH_SH               74        4087           452               31


session_id    cpu_time total_elapsed_time
----------  ----------- ------------------
        52     2583595         2786682 (46:33)
```

The CXPACKET wait is gone, so you're not using parallel queries any more. You now have WRITELOG as the top wait, which means that the transaction log file is now the top bottleneck. The total elapsed time has jumped from 40 minutes 21 seconds to 46 minutes 33 seconds, and the signal waits still indicate a concern for CPU time. Simply disabling parallelism or even reducing max degree of parallelism to half the number of processors is a quick and effective way to reduce an overall CPU bottleneck at the expense of a longer execution time.

We've been called out to Microsoft customer sites with a "Severity A - Server Down" support case (what we call a critsit) where all the CPUs are running at 100 percent in a large OLTP system to fulfil a parallel execution. The server cannot serve any other requests so in effect the system is down. In that situation disabling parallelism doesn't tackle the root cause, but it does bring the system back to a usable state for a more leisurely investigation of the parallel query.

However, for our scenario we know where the parallel execution is coming from, so we can tackle it directly. Run this script again to re-enable parallelism:

```
SP_CONFIGURE 'max degree of parallelism', 0
GO
RECONFIGURE
```

We do this so we know that SQL Server is *choosing* not to do a parallel execution instead of preventing it.

There is a table scan in the execution plan, which is bad because it means that it has to read all the rows in the table. You can see in Figure 4-7 that the estimated number of rows returned is 1. On a 250,000 row table, this is just crying out for a visit to Chapter 11 to read about indexing, but as a quick fix let's just add a non-clustered index to the column we're searching on — people.personId:

```
CREATE NONCLUSTERED INDEX idx_personID
ON people(personID)
```

After running the workload script again:

waitType	waitingTasks	waitTimeMs	maxWaitTimeMs	signalWaitTimeMs
WRITELOG	11799	81136	655	5288
PAGEIOLATCH_UP	1803	15272	546	31
SOS_SCHEDULER_YIELD	276910	6505	171	6396

session_id	cpu_time	total_elapsed_time
52	831829	991306 (16:36)

You can see a dramatic overall improvement with a significant reduction in CPU time and WRITELOG is now the top wait with PAGEIOLATCH_UP in second place. You can look at the execution plan in Figure 4-8 and see that the table scans are now index seeks, which accounts for the dramatic increase in performance to 16 minutes 36 seconds. There could still be some CPU time reduction to be had by looking at indexes thoroughly by following Chapter 11, but the top bottleneck points to the transaction log, so we're going to look at that first.

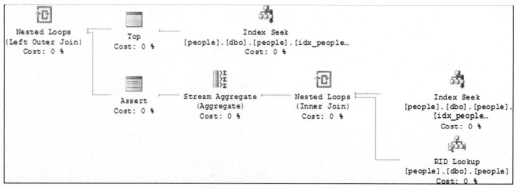

Figure 4-8

The transaction log for the people database is on the C: drive on my laptop (as well as everything else) so it's not surprising that it's slowing the workload down. I have an external hard disk connected by USB to my laptop that I'm going to move the transaction log to see if that helps.

Run the following script to relocate the people database transaction log file, replacing H:\ with your drive letter:

```
USE master;
GO
ALTER DATABASE people
MODIFY FILE(NAME = people_log,FILENAME = N'h:\people_log.ldf')
GO
ALTER DATABASE people SET OFFLINE
GO
ALTER DATABASE people SET ONLINE
```

And run the workload script again:

```
waitType              waitingTasks  waitTimeMs maxWaitTimeMs signalWaitTimeMs
-------------------- ------------- ---------- ------------- ----------------
WRITELOG                    11796       26379           421             2761
SOS_SCHEDULER_YIELD        244447        3650            31             3556
PAGEIOLATCH_UP               1807        3432           546                0


session_id     cpu_time total_elapsed_time
---------- ----------- ------------------
        52      857615             965589 (15:25)
```

You can see that we've taken over a minute off the elapsed time and we've reduced the wait on WRITELOG from 81 seconds down to 26 seconds. On a server with faster disks this will be much lower again.

The next step in tuning this system would be to look at the indexing strategy.

Locking and Blocking

No chapter on waiting is complete without a discussion on locking and blocking. To understand why, you need to understand a few core concepts: Concurrency, transactions, isolation levels, blocking locks, and deadlocks.

Concurrency

Concurrency is the ability for multiple processes to access the same piece of data at the same time. There are two approaches to managing this effectively: Pessimistically and optimistically. The pessimistic approach takes the view that different processes will try to simultaneously read and write to the same data and acquires locks to prevent conflicts from occurring. When a process reads data, a lock is placed to prevent another process from writing to it, and when a write occurs a lock is placed to prevent another process reading it. Thus, readers block writers and writers block readers. The optimistic approach takes the view that it's unlikely that readers and writers will cross paths and doesn't lock the data. This means that readers don't block writers and writers don't block readers.

The default in SQL Server is pessimistic concurrency, so a system of locking and un-locking resources is used to enable applications to have high concurrency. However, with the release of SQL Server 2005, you have the ability to adopt an optimistic strategy, which is possible because SQL Server is now able to use *row versioning*. This allows a reader to read the data as it was before the start of a modification from a writer. We will come back to row versioning later (and the isolation level that uses it) after looking at what anomalies can occur with concurrency and the different isolation levels you can use to prevent them.

Lost Updates

A lost update occurs when two processes read the same data and both try to update the original value. Imagine if you share a bank account and you go into a branch to deposit $400 in cash while your partner who works on the other side of town goes into a different branch to deposit $500 in cash. The bank teller at each branch simultaneously reads the current balance as $1000. Your bank teller adds $400 to $1000 and updates the balance to $1400 and your partner's bank teller adds $500 to the $1000 that they originally read and updates the balance to $1500. You just lost $400 because of a lost update. Clearly, this is an unacceptable side effect.

Dirty Reads

A dirty read is a read of uncommitted data. One process modifies data and then cancels before committing the new value, but another process has already read the changed value and started using it. For example, you tell a real estate agent that you'd like to sell your house and she adds it to the list of available properties. You change your mind before you complete the paperwork and it gets taken off the list. However, before it was taken off, another agent found a buyer because their list included properties without completed paperwork. The second agent read *dirty* or *uncommitted* data and took an action based on the value that shouldn't have been possible.

Non-Repeatable Reads

A non-repeatable read is when a process that reads data twice within a transaction might get different results on the second read. For example, you add up all the money in ten cash registers in your store one by one and then do it again to double-check your sums only to find the results to be vastly different. As you finished adding up one register, it started taking money again, so when you came back around to read it a second time, you got a different figure. Your initial reads were non-repeatable.

Phantoms

Phantoms occur when a row is inserted or deleted by one transaction into a range being read by another transaction. For example, you search a recruitment website for DBA positions in your area and get 12 results. You create 12 cover letters for your resume and search the website again to get the e-mail addresses. You get 13 results back but you've only got 12 covering letters. The extra position you got that you didn't get in the first search is a phantom row.

These anomalies aren't always un-wanted and which ones could occur depends on the *isolation* level of your *transaction*.

Transactions

A transaction is one or more actions that are defined as a single unit of work. In the Relational Database Management System (RDBMS) world they also comply with ACID properties:

❑ **Atomicity:** An atomic transaction means either all the actions happen or none of them. If an action fails half-way through a transaction, then all previous actions in the transaction must be rolled back as if they never happened.

❑ **Consistency:** A transaction cannot break the integrity rules of the database; it must leave the database in a consistent state. For example, you might specify that stock levels cannot be a negative value, a spare part cannot exist without a parent object, or the data in a sex field must be male or female.

❑ **Isolation:** SQL Server is designed to service many concurrent users, but from the viewpoint of each user, the data set must look like the user is the only one on the system. Each transaction must be entirely self-contained, and changes it makes must not be readable by any other transaction. SQL Server allows flexibility in the degree of isolation you can specify for your transaction so that you can find a balance between the performance and business requirements.

❑ **Durability:** When a transaction is committed, it must persist even if there is a system failure immediately afterwards. When you commit a transaction in SQL Server, the information needed to replay it is physically written to the transaction log before the commit is returned to the user as successful.

Atomicity, consistency, isolation, and durability are inherent properties of SQL Server transactions. Isolation has a degree of flexibility and is a choice which requires a more detailed understanding, so we will explore it further in the following section.

Isolation Levels

There are five transaction isolation levels available in SQL Server 2005 that provide increasing levels of isolation.

❑ **Read uncommitted:** This is the least isolated and best performing level, but it does allow dirty reads, non-repeatable reads, and phantoms. It can be used when you don't care about dirty reads and you want to read the data with the lightest touch possible. It doesn't hold any locks on the data when reading.

❑ **Read committed:** This is the default isolation level for SQL Server and usually provides the best balance between performance and business requirements. It does not allow dirty reads, but non-repeatable reads and phantoms are still possible. Any locks held are released when the statement that caused the read operation is complete, even within a transaction. SQL Server 2005 also has a new flavor of read-committed based on row versioning called read-committed snapshot which is covered later in this chapter.

❑ **Repeatable read:** A repeatable read is possible by holding read locks for the duration of a transaction to prevent other transactions from modifying the data so you can have a repeatable read. It prevents dirty reads and non-repeatable reads but phantoms can still occur.

❑ **Serializable:** This serializes access to data and prevents all of the side effects by holding locks for the duration of the transaction and effectively locking rows that don't even exist yet through key range locks. This is the most isolated level and the most damaging to high concurrency.

❑ **Snapshot:** The snapshot isolation level is the only optimistic isolation level available and uses row versioning rather than locking. It prevents all of the previously mentioned side effects just like serializable, but it does allow for an update conflict to occur that wouldn't if transactions were run serially. This conflict occurs when data to be changed inside a snapshot transaction is changed concurrently by another transaction. Detection occurs automatically and causes a rollback of the snapshot transaction to prevent a lost update. Snapshot and row versioning will be covered in more depth after looking at locking in more detail.

Table 4-1 summarizes the isolation levels and possible anomalies.

Table 4-1: Isolation Levels and Possible Anomalies

Isolation level	Dirty Read	Non-Repeatable Read	Phantom Read	Update Conflict	Concurrency Model
Read Un-Committed	Yes	Yes	Yes	No	Pessimistic
Read Committed					
1 – Locking	No	Yes	Yes	No	Pessimistic
2 – Snapshot	No	Yes	Yes	No	Optimistic
Repeatable Read	No	No	Yes	No	Pessimistic
Snapshot	No	No	No	Yes	Optimistic
Serializable	No	No	No	No	Pessimistic

To use a transaction isolation level other than the default read-committed, run the SET TRANSACTION ISOLATION LEVEL T-SQL command. For example:

```
SET TRANSACTION ISOLATION LEVEL REPEATABLE READ
GO
```

Locks and Locking

Locks are necessary for concurrency in whatever model you choose (assuming you need to read *and* write to the database). SQL Server handles locks automatically for you. There are three basic levels of granularity: row, page, and table. Which one SQL Server uses depends on the isolation level of the transaction. Each lock acquired takes a certain amount of system resources, so there comes a point at which it would be more efficient to use a single larger lock rather than many of locks of a smaller granularity. When this occurs SQL Server will *escalate* the locks to a table lock.

The process is called lock escalation and it doesn't happen very frequently. When a single statement within a transaction holds more than 5000 (roughly) locks on a single object, SQL Server will try to escalate to a table lock. SQL Server will also try to escalate locks when coming under memory pressure. Escalation is *always* to a table lock, but most of the time the Query Optimizer will choose the most appropriate granularity of locking when it creates the execution plan, so you shouldn't see escalations often. The Microsoft Knowledge Base article "How to Resolve Blocking Problems that Are Caused by Lock Escalation in SQL Server" at `http://support.microsoft.com/kb/323630` discusses what you can do if they are a problem on your system.

Lock Modes

There are two main locking modes: Shared and exclusive. *Shared locks* are used when reading data to prevent a process from changing the data while it is being read, but they don't prevent other readers. An *exclusive lock* is required to perform an insert, update, or delete and only one exclusive lock can be held on data at a time.

The other locking modes either are hybrids of these two or are used in support of them. The main two you will see are update locks and intent locks.

Update locks are used to prevent deadlocks due to updates and are taken when a processes needs to read data before updating it. Conversion from an update lock to an exclusive lock will then occur. Only one process can hold an update lock, and the one that does will be the only one able to get an exclusive lock. Update locks do not block shared locks.

Intent locks are used to indicate that locks are present at a lower level of granularity. For example, a shared lock on a row will also hold an intent shared lock on the page and table it belongs to. Anyone trying to get an exclusive lock on the table will be blocked by the intent shared lock, which indicates that a resource in the table is already locked. Exclusive locks are not compatible with any other locks. Searching SQL Server 2005 Books Online for "Lock Compatibility" reveals a matrix that shows which locks can be held together on a resource.

Locking Problems

Locking can be a problem in one of two scenarios. The first is a *blocking lock* whereby one process is blocked from locking a resource because another process has already locked it. This behavior is obviously "as designed" but it creates a performance problem if the first process has to wait too long to acquire a lock. It can also create a chain of blocked processes each waiting to acquire a lock. This can occur thousands of times in a busy system, and you'll know it's a problem when users complain and you start to see locking high on your wait statistics.

The second issue is called a *deadlock*. This occurs when two processes each hold a lock that the other needs to continue and if left alone they would wait on each other indefinitely. Fortunately, SQL Server has built-in deadlock detection and resolution. Every five seconds the lock monitor checks for deadlock situations and this check becomes more frequent if deadlocks are found. SQL Server resolves deadlocks by choosing the process that is the least expensive to roll back and terminates it. This is known as the deadlock victim.

Locking in Action

To review the core concepts, you're going to use the people database again. Open a new window and run the following statement:

```
SET TRANSACTION ISOLATION LEVEL REPEATABLE READ
GO
```

```
BEGIN TRANSACTION
SELECT * FROM people
WHERE personid = 'B95212DB-D246-DC11-9225-000E7B82B6DD'
```

Obviously, your settings, system, and results probably won't be identical to mine. However, it is still helpful to work through the example, as the general principles will work the same way.

You'll need to replace the value for personid with a value that exists in your version of the table.

This starts a transaction without closing it so you can look into what locks it has open. The select statement will require a shared lock. However, under the default isolation level (read committed), shared locks are only held for the duration of the *statement*, and as the statement completes quickly it doesn't make for a good demo. The script changes the isolation level to repeatable read, which holds locks for the duration of the *transaction* to make it easier to see what's going on. Open locks can be viewed by querying the sys.dm_tran_locks DMV.

```
SELECT  request_session_id AS Session,
        resource_database_id AS DBID,
        Resource_Type,
        resource_description AS Resource,
        request_type AS Type,
        request_mode AS Mode,
        request_status AS Status
FROM sys.dm_tran_locks


Session DBID Resource_Type Resource       Type  Mode  Status
------- ---- ------------- -------------- ----- ----- -------
58      7               KEY (2f024a673f11) LOCK    S   GRANT
58      7              PAGE       1:24892  LOCK   IS   GRANT
58      7            OBJECT                LOCK   IS   GRANT
```

From the results you can see that there is a shared lock (S) on the row that's being selected. More accurately, it is on the clustered index *key* of the selected row, so you know there is a clustered index on the table. There is also an intent shared lock (IS) at the page and table level.

If you start a different query window and run an update statement to set the dob column to zero:

```
UPDATE people SET dob = 0
```

sys.dm_tran_locks will now look something like this:

```
Session DBID Resource_Type Resource       Type  Mode  Status
------- ---- ------------- -------------- ----- ----- -------
     53   7               KEY (410248acfd12) LOCK    S   GRANT
     53   7              PAGE       1:16960  LOCK   IS   GRANT
     53   7            OBJECT                LOCK   IS   GRANT
     54   7              PAGE       1:16960  LOCK    U   GRANT
     54   7              PAGE       1:16960  LOCK    X CONVERT
     54   7            OBJECT                LOCK   IX   GRANT
```

The new query window connected as session 54, and you can see that an *update* (U) lock has been granted on the same *page* that session 53 has an *IS* lock on. U lock and IS locks don't conflict, so the U lock was granted. As previously discussed, update locks are used to read the data before changing it, so the next lock is a conversion to an *exclusive* (x) lock on that same data page. Refreshing the sys.dm_tran_locks view will show that nothing is changing so have a look at sys.dm_os_waiting_tasks:

```
SELECT session_id,wait_duration_ms,wait_type,
blocking_session_id,resource_description
FROM sys.dm_os_waiting_tasks
WHERE session_id = 54

session_id wait_duration_ms wait_type blocking_session_id
---------- ---------------- --------- -------------------
54                 5750212   LCK_M_X                    53
```

This confirms that the update statement is waiting on an exclusive lock (LCK_M_X) which is blocked by session 53.

Issuing a COMMIT TRANSACTION statement from session 53 clears the shared and intent shared locks and allows session 54 to get an exclusive lock and complete the update operation.

Row Versioning

Row versioning is the SQL Server 2005 mechanism employed to enable the new snapshot based isolation levels. It allows for an optimistic concurrency approach based on versioning as opposed to the pessimistic approach with locking that was previously the only option. SQL Server 2005 also brings a new flavor of read-committed: the read-committed snapshot. The snapshot and the read-committed snapshot have been introduced to provide increased concurrency for OLTP environments by preventing writers from blocking readers and readers from blocking writers.

> *Row versioning is also used to support the Trigger, Multiple Active Result Sets (MARS) and Online Indexing features in SQL Server 2005.*

To use Snapshot isolation in a database, you must first set an option in the database to enable it. Enable it by using the ALTER DATABASE command:

```
ALTER DATABASE people
SET ALLOW_SNAPSHOT_ISOLATION ON
```

This doesn't mean that it will now start working as the default. After enabling it you still have to set it at the session level by using:

```
SET TRANSACTION ISOLATION LEVEL SNAPSHOT
```

The read-committed snapshot isolation level is enabled in a similar way but actually replaces the behavior of the default read-committed isolation and doesn't need to be explicitly set. This means no applications changes are required.

```
ALTER DATABASE people
SET READ_COMMITTED_SNAPSHOT ON
```

Once enabled, all subsequent transactions running at the read-committed isolation level will default to snapshot behavior and use versioning for reads rather than locking. Readers will see the previously committed value (version) when a resource is locked for update, which can dramatically reduce locking and deadlocking problems without the need to change any applications. For inserts, updates, and deletes, there is no behavior change and locks are acquired as normal.

As Table 4-1 earlier stated, the full snapshot isolation level supports repeatable reads and doesn't allow phantoms. The downside is that update conflicts can occur when the data to be changed inside a snapshot transaction is changed concurrently by another transaction. Conflicts are detected automatically though, and the snapshot transaction is rolled back to prevent a lost update.

Versioned rows have an overhead of 14 bytes (see Figure 4-9), which is used to store an instance-wide unique identification of the transaction that made the change called *XSN* and a row identifier (RID). Only the modified rows are stored, not the entire page. Rows from different tables may be stored together on the same page in the version store. Multiple versions of a row are tracked by the incremental XSN.

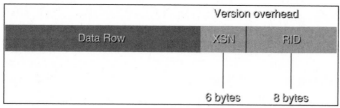

Figure 4-9

The version store is in TempDB so if you do switch to using snapshots make sure that you have it sized well and on a fast disk subsystem. Snapshot isolation can benefit applications that have heavy read/writer blocking but if there isn't much on the system before switching then the overhead of versioning may prove to affect performance negatively.

Monitoring for Deadlocks

By default deadlock messaging is quite minimal. Deadlocks are reported back to the deadlock victim with the following error message, but nothing is written to the SQL Server errorlog.

```
Msg 1205, Level 13, State 51, Line 1
Transaction (Process ID 52) was deadlocked on lock resources with another pro-
cess and has been chosen as the deadlock victim. Rerun the transaction.
```

If you experience frequent deadlocking, you can enable trace flag 1222, which prints full deadlock information to the error log (-1 means apply the flag to all connections):

```
DBCC traceon (-1,1222)
```

Trace flag 1222 is new to SQL Server 2005. It enables a more complete deadlock detection output than the 1204 flag that was used in SQL Server 2000, although both will work in SQL Server 2005.

A deadlock output looks like this:

```
    deadlock-list
     deadlock victim=process988f28
      process-list
     process id=process988b68 taskpriority=0 logused=236 waitresource=PAGE: 9:1:110
waittime=4718 ownerId=6233 transactionname=user_transaction lasttranstarted=2007-09-
03T23:14:56.530 XDES=0x58a07f0 lockMode=S schedulerid=2 kpid=4212 status=suspended
spid=54 sbid=0 ecid=0 priority=0 transcount=1 lastbatchstarted=2007-09-03T23:15:39.
530 lastbatchcompleted=2007-09-03T23:14:56.530 lastattention=2007-09-03T22:54:53.497
clientapp=Microsoft SQL Server Management Studio - Query hostname=STUDYPC host-
pid=5312 loginname=STUDYPC\Christian isolationlevel=read committed (2) xactid=6233
currentdb=9 lockTimeout=4294967295 clientoption1=671090784 clientoption2=390200
        executionStack
         frame procname=adhoc line=1 stmtstart=36
sqlhandle=0x02000000978fb129ee9e7073d169972d3459d9183f365a2b
     SELECT * FROM [people] WHERE [personid]=@1
           frame procname=adhoc line=1
sqlhandle=0x02000000bc719c0327c935dde5ab234e257b5956e3670e69
     SELECT * FROM people
     WHERE personid = '63E3D4B0-8155-DC11-9676-00138F9F2378'
          inputbuf
     SELECT * FROM people
     WHERE personid = '63E3D4B0-8155-DC11-9676-00138F9F2378'
     process id=process988f28 taskpriority=0 logused=216 waitresource=RID: 9:1:109:12
waittime=15109 ownerId=5438 transactionname=user_transaction lasttranstarted=2007-
09-03T23:11:30.483 XDES=0x58a0250 lockMode=S schedulerid=2 kpid=2504 status=suspended
spid=53 sbid=0 ecid=0 priority=0 transcount=1 lastbatchstarted=2007-09-03T23:
15:29.153 lastbatchcompleted=2007-09-03T23:11:30.497 clientapp=Microsoft SQL Server
Management Studio - Query hostname=STUDYPC hostpid=5312 loginname=STUDYPC\Christian
isolationlevel=read committed (2) xactid=5438 currentdb=9 lockTimeout=4294967295
clientoption1=671090784 clientoption2=390200
        executionStack
         frame procname=adhoc line=1 stmtstart=36
sqlhandle=0x0200000033c24915c37a771dd564c5d67e9332074c7f9fe9
     SELECT * FROM [lastnames] WHERE [name]=@1
           frame procname=adhoc line=1
sqlhandle=0x0200000078b28408ba6b06d21cbf6fadedf220ceffbb6c4d
     SELECT * FROM lastnames
     WHERE name = 'EKGLIMGIJYALXAYC'
          inputbuf
     SELECT * FROM lastnames
     WHERE name = 'EKGLIMGIJYALXAYC'
       resource-list
        ridlock fileid=1 pageid=109 dbid=9
objectname= people.dbo.lastnames id=lock3ca4f40 mode=X
associatedObjectId=72057594041663488
          owner-list
           owner id=process988b68 mode=X
```

```
        waiter-list
          waiter id=process988f28 mode=S requestType=wait
          pagelock fileid=1 pageid=110 dbid=9
objectname=people.dbo.people id=lock3ca5300 mode=IX
associatedObjectId=72057594041466880
          owner-list
            owner id=process988f28 mode=IX
          waiter-list
            waiter id=process988b68 mode=S requestType=wait
```

We've highlighted the parts of interest to build a picture of the deadlock. From these we can summarize the following:

```
SPID 54
Had an Exclusive lock on people.dbo.lastnames
Blocked by 53. Waiting for a Shared lock on people.dbo.people to fulfill this state-
ment:
    SELECT * FROM people WHERE personid=@1

SPID 53
Had an Intent Exclusive lock on people.dbo.people
Blocked by 54. Waiting for a Shared lock on people.dbo.lastnames to fulfill this
statement:
    SELECT * FROM lastnames WHERE name=@1

SPID 53 was chosen as the deadlock victim.
```

The two select statements were blocked by existing Exclusive locks held by the other connection. Unfortunately, you can't see what the statement was that generated the exclusive lock without a corresponding Profiler trace captured during the deadlock. Alternatively, if the statements were part of a stored procedure and not ad hoc T-SQL as they are here, you'd also see the procedure name, which might help to locate the source of the exclusive locks.

Even without that information you have quickly identified:

- ❑ The connections involved
- ❑ The code that caused the deadlock
- ❑ Which resources were locked
- ❑ Who was rolled back

This is enough to help you move forward with resolving the deadlock using the methods described in Chapter 9.

SQL Server Profiler also has a deadlock graph event that displays exactly the same deadlock information as trace flag 1222 but in an easy-to-read chart. You can even hover the mouse over each node to get the T-SQL that was run. Figure 4-10 shows a deadlock graph from exactly the same deadlock scenario as above.

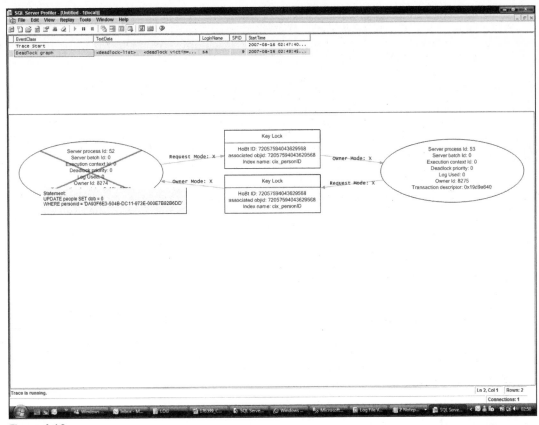

Figure 4-10

Monitoring for Blocking Locks

You've already seen how to view and troubleshoot blocking locks using DMVs. Monitoring of a busy system needs a bit more forethought than just viewing dynamic locking or reactively troubleshooting. Historic data is the most valuable asset to have when troubleshooting, and proactively gathering a baseline of locking activity can yield positive results when you analyze the output.

Microsoft knowledge base article 271509 contains a script to create a stored procedure called sp_blocker_ pss80, which is often called simply *the blocker script*. It was created for SQL Server 2000 and gathers all the information you need to analyze blocking issues. You need to run the stored procedure in a loop and output the information to a file at set intervals. The article can help you to set this up.

The blocker script is used by Microsoft support staff to monitor locking over a certain period and then take the results to analyze offline. It also works for SQL Server 2005 but doesn't make use of the new features and DMVs. For SQL Server 2005 they decided to take a wider performance tuning approach that encompasses locking. They have released a SQL Server 2005 Performance Statistics script via their blog:

❑   How to monitor blocking in SQL Server 2005 and in SQL Server 2000: `http://support.microsoft.com/kb/271509`

❑   SQL Server 2005 Performance Statistics Script: `http://blogs.msdn.com/psssql/archive/2007/02/21/sql-server-2005-performance-statistics-script.aspx`

The output from these scripts is intended to help troubleshoot the most complex issues, so they can provide too much information for the casual tuner of locking issues. Easy reviewing of historic locking behavior can be had from the locking report supplied with DMVStats, which is described near the beginning of the chapter. Figure 4-11 shows the Analyze Block Info report.

SQL Server 2005 also has a nice little Profiler event called *blocked process report*, which contains all the blocking information for blocked processes that have been waiting for a period of time determined by the *blocked process threshold*, which is configured with `sp_configure`. It's off by default but when configured will trigger blocked process report events that can be picked up by Profiler.

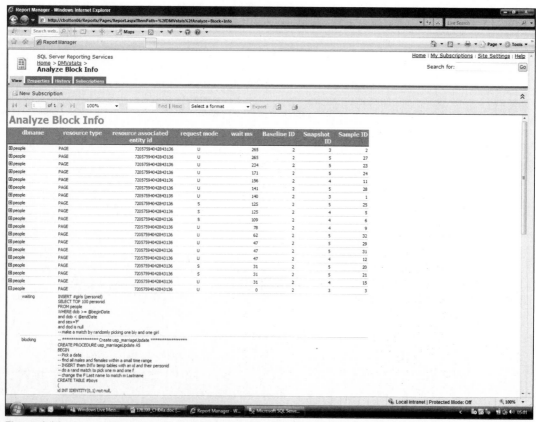

Figure 4-11

However you choose to look at locking within SQL Server, being as familiar with the architecture as you can will yield great benefits when a high-priority problem occurs and you don't have to stop and read up on how it all works. SQL Server 2005 Books Online is a great resource to continue your reading on the subject.

Summary

This chapter has described the concept behind a SQL Server wait and covered the architecture to provide an understanding of why they can be useful to monitor. It detailed the different ways that wait information can be gathered, showed you how to interpret the information, and looked at a free performance data warehouse application called DMVStats, which has been released by Microsoft. The final part of the chapter focused on locking and blocking within SQL Server. It described why locking is employed, how it works, how to view locking with DMVs, and what methods there are to monitor and troubleshoot locking over an extended period.

Now that you know how to find and monitor for blocking problems you can turn to Chapter 9 for details on how to minimize and resolve blocking through sensible coding strategies or continue with the next chapter, which maintains the theme of troubleshooting tools and techniques with a closer look at SQL Profiler.

5

Finding Problem Queries with SQL Profiler

The previous chapters provide the knowledge, tools, and resources for finding Windows and SQL server bottlenecks. Tracing database activities and collecting information are critical steps in troubleshooting, tuning, and optimizing a database. SQL Profiler is a valuable investigative tool for measuring query performance and troubleshooting database applications.

In this chapter, you will see how and when to use SQL Profiler to collect and analyze query performance data. SQL Trace is a server-side component for tracing. SQL Profiler is a graphical user interface for SQL Trace. Profiler is used for monitoring an instance of the Microsoft Database Engine or Analysis Services. This chapter focuses mainly on using Profiler to solve performance issues. SQL Trace provides a set of system-stored procedures that can be used from within your own applications to create traces manually. This allows you to write custom applications specific to the needs of your enterprise.

Performance issues can be very specific or vague. Capturing the right amount of reliable event data at the right time with minimum costs presents a challenge for most database administrators. There are many SQL Profiler features and details, which need to be considered before starting a trace. You will see some important options and concerns. You will use appropriate scenarios to examine the processes involved in setting up a Profiler trace and a server-side trace. Toward the end of this chapter, you will see how to correlate SQL Profiler trace data and Windows performance counter data.

Upon finishing the chapter, with some practice, a database administrator should be able to set up an optimal Profiler trace based on a given scenario.

Preparations for Setting Up a Trace

Setting up a useful trace requires proper planning. The purpose of a trace should be clearly defined. Selecting SQL trace events in a trace requires a good understanding of both SQL trace event classes and terminologies. This section will provide you with what you should know for setting up a trace.

Checking for a Complete "Issue" Statement

A well-prepared issue statement will help to define the scope of a trace. Issues can be described in many forms; at the minimum, the following information is required:

❑ **Who:** This information confirms the status of the issue.

❑ **What:** These symptoms of the performance issue will help determine which SQL trace template or events to use for a trace.

❑ **When:** When did the issue occur? Does the issue persist? This information will determine when to schedule the next trace.

❑ **System environment description:** Operating system, SQL Server editions, and service pack levels.

❑ **Error messages:** Do you have system, application, or other related logs documented as evidence?

❑ **Service Level Agreement (SLA):** Do you have related measurable descriptions in the SLA for the issue?

Profiler trace setup requires many detailed decisions: how to connect to a SQL instance, how to save trace results, when to start and stop a trace, what events to select, and how to filter data for a specific need. Information in the issue statement may help to make these decisions.

Best Practice

Each Profiler trace should have a specific purpose, whether it is gathering data for specific troubleshooting, performance tuning, or a baseline. When you design a trace, obtain all the information you can about what to collect, when to collect, how to process the trace data, and who can benefit from your trace analysis.

Searching for Related Known Issues

Sometimes known issues have already been found and documented for specific OS, SQL Server editions, and patch levels by other people. A quick search, using common Internet search engines, can divulge useful information.

Thinking in Terms of SQL Trace Terminologies

To effectively set up a trace, you need to understand the technical issues you are dealing with and SQL trace terminology. The following are common terms used in SQL Profiler and SQL Trace:

❑ **Server instance:** For a Profiler trace to connect to an instance of SQL server, the name of the instance is required. If SQL Server is running under Windows clustering, the virtual name is required.

❑ **Applications and user logins:** If a specific issue is involved in an application or user login, you can use this information to filter trace events.

❑ **SQL trace events:** Matching issue symptoms with SQL trace events accounts for a major part of the trace setup. A trace event might represent various activities generated by SQL Server: a stored procedure executed, a scheduled SQL agent job started, or a database lock acquired. Matching issue symptoms with traceable events is a non-trivial task. This requires knowledge of the system environment, including hardware, OS, and application software. Actual working experience is essential to the success of a trace. Being familiar with common scenarios and commonly used trace events are good starting points.

❑ **Event category:** Within SQL Profiler, an event category groups event classes. For example, all lock event classes are logically grouped into the Locks event category (see Figure 5-1). The event class corresponds to a predefined traceable event in SQL server.

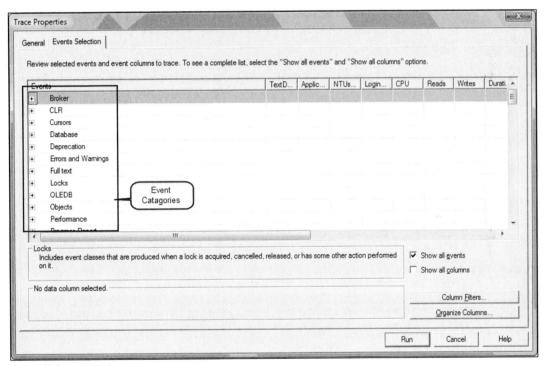

Figure 5-1

❑ **Event class:** An event class is a specific type of event that can be traced by a SQL Server instance. The event class contains all of the data that describes an event. There are approximately 200 event classes in SQL Server 2005. In SQL Profiler, event classes are organized under event categories. Each event class is associated with its own set of data columns (TextData, ApplicationName, LoginName, CPU, and so on), as shown in Figure 5-2.

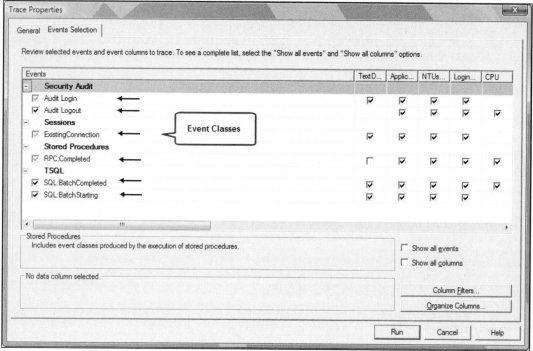

Figure 5-2

- ❑ **Event number:** Writing a script or stored procedure for a server-side trace requires using an event number to reference an event class. Corresponding event numbers can be found with respect to event classes in the SQL Book Online (BOL) under the system-stored procedure sp_trace_setevent. For example, the event class RPC:Completed corresponds to event number 10 (see Table 5-1).

- ❑ **Data column:** A data column is associated with an event class captured in a trace. It is an attribute of an event class. A single event class will have multiple related data columns. SQL Server 2005 Profiler has an internal built-in logic that handles data column dependencies; this logic only displays relevant data columns for a given event class. Because the event class determines the type of data that can be collected, not all data columns are applicable to all event classes. For example, in the SQL:BatchStarting event class, the CPU, Reads, Writes, and Duration data columns do not contain values because they are not applicable to the SQL:BatchStarting event class. However, these data columns *are* applicable to the SQL:BatchCompleted event class.

- ❑ **Trace:** Typically, trace refers to a collection of traceable event classes and data that are returned by an instance of SQL Server. Trace, as an action, refers to collecting and monitoring event classes in an instance of SQL Server. A trace captures data based on selected event classes, data columns, and filters. SQL Server provides two ways to trace an instance of SQL Server: you can trace with SQL Server Profiler, or you can trace using system-stored procedures.

Table 5-1

Event Number	Event Name	Description
0–9	Reserved	
10	RPC:Completed	Occurs when a remote procedure call (RPC) has completed.
11	RPC:Starting	Occurs when an RPC has started.
12	SQL:BatchCompleted	Occurs when a Transact-SQL batch has completed.
13	SQL:BatchStarting	Occurs when a Transact-SQL batch has started.
14	Audit Login	Occurs when a user successfully logs in to SQL Server.
15	Audit Logout	Occurs when a user logs out of SQL Server.

❑ **Trace file:** A trace file is an output file created by SQL Trace. Either SQL Profiler or a server-side trace script can create this file.

❑ **Trace table:** A trace table refers to a database table into which the trace data will be saved. From SQL Profiler, you can configure trace data to be saved into a specific database table.

❑ **Filter:** When creating a trace or template, you must define criteria to filter the data collected by the event. To keep traces from becoming too large, filter them so that only a subset of the event data is collected. For example, filter user names to a specific group of users, thereby reducing the output data. If a filter is not set, all events of the selected event classes are returned in the trace output (file, table, or screen).

❑ **Template:** A template defines the default configuration for a trace. The template includes the event classes that need to be monitored by SQL Server Profiler. For example, create a template that specifies which events, data columns, and filters to use. A template is not executed, but rather it is saved as a file with a .tdf extension. Once saved, the template controls the trace data that is captured when a trace based on the template is launched.

❑ **Common trace scenarios:** Table 5-2 contains common trace scenarios with their suggested event classes.

Best Practice

Try to minimize the system impact by selecting only the trace events needed. A catch-all trace will slow down the overall system performance, consume unnecessary disk space, and add complexity to the task that processes the trace output data.

If you are working with another party and are instructed to collect a large set of trace data, be sure to get an estimate on the overall system impact first.

Table 5-2

Scenario	Suggested Event Classes	What To Do
Monitoring long-running queries by execution time	RPC:Completed SQL:BatchCompleted	Capture all completed stored procedure calls and Transact-SQL statements submitted to SQL Server by clients.
		Include all data columns in the trace, group by Duration, and specify event criteria. For example, specify that the Duration of the event must be at least 500 milliseconds; you can eliminate short-running events from the trace. The Duration minimum value can be increased as required.
		Available template: TSQL_Duration
General Performance Tuning	RPC:Completed SP:StmtCompleted SQL:BatchCompleted Showplan XML	Capture information about stored procedures and Transact-SQL batch execution.
		Trace output can be used as a workload to Database Engine Tuning Advisor tool.
		Available template: Tuning
Identify the cause of a deadlock	RPC:Starting SQL: BatchStarting Lock:Deadlock Lock:Deadlock Chain Deadlock Graph	Include all data columns in the trace and group by Event Class. If you want to monitor only one database at a time, specify a value for the Database ID event criteria.
Blocking	Blocked Process Report	Include all data columns.
Audit login activity	Audit Login Event Sessions	Output data can be used for legal purposes to document activity and for technical purposes to track security policy violations.
Benchmark or replay a trace workload	CursorClose CursorExecute CursorOpen CursorPrepare CursorUnprepare Audit Login Audit Logout Existing Connection RPC Output Parameter RPC:Completed RPC:Starting Exec Prepared SQL Prepare SQL SQL:BatchCompleted SQL:BatchStarting	Use to perform iterative tuning, such as benchmark testing.
		If output data will be used for a trace replay, capturing detailed information about Transact-SQL statements will be required.
		Available template: TSQL_Replay

SQL Trace Options and Considerations

SQL Server provides many options to choose from when you trace database events. Some of these are beneficial for specific use case scenarios. Using a trace in a production environment is sensitive to how much system resources the trace will consume. The following sections discuss and compare some of the trace options available. Understanding these options will help you develop and optimize your trace solutions.

SQL Profiler and Server-Side Trace

There are two ways to collect event data. The most common way is to use a SQL Profiler trace; the second way is to use a server-side trace. Understanding the differences between the two and applying them to suitable environments can effectively reduce overhead and increase the quality of data collection.

- ❑ **Overhead:** SQL Profiler is a client Windows application that has a graphical user interface. When Profiler starts, it internally executes a set of system-stored procedures to create traces. After a trace event occurs, Profiler takes the event from the SQL Trace queue and displays the results of it.

- ❑ Server-side trace does not have a display feature; it moves events from the queue to file using buffered I/O. Since server-side trace does not require a display feature, it is the most efficient and low-cost way to collect SQL event data.

- ❑ **Ease of use:** SQL Profiler provides a user-friendly and real-time monitoring environment. To use the server-side trace, a written application or script is required. The server-side trace is not as easy as Profiler is.

- ❑ **Efficiency:** On a busy server, Profiler cannot guarantee the collection of every single event unless you save the data to a file on the server side and enable the server processes trace data option. Since the server-side trace does not display events during the data collection, it is more efficient.

- ❑ **Reusability:** The reusable parts of SQL Profiler are the pre-defined templates and user-defined templates. The server-side trace offers only a programming environment to create customized reusable scripts.

- ❑ **Schedule to start and stop:** SQL Profiler command utility (`Profiler90.exe`) has a feature to set a stop time for a Profiler trace; however, Microsoft documentation of the utility mentions that `Profiler90.exe` is not intended for scripting traces. The server-side trace can be scheduled to start and stop by using the system-stored production sp_trace_setstatus.

SQL Server 2005 provides a system view sys.traces that maintains detailed data for each live trace. In the following code example, the script pulls information from the sys.traces.

```
USE MASTER
GO
SELECT
      ID,                    -- Trace ID
      STATUS,                -- Trace Status, 0 = stopped, 1 = running
      IS_ROWSET,             -- 1 = rowset trace.
      BUFFER_COUNT,          -- Number of in-memory buffers used by the trace.
      BUFFER_SIZE,           -- Size of each buffer (KB).
      EVENT_COUNT,           -- Total number of events that occurred.
      PATH,                  -- Path of the trace file. Null means rowset trace.
      MAX_SIZE               -- Maximum trace file size limit in megabytes (MB).
```

```
FROM SYS.TRACES
WHERE ID <> 1                    -- Id 1 is default SQL black box trace.
```

Figure 5-3 shows that there were two traces created on the server instance. From the query results, the IS_Rowset column shows indicator flags, the number 0 indicates a server-server trace, and the number 1 indicates a Profiler trace. BUFFER_COUNT is the number of in-memory buffers used by a trace. Since these two traces were not started at the exact same time, the Event_COUNT had different numbers.

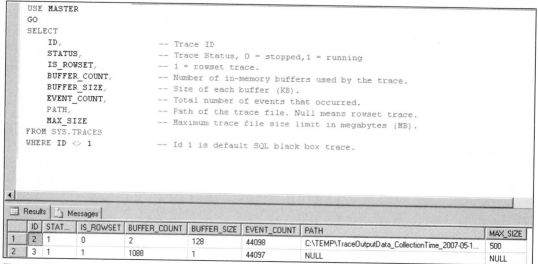

Figure 5-3

The following query displays all current running traces with similar information.

```
select * from fn_trace_getinfo(NULL)
```

Tracing in a Production Environment

In a production environment, if critical events must be monitored or confirmed in real time for a short period, SQL Profiler is one of the best tools to use.

SQL Profiler is a client application; its graphical interface utilizes server resources. Since dedicated SQL Servers in a production environment are adjusted to achieve greater performance of background services, it is not good practice to run the Profiler directly on a production SQL Server.

Running Profiler from another machine is the best practice; however, you need to consider the following factors. Because SQL Profiler is a process that is separate from the SQL Server process, transferring each event of a monitored SQL instance to a SQL Profiler will take some time. If you run SQL Profiler on a different computer, this process may take longer due to network latency. Therefore, performance of the SQL Server instance can be affected.

The disk space should also be monitored. Profiler trace displays trace results; in the mean time, it saves the results in a temporary file until the Profiler is closed. The file location depends on how the environment variable TMP is set for the user's account. For example, if the TMP environment variable is set to %USERPROFILE%\Local Settings\Temp, then the Profiler temporary files will be written to this folder until the Profiler is closed.

If trace data needs to be collected regularly for other purposes (auditing, workload baseline, performance tuning, or troubleshooting) then the server-side trace is the most efficient and low-cost approach.

Options of Configuring SQL Trace Output Data

Table 5-3 shows five options where trace output data can be saved.

Table 5-3

Option	SQL Trace	Profiler Screen	Trace Output File	Trace Database Table
1	SQL Profiler	✓		
2	SQL Profiler	✓	✓	
3	SQL Profiler	✓		✓
4	SQL Profiler	✓	✓	✓
5	Server-Side Trace		✓	

Here are the options examined more closely:

❑ **Option 1: Use SQL Profiler to trace without saving data:** The Profiler collects events from an instance of SQL Server locally (or remotely). Trace output data will be displayed on the SQL Profiler screen as soon as a configured event class occurs on the connected instance of SQL server.

After a trace is started, trace events will be displayed on the Profiler screen in near real time. This setup provides an excellent environment to learn SQL Profiler features and become familiar with traceable events.

However, this option is not an efficient setup for tracing in a production environment with high database transaction volumes. When a server is under resource stress, a server-side trace is preferable to SQL Profiler to guarantee the collection of every event without missing data.

In general, Profiler is an excellent choice for a non-production environment.

❑ **Option 2: Use SQL Profiler to trace and save data to a file system:** This setup has the same benefits and drawbacks as option 1. In addition, option 2 saves trace data to a Windows file system. This adds overhead.

❑ **Option 3: Use SQL Profiler to trace and save data to a database table:** This setup has the same benefits and drawbacks as option 1. In addition, it saves trace data to a database table for future data analysis. However, this process adds overhead directly to the monitored SQL Server.

❑ **Option 4: Use SQL Profiler to trace and save data to both the file system and the database table:** There might be special circumstances when this redundancy is useful. Otherwise, it is not advised to use this option.

❑   **Option 5: Use server-side trace and save data to a file system:** If monitoring real-time events is not required, a server-side trace provides the most efficient way to collect events for database performance tuning and troubleshooting. Server-side trace handles trace output data to a file using buffered I/O.

> A server-side trace can be executed manually or automatically from a scheduled SQL batch job.

Impacts on Where to Start Profiler and File Options

SQL Profiler can be connected to a monitored server locally or remotely. Where to start Profiler Trace and how to save the results will be determined by the following two important factors:

❑   SQL Profiler overhead impact on the monitored SQL Server

❑   Missing trace events' impact on trace data collection

SQL Profiler is nothing more than a GUI front end that invokes a set of T-SQL functions and system procedures collectively. When you start SQL Profiler, you start a Windows client application with the process name PROFILER90.exe. The overhead of each running PROFILER90.exe can be measured by the System Performance monitor. To minimize Profiler trace overhead on the SQL Server to be monitored, start your Profiler from a remote server (or workstation).

To ensure the collection of all trace events without missing data, select the option Server Processes Trace Data. (Later, in the Setup section, you will see in Figure 5-15 a check box named Server Processes Trace Data located in the middle section of the Trace Properties screen.) This option requires you to create a file (or rollover files) on the SQL Server that is being monitored. This way, even when the server processes trace data under stressful conditions, no events will be skipped. However, server performance may be affected.

Table 5-4 shows common configurations, pros, and cons.

Selecting a Data Collection Timeframe

Since collecting event data adds overhead to the system, targeting a specific timeframe for a clearly defined purpose will help to minimize system overhead.

For troubleshooting scenarios, if you have a known timeframe when the performance issue occurred, you can target that specific timeframe. Otherwise, try short trace intervals.

In collecting event data for baseline purposes, consider the purpose and the frequency. Be specific. Table 5-5 provides examples.

Duration Column Configuration

In the previous versions of SQL Profiler, the Duration column was measured in milliseconds regardless of whether the duration data was displayed on the Profiler screen, saved to an output file, or saved to a database table. However, in SQL 2005 Profiler, if a trace is saved to either a file or a database table, this column is defaulted to microseconds (one millionth, or 10^{-6}, of a second). It is important to recognize that in SQL Server 2005, while saving the trace output file, the measurement of the Duration column is microseconds and not milliseconds (as it was with previous versions). Without knowing about this new feature, your analysis for the Duration data may potentially be inaccurate.

Table 5-4

	Local or Remote	File Options	Comments
1	Start a Profiler trace from **the same server you are monitoring.**	1. Do not save data to files. 2. Save trace data to the local file system or a file share, but do not select the **Server processes SQL Server trace data** option.	**This option provides a simple trace environment for developing and troubleshooting database applications on a non-production and low-load server.** **This configuration is convenient to calibrate a very small trace or verify your trace configurations.**
2	Start a Profiler trace from **the same server you are monitoring.**	Save trace data to the local system or a file share, and select the **Server processes SQL Server trace data** option.	Pros: SQL Profiler is guaranteed to collect all configured trace events. Cons: This option adds extra overhead to the monitored server.
3	Start a Profiler trace from **a remote server or workstation.**	1. Do not save data to files. 2. Save trace data to the remote file system or a file share, but do not select the "**Server processes SQL Server trace data**" option.	Pros: Low overhead on monitored SQL Server. Cons: On a busy monitored SQL Server, the Profiler may lose event data.
4	Start a Profiler trace from **a remote server or workstation.**	Save trace data to the monitored SQL server by selecting the **Server processes SQL Server trace data** option.	Pros: SQL Profiler is guaranteed to collect all configured trace events. The Profiler load is on the remote node. Cons: The monitored SQL Server has to send one event stream to the Profiler GUI and the other event stream to the local file system. If you have to use Profiler to trace on a busy production server without missing events, then consider this configuration.

Table 5-5

Baseline Type	Timeframe	Frequency	Purpose
Peak Hours	10:00 am to 11:00 am	Weekly	Captures daily high transaction volumes during a weekday.
24-Hour	A full 24 hours	Monthly	Captures core database transition distributions over 24 hours on the 15th of the month.
Seasonal Events	A full 24 hours	Holiday shopping season, managerial reporting season	Captures seasonal high-transaction volumes over a 24-hour timeframe during the season.

With SQL Server 2005 Profiler, you can optionally configure the Duration column to be set in microseconds so that the Duration measurement will be consistent among the graphical user interface, file, or database table. To do this, select Tools ⇨ Options from the Profiler menu, and then select the check box Show values in Duration column in microseconds (SQL Server 2005 only), as shown in Figure 5-4.

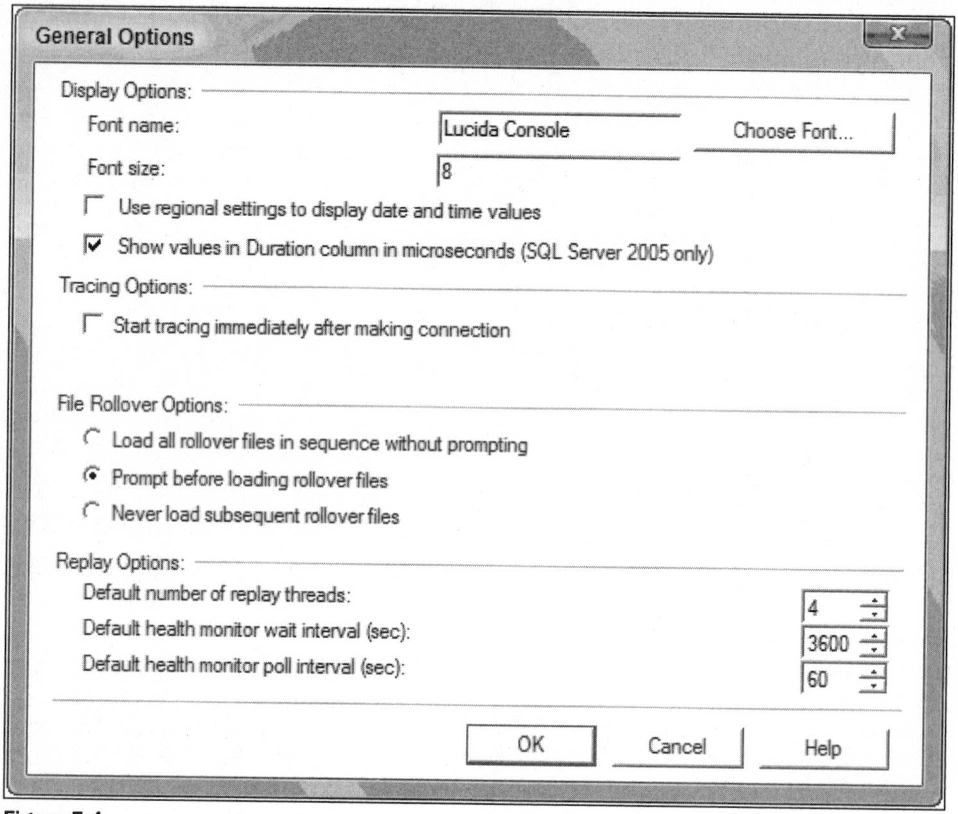

Figure 5-4

Capturing Blocking Events

Prior to SQL 2005, there were many scripts made available from various sources to capture what processes are blocking and what processes are being blocked. However, these scripts require manual execution. The sp_blocker (and its variation) is an example.

To configure Profiler, you only need the new SQL Trace event class listed below and must configure a threshold value in SQL Server for detecting blocking events.

❑   **Blocked Process Report:** This indicates that a task has been blocked for more than a specified amount of time. This event class does not include system tasks or tasks that are waiting on non–deadlock-detectable resources. Figure 5-5 is an example of this configuration.

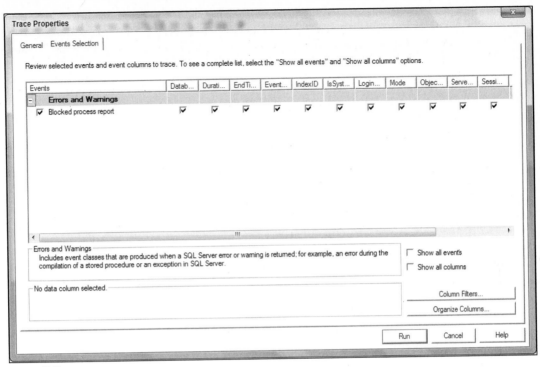

Figure 5-5

To configure the threshold and frequency at which reports are generated, use the `sp_configure` command to configure the blocked process threshold option, which can be set in seconds. By default, no blocked process reports are produced. In the following code example, the blocked process threshold is configured to report the blocking event every 10 seconds. After the configuration, execute `sp_configure` again to verify the setting of "blocked process threshold" (see Figure 5-6).

```
sp_configure 'show advanced options', 1
GO
RECONFIGURE
GO

-- The blocked process report threshold is the number of seconds the block is
-- in effect after which you get an event firing.
-- For example, setting this to 10 tells SQL Server to fire an event whenever
-- a block is 10 seconds old or 20 seconds or 30 seconds etc...
-- If the block lasted 40 seconds then you'd get 4 events.
sp_configure 'blocked process threshold', 10 -- 10 seconds
GO
RECONFIGURE
GO
```

To see a blocking event from Profiler, you will use the SQL Server sample database Adventureworks and open two query windows.

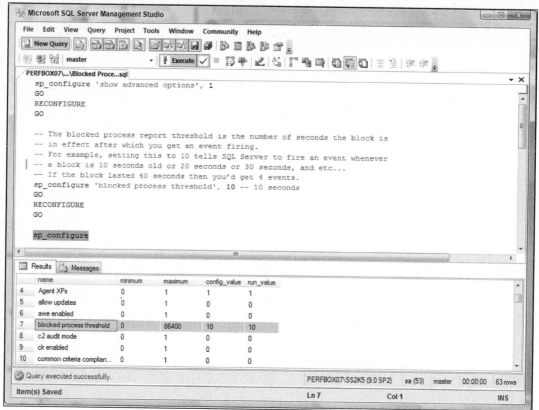

Figure 5-6

Start the Profiler as configured in Figure 5-5.

From the first query window, execute the following UPDATE to modify a data row in the Address table of the SQL Server sample database Adventureworks. You are intentionally leaving the transaction open so that you can trigger the blocking event.

```
--Connection A
BEGIN TRAN
UPDATE Adventureworks.Person.Address
SET AddressLine1 = '40 Ellis Street'
WHERE AddressLine1 = '40 Ellis St.'
AND City = 'Bothell'
AND PostalCode = '98011'
```

From the second query window, execute the following query to display the same data row. Since the data has been blocked by the UPDATE transaction, this query will be blocked.

```
--Connection B (open another session)
SELECT *
FROM Adventureworks.Person.Address
```

```
WHERE AddressLine1 = '40 Ellis St.'
AND City = 'Bothell'
AND PostalCode = '98011'
```

After the threshold value (10 seconds in your sp_configure setting) of a blocking event has been met, Profiler captures every blocking event. For each blocking event captured in Profiler, it records execution statements for the blocker. It pinpoints who the blocker is and which process is being blocked. This data is displayed in XML format as seen in Figure 5-7.

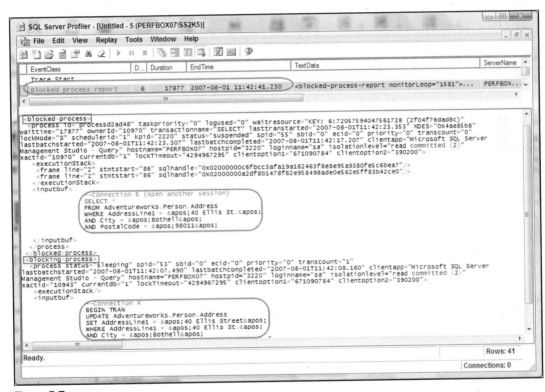

Figure 5-7

Configuring Profiler to capture blocking events makes performance monitoring and tuning tasks much simpler than ever before. Measuring the frequency of blocking events and number of blocking events per day will provide you with a quantified measure of performance data.

Capturing Showplan XML Data

One of the new SQL trace events worth mentioning is the Showplan XML event class. In the case of tuning T-SQL statements or stored procedures, the output of XML data with execution statistics is very useful.

To configure the Profiler, use the new event class Showplan XML, which includes the following events settings:

- ❑ **Showplan XML:** Occurs when Microsoft SQL Server executes a SQL statement. Include the Showplan XML event class to identify the Showplan operators. This event class is under the Performance event category (see Figure 5-8). The XML Showplan output can be stored as a separated file as indicated in Figure 5-9.

- ❑ **RPC:Completed:** Indicates that a remote procedure call has been completed.

- ❑ **SQL:BatchCompleted:** Indicates that the Transact-SQL batch has completed.

When the Showplan XML event class is included in a trace, the amount of overhead will significantly slow down performance. To minimize the overhead incurred, limit use of this event class to trace specific problems for brief periods.

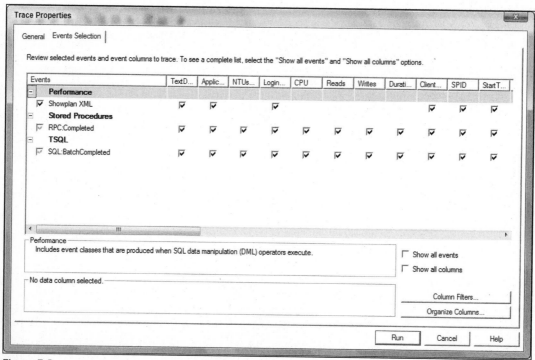

Figure 5-8

Figure 5-10 displays data from an Adventureworks database view called HumanResources.vEmployee. Profiler captured the query plan used. The actual plan used for the query and statistic data reveals valuable information for a query tuning (see Figure 5-10).

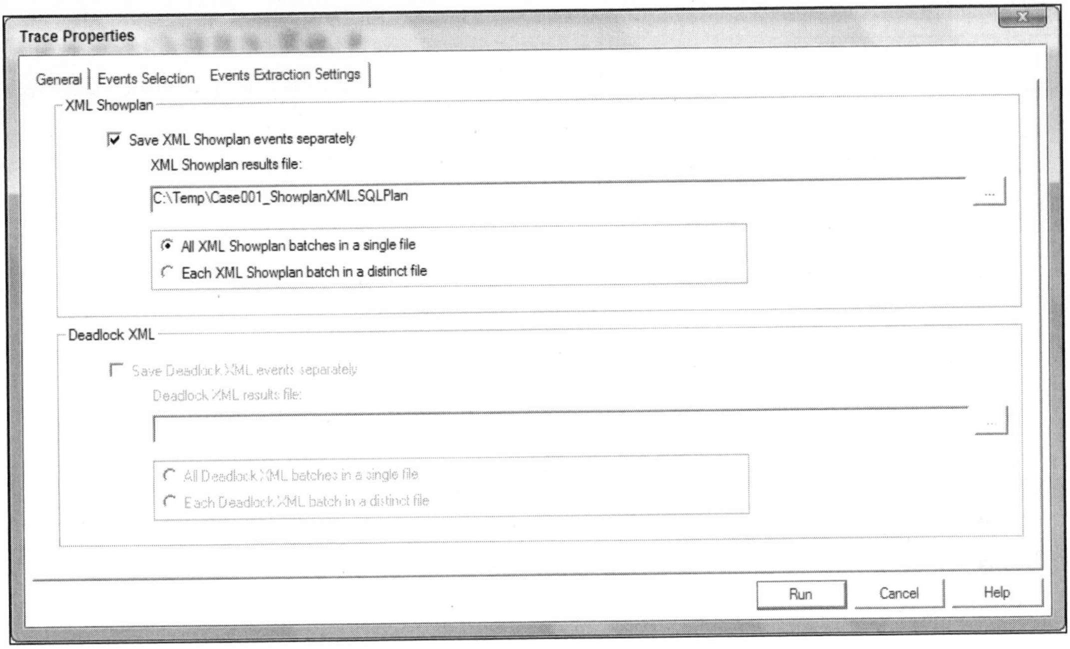

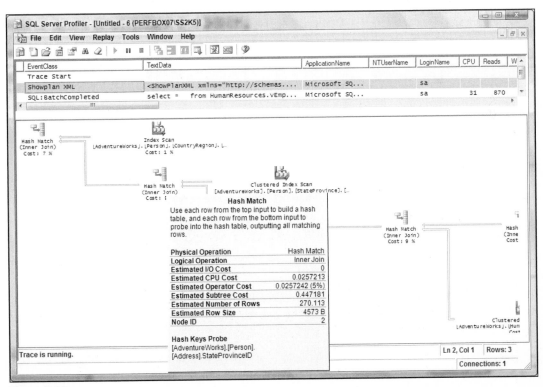

Figure 5-9

Figure 5-10

Capturing Deadlock Graphs

Because each process is preventing the other process from getting a required resource, a deadlock occurs when two SQL Server system process IDs (SPIDs) are waiting for a resource and neither process can proceed.

SQL Server has a lock manager thread that checks for deadlocks. When a deadlock is detected, in order to break the deadlock, the lock manager will choose one of the SPIDs as a victim. The lock manager then cancels the current batch for the victim, rolls back its transaction, and issues an error message as in the following example:

```
Transaction (Process ID 53) was deadlocked on lock resources with another
process and has been chosen as the deadlock victim. Rerun the transaction.
```

If deadlocks happen frequently, database applications suffer. SQL Server Profiler can create a trace to capture deadlock events for analysis. Use the following event classes to configure a Profiler trace (also, see Figure 5-11):

- ❑ **Lock:Deadlock Chain:** Monitors when deadlock conditions occur.
- ❑ **Lock:Deadlock:** Identifies which SPID was chosen as the deadlock victim.
- ❑ **Deadlock Graph:** Provides an XML description of a deadlock. This class occurs simultaneously with the Lock:Deadlock event class.
- ❑ **RPC:Completed:** Indicates that a remote procedure call has been completed.
- ❑ **SQL:BatchCompleted:** Indicates that the Transact-SQL batch has completed.

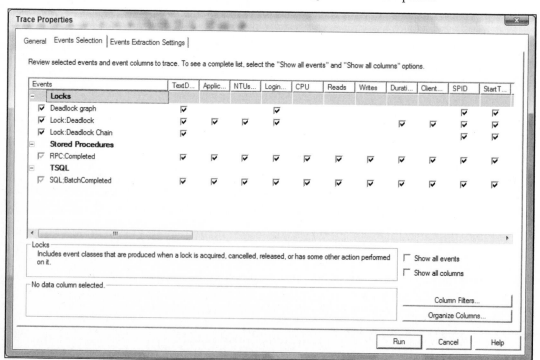

Figure 5-11

To simulate a deadlock event, you will create a simple testing database with a single table. The source code can be downloaded from the publisher's web site.

```
CREATE DATABASE TestingDeadlockDB
GO

USE TestingDeadlockDB
CREATE TABLE tbl_deadlock (id int IDENTITY(1,1), Comments VARCHAR(30))

INSERT INTO tbl_deadlock values ('Simulating Deadlock Event')
INSERT INTO tbl_deadlock values ('Simulating Deadlock Event')

CREATE UNIQUE NONCLUSTERED INDEX [CI_id] ON [dbo].[tbl_deadlock]
( [id] ASC )ON [PRIMARY]
GO
```

Next, you will use a simple script to trigger a deadlock. The purpose is to show that the Profiler is now fully capable of capturing deadlock events and providing useful information. Open a new query window (in the following example, you refer to it as connection 1) and type in the following code:

```
-- Open a new SQL Query Window from SQL Management Studio (connection 1)
USE TestingDeadlockDB
SET NOCOUNT ON
SELECT @@SPID AS SPID

BEGIN TRAN
  UPDATE tbl_deadlock
  SET Comments = 'Simulating Deadlock Event 2.'
  WHERE id = 2

WAITFOR DELAY '00:0:20'

UPDATE tbl_deadlock
SET Comments = 'Simulating Deadlock Event 1.'
WHERE id = 1
```

There are two T-SQL UPDATE statements in one transaction. The first UPDATE modifies the data row with id=2 and waits for 10 seconds; the second UPDATE modifies the data row with id=1. Do not execute the code yet.

Open another query window (you refer to it as connection 2) and type in the following code. The code logic is similar to the previous code except it modifies the data row with id=1 first and then the data row with id=2. Do not execute the code yet.

```
-- Open another SQL Query Window from SQL Management Studio (connection 2)
USE TestingDeadlockDB
SET NOCOUNT ON
SELECT @@SPID AS SPID

BEGIN TRAN
  UPDATE tbl_deadlock
  SET Comments = 'Simulating Deadlock Event 1.'
  WHERE id = 1
```

```
WAITFOR DELAY '00:0:20'

UPDATE tbl_deadlock
SET Comments = 'Simulating Deadlock Event 2.'
WHERE id = 2
```

At this point, perform the following:

1. Start the Profiler as configured in Figure 5-11.

2. Execute code from the connection 1 screen.

3. Then go to the connection 2 screen and execute the code you have prepared within 20 seconds after the previous step.

Wait for about 20 seconds and you will see the query result from connection 1 completed successfully. In this example, the SPID number is 53 (see Figure 5-12). However, the query result from connection 2 will be encountered with a deadlock error message as indicated in Figure 5-13.

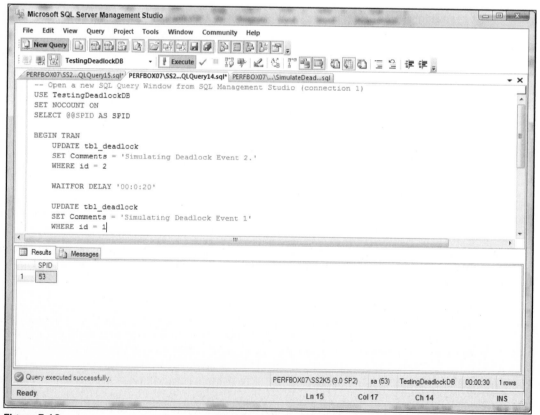

Figure 5-12

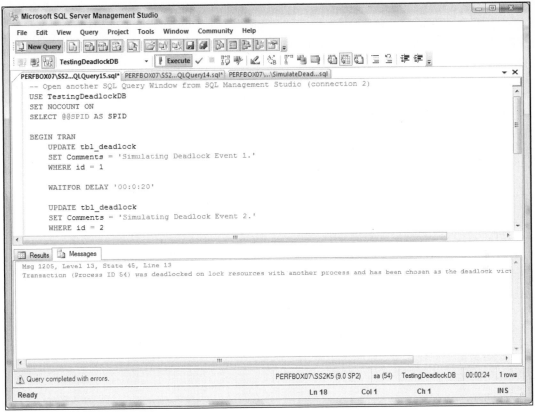

Figure 5-13

Profiler captures the deadlock event with the following information (see Figure 5-14). Let's go over events captured in Profiler one by one:

- ❑ **Line 1:** Trace Start.

- ❑ **Lines 2 and 3:** The SQL Server lock manager thread (SPID 5) detected a circular blocking chain with SPID numbers 53 and 54. The database name is TestingDeadLockDB.

- ❑ **Line 4:** The transaction from SPID 54 was canceled and rolled back. A detailed execution query statement was captured in the TextData column. The confirmation is indicated in the Deadlock graph event.

- ❑ **Line 5:** The transaction from SPID 53 was completed.

- ❑ **Line 6:** A deadlock graph was produced. From the graph, it is clearly indicated that the SPID 54 was the victim (because it is crossed out). If you move a mouse over any symbol on the graph, execution statements encountered are displayed.

Prior to SQL Server 2005, to get a deadlock graph, it was necessary to turn on deadlock trace flags and collect deadlock data from the SQL Server error log. Now, Profiler provides a much easier way to capture all deadlock events. For troubleshooting and deadlock scenarios, the deadlock graph provides not only a visual presentation of a circular blocking scenario but also the execution statements involved.

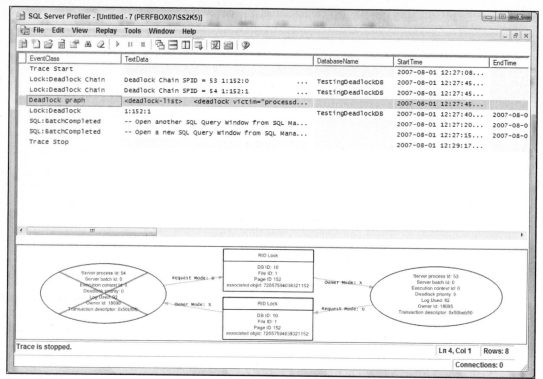

Figure 5-14

In your sample test, if you re-arrange the two UPDATE statements that access the database resource from one connection in the same chronological order as the other connection, the deadlock issue will be resolved. For more information on resolving deadlocks, see the SQL Server technical bulletin "How to resolve a deadlock" at http://support.microsoft.com/kb/832524.

Identifying Long-Running Queries Using SQL Profiler

Many situations require monitoring long-running queries. For example, an existing Service Level Agreement (SLA) might require that some items need to be measured by query response time. Database users might complain that some of the queries have inconsistent response time behaviors. Sometimes queries can execute slowly or cause application time-outs.

SQL Profiler is one of the most valuable graphical user interface (GUI) tools in determining which queries take the longest time to execute or confirming which specific queries run slowest. SQL Profiler can monitor query activity as it occurs.

The following simple scenario will walk through the process of identifying long-running queries.

Simulating a Scenario and a Sample Database

The purpose of this scenario is to have SQL Profiler identify the longest running queries in a workload. To simulate a set of long-running queries, you first create a sample database.

To create the sample database (people2), you can download source code from the publisher's web site at www.wrox.com. All T-SQL scripts are stored in the People2 folder. Instructions are provided in the readme.txt file. You will execute Step1_CreatePeople2Database.sql to create the sample database, and then execute Step2_CreateTablesProcs.sql to create database tables and stored procedures. Lastly, execute Step3_InitializeNames.sql to initialize the testing data for our scenario.

The database has a key table called people that you want to generate about 400,000 rows. Each row contains data for the first name, last name, and date of birth. A T-SQL script called populate.sql will find a male entry and update a female entry to match the male last name.

Depending on your server speed, the populate.sql *script may take about 3–4 minutes to finish.*

Analyzing the Issue

The definition of long-running queries can be arbitrary. For example, the threshold value may be defined by a set of business requirements. Using SQL Profiler to identify the top 10 long-running queries is not difficult. In this scenario, you will use a T-SQL script populate.sql to generate long-running queries.

The first challenge is to match event classes with the issue. Please reference Table 5-1 for suggested event classes. Use the following event classes. A query execution time is recorded in the duration column.

❑   **RPC:Completed:** Indicates that a remote procedure call has been completed. This event will capture stored procedure calls from client connections.

❑   **SQL:BatchCompleted:** Indicates that the Transact-SQL batch has been completed.

❑   **SP:StmtCompleted:** Indicates that a Transact-SQL statement within a stored procedure has been completed.

The second challenge is to set up a filter to collect the right amount of data. Calibrate a small sample workload first. After analyzing the sample workload, this new information will help to determine what exact filters to use and what threshold values to apply.

For this scenario, you will launch the Profiler on the same server and not use the Save To File option to save trace data to a file, since you will be monitoring the activities.

Setup

The following steps include initial setup, validation, and finding filter criteria:

1.   Start SQL Profiler. In SQL Server Management Studio, click the Tools menu, then select SQL Server Profiler. (Alternatively, start SQL Profiler by clicking Start ➪ Run, then type in **Profiler90**).

2.   From the File menu, click New Trace.

3. Specify the relevant connection details to connect to an instance of SQL Server. The Trace Properties dialog box will then appear.

4. In the General tab, fill in the appropriate information, making sure to select the Standard template (see Figure 5-15).

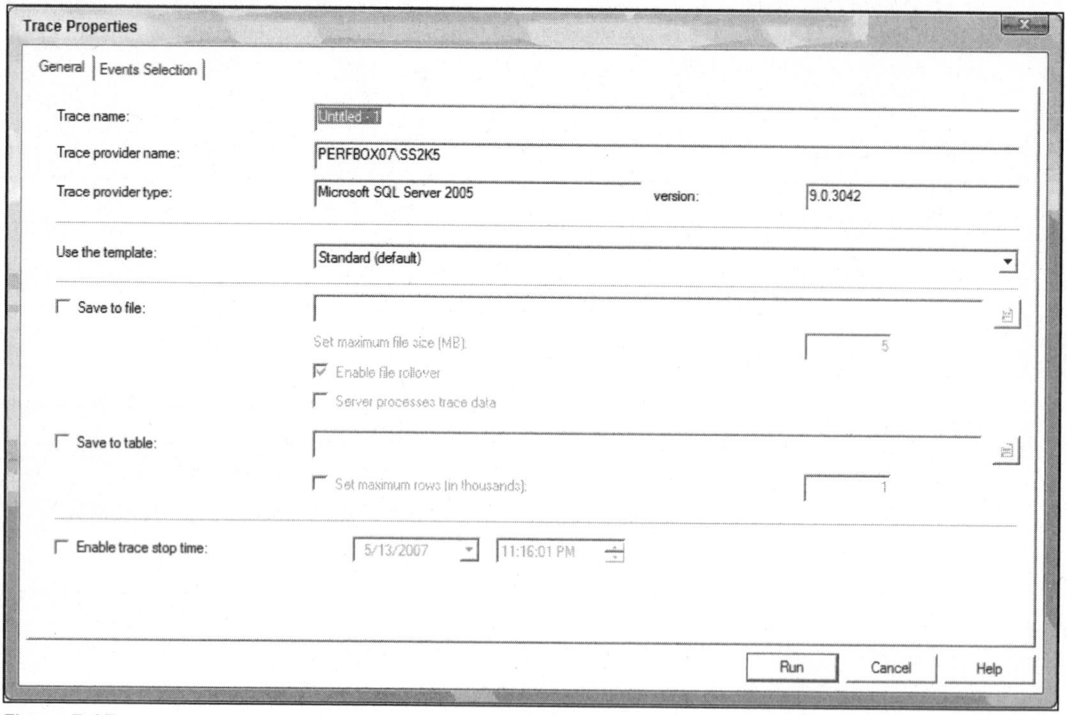

Figure 5-15

5. Click the Events Selection tab. Select the three event classes chosen in the upfront analyzing process (see Figure 5-16).

6. Click the Column Filters button on the bottom right, then highlight the Duration column on the left; expand the Greater Than Or Equal label by clicking the plus sign in front of it and type in an initial value of 2 for this case. (In a real production environment, a long-running query is determined by a specific business requirement, such as an SLA).

7. Click the Organize Columns button, also on the bottom right corner of the Trace Properties dialog box. Highlight Duration (see Figure 5-17), which is under the Columns header, and click the Up button to move it all the way up to be under the Groups header. Click OK.

8. Click Run to start the trace.

9. Now, open the event generation script named `populate.sql` to generate database transactions from a Query Window within SQL Server Management Studio. Execute the script by pressing F5.

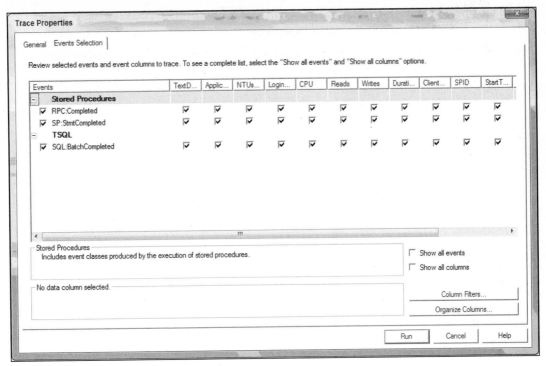

Figure 5-16

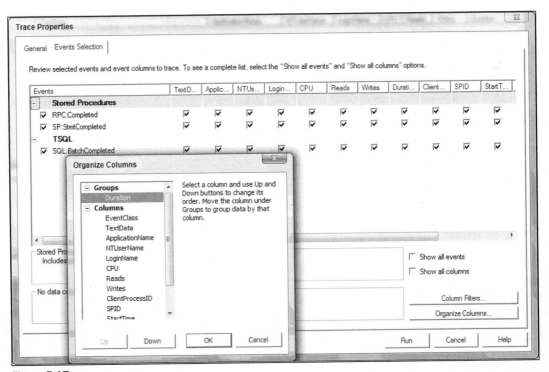

Figure 5-17

10. In about a minute, you should see the events that are captured. Once the events have been captured, stop the trace (see Figure 5-18).

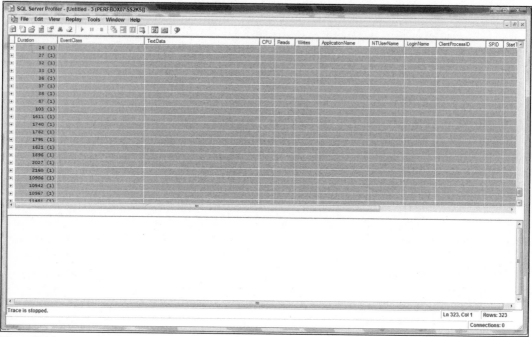

Figure 5-18

11. The populate.sql script generated the workload sample. From Figure 5-18, under the Duration column, the longest running queries are arranged from the bottom to the top of the screen. You also see that most entries (starting from the bottom of the screen) in the duration column are longer than 2000 milliseconds. From this information, you can re-adjust the duration filter criteria accordingly. In this case, you update the Duration filter (defined in the step 6) from the value 2 to 2000 (under the Greater Than Or Equal label).

12. Save the Trace to a template.

Tracing

Your trace has been defined, validated, and saved into a template. You can now begin to trace for the duration of your simulations.

1. From SQL Profiler, open and run the trace template you saved from the previous step (Step 12 in the previous section). Re-start the event generation script populate.sql.

2. After the script is completed, stop the trace.

3. Click the View menu, click Grouped View, and you should see results similar to Figure 5-19. Please note actual results depend on the speed of the system hardware.

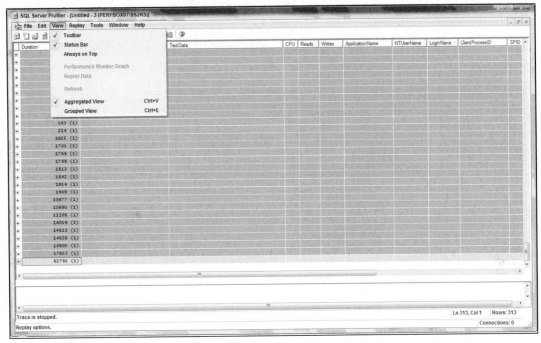

Figure 5-19

Now you have received Profiler tracing results. In the next section, you will see result analysis and brief tuning.

Analysis and Tuning

The very last event in Figure 5-20 is the query statement from your simulation script, so you ignore it. The Duration column is sorted in a descending order. The highlighted portion in the second-to-last row indicates a duration of 17582 milliseconds, and an exec marriage query statement under the TextData column, showing that it is one of the longest queries in this trace.

Now, based on the trace information, you can start to investigate tuning opportunities for identified long-running queries.

For a quick illustration on how to find obvious tuning opportunities, you will use SQL Server 2005 Database Tuning Advisor (DTA). Type **exec marriage** from a new Query session within SQL Server Management Studio, and then right-click Analyze Query in Database Tuning Advisor (See Figure 5-21).

Enter a session name for a future reference, and then click Start Analysis (see Figure 5-22).

If you were connected to the SQL Server in the SQL Server Management Studio by using SQL Server authentication, you will have to re-connect to a server instance and select a database to tune before you can click Start Analysis. Otherwise, if your used Windows Authentication, you will not be asked to re-connect to the server instance again.

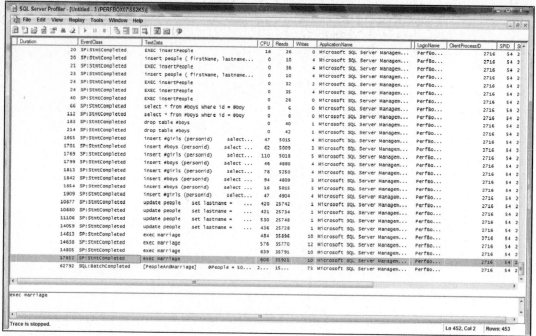

Figure 5-20

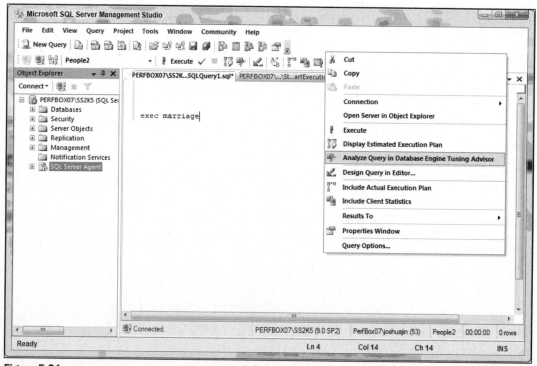

Figure 5-21

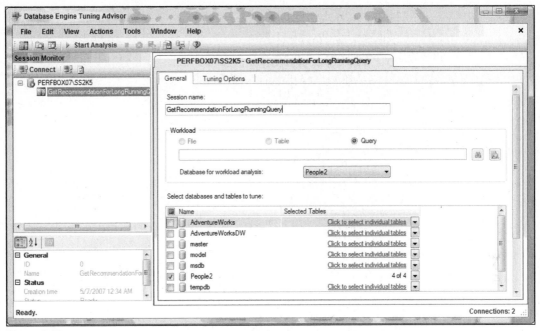

Figure 5-22

Wait for a while and some suggestions will be displayed under the Recommendations tab; scroll the Windows horizontal bar to the right and find some entries under the Definition column (see Figure 5-23).

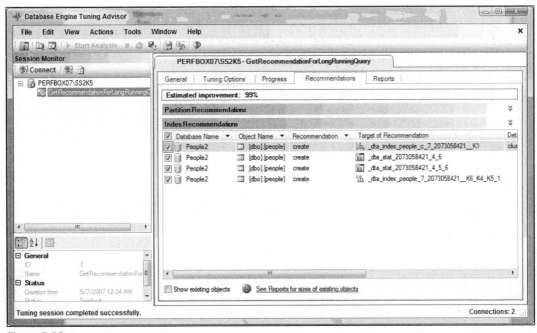

Figure 5-23

Click the first entry. You see DTA made a suggestion to add a clustered index for the `people` table (see Figure 5-24).

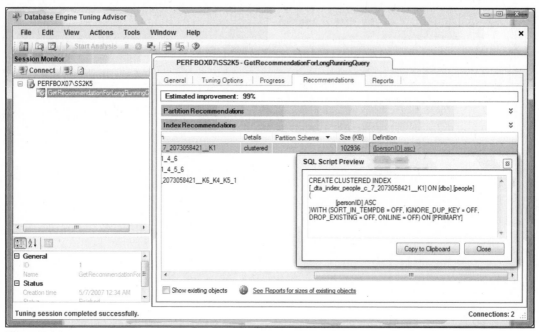

Figure 5-24

After carefully studying the logic in the stored procedure `marriage`, you found that all index suggestions are valid. After implementing new indexes, the performance increases dramatically.

Case Summary

In this case scenario, you used Profiler to identify long-running queries directly; long-running queries were sorted by Profiler in ascending order. After long-running queries were identified, you demonstrated that the SQL DTA tool could provide valuable information for tuning opportunities.

Tracing Costly Queries by Using Profiler to Generate Server-Side Trace Code

Proactive database administrators want to keep track of costly database queries in order to analyze them. Costly queries have symptoms of high CPU and I/O utilizations.

In the following scenario, you want to capture costly queries in stored procedures or SQL statements. For this, you need to have CPU, Reads, Writes, and Duration information in your trace file for analysis. You will use SQL Profiler to generate a server-side trace code.

Using Profiler to Generate Server-Side Trace Script

You can use SQL Profiler to define a trace to meet your requirements. Start Profiler, make a connection to a SQL 2005 instance, select the Standard template, check the box for Enable trace stop time, and then click the Event Select tab. Unselect all events but RPC:Completed and SQL:BatchCompleted, as shown in Figure 5-25. Depending on who processes the trace data and what the purpose is of collecting the trace data, it is also a common practice to include the SP:StmtCompleted event. If you include the SP:StmtCompleted event, you can get to the individual statement in the stored procedure that is causing the problem. The downside is that you will have more data to process and the size of the trace output file will be larger.

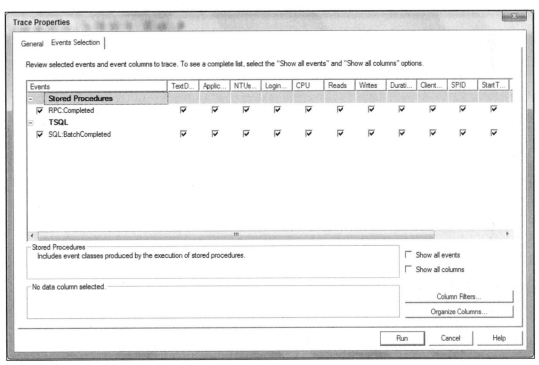

Figure 5-25

Set the CPU filters to greater than 50 (ms). Set the Duration filter to greater than 2000 (ms), as shown in Figure 5-26.

After defining the filters, click Run to start the trace, and then immediately stop the trace. Click File ⇨ Export ⇨ Script Trace Definition ⇨ For SQL Server 2005, as shown in Figure 5-27. Save the script to a file. The server-side trace code is then generated.

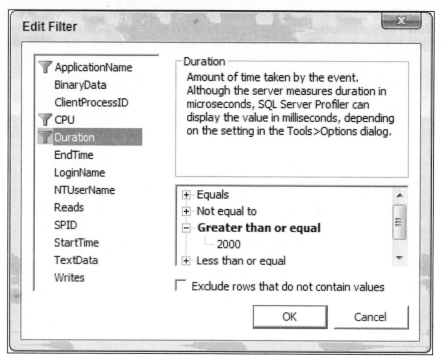

Figure 5-26

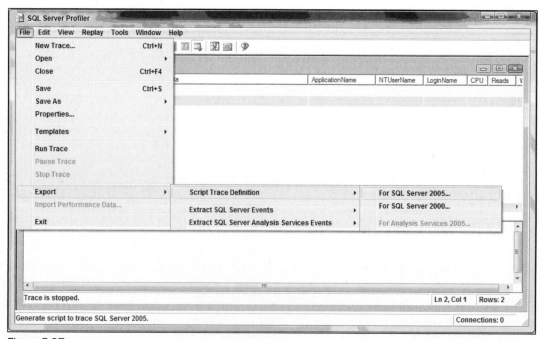

Figure 5-27

Before you execute the server-side trace, you need to open the server-side trace file to make minor modifications. Within the top portion of the script, you need to define a time for the trace to stop itself, and provide a new file name for the trace to save its output data using the following code:

```
-- Create a Queue
declare @rc int
declare @TraceID int
declare @maxfilesize bigint
declare @DateTime datetime
```

```
set @DateTime = '2007-05-12 10:22:14.000'
```

```
set @maxfilesize = 5
```

```
-- Please replace the text InsertFileNameHere, with an appropriate
-- filename prefixed by a path, e.g., c:\MyFolder\MyTrace. The .trc extension
-- will be appended to the filename automatically. If you are writing from
-- remote server to local drive, please use UNC path and make sure server has
-- write access to your network share
```

```
exec @rc = sp_trace_create @TraceID output, 0, N'InsertFileNameHere', @maxfile-
size, @Datetime
```

```
if (@rc != 0) goto error
```

```
-- Client side File and Table cannot be scripted
```

Assuming the trace will be started at '2007-05-14 09:00:00.000' for a 15-minute trace, you need to change the @DateTime to '2007-05-14 09:15:00.000' as shown here:

```
set @DateTime = '2007-05-14 09:15:00.000'
```

For the file name you substitute the N'InsertFileNameHere' with a legitimate file name, for example, c:\temp\myServerSideTraceOutput_CostlyQueries. This file name has to be unique.

The default file extension is .trc.

The second input parameter was 0, which you will change to 2. The value 2 indicates that the output file is a rollover file. It also specifies that when the maximum_file_size is reached, the current trace file will be closed and a new file will be created. (All new records will be written to this new file.) The new file will have the same name as the previous file, but an integer will be appended to indicate its sequence. You also added the last parameter file count and specified a value of 10. This indicates that the maximum number of rollover files is 10.

```
exec @rc = sp_trace_create @TraceID output,
    2,
    N'c:\temp\myServerSideTraceOutput_CostlyQueries',
    @maxfilesize,
    @Datetime,
    10
```

As with any scripting code development, after you modify the original code, you should test and validate it.

Open a query window, connect to a SQL Server instance, open the server-side script file, and execute it to start a server-side trace. If the code has no defect, a new trace ID will be created, as seen in Figure 5-28. The output trace file in this example will be created on the server side, which resides on the monitored SQL server. Use the following statement to query all traces on the server.

```
select * from ::fn_trace_getinfo(NULL)where traceid <> 1
```

```
select * from ::fn_trace_getinfo(NULL)where traceid <> 1
```

	traceid	property	value
1	2	1	2
2	2	2	c:\temp\myServerSideTraceOutput_CostlyQueries.trc
3	2	3	5
4	2	4	2007-05-14 09:15:00.000
5	2	5	1

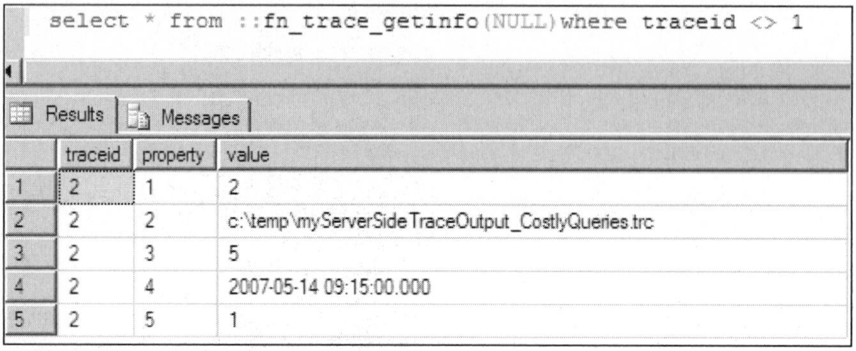

Figure 5-28

After the validation, stop and remove the trace that was just created and delete the trace output file. Using the following command, replace <traceID> with the trace ID created from your testing:

```
EXEC sp_trace_setstatus <traceID>, 0 -- To stop a trace
EXEC sp_trace_setstatus <traceID>, 2 -- Closes and deletes the specified trace
```

Executing Server-Side Scripts

When it is time to start the trace, you can either schedule a SQL agent job to start the trace at '2007-05-14 09:00:00.000' or alternatively wait until the starting time to manually execute the trace script from a SQL Query Window.

In this example, you use the same populate.sql script as before to generate database queries.

Handling Trace Files and Analyzing Trace Data

After the server-side trace stops, you can now analyze the resulting trace data.

Opening Trace Rollover Files into SQL Profiler

Since your output trace data is a set of rollover files, you want to configure the SQL Profiler to load all these files in sequence without prompting. To do this, select Tools ⇨ Options from the Profiler menu to bring up the General Options screen and then select the option Load All Rollover Files In Sequence Without Prompting, as shown in Figure 5-29.

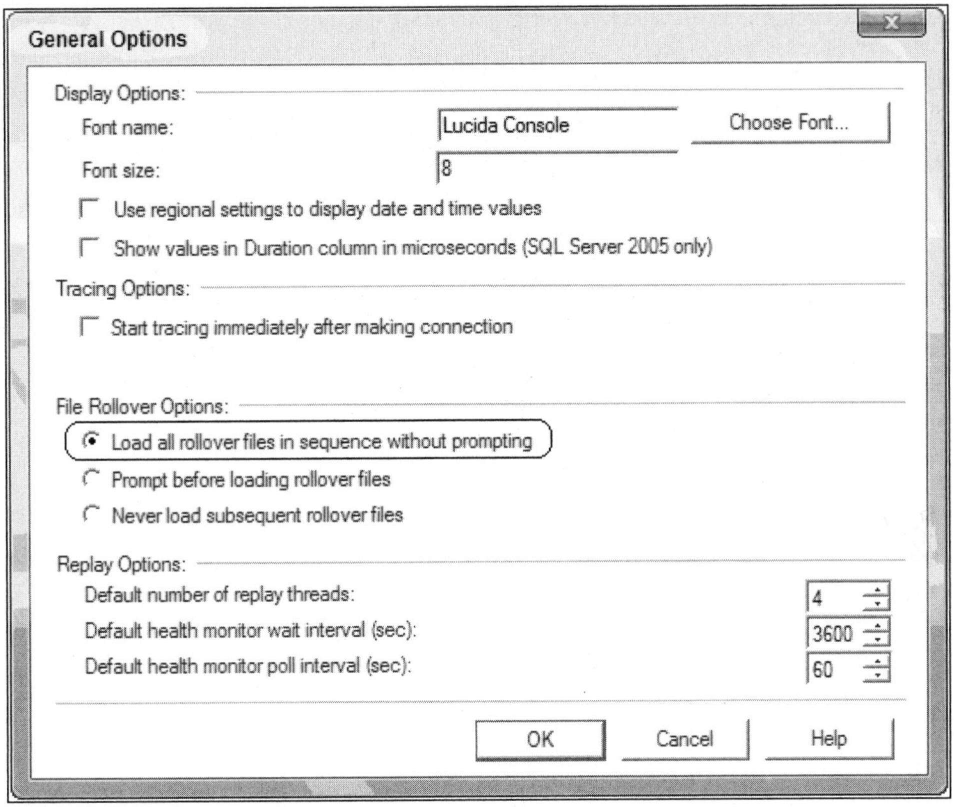

Figure 5-29

Importing Trace Data to a Trace Table

The SQL Server function `fn_trace_gettable` returns the content of one or more trace files in tabular form. Use this function to read trace files directly and insert data into a user database table for analysis.

```
SELECT *
INTO temp_trace_table_001
FROM ::fn_trace_gettable('c:\temp\myServerSideTraceOutput_CostlyQueries
   .trc', default)
```

The function `fn_trace_gettable` returns a table specified with the columns valid for the specified trace.

The function `fn_trace_gettable` has two arguments. The first argument, *filename*, specifies the initial trace file to be read. The second argument, *number_files*, specifies the number of rollover files to be read; this number includes the initial file specified in *filename*. If *number_files* is specified as default, `fn_trace_gettable` will read all the rollover files until it reaches the end of the trace.

One minor issue that will need to be resolved is that the data type of the TextData column created by the function is a SQL NTEXT data type. Many string functions do not support the NTEXT data type.

According to SQL 2005 BOL (February 2007), the NTEXT data types will be removed in a future version of Microsoft SQL Server. See more details in the article: `http://msdn2.microsoft.com/en-us/library/ms187993.aspx`.

To get around this, convert the TextData column from the NTEXT data type to a string function friendly data type: VARCHAR, NVARCHAR, VARCHAR(MAX), or NVARCHAR(MAX). For example, use NVARCHAR(MAX).

```
ALTER TABLE temp_trace_table_001
    ALTER COLUMN TextData NVARCHAR(MAX)
```

Now you will be able to write a query and analyze trace data. The following query statement will report the top 50 longest queries. Some queries are executed multiple times. Since the default measurement in the duration column of the trace file is in microseconds, the following query statement will convert the duration time to milliseconds to be consistent with the CPU measurement. Figure 5-30 shows the query result.

```
SELECT TOP 50
    COUNT(*) AS NumberOfExecutions,
    TextData,
    SUM(Duration)/1000 AS Total_Duration_MilliSeconds,
    SUM(CPU) AS Total_CPU_Time_MilliSeconds,
    SUM(Reads) AS Total_Logical_Reads,
    SUM(Writes) AS Total_Writes
FROM temp_trace_table_001
WHERE TextData IS NOT NULL
GROUP BY
    TextData
ORDER BY Total_Duration_MilliSeconds DESC
```

If your trace data collection has procedures called multiple times with different parameters or simple query statements with different filters, the above GROUP BY TextData clause will not work well. In that case, a simple solution is to modify the query to use string functions (substring, charindex) to filter the TextData in the query statement. In the following example, the query uses a substring function to get the first 15 character data from the TextData. You can change the substring function to extract a different set of character strings based on your requirements. There are many ways to tokenize TextData, but to cover them all is beyond the scope of this book.

```
-- As a reminder, you have converted the TextData to NVARCHAR(MAX) data type.
SELECT TOP 50
    ...,
    SUBSTRING(TextData,1,15),
    SUM(Duration)/1000 AS Total_Duration_MilliSeconds,
    ...
FROM temp_trace_table_001
WHERE TextData IS NOT NULL
GROUP BY
    SUBSTRING(TextData,1,15)
ORDER BY Total_Duration_MilliSeconds DESC
```

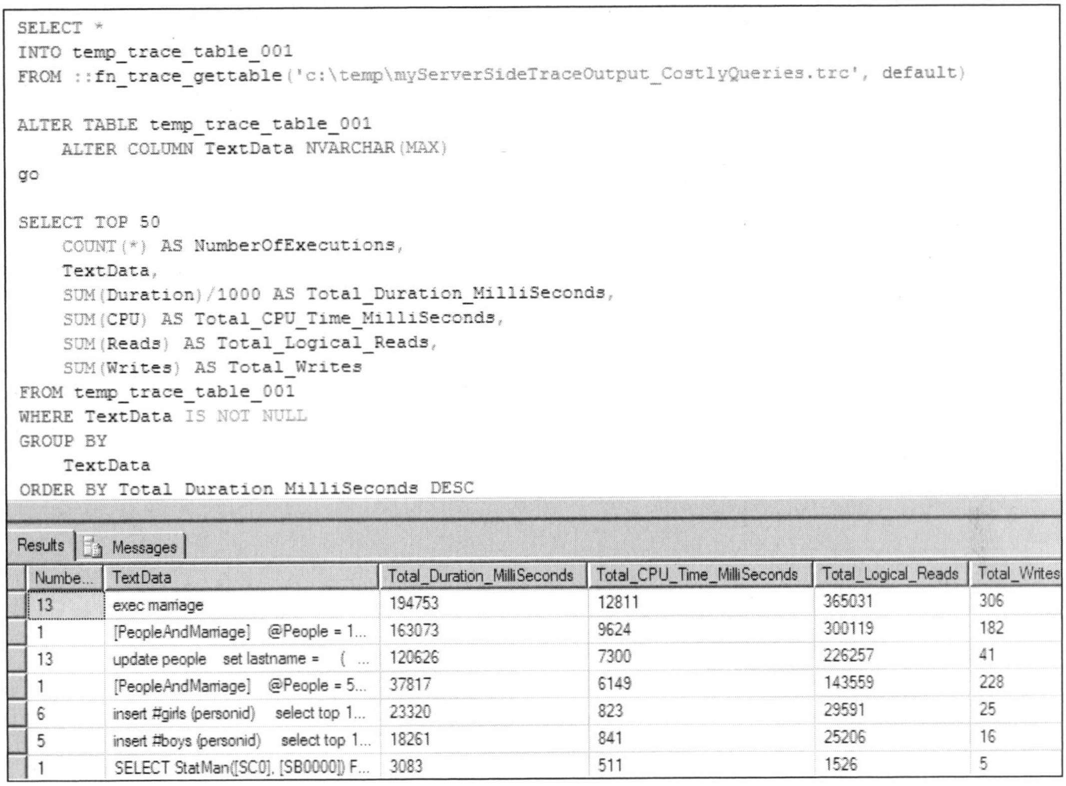

```
SELECT *
INTO temp_trace_table_001
FROM ::fn_trace_gettable('c:\temp\myServerSideTraceOutput_CostlyQueries.trc', default)

ALTER TABLE temp_trace_table_001
    ALTER COLUMN TextData NVARCHAR(MAX)
go

SELECT TOP 50
    COUNT(*) AS NumberOfExecutions,
    TextData,
    SUM(Duration)/1000 AS Total_Duration_MilliSeconds,
    SUM(CPU) AS Total_CPU_Time_MilliSeconds,
    SUM(Reads) AS Total_Logical_Reads,
    SUM(Writes) AS Total_Writes
FROM temp_trace_table_001
WHERE TextData IS NOT NULL
GROUP BY
    TextData
ORDER BY Total_Duration_MilliSeconds DESC
```

Numbe...	TextData	Total_Duration_MilliSeconds	Total_CPU_Time_MilliSeconds	Total_Logical_Reads	Total_Writes
13	exec marriage	194753	12811	365031	306
1	[PeopleAndMarriage] @People = 1...	163073	9624	300119	182
13	update people set lastname = (...	120626	7300	226257	41
1	[PeopleAndMarriage] @People = 5...	37817	6149	143559	228
6	insert #girls (personid) select top 1...	23320	823	29591	25
5	insert #boys (personid) select top 1...	18261	841	25206	16
1	SELECT StatMan([SC0], [SB0000]) F...	3083	511	1526	5

Figure 5-30

Querying Trace Data Directly

If it is not necessary to save the trace data to a database table, you can directly query against a set of rollover trace files. With the NTEXT datatype issue, you can use a T-SQL CAST function to convert the TextData data from NTEXT to NVARCHAR. The following query uses the fn_trace_gettable function to return data directly from the trace output file. Figure 5-31 shows the query result.

```
SELECT
    COUNT(*) AS NumberOfExecutions,
    CAST (TextData as nvarchar(max)) AS TextData,
    SUM(Duration)/1000 AS Total_Duration_In_MilliSeconds,
    SUM(CPU) AS Total_CPU_Time_In_MilliSeconds,
    SUM(Reads) AS Total_Logical_Reads,
    SUM(Writes) AS Total_Writes
    FROM ::fn_trace_gettable('c:\temp\myServerSideTraceOutput_CostlyQueries
.trc', default)
WHERE TextData IS NOT NULL
GROUP BY
    CAST (TextData as nvarchar(max))
ORDER BY Total_Duration_In_MilliSeconds DESC
```

```
SELECT
    COUNT(*) AS NumberOfExecutions,
    CAST (TextData as nvarchar(max)) AS TextData,
    SUM(Duration)/1000 AS Total_Duration_In_MilliSeconds,
    SUM(CPU) AS Total_CPU_Time_In_MilliSeconds,
    SUM(Reads) AS Total_Logical_Reads,
    SUM(Writes) AS Total_Writes
    FROM ::fn_trace_gettable('c:\temp\myServerSideTraceOutput_CostlyQueries.trc', default)
WHERE TextData IS NOT NULL
GROUP BY
    CAST (TextData as nvarchar(max))
ORDER BY Total_Duration_In_MilliSeconds DESC
```

Results | Messages |

Numbe...	TextData	Total_Duration_In_MilliSeconds	Total_CPU_Time_In_MilliSeconds	Total_Logical_Reads	Total_Writes
13	exec marriage	194753	12811	365031	306
1	[PeopleAndMarriage] @Peop...	163073	9624	300119	182
13	update people set lastname ...	120626	7300	226257	41
1	[PeopleAndMarriage] @Peop...	37817	6149	143559	228
6	insert #girls (personid) select...	23320	823	29591	25
5	insert #boys (personid) selec...	18261	841	25206	16
1	SELECT StatMan([SC0], [SB0...	3083	511	1526	5

Figure 5-31

Best Practice

Process your output trace data on a non-production server. Processing trace events can be CPU intensive if you use T-SQL to parse and aggregate the trace events collected.

Analyzing Costly Queries — Single Execution vs. Multiple Executions

Costly queries can be classified in several ways. For example, most people capture and report the Top 30 (or N) costly queries with high I/O or CPU cost. Analyzing both the single longest query and a query with multiple executions is advisable.

Queries with multiple executions form an overall database load. It is crucial to analyze load patterns on a regular basis. If a stored procedure is executed in 200 milliseconds, it may not look bad at all. However, if this stored procedure is executed two million times a day, you certainly need to pay more attention to it and optimize it to the max. Compared to a single long-running query, queries with multiple executions may deserve more attention.

From the example results in Figure 5-31, the stored procedure [marriage] has the greatest overall impact on the system in terms of accumulated CPU and I/O usages. It has been executed 13 times.

If you evaluate the most costly query based on a single execution, it is [PeopleAndMarriage]. This query used 9624 milliseconds of CPU and 300119 reads.

Server-Side Trace Code Walk-Through

What are the benefits of getting familiar with the syntax and structure of generated code? A server-side trace script generated by SQL Profiler is efficient, consistent, easy to maintain, and reusable. In the earlier section, "Using Profiler to Generate Server-Side Trace Script," you used SQL Profiler to generate the server-side trace script and saved it to a file. Now you will open the file and examine the details of the script.

The following is the entire code listing. The script only provides limited comments; fortunately, it is easy to read. The script can be divided into the following sections: declaration and initialization, create a trace, set trace events, set filters for trace events, start the trace, and display the trace. In the next section, you will examine all the details.

```
-- Create a Queue
declare @rc int
declare @TraceID int
declare @maxfilesize bigint
declare @DateTime datetime

set @DateTime = '2007-05-14 09:15:00.000'
set @maxfilesize = 5

-- Please replace the text InsertFileNameHere, with an appropriate
-- filename prefixed by a path, e.g., c:\MyFolder\MyTrace. The .trc extension
-- will be appended to the filename automatically. If you are writing from
-- remote server to local drive, please use UNC path and make sure server has
-- write access to your network share

exec @rc = sp_trace_create @TraceID output,
    2,
    N'c:\temp\myServerSideTraceOutput_CostlyQueries',
    @maxfilesize,
    @Datetime,
    10
if (@rc != 0) goto error

-- Client side File and Table cannot be scripted

-- Set the events
declare @on bit
set @on = 1
exec sp_trace_setevent @TraceID, 10, 15, @on
exec sp_trace_setevent @TraceID, 10, 16, @on
exec sp_trace_setevent @TraceID, 10, 1, @on
exec sp_trace_setevent @TraceID, 10, 9, @on
exec sp_trace_setevent @TraceID, 10, 17, @on
exec sp_trace_setevent @TraceID, 10, 2, @on
exec sp_trace_setevent @TraceID, 10, 10, @on
exec sp_trace_setevent @TraceID, 10, 18, @on
exec sp_trace_setevent @TraceID, 10, 11, @on
exec sp_trace_setevent @TraceID, 10, 12, @on
```

```
exec sp_trace_setevent @TraceID, 10, 13, @on
exec sp_trace_setevent @TraceID, 10, 6,  @on
exec sp_trace_setevent @TraceID, 10, 14, @on
exec sp_trace_setevent @TraceID, 45, 16, @on
exec sp_trace_setevent @TraceID, 45, 1,  @on
exec sp_trace_setevent @TraceID, 45, 9,  @on
exec sp_trace_setevent @TraceID, 45, 17, @on
exec sp_trace_setevent @TraceID, 45, 10, @on
exec sp_trace_setevent @TraceID, 45, 18, @on
exec sp_trace_setevent @TraceID, 45, 11, @on
exec sp_trace_setevent @TraceID, 45, 12, @on
exec sp_trace_setevent @TraceID, 45, 13, @on
exec sp_trace_setevent @TraceID, 45, 6,  @on
exec sp_trace_setevent @TraceID, 45, 14, @on
exec sp_trace_setevent @TraceID, 45, 15, @on
exec sp_trace_setevent @TraceID, 12, 15, @on
exec sp_trace_setevent @TraceID, 12, 16, @on
exec sp_trace_setevent @TraceID, 12, 1,  @on
exec sp_trace_setevent @TraceID, 12, 9,  @on
exec sp_trace_setevent @TraceID, 12, 17, @on
exec sp_trace_setevent @TraceID, 12, 6,  @on
exec sp_trace_setevent @TraceID, 12, 10, @on
exec sp_trace_setevent @TraceID, 12, 14, @on
exec sp_trace_setevent @TraceID, 12, 18, @on
exec sp_trace_setevent @TraceID, 12, 11, @on
exec sp_trace_setevent @TraceID, 12, 12, @on
exec sp_trace_setevent @TraceID, 12, 13, @on


-- Set the Filters
declare @intfilter int
declare @bigintfilter bigint

exec sp_trace_setfilter @TraceID, 10, 0, 7, N'SQL Server Profiler - 0dc223b7-b4ef-
48b2-9901-b4091f703729'
set @bigintfilter = 2000000
exec sp_trace_setfilter @TraceID, 13, 0, 4, @bigintfilter

set @intfilter = 50
exec sp_trace_setfilter @TraceID, 18, 0, 4, @intfilter

-- Set the trace status to start
exec sp_trace_setstatus @TraceID, 1

-- display trace id for future references
select TraceID=@TraceID
goto finish

error:
select ErrorCode=@rc

finish:
go
```

The script begins by declaring the needed variables. The variable `@rc` is declared as a return code for error handling purposes. The variable `@TraceID` will be used to store a number assigned by a new trace.

The variable `@DateTime` specifies the stop time of the trace. In this code, it is initialized at `'2007-05-14 09:15:00.000'`. The variable `@maxfilesize` specifies the maximum size in megabytes (MB) a trace file can grow; it is initialized at a value of 5.

```
-- Create a Queue
declare @rc int
declare @TraceID int
declare @maxfilesize bigint
set @maxfilesize = 5

set @DateTime = '2007-05-14 09:15:00.000'
set @maxfilesize = 5
```

The next program statement is to create a new trace. The store procedure `sp_trace_create` creates a new trace definition. There are several input and output parameters followed by the stored procedure:

```
exec @rc = sp_trace_create @TraceID output,
    2,
    N'c:\temp\myServerSideTraceOutput_CostlyQueries',
    @maxfilesize,
    @Datetime,
    10
```

❑   **@TraceID output:** An output returned by `sp_trace_create`. This trace identification number will be used by other stored procedures in the script. It is used to identify a specific SQL Trace.

❑   **2:** This corresponds to the second parameter, `@options`. The value 2 specifies that when the max_file_size is reached, the current trace file will be closed and a new file will be created. All new records will be written to the new file. The new file will have the same name as the previous file, but an integer will be appended to indicate its sequence. For example, if the original trace file is named `filename.trc`, the next trace file will be named `filename_1.trc`, and following that trace file will be `filename_2.trc`, and so on.

❑   **N'c:\temp\myServerSideTraceOutput_CostlyQueries':** This corresponds to the `@trace_file` parameter. The trace file can be either a local directory (such as N 'C:\MSSQL\Trace\trace.trc') or a UNC path (Uniform Naming Convention) to a shared drive (N'\Servername\Sharename\Directory\trace.trc'). A local directory means that it resides on a monitored server.

❑   **@maxfilesize:** The fourth parameter specifies the maximum size in megabytes (MB) a trace file can grow. In the beginning of the script, it was initialized at 5 (set @maxfilesize = 5).

❑   **@Datetime:** This corresponds to the fifth input parameter, `@stoptime`. How does a trace stop time work? If NULL is specified, the trace will run until it is manually stopped or until the server shuts down. If both `stop_time` and `max_file_size` are specified, and `TRACE_FILE_ROLLOVER` is not specified, the trace will stop when either the specified stop time or maximum file size is reached. If `stop_time`, `max_file_size`, and `TRACE_FILE_ROLLOVER` are all specified, the trace will stop at the specified stop time, assuming the trace does not fill up the drive first.

❑   **10:** This corresponds to the last input parameter `max_rollover_filers`. It specifies the maximum number or trace files to be maintained with the same base file name.

Next, you will see how event classes and data columns are configured. The stored procedure sp_trace_setevent facilitates this task. It adds or removes an event class or data column to a trace. You will look at the first execution statement exec sp_trace_setevent @TraceID, 10, 15, @on.

```
-- Set the events
declare @on bit
set @on = 1
exec sp_trace_setevent @TraceID, 10, 15, @on
```

❑   **@TraceID:** In the sp_trace_setevent, the @TraceID is an input parameter, which is generated from the sp_trace_create stored procedure call.

❑   **10:** This corresponds to the second parameter, @eventid. Use an event number to setup the @eventid. The event number 10 refers to the event class RPC:Completed.

❑   **15:** This corresponds to the third parameter, @columnid. Here you will use a column ID to refer to an event data column. For example, 15 is the EndTime.

❑   **@on:** This specifies whether to turn the event ON (1) or OFF (0). In this code example, the variable @on is initialized to 1 before the stored procedure call, meaning that the event class (specified in the @eventid) is set to be ON, and the data column (specified in the @columnid) is set to ON if the column ID is not null.

After the event classes and data columns are configured, the next step is to set the data column filter. A stored procedure is used to apply a filter to a trace. There are four input parameters for this stored procedure.

```
-- Set the Filters
declare @intfilter int
declare @bigintfilter bigint

exec sp_trace_setfilter @TraceID, 10, 0, 7, N'SQL Server Profiler - 0dc223b7-b4ef-
48b2-9901-b4091f703729'
```

❑   **@TraceID:** The @TraceID is an input parameter, which is generated from the sp_trace_create stored procedure call.

❑   **10:** The second parameter is the column ID parameter. Id value 10 corresponds to the event data column ApplicationName.

❑   **0:** This logical_operator specifies whether the AND (0) or OR (1) operator is applied. In this case, a logical AND operator is used.

❑   **7:** This comparison_operator specifies the type of comparison to be made. The value 7 is used to symbolize a "Not Like" operator.

❑   **N'SQL Server Profiler - 0dc223b7-b4ef-48b2-9901-b4091f703729':** This specifies the value to be filtered.

The preceding input parameters instruct the event filter procedure to filter out all events generated from the SQL Server Profiler application.

Next, you will see the setting of two more similar event filters. The two event filters statements were generated when you set the Duration filter to greater than 2000 milliseconds and CPU filter to greater than 50 milliseconds (see Figure 5-26).

```
set @bigintfilter = 2000000
exec sp_trace_setfilter @TraceID, 13, 0, 4, @bigintfilter
```

❏   **@TraceID:** The @TraceID is an input parameter, which is generated from the sp_trace_create stored procedure call.

❏   **13:** The second parameter is the column ID parameter. ID value 13 corresponds to the event data column Duration.

❏   **0:** This logical_operator specifies whether the AND (0) or OR (1) operator is applied. In this case, a logical AND operator is used.

❏   **4:** This comparison_operator specifies the type of comparison to be made. The value 7 is used to symbolize a Greater Than Or Equal operator.

❏   **@bigintfilter:** This specifies the value to be filtered. The T-SQL variable @bigintfilter was initialized to 2000000 right before calling this event filter stored procedure.

With the preceding input parameters, the event filter procedure will catch trace events that have a duration greater than or equal to 2000000 microseconds (2000 milliseconds).

```
set @intfilter = 50
exec sp_trace_setfilter @TraceID, 18, 0, 4, @intfilter
```

❏   **@TraceID:** The @TraceID is an input parameter, which is generated from the sp_trace_create stored procedure call.

❏   **18:** The second parameter is the column ID parameter. ID value 18 corresponds to the event data column CPU.

❏   **0:** This logical_operator specifies whether the AND (0) or OR (1) operator is applied. In this case, a logical AND operator is used.

❏   **4:** This comparison_operator specifies the type of comparison to be made. The value 7 is used to symbolize a Greater Than Or Equal operator.

❏   **@intfilter:** This specifies the value to be filtered. The T-SQL variable @bigintfilter was initialized to 50 before calling this event filter stored procedure.

With the preceding input parameters, the event filter procedure will catch trace events that have CPU greater than or equal to 50 milliseconds.

Since all three filters used logical AND (0) operators, the three filters will be linked together using the AND logic. In this setup, SQL Trace will catch all events that must satisfy the three filter conditions at the same time. The three filter statements listed above are not easy to comprehend. However, they become clearer after translating them into T-SQL syntax. The key is to look for how the filters are connected. In this example, the logic operator AND is used.

```
-- To translate the above section of code into the T-SQL syntax for a comparison
-- purpose only.
SELECT <related data columns>
FROM <EventQueue>
WHERE TraceID = @TraceID
AND ApplicationName NOT LIKE N'SQL Server Profiler - 0dc223b7-b4ef-
```

```
48b2-9901-b4091f703729'
AND Duration >= 2000000
AND CPU >= 50
```

Once event classes and data columns are chosen and the data columns are applied, the next step is to start the trace. Again, a stored procedure is used. The `sp_trace_setstatus` procedure modifies the current state of the specified trace.

```
-- Set the trace status to start
exec sp_trace_setstatus @TraceID, 1
```

❑   **@TraceID:** It is the ID of the trace to be modified.

❑   **1:** It specifies the action to the trace. The value 1 means to start the specified trace.

The last `select` statement is used to display the trace ID number.

```
-- display trace id for future references
select TraceID=@TraceID
goto finish

error:
select ErrorCode=@rc

finish:
go
```

To list all the traces on an instance of SQL Server, you can use the either of following two queries:

```
select * from ::fn_trace_getinfo(null)
select * from sys.traces
```

In a SQL Server 2005 instance, the SQL default trace has an ID of the number 1. The default trace provides troubleshooting assistance to database administrators by ensuring that they have the log data necessary to diagnose problems (see SQL Books Online for details). In SQL Server 2000, a similar trace is called Blackbox trace.

If SQL Profiler is used to generate a server-side trace for two different scenarios and the generated codes are compared, some commonalities will appear in the code logic and structures. There are many ways to customize previously generated codes to make them more reusable and meet your specific needs.

Best Practice

In a production environment, use server-side traces to collect data. A server-side trace consumes fewer system resources than a Profiler trace. Develop a set of reusable server-side traces if you can.

Case Summary

To summarize our activities:

- ❑ You used SQL Profiler as a code generator to generate a server-side trace.
- ❑ You made minor code modifications: reset a stop time, specified a unique output file name, and specified a set of output rollover files to a maximum of ten files.
- ❑ Tested the server-side trace and scheduled it.
- ❑ Simulated database events.
- ❑ After the trace stopped, you used a pre-prepared T-SQL script to analyze your trace data.

Based on trace data you collected by measuring CPU usage per single or multiple execution, the result indicates that the stored procedure marriage is the most costly query.

Correlating a Profiler Trace with System Monitor Performance Counter Data

Prior to SQL Server 2005, there were no available tools or utilities to correlate SQL Trace event data with Windows System Performance (Perfmon) counter data. However, SQL Server 2005 has added a new feature that correlates these two sources of performance data and displays them in Profiler. All you need to do is to load these two sources of data; Profiler will synchronize these two sources of data via timestamps. Using this new feature, you can evaluate query performance with system resource utilizations visually.

Once Profiler trace and System Monitor performance data are colleted, launch SQL 2005 Profiler.

Open trace file from Profiler and load event data (see Figure 5-32).

From Profiler, import System monitor performance data and select system performance counters to load (see Figure 5-33).

After all data is loaded, the system performance data will be displayed in the middle section of the Profiler.

By clicking a trace event, the corresponding performance data will be highlighted by a vertical line. This is useful when you investigate a long-running query and want to find out how this query affects system resources. Conversely, by clicking on any place on the performance counter graphs, the corresponding trace event will be highlighted.

Performance counter data can be zoomed in and out; this allows you to see system resource utilizations for a narrowed period or an entire period (see Figure 5-34). With the integrated data in Profiler, you can quickly pinpoint a problem area for detailed troubleshooting or a root-cause analysis.

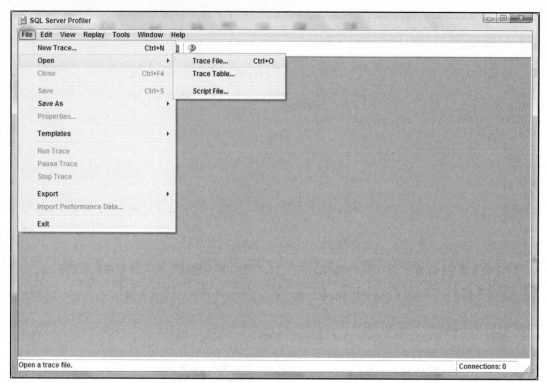

Figure 5-32

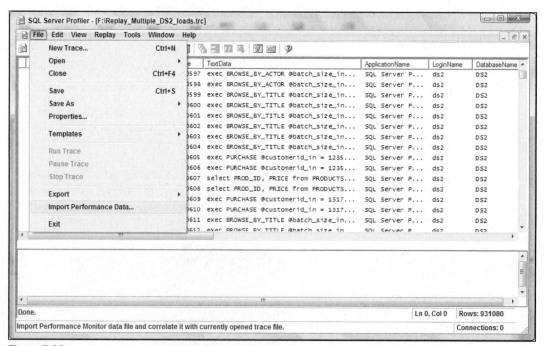

Figure 5-33

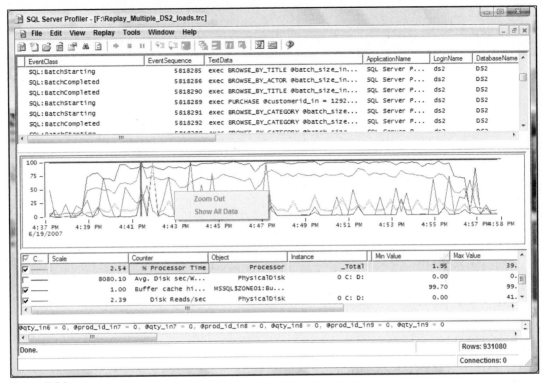

Figure 5-34

Summary

This chapter began with preparations for setting up a SQL trace. You learned what to look for in an `issue` statement, what trace options you have in SQL Server 2005, and important factors to consider when minimizing the overhead associated with a trace. You reviewed Profiler usage scenarios for capturing blocking events, Showplan XML data, deadlock graphs, and identifying long-running queries. You examined the steps needed to generate a server-side trace code and examined the server-side trace code in detail. Finally, you reviewed the new feature of correlating SQL trace data with Windows performance counter data.

In Part 2 of this book, you will be looking at resolving bottlenecks with tuning.

Part CXLII
Removing Bottlenecks with Tuning

Choosing and Configuring Hardware

6

The previous chapters have focused on how to monitor and troubleshoot a SQL Server system. From this chapter forward you'll look at what you can do to resolve the bottlenecks and tune any performance problems. Your SQL Server system may consist of multiple servers hosting multiple applications or just a single server running everything. Either way, there are lots of moving parts, each of which must work together efficiently to provide the highest level of performance. If you think of each resource as a link in a chain, the weakest link really can weaken or even break the chain.

This chapter covers selecting and configuring the environment that SQL Server runs in; namely Windows and the server hardware itself. You will also learn how you should proactively design your environment using best practices to avoid performance problems later on.

First you'll look at which resources can become a bottleneck and what can be the cause. It is important to know where your system's weaknesses are likely to occur so you can proactively monitor the resources using what you've learned in Chapters 2 and 3. Read the first section of this chapter to understand the scope of what you're going to tune.

You will then look at what you need to consider to make the correct server configuration choices and how your choice can impact SQL Server performance. Taking into account the requirements of all the applications running on the infrastructure is absolutely necessary to avoid service outages later on. You can read this section to guide your decisions when designing a new system or to help you proactively review an existing environment to ensure you're getting the most from your setup.

Server Bottlenecks

There are three server resources that you should be concerned about when trying to identify and resolve bottlenecks. You should review them in the following order: Memory, I/O, CPU. This section looks at each of these in turn and you'll also learn why you should look at them in this order.

Memory

Memory very often drives the overall performance of a system and lack of it often creates a greater perceived performance impact than the lack of any other resource. Lots of spare memory can also mask bottlenecks in other areas so it's important to know how your memory is being used before looking at anything else. This is covered in Chapters 2 and 3.

Effect on I/O

Lack of physical memory has a greater effect on I/O than anything else because paging activity will be high, which means high disk activity. Obviously, when you notice your I/O throughput reducing in this scenario, the wrong approach to take would be to buy faster disks.

Effect on CPU

The goal for CPU usage is to spend as much time as possible executing in user mode. Kernel mode represents time spent working on system processes and not your application, so a lack of physical memory will cause high CPU utilization in kernel mode because the server has to work harder to manage what little memory it has. Again, the wrong approach to take would be to buy faster CPUs, but could be easily done if you only looked at CPU utilization in isolation. User mode and kernel mode are covered in more detail in Chapter 2.

> ### Best Practice
> Memory is very cheap these days so you shouldn't have any servers with less than 2 GB of RAM. Having 4 GB of RAM or more requires a bit of thought as to how to configure the server to use it and this is covered in the "Configuring the Server" section later in this chapter.

I/O

Disk I/O is the next most likely resource to be a bottleneck on your server and is particularly important to SQL Server because its job is to serve data from a database stored on disk. Identifying disk bottlenecks is covered in Chapter 2, how to configure your storage for optimal performance is covered in the "Configuring the Server" section of this chapter, and Chapter 10 details how to benchmark and fully test your I/O subsystem.

CPU

CPU can often be driven by the other two subsystems, so a bottleneck in memory or disk I/O will very often manifest itself as a CPU bottleneck. This is why you should analyze memory first, then the I/O subsystem, followed by the processor. As discussed above, lack of memory will drive the CPU and I/O subsystem, and I/O operations account for a significant percentage of kernel mode CPU time.

> ### Best Practice
> Buy multi-core processors with large amounts of cache. This is discussed in great detail in the next section.

Configuring the Server

The three key resources on the server are: Memory, I/O, and CPU.

Let's start with memory. It's easier to add or remove memory (RAM) than it is to change the number or type of processors in a server. SQL Server 2005 even supports adding additional RAM to a server without rebooting (we call it hot-add memory, but more on that later). When you initially configure the server, you should have some idea how much memory you might need, and this may even determine the type of CPU you purchase. On 32-bit systems, for example, there are a number of switches you can add to boot.ini that can affect the memory configuration. If you've never seen boot.ini before, it's a hidden file on the root of your boot drive, usually c:\. Here is an example from Windows Server 2003 Enterprise Edition:

```
[boot loader]
timeout=30
default=multi(0)disk(0)rdisk(0)partition(1)\WINDOWS
[operating systems]
multi(0)disk(0)rdisk(0)partition(1)\WINDOWS="Windows Server 2003, Enterprise"
/noexecute=optout /fastdetect /PAE /3GB
```

/PAE enables the operating system to use more than 4 GB RAM and /3GB allows you to increase the virtual memory address space for applications at the expense of the kernel. You'll look at these switches plus some others in more detail later, so don't worry if it sounds strange at this point.

In many ways I/O performance is perhaps the most important part of the server configuration to get right. The reason for this is that everything you do lives on the disk. All the code you run in the operating system, SQL Server, and any other applications, starts off as files on the disk. All the data you touch in SQL Server lives on the disk. It starts out life there, gets read into memory, and then has to be written back to disk before it's a permanent change. Every change you make in SQL Server is written to the SQL log file, which lives on disk. All these factors make a good I/O configuration an essential part of any SQL Server system.

I/O configuration is a big enough subject that it really requires a book all of its own to cover. We're going to introduce you to some of the options available and then walk through several scenarios to provide some insight into how to make the right storage configuration decisions.

There aren't a lot of options to play with when dealing with CPUs, so you need to make sure that you make an informed decision when choosing them to begin with. SQL Server 2008 will enable "hot-add CPUs" (similar to the "hot-add memory" support in SQL Server 2005) but the feature requires specialized hardware to work. Ironically, this means you'll still need to plan to eventually need more CPUs.

Before you go any further, put each of the three server resources back into perspective in terms of their relative performance. The following is an outline that's relevant to today's systems. As systems change at some time in the future, you can easily pencil in the current state of processor, memory, and I/O performance to see how the relative speeds of different pieces have changed.

Typical speeds and throughput for system resources are:

❑ A CPU speed of 2 GHz results in 8 GB/Sec

❑ Memory speed of 500 MHz results in 2 GB/Sec

❑ A reasonable single hard disk results in 40 MB/Sec

Use these numbers to do the math for throughput for a 10 GB table:

❑   A 2 GHz CPU with a throughput of 8 GB/Sec would read 10 GB of data in 1.2 seconds

❑   500 MHz memory with a throughput of 2 GB/Sec would read 10 GB of data in 5 seconds

❑   Disks with a throughput of 40 MB/Sec would read 10 GB in 256 seconds

Graphically, this might look something like Figure 6-1.

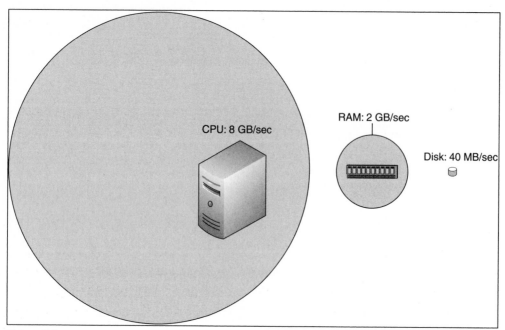

Figure 6-1

Unfortunately we can't draw the disk small enough or the CPU big enough to make this to-scale given the relative difference between CPU speed and disk speed. The lesson here is that disk access is much slower than memory access, which is slower than the CPU. So the key is to get as much data as you can into memory, and then as much of that onto the CPU as you can.

With SQL Server there isn't much you can do to alter how much of your data is being operated on by the CPU. That's controlled by the developers who wrote SQL Server. What you can do, however, is:

❑   Buy processors with larger cache and a higher clock speed (GHz).

❑   Add more memory at a faster speed.

❑   Design your storage sub-system to deliver the fastest performance possible within your requirements for speed, capacity, and cost.

Now let's drill down further to help clarify these options.

Memory

In this section you are going to look at server memory, some of the issues associated with memory, the options you can use, and how they can impact the performance of the server. You'll start with a basic introduction to operating system memory and then jump into the details of how to configure a server for different memory configurations.

Physical Memory

Physical memory is the RAM you install into the server. You are probably already familiar with the SIMMs and DIMMs that go into desktop PCs and servers. This is the physical memory or RAM. This memory is measured in megabytes or gigabytes. Windows Server 2003 Data Center edition with SP1 even supports up to 2 TB of RAM and future editions of the operating system will increase this as customers demand ever more powerful systems to solve ever more complex business problems.

Physical Address Space

The physical address space is the set of addresses that the processor uses to access anything on its bus. On a 32-bit processor, this is limited to 4 GB of total addresses. On a 32-bit Server with PAE (PAE allows more than 4 GB of memory to be addressed and is discussed further in the section "32-bit System Memory Configuration"), the address bus is actually 36 bits, which allows the processor to address 64 GB of addresses. On a 64-bit processor, you would think the address bus would be 64 bits, but because there isn't a need for systems that can address 18 Exabytes (1,048,576 TB) of memory yet (nor the ability to build a system that large), the manufacturers have limited the address bus to 44 bits, which is enough to address 2 TB.

Virtual Address Space

On a 32-bit system, each process running on the system has a total of 4 GB of virtual address space (VAS), which is used to store program code and data used by applications. There are two important things to note about this: it's virtual memory (not physical memory) and it's only space (not actual memory).

The 4 GB of VAS is shared between the kernel and your process, split in the middle giving 2 GB for user-mode address space and 2 GB for kernel-mode address space. However, if you enable /3GB or /USERVA, the boundary can be moved from 2 GB anywhere up to 3 GB. You can find more information on /3GB and /USERVA in the "32-bit System Memory Configuration" section later in this chapter.

What this means is that there is no memory in the VAS until you either ask for memory or try to load something. In both cases, the OS takes your request and links a block of virtual address space with actual memory. Note that the actual memory isn't guaranteed to always be there as the Virtual Memory Manager can take the memory away and put it into the page file. This is completely transparent and you won't be aware of it until the next time you try to access that piece of memory. Then it will be really slow because you will have to wait for the Virtual Memory Manager (VMM) to go and read the page from the Page File, put it back into a page of memory, and then map that page back into your VAS.

Virtual Memory Manager

The Virtual Memory Manager (VMM) is the part of the operating system that manages all the physical memory and shares it between all the processes that need memory on the system. Its job is to provide each process with the illusion that it has 4 GB of VAS and that it has memory when it needs it while having to juggle the limited physical memory between all the processes running on the system at the same time.

The VMM does this by managing the virtual memory for each process. When necessary it will take the physical memory behind virtual memory and put the data that resided in that memory into the page file so that it is not lost.

When the process needs to use that data again, it needs to be re-loaded into physical memory. This is called a *hard page fault*, and to fix it the VMM will go and get the data from the page file, find a free page of memory either from its list of free pages or from another process, write the data from the page file into memory, and map the new page back into the process's VAS.

On a system with enough RAM to give every process all the memory it needs, the VMM doesn't have to do much other than give out memory and clean up after a process is done with it. On a system without enough RAM to go around, the job is a little more involved. The VMM has to do some work to provide each process with the memory it needs when it needs it. It does this by using the page file to temporarily store data that a process hasn't accessed for a while. This process is called *paging* and the data is often referred to as having been *paged* or *swapped* out to disk. Figure 6-2 shows two processes with various pages swapped into memory and out to disk.

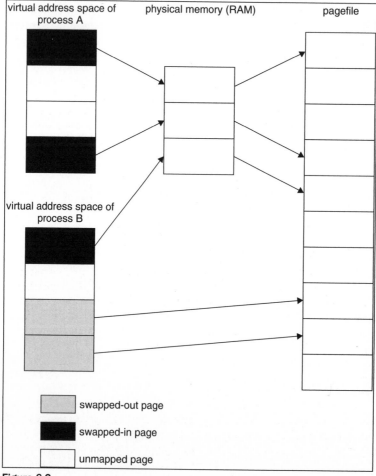

Figure 6-2

32-Bit System Memory Configuration

There are several options with 32-bit systems that have been introduced over the years as ways to get around the basic limitation that 32-bit has with only having 4 GB of VAS. You'll get a chance to review each option over the next few pages so you can choose the right configuration for your environment.

/3GB

One way to increase the amount of memory a 32-bit process can use is to take some of the space assigned to the kernel and use it for *user-mode address space*. You can do this by specifying either the /3GB or /USERVA options in the boot.ini file. This is also called 4-gigabyte tuning (4GT).

The /3GB option moves the boundary to be at 3 GB, giving each process an additional 1 GB of VAS. This does mean that the kernel now only has 1 GB of virtual memory to use. This can sometimes be a problem that can result in the server crashing when the kernel runs out of VAS and can't free it quickly enough.

The /USERVA option is new with Windows Server 2003 and provides a way you to specify a different amount of address space to be taken from the kernel. It's used in conjunction with /3GB, and you can specify any value between 2 GB and 3 GB as the boundary between user and kernel address space. This has the same effect of increasing each process's virtual address space and reducing the kernel's address space as setting /3GB, and can have the same consequences if the kernel ends up running out of memory space.

One of the limitations with reducing the amount of memory available for the kernel is that it reduces the amount of memory available for the kernel to track physical memory. This is why when you turn on /3GB the operating system is limited to using a maximum of 16 GB of RAM. If your server has 16 GB of RAM or more installed, you shouldn't even try using /3GB. Figure 6-3 shows the virtual address space layout with and without /3GB enabled.

Best Practice

Don't use /3GB if you have 16 GB or more of RAM.

/PAE (Physical Address Extensions)

Intel introduced a way to get around the 4 GB limitation of a 32-bit address bus by physically extending the address bus to 36 bits. This extension is called *Physical Address Extension* (PAE). It allows a 32-bit operating system to access up to 64 GB of memory but requires an Enterprise Edition or greater version of Windows Server. It's also worth noting that 64 GB is only supported on servers running Windows 2003 SP1 and greater.

PAE is enabled by setting the /PAE flag in the boot.ini file to tell the operating system to use the version of the kernel that can take advantage of those extra four bits of address bus. It also allows a 32-bit Windows system to use more than 4 GB of memory.

There are some cases where you will end up running the PAE kernel even if you don't enable it in boot.ini. This is the case if you are running a DataCenter edition of the OS and the hardware is hot-swap memory enabled. In this case, because the server may have additional memory added at any time that could exceed the 4 GB limit of 32-bit addresses, the OS always uses the PAE kernel just in case it ever has to deal with more than 4 GB of physical memory.

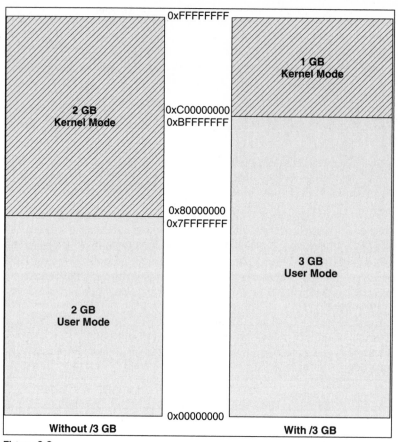

Figure 6-3

PAE just enables Windows to see memory above 4 GB. For applications to use it, they have to be written specifically to take advantage of it.

> **Best Practice**
> Enable PAE if you have more than 4 GB of RAM.

AWE (Address Windowing Extensions)

AWE is a Windows API that allows a 32-bit process to map memory from outside its Virtual Address Space. It enables a process to use physical memory to store data, but to use the data it has to be mapped into the process's VAS. Think of it like the page file in windows, only because it's a memory-to-memory transfer, it's much quicker. It allows a process to use more than 2 GB of memory (or 3 GB if /3GB is on) but you're still limited by 4 GB that 32-bit can address. For this reason it's most commonly used in combination with PAE on servers with more than 4 GB of memory.

SQL Server has been written to use the Windows AWE API. You enable it by setting the Advanced Configuration option AWE to 1 using sp_configure. It also requires the Windows Advanced User Right

Lock Pages in Memory option, which is automatically granted to the service account on install or if you change the service account using SQL Server Configuration Manager.

Given what you know about memory and AWE, it would seem that there is no reason for using AWE on a 64-bit system. After all, a 64-bit system has enough address space to address as much memory as it needs, so why would you want AWE on a 64-bit system? You can't even enable AWE in a 64-bit version of SQL Server; the option is disabled in the user interface.

It turns out that there are some great reasons for using AWE to access your memory, even on a 64-bit system. The SQL Server team realized that on 64-bit systems they could improve overall performance by using AWE in a 64-bit environment. They found that using AWE memory allows memory to be allocated and accessed a lot faster. In addition, the memory cannot be paged out by the operating system.

Because of this, 64-bit SQL Server was changed so even though you can't enable AWE on 64-bit versions of SQL Server, if the SQL Server service account has the Lock Pages in Memory advanced user right, SQL Server will automatically use AWE to access buffer pool memory.

There have been numerous support cases for 64-bit where huge areas of SQL Server memory have been paged out unnecessarily by the operating system, which is why the standard recommendation is to give the service account Lock Pages in Memory as above. Figure 6-4 shows the AWE window through which data is mapped into memory outside the normal virtual address space.

Best Practice

Use AWE in conjunction with PAE on 32-bit systems with more than 4 GB of memory. For 64-bit SQL Server, give the SQL Server service account the Lock Pages in Memory advanced user right in Windows to stop SQL Server memory being paged out.

/3GB or /PAE or AWE?

This is a question that gets asked very frequently: a customer has a number of systems with between 2 GB and 16 GB of RAM and they want to know if they should use /3GB, /PAE, AWE, or even all three. One thing to remember is that this has to be a 32-bit operating system running 32-bit SQL Server 2005. In any other scenario this question isn't relevant, and you'll see why in the next section.

There are three categories of answers to this question, each becoming more prescriptive than the last, and your business environment may dictate a favorite:

❏ **Supported by Microsoft:** All combinations of the above are actually supported except when physical memory is 16 GB or greater, which makes using /3GB and /PAE together unsupported. This is because the Operating System requires more than the 1 GB kernel address space that /3GB leaves you with to manage 16 GB of memory.

❏ **Recommended Best Practice:** Don't use /3GB and /PAE together at all because they both modify the amount of resources that are dedicated for various functions. For example, /3GB reduces the non-paged pool from 256 MB to 128 MB. PAE doesn't reduce the non-paged pool size, but it does double the size of each allocation from 4 bytes to 8 bytes. Using them both together actually throttles the system twice.

❏ **Keep It Simple:** Use these easy rules whenever possible to reduce risk and support costs:

    ❏ **Less than 4 GB RAM:** Don't use any of the above.

151

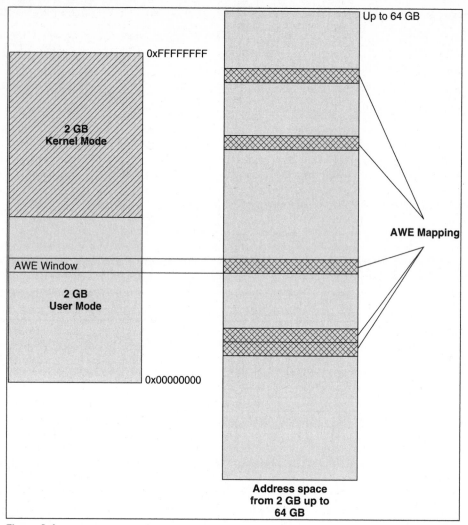

Figure 6-4

❑   **4 GB RAM:** Use /3GB if memory is a bottleneck for SQL Server.

❑   **More than 4 GB RAM:** Use /PAE and AWE.

❑   If you need more than 4 GB because something other than the data cache (Buffer Pool) is constrained, then go to 64-bit.

❑   There are of course exceptions to all prescriptive guidance, but armed with the information provided in this chapter you should be able to work out when it's appropriate to "stray off the path." A lot of customers use the Keep It Simple guidelines to reduce the complexity and risk of managing large numbers of SQL Servers.

64-bit System Memory Configuration

*x*64 and IA64 have a slightly different memory layout from each other and provide each process with a slightly different amount of VAS. It's roughly 7 TB for IA64 and 8 TB for *x*64. Note that Windows Server 2003 SP1 currently only supports a maximum of 2 TB of physical memory.

What this means for SQL Server is that you don't have to worry about using /PAE or /3GB. SQL Server will have 7 or 8 TB of Virtual Address Space as opposed to 2 or 3 GB in a 32-bit environment.

I/O

I/O encompasses both network I/O and disk I/O. In most cases with SQL Server, you are primarily concerned with disk I/O, as that's where the data lives. However, you also need to understand the effect that poor network I/O can have on performance.

Configuring I/O for a server storage system is perhaps the place where you have the most options, and can have the largest impact on the performance of your SQL Server system. When you turn off your computer, the only thing that exists is the data stored on your hard drive. When you turn the power on, the processor starts running, the OS is loaded, and SQL Server starts up. All this happens by reading data and code from the storage subsystem.

This basic concept is true for everything that happens on a computer. Everything starts on the disk, and has to be read from the disk into memory. From there it moves through the various processor caches before it reaches the processor and can be used either as code or data. Any results the processor arrives at have to be written back to disk in order to survive any system shutdown or power cycle (failure, maintenance, or shutdown).

SQL Server 2005 is very sensitive to disk performance, more so than many applications, because of the nature of what it does in managing large amounts of data in user databases. Many applications have the luxury of being able to load all their data from disk into memory and then being able to run for long periods of time without having to access the disk again. SQL Server strives for that model as it's by far the fastest way to get anything done. Unfortunately, when the requested operation requires more data than can fit into memory, SQL Server has to do some shuffling around to keep going as fast as it can, and it has to start writing data back to disk so it can use that memory for some new results.

Network I/O

The network is a key component in any SQL Server system. The network is the link over which SQL Server receives all its requests to do something and by which it sends all its results back to the client. In most cases today's high-speed networks provide enough capacity to drive a SQL Server system to use all its other resources (CPU, memory, and disk) to their maximum potential before the network becomes a bottleneck.

There are some systems where the type of work being done on the SQL Server is relatively small compared to the number of requests being sent to the server or to the amount of data being returned to the client. In either of these cases, the network can be a bottleneck.

Network bottlenecks can occur anywhere in the network. This fabric consists of many pieces of network infrastructure, from the simplest system, where two machines are connected over a basic local area network, to the most complex network interconnected systems in either the Internet or a global corporate wide area network. In these larger, more complex, interconnected systems, much of the network can be beyond your control and may have bandwidth or latency issues outside of acceptable limits, but that you have no control over. In these cases you can do little more than investigate, document, and report your findings.

There is actually very little that you can or need to do to optimize the network on the physical server. If you have no reported problems with your network interface card (NIC), you have the latest drivers, and you still find network I/O to be your bottleneck, then best approach to take is to optimize your application. If you have too many requests going to a single server, then maybe you could think about how to split some of the logic and spread the load across multiple servers, or if you have large datasets being sent to a middle-tier server to process business logic, you could look at utilizing some of the SQL Server 2005 features to move the business logic down to the SQL Server.

The fact that SQL Server 2005 can host the .NET CLR (Common Language Runtime) means that you can write stored procedures and functions in C# or Visual Basic .NET, which creates new options for you to locate business logic that could only be run on a middle-tier application server previously. This brings its own set of caveats and challenges that are beyond the scope of this book, but you should be aware of the option.

Disk I/O

The other piece of I/O and the one that first comes to mind is disk I/O. With earlier versions of SQL Server, disks were pretty simple. You had few options for what you could do with disks and in most cases you only had a handful to deal with. Large enterprise systems have long had the option of using SAN storage, whereas medium to large business systems have been able to use external disk subsystems using some form of RAID and most likely utilizing a SCSI interface.

These days the landscape has changed for storage and thankfully so has our understanding of our requirements and best practices for design and configuration.

Storage Design

Good performance comes from good design. Although this isn't a storage design book, awareness of the terminology associated with modern storage products is important to be able to articulate requirements and the reasoning behind the best practices.

Disk Drives

Fundamentally there are two types of disk drives that are available today: SCSI or ATA. SCSI has traditionally been the choice for the enterprise and ATA for the lower end of the market and desktop computing. The value proposition for ATA drives is low cost, low power, high capacity storage. ATA is a great choice to meet these requirements.

SCSI drives are very high cost and have much lower capacity, but the value proposition is data integrity, performance, scalability, reliability, and high duty cycle. Duty cycle is a storage term used to denote the expected drive usage. A high duty cycle means that the drive is designed for constant 24-7 use.

Serial-ATA (SATA) and Serial-SCSI (SAS) are the most common new drives sold today and *serial* refers to the interface to the disk drive. Fundamentally, the disks are the same as their historic parallel based relatives (which are known as ATA, or sometimes PATA); it's just a new high-speed interface built into the drive. The same also applies to Fibre Channel (FC) drives, which are just SCSI disks with an FC interface instead of SAS.

Due to the huge capacity SATA disks available today at very low prices, you might start to see them appearing in organizations as storage for infrequently accessed data like archives. As I write this the largest SAS disk I can find to buy is 300 GB, and the largest SATA disk is 1 TB and costs 80 percent less. If you can find the right use for them, SATA disks can bring substantial cost savings.

Additionally, a new disk interface card that supports SATA is emerging on the market, that claims a sustained transfer rate of 1.2 GB/s. For smaller organizations, using SATA is definitely a possibility, especially if on a budget.

Best Practice

Use SAS for most if not of all of your storage requirements if you can afford it and consider SATA for infrequently accessed data like archives if you're on a budget.

Direct-Attached Storage

Direct-attached storage (DAS) simply means that one server is connected directly to a disk array without a storage network in between. A few years ago it was the predominant choice for storage and still in many cases yields the best performance because it's a direct relationship. The problem with DAS becomes apparent in enterprise organizations where they have dozens or hundreds of servers. Each server has different disk space requirements but you're limited to the disk size in what you can provision. The result is that TBs of storage space throughout the organization sit unused and wasted.

Storage Area Network

A storage area network (SAN) provides a common storage pool for an organization providing highly robust and dynamic storage without the wasted disk space you see in an enterprise deployment of DAS. A common mistake is to refer to the box that holds all the disks as the SAN; that is just the disk array. The SAN is the entire network that supports the storage platform. Figure 6-5 shows a simple SAN to help understand some of the terminology.

❑   The host bus adapter (HBA) is the storage equivalent of an Ethernet network card.

❑   The switches operate in much the same way as network switches routing traffic.

❑   A *fabric* refers to a collection of switches that together provide the link between the server and the disk array.

There is a common perception that SANs give greater performance than DAS and although that can be true, it isn't the key driver for moving to a SAN. Storage consolidation is the value proposition but of course it would be useless without a good performance baseline. To help offset the overhead inevitable with the complexity and concurrency requirements of a SAN they can be installed with a very large cache. I worked with a banking customer in London on one of their trading platforms that used a large SAN. They had two 32 GB caches installed, which meant that I/O requests were never served from disk 99 percent of the time. The I/O performance was incredible.

Having said that it's worth clarifying that the example above came at a huge price (millions of dollars) both in the cost of the hardware and the specialist skills required to design and maintain the solution.

SANs and DAS both have their place as storage solutions for SQL Server, and which one you choose will depend on your budget and the scope of the solution you're designing.

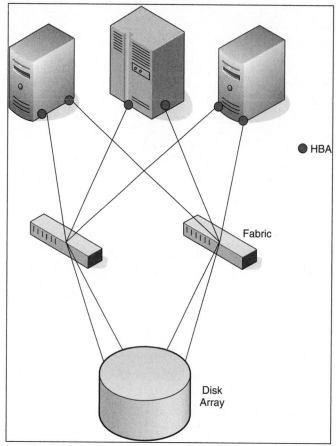

Figure 6-5

HBA Queue Depth

The queue depth on a HBA is a limit on the number of requests that can be "in-flight" on your storage network and by default will be between 8 and 32. You've already established that SQL Server is I/O intensive so the default queue depth is usually sub-optimal. A setting of 64 or greater will provide better results in I/O intensive periods but will make the SAN work harder, which could in turn affect the performance of other systems that use the SAN.

> **Best Practice**
>
> If no other servers use the SAN, then set the queue depth to 64 or 128 using windows device manager. If you're concerned about the performance impact on other systems, then increase the queue depth gradually until you reach an acceptable balance.

HBA Drivers

There are two types of HBA driver available: SCSIPort and StorPort. SCSIPort is based on older technology and will yield less performance and options than the newer StorPort drivers. You should always use the latest drivers from your storage vendor and hopefully they will have a StorPort driver available.

> **Best Practice**
>
> Use StorPort drivers instead of SCSIPort.

RAID

We won't spend too much time here on RAID because there are plenty of other books that cover it in detail but we will cover what RAID levels we recommend and why. Historically RAID5 is always recommended for data files and RAID1 for log files. That still might be an option for you if you're limited on disks or need to maximize available disk space.

RAID5 has relatively good performance because the data is striped and you have redundancy to the effect that you can lose one disk and keep working with no loss of data. It manages to do this by creating a parity bit so that all the drives together contain the information to rebuild a single disk but there is an overhead to creating the parity that impacts performance. If you lose a disk all the other disks have to work much harder, which can impact performance so much that it could be as crippling as if the server was down.

RAID1 has good redundancy because the disk itself is mirrored, which means low overhead, but the reason Microsoft recommended it for transaction logs was because a transaction log I/O pattern is mainly sequential writes and the disk will write faster if the head is still in the correct position. The downside to RAID1 is that you only really get the same performance as a single disk because all activity will be serviced by one of mirrored pairs. There are exceptions where you can get controllers that allow some reads to be serviced by the mirror, but that's not the case in most setups.

The most up-to-date recommendation is to use RAID10 (sometimes known as RAID1+0, which is not the same as RAID 0+1) for both data files and transaction log files. RAID10 combines the availability benefits of RAID1 (by first mirroring your writes) with the performance of RAID0 by striping your writes across multiple disks after they've been mirrored. The downside of this is the number of physical drives required to support it. You need an even number of drives and will lose half of the storage space to support the mirrored data.

> **Best Practice**
>
> Use RAID10 for SQL Server data files and transaction log files. This is not the same as RAID0+1, which provides less redundancy.

Database File Placement

This is a frequently raised topic these days primarily because of the widespread adoption of SANs with very clever disk arrays. The recommendation used to be simple and it still is really, it's just harder to follow than it used to be: "Put your database data files, database log files, and TempDB on separate physical spindles." That's easy to follow when you have a small disk array with 12 disks, for example. In that scenario 3 x RAID10 volumes of 4 disks each would be a safe option.

It gets more difficult when you have a large SAN. More than likely if you have a SAN you have somebody (or a team) that looks after it and presents the logical unit numbers (LUNs) of a size you specify to your SQL Server, which you can then use. (An LUN is how you refer to a volume on a disk array.) The issue is that they can't guarantee that your LUNs will be on separate spindles because they carve out your LUN from free space on the array and they don't know how many or which spindles are yours. The idea is that the arrays are monitored at the disk level to look for "hot disks" that are overworked so the data can then be moved and spread around disks that aren't so busy. So even if you could work out which spindles were yours, there's no guarantee they'll stay yours.

The question that then follows from that is, "Are there any benefits to following the traditional recommendations if you can't get separate spindles?" The answer is yes, but the benefits are mainly from a manageability perspective rather than performance:

❑   If you keep your databases on separate LUNs, you can manage how much disk space each one can grow into without affecting the others.

❑   If you move TempDB to a separate LUN, you can specify the size to be as big as the drive without losing performance, so you'll never have to worry about growing TempDB.

I know of at least one of the SQL Servers that Microsoft IT runs for an internal application that has a 200 GB TempDB on a 200 GB LUN with autogrow disabled. It's more than they'll ever need but TempDB space will never be a concern and the size doesn't impact performance.

Another question I've been asked in the past is whether or not there is a performance benefit from a Windows perspective by having multiple drive letters to multiple LUNs rather than 1 drive letter to 1 LUN. I could find no evidence theoretical or practical that would suggest that Windows benefits from having multiple drive letters.

Best Practice

If you can put your data, transaction log and TempDB files on separate physical spindles it will improve performance. If you can't guarantee separate spindles then separate the files across partitions for manageability purposes.

Provisioning a Partition

After installing the disks, you need to configure them and the first step with a new disk is to consider the partitions you wish to create. There are two choices of partition style currently available: the classic MBR (Master Boot Record) and the new GPT (GUID Partition Table). Eventually GPT will take over as the default choice as MBR only supports partitions up to 2 TB. However, there are very few scenarios today that require this much space in a single partition and support for GPT has only just become available in Windows Server 2003 SP1, so it's still relatively new and not yet supported for shared disks in Windows Failover Clustering. MBR remains the recommended choice for all but the most unusual of requirements.

Sector Alignment

Sector Alignment is a little-known performance optimization tip that is documented for Exchange at `http://technet.microsoft.com/en-us/library/aa998219.aspx` (but not very well described). It is equally valid for SQL Server. There are a few blog postings that try to measure the performance difference for SQL Server, but why it can cause a problem is not detailed very well. It should be performed on any NTFS partition that is created on a RAID array to avoid misalignment with stripe units and caching, which can cause performance degradation. Let's look in a bit more detail about what that actually means.

First of all, some disk terminology. What you're interested in for the purpose of explaining sector alignment are sectors, tracks, and blocks.

❑   A sector is the smallest unit of storage space on disk and is typically 512 bytes.

❑   A track is the circular path of sectors that sit around a single circumference of the disk. There are 63 sectors per track, numbered 1–63 on each track.

❑   A block is how you usually refer to sectors to make things easier for you. You start at the beginning of the disk and increment until the end of the disk. Blocks start from 0.

Partitions always start at the first sector on a track, so for the first partition that means Track 2 Sector 1 (because the MBR is on Track 1), which equates to Block number 63 (blocks start from 0). Misalignment occurs because the storage vendors define tracks differently. On an EMC Symmetrix, for example, a track is considered to be 64 blocks and the cache is also based on this.

A Symmetrix DMX RAID5 array uses a stripe size of 4 tracks, which totals 256 blocks. 64 KB is the largest single write that Windows can make, so using the default partition location means that the first 64 KB write will be fine but the second will straddle 2 stripes causing both to be updated, which impacts performance. Figure 6-6 illustrates an un-aligned partition.

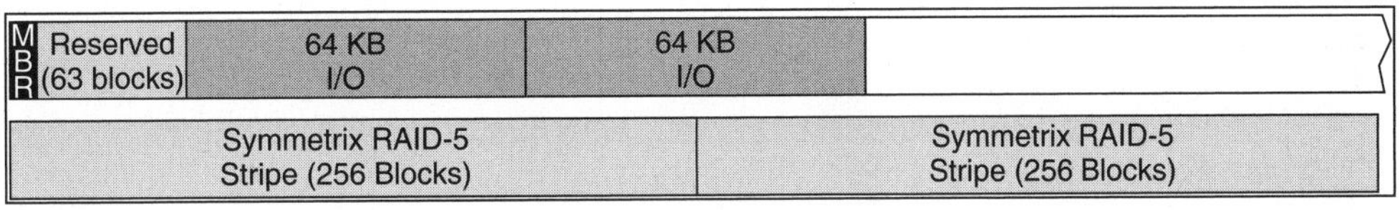

Figure 6-6

If you align the partition to 128 blocks (or 64 KB as each block is 512 bytes) then you don't cross a track boundary and therefore issue the minimum number of I/Os. Figure 6-7 illustrates an aligned partition.

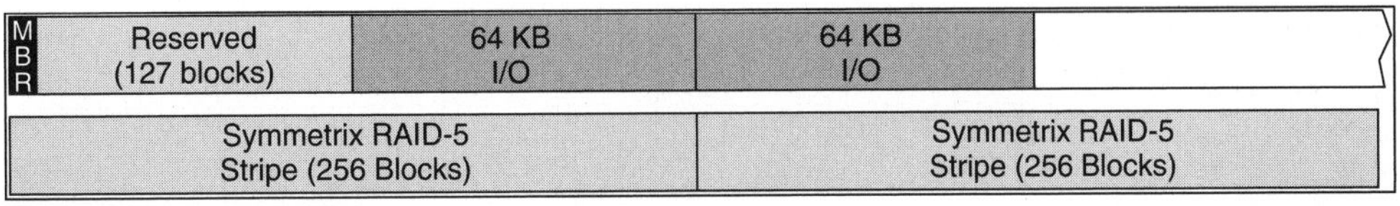

Figure 6-7

There are two methods of aligning your partition and it's quite simple. Diskpar is a tool that's been available for a while to enable you to align partitions but as of Windows 2003 SP1 the preferred method is Diskpart (note the extra *t*). The main difference between the two methods is that you specify the alignment value in blocks using Diskpar and in KB using Diskpart.

Figure 6-8 is a screenshot of a command prompt window where I created a new partition aligned to 64 KB using diskpart in Windows Server 2003.

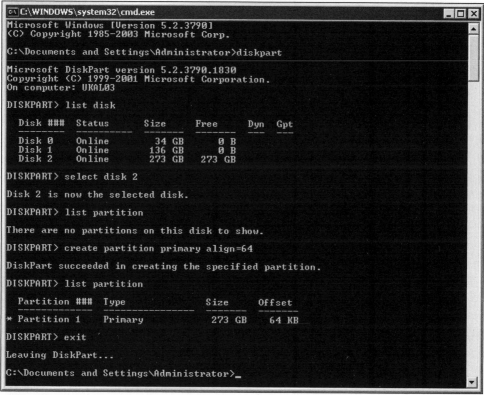

Figure 6-8

Best Practice

You should get the optimal alignment value from your array vendor but in the absence of that information Microsoft has traditionally recommended aligning to 64 KB. However, Windows Vista and Windows Server 2008 automatically align partitions to 1024 KB (for volumes over 4 GB) to optimize for pretty much any stripe size so it might be worth taking that approach also.

Type of Volume

Fundamentally a volume is a logical abstraction of a disk partition. When you format a drive it's the volume that you're formatting and there are two types to choose from. A *basic volume* provides a simple and efficient storage solution that's been around for years. *Dynamic volumes* were introduced with Windows 2000 and enable additional features like spanned and extendable volumes and software driven RAID.

With the better performing hardware driven RAID so affordable these days you don't often see dynamic disks in the field. Also, dynamic disks are not supported for Windows Failover Clustering so basic disks are the only option if you're going to be building a cluster.

> ### Best Practice
>
> Don't convert your disks to dynamic disks unless you have a specific reason to do so. Only basic disks are supported on a Windows Failover Cluster. Use hardware-based RAID for better performance.

NTFS Allocation Unit Size

You specify the NTFS allocation unit size when you format a partition in windows. Tests in the Microsoft labs indicate that 64 KB is the best size for partitions containing SQL Server data files or transaction log files because it's the most common size of reads and writes from SQL Server. However, the performance benefit is usually marginal, so you should only implement it on new drives or when re-formatting for other reasons. You shouldn't request server downtime to change it. The default is 4 KB and this size is required if you want to use the NTFS compression feature in Windows. Although NTFS compression is not recommend for SQL Server database files it is supported for read-only data so you should bear in mind that it requires the default NTFS allocation unit size.

> ### Best Practice
>
> Format the partitions holding your SQL Server data and transaction log files with an NTFS Allocation Unit Size of 64 KB.

Disk Fragmentation

Any discussion on disks would not be complete without a discussion of fragmentation. Fragmentation can occur in two forms with SQL Server:

❏ Internal fragmentation occurs when data gets old and has been subject to many inserts, updates, and deletes. This is covered in Chapter 11.

❏ External file fragmentation occurs when a file is created and the file system doesn't have enough contiguous disk space to create the file in a single fragment. You end up with a single file spread across multiple file fragments on the surface of the disk.

An important point to consider is that SQL Server files don't become more fragmented once they have been created. If files are created when there isn't enough contiguous free space, they are created in multiple fragments. If the disk is defragmented (and the OS has enough space to fully defragment all files) right after the files are created, then the files are no longer fragmented and won't ever become fragmented.

The ideal scenario is that you have dedicated disks for your SQL Server files, can size each file correctly, and disable autogrow. In this situation, you start with clean disks, create one or two files that aren't fragmented, and they stay that way forever. Then you only need to deal with internal fragmentation.

The most common scenario, however, is that autogrow is enabled and is relied upon to continue growing the database files as needed. Autogrow as a feature is great to help you avoid the emergency of running out of space in a file and having to manually add more space. However, it should only be there as a last resort as it could create fragmented files on disk, which will impact performance.

I attended a CritSit once where a customer was "autogrowing" their database in 10 MB increments throughout the day and then archiving data at night and shrinking the file again. Performance was dire due to the constant autogrow events and the heavily fragmented database files.

If you don't have dedicated drives for the databases and you're starting from scratch the best method is:

1. Install the OS.

2. Defragment the disk.

3. Install any applications (SQL Server).

4. Defragment the disk.

5. Create data and log files at max size.

6. Stop SQL Server, check for fragmentation, and defrag if necessary.

7. Disable autogrow or at least make the increment large so it happens rarely.

8. Routinely defragment the disk to preserve contiguous free space in the event you ever need to add more SQL Database files.

In most cases the operating system's disk defragmenter does a great job and is all you need, but there are various third-party tools that can give you more control, speed, and centralized management for coordinating defragmentation of multiple servers.

If you have a large database on a dedicated drive and you're concerned about file fragmentation, copying it off the drive and then back again will remove any fragmentation. This requires enough free disk space of course to copy the database somewhere, so if that isn't available then stop SQL Server (to close the database files) and use the OS defragmenter to fix the problem.

Best Practice

Plan your database growth rate and size the files appropriately so you can switch off autogrow.

CPU

SQL Server 2005 operates in a very different environment than previous versions of SQL Server. When SQL Server 2000 was launched, a large server used for SQL Server might have two or maybe even four processors. Today SQL Server 2005 is commonly run on 8 or 16 processors and is able to run on the largest servers with 64 processors, and up to 2 TB of RAM running Windows Server 2003 Data Center Edition with SP1. Today there is a bewildering array of processor options to consider when thinking about a new system. SQL Server 2005 can run on all the mainstream processors available today.

❑   32-bit processors: *x86*

❑   32-bit with 64-bit extension processors: *x64*

❑   64-bit processors: IA64

What follows is a short introduction to these different processor families along with a short discussion of some of the factors that influence making a decision on which processor you should use.

32-bit x86 Processors

32-bit systems are fast becoming replaced by 64-bit systems. About the only reason for purchasing a 32-bit system today is cost, and the clear knowledge that the system will never need more than 2 to 4 GB of physical memory. In fact you would find it very hard to find new 32-bit-only processors these days so your decision is really about whether or not to run 32-bit or 64-bit software.

Multi-Core

A common interpretation of Moore's Law is that processor power will double every 18 months. That has pretty much held true since 1975 and can be seen in the increase in processor speed over the years. However, it wasn't expected to continue forever and the processor manufacturers have now pretty much reached the physical limitations of the processor components, resulting in maximum speeds of about 3.8 to 4.0 GHz. The big question now is how to significantly increase processor performance when you're unable to increase processor speed. The answer appears to be multiple CPU cores.

Multi-core effectively means more than one CPU on the same chip so when you buy a dual-core processor you're actually buying two CPU cores, Windows will see two CPUs, and you should treat it for capacity planning purposes like two single-core CPUs. It gets even better from a licensing perspective because Microsoft per-processor licensing is per socket, not per core. *Socket* refers to the physical socket that you plug the processor into (see Figure 6-9 for an illustration). This licensing model gives Microsoft a competitive advantage over its competitors in the database market, where others charge customers a license fee per core. This is great news for SQL Server customers because a server with four dual-core CPUs will perform comparably with an eight single-core server but at half the license cost.

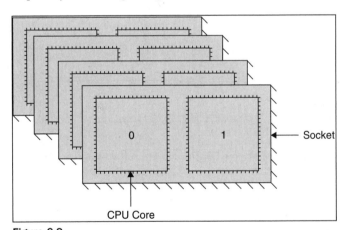

Figure 6-9

At the time of writing, quad-core CPUs are available but not really mainstream and 8-core CPUs are on the processor manufacturer's short-term roadmap.

Best Practice

Multi-core processors are only licensed per socket so if you can get an 8-core processor you'll only need a Windows and SQL Server license for 1 socket!

Hyper-Threading

The most commonly asked question about Hyper-Threading and SQL Server is, "Should I enable it or disable it?" This is a difficult question and the best answer of course is to test it yourself using your workload and your hardware to see if it gives you a performance increase or even a performance *decrease*. This is the cause of all the concern; it may actually impact your SQL Server's performance depending on your usage and workload. Before you decide whether to use it on your server, have a look at what Hyper-Threading actually is and what the theoretical performance benefits are.

First of all let's define what a thread is; a thread is a unit of execution that runs on a CPU that can only execute one thread at a time. However, a CPU is very good at switching between threads very quickly to share its power, giving the illusion of simultaneous execution.

Hyper-Threading is a technology found only on Intel processors, that tries to make more efficient use of the CPU by duplicating the architectural state to provide two logical CPUs. This allows more than 1 thread to be scheduled and enables simultaneous execution when the threads require different processor functions. The effect of this is that you will see two logical CPUs to which the operating system can assign different threads. However, it is only the architectural state that is duplicated, not the physical execution engine. Figure 6-10 shows a 4 dual-core system with Hyper-Threading enabled, giving 16 logical processors.

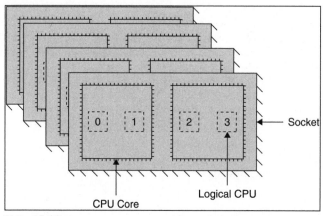

Figure 6-10

The first step when considering Hyper-Threading is to understand the maximum performance benefit that you might get. Intel's documentation reveals that the maximum theoretical performance gain from Hyper-Threading is 30 percent. Many people running with Hyper-Threading enabled for the first time expect to see double the performance because the operating system shows two processors. You should understand that Hyper-Threading is only ever going to give you a maximum of 1.3 times non-Hyper-Threaded performance and in practice it will be closer to 1.1 to 1.15 times. This knowledge helps put any decision about enabling it back into perspective.

There are a couple of places where Hyper-Threading won't provide any benefit. In any workload where the code is running a tight loop entirely from cache, Hyper-Threading won't provide any benefit, because there is only a single execution engine. This can show a performance decrease as the operating system tries to schedule activity on a CPU that isn't physically there.

Another place where Hyper-Threading can directly affect SQL Server performance is any time a parallel plan might be chosen. One of the things a parallel plan does is to split the available work across the available processors with the assumption that each processor will be able to complete the same amount of work in the given time. In a Hyper-Threading scenario, any thread that's not currently executing will be stalled until the other thread on that processor completes.

If you do have the time to test it and you think the performance benefit will be worth it, then there are a couple of things you should be aware of to give you the best chance for a performance gain. First, the operating system can make a big difference; Windows Server 2000 isn't Hyper-Threading aware and Windows Server 2003 is. The effect of this is that Windows 2003 in theory will schedule threads on one logical processor per core before utilizing the other logical processor on each core.

Windows Server 2003 Service Pack 1 added more Hyper-Threading optimizations, so make sure you're running at least Service Pack 1.

Something else to consider is that Hyper-Threading itself has been evolving and feedback from customers running SQL Server seems to indicate that it's getting better with each generation of processors. So a customer trying it on an older server may not see as much benefit as if they run on a server with the very latest generation of processors.

Admittedly, there is a chance of getting a performance benefit from Hyper-Threading on SQL Server but due to the cost of testing each SQL Server application and the relative low reward, most customers choose to switch it off as default, particularly if they have dozens or even hundreds of SQL Servers in their environment.

Best Practice

Disable Hyper-Threading unless you have the time to test it thoroughly. Don't use it on Windows 2000 as it's not Hyper-Threading aware.

64-Bit

If you're considering purchasing new servers today you're pretty much guaranteed to get 64-bit capable hardware so you should be considering 64-bit Windows. Even if the server is only going to run 32-bit applications, the ability to increase memory beyond 4 GB without resorting to PAE means that a 64-bit system should be the first choice. You should take the approach of making 64-bit the default and 32-bit an option requiring justification rather than the other way around.

However, before jumping in with both feet it's worth noting a potential drawback with 64-bit systems, and that's a lack of 64-bit drivers; any driver that runs in kernel mode needs to be compiled for 64-bit. That predominantly means hardware and most hardware vendors have written 64-bit drivers for their new products but there are some out there who still haven't written them. If you're purchasing hardware on a budget, you may end up with older model hardware and then find that the vendor has no intention of writing a 64-bit driver for your brand new NIC, disk adapter, and so on. Check for full 64-bit support before you buy.

SQL Server 2008 will be released for both 32-bit and 64-bit, but it's a distinct possibility that the version after that will be 64-bit only.

Best Practice

Go for 64-bit for your default environment and justify any need to go for 32-bit.

---

x64 or IA64

First, a bit of history; *x64* was created by AMD as an alternative to the strictly patented IA64 platform from HP and Intel and became a feature in all of their processors. Then Microsoft announced the development of Windows XP Professional *x64* Edition to take advantage of this new computing environment on the desktop and Intel finally responded to the competitive pressure by releasing *x64* compatible extensions to their processors called EM64 T. AMD renamed their technology AMD64 and Intel renamed theirs Intel64. We use the *x64* term today as a vendor neutral way to refer to either platform.

The key factors when deciding between *x64* and IA64 are cost, availability, scalability, and performance.

It's always dangerous to generalize, but today most *x64* processors have faster clock speeds than IA64 systems. The current state of processor clock speed is that *x64* processors are running over 3 GHz, whereas IA64 processors have stayed around 1.6 GHz for some time now.

However, processor speed alone can be misleading as the most recent IA64 processors have larger cache sizes than *x64* processors. The larger cache can help minimize the disadvantage of slower processor speeds and is very beneficial when you have many processors in a server. *x64* processors are typically available in a wider range of servers than IA64 systems, which are increasingly only found in specialized machines, either high performance workstations, or very large highly scalable systems from a few specialist vendors.

Cache

The reason modern processors need cache is because the processor runs at 2 to 3 GHz and main memory simply cannot keep up with the processor's appetite for memory. To try and help this, the processor designers added several layers of cache to keep recently used data in small fast-memory caches so that if you access it again it might already be in cache. To make this process more efficient it doesn't just load the byte requested, but the subsequent range of addresses as well.

The cache on modern processors is typically implemented as multiple layers commonly known as L1, L2, and L3. Each layer is physically further from the processor core, and gets larger and slower until you are back at main memory. Some caches are general purpose and hold copies of any memory (L2 and L3). Other caches are very specific and hold only address lookups, data, or instructions. Typically L1 is smaller and faster than L2, which is smaller and faster than L3. L3 cache is often physically located on a separate chip, so is further away from the processor core than L1 or L2 but still closer and faster than main memory. Figure 6-11 illustrates an example of CPU cache implementation.

Processor Cache is implemented as a transparent look-thru cache. This means that there are controlling functions on the chip that manage the process of filling the cache and managing cache entries.

Now onto some SQL Server specifics; SQL Server 2005 is a considerably more complex product than SQL Server 2000 and building in all this additional complexity comes at the cost of additional lines of code. This can be seen as additional bytes in the size of the final executable (EXE) file, Sqlservr.exe. The executable for SQL Server 2000 is 8.9 MB. The executable for SQL Server 2005 has grown considerably and is now at 28 MB. Not just that, but simply starting the service requires more system resources. SQL Server 2000 runs in about 29 MB of memory (you can easily see this by using Task Manager and looking at the Mem Usage column for SQL Server. The Mem Usage column provides an approximation of the working set for the process). Connecting with SQLCMD and issuing a simple query, such as select name from master..sysdatabases, adds another 0.5 MB to that number. SQL Server 2005 uses around 50 MB of memory just to start. On our test server, Task Manager Mem Usage reports 49,604 KB. Connecting with SQLCMD and issuing the same command makes that grow to 53,456 KB.

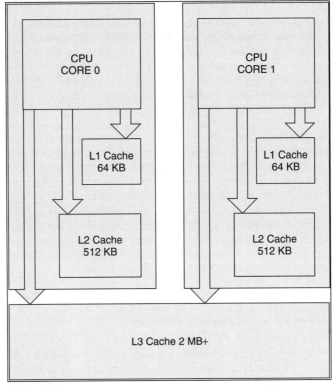

Figure 6-11

All this increased complexity results in a lot more code being run inside SQL Server to enable you to do the same operations in SQL Server 2005 than in SQL Server 2000. It's not all bad though; additional security features, for example, can take some of the stress away from having to build security into SQL Server yourself and even though you might see an increase in the time it takes to compile a query it is likely that the execution time will be faster. This means that the first time a new query is run, there is a chance that it may actually take longer to run than in SQL 2000. However, future executions of the plan from cache will execute considerably faster.

This is an excellent reason to use any feature that allows you to re-use a plan. After SQL Server has taken all that time to figure a fast way to get you your data, re-use that plan as much as you can before it's thrown away. This way you are making use of the time SQL Server took to figure out a great plan for you.

All this extra code manifests itself as an increase in sensitivity to cache size. So the smaller the cache, the slower you might run and vice versa. The result of this is that if you have a choice between two processors running at the same speed opt for the one with the largest cache. Unfortunately, the increased cache comes at a premium. Whether or not that additional cost is worthwhile is very difficult to quantify; if you have the ability to run a test on both processors, this is the best way to determine the potential improvement. Try to come up with a test that delivers a specific metric that you can factor against the cost to deliver a clear indication of the cost benefit of larger cache.

System Architecture

Another key purchasing decision has to be around the machine architecture. For systems up to eight processors there really isn't much choice. Single-socket, dual-socket, quad-socket, and even most eight-way systems are only available in Symmetric Multi-Processing (SMP) configuration. It's only when you move to 16-, 32-, or 64-way systems that you need to consider the options of SMP versus NUMA. This isn't something you really need to configure but rather something you need to understand as an option when considering the purchase of one type of system over another.

SMP

Symmetric multi-processing (SMP) is a computer architecture where multiple processors are connected to a single shared memory through a system bus. This is the most common computer architecture today and allows for any processor to work on any task regardless of where in memory the data is located. Windows and SQL Server have been designed to take advantage of this by splitting work into separate tasks where possible so that work can be evenly distributed between processors. The downside, which you already read about at the start of this section, is that memory is much slower than the processors accessing it and SMP compounds the problem because only one processor can access memory at a time. To try and lessen the performance hit processors use local cache as described above. Figure 6-12 shows the relationship between memory and CPU in an SMP-based server.

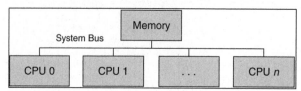

Figure 6-12

SMP is an efficient architecture where you have a small number of CPUs but when you start counting them in dozens the system bus becomes a bottleneck and you have to look at alternatives.

NUMA

Non-Uniform Memory Access (NUMA) is an architecture designed to exceed the scalability of SMP. The SMP architecture connects the memory to all the processors symmetrically via a shared bus whereas the NUMA architecture has multiple system buses and limits the number of processors on each system bus to four. Each group of four processors with its own system bus is called a *node* and each node has access to its own pool of local memory. Each node is connected to every other node's memory through a high-speed interconnect, but access to this "foreign" memory is considered to be four times slower than access to local memory. Figure 6-13 shows the relationship between nodes in a NUMA-configured server.

The goal on a NUMA system is to maximize the amount of data that you get from the local memory rather than the memory from another node but applications need to be NUMA-aware to take advantage of this. Windows 2003 and SQL Server 2005 have been designed to be NUMA-aware but SQL Server 2000 is not. If you have to run SQL Server 2000 on a NUMA machine it should be configured as interleaved-NUMA, which I will explain momentarily.

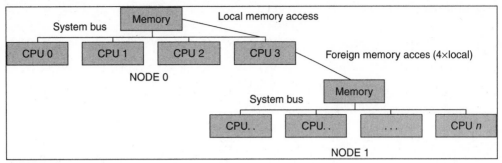

Figure 6-13

You can see if SQL Server is using NUMA buy running the following query or checking the startup messages in the SQL Server errorlog:

```
SELECT DISTINCT memory_node_id FROM sys.dm_os_memory_clerks
```

The query shows the number of memory nodes that SQL Server is using. If you return a zero then you're only using one node and no NUMA. If you're running on an AMD processor, however, you might get an unexpected result; all AMD processor architectures (as far as I'm aware) are implemented as NUMA, so if you have a dual-core AMD and run the above script you'll see two NUMA nodes reported.

When an application isn't NUMA aware you can configure the server to emulate an SMP architecture. This means that each node doesn't distinguish between local and foreign memory. We call this interleaved-NUMA and it is illustrated in Figure 6-14.

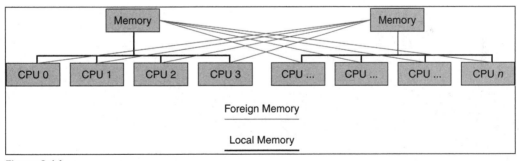

Figure 6-14

> ### Best Practice
> SQL Server 2000 should only use interleaved-NUMA. I see lots of customers with SMP servers up to 16 processors and most go for NUMA when looking at 32+ processors.

Soft NUMA

Soft NUMA is a SQL Server 2005 feature that was developed to help the Microsoft test teams to run use case scenarios simulating NUMA hardware. It soon became apparent, however, that there were customer scenarios that would benefit from simulated NUMA, so it became a supported feature. It allows you to group CPUs into soft-NUMA nodes, which can help with performance if you have lots of CPUs and no hardware NUMA. For example, SQL Server has one I/O thread and one Lazy Writer thread per NUMA node, which can become a bottleneck on a non-NUMA system, so if you have an eight CPU machine then configuring 4 × 2-CPU soft-NUMA nodes would make SQL Server use 4 × I/O threads and 4 × lazy writer threads without using hardware NUMA.

Best Practice

Use Soft-NUMA to allocate groups of CPUs to specific tasks even when you don't have hardware NUMA. You can even create soft-NUMA nodes within hardware NUMA nodes to further control what your CPUs work on.

Summary

This chapter covered a lot of ground that might not be a core skill for the SQL Server Professional but plays a very important part in SQL Server's performance. These topics need to be understood and taken into consideration at both the design stage and when supporting a live system.

The chapter centered on the three key server resources: Memory, I/O, and CPU, and covered design choices and configuration best practices for each area.

For memory, we covered architecture and discussed the configuration options for large memory support: /3GB, /PAE, and AWE. We talked about how to decide which options to use and gave prescriptive guidance to use as a baseline.

For I/O, we briefly covered network versus disk I/O and discussed types of hard disks, SAN and DAS solutions, storage configuration best practices, and SQL Server file placement.

For CPU, we discussed 32-bit versus 64-bit, multi-core, Hyper-Threading, CPU cache, and NUMA versus SMP to help you understand how to make an informed decision when purchasing a processor or computer architecture.

In the next chapter we will look at tuning the database schema to make more efficient use of server resources to help avoid bottlenecks.

7

Tuning SQL Server Configuration

Unlike other major RDBMS products on the market such as Oracle 9i and 10g, which have hundreds of parameters to tweak, SQL Server, for the most part, is self-configuring. That means that the default setting will work best for most scenarios.

Having said that, there are some configuration settings you can tweak, after careful analysis of the application, performance counters, SQL traces/profiling, and DMVs data, that warrant such action. If you need help with performance monitoring, SQL Server trace and profiling, and DMVs, please refer to the relevant chapters in this book for detailed discussion on those subjects.

In this chapter, we will discuss ways on how to tweak some advanced SQL Server settings to maximize performance. We will start from where and how to find existing SQL Server configuration settings. Next we will examine some important server settings, what they mean, and implications of changing them to different values.

As mentioned earlier, SQL Server is self-tuning for the most part. Only change server configuration settings when you have solid evidence that it really helps performance.

Considerations before Adjusting Server Level Settings

Throughout the book, we've talked about many aspects of performance tuning for SQL Server. Normally, you should try not to tinker too much with server settings, as SQL Server is self-configuring for the most part.

A common approach many people take when they are asked to troubleshoot a performance issue is to jump right into things, and they forget to look into some more obvious areas. Instead, there are some things to keep in mind before you dive right into the problem. Depending on the situation you are facing, you may ask some other seemingly obvious questions just to confirm or rule out various considerations:

1. Is SQL Server the only application running on the server box? Running SQL Server is a memory- and CPU-intensive process. If you share it with a domain controller, Exchange, HR, or some other enterprise applications, it probably cannot perform optimally.

2. Have you analyzed some CPU, Memory, and I/O counters? If you are running a mission-critical, resource-intensive database on an underpowered server, no amount of server tweaking and tuning can fix the problem.

3. Related to the question above, do you have a good physical design of the data? Is data placed appropriately on different spindles and I/O paths so you can maximize simultaneous I/O? Is your application designed appropriately (having short transactions, appropriate isolation levels, set operations as opposed to processing one row at a time, useful indexes, and so on)?

4. Is there anti-virus software on the server? Normally, database boxes are behind the firewall and properly patched. Performance-wise, it is not always a good idea to have virus-scanning software on the database box. Sometimes there is no other way around it. If that is the case, is the scanning scheduled to occur during less busy times? Have the database files, the ones having `.mdf`, `.ndf`, and `.ldf` extensions, been excluded from the scanning process? Another way to achieve that is to exclude the database folder from the scanning list.

5. Is the firmware on your hardware up-to-date? This includes the BIOS, disk controller firmware, fire-channel drivers, and other storage devices and their respective drivers. Most, if not all, of the hardware requires the latest version of firmware or drivers to function properly and at the optimal level. So it is very important to keep them up-to-date.

Now that the disclaimer is out of the way, it is time to get started with server-level configuration settings.

Inspecting Current SQL Server Settings

For all things SQL Server, there are generally two ways to do things: via the graphical user interface (GUI) (whether it is SQL Server Management Studio, Configuration Manager, or others) or via scripts. You will take a look at inspecting server settings via the GUI interface first.

Inspecting Server Settings with SQL Server Management Studio

For most server parameters, you can see and change their values using SQL Server Management Studio. Here are the steps to do it:

1. Connect to the database server in question with Management Studio.

2. Within Object Explorer, right-click the server itself, and select Properties from the context menu.

3. You will see the Server Property window (shown in Figure 7-1). From here, you can inspect your server parameter settings. Click different sections in the Select a Page Frame, and you will see settings pertaining to the property you select.

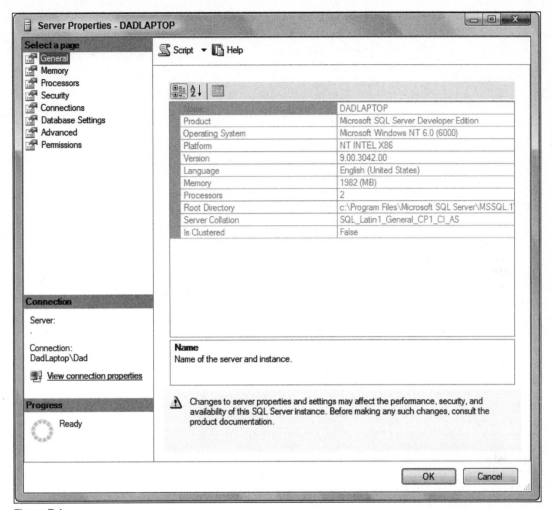

Figure 7-1

Note that anybody who can connect to the server will be able to view these settings this way. However, to change any of them, the user must have the ALTER SETTINGS permission. By default, a user with the sysadmin or serveradmin fixed server role has this right.

Inspecting Server Settings with Scripts

Another way to inspect server settings is to use scripts. You can use DMVs to get some of those settings, but the best way to do it is through sp_configure.

Open a Query window, connect to the server in question, and enter the following command:

```
sp_configure
go
```

If you run this query, you will get a result similar to the one shown in Figure 7-2.

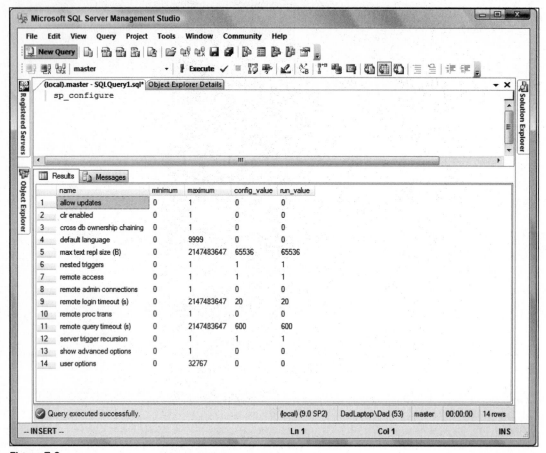

Figure 7-2

To see the individual running value of any single parameter, such as whether CLR is enabled, you can run `sp_configure` on it, as in the following statement:

```
sp_configure 'clr enabled'
```

In Figure 7-2, you only see 14 parameters listed. You might expect there should be more. In fact, there are. We will talk about how to view and change them next.

Inspecting Advanced Settings and Changing Their Values

Look closely at Figure 7-2. You can see that the run_value for the Show Advanced Options setting (row 13) is 0, which means off.

Now run the following statement:

```
sp_configure 'show advanced options', 1
go
```

You will get the following message:

```
Configuration option 'show advanced options' changed from 0 to 1. Run the
RECONFIGURE statement to install.
```

If you run sp_configure 'show advanced options', you will see that the config_value is 1 whereas the run_value is 0:

name	minimum	maximum	config_value	run_value
show advanced options	0	1	1	0

You can then run the following code:

```
reconfigure
go
```

Now if you run sp_configure again, you should see many more parameters to play with. Changing values for parameters works exactly the same as you just saw for show advanced options.

Here is one very efficient shortcut: When specifying the parameter, you don't need to type the whole string. You just need to type enough letters for SQL Server to uniquely identify it. For example, typing sp_configure 'show' works the same as typing sp_configure 'show advanced options'.

Important Server Settings: CPU, Memory, and I/O

Generally speaking, an application needs to have a solid design and architecture for it to perform and scale well. However, if you are tasked with putting out fires and improving the performance of an existing application in short order, simply complaining about bad design and sloppy code is not going to cut it. One area you can look at is server configuration parameters. Application refactoring and enhancement will come later, hopefully. On the server side of things, from a high level, there are three areas you need to focus on: CPU, memory, and I/O. They will be the focus of this section.

CPU

CPU obviously can have a big impact on database server performance. Since we are talking about SQL Server, when the server allocates processor resources, it should naturally favor background processes such as SQL Server Service. To verify this, go to the properties page of your server (right-click My Computer and pick Properties) and then pick the Advanced tab, as seen in Figure 7-3.

Now click Settings within the Performance box, and you will see the Performance Options window. Click the Advanced tab (see Figure 7-4).

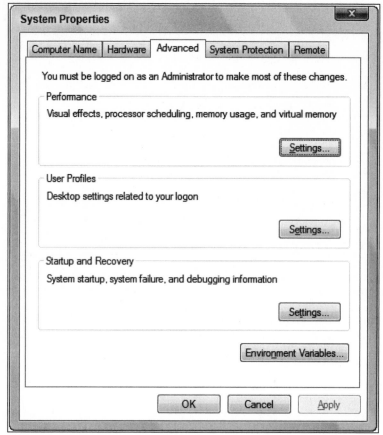

Figure 7-3

Take a look at Processor scheduling box. Ensure that the Background services option is selected, as a SQL Server box should favor background processes.

In addition, you might also want to select the Boost SQL Server priority check box on the properties page of the server, under the Processors page, when there are other applications running on the server box (see Figure 7-5).

There are many terminologies surrounding this area: hyper-threading versus non hyper-threading, 64-bit vs. 32-bit, degree of parallelism, CPU affinity. Now you will look at them in that order.

Hyper-Threading versus Non Hyper-Threading

Starting with Pentium 4, Intel introduced an enhancement to its processors called *hyper-threading*. Here is the basic idea behind it: Due to cache miss, branch mis-prediction, or other reasons, a physical processor may stall, therefore not doing real work at any given time. To improve processing efficiency, certain sections of the processor can be duplicated, so when a stall happens, the processor can work on another scheduled task, instead of idling. This makes one physical processor appear as two logical processors to the operating system. As a result, both logical CPUs will be used to schedule and process tasks.

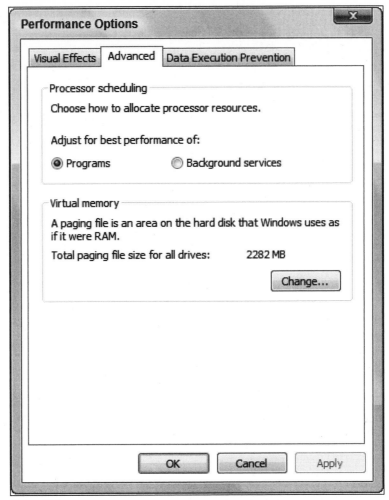

Figure 7-4

Research from processor vendors show that at a maximum, hyper-threading can improve performance by 30 percent. And the performance increase is not guaranteed. In some cases, performance may degrade, because the operating system may accidently schedule a lot of tasks to what it thinks are two separate processors, but those two logical processors maybe just one physical processor. It all depends on how your application is written.

If you want to use hyper-threading, here are two rules to follow:

❑ Since hyper-threading is a relatively new technology, Windows Server 2000 does not have additional features built-in to provide extra support for this feature. You might want to get the latest Windows Server operating system with the latest patch.

❑ Conduct before and after testing to confirm whether hyper-threading works for your application. Don't blindly assume that hyper-threading will deliver you out of your predicaments. Let your performance data tell you if it needs to be turned on or not.

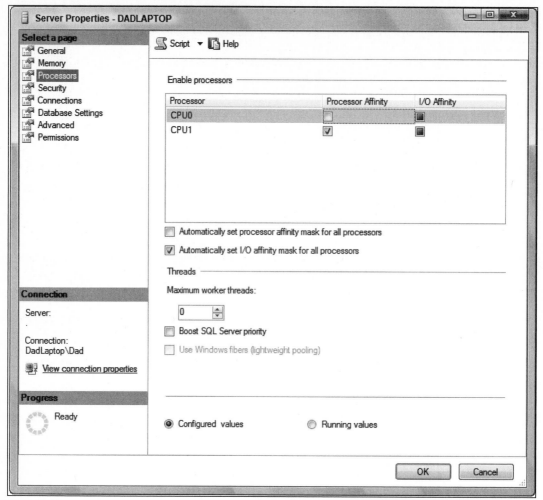

Figure 7-5

In the server's BIOS, you can turn hyper-threading on or off.

NUMA

Non-uniform memory access (NUMA) is a hardware design enhancement to better handle the ever increasing load on your database servers.

In traditional symmetric multiprocessing (SMP) architecture, all memory usage by all available processors is done through the shared system memory bus. This is sufficient when the load is not too heavy on the database server system. However, as you try to scale things vertically, there could be contention issues for system memory bus. The emergence of multi-core systems would only exacerbate this even further, with the existing shared memory bus architecture. NUMA can help reduce the latency on the memory bus, especially for servers with more than 32 CPUs.

Hardware NUMA

To prevent memory bus contention problems and enhance overall performance, newer systems have incorporated more than one system bus, each accommodating one or more processors. Each processor group has its own memory, called local memory. Processors within the group use the local memory first. This group is called one NUMA node. Processors within one node can, when necessary, access memory in a foreign node, but local memory access is significantly faster than accessing memory in a foreign node.

SQL Server 2005 is NUMA-aware. At service startup, SQL Server 2005 detects the underlying hardware architecture and will automatically take advantage of the underlying hardware design. You do not need to do anything special, unlike with SQL Server 2000, where you have to turn on a trace flag to use it.

Software NUMA

As mentioned earlier, if your server box is of NUMA design, then SQL Server automatically configures itself to take advantage of that feature. However, for non-NUMA hardware such as traditional SMP boxes, if you have multiple processors to play with, you can still divide processors into different nodes, thus allowing SQL OS and SQL Server network interface to use them properly. That can potentially alleviate I/O and lazywriter (a periodic process that checks and evaluates the status of Buffer Pool buffers) bottlenecks.

For example, suppose you have eight SMP processors. By default, there will be one single lazywriter and one single I/O thread for all eight processors. In NUMA, each node has its own single lazywriter and I/O thread. If you sub-divide those eight processors into four soft-NUMA nodes, you will gain three additional I/O threads and three additional lazywriter threads, which could increase your server performance.

Soft-NUMA is configured within the registry. Following are the registry entries for the previous example's configuration:

```
[HKEY_LOCAL_MACHINE\SOFTWARE\Microsoft\Microsoft SQL
Server\90\NodeConfiguration]
[HKEY_LOCAL_MACHINE\SOFTWARE\Microsoft\Microsoft SQL
Server\90\NodeConfiguration\Node0]
"CPUMask"=dword:00000003
[HKEY_LOCAL_MACHINE\SOFTWARE\Microsoft\Microsoft SQL
Server\90\NodeConfiguration\Node1]
"CPUMask"=dword:0000000C
[HKEY_LOCAL_MACHINE\SOFTWARE\Microsoft\Microsoft SQL
Server\90\NodeConfiguration\Node2]
"CPUMask"=dword:00000030
[HKEY_LOCAL_MACHINE\SOFTWARE\Microsoft\Microsoft SQL
Server\90\NodeConfiguration\Node3]
"CPUMask"=dword:000000C0
```

Note that you can configure soft-NUMA on both SMP and NUMA hardware. In other words, you can divide the hardware nodes even further into soft-NUMA nodes. One important thing to remember is that the soft-NUMA node should be fully contained with the hardware NUMA node.

When soft-NUMA is configured, you can use network connection affinities to distribute different application loads to different processors. See the section "Network Connection Affinity" later in this chapter on how to set that up.

Here is a sample script to determine if NUMA is enabled on your system:

```
select
        CASE count( DISTINCT parent_node_id)
        WHEN 1 THEN 'NUMA disabled'
        ELSE 'NUMA enabled'
        END
from
        sys.dm_os_schedulers
where parent_node_id <> 32
```

64-bit vs. 32-bit

64-bit boxes appeared in the Windows Server market a few years ago. Now we've reached the tipping-point where 64-bit servers will gradually replace 32-bit machines. For new projects or server upgrades, there is really no point in getting 32-bit boxes nowadays. For one thing, 32-bit Windows OS and 64-bit Windows OS cost the same, as does SQL Server 2005 software. More importantly, with 64-bit machines, the virtual memory space is much, much larger than that of 32-bit system.

The 32-bit system has a maximum of 4 GB of virtual address space. That leaves 2 GB of virtual memory space for application use, because the other half is reserved for the operating system. When you have memory pressure, you sometimes use the /3GB, /PAE, or AWE option to tweak the system so you can give more memory to SQL Server's data cache. This can help, but it is far from being optimal.

With a 64-bit system, the addressable virtual memory is vastly expanded. To put things into perspective, the VAS on a 64-bit system is about 10 million times bigger than that of 32-bit. So you will definitely have more header room to grow, expand, and scale.

Parallel Processing

Most servers nowadays have more than one physical processor. By default, SQL Server makes the decision on which processor to use and how many to use. As mentioned earlier, in most cases, this is a good approach.

However, in some cases, parallel query processing can hurt performance, because of the excessive wait involved. To verify this, you can run the following query:

```
select * from sys.dm_os_wait_stats order by wait_time_ms desc
```

Inspecting the results, if you find wait type CXPACKET within the top 10 rows, it may be a cause of concern. You will then need to test the degree of parallelism thoroughly to see if that is the cause of your performance problems.

You can set the max degree of parallelism at the sever level. To do this, you can use the following script:

```
sp_configure 'max degree of parallelism', SomeInteger
```

By default, the value for 'max degree of parallelism' is 0, meaning the query processor could potentially use all available processors. If you set it to 1, then the query processor will not use parallel processing at all. The recommended approach is to set it to the number of physical processors minus 1. You will need to conduct some testing to find the optimal value for your application. Note that you can bypass this setting by using query hints.

Another way to get around this is to use a query hint called MAXDOP. For example, the following script will only use two processors at the most, when and if the query processor decides multiple CPUs are beneficial:

```
select * from orders option (maxdop 2)
```

Windows Fibers/Lightweight Pooling

You can put your SQL Server on a diet, that is, let it run in fiber mode, to see if it improves performance. Similar to any popular dietary regimen, this may not necessarily work. So, you should test it to verify if it improves or hurts performance, just like the way you deal with parallel processing.

Put simply, fibers are simple lighter execution units that run off of a thread. When fiber mode is enabled in SQL Server 2005, a fiber runs just like a thread, but it is running under user mode, not kernel mode. Therefore, it can be advantageous, especially when there are way too many context switches involved. You control the number of fibers used by setting the proper worker threads. SQL Server 2005 also identifies fiber usage as lightweight pooling. You can set it all up within the properties page, accessible via the Server Properties page from Object Explorer within Management Studio, as shown earlier in Figure 7-5.

CPU Affinity

For a dedicated, single instance SQL Server box, you should leave this parameter at its default value. This parameter comes into play when you have multiple instances or other applications running on the same server as your SQL server box.

Another situation in which CPU affinity can be useful is when you have applications with different network I/O. In that case, you can set network CPU affinity with SQL Server Configuration Manager. See the section "Network Connection Affinity" later in this chapter for details.

Simply put, CPU affinity determines which processors SQL Server uses. The default value allows SQL Server to use all available processors. However, if you have multiple instances on the box, you can use this parameter to designate unique CPUs to different instances, thereby decreasing the CPU contention. You can also use this parameter if you run other applications on the database box. Normally, you would like your database box to be a dedicated single instance server; therefore, the default setting for it would be ideal.

It is not difficult to set it using Management Studio, as seen earlier in Figure 7-5.

To determine CPU affinity, you can use this quick script:

```
select
       scheduler_id,
       CAST (cpu_id as varbinary) AS scheduler_affinity_mask
from
sys.dm_os_schedulers
```

I/O Affinity

As seen earlier in Figure 7-5, right next to the Processor Affinity check box in your properties page, there is one additional column called I/O Affinity. This is one additional area that you can tweak to potentially increase server performance.

The I/O Affinity property binds I/O operation to some particular subset of processors. By default, SQL Server I/O operation is allowed on all available processors. In high volume OLTP environments, grouping I/O tasks on dedicated resources could improve performance, since it can maximize data usage within local memory to those processors and decrease unnecessary system bus traffic.

Like all other advanced server settings, use this with caution. Ideally, you would conduct a before and after test to collect performance data to confirm that this could really help your operation. You should also be careful not to overload any single processor with tons of tasks. Refer to Figure 7-5 for details.

Memory

SQL Server is a very memory-intensive application. Generally speaking, the more physical memory you can afford, the better it will perform. As discussed earlier, you generally should go with 64-bit servers, as they provide much more virtual address space than a 32-bit system does. Therefore, it provides a bigger headroom to scale up. For 32-bit systems, if you have enough memory, you can use the /PAE switch in the boot.ini file under c:\ and enable AWE using sp_configure to allocate more memory for SQL Server consumption. The following code demonstrates how to enable AWE in SQL Server:

```
sp_configure 'show advanced', 1
reconfigure

sp_configure 'awe enabled', 1
reconfigure
```

Specifically, if you have a 64-bit system, it is very important that you grant the Lock pages in memory right to SQL Server's startup account. That is done via the group policy editor snap-in called gpedit.msc (see Figure 7-6).

Please refer to Chapter 6 for more information on locking pages in memory.

In addition, there are a couple of other memory parameters to tinker with. For example, you can set the minimum size and maximum size of memory SQL Server can use. You can give SQL Server a fixed size memory to use, by setting the minimum and maximum memory size to the same value. If you so, keep in mind that SQL Server memory grows until it reaches the minimum memory setting and then it does not release it. You can do all these with script by using sp_configure. However, Figure 7-7 shows you how to change it in the graphical user interface.

Once again, if SQL Server is not sharing resources with other SQL Server instances or applications, it is best to leave these memory settings at their default value. However, if you are sharing resources with other applications on the server, you may set the memory size for SQL Server so it has enough memory to work with and yet not over-allocate to the point that the other applications are starved for memory.

Network I/O

I/O can be further classified as network I/O and disk I/O. Disk I/O and its comparison to network I/O is discussed in Chapter 6. Please refer to it if you need additional information in that area. We will focus on network I/O in this chapter.

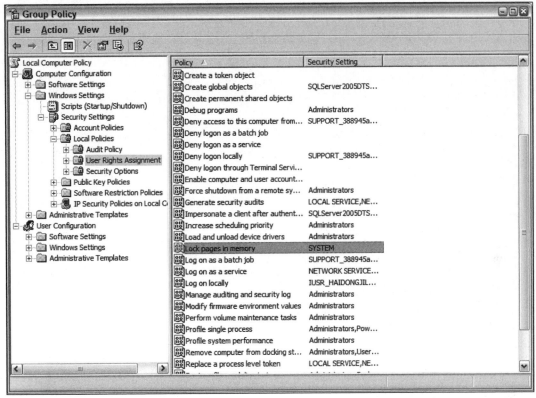

Figure 7-6

Network Packet Size

By default, network packet size is 4096 bytes. Once again, this has proven to work well in most scenarios. However, if your application sends a lot of text or image data to SQL Server, it may be beneficial to adjust the parameter to a bigger size, due to fewer network read and write operations.

By now you should be familiar with adjusting parameters with scripts. You can use `sp_configure` to adjust network packet size to a size of your choosing. Alternatively, Figure 7-8 shows the properties page where you can change it with the UI.

As with all other server parameters, test and verify that the change will result in performance improvement before you apply it to production.

Network Connection Affinity

Network connection affinity is an advanced feature that is only available for TCP/IP network connections, which, fortunately for SQL Server, are the dominant network protocol nowadays. The idea is that a different end point, which essentially is a port on the server, can be created. The new end point can then be bound to CPUs on the server. This can be very useful to spread the load to different processors on the server.

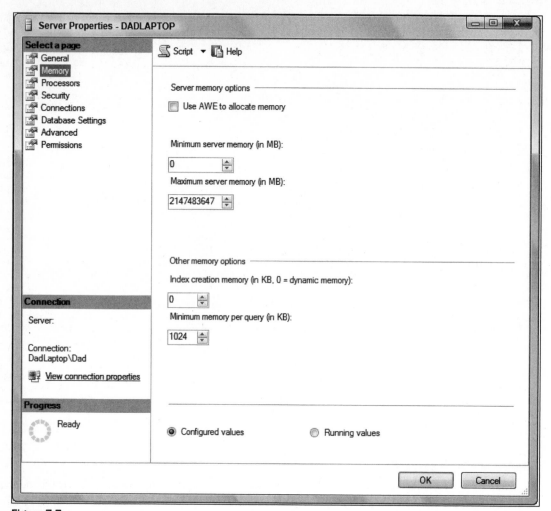

Figure 7-7

For example, suppose you have a number of applications that all use your dedicated database server. Those applications serve ordering, reporting, and HR functions, listed in the order of importance to the company, from the most important to the least important. Suppose you have eight processors on your database server. Ideally, you'd like to have the reporting and HR application defer to the ordering application, so that the mission critical application always receives the highest priority.

You can create three separate end points for this purpose. One end point is just for ordering application connections, where you assign five processors to it. You can then create another end point, which you assign two processors to. And finally, for the HR application, you will have an end point, which will only have one processor to use.

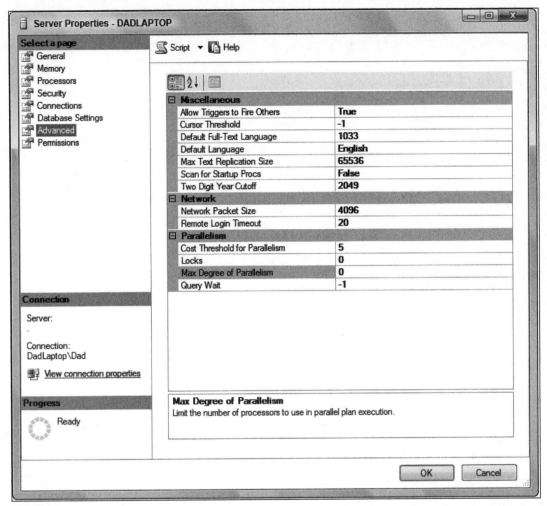

Figure 7-8

To set this up, you will need to use SQL Server Configuration Manager. You need to select SQL Server 2005 Network Configuration, and configure Protocols for your SQL Server instance (see Figure 7-9).

Next, right-click the TCP/IP protocol on the right pane, and then select Property from the context menu. You can configure your network connection affinity here.

Click the IP Addresses tab (see Figure 7-10).

You will need to put the CPU node number into a square bracket right after the port number. Now, in your application database connection setting, you just point it to the right port on the server. That application will only use the processors you designated earlier.

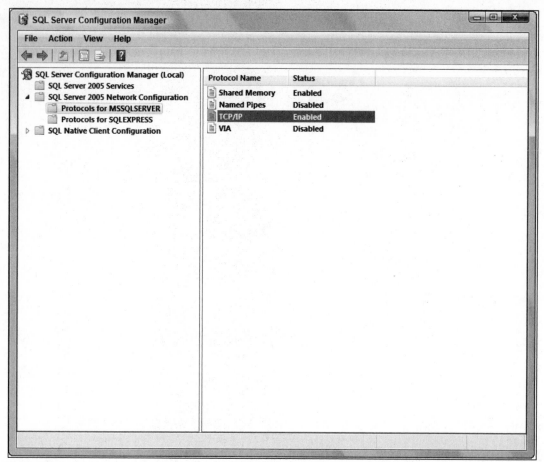

Figure 7-9

For example, if you want to bind your `sqlcmd` command line application to a particular CPU node, you can issue the following statement in a command prompt:

```
sqlcmd -E -Sservername,1438
```

Similarly, you can put the port number into your connection string for any specific application. That application will be bound to the CPU nodes you defined in SQL Server Configuration Manager.

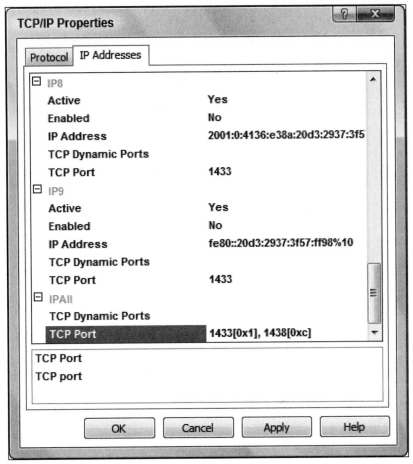

Figure 7-10

Summary

In this chapter, we discussed a few important server parameters that you can tweak to potentially improve your database overall performance, such as CPU affinity, hyper-threading, parallel processing, memory settings, and some network advanced settings. Be careful when adjusting them because most of these parameters work best with their default settings. You only want to adjust them when performance analysis demonstrates that the changes result in performance improvements.

8

Tuning the Schema

A key component in creating a high-performance database or improving one that is performing inadequately lies in the schema. The schema refers to both the general and specific design of a database. General aspects include items such as normalization and database style (OLTP, OLAP). Specific aspects include items such as data types, foreign key relationships, table definitions, and so on. This chapter serves as a guide, describing the techniques and methodologies addressing both areas.

Data Quality

The quality of data simply means how dependable the data is. Obviously, you want your organization's data to be as dependable as possible. This section covers topics of normalization, defining columns, stored procedures, and triggers. All of these areas have a great impact on dependability of data.

Normalization

This is a term you've probably heard before, but may not fully understand. Exacerbating this misunderstanding are textbooks and references that tend toward heavy use of jargon and mathematical symbology. Therefore, clear explanations of the issues that normalization addresses and the techniques used are necessary. First, the primary problems addressed concern data quality. Data inconsistencies and anomalies lead to poor data quality. In order to eliminate or at least minimize that situation, a proven process of reorganization is needed. Edgar F. Codd, the pioneer of relational database methodology, first described this process, which he defined as normalization. He described it as a method in which non-simple domains are decomposed to the point that the elements are atomic values (no further decomposition is possible).

The best way to understand these issues is with an example. A data set is presented. Next, the anomalies that can occur on that set are described. Finally, the data set will be reorganized using proven normalization rules.

Example Data Set

Suppose the following dataset is used by the FCC to keep track of amateur radio license information. Included in this information are things like the Class of license, Callsign of operators, Frequency privileges, and so on. See Table 8-1 below.

Table 8-1: Example Data

Name	Callsign	Examiner	Examiner Callsign	LicenseClass	Frequency 1...n	Region	Region Coordinator
Bob	KE4IOR	Ted	A4GH	Amateur Extra	3, 7, 14, 20, 28, 30	Southeast	Jim
Mike	KF4DGK	John	W4NBV	Technician	3, 7, 14	Southeast	Jim
Billy	N4UF	Steve	WA4B	Amateur Extra	3, 7, 14, 20, 28, 30	Southeast	Jim
David	K2NXT	Sam	K5RTY	General	3, 7, 14, 20	Northeast	Bill
Emily	W5TX	James	N1ZZT	Advanced	3, 7, 14, 20, 28	Southwest	Jim
Ray	W9UTQ	Jane	W0FDK	General	3, 7, 14, 20	Northwest	Carol

Anomalies

The data anomalies that can occur are broken down into several different categories.

- ❑ **Redundancy:** In the sample notice that the License Class and Region are repeated for the corresponding LicenseClass.

- ❑ **Insert anomaly:** This occurs because the table in which a row should be inserted can't accept the insert. Using the sample dataset, suppose the FCC wants to create a new class of license called *Novice*. A row cannot be inserted until someone is actually issued a *Novice* license.

- ❑ **Update anomaly:** The same information is repeated on multiple rows, which opens the door for updates that might result in data inconsistencies. Suppose David upgrades his license class from General to Advanced. Changing David's LicenseClass to Advanced will cause the data to show that the Advanced class has two different privileges. Another variation of an update anomaly occurs when a change needs to be made to all rows, but for some reason the update operation doesn't completely succeed. Suppose you want to change the region coordinator from Jim to Jason. If the update operation is entirely successful then some rows would have both Jim and Jason as section coordinators. In either case, interrogating the table to find a particular privilege or region coordinator would result in multiple values (and it is usually impossible to determine which value is correct).

- ❑ **Deletion anomaly:** Deleting data that represents one piece of information requires the deletion of other data that represents a different piece of information. Suppose the FCC decides to discontinue the General license class. Deleting the rows in the sample will cause a loss of operator names, callsigns, and other information where the license class equals General. Thus, data that is unrelated to the license class is lost.

Functional Dependencies and Forms of Normalization

Before describing the method for normalizing a table some background information on normal forms and functional dependencies is needed.

A functional dependency means that knowing the value of one attribute is sufficient to find the value of another attribute. In relational algebra notation this is written as: $X \rightarrow Y$. This translates as X determines Y. This can be extended to something called mutivalue dependency. This is written as: $X \twoheadrightarrow Y$. This translates as X determines several Ys.

Normalizing is the act of classifying a table based on its functional dependencies. The first three normal forms can be informally understood knowing that all non-key columns are wholly dependent on the key. Fourth normal form deals specifically with many-to-many and one-to-many relationships.

- ❏ **First Normal Form (1NF):** This means that a table does not have any repeating groups. Another way to state this is that every column contains singular (or atomic) values. Lists of values are not allowed. The sample fails to satisfy this condition because the Frequency column contains a list of values for each row.

- ❏ **Second Normal Form (2NF):** This means that a table meets the requirements of 1NF and only has full key dependencies. All the columns that compose the key for the table determine all the non-key columns. Suppose a table had three columns that constituted the key for the table. Second normal form means that all three key columns determine the non-key columns in the table. Conversely, if two of the key columns also determine the non-key columns then a table does not meet this requirement.

- ❏ **Third Normal Form (3NF):** This means that none of the non-key columns of a table can depend on any other non-key column. Therefore, all the non-key columns are independent of each other. A non-key column cannot depend on another non-key column. There are no functional dependencies between non-key columns.

- ❏ **Fourth Normal Form (4NF):** This means that a table does not have more than one multi-valued dependency. Multiple multi-valued dependencies are not allowed.

There are other normal forms, but this chapter focuses on the four core normal forms.

Rules of Normalization

Now that the explanation of functional dependencies and normal forms is behind you, it's time to describe rules for normalizing a table. Earlier I stated that clear explanations are necessary for understanding normalization, and the problems it solves. Equally necessary is a clear process for normalizing datasets. There are many explanations and methodologies that work well, yet are fairly complex or difficult. However, there's one methodology that is clear, concise, and best of all easy to follow.

The idea is a simple process. First, seek to eliminate redundancy, both within rows and columns. Next, endeavor to create all tables for a single purpose. Don't have multi-purpose tables. Simply apply these rules to a dataset until all the tables fit the definition. Also, as you create tables give each table a key column. That way you'll have a way to easily relate the tables together as you work through this process. A few iterations may be necessary before you finish. That's OK; hang in there. Just keep iterating over your tables until they're all single-purpose tables, and the redundancy has been eliminated or reduced.

As you'll see later in the section on denormalization, in some cases data redundancy is good to minimize the number of joins.

To refresh, the sample dataset has the following structure:

```
Name
Callsign
Examiner
ExaminerCallsign
Region
RegionCoordinator
LicenseClass
Frequency1...n
```

So let's start by organizing these attributes in single-purpose groups. If you don't get it right the first time, don't worry! You're going to keep doing this until all the tables meet the requirements.

Regroup these attributes as shown in Figure 8-1.

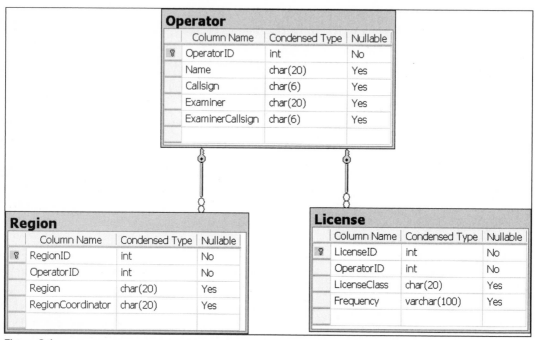

Figure 8-1

Oops! It appears that the operator table is a multi-purpose table. It's currently holding information for both an operator and an examiner. You know what's next. Subdivide the Operator table into two single-purpose tables (see Figure 8-2).

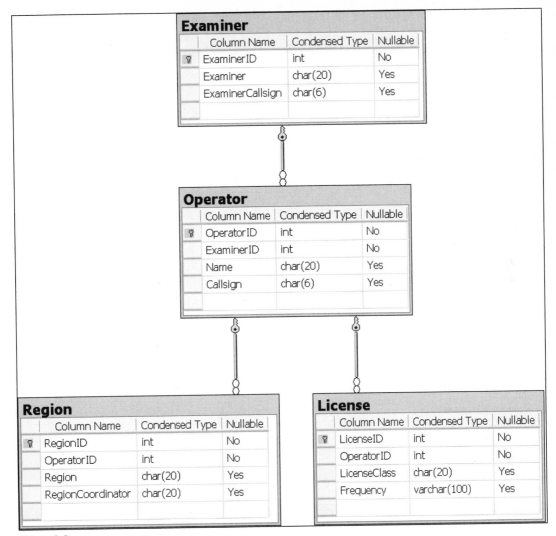

Figure 8-2

Oops again! By putting the OperatorID in the License and Region tables, I've made those tables multi-purpose tables. A quick re-shuffling of the key columns will fix that (see Figure 8-3).

Now the tables have been rearranged as single-purpose tables. Next, turn your attention to redundancy. The Region and License tables have some redundancy in the column values. In Region, the RegionCoordinator can appear more than once. In License, the LicenseClass can appear more than once because of the multiple values for Frequency. Again, split those tables (see Figure 8-4).

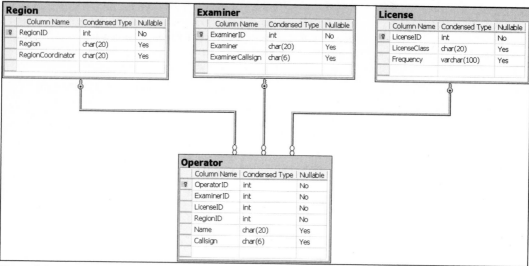

Figure 8-3

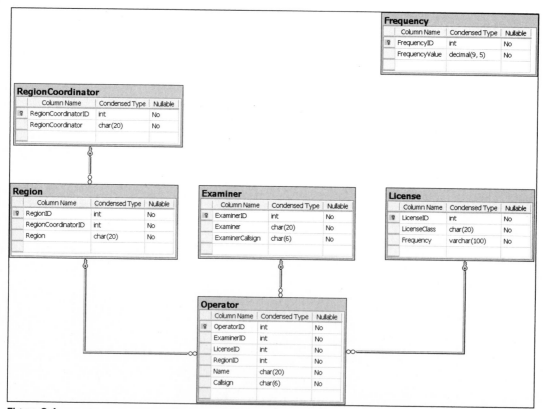

Figure 8-4

Note that in the License and Frequency tables there's no reference of the other table's key. This is because License and Frequency have a many-to-many relationship with each other. This means that many license classes can reference many frequency values. Likewise, many frequency values can reference many license classes. The only way to accommodate these relationships is through the use of a third table. This table will contain nothing but the key columns of both base tables. Hence, a LicenseFrequency table with the structure shown in Figure 8-5.

LicenseFrequency

	Column Name	Condensed Type	Nullable
🔑	FrequencyID	int	No
🔑	LicenseID	int	No

Figure 8-5

Thus, the final structure as shown in Figure 8-6.

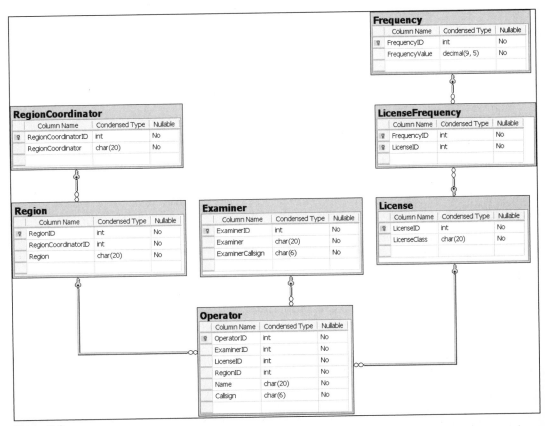

Figure 8-6

Denormalization

No description of normalization can be complete without including a word about denormalization (or as I like to call it ab-normalization!). This term is somewhat misleading. It doesn't mean that a table will or can be created outside the rules of normalization. It means that a schema can be "downgraded" from a higher normal form (say 4NF) to a lower normal form (say 2NF).

Denormalizing a group of tables should be carefully considered before proceeding. The reason is that as the schema descends the normalization scale, the anomalies which normalization seeks to eliminate start ascending. In short, denormalization can be interpreted to mean that data quality is less important than data retrieval.

However, there is certainly a place for denormalized data structures, which is typically in support of decision support systems or data warehouses. Any system that provides a high degree of reporting and data retrieval is a prime candidate for denormalization. In these applications, data retrieval takes priority over data writing. Therefore, the anomalies that normalization seeks to squelch aren't deemed to be an issue.

In fact, many organizations will have both types of databases present. They'll have a highly normalized database, known as an online transactional process (OLTP) style. They'll also have a highly denormalized database, known as an online analytical process (OLAP) style. These organizations will use the OLTP database to populate the OLAP database. This provides the best of both worlds. The OLTP database will function to quickly and accurately capture the data, and the OLAP database will function to quickly and accurately produce reports, queries, and analytical capabilities.

For a quick illustration of these differences consider the model of a normalized structure shown in Figure 8-7 and the model of a denormalized structure shown in Figure 8-8.

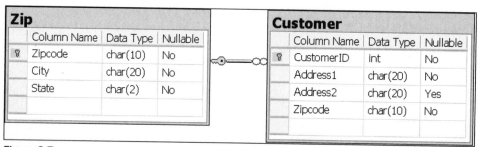

Figure 8-7

Notice that in the second structure the Zip table has been removed entirely. The City and State columns have been moved into the Customer table. Because of this, those columns are prone to writing anomalies, which isn't an issue in the first structure. However, querying and retrieval are simpler in the second structure. Conversely, that is a more difficult task with the first structure because of the need for joining two tables.

One of the main reasons for denormalizing is to provide a performance edge when retrieving data. Denormalization means that there will be fewer tables in the schema, therefore fewer joins. The idea is that fewer joins will result in better performance. For example, if the data is in four tables as opposed to being in a single row of one table, you will incur four physical I/Os, four pages in buffer pool, and so on.

Customer			
	Column Name	Data Type	Nullable
🔑	CustomerID	int	No
	Address1	char(20)	No
	Address2	char(20)	Yes
	Zipcode	char(10)	No
	City	char(20)	No
	State	char(2)	No

Figure 8-8

In summary, denormalizing a structure should be carefully considered. Remember that the purpose of normalization is to minimize data anomalies. Therefore, as you denormalize a structure, it becomes more susceptible to those anomalies.

Wrap Up

A few more words about normalization are in order. In applications of any size, there's usually one or more DBAs and developers. These two groups have very different opinions concerning normalization. Generally speaking, the more normalized a database is, the more difficult it is to program against. Let's face it: programming against one table is easier than programming against three. Therefore, some developers advocate less normalized forms of data structures.

Please realize that making a developer's job easier is not the goal. The goal is to make a high performance database structure that is durable and scalable.

Also realize that application design and database design are two different but interconnected activities. Relational database design is founded on the mathematical principles of set theory. Application design is founded on object-oriented principles. These foundations are not the same. In fact, this difference has become known as the object-relational impedance mismatch. The Wiley publication *Agile Database Techniques* by Scott Ambler explores this topic in great detail. The point is that when designing a robust, durable system both application designers and database designers share an equal part in delivering a successful product. This means that application designers should not dictate database structures, and equally true database designers should not dictate object design.

Defining Columns

The next step in maximizing data quality concerns defining columns. Issues such as data types, nullability, primary and foreign key constraints, as well as several others are covered in this section.

Data Types

One of the most important aspects of designing a database is choosing the correct data type for the columns. This may seem trivial, but choosing the right type can make a huge difference in storage and processing requirements. The goal is to maximize the number of rows that can fit onto one data page. There are a few points to remember when it comes to choosing the correct data type.

❑ First, choose the smallest data type available that will satisfy the needs for column. For example, use a smalldatetime instead of a datetime if the smalldatetime will suffice for the column in question.

❑ Second, favor the non-variable data types over the variable ones. For example, use CHAR instead of VARCHAR when possible. Note that this doesn't mean that variable data types shouldn't be used. When column data is going to vary significantly in length from row to row, then variable length data types should definitely be used.

For SQL Server 2005, Microsoft has organized the data types into the following groups (see Table 8-2):

❑ Exact numerics

❑ Approximate numerics

❑ Date and time

❑ Character strings

❑ Unicode character strings

❑ Binary strings

❑ Other

With SQL Server 2005 SP2, Microsoft introduced the VARDECIMAL storage format. This is not a data type. Rather it is a mechanism for storing decimal data in a variable-length structure. It is activated first by enabling the feature at the database level. This is done using the sp_db_vardecimal_storage_ format *command. Once that is done, each table for which you want to enable vardecimal storage must also have it enabled. This is done by using the* sp_tableoption *command. For further details see BOL.*

Table 8-2: Data Types

Group	Type name	Range	Storage	Comments
Exact numerics	Tinyint	0 to 255	1 byte	n/a
	Smallint	−32,768 to 32,767	2 bytes	n/a
	Int	−2,147,483,648 to 2,147,483,647	4 bytes	n/a
	Bigint	−9,223,372,036, 854,775,808 to 9,223,372,036, 854,775,807	8 bytes	n/a
	Bit	0 or 1 (also NULL)	1 byte for every 8 bit columns	n/a
	Decimal (p, s) or Numeric (p, s)	$-10^{38} + 1$ to $10^{38} - 1$	Precision Storage 1–9 5 bytes	P (precision) The maximum number of digits that can be stored.

Table 8-2: Data Types (continued)

Group	Type name	Range	Storage	Comments
			10–19 9 bytes 20–28 13 bytes 29–38 17 bytes	S (scale) The maximum number of digits to the right of the decimal point.
	Money	−922,337,203,685, 477.5808 to 922,337,203, 685,477.5807	8 bytes	n/a
	smallmoney	−214,748.3648 to 214,748.3647	4 bytes	n/a
Approximate Numerics	Float(n)	−1.79E + 308 to −2.23E−308, 0 and 2.23E − 308 to 1.79E + 308	N value Storage 1–24 4 bytes 25–53 8 bytes	n/a
	Real	−3.40E + 38 to −1.18E − 38, 0 and 1.18E − 38 to 3.40E + 38	4 bytes.	n/a
Date and time	Datetime	January 1, 1753, to December 31, 9999	8 bytes total. Stored as 2 4 byte integers.	Accuracy is 3.33 milliseconds
	smalldatetime	January 1, 1900, to June 6, 2079	4 bytes total. Stored as 2 2 byte integers.	Accuracy is 1 minute
Character	Char(n)	Non-Unicode characters.	n bytes	Fixed length. Always occupies n bytes, even if some bytes are unused. Valid values for n range from 1–8000.
	Varchar(n)	Non-Unicode characters	1 byte for each stored character.	Variable length. Valid values for n range from 1–8000. If n is omitted the default is 1. Unused bytes do not occupy storage space. However, 2 additional bytes are added. These are used as an offset indicating the location of the string's end. See "Row Overflow Considerations."

Continued

Table 8-2: Data Types (continued)

Group	Type name	Range	Storage	Comments
	Varchar(max)	Non-unicode characters	Up to $2^{31} - 1$ bytes	See "Large Value Data Types."
	text	Non-unicode characters	16-byte pointer is stored in the row. Up to $2^{31} - 1$ bytes.	See "Large Value Data Types."
Unicode Character	Nchar(n)	Unicode characters	$(2 \times n)$ bytes	Fixed length. Always occupies $(2 \times n)$ bytes, even if some bytes are unused. Valid values for n range from 1–4000.
	Nvarchar(n)	Unicode characters	2 bytes for each stored character.	Variable length. Valid values for n range from 1–4000. If n is omitted the default is 1. Unused bytes do not occupy storage space. However, 2 additional bytes are added. These are used as an offset indicating the location of the string's end. See "Row Overflow Considerations."
	Nvarchar(max)	Unicode characters	Up to $2^{31} - 1$ bytes. 2 bytes for each stored character.	The storage size, in bytes, is 2 times the number of characters saved. Unused bytes do not occupy storage space. However, 2 additional bytes are added. These are used as an offset indicating the location of the string's end. See "Large Value Data Types."
	ntext	Unicode characters	16-byte pointer is stored in the row. Up to $2^{30} - 1$ bytes.	Storage size is 2 times the characters saved. See "Large Value Data Types."

Continued

Table 8-2: Data Types (continued)

Group	Type name	Range	Storage	Comments
Binary Strings	Binary(*n*)	String of bits	*n* bytes.	Fixed length. Always occupies n bytes, even if some bytes are unused. Valid values for n range from 1–8000.
	Varbinary(*n*)	String of bits	1 byte for each stored character.	Variable length. Valid values for n range from 1 - 8000. If n is omitted the default is 1. Unused bytes do not occupy storage space. However, 2 additional bytes are added. These are used as an offset indicating the location of the binary string's end. See "Row Overflow Considerations."
	Varbinary(max)	String of bits.	Up to $2^{31}-1$ bytes	See "Large Value Data Types."
	image	String of bits.	16-byte pointer is stored in the row. Up to $2^{31}-1$ bytes	See "Large Value Data Types."
Misc. types	Xml	This allows storage of complete or partial XML documents	Up to 2 GB.	These documents can be either typed or untyped. See BOL for details about creating a typed column. See "Large Value Data Types."
	Sql_variant	See entries for base datatypes.	???	This allows storing values of various data types, except text, ntext, image, timestamp, and sql_variant. See "Row Overflow Considerations."
	Sysname	Unicode characters	2 bytes for each stored character.	Equivalent to nvarchar(128)

Continued

Table 8-2: Data Types (continued)

Group	Type name	Range	Storage	Comments
	Timestamp	A non-nullable timestamp column is equivalent to a binary(8) column. A nullable timestamp column is equivalent to a varbinary(8) column.	8 bytes	Each database has a counter for each insert or update performed on a table. Only one per table is allowed. Synonymous with ROWVERSION.
	Uniqueidentifier	A GUID	16 bytes	See "Using Uniqueidentifier datatypes."
Non-persisted types	table	—	—	Available only for T-SQL variables. It cannot be saved or used as a data type when defining a column. Can be used instead of a temporary table. Holds result sets for later processing.
	Cursor	—	—	Available only for T-SQL variables. It cannot be saved or used as a data type when defining a column.

Character notes: When using CAST or CONVERT if *n* is not specified then the default length is 30. Use char and nchar when the size of data entries for a column are relatively uniform. Use varchar and nvarchar when the size of data entries for a column widely vary *and* the column needs to be fairly wide. Personally, I recommend using the CHAR or NCHAR data type for lengths of 20 or less. Use varchar(max) and nvarchar(max) when the sizes of data entries for a column vary considerably, and the size is more than 8000 bytes. Also note that Microsoft recommends migrating away from the text and ntext data types, because they plan to remove them from future versions of SQL Server.

Unicode notes: Unicode was created to address the need to accommodate characters from different languages, such as German and Russian. Unicode uses 2 bytes per character, which is why the limits for these data types is half what it is for their non-unicode counterparts. So, unless requirements mandate international support use the non-unicode types. They take up less storage to store the same amount of data.

Binary notes: When using CAST or CONVERT if *n* is not specified then the default length is 30. Use binary when the size of data entries for a column are relatively uniform. Use varbinary when the size of data entries for a column needs to be fairly wide. Personally, I recommend using the binary data type for lengths of 20 or less. Use varbinary(max) when the sizes of data entries for a column vary considerably, and the size is more than 8000 bytes. Also note that Microsoft recommends migrating away from the image data type, because they plan to remove from future versions of SQL Server.

Large Value Data Types

A large value data type will hold values larger 8 KB. With SQL Server 2005 Microsoft has created three new data types for large values: VARCHAR(MAX), NVARCHAR(MAX), and VARBINARY(MAX). These new types are positioned to replace the older TEXT, NTEXT, and IMAGE types.

The new types are generally easier to work with than their older counterparts. Anything you can do with a regular varchar, nvarchar, or varbinary column can be done with the max variation.

Storage Considerations

For both the older and newer groups of large value data types it is possible to control where the values are stored. The data can either be stored in the data row or outside the row. Knowing which option to use is difficult to determine. To make matters more confusing the default behavior is different for the old and new types. The old types default to storing the data outside the data row, and the new types default to storing the data in the data row.

When storing data outside the data row, a two-part scheme is used. First, a 16-byte pointer is stored with the row on the data page. Second, this pointer redirects SQL Server to additional data pages, which contain the actual data.

When first creating tables with these data types, it's recommended to start out by storing these values outside the data row. In order to force Large Value Data Types to be stored outside the data row use the following commands.

```
For VARCHAR(MAX), NVARCHAR(MAX), VARBINARY(MAX), & XML data types
sp_tableoption 'tablename', 'large value types out of row', 'ON'

For TEXT, NTEXT, & IMAGE data types
sp_tableoption 'MyTable', 'text in row', 'OFF'
```

Note that it's not possible to control this on a column-by-column basis. Once you disable in-row storage, it's disabled for all columns of the same large value data type family. There are two reasons for starting out this way. First, putting these values outside the data row allows the data row to remain relatively small, which in turn allows the data page to hold more rows. Second, SQL Server's management of in-row data can become quite complex. Without going into great detail, SQL Server must handle the possibility that the data won't fit into a data row. This means that SQL Server has to revert to the two-part scheme described above. Also, in the event that the data is updated to a shorter value that would fit into the row, SQL Server will shuffle that data back into the data row. The downside of storing the data outside the data row is that retrieval performance suffers. The additional overhead of getting the data by using the pointers can get expensive.

Once a table has been created and is in use consider two aspects when determining where to store large value data. First, take into account the percentage of rows storing data outside the data row. Second, consider the likelihood that this data will be queried. Table 8-3 will serve as a guide.

Using the Uniqueidentifier Data Type

Using the uniqueidentifier data type requires a deeper understanding than most other data types. First, you need a good definition for them. BOL defines the uniqueidentifier as, "A globally unique identifier

(GUID)." Uniqueidentifiers occupy 16 bytes of storage. They're also touted as universally unique. In some instances a uniqueidentifier can be a good choice.

Table 8-3: Large Data Type Location Matrix

Percentage of outside data row storage	Frequency of retrieval	Recommendation
Low	Low	In-row storage. The low percentage of overflowing rows makes storing the data in the data row acceptable.
High	Low	Out of row storage. By always forcing this data to be stored outside the data row, you're eliminating the burden on SQL Server to determine how to store the data. Also, since the data in question is rarely retrieved the occasional performance degradation is acceptable.
Low	High	In-row storage. Since the rows are not likely to require out of row storage and these columns are frequency accessed they should be stored in the data row.
High	High	Unknown. Try to avoid this scenario. There's no solid direction when this occurs. Instead try splitting the table into multiple tables. The goal would be to make all the new tables fall into one of the three previous categories.

However, some objections have been given against using them:

❑ They're too large to be an effective index: Uniqueidentifiers are 16 bytes long, which some believe is too long for columns used in indexes or primary keys. Instead, using an integer or even bigint is advised because they're only 4 or 8 bytes long, respectively. Although this is true, this alone isn't compelling enough to warrant not using them.

❑ They're too hard to remember: When displaying a uniqueidentifier value in SSMS, it appears as a 36-character string of letters and numbers. For example, 53F001FE-5CBF-4141-87FC-C42B634FF464 is a valid uniqueidentifier. Again, although this is true, they're not really meant for "human" consumption. They're really only meant for the computer.

Next, are some reasons they should be used:

❑ **Merge replication:** Uniqueidentifiers are used with merge replication. If the environment you work in involves Merge Replication, you're already using uniqueidentifiers. SQL Server manages merge replication by adding a uniqueidentifier column (with the rowguid property set to yes) to a table, if it's not already there. Allowing SQL Server to automatically alter a table and add a column could be very problematic.

❑ **Data entry (OLTP) applications:** For a table that experiences a high degree of row inserts such as a traditional data entry or OLTP type of application, uniqueidentifers can be a tremendous enhancement. The reason is the uniqueidentifier value can be generated at the client *before* the insert occurs. That's not possible with identity columns. In the ubiquitous Order-Order Detail example, using a uniqueidentifier as the primary key on the Order table means that a new order can be created (including primary key) entirely on the client. Thus, there is no need for a round trip to the server to get the ID of the newly inserted Order row. This is a huge advantage.

❑   Here's some sample .NET code to generate a GUID value.

```
C#
System.Guid g;
g = System.Guid.NewGuid();
txtGUID.Text = g. ToString();


VB.NET
Dim g As System.Guid
g = System.Guid.NewGuid()
```

Computed Columns

Computed columns are not physically stored in a table (unless it's marked PERSISTED). They are expressions that usually use other columns in the same table. They can also utilize functions such as GETDATE() or user defined functions. For example, a table may contain columns for length, width, and depth. A computed column called volume could be defined as length × width × depth. The volume column wouldn't take up any storage space in the table.

Every time a query retrieves a computed column, SQL Server must calculate the result first. In some instances, however, this may be desirable. The computation takes place within the SQL Server, not the query processor. Also, the computation is defined in one place, so it's easier to maintain and provides greater consistency.

Computed columns cannot be used as foreign keys. They can be used in an index or as part of a primary key if the value is deterministic and precise.

In SQL Server 2005 a computed column can be defined with the PERSISTED option. This means that SQL Server will actually store the value. This does take up storage space. This might be desirable if the server is overworked by continually calculating computed column results. Also, persisting a computed column allows it to be indexed if it's not precise (it still has to be deterministic). Finally, this would be a good way to define a calculated field once, instead of possibly multiple times in an application tier.

I/O is usually the most common cause of poor query performance. Computed columns can help alleviate that because the value of the column isn't actually stored (except for PERSISTED computed columns), which means that less I/O is needed to retrieve data. However, SQL Server will have to evaluate the computed column when it's retrieved. The reduction in I/O will usually more than offset the cost of this evaluation.

Also, computed columns aren't evaluated unless they're included in a query. Therefore, you should make sure that queries don't unnecessarily retrieve them.

Another interesting aspect of computed columns is that they can sometimes be used in an index. This is also a technique for providing the same functionality that Oracle provides with its function-based index. Sometimes you may need to create queries which apply a function to a column in a where clause. For example, you may write a where clause that uses the YEAR function on a date column. Once you do this, the query optimizer will have to revert to scanning the table. However, by combining a computed column with an index the query optimizer will use the index instead of a scan.

Consider the following query and plan (shown in Figure 8-9) against the SalesOrderHeader table in AdventureWorks.

```
SELECT    YEAR(OrderDate) OrderYear, COUNT(*)
FROM      Sales.SalesOrderHeader
WHERE     MONTH(OrderDate) = 4 AND YEAR(OrderDate) = 2002
GROUP BY  YEAR(OrderDate)
```

Figure 8-9

Next, apply the following changes to the table and look at the new query plan (shown in Figure 8-10).

```
ALTER TABLE Sales.SalesOrderHeader ADD
OrderYear AS YEAR(OrderDate),
OrderMonth AS MONTH(OrderDate)

CREATE INDEX IX_OrderYear ON Sales.SalesOrderHeader (OrderYear)
CREATE INDEX IX_OrderMonth ON Sales.SalesOrderHeader (OrderMonth)
```

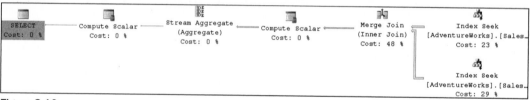

Figure 8-10

Notice how the optimizer now picked up on the indexes created on the newly added computed columns. With a very small use of additional disk space by the indexes, this query has gained a substantial performance improvement.

Column Options

Choosing the correct data types, normalizing tables, defining primary keys, and so on contributes to improving the quality of your data. However, your work in this area isn't finished. Another aspect of quality has to do with the integrity of the data. Ensuring this integrity doesn't come for free. Ensuring that data meets all the requirements for accuracy can be detrimental to performance. For example, inserting a new row into a table with a foreign key constraint requires that the SQL Server engine check that the key value is valid, based on values in the parent table. This will be slower than if the foreign key constraint didn't exist.

To illustrate this consider the tables shown in Figure 8-11.

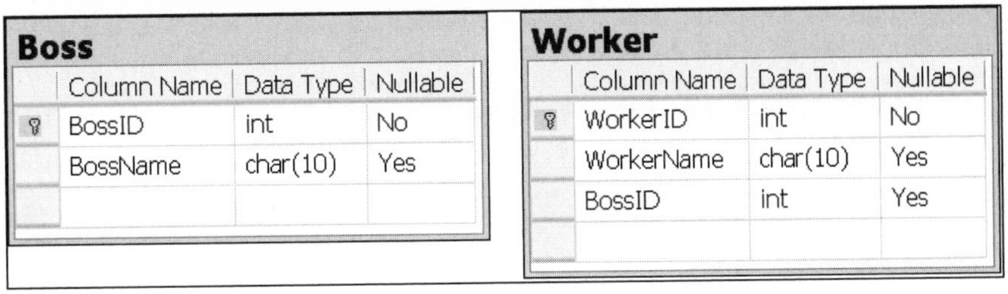

Boss		
Column Name	Data Type	Nullable
🔑 BossID	int	No
BossName	char(10)	Yes

Worker		
Column Name	Data Type	Nullable
🔑 WorkerID	int	No
WorkerName	char(10)	Yes
BossID	int	Yes

Figure 8-11

Now look at the query plan (shown in Figure 8-12) for populating the table Worker with the following query, which doesn't include referential integrity:

```
DECLARE @I int
DECLARE @BossID INT
SET @BossID = 1
SET @I = 1
WHILE @I <= 1000
BEGIN
    IF @I <= 100
    BEGIN
        SET @BossID = @I
    END
    ELSE
    BEGIN
        SET @BossID = @I%100
        IF @BossID = 0
            SET @BossID = 100
    END
    INSERT INTO dbo.Worker VALUES (@I, 'Adam', @BossID)
    SET @I = @I + 1
END
```

Now, with the statement, ALTER TABLE dbo.Worker ADD CONSTRAINT FK_Worker_Boss FOREIGN KEY (BossID) REFERENCES dbo.Boss (BossID), let's add the foreign key constraint on the Worker table for the BossID column and re-evaluate the query plan.

As you can see in Figure 8-13, the second plan has added a clustered index seek operation. This is necessary to provide the integrity that's defined by the constraint.

However, this overhead is generally deemed an acceptable price to pay to ensure the data quality. Additionally, defining these integrity mechanisms at the database level is better than attempting to define it in the front-end applications. The reason is that there may be several different applications that can operate against a common table. Coding the integrity checks in all those applications is impractical.

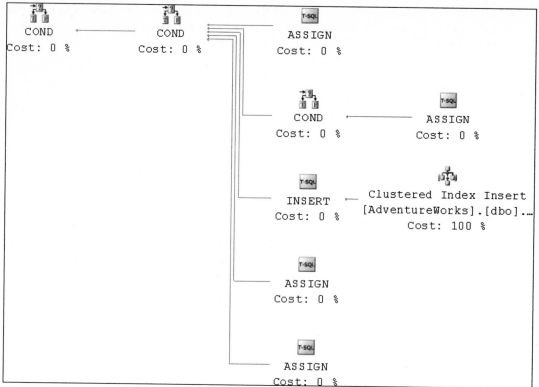

Figure 8-12

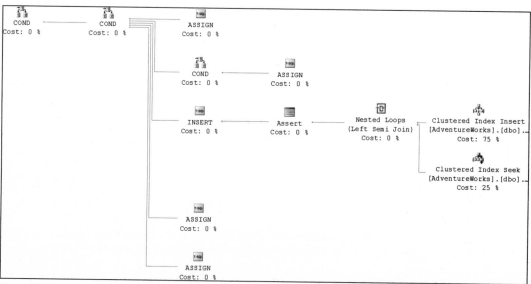

Figure 8-13

SQL Server provides several paths for enforcing the integrity of the data in a column. Those are: Primary key constraints, foreign key constraints, unique constraints, check constraints, default definitions, and nullability.

Primary Key Constraints

A primary key is one or more columns of a table that uniquely identify a row in the table. In some cases a table may have more than one column that could fulfill this requirement. These are called candidate keys. In other cases a table may not have any column that uniquely identifies a row in the table.

Another aspect of primary keys is choosing a technique for defining the key. One technique involves using the existing columns of a table, which is known as a natural key. The other technique involves inserting a new, independent column in the table whose sole purpose is to provide a unique handle for all the rows in the table. This is known as a surrogate (or as I call it, artificial) key.

I recommend using surrogate primary keys over natural primary keys for the following reasons:

❑ The primary key in one table generally becomes foreign keys in other tables. Therefore, it's much easier on the SQL Server environment to have one key column per table.

❑ Surrogate keys usually consist of one column with a small footprint. Natural keys often are comprised of multiple columns.

❑ Surrogate keys are independent of the other columns. They are not logically linked to the other columns in a table.

❑ Surrogate key values are immutable. Once a surrogate key value has been generated, it never has to be changed. In some cases with natural keys, they may need to change. I once worked on a project that used SSN as a primary key for employees. This key was also a foreign key in 12 other tables. In the case where the SSN had to be changed (and it did occur mainly due to data entry error) an elaborate and complex update process had to be concocted. All 12 tables and the employee table had to be updated.

Consider the table structures for an insurance company as shown in Figure 8-14.

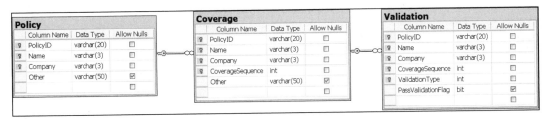

Figure 8-14

Note that the Validation table has 6 columns and 5 of them act as the primary key. The sixth column is a bit column that indicates whether or not the policy coverage has passed its validation requirements.

Now consider the same table structure using surrogate keys instead of natural keys, as shown in Figure 8-15.

Now notice the difference. The policy table now has one additional column, which adds 4 bytes of storage requirement. However, the Coverage table has one less column, and has a 62 byte storage requirement. The previous version required up to 80 bytes of storage. Finally, the Validation table has two fewer columns and the storage requirements went from up to 35 bytes of storage to 13 bytes.

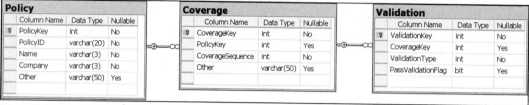

Figure 8-15

Also, note that the new keys are all fixed length types, not variable length. This means that there is no need for the 2-byte offset that's required by all the variable length data types. That translates to better performance and lessens the workload imposed on the server.

Foreign Key Constraints

Recall that the main section is called Data Quality. A fundamental way for enforcing this is through the use of foreign keys. A foreign key is a column or columns used to link two tables. Preserving the quality of this link is the job of the foreign key constraint. The classic example of a foreign key is through Order and OrderDetail tables, as shown in Figure 8-16.

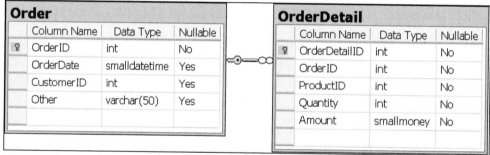

Figure 8-16

```
CREATE TABLE [OrderDetail](
  [OrderDetailID] [int] IDENTITY(1,1) NOT NULL,
  [OrderID] [int] NULL DEFAULT(-1),
  [ProductID] [int] NOT NULL,
  [Quantity] [int] NOT NULL,
  [Amount] [smallmoney] NOT NULL,
  PRIMARY KEY NONCLUSTERED ([OrderDetailID] ASC)
GO


ALTER TABLE [OrderDetail]
  ADD CONSTRAINT [FK_Order_OrderDetail] FOREIGN KEY([OrderID])
        REFERENCES [Order] ([OrderID])
GO
```

In this example the OrderDetail table contains a column called OrderID. It is linked to the the OrderID column in the Order table. Adding this constraint has several effects. First, whenever a new row is inserted into the OrderDetail table that row must contain a value for OrderDetailID. Also, that value must exist in the Order table. For example, suppose the Order table contained OrderID values between 1 and 10. If you attempt to insert a row in the OrderDetail table where the OrderID value is 25, an error will occur and the insert will fail.

Another aspect of the constraint affects the Order table. If you attempt to delete a row from this table, and that row's OrderID value is used in the OrderDetail table, the delete will fail. That's because allowing the delete to succeed would mean that an OrderDetail row would be "orphaned" from its parent Order row.

One way around this is by defining cascading rules for the foreign key constraints. This gives you the ability to define the actions that SQL Server 2005 takes when deleting or updating a foreign key.

The REFERENCE clause in the example above support ON DELETE and ON UPDATE options. The valid options for these statements are: NO ACTION, CASCADE, SET NULL, SET DEFAULT.

- ❑ **NO ACTION:** This is the default. This should be self-explanatory, this option means that the natural behavior of the foreign key will apply.
- ❑ **CASCADE:** This means that the change will be cascaded through the foreign key relationship.
- ❑ **SET NULL:** This means that the foreign key column will be reset to NULL if possible.
- ❑ **SET DEFAULT:** This means that the foreign key column will be reset to the default value defined for the column.

Given the previous action, the following options are available:

- ❑ **On Delete Cascade:** Adding the option ON DELETE CASCADE to the OrderDetail foreign key would mean that if a row in the Order table was deleted, then ALL the rows in the OrderDetail where the OrderID matched the deleted row's OrderID would also be deleted.
- ❑ **ON DELETE SET NULL:** All the values in the foreign key column are reset to NULL. In the OrderDetail example, when a row is deleted from Order all the rows in OrderDetail where the OrderID equals the OrderID from the deleted row would get a NULL.
- ❑ **ON DELETE SET DEFAULT:** All the values in the foreign key column are reset to default value. In the OrderDetail example, when a row is deleted from Order all the rows in OrderDetail where the OrderID equals the OrderID from the deleted row would get the default value defined for the column, in this case −1.
- ❑ **ON UPDATE CASCADE:** Any change made to the key column is percolated down to all foreign keys. Again, using the OrderDetail constraint. If an ON UPDATE CASCADE was added to the constraint definition then any change to the OrderID value in the Order table would be performed on any OrderDetail rows where the OrderID values matched. For example, suppose you wanted to change the OrderID value in Order from 5 to 15. Updating the value in Order would also cause the value of OrderID in OrderDetail to be updated where the OrderID was 5.
- ❑ **ON UPDATE SET NULL:** All the values in the foreign key column are reset to NULL. In the OrderDetail example, when a row is updated in the Order table all the rows in OrderDetail where the OrderID equals the OrderID from the updated row would get a NULL.

❑ **ON UPDATE SET DEFAULT:** All the values in the foreign key column are reset to default value. In the OrderDetail example, when a row is updated in the Order table then all the rows in OrderDetail where the OrderID equals the OrderID from the updated row would get the default value defined for the column, in this case −1.

Unique Constraints

A unique constraint on a column ensures that no two values can be the same for all the rows in a table. Unique constraints and primary keys are very similar; however, there are a few differences to be aware of:

❑ First, a table can only have one primary key. It can have many unique constraints, though.

❑ Second, a unique constraint can allow for a NULL value. A primary key cannot. Note that the table can only have one row where the column value is NULL.

Unique constraints are sometimes known as alternate keys. Because of their unique nature they can also participate in a foreign key constraint.

Check Constraints

Check constraints enforce integrity by limiting values that are allowed in a column. These are similar to foreign keys. The difference is that foreign keys get their list of valid values from another table. Check constraints get their list of valid values from the column definition.

Check constraints are expressions that must evaluate to true or false. They can be defined on a single column of a table or multiple columns. A constraint that operates on multiple columns is known as a table-level constraint.

A column-level constraint might restrict entries to certain values. Suppose you have a table with a Gender column in it. You only want to allow two values: M or F. A constraint can be created: Gender = M OR Gender = F.

For a table-level constraint, suppose you have the table shown in Figure 8-17.

Shipment

	Column Name	Data Type	Nullable
🔑	ShipmentID	int	No
	ArrivalDate	smalldatetime	No
	DepartureDate	smalldatetime	No

Figure 8-17

You might create a constraint such that (DepartureDate > ArrivalDate).

Nullability

Columns can either allow nulls or not. A null is not the same thing as zero or blank. Null indicates that a value is unknown or doesn't exist. It's generally recommended that columns shouldn't allow nulls.

In fact a colleague believes that during the normalization process all columns should start out with not allowing null. One reason that nullable columns are not recommended is that they can be confusing. The definition of NULL is that the value for a data item is unknown. Thus, if a table contains null columns, it could mean that the value for the column is not known at the moment, but it could also mean that the column doesn't apply to the row. Null columns can also be misleading in aggregate functions. For example, suppose you included COUNT(columnname) in a query, and that the columnname is nullable. The result would be a count for all the rows where the column value was null.

Furthermore, there's certainly additional complexity with handling nulls. For example suppose you use this query:

```
SELECT    *
FROM      tableName
WHERE     columnA = columnB
```

Further, suppose that both columnA and columnB are both NULL. This query will not yield any results because when comparing two nulls SQL Server evaluates that to false. One way to change this behavior is by using the SET ANSI_NULLS option. If the SELECT statement above were preceded with SET ANSI_NULLS OFF, then the query would yield results. Other useful functions for handling NULLS are ISNULL and COALESCE.

ISNULL takes two arguments, check_value and replacement_value. In the previous example, columnA could be replaced with ISNULL(columnA, 'None'). This means that if the value of columnA is not null then it is returned. If it is null then None is returned. Note also that the data type of ISNULL will match the data type of columnA.

COALESCE takes n number of arguments. It returns the first non-null value in the list of arguments. For example, COALESCE(columnA, columnB, columnC, columnD) will return the first value from these columns which is not null. If they're all null then the return value is also null.

Default Values

Columns will either have a valid value or NULL. However, if you set a column's nullability as not allowed then you may have a situation where the column's value isn't supplied when a row is created. The solution to that is to define a default value for that column. The default value is defined when the table is created. This means that whenever that column is updated, anytime the new value is NULL it will be replaced by the default definition. For example, suppose you have an Amount column in a table. You may define the column to have a default value of 0. This way any attempt to put a NULL in the Amount column will instead put in a 0. Also, the default value doesn't have to be defined with a static value. A scalar function can also be used as a default. Consider the following table definition:

```
CREATE TABLE Billing
(BillingID      int identitify(1, 1) NOT NULL,
BillTS   smalldatetime NOT NULL,
BillAmount      smallmoney NOT NULL,

.
.
.

InsertUID       varchar(30) NOT NULL DEFAULT suser_sname(),
InsertTS        smalldatetime NOT NULL DEFAULT getutcdate(),
UpdateUID       varchar(30) NULL,
UpdateTS smalldatetime NULL,
```

```
DeleteUID           varchar(30) NULL,
DeleteTS smalldatetime NULL,
PRIMARY KEY NONCLUSTERED (BillingID))
```

In this table, the CreateUID, and CreateTS columns have default values defined. Note, however, that those defaults are actually scalar functions. This is actually a handy way to create auditing columns in your tables, which can be useful for a variety of reasons. Note that the additional audit columns UpdateUID, UpdateTS, DeleteUID, DeleteTS in this table definition will be discussed in the following section covering triggers.

In Practice

With all this discussion of constraints you may be asking if defining constraints has a negative impact on performance. I have to painfully acknowledge that it does. However, removing or not including constraints for performance purposes should be done as the *very last resort*! Once you've exhausted *every* technique and recommendation in this book, as well as the technical resources of Microsoft, removing constraints might be a consideration. However, sacrificing the protection constraints provide for data integrity requires significant consideration. Please *do not* remove constraints unless there is absolutely no other way to improve performance.

Stored Procedures

Stored procedures should be familiar to you. Therefore, extensive background description won't be given. For anyone needing in-depth education concerning stored procedures, start with BOL. That being said, there is some material to be discussed here. First, know that there are two types of stored procedures. Those are Transact-SQL and CLR.

There are some definite advantages for using stored procedures. First, a stored procedure is syntax checked and compiled only the first time it is executed. SQL Server will store the compiled version of the stored procedure in its memory cache. Subsequent executions will then use that. Another benefit is a reduction in network traffic. The call for a stored procedure will simply include the procedure name and any parameter values. Compare that to sending an entire T-SQL batch. Also, the procedure can limit output returned so that only data that really needs to be sent back to the caller will be sent. Yet another advantage of procedures deals with security administration. Applying the appropriate security settings on a procedure is much easier than trying to apply those same settings on all the underlying SQL objects, for any given user or group. Finally, another advantage is maintainability. Because the stored procedure resides within a database it can be updated easily and independent of any calling code. Thus, once the procedure is updated, all calling programs will get the change.

There are a couple of disadvantages of stored procedures that should also be mentioned. The maintainability aspect mentioned above is a dual-edged sword. A change in a stored procedure will be felt by every bit of code that calls the procedure. If the change turns out to be undesirable, then the scope would be much wider than if the change were limited to specific code instances. Another disadvantage has to do with network traffic. Stored procedures return messages to the calling program. Most of the time, this isn't a problem. However, in some instances those messages become overwhelmingly numerous. Unless the procedure is modified to curb those messages (which is described in the "NO COUNT" section later), they can cause performance problems.

Transact-SQL

This type of stored procedure has been around a long time in SQL Server. It's simply a single T-SQL statement or multiple T-SQL statements. They can take parameters and optionally return parameter output values. They can also return resultsets. In fact, a single stored procedure can return multiple resultsets. They may not return anything at all. Also, they can be used to pump output into a table which can then be used for later analysis.

CLR

CLR-based stored procedures are new to SQL Server 2005. They are based on the Microsoft .NET common language runtime (CLR). They are implemented as public static methods on a class written in a supported .NET programming language, such as C# or Visual Basic .NET. The method type can either be void or return an integer.

One thing to consider concerning stored procedures is which type you should use. Choosing the correct type can make a huge difference in performance. If your stored procedure will manipulate a lot of data, then use a T-SQL procedure. If your stored procedure contains a great deal of logic, or complex calculations with little data access, then use a CLR procedure.

I'm not going to discuss any techniques concerning bottlenecks caused by CLR-based stored procedures. The Wrox publication *SQL Server 2005 CLR Programming* tackles that topic in great detail.

Implementing Stored Procedures

For T-SQL–based stored procedures there are some techniques to describe. One of the first things to discuss is why you should use stored procedures at all. After all, it's quite possible (and I remember the days before stored procedures, which left no alternative) to write an application that generates all the necessary SQL statements in-line. Consider the steps involved when SQL Server has to manage a group of T-SQL statements.

1. The statements are checked for proper syntax, and the statements are translated into a query tree. This is similar to compiling a program. The program is checked for syntax errors and then translated into executable objects.

2. From the query tree an execution plan is determined. This step involves optimizing the queries, checking security, checking constraints, and incorporating any triggers in the process.

3. Finally, the statements are executed.

Now consider putting those same statements in a stored procedure. By doing this, the first step above is only done once, when the procedure is created. Next, when the procedure is executed an execution plan will be built just as in Step 2. However, subsequent calls to the procedure may be able to skip this step because an existing execution plan will be in cache. (Cache management is covered in Chapter 9.)

So a stored procedure will save time by performing the syntax checking only once. Also, execution plans will likely be available for subsequent calls for a given procedure, thus saving time as well. This just leaves the actual execution of the procedure as the only step that must be repeated.

Another benefit of using stored procedures is minimizing the length of the command text that an application sends over the network. Imagine the overhead of sending a group of T-SQL statements that are several hundred or even thousands of lines long over a network. Now imagine calling a stored procedure, which would only require one line of code to be sent over a network, and still perform the same task.

Some helpful information concerning improving T-SQL stored procedure performance is given below.

NOCOUNT

When I first started working with SQL Server many stored procedures I saw would have the statement, SET NOCOUNT ON, as the first line. A colleague explained that this was to help improve the performance of the stored procedure. I didn't understand how this would help. After all, the only effect I knew of was that this would cause the number of rows affected by a T-SQL statement to be suppressed. This hardly seems to be a performance concern. However, I later learned that this statement has another effect. It also causes the suppression of sending of DONE_IN_PROC messages to the client. If a stored procedure has multiple statements, and NOCOUNT is off (which is the default) it will send this message every time one of the statements completes. You can imagine that if a stored procedure executes statements hundreds or even thousands of times perhaps via loop or cursor structures, these messages could become a significant source of network traffic. Additionally, most applications don't need these messages, so why send them. Therefore, disabling them can greatly improve performance by reducing network traffic. I even heard of an application that had an order-of-magnitude performance improvement by setting NOCOUNT ON. So, always include SET NOCOUNT ON as the first line in *every* stored procedure you write. Note that setting NOCOUNT ON does *not* effect the use or population of the system variable @@ROWCOUNT.

Avoiding Unnecessary Database Access

This sounds obvious, but I've seen plenty of examples where this isn't done. Since stored procedures are similar to code modules in a programming language, you can use some of that functionality to minimize impact to the database. Use variables, loop structures, conditional checks, and control-of-flow when possible. The following example illustrates this.

Perhaps the most common problem concerns stored procedures that save data to a table. For example, suppose you need to create a stored procedure to save data to the Billing table listed earlier in the section "Default Values." A typical procedure would be:

```
CREATE PROCEDURE saveBilling    (@BillTS AS SMALLDATETIME,
                                 @Amount AS SMALLMONEY,
                                 @BillingID AS INT NULL) AS
SET NOCOUNT ON
IF (SELECT COUNT(*) FROM Billing WHERE BillingID = @BillingID) = 0
BEGIN
        INSERT INTO Billing(BillTS, BillAmount) VALUES (@BillTS, @Amount)
END
ELSE
BEGIN
        UPDATE Billing
        SET     BillTS = @BillTS,
                BillAmount = @Amount
        WHERE   BillingID = @BillingID
END
```

However, this procedure can be rewritten as follows:

```
CREATE PROCEDURE saveBilling2   (@BillTS AS SMALLDATETIME,
                                 @Amount AS SMALLMONEY,
                                 @BillingID AS INT NULL) AS

SET NOCOUNT ON
UPDATE Billing
SET    BillTS = @BillTS,
       BillAmount = @Amount
WHERE  BillingID = @BillingID

IF @@ROWCOUNT = 0
BEGIN
       INSERT INTO Billing(BillTS, BillAmount) VALUES (@BillTS, @Amount)
END
```

By using the @@ROWCOUNT system variable you've eliminated the SELECT COUNT(*) . . . query from the first procedure. Some argue that saveBilling2 will run an UPDATE statement, which won't update any rows, thus causing the procedure to run two queries. This is true, however, if the UPDATE does update rows then the INSERT statement will be skipped altogether. In short, there's a chance that saveBilling2 will only run one SQL statement, however, saveBilling will *always* run two SQL statements.

Temp Tables versus Table Variables

Another technique to minimize database access is using table variables instead of temporary tables. Temporary tables, which are preceded by # or ## are stored in tempDB. They are physically created and stored. Table variables are also created in tempDB. However their creation is not part of a user transaction. They also require fewer locks and recompilations. Thus, they can perform much better than temporary tables.

There are a few issues with table variables which would make them less optimized than temporary tables. First, if there is sufficient memory pressure, the table variable will be stored on disk. Also, other than defining a primary key, table variables can't be indexed. Temporary tables can have all the same features and options that a regular table can have. A temporary table can have multiple indexes.

Minimizing Cursor Usage

Another technique for stored procedures is one that minimizes the use of cursors. Cursors are fully explained in BOL. SQL Server is geared to operate on sets of data (rows). However, sometimes you may have occasion to operate on a single row at a time. In that instance a cursor can be used. Note, however, that operating on one row at a time is inefficient. So, whenever possible use SQL Server's natural ability to operate on sets of data, instead of a single row at a time.

Naming Convention for Stored Procedures

Finally, a technique for enhancing stored procedures has to do with their names. A common convention for naming stored procedures is one that includes a prefix of sp_. This should be avoided for stored procedures you create. The reason is that this prefix is treated specially. Whenever SQL Server receives a command to execute a stored procedure that begins with sp_, it will first look in the master database for the procedure. If it's not found, the engine will then search in the connected database for the procedure.

Thus, you can prevent SQL Server from unnecessarily checking the master database simply by using a different prefix for your stored procedure names.

Triggers

SQL Server supports two different types of triggers. They are Data Manipulation Language triggers, and Data Definition Language triggers. Triggers are special types of stored procedures. They execute whenever certain actions occur against a table. They also include two special structures known as the pseudo-tables "inserted" and "deleted."

DML

A DML trigger executes whenever a DML event occurs. These events are: UPDATE, INSERT, or DELETE statements. This type of trigger is used to enforce rules whenever data is modified. Another purpose of this type of trigger is to extend integrity enforcement.

There are two types of DML triggers. They are: AFTER triggers and INSTEAD OF triggers.

AFTER

This type of trigger occurs after the specified event (Insert, Update, or Delete) occurs. Using the Billing table example, here's an AFTER trigger defined on the Billing table for UPDATE. This trigger will fill in the UpdateUID, and UpdateTS columns for rows in the Billing tables which get updated.

```
create trigger UpdateAuditCols on Billing for UPDATE as
begin
        Update  T
        SET     UpdateUID = SUSER_SNAME(),
                UpdateTS = GETUTCDATE()
        FROM    BillingCase T
                INNER JOIN inserted i ON T.BillingID = i.BillingID
    end
go
```

INSTEAD OF

INSTEAD OF triggers execute in place of the event that originally initiated the operation. For example, define an INSTEAD OF trigger on a table for the Delete event. Next, try to delete some rows. The INSTEAD OF trigger will prevent the rows from getting deleted. Again, using the Billing table as an example consider the following INSTEAD OF trigger:

```
create trigger DeleteAuditCols on Billing INSTEAD OF DELETE as
begin
        Update  T
        SET     DeleteUID = SUSER_SNAME(),
                DeleteTS = GETUTCDATE()
        FROM    BillingCase T
                INNER JOIN deleted d ON T.BillingID = d.BillingID
    end
go
```

This trigger will prevent the rows from actually being deleted from the Billing table. However, it will mark those rows with deleted information.

Execution Order

The AFTER and INSTEAD OF triggers have an order of execution, which you need to be aware of. The order is: INSTEAD OF triggers, Constraint checks, AFTER triggers. Because of this order, whenever a constraint check fails, any subsequent AFTER triggers will not run.

Also some notes about INSTEAD OF triggers. Because they occur before any constraint checking occurs an INSTEAD OF trigger could be used as type of pre-processor. Any items that might fail the constraint checks could be fixed in the INSTEAD OF trigger. Another aspect of INSTEAD OF triggers is that if the trigger executes statements against the table the trigger is defined for, the trigger won't fire again. If it did, SQL Server would get into an infinite calling loop.

Multiple Triggers

A table can have multiple AFTER triggers. If you wanted to you could define 3 UPDATE triggers for a single table, as long as each trigger had a unique name.

A table can only have one INSTEAD OF trigger for each type: UPDATE, DELETE, and INSERT.

DDL

A DDL trigger executes whenever a DDL event occurs. DDL event groups include operations: CREATE, ALTER, and DROP. These actions can occur on many database objects such as tables, indexes, and procedures. See the BOL topic "DDL Events for Use with DDL Triggers" for a complete list of all the events that can be used to define this type of trigger.

Scope

DDL triggers have two different scopes. They are: database and current server. Database-level scope triggers fire from actions that modify the database schema. For example, a CREATE TABLE statement might fire a DDL trigger. These triggers are stored in the database.

Sever-level scope triggers fire from server changes. These triggers are stored in the master database.

DDL Trigger Usage

Some of the reasons you may want to use a DDL trigger include:

- ❑ Preventing or logging changes to your database. You may need to log or even prevent changes made to a database. A DDL trigger can aid in that goal.
- ❑ Enforcing standards. You may have standards such as naming conventions or comment requirements for your database objects. DDL triggers can enforce them by applying those standards to new objects, such as tables, views, or stored procedures.

Nested Triggers

Triggers can be nested together to create a trigger chain. Triggers can be nested up to 32 levels deep. Any trigger in the chain that starts an infinite loop of firing triggers will terminate once the 32 limit is exceeded. These are enabled by default. However, you can change the setting using the sp_configure command. For nested triggers the syntax would be:

```
Sp_Configure 'nested triggers', 0|1
```

Recursive Triggers

Triggers can also run recursively. They only apply to AFTER triggers. The recursion is either direct or indirect. These are enabled by default:

❑ **Direct:** Suppose a table has an update trigger called UpdateTableA. Inside this trigger is an update statement which runs against TableA. This will cause UpdateTableA to fire again. This is known as direct recursion.

❑ **Indirect:** Suppose a table has an update trigger called UpdateTableA. Inside this trigger is an update statement that runs against TableB. However, TableB has its own update trigger called UpdateTableB. This trigger runs an update statement against TableA. This is an example of indirect recursion.

To allow recursion, again use the `sp_configure` command. The syntax is:

```
Sp_configure 'server trigger recursion', 0|1
```

Note that turning this option off only prevents direct recursion. In order to turn off indirect recursion you must also turn off the nested triggers option as well.

Triggers in Practice

Now that the basics of triggers have been covered it's appropriate to discuss their usage and the potential bottlenecks they may introduce. It should be apparent from the details about triggers that they can quickly become performance bottlenecks. Imagine a trigger chain that includes both nesting and recursion. These can become particularly troublesome. Not only can they slow performance to a crawl, but they can be devilishly difficult to debug. Also, triggers are essentially stored procedures. Therefore, the complexity that you can code in a stored procedure can be coded in a trigger. In fact, the potential for bottlenecks makes some DBAs shun triggers altogether.

A couple of experiences come to mind considering trigger usage.

First, I had triggers set up similar to the UpdateAuditCols trigger defined above on some summary tables in a data warehouse. Whenever, I ran the weekly load process, the code that loaded these tables was unacceptably slow. The solution was simple. I disabled the trigger before I updated the table, and I altered the update process to also update the UpdateUID and UpdateTS columns. After the update completed I re-enabled the trigger. This way if the table was ever updated outside the normal load process (which was rare), these columns would get a value. Yet whenever the table was updated using the load process (which was common) the columns were still maintained.

Second, another place I worked used triggers to track changes to all data rows. For those of you familiar with the Sarbanes-Oxley law, this scenario should be familiar. At this company, the triggers would save the rows from both the inserted and deleted pseudo-tables in an audit table. However, this company had a nightly load procedure for some of their tables. The audit triggers made that load process too long. The solution here was two-fold. The triggers were disabled just as before. However, special stored procedures were written to check for new or changed rows in the main table that didn't exist in the corresponding audit table. If any rows were found they were then inserted into the audit table. The triggers were again enabled after this step finished. Again, the result was that during the special process of the nightly load a different set of steps was followed in order to achieve the desired results in a more timely manner. However, the normal process of the business application caused the triggers to track these changes.

Data Performance

The performance of data simply means how well the data will perform under a load. Obviously, you want to have as much performance as possible. This section will cover pages, partitioning, indexing, and other topics that have a great impact on data performance.

Pages

Most everything covered so far culminates here with a discussion about pages. SQL Server 2005 utilizes eight different page types; here we'll only discuss data pages. Intimately understanding data pages is a key for optimizing performance. The reason it's key is that the page is the fundamental unit of storage within SQL Server. Disk I/O occurs at the page level. SQL Server's locking mechanism defaults to the page level.

Data Pages

Data pages will be described first. These pages contain all the data, with the possible exception of the large value data types, described earlier, which may be stored on Text/Image pages (described later). Data pages are 8 KB (8,192 bytes) in size. The data page is divided into three main sections. The first section is a 96-byte header, which contains information about the page. The next section contains the data rows themselves. The final section is a row offset array (see Figure 8-18).

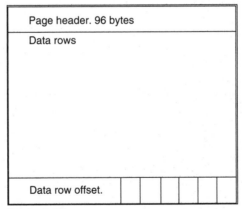

Figure 8-18

Page Headers

Table 8-4 describes the content of the page header.

Data Rows

The table's actual data rows are next on a page. A single data row can't be more than 8,060 bytes. A data row doesn't usually span a page. The exception to this is the large value data types. Those elements can be relegated to other pages. The number of rows stored on a given page will vary.

A table that doesn't have any variable-length columns will store the same number of rows on each page, assuming the pages are fully packed. However, a table that has some variable-length columns will likely store a different number of rows on each page. The idea to keep in mind when designing a table is to make the pages hold as many rows as possible. Keeping row lengths as short as possible is the way to achieve this goal. I refer to the number of rows per page as page density. The higher the density, the better. That's because more rows per page translates into fewer pages. That means that disk I/O can be reduced and the cache-hit ratio should improve.

Table 8-4: Page Header Content Details

Column	Purpose
pageID	File and page number of the current page in the database.
nextPage	File and page number of the next page, if the current page is part of a chain of pages.
prevPage	File and page number of the previous page, if the current page is part of a chain of pages.
objID	ID of the object to which the page belongs.
lsn	Log sequence number (LSN) value used for changes and updates to the page.
slotCnt	Total number of slots used on the page.
level	Level of the page in an index (always 0 for leaf pages).
indexId	Index ID of the page (always 0 for data pages).
freeData	Byte offset of the first free space on this page.
Pminlen	Number of bytes in fixed-length portion of rows.
freeCnt	Number of free bytes on page.
reservedCnt	Number of bytes reserved by all transactions.
xactreserved	Number of bytes reserved by the most recently started transaction.
tornBits	1 bit per sector for detecting torn page writes.
flagBits	2-byte bitmap that contains additional information about the page.

Data Row Structure

There's more to a data row than just the data. Each row has its own collection of "housekeeping" items. Table 8-5 provides the general structure of a data row.

Note that for a table that only has fixed-length columns the last three segments won't exist.

Page Row Offset Arrays

The row offset array is a series of 2-byte entries. Each entry indicates where on the page the corresponding data row begins, and every row has an entry. Even though these bytes aren't stored with the data row, they do play a part in determining how many rows will fit on a page.

Table 8-5: Row Layout Details

Information	Handle	Size	Purpose
Status Bits A	StatusA	1 byte	Internal. Ignore.
Status Bits B	StatusB	1 byte	Internal. Ignore.
Fixed-length size	FS	2 bytes	Total storage occupied by all the fixed-length columns.
Fixed-length data	FD	FS – 4	All the fixed-length data.
Number of columns	NC	2 bytes	Number of columns in the table.
NULL bitmap	IsNull	Ceiling (NC / 8)	1 byte for each column. A 1 indicates that the column is NULL.
Number of variable-length columns	VC	2 bytes	Indicates the number of variable length columns in the table.
Variable column offset array	VO	2 * VC	Each variable-length column contains an offset value. This is a 2-byte entry which indicates the position in the data row where the column ends.
Variable-length data	VD	VO[VC] – (FS + 4 + Ceiling (NC / 8) + 2 * VC)	All the variable-length column data.

The row offset array indicates the logical order of rows on a page. For tables that have a clustered index, the logical order is dictated by the clustered key. Note that SQL Server will not physically store the rows on the page in the order of the key. However, the first slot in the offset array will refer to the first row in the key order, the second slot will refer to the second row, and so on. For tables that don't have a clustered index, the logical order is the order in which the rows are inserted.

Extent Pages

You may have heard or read the term extent pages. This terminology is somewhat confusing. Extent pages aren't some special type of data page. Instead, they're simply eight logically contiguous data pages. When SQL Server allocates storage to a table, it doesn't allocate just one page. Instead, it allocates eight. Likewise, when SQL Server reads a data page it doesn't read just one, it reads eight. There are two types of extents:

❏ **Mixed extents:** These are shared by up to eight tables.

❏ **Uniform extents:** These are owned by a single table.

A new table or index is allocated pages from mixed extents. However, when the table grows to require eight pages for itself, it shifts to use uniform extents. Also, once a table begins using uniform extents it will never go back to using mixed extents.

As you can tell from this information about pages, it's imperative that you design your tables to maximize page density. This means using the smallest data type that will accommodate the needs of a column. This also means using variable-length data types wisely. The space saved by variable-length data types can be substantial. However, there's additional overhead surrounding variable-length data types. If a column's data doesn't vary greatly within the rows of a table, then a variable-length data type shouldn't be used.

Partitioning

The purpose of partitioning is simple. The idea is to segregate a table's rows and columns based on popularity. A table's most popular rows and columns are known as *hot*. The goal is to group those rows and columns together so that access can be fast. Furthermore, the counter-goal is to get the least popular rows and columns out of the way. Let's face it, year-old order information in an order-entry system is less useful than week-old information. Partitioning tables has always been possible with SQL Server. However, SQL Server 2005 adds some tools and utilities, which make the task much easier. There are two types of partitioning which can be applied to a table. They are horizontal and vertical partitioning.

Vertical

Vertical partitioning involves splitting a table's columns into multiple tables. Splitting one table into multiple tables for the purpose of grouping the columns does not violate the idea of normalization. Remember that normalization essentially means that tables should have a single purpose. If the table you're splitting has a single purpose, then the resulting "sub-tables" should also have a single purpose.

Let's revisit the "Operator" table from the normalization example. See Figure 8-19.

Operator

	Column Name	Data Type	Nullable
🔑	OperatorID	int	No
	ExaminerID	int	No
	LicenseID	int	No
	RegionID	int	No
	Name	char(20)	No
	Callsign	char(6)	No

Figure 8-19

Suppose that you learn that the Name and Callsign columns are very popular and the LicenseID, ExaminerID, and RegionID aren't. You might split the table into two, as shown in Figure 8-20.

Now to round out the change a view called Operator can be created that mimics the original table. This would allow any existing coding against the Operator table to work unaltered. Also, if the columns in the second table aren't referenced in a query they won't be accessed.

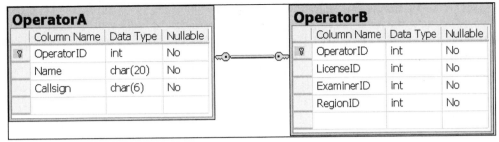

Figure 8-20

Horizontal

Horizontal partitioning involves moving rows into separate tables. This is the area where SQL Server 2005 has improved the support for partitioning. However, this is only available in the Enterprise and Developer editions. Advantages to doing this can make large tables or indexes more manageable, because it gives you the option of managing subsets of data instead of all of it. Another advantage is that the individual partitions are associated with one file group. This means there can be multiple file groups matching the number of partitions. Also note that a partitioned table or index work just like their unpartitioned counterpart. In fact, according to BOL SQL Server treats all tables as partitioned, even if the table only has one partition.

When to Partition

Creating horizontal partitions is usually done for one of two reasons. One reason is to allow easy management of subsets of data. The other reason is to improve query performance. Note that a query that will cause more than one partition to be referenced may have an impact on performance. This is because these types of queries only use one thread per partition.

Partitioning for Subsets of Data

By dividing a table into multiple partitions allows you to easily move those partitions from one table to another. You can easily add an existing table to another partitioned table. You can also switch partitions from one partitioned table to another.

Partitioning for Performance

One obvious use for partitions is performance. However, there are a few things to keep in mind here. Otherwise it's possible to create a partition plan that actually hurts performance instead of enhancing it.

The first issue involves frequently joining two or more partitioned tables. In this case the tables should have the same partition column as the column on which the tables are joined. Also, these partitioned tables should be located together. The easiest way to do that is for each table to use the same partition function. Doing this allows the query optimizer can process the join faster, because the partitions themselves can be joined. Beware however, that if a query joins two tables that are not located together or are the partition column and the join column are different, the presence of partitions may actually hinder performance instead of enhancing it.

Another issue to be aware of is the idea of placing your defined file groups on separate hard drives in an effort to improve I/O performance. According to BOL, when SQL Server performs data sorting for I/O operations, it sorts the data first by partition. This means that the database engine accesses one drive at a time, which may negatively impact performance. In this case it's better to stripe the data files across a RAID configuration. This way, when the database engine sorts the data by partition, it can access all the drives of each partition at the same time.

Utilizing Partitions

Once you've decided that you need to create a partition for a table, there's a few things you'll have to create. The first thing is file groups, the next item is a partition function, and finally a partition scheme must be created.

File Groups

File groups are nothing more than named collections of the database files. We're not going to go into any detail about defining file groups. BOL has plenty of documentation in that regard. However, know this; when you're going to partition a table, you'll typically have one file group for each partition. Thus, if you want to create three partitions for a table, you should create three file groups.

Partition Function

A partition function defines how the rows of a table or index are split among a set of partitions. This splitting is based on the values of specified column. Note that you can only specify one partition column. For example, an Order table may be split into multiple partitions based on the OrderDate column.

There are two things to consider when you plan a partition function. Choosing the appropriate partitioning column, and setting the range of values of the partitioning column for each partition. The range of values determines the number of partitions that make up your table. Note, however, that there's a limit to the number of partitions a table can have, which is 1,000 partitions.

Choosing the appropriate partitioning column and the range of values for each partition are the keys to creating useful partitions.

Creating a partition function specifies how the table or index is partitioned. The function maps the domain into a set of partitions. Creating a partition function involves specifying the number of partitions, the column to partition on, and the range of values that the partition column will use on each partition. If you want to use a computed column as a partitioning column it must be marked as persisted. Furthermore, the following datatypes are not allowed for a partitioned column: timestamp, ntext, text, image, xml, varchar(max), nvarchar(max), or varbinary(max). Also, CLR user-defined type and alias data type columns cannot be specified.

Partition Scheme

A partition scheme simply assigns each partition defined by the partition function to a file group. The main reason for putting partitions on separate file groups is that backing up those file groups can be done independently of one another.

Creating a Partitioned Table

With the previous three database objects defined you can now create a table that is partitioned. This is done using the ON clause of the CREATE TABLE statement. The ON clause will designate which partition scheme to use and which column acts as the partitioning column. Again, BOL has the detailed syntax for this.

Example

With all that in mind let's look an example using the Operator table from the normalization section. Suppose you want to split this table on the LicenseID column. You also want four partitions.

1. Create four file groups called fgOperator1, fgOperator2, fgOperator3, fgOperator4. Again, see BOL for syntax details.

2. Create the partition function. `CREATE PARTITION FUNCTION pfLicenseID (int) AS RANGE LEFT FOR VALUES (1, 2, 3)`. This will set up a partition as shown in Table 8-6.

Table 8-6: Partition Scheme

Partition	1	2	3	4
Value	Col <= 1	Col > 1 and Col <= 3	Col > 3 and Col <= 4	Col > 4

3. Create the partition scheme. `CREATE PARTITION SCHEME psLicenseID AS PARTITION pfLicenseID TO (fgOperator1, fgOperator2, fgOperator3, fgOperator4)`. This results in rows being redirected into their respective file groups based on the range.

4. Finally, create the Operator table:

```
CREATE TABLE OPERATOR(OperatorID int,
Name varchar(20),
Callsign char(6),
LicenseID int,
ExaminerID int,
RegionID int) ON psLicense(LicenseID)
```

Once created, SQL Server will transparently redirect operations on the table to the appropriate partition.

Concurrency and Locking (and Blocking)

At this point most of the information concerning table design has been covered. However, we're going to shift focus a bit to discuss the utilization of those the tables. Concurrency is simply the notion that the same group of data is accessed simultaneously. However, that access has to be managed in such a way that undesired effects on the data don't occur. That management is handled by SQL Server's lock manager.

This is a complex and arduous topic. BOL covers these issues in great detail, and we recommend you constantly have to return to that for reference.

Transaction Refresher

Before describing concurrency and locking, a brief description of transactions is warranted. Simply stated, transactions define the beginning and ending of a unit of work. Several statements can comprise a unit of work. The beginning of the unit of work is created by a BEGIN TRANSACTION SQL statement, and the unit of work ends with either a ROLLBACK or COMMIT TRANSACTION statement.

Concurrency Effects

As stated earlier, concurrency deals with the simultaneous access of a set of data. If the database engine did not control concurrency, there could be several unwanted side effects. Those are lost updates, dirty reads, non-repeatable reads, and phantom reads.

A lost update means that two transactions update the same piece of data and only the last transaction's update of the data is captured.

Dirty reads refer to the notion that a piece of data is in the processing of being updated by a transaction. However, before that update is committed, a second transaction reads the same piece of data. If this transaction gets the uncommitted data, there's a possibility that the transaction updating the data will change something, and the second transaction's copy of the data won't match what's been written.

Non-repeatable reads are similar to dirty reads with the following difference. In this case, the data read by the second transaction does read committed data from the first transaction. The other factor here is that the second transaction reads the same piece of data two or more times, and gets different results. Thus, the second transaction is unable to repeat the read. Avoiding this is accomplished by not allowing any other transactions to read the changing piece of data until the last of the modifications are saved and the transaction is committed.

Finally, phantom reads happen when a row is inserted or deleted by one transaction into a range of rows being read by a second transaction. When another read is executed against the same range of rows there appears to be fewer or more rows than with the original read. Like non-repeatable reads this can be avoided by restricting access to the piece of data from readers until all the writing is completed.

Concurrency Control

Controlling concurrency in order to address the issues above concerning the effects is the next order of business. There are two types of concurrency control: pessimistic and optimistic.

Pessimistic control tends to ensure that read operations access current data. This means that a transaction reading a piece of data will create a lock that prevents other transactions from modifying that data until the read operation is completed.

Optimistic control tends toward minimizing the blocking that can occur among reader and writer transactions of the same piece of data. This is accomplished by the fact that read operations don't acquire locks that would prevent other transactions from modifying the piece of data.

Isolation Levels

Along with maximizing row density, the mechanism for implementing concurrency control is through setting isolation levels. Isolation levels are designated on a transaction occurring against a database. They are either pessimistic or optimistic. The idea here is that one transaction is being isolated from other transactions in varying degrees. The isolation levels dictate which of the concurrency effects listed above are allowed. Also, it's important to realize that setting an isolation level only controls read operations. Additionally, that level essentially dictates what's allowed for data modification by other transactions.

There are 5 isolation levels available in SQL Server. Each level dictates which of the concurrency effects are allowed.

❑ **READ UNCOMMITTED:** This level means that a transaction can read rows that have been modified by other transactions but haven't been committed. This is the least restrictive level. It allows dirty reads, non-repeatable reads, and phantom reads.

❑ **READ COMMITTED:** This level means that a transaction cannot read rows that have been modified but not committed by another transaction. It allows non-repeatable reads, and phantom reads. It does not allow dirty reads. This is the default isolation level. It usually provides the best balance between the allowed concurrency effects and the overhead of required for providing this level of isolation.

❑ Note that READ COMMITTED has a new option with SQL Server 2005. In this version, Microsoft introduced the READ_COMMITTED_SNAPSHOT database option. When this option is off, which is the default, SQL Server uses shared locks to prevent other transactions from modifying rows while the current transaction is executing a read operation. This is the traditional behavior for READ COMMITTED.

❑ However, when this option is on, SQL Server uses row versioning so that each statement has a consistent snapshot of the data as it existed when the statement began.

❑ **REPEATABLE READ:** This level means that a transaction cannot read rows that have been modified but not committed by another transaction. Also, no other transaction can change the rows that have been read by the initial transaction until it completes. It allows phantom reads. It does not allow dirty reads or non-repeatable reads.

❑ **SNAPSHOT:** This level means that when a transaction starts, any rows read will be a version of the rows before the transaction started. Any changes that take place on those rows by other transactions will not be available to the first transaction. It does not allow dirty reads, non-repeatable reads or phantom reads. Note that the ALLOW_SNAPSHOT_ISOLATION database option must be enabled before you can utilize the SNAPSHOT isolation level.

❑ **SERIALIZABLE:** This level means that a transaction cannot read rows that have been modified but not committed by another transaction. Also, no other transaction can change the rows that have been read by the initial transaction until it completes. Finally, other transactions cannot insert new rows which might fall in the range of rows that the current transaction has read until the current transaction is completed. It does not allow dirty reads, non-repeatable reads, or phantom reads.

Locks

The discussion of isolation levels and concurrency lead to the topic of locks. As stated earlier, locking is the mechanism that SQL Server employs to carry out the concurrency controls dictated by the isolation level. This mechanism is very complex and resource intensive. Generally speaking, as the isolation level increases in restrictiveness the amount of resources required also increases.

I'm going to attempt to describe that complexity in a simplified and (somewhat) concise manner. Not everything will be described. For a complete description, see BOL.

First, know that there are varying levels of granularity for locks. They range from row-level locking all the way up to database-level locking. Also, know that SQL Server takes a dynamic approach to determine a locking strategy, which is based on the most cost-effective (that is, least amount of resources) plan.

Granularity

Granularity refers to the resource that a lock applies to. A partial list of the resources that can be locked includes:

- ❏ Row
- ❏ Page
- ❏ Table
- ❏ Database

Lock Modes

The type of lock applied to the resources listed above is known as the lock mode. SQL Server provides several modes for locks. Following is a list of the lock modes:

- ❏ **Shared:** These are used for read operations.
- ❏ **Update:** Used on updatable resources.
- ❏ **Exclusive:** These are used for write operations (insert, update, delete).
- ❏ **Intent:** These are used to establish a lock "hierarchy."
- ❏ **Schema:** These are used when an operation that is dependent on a table's schema is operating.
- ❏ **Bulk Update:** These are used when bulk copying data is occurring, and the TABLOCK hint is enabled.
- ❏ **Key-range:** These are used to protect a range of rows read by a query that is in a serializable transaction.

Lock Compatibility

Sometimes a transaction will attempt to lock a resource that is already locked. If the modes of the locks are compatible then the new lock can be granted without interference. However, if the modes are not compatible then the transaction requesting the new lock will be forced to wait until the first lock is released. Obviously exclusive locks are not compatible with any other lock modes. However, many lock modes are compatible. For a complete listing of compatible lock modes see BOL.

Lock Escalation

Whenever possible, SQL Server will convert fine-grain locks into coarse-grain locks. This process is known as lock escalation. Note that when SQL Server escalates locks it does so by promoting both row and page level locks to the table level. It does not promote row-level locks to page-level. When the database engine acquires a lock on a resource it will place an intent lock on that resource's parent object. For example, when a row lock is placed on a data row, that row's page receives an intent lock.

When successful, all lower-level locks can be released, thereby reducing overhead for the lock manager.

Finally, note that SQL Server attempts lock escalation after acquiring 5000 locks on the rowset. It also attempts lock escalation under memory pressure.

Dynamic

SQL Server manages locking in a dynamic manner. This means that the engine determines what granularity and mode are appropriate when the query is executed. By allowing SQL Server to manage the locking mechanism autonomously this shifts the responsibility from the database administrator or developer.

Blocks

As stated earlier, an existing lock can block an attempt to lock the same resource. This is a normal and usually temporary condition. The existing lock will be released and the new lock will be granted. You can surmise from the previous discussion of locking that blocking is a fact of life within the operation of SQL Server. However, blocks can sometimes conflict with each other. This leads to a condition known as deadlock.

Deadlocks

One of the most common situations for deadlocks is when transaction A is holding a lock on a resource that transaction B wants to change. Additionally, transaction B has a lock on a resource that transaction A wants to modify. If left unattended this condition will live on indefinitely. However, SQL Server monitors for deadlocks and will manage them. When the database engine detects a deadlock it will choose one of the transactions as a deadlock victim. The engine will then roll back the changes made by that transaction. When this occurs the only option is to re-execute the original statement.

Deadlocks are certainly something you want to minimize. We'll look at some guidelines for that in the next chapter, on SQL tuning.

In Practice

At this point you may be wondering how all this talk of concurrency and locking leads to relieving bottlenecks. First, it's important that you have a decent understanding of these areas. Ensuring that you're using the appropriate concurrency controls can't be done unless you understand what your options are. Using the proper isolation level is a key to achieving this goal. Second, as far as locking is concerned, there's little that can be done to directly control the lock manager. SQL Server manages locking automatically. However, you should have a good appreciation for the amount of effort that SQL Server has to exert when managing locks.

Both these areas lead to what should be clearly an underlying theme with this chapter. Designing tables that provide the highest row density as practical is paramount. The benefits you'll reap for this are numerous. Conversely, by not doing this the results can be severe.

In fact, let me tell you a story that illustrates this principle. Several years ago I inherited a data warehouse database that had been hastily designed and implemented. When it was first implemented it performed well enough. However, after about 15 months, the database had become problematic. Because the tables didn't have very many rows per page, the DB quickly grew to about 90 GB. In addition to that, the nightly load on this database took about 6 hours. The lack of density caused the database size to grow rapidly. Furthermore, this also led to overburdening the lock manager. Since the density was so low, the data pages and row counts were almost one to one. I vividly remember watching the statistics of one of the table loads. This particular load included about 100,000 rows, and the lock manager generated about

80,000 locks (page level). That's almost a one-to-one ratio of rows to locks. In fact, row-level locking in this example wouldn't have performed that much worse than page-level.

So, a colleague and I redesigned the database using the principles described earlier. We normalized where we could, and most importantly we used the right data types for the columns. The end result was a database that was about 30 GB in size. Also the 6-hour load process was reduced to about 45 minutes.

Indexing

Poorly designed indexes or missing indexes can be a major contributor to bottlenecks. There are several factors that go into designing proper indexes. However, the task is generalized by the need to balance fast executing queries with fast updates. This section covers some general techniques for designing indexes. It also describes the different types of indexes and provides some examples.

General Structure

An index is a B-tree structure. In general it looks something like Figure 8-21.

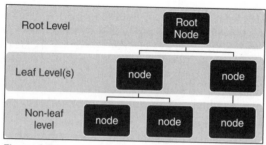

Figure 8-21

The top level is known as the root level. The intermediate levels are known as the leaf levels. The bottom level is known as the non-leaf level.

General Techniques

Tables generally fall into two categories. One is a table that experiences a great deal of data changing (or writing). The second type of table is one that is primarily used to read data from.

For write-oriented tables, indexes must be used carefully. Every time an insert, update, or delete occurs on a table all the indexes associated with that table will need to be updated as well. As you can imagine, a write-oriented table that is laden with indexes may well perform poorly.

For read-oriented tables with large amounts of data, the opposite is true. Copious use of indexes is usually beneficial. Since this table doesn't experience high amounts of changes, it can have more indexes.

Another issue with indexes is table size. For small tables, say a few hundred rows or less, indexes are unnecessary. In fact they can actually impede performance. Traversing an index on a table with few rows can take longer than simply allowing SQL Server to perform a table scan on the table. Also, as always, the indexes have to be maintained whenever an insert, update, or delete occurs.

Also, keep indexes as narrow as possible. Use as few columns as possible. Furthermore, use columns that have known sizes over variable-sized columns. Variable length columns such as VARCHAR aren't as efficient as the non-variable length columns. Favor integer, non-null columns when possible.

Selectivity

A key concept in designing indexes is selectivity. This is defined as the ratio of the number of distinct values in an index's column(s) to the number of rows in the table. The highest possible selectivity is 1. This would occur when the number of distinct values in the index column(s) equals the number of rows in the table. This will occur with primary keys and any other unique keys defined for a table.

Imagine a table having 100,000 rows and one of its indexed columns has 75,000 distinct values. The selectivity of this index is 75,000 / 100,000 = 0.75.

Now suppose that same table of 100,000 rows had an index whose column only had 500 distinct values. This index's selectivity is 500 / 100,000 = 0.005.

Note that SQL Server also defines something called density, as related to indexes (don't confuse this with row density.) Density is the inverse of selectivity. Therefore, a low density implies a high selectivity and vice versa.

So, you may be wondering what this has to do with creating indexes. The idea is simple; when you create an index, use columns which are highly selective. An extension to this applies to multi-column indexes. As you add columns to an index, do so such that the additional columns help to increase the selectivity of the index. Otherwise, there's no point. This leads to another experience, which bears inclusion here.

Remember the 90 GB database I mentioned earlier? Well one of the actions I took in reducing that size was cutting out the plethora of superfluous indexes. As I stated earlier, a unique key index will have a selectivity of 1. Therefore adding additional columns to this index won't improve its selectivity at all. This database was peppered with indexes such that the unique column was first in the list, then a second (or third or fourth) column was listed. Those indexes did nothing for the query optimizer (which is really the "consumer" of all indexes). However, they certainly had a negative impact on the size and load times!

Another aspect of indexes is type. SQL Server recognizes two types of indexes. One is a clustered index. The other goes by the truly uninspired name of non-clustered index.

Clustered Indexes

Clustered index is a somewhat unfortunate term. The reason is that a clustered index is more than an index. In fact, the main attribute of a clustered index isn't the fact that it's an index. The most important aspect of a clustered index is the fact that it dictates where the incoming rows will be stored.

The purpose of clustered indexes is to provide greater read performance. In fact, a clustered index should always outperform a similarly defined non-clustered index. This performance boost comes from the fact that the bottom of the index structure (known as the leaf level) are actually the data pages.

For non-clustered indexes, the bottom of the index structure is the pointer to the data pages. (However, if a clustered index is present, then it will point to the clustered index.) Therefore, when traversing a non-clustered index SQL Server will have to make one extra operation to retrieve the data. However, traversing a clustered index won't incur that because the data page is already at hand.

Another unfortunate aspect of clustered indexes is their overuse. Most publications on this subject advise that every table should have a clustered index. In fact, when you define a primary key, SQL Server defaults that key as a clustered index. The remainder of this section will discuss some techniques you can use to determine when to define a clustered index on your tables.

If you've worked with SQL Server any length of time you've probably heard or read statements that claim that every table should have a clustered index. This is simply wrong and a quick example with the following table schema will bear that out:

```
CREATE TABLE Product
  (ProductID      uniqueidentifier      NOT NULL,
   SupplierID     uniqueidentifier      NULL)

CREATE UNIQUE CLUSTERED INDEX bad_cluster
ON Product (ProductID)
```

The ProductID column is defined as a uniqueidentifier data type, and a clustered index. A uniqueidentifier column shouldn't be used for a clustered index.

Therefore, not all tables will benefit from a clustered index. The question then becomes, "Is this example the only one where a clustered shouldn't be used, or are there others?" The remainder of this section will address that question.

Using the following approach will help identify tables deriving benefit from a clustered index. If the table in question doesn't meet all the requirements, don't create a clustered index.

Don't Create a Clustered Index on an Artificial Column

An artificial column is one whose value is generated by the database engine. In SQL Server, this is most commonly achieved by two methods:

❑   Designate a column as an identity column.

❑   Define a column's data type as uniqueidentifier and set its default value equal to NEWID().

Consider the second type of artificial column. A uniqueidentifer is the same thing as a GUID. They are globally unique and random, thus one value has absolutely no relation to another value. Defining a clustered index on a uniqueidentifier column forces the server to order the rows physically in the table based on a column whose values are totally random and unrelated to one another.

Now consider the first type of artificial column. The reason for excluding this requires a little understanding of SQL Server data page management. SQL Server recognizes two types of tables: heap and clustered. Any table that doesn't have a clustered index is a heap table. Any table that has a clustered index is a clustered table. When inserting rows into a heap table the server will simply add the new row at the end of the table's data pages. However, when inserting rows into a clustered table the server must find the proper data page to place the new row. When using a typical identity column the proper data page will always be the last one. Therefore, defining a clustered index on an identity column forces the server to go through the process of determining the proper data page to store a new row — even when this location will be the last page. If the clustered index were removed then the heap nature of the table will naturally cause new rows to be stored on the last data page, without having to go through the process of determining where.

One exception to this is if you're going to use that identity column for range-based queries. For example, suppose you have a table Order with an OrderID identity column. You may have queries that retrieve rows where OrderID is between 100 and 200. A good example of this is in the world of web applications. Those applications usually return only a fixed amount of rows at a time, say 20.

The Table Must Be Relatively Large

Classifying a table as large is, well...relative. To paraphrase a popular expression, "one man's large table is another man's small table." Everyone will have to determine the meaning of large. A good yardstick to use is page count. Additionally, use multiples of 8, that is, 8, 16, 32, and so on. The reasoning for this is that SQL Server reads or allocates 8 pages at a time. Thus, when a row is retrieved from a table, the page containing the row, as well as the next 7 pages, is read. Likewise, when SQL Server allocates new data pages to a table, it will actually add 8 of them, not just one. Therefore, choose a number such as 256. Then any table that contains more than 256 data pages is considered large, thereby making it a candidate for clustered indexing. Conversely, any table with fewer than 256 pages wouldn't be a candidate for clustered indexing. Note that if the table under consideration is currently empty, then use an estimate of the table's data page requirements.

The Table Must Be Relatively Static

Again, classifying a table as static is also relative. This is the most important tenet of these guidelines. The purpose here is to determine the frequency of inserts that a table experiences. As this frequency increases, the prospect for a clustered index decreases. If the table under consideration experiences frequent inserts, such as an OLTP-style transaction table, then it's not a candidate for a clustered index. However, if the table experiences infrequent inserts, as with most data warehouse tables, then it is a candidate.

The Table Should Generally Be Queried Using the Same Column

This means that for the table being considered; when filtering rows, or joining the table to others, those operations are typically done with the most frequently used column(s). Perhaps a better way to state this is that a clustered index should only be defined using the table's most popular column(s). If no column(s) stand out as being the most popular then don't create a clustered index.

Clustered Index Summary

To summarize, these guidelines lead to one underlying principle. When contemplating a clustered index on a table, you must first determine the most important operation for the table. If the most important operation is reading, which is the case in most data-warehouse tables, the table should probably have a clustered index. Remember to keep in mind all the preceding guidelines. However, if the most important operation is inserting, which is the case in most OLTP tables, the table probably shouldn't have a clustered index. Following these guidelines will lead to effective use (and non-use) of clustered indexes.

Again, another real-world experience comes to mind. A colleague had a classic Order-OrderDetail table arrangement in his application. His application had an end of day report, which took about 30 minutes to run, and he wanted to improve that time. One of the DBA's recommended that a clustered index be created on the OrderID column in the OrderDetail table. After creating this index the end of day report improved to about 5 minutes. However, the next day when the order entry clerks started using the application, it quickly ground to a halt. The reason was that the clustered index slowed down the inserting and updating operations to the point that the system became unusable.

Non-Clustered Indexes

Non-clustered indexes don't dictate the storage as do clustered indexes. Also, a table can have several non-clustered indexes, whereas it can only have one clustered index. If you've applied the rules listed above for clustered indexes and find that the index you want to create shouldn't be a clustered index, then your only choice is to make it non-clustered.

All the design rules given at the beginning of this section apply to non-clustered indexes. Keep them small, use non-variable length columns whenever possible, and use the most selective columns you can.

For non-clustered indexes, the bottom of the index structure are pointers to the data pages. Therefore, when traversing a non-clustered index, SQL Server will have to make one extra operation to retrieve the data.

Covering Indexes

A covering index includes all of the columns referenced in the SELECT, JOIN, and WHERE clauses of a query. Thus, the index contains all the data and SQL Server doesn't have to go to the data pages to get it. It's all in the index.

Covering indexes have to be used carefully. If they have too many columns, they can actually increase I/O and negatively impact performance. A couple of guidelines for covering indexes are listed below:

- ❏ First, make sure that the query you're creating for the covering index is frequently run. If it's not then don't create a covering index.
- ❏ Don't add too many columns to an existing index to get a covering index.
- ❏ The covering index must include all columns found in the query. That includes the SELECT, JOIN, and WHERE clauses of the query.

Include Indexes

Include indexes are new to SQL Server 2005. They provide an additional method of creating covering indexes. An example statement that creates an include index from the AdventureWorks database is:

```
CREATE INDEX IX_Address_PostalCode
ON Person.Address (PostalCode)
INCLUDE (City, StateProvinceID)
```

This works by placing the columns listed in the INCLUDE clause on the leaf level nodes of the index. All the other nodes at the non-leaf level won't have those columns. Also, those columns won't be used when calculating the number of index key columns or index key size.

This is really the way to create covering indexes in SQL Server 2005 because these non-key columns won't take up unnecessary space in the index key. However, when data is retrieved it can still be done from the index, and the data won't have to be read from the data pages.

Summary

You should realize that delivering a high performance database that will also scale is largely dependent on proper schema design. The highlights of this chapter are:

❑   Using normalization you can minimize the amount of storage required as well as mitigate several data quality anomalies.

❑   Understanding the data page will serve as a constant guide as you design your tables.

❑   Choosing the smallest data types that will fit the need will provide tremendous benefits for your tables. This will go a long way to maximizing row density, which is key.

❑   Placing large value data types in the right place, either in-row or out-of-row, will also contribute to getting the most out of your data pages.

❑   Use partitioning can also reap many benefits.

❑   Adding constraints will enforce data quality.

❑   Create stored procedures to minimize recompiling and execution plan generation.

❑   Use triggers to augment constraints as well as providing a place to put complex business logic.

❑   Use concurrency properly. Relieve the lock manager from any unnecessary work.

❑   Use indexes properly, especially clustered indexes.

9

Tuning T-SQL

Tuning T-SQL statements for performance is a primary task for most DBAs. The task is essentially a contest between a human being and SQL Server's query optimizer. An analogy can be seen in the world of chess. Numerous chess-playing computer programs have been developed over the years. Early chess programs were weak. However, the programs got better and began to surpass most people's ability to play. Yet there are human players who can still beat the best chess programs in the world.

The world of T-SQL tuning is no different. In the early days of database engines, the query optimizers were weak. In fact, an early tuning technique was a simple re-arrangement of table order in a query. By simply reordering the tables, vast improvements could be made. However, over the years optimizers have gotten better and can now automatically handle situations that previously had to be handled by a person. Don't make the mistake of expending large amounts of effort to create a report that torpedoes thousands of write operations. The days of tweaking an existing query to get large gains in performance are rapidly diminishing, so this type of tuning really isn't an option anymore.

In the first section, like the two different approaches that machines and humans take to playing chess, you'll look at the algorithmic approach to playing chess — how to analyze the cost components of each step in a query execution process. You'll examine in detail the pieces of the game as the optimizer sees them. In the second section, you'll apply human intelligence that is agile and can apply abstractive reasoning. You'll discover the things that you can do to avoid expensive operations, techniques for reducing specific cost components, and how to go about examining the performance data you'll need to tune your T-SQL for performance.

Opening Move: The Optimizer's Gameplan

SQL is a declarative language — at least it is supposed to be, although it isn't always. The idea is that you should use the language constructs to describe what you want. It is the job of the algebrizer and optimizer to figure out how to best get what you want. Performance issues can be created by poorly written T-SQL that cannot be optimized or, conversely, the incorrect optimization of well-written

T-SQL. Where the optimizer makes poor decisions, it is helpful to understand the severe restrictions that the optimization componentry has

❏ Examining alternate plans in a limited to small time frame

❏ Executing test queries to gather actual meaningful statistics or key performance indicators (KPIs) is not allowed

❏ Predicting costs based on imperfect cost plan data

❏ Throwing out edge-case scenarios evaluation

❏ Ignoring advantageous database schema changes to tables or indexes (it can't make them)

Many turn this into a mortal battle of us against the optimizer. It's not much of a battle, because you actually have the unfair advantage. You have unlimited time to execute alternative queries, capture real KPI metrics, and evaluate edge cases to figure out the best query plans for your purposes. You can rearrange tables and alter index schemes. You should never lose against the optimizer. Tie? That should be the worst case scenario. Learn the ways of the optimizer — not to beat it, but to provide the most efficient communication of your SQL-based intentions.

Cost-Based Optimization

Cost-based optimization is a process of examining a tree of possible permeations, determining the best plan out of the possibilities, and attaching an estimated cost on each step of a plan. However, for the sake of speed it is not guaranteed that all the possibilities are examined. The cost model determines possible predicate results from stored statistics and applies complex algorithms to the results to come up with an estimated CPU and I/O cost. When you are examining the execution plan, every operator has a cost associated with it, but don't get hung up thinking that these numbers represent specific resource utilization or actual query runtimes. These numbers are the result of row count estimates and internal formulas for typical disk I/O and sort time per row and other heuristics. The actual runtimes of a query depend upon many things like caching, other requests on same resources, and locking, among other things. (See the following sections on minimizing caching effects in your tuning process.) Table 9-1 contains the important things to remember about cost-based optimization and the effects on your tuning process.

Table 9-1: Cost versus Performance

Cost Model Element	Performance Tuning
Use of statistics for indexes and tables.	If statistics are not up-to-date, optimizer gets incorrect row counts and may choose suboptimal joins or access methods.
Selectivity Formulas to estimate predicate results.	Statistics are also heavily used here. Provide more information about relations between tables. For example, a.A=b.A AND b.A=c.A AND a.A=c.A.
Formulas to estimate cost per Operator. Order of existing data and requested data streams are considered.	Ordering of results can alter join options that optimizer can use.

Reading Index Statistics

Index statistics are so important to the correct costing of query execution plans that it is worth a second to refresh your memory on how to read this statistical treasure trove. There are many ways to retrieve this information but one of the best is to use the DBCC SHOW_STATISTICS command like this:

```
DBCC SHOW_STATISTICS('Sales.SalesOrderheader', IX_SalesOrderHeader_SalesPersonID)
```

This produces three result sets of which only partial results are shown in the following explanations, for brevity's sake. The first result set is at the index level. Here you can find when the statistics were last updated for the index, the total number of rows, and rows sampled to build the statistics.

Updated	Rows	Rows Sampled
May 31 2007 10:26PM	31465	31465

If the date the statistics were last updated is too old or if the number of rows indicated in the statistics metadata is not close to the current row count, then it is time to rerun statistics on this table (or better yet, to enable auto-create statistics to do this for you). If the number of rows sampled is less than 80 percent of the actual row count of the table, you'll need to increase the probability of accurate plan creation in the optimizer by running the update statistics command using the FULLSCAN option. This next result set provides density information at the column level in the index. Density is a measure of the selectivity of any one value in the column being found in any of the rows sampled. A value of 100 percent would indicate that all columns have the same value or density. This information is used in the first step of the optimizer. In the sample below, from the perspective of the optimizer, 5 percent of the table needs to be read to select any one SalesPersonId.

All density	Average Length	Columns
0.05555556	0.4838392	SalesPersonID
3.178134E-05	4.483839	SalesPersonID, SalesOrderID

The next result set has the interesting histogram data. This data is calculated at the same time that the statistics are updated, so pay attention to how current your statistics are for the best performance. The histogram is used when the predicates of your T-SQL statement are evaluated to predict row counts (partial results shown).

RANGE_HI_KEY	RANGE_ROWS	EQ_ROWS	DISTINCT_RANGE_ROWS	AVG_RANGE_ROWS
268	0	48	0	1
275	0	450	0	1
...				
288	0	16	0	1
289	0	130	0	1
290	0	109	0	1

This histrogram is easy to read. The RANGE_HI_KEY column contains actual values of the SalesPersonId column. The EQ_ROWS column counts the number of rows that contain this exact number of rows. The in-between column RANGE_ROWS is 0. This means that there are 0 rows containing values between 268 and 275 for SalesPersonId. There are also 0 distinctly different values and only 1 average value between 268 and 275. You can see a more range-based histogram if you look at the index for CustomerId.

```
RANGE_HI_KEY RANGE_ROWS      EQ_ROWS        DISTINCT_RANGE_ROWS
AVG_RANGE_ROWS
------------ -------------- -------------- -------------------- --------------
1            0              4              0                    1
19           119            1              16                   7.4375
54           190            12             31                   6.129032
75           103            12             18                   5.722222
126          288            11             47                   6.12766
...
(Partial Results Shown)
```

The interpretation of this histogram is that between the step for RANGE_HI_KEY values of 75 and 126 there are 288 rows. Eleven rows are exactly equal to the range key of 126. There are 47 distinct other values in the step, with about 6.12 rows per value. Sometimes after explaining this data, light bulbs go off. It can't be overstated how important this set of data is to the optimizer to determine how many pages are going to be needed and make guesses about how many rows will be filtered by the predicates provided.

Include Actual Execution Plan Misconception

There is a common misconception that the Include Actual Execution Plan menu option in the SSMS UI renders the cost estimates as actual cost numbers. That is incorrect. Cost estimates are still cost estimates — not actuals (see the section "Cost-Based Optimization"). What this option does is include effects of current server operations. Typically, the cost estimates are the same regardless of whether you select this menu option or the Display Estimated Execution Plan menu option. The only difference is that selecting the former will result in actually executing the plan and providing accurate row count numbers.

Use sp_helpindex to Examine Indexes

This system-stored procedure is essential if you are writing T-SQL queries. It allows you to see the indexes available on a table and the columns that make up that index. Figure 9-1 describes the indexes on Sales.SalesOrderDetail when this query is run:

```
sp_helpindex 'Sales.SalesOrderDetail'
```

	index_name	index_description	index_keys
1	AK_SalesOrderDetail_rowguid	nonclustered, unique located on PRIMARY	rowguid
2	IX_SalesOrderDetail_ProductID	nonclustered located on PRIMARY	ProductID
3	PK_SalesOrderDetail_SalesOrderID_SalesOrderDeta...	clustered, unique, primary key located on PRIMARY	SalesOrderID, SalesOrderDetailID

Figure 9-1

You should now have an understanding of the query optimizer's function, as well as the components it draws upon to fulfill its mission. Armed with that knowledge, you'll move on to gathering facts concerning those components. Finally, you'll use that information to formulate your own optimized query.

Middle Game: Gathering the Facts

At this point you need to gather information about the queries you need to tune. The major component of this involves generating and interpreting query plans. Once you've gathered the facts, and understand how SQL Server is handling the queries, you'll be able to move to the last stage — the end game.

Query Plans

Some DBAs start tuning an offending query by running the query through the Database Tuning Advisor. However, a better approach is to start by generating an execution plan. Once you've done that you should be able to find specific places to start.

There are two types of query plans you can generate. One is a graphical plan, and the other is text-based. Both types are useful.

Figure 9-2 is a typical graphical query plan. In order to generate this you can do this a couple of ways. The easiest is to press Ctrl-L in the Microsoft SQL Server Management Studio. Another option is to choose Display Estimated Query Plan from the Query menu option.

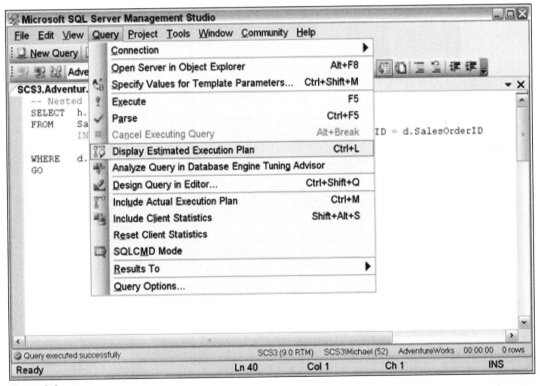

Figure 9-2

Finally, you can click the Include Actual Query Plan button on the toolbar (see Figure 9-3).

Figure 9-3

Figure 9-4 shows a typical query plan.

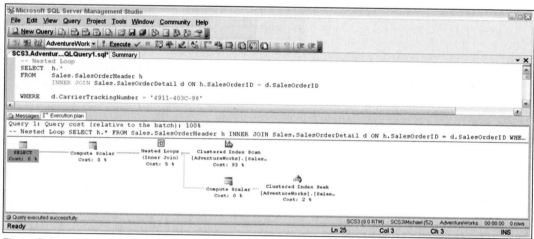

Figure 9-4

Note that execution plans cannot be generated for encrypted stored procedures, triggers, or if your stored procedure makes use of temporary tables.

Query Plan Essentials

Now that you've generated a plan, there is a lot to take in. First, know that graphical query plans are read right to left, and generally bottom to top. Thus, the top-left step is the last step in the plan.

Here are a few things to keep in mind when looking at a graphical plan:

❑ Each step in the plan will be indicated by an icon. These icons have very specific meanings. The following section contains the entire list of possible icons.

❑ Each step in the plan will receive a cost expressed as a percentage.

❑ The query plan will show an execution plan for every statement in the query pane. These plans will be listed sequentially in the result pane. Each plan will have a cost relative to the batch. This is expressed as a percentage.

❑ The steps are connected by arrows showing the order taken by the query when it was executed.

❑ Hovering the mouse over any of the steps shows a pop-up information box giving detailed information about the specific step.

❑ Hovering the mouse over any of the arrows shows a pop-up information box showing how many records are affected.

❑ The arrows that connect steps have different thicknesses. The thickness indicates the relative cost in the number and size of rows of the data moving between each step. Thicker arrows indicate more relative cost. This indicator is a quick gauge as to what is happening within the query plan. Thicker lines on the left side than the right can be an indicator of trouble. Either too many rows are being returned, or the query plan may not be optimal.

Typically, you may need to improve a stored procedure, which has multiple statements. Each statement will have a cost relative to the total. As you can imagine, a small group of SQL statements can generate an enormous execution plan. Therefore, you need to narrow down your analysis and focus on the most offensive portions of the batch of SQL statements. Therefore, start with the statement that has the highest relative cost. Next, each step in that plan has a cost associated with it. Again, find the step with the highest cost. You now have a very specific and narrow area to concentrate on.

Tables 9-2 through 9-6 show excerpts from Books Online (BOL). They show all the operators you might see in a query plan. Also listed are detailed information items that the operators may contain.

Table 9-2: Query Plan Operators

Icon	Operator	Icon	Operator
$\frac{A}{(B+C)}$	Arithmetic Expression (SQL Server 2000 Only)		Clustered Index Seek
	Assert		Clustered Index Update
	Bitmap		Collapse
	Bookmark Lookup		Compute Scalar
	Clustered Index Delete		Concatenation
	Clustered Index Insert		Constant Scan
	Clustered Index Scan		Delete (Database Engine)

Continued

Table 9-2: Query Plan Operators (continued)

Icon	Operator	Icon	Operator
	Deleted Scan		Inserted Scan
	Eager Spool		Iterator Catchall
	Filter (Database Engine)		Lazy Spool
	Hash Match		Log Row Scan
	Hash Match Root (SQL Server 2000 Only)		Merge Interval
	Hash Match Team (SQL Server 2000 Only)		Merge Join
	Nonclustered Index Delete		Nested Loops
	Nonclustered Index Insert		Online Index Insert
	Nonclustered Index Scan		Parameter Table Scan
	Nonclustered Index Seek		Remote Delete
	Nonclustered Index Spool		Remote Insert
	Nonclustered Index Update		Remote Query
	Insert (Database Engine)		Remote Scan

Table 9-2: Query Plan Operators (continued)

Icon	Operator	Icon	Operator
	Remote Update		Switch
	RID Lookup		Table Delete
	Row Count Spool		Table Insert
	Segment		Table Scan
	Sequence		Table Spool
	SequenceProject		Table Update
	Sort		Table-valued Function
	Split		Top
	Spool		UDX
	Stream Aggregate		Update (Database Engine)

Table 9-3 shows the various types of cursor operators.

Table 9-4 shows the various parallelism operators.

Table 9-5 shows the various T-SQL operators.

Table 9-6 provides detailed information about the operators shown in the previous tables. Each operator above will have specific information associated with it, although not all operators contain all the items listed. Furthermore, you can see this information by simply hovering the mouse cursor over the operator.

Table 9-3: Cursor Operators

Icon	Cursor Physical Operator	Icon	Cursor Physical Operator
	Cursor Catchall		Population Query
	Dynamic		Refresh Query
	Fetch Query		Snapshot
	Keyset		

Table 9-4: Parallelism Operators

Icon	Parallelism Physical Operator	Icon	Parallelism Physical Operator
	Distribute Streams		Gather Streams
	Repartition Streams		

Table 9-5: T-SQL Operators

Icon	Language Element	Icon	Language Element
A←B	Assign		Intrinsic
	Convert (Database Engine)	T-SQL	Language Element Catchall
A→	Declare		Result
	If		While

Table 9-6: Operator Details

ToolTip item	Description
Physical Operation	The physical operator used, such as Hash Join or Nested Loops. Physical operators displayed in red indicate that the query optimizer has issued a warning, such as missing column statistics or missing join predicates. This can cause the query optimizer to choose a less efficient query plan than otherwise expected. When the graphical execution plan suggests creating or updating statistics, or creating an index, the missing column statistics and indexes can be immediately created or updated using the shortcut menus in SQL Server Management Studio Object Explorer.
Logical Operation	The logical operator that matches the physical operator, such as the Inner Join operator. The logical operator is listed after the physical operator at the top of the ToolTip.
Estimated Row Size	The estimated size of the row produced by the operator (bytes).
Estimated I/O Cost	The estimated cost of all I/O activity for the operation. This value should be as low as possible.
Estimated CPU Cost	The estimated cost of all CPU activity for the operation.
Estimated Operator Cost	The cost to the query optimizer for executing this operation. The cost of this operation as a percentage of the total cost of the query is displayed in parentheses. Because the query engine selects the most efficient operation to perform the query or execute the statement, this value should be as low as possible.
Estimated Subtree Cost	The total cost to the query optimizer for executing this operation and all operations preceding it in the same subtree.
Estimated Number of Rows	The number of rows produced by the operator.

I'm not going to cover all the operators listed in these tables. However, the most common ones will be addressed. Those include the various join operators, spool operators, seek and scan operators, and lookup operators.

Join Operators

SQL Server employs three types of join strategies. The first is the Nested Loop Join Operator. Prior to SQL Server version 7, this was the only join operator available. The other two are known as *merge joins* and *hash joins*. When the query optimizer encounters a join it will evaluate all three join types and select the strategy with the lowest cost. Note that the tables to be joined are known as the join inputs.

In order to show the three types of join operators the following changes to the AdventureWorks database were made:

❑ The SalesOrderID column was removed from the primary key definition of Sales.SalesOrderDetail. This left only the SalesOrderDetailID as the primary key.

❑ A new index was created on Sales.SalesOrderDetail called IX_SalesOrder. This index included the SalesOrderID.

Nested Loop Joins

This is the default strategy for processing joins. SQL Server will evaluate this technique first. This works by taking a row from the first table, known as the *outer table*, and uses that row to scan the second table, known as the *inner table*. Be aware that this scan is not a table scan; it's usually done with an index. Furthermore, if no appropriate indexes are available in the inner table, a nested loop join won't typically be used. Instead a hash match join will be used. See Figure 9-5 for an example of a query plan with a nested loop join.

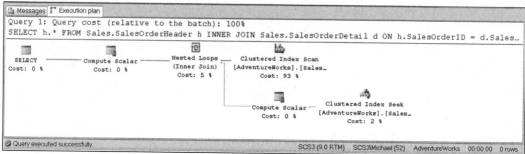

Figure 9-5

Using the AdventureWorks database with the previous changes, the following query will use a Nested Loop Join.

```
SELECT  h.*
FROM    Sales.SalesOrderHeader h
        INNER JOIN Sales.SalesOrderDetail d
ON h.SalesOrderID = d.SalesOrderID
WHERE   d.CarrierTrackingNumber = '4911-403C-98'
```

In this case the optimizer designated the SalesOrderDetail table as the outer table. The reason is that the where clause limits the SalesOrderDetail table to just a few rows. Thus, the optimizer determined that using a few rows to apply to the inner table, in this case SalesOrderHeader, will be the lowest cost.

This scenario is ideal for Nested Loop joins. However, this is also the fallback option for the optimizer. This means that if the other two join operators are unavailable then this option will be used. Sometimes this isn't desirable.

If the outer table contains a high number of rows, then this option performs poorly. This usually indicates that an index is needed on the inner table. If the inner table had an appropriate index, then the other two options would usually be a better option.

Note that the cost of a nested loop join is easily determined. Simply multiply the size of the outer table by the size of the inner table.

Merge Joins

A merge join will be used when the two join inputs are both sorted on the join column. The following query will use a Merge Join and the query plan is shown in Figure 9-6:

```
SELECT   h.*
FROM     Sales.SalesOrderHeader h
INNER JOIN Sales.SalesOrderDetail d WITH (INDEX(IX_SalesOrder))
  ON h.SalesOrderID = d.SalesOrderID
```

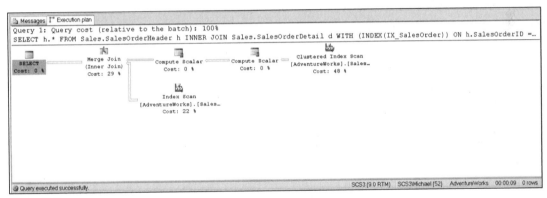

Figure 9-6

Note that the optimizer is forced to use a merge join by including the following table hint:

```
WITH (INDEX(IX_SalesOrder)).)
```

Essentially, a merge join works by taking two sorted lists and merging them into one. In this example, there are two stacks of sales information. The first stack contains header information about a sale such as the salesman, customer, and due date. The second stack contains the details of each sale, such as the product number and quantity. In this example, both stacks are sorted by SalesOrderID. The result is that each customer's sales include the details of the products purchased. Because both stacks are sorted by the same column, there only needs to be one pass through each stack.

The cost of a merge join can be calculated as the sum of the number of rows in the inputs. Thus, the fact that the cost of a merge join is the sum of the row counts of the inputs and not a product means that merge joins are usually a better choice for larger inputs.

The optimizer will generally choose a merge join when both join inputs are already sorted on the join column. Sometimes, even if a sort must be done on one of the input columns, the optimizer might decide to do that and follow up with a merge join, rather than use one of the other available join strategies.

Hash Joins

Hash joins are used when no useful index exists on the join column in either input. They're also used when one table is much smaller than the other. Also, hash joins work well when SQL Server must perform joins of very large tables. See Figure 9-7 for an example of a query plan with a hash join.

```
SELECT   *
FROM     Sales.SalesOrderHeader h
         INNER JOIN Sales.SalesOrderDetail d
ON h.SalesOrderID = d.SalesOrderID
```

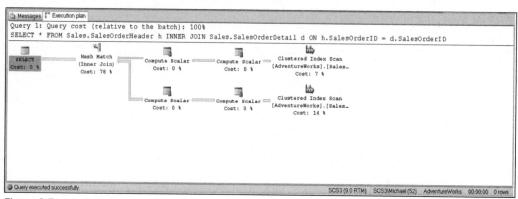

Figure 9-7

SQL Server performs hash joins by completing two phases. The first phase is known as the build phase, and the second phase is known as the probe phase.

In the build phase all rows from the first input, known as the build input, are used to build a structure known as a hash table. This hash table will be built using a hashing function based on the equijoin columns. The hash table will contain some number of buckets in which data can be placed. Also, note that the hash table is created in memory if possible. In fact, SQL Server stores these buckets as linked lists. The key to an effective hash table is using a hashing function that will divide the data in sets of manageable size with roughly equal membership. Also note that SQL Server will attempt to use the smaller of the two query inputs as the basis for the build phase.

After the hash table is built, the second phase can begin. This is the probe phase. It works by taking one row at a time and trying to find a match in the hash table. If a match is found, then it is output.

A simple example will help illustrate the concepts of a hash join. Using the Production.Product-Category and Production.ProductSubcategory tables in the AdventureWorks database, consider the following query:

```
SELECT  pc.Name as Category,
        ps.Name as Subcategory
FROM    Production.ProductCategory pc
INNER JOIN Production.ProductSubcategory ps
ON pc.ProductCategoryID = ps.ProductCategoryID
OPTION (HASH JOIN)
```

Since Production.ProductCategory is the smaller input, it will be used for the build phase. Thus, a hash table as shown in Table 9-7 may be generated.

Table 9-7: Hash Table

0	→	2 Components	4 Accessories
1	→	1 Bikes	3 Clothing

Now that the build phase is complete, the probe phase can begin. SQL Server will compute the hash values on the probe input's equijoin columns using the same hash function that was used in the build phase. SQL Server will then check the appropriate hash bucket to see if there are any matches. If it finds a match, then that will be output.

The pseudo code for the hash operation applied to our example is:

```
for each row in the Production.ProductCategory table (build input)
   begin
         calculate hash value on
 Production.ProductCategory.ProductCategoryID
         insert ProductCategory.Name and ProductCategory.ProductCategoryID
         into the appropriate hash bucket
   end

   for each row in the Production.ProductSubcategory table (probe input)
   begin
         calculate hash value on
         Production.ProductSubcategory.ProductCategoryID
         for each row in the corresponding hash bucket
             if node in the hash bucket joins with the probe input row on
         the key columns then output the contents of the hash node and
         the probe columns
   end
```

As you've probably determined by now, hash joins are the most intensive of the three join types. There are several issues concerning hash joins. First, the build process is a blocking process. The build phase has to completely finish before any rows can be returned. Second is the hash function. SQL Server uses hash functions that are considerably more complex that the example here. Coming up with a good hash function is both science and art (and prayer doesn't hurt either). The hash function must divvy up the build input into evenly distributed hash buckets. This is easier said than done. Another issue is using the smaller input for the build phase. Sometimes SQL Server will choose a build input that turns out to be the larger input. When this occurs SQL Server will switch the roles of the build and probe inputs in a process called role reversal. Also, if the hash table is too big to fit into memory it will be spooled to tempdb in partitions. The partitions will then be pulled into memory when needed. This significantly increases the amount of I/O and CPU usage.

Thoughts on Join Types

Before SQL Server version 7, the only type of join was the nested loop join. At that time this was adequate for most database designs. OLTP type databases dominated the landscape. The record-to-record navigation needed was well served by this technique.

As decision support systems became more and more prevalent, additional join techniques were warranted. Another issue is indexing. As systems became more complex, creating effective indexes for a given query workload became impossibly difficult. Thus, adding different join techniques to SQL Server became necessary.

Merge joins were the first logical step. This technique provides better performance for larger join inputs.

Finally, hash joins were added. They can support very large join inputs. However, it does come at a price. The requirements for CPU, memory, and possibly disk make hash joins resource intensive. So, given the resource requirements for hash joins, it seems reasonable to ask how they can ever be worth it. Interestingly, Microsoft has done some testing to answer this question. They learned that for large join inputs, merge joins average about 40 percent slower than hash joins. The reason has to do with indexes. If there are very few indexes in the database or the indexes don't serve a particular query, then hash join often works well. In fact, hash join can be thought of as an in-memory, on-demand index.

Spool Operators

Spool operators in a query plan are there to temporarily retain intermediate results of a complex query. For example, large subqueries or remote scans such as querying a linked server. The spool operator takes the rows produced by its previous operators and stores them in a table in tempdb. This table only exists for the lifetime of the query.

There are a couple of concepts to know about when it comes to spool operators. First, spool operators usually sit between two other operators. The operator on the left of the spool operator is the *parent* operator and the operator on the right is the *child* operator.

The other concepts are rewind and rebind. A *rewind* means that the result set from the child operator can be reused by the parent operator. A *rebind* means that the result set from the child operator cannot be reused by the parent operator. Therefore, the result set from child operator has to be reevaluated and the tempdb table has to be rebuilt.

Finally, there is the concept of physical versus logical operators. All operators, not just spool operators, are classified as logical or physical operators.

A logical operator is a conceptual mechanism for describing a query processing operation. An example of this is an INNER JOIN.

A physical operator actually implements the logical operator using some actual method or technique. A Nested Loop Join is a physical operator, which implements the logical operator INNER JOIN.

Spool operators can be either logical or physical. The following is a list of physical spool operators:

❑ **Table Spool:** The table spool operator scans the input (from the child operator) and places a copy of each row in a table in tempdb. The entire input from the child operator is written into the tempdb table before proceeding. If the parent operator is rewound, such as a Nested Loop operator, and no rebinding is needed, the spool table can be used with no further processing.

❑ **Non-clustered Index Spool:** The Index Spool operator scans its input rows (from the child operator) and places a copy of each row in a table in tempdb. The entire input from the child operator is written into the tempdb table before proceeding. It then builds a non-clustered index on the rows. This allows the system to use the seeking capability of indexes. If the parent operator is rewound, such as a Nested Loop operator, and no rebinding is needed, the spool table can be used with no further processing.

❑ **Row Count Spool:** The Row Count Spool operator scans its input rows (from the child operator), and counts the rows. The rows are also returned without any data in them. This is useful when checking for the existence of rows, rather than the data itself. For example, a query may include an EXISTS or NOT EXISTS predicate. Thus, the content of the data isn't important, only the fact that a row does or does not exist.

The following is a list of logical spool operators:

❑ **Eager Spool:** The Eager Spool operator scans its input rows (from the child operator), and places a copy of each row in a table in tempdb. The entire input from the child operator is written into the tempdb table before proceeding. If the parent operator is rewound, such as a Nested Loop operator, and no rebinding is needed, the spool table can be used with no further processing. If rebinding is needed, the spooled table is thrown away and the spool table is rebuilt by rescanning the input (from the child operator).

❑ When the eager spool's parent operator asks for the first row, the spool operator builds its spool table by writing all the rows from the input (from the child operator).

❑ **Lazy Spool:** The Lazy Spool operator builds its spool table in an "as requested" manner. That is, each time the spool's parent operator asks for a row, the spool operator gets a row from its input operator and stores it in the spool table. This is different from the eager spool, which must gather all the rows from the input operator before proceeding.

Sometimes, spooling intermediate results to tempdb is cheaper than retrieving all of the rows from the child operators. Spools can provide a lot of benefit, especially when processing a complex query is necessary. However, they can also generate performance robbing I/O while they manage the tempdb table. For example, an eager spool, which has to be repeatedly reprocessed because of rebinding, can be particularly nasty.

When you have a spool operator in a query plan that you think is causing a bottleneck, you have a couple of options. First, try rewriting the query such that spools aren't necessary. Another option is to try and perform the spool operation yourself. Sometimes creating and populating your own tempdb will perform better than letting SQL Server do it. You'll have more control over indexing and ordering. Also, if you're tuning a stored procedure, which generates the same spool operator for multiple queries, you would definitely be better off creating the tempdb table once, rather than allowing SQL Server to create the same table over and over. Another idea is to see if creating a table variable to hold the intermediate results would help. For smaller result sets, the table variable may be a better option because the data won't have to be physically saved to disk. This would save on I/O activity. Finally, for queries that must spool (and you're likely to have some, if not several) make sure you have adequate tempdb space and also ensure that the tempdb is properly designed from a hardware and performance perspective.

Seek and Scan Operators

The next group of operators to discuss are seek and scan operators. These two operators apply to both clustered and non-clustered indexes. However, only the scan operator applies to tables.

These operators provide the mechanism that SQL Server employs to read data from tables and indexes. The difference between scans and seeks is that scans return the entire table or index, whereas seeks return rows using an index and a filter predicate. Consider the following query for the AdventureWorks database:

```
SELECT   *
FROM     Sales.SalesOrderDetail sod
WHERE    ProductID = 870
```

Scan

With a scan, *all* rows in the SalesOrderDetail table are read. Each one is then evaluated based on the where clause "where ProductID=870". If the evaluation is true then the row is returned. Because scans examine every row in the table, whether it qualifies or not, the cost is relative to the total number of rows. Therefore, a scan is effective if the table is small or a large percentage of rows qualify for the evaluation. Conversely, if the table is large and most of the rows don't qualify, then a scan is not a good option.

Seek

In the example, there's an index on the ProductID column. Thus, in many cases a seek operation will be a better plan. A seek will use the index to go directly to the rows that evaluate to true in the where clause. A seek only retrieves rows that qualify. Thus, the cost is proportional to the number of qualifying rows (actually pages) with the total number of pages. A seek is usually more efficient if the WHERE clause is highly selective. This will effectively eliminate a large portion of the table.

Table Scan

Table Scan is a logical and physical operator. Table Scan operator works against a table. All rows are evaluated against the WHERE clause (if there is one). Any matching rows will be output. Contrary to popular rumor, table scans aren't always bad. If the table is small, say less than 64 data pages, SQL Server can scan the table just as quickly as using an index. Queries that aren't executed very often may be better off using table scans. The frequently incurred cost of an update, insert, or delete may ultimately be more expensive than allowing a seldom-run query to utilize a table scan. Also, no matter how large the table, if the query retrieves a significant percentage (anything above about 25 percent for SQL Server) of the table, that, too, makes table scans appropriate.

Index Scan

Index Scan is a logical and physical operator. The Index Scan operator works against a non-clustered index. Just like the table scan, it retrieves all rows, except this time it from a non-clustered index. If a WHERE clause is present then each row is evaluated based on the WHERE clause. All evaluations returning true will allow the row to be returned.

Index Seek

Index Seek is a logical and physical operator. The Index Seek operator uses the power of indexes to retrieve rows. SQL Server uses the index to choose only those rows that match the specified predicate. Unlike the Index Scan, not all the rows in the index need to be evaluated. Only the rows that match the search predicate are chosen. Those matches are then outputted.

Clustered Index Scan

Clustered Index Scan is a logical and physical operator. The Clustered Index Scan operator works against the clustered index of a table. Just like the table scan, it retrieves all rows, except this time it retrieves the rows from the clustered index. If a WHERE clause is present then each row is evaluated based on the WHERE clause.
All evaluations returning true will allow the row to be returned.

Clustered Index Seek

Clustered Index Seek is a logical and physical operator. The Clustered Index Seek operator uses the power of indexes to retrieve rows. SQL Server uses the index to choose only those rows that match the specified predicate. Unlike the Clustered Index Scan, not all the rows in the index need to be evaluated. Only the rows that match the search predicate are chosen. Those matches are then output.

Lookup Operators

A lookup operator performs the task of locating a row of data in the data pages.

Bookmark Lookup (2000 Only)

Bookmark Lookup is no longer supported in SQL Server 2005. Instead, for heap tables, the RID Lookup has taken its place. For clustered tables this is replaced by a clustered index seek that includes a lookup operation.

RID Lookup

RID Lookup is a physical operator. RID Lookup is a lookup on a heap table only. It does not apply if the table has a clustered index. This operator actually looks up the rows in a table's data pages by using a row identifier. This can be an expensive operation. The reason is that iterating through the input will force the lookup to perform random I/O operations. These are expensive because more physical interaction between the hard drives and SQL Server has to occur.

Interpreting a Query Plan

Now that the highlights of the graphical plan have been described, you should be well equipped to start using this information to interpret plans.

First, look at the join types, and make sure the right join type has been chosen. For example, nested loop joins work best when uniting two relatively small inputs. If you see a nested loop join operating against two large inputs, then something's wrong. Try creating indexes that will prompt the optimizer to choose another join type. You could also force the query to use a specific join type, but only when you're *sure* it's the right thing to do.

Second, in a graphical plan, arrows have different thicknesses to indicate the number of rows returned. Also recall that graphical plans are read from right to left. Therefore, in most cases, moving from right to left, the arrow thickness should lessen. However, if you notice an arrow near the left that is very thick, and the previous arrows where not as thick, that's a visual indicator that your query may be sub-optimal. As you move toward the end of the query the arrows should diminish in thickness. If you notice that the opposite has happened, or that the arrow sizes were trending then suddenly one arrow is noticeably thick that may indicate a problem.

Also, look for scans, spools (especially a rebinding eager spool), and RID lookups. All these operations can cause some major degradation due to excessive I/O. Try rewriting the query to minimize these operators. You may also be able to create some indexes that would cause some of these operators to not be used.

Other Query Plan Display Modes

Another option for displaying query execution plans is through the use of T-SQL SET SHOWPLAN statements. The various SHOWPLAN statements are described below. However, note that when using some of these statements the queries submitted aren't actually executed. This can be an issue if the queries you want to analyze contain temp tables that are created in an initial statement, then referenced later in subsequent statements. SQL Server analyzes the query and returns the results of that analysis.

Set Showplan_XML

When this option is enabled SQL Server returns then plan information for a query in a well-formed XML document. Consider the following query for the AdventureWorks database:

```
SELECT ProductID FROM Sales.SalesOrderDetail
```

When using SHOWPLAN_XML, the following output is generated. As you can see, the simplest query will generate a fairly large XML plan.

```
<ShowPlanXML xmlns="http://schemas.microsoft.com/sqlserver/2004/07/
    showplan" Version="1.0"
Build="9.00.1406.00">
  <BatchSequence>
    <Batch>
      <Statements>
        <StmtSimple StatementText="SELECT&#x9;ProductID FROM&#x9;Sales
          .SalesOrderDetail &#xD;&#xA;" StatementId="1" StatementCompId="1"
          StatementType="SELECT" StatementSubTreeCost="0.303397"
          StatementEstRows="121317" StatementOptmLevel="TRIVIAL">
          <StatementSetOptions QUOTED_IDENTIFIER="false" ARITHABORT="true"
            CONCAT_NULL_YIELDS_NULL="false" ANSI_NULLS="false" ANSI_PADDING="false"
            ANSI_WARNINGS="false" NUMERIC_ROUNDABORT="false" />
```

```
<QueryPlan CachedPlanSize="9">
  <RelOp NodeId="0" PhysicalOp="Index Scan" LogicalOp="Index Scan"
      EstimateRows="121317" EstimateIO="0.169792" EstimateCPU="0.133606"
      AvgRowSize="11" EstimatedTotalSubtreeCost="0.303397" Parallel="0"
      EstimateRebinds="0" EstimateRewinds="0">
    <OutputList>
      <ColumnReference Database="[AdventureWorks]" Schema="[Sales]"
          Table="[SalesOrderDetail]" Column="ProductID" />
    </OutputList>
    <IndexScan Ordered="0" ForcedIndex="0" NoExpandHint="0">
      <DefinedValues>
        <DefinedValue>
          <ColumnReference Database="[AdventureWorks]" Schema="[Sales]"
              Table="[SalesOrderDetail]" Column="ProductID" />
        </DefinedValue>
      </DefinedValues>
      <Object Database="[AdventureWorks]" Schema="[Sales]"
          Table="[SalesOrderDetail]" Index="[IX_SalesOrderDetail
          _ProductID]" />
    </IndexScan>
  </RelOp>
</QueryPlan>
</StmtSimple>
</Statements>
</Batch>
</BatchSequence>
</ShowPlanXML>
```

Showplan_Text

When this option is enabled, it returns the operation for each step in the query. The previous query will yield the following output:

```
|--Index Scan(OBJECT:([AdventureWorks].[Sales].[SalesOrderDetail]
   .[IX_SalesOrderDetail_ProductID]))
```

Note that this only shows the operation of each step. In order to get more information use the SHOWPLAN_ALL option.

Showplan_All

In addition to the operation step that SHOWPLAN_TEXT produces, this option also produces additional columns, such as Estimated IO, Estimated CPU, and Estimated Rowcount. The results of this are too large to include in this text. However, the results from this are easily copied into Excel. There you sum up the EstimatedIO and EstimatedCPU to quickly see which seems to be problematic. Also, you can easily sort the results to find the operation that is taking the most I/O or CPU.

Statistics XML

When this option is enabled SQL Server returns the plan information for a query in a well-formed XML document. The difference between this option and SHOWPLAN_XML is that this option actually executes the statements. Using our previous example, the following results are generated when this option is enabled.

```
<ShowPlanXML xmlns="http://schemas.microsoft.com/sqlserver/2004/07/showplan"
    Version="1.0" Build="9.00.1406.00">
  <BatchSequence>
    <Batch>
      <Statements>
        <StmtSimple StatementText="SELECT&#x9;ProductID FROM&#x9;Sales
          .SalesOrderDetail &#xD;&#xA;" StatementId="1" StatementCompId="1"
          StatementType="SELECT" StatementSubTreeCost="0.303397"
          StatementEstRows="121317" StatementOptmLevel="TRIVIAL">
          <StatementSetOptions QUOTED_IDENTIFIER="false" ARITHABORT="true"
            CONCAT_NULL_YIELDS_NULL="false" ANSI_NULLS="false" ANSI_PADDING="false"
            ANSI_WARNINGS="false" NUMERIC_ROUNDABORT="false" />
          <QueryPlan DegreeOfParallelism="0" CachedPlanSize="9">
            <RelOp NodeId="0" PhysicalOp="Index Scan" LogicalOp="Index Scan"
              EstimateRows="121317" EstimateIO="0.169792" EstimateCPU="0.133606"
              AvgRowSize="11" EstimatedTotalSubtreeCost="0.303397" Parallel="0"
              EstimateRebinds="0" EstimateRewinds="0">
              <OutputList>
                <ColumnReference Database="[AdventureWorks]" Schema="[Sales]"
                  Table="[SalesOrderDetail]" Column="ProductID" />
              </OutputList>
              <RunTimeInformation>
                <RunTimeCountersPerThread Thread="0" ActualRows="121317"
                  ActualEndOfScans="1" ActualExecutions="1" />
              </RunTimeInformation>
              <IndexScan Ordered="0" ForcedIndex="0" NoExpandHint="0">
                <DefinedValues>
                  <DefinedValue>
                    <ColumnReference Database="[AdventureWorks]" Schema="[Sales]"
                      Table="[SalesOrderDetail]" Column="ProductID" />
                  </DefinedValue>
                </DefinedValues>
                <Object Database="[AdventureWorks]" Schema="[Sales]"
                  Table="[SalesOrderDetail]" Index="[IX_SalesOrderDetail
                  _ProductID]" />
              </IndexScan>
            </RelOp>
          </QueryPlan>
        </StmtSimple>
      </Statements>
    </Batch>
  </BatchSequence>
</ShowPlanXML>
```

Note that this result includes a section called RunTimeInformation. This section gives details about the actual execution of the query.

Statistics Profile

When this option is enabled, SQL Server returns the same results as it does when using SHOWPLAN_ALL. However, there are a couple of differences. First, this option will actually execute the statements. Second, the results will include columns Rows and Executes. The Rows column gives the actual (not an estimate) number of rows produced by the step. The Executes column gives the number of times the step was executed.

Statistics IO

When this option is enabled, SQL Server shows the disk activity that is generated by queries. The queries are executed, and the results are generated. However, at the end of the results is a message that includes information about the disk access. The previous example query will include this message when this option is turned on.

```
Table 'SalesOrderDetail'. Scan count 1, logical reads 1238, physical reads 3, read-
ahead reads 1234, lob logical reads 0, lob physical reads 0, lob read-ahead reads 0.
```

Most of these are self-explanatory. However, a few need further explanation:

- ❑ **Read-ahead reads:** Number of pages placed into the cache.
- ❑ **LOB logical reads:** Number of large object types, such as text, image, or varchar(max) pages read from the data cache.
- ❑ **LOB physical reads:** Number of large object types, such as text, image, or varchar(max) pages read from the disk.
- ❑ **LOB read-ahead:** Number of large object types, such as text, image, or varchar(max) pages placed into the cache.

Statistics Time

When this option is enabled, SQL Server shows the time used to parse, compile, and execute the queries. The queries are executed and the results are generated. The previous example query will include this message when this option is turned on:

```
SQL Server parse and compile time:
    CPU time = 30 ms, elapsed time = 666 ms.

(121317 row(s) affected)

SQL Server Execution Times:
    CPU time = 50 ms,  elapsed time = 1855 ms.
```

Note that these last two options, STATISTICS TIME and STATISTICS IO, can both be enabled at the same time. This allows you to get both I/O and time statistics. The other options can only be used by themselves. They cannot be combined with one another.

Best Practice: Using SHOWPLAN

In many ways the results that you can get from the SHOWPLAN options are more useful than what you get from the graphical plan. Operator steps from SHOWPLAN are easier to read with better detail than when hovering over the same step in the graphical plan. The ability to easily put the SHOWPLAN results into an Excel spreadsheet is very handy. Putting the results into an Excel spreadsheet will give you the capability to quickly summarize and sort on expensive operations in your query. This lets you quickly analyze and focus in on a very specific portion of the query.

Retrieving a Query Plan from a Plan Cache

In SQL Server 2005, you have the ability to retrieve plans from SQL Server's plan cache. Using DMVs and functions, you can actually retrieve a plan that was used by SQL Server. This query will retrieve all the SQL statements and query plans you might want to troubleshoot.

```
Select  st.text, qp.query_plan
From    sys.dm_exec_query_stats qs
 cross apply sys.dm_exec_sql_text(qs.sql_handle) st
 cross apply sys.dm_exec_query_plan(qs.plan_handle) qp
```

The Text column is the SQL statement, and the query_plan column is an XML representation of the plan, just like it was generated from SHOWPLAN_XML. Next, save the query_plan column in a file with an extension of .sqlplan. You can now use SQL Server Management Studio and open the file. You will see a graphical plan!

This is very useful because you can get a plan that was actually used by SQL Server to execute the query. Many times you'll be tasked with troubleshooting a query that has sporadic performance problems. This is especially true if you have stored procedures that accept parameters and in turn use the parameters as filters on a select statement. When SQL Server generated a plan for this procedure it may not have created a plan that works well with all parameter values. Therefore, sometimes the procedure will run fine, and other times it won't. By retrieving the plan from cache, you'll be able find out what SQL Server actually did.

With the plan handle, you can examine the graphical query execution plan, the T-SQL text, or certain attributes about the plan. Table 9-8 describes the different TVFs you'll need for interpretation of these plans.

You'll need VIEW SERVER STATE permission to use these functions and DMVs.

Table 9-8: DMV List for Retrieving a Plan from the Plan Cache

Command	Returns Cached Plan
sys.dm_exec_query_plan	XML Showplan information
Sys.dm_exec_sql_text	T-SQL statement
Sys.dm_exec_plan_attributes	Set of Code-Value pairs containing cached counters and values.

Another great place to look at performance related to cached plans is in the sys.dm_exec_query_stats DMV. The result set returned from this DMV contains counters for worker thread time, all I/O activity, common language runtime counters, and general time counters. You can use this query to monitor all of this in one shot and translate the plan_handle and sql_handle values.

```
SELECT qplan.Query_Plan, stext.Text, qstats.*, plns.*
FROM sys.dm_exec_cached_plans plns
JOIN sys.dm_exec_query_stats as qstats
```

```
ON plns.plan_handle = qstats.plan_handle
CROSS APPLY sys.dm_exec_query_plan(qstats.plan_handle) as qplan
CROSS APPLY sys.dm_exec_sql_text(qstats.plan_handle) as stext
WHERE qplan.query_plan is not null
```

Buffer Pool

SQL Server 2005 has a pool of memory known as the buffer pool. All the memory components utilized by SQL Server are drawn from this pool. SQL Server utilizes something called the Memory Broker, which manages these components. The Memory Broker works by monitoring the behavior of each memory component. This information is then communicated to the individual components, which they can use to adapt their own memory usage.

When SQL Server starts up it computes the size of the virtual address space (VAS). This size depends on the server type (32 or 64 bit) and the OS (again, 32- or 64-bit based). Note that this is not dependent on the amount of physical memory installed.

One recommendation concerning tuning is to use a 64-bit solution. Memory management is much easier using the 64-bit architecture, for both the DBA and SQL Server (the humans and non-humans). It's easier for the DBA because special startup flags and memory options, such as AWE, don't have to be used. (Note, however, that with a 64-bit setup, the AWE can be used for creating a non-paged pool.) It's easier for SQL Server because there's so much more allowable virtual address space.

Even though there are several memory components, the two most concerned with performance are the procedure cache and data cache. No doubt you've deduced that SQL Server has to perform a delicate balancing act in order to provide adequate memory resources for both. The procedure cache holds all the query plans that SQL Server has generated through its optimization process. The data cache contains the latest data that SQL Server has read or written. It's easy to understand the dilemma that SQL Server must address. Generating optimized query plans is not a trivial task. Therefore, once a plan has been created, SQL Server will attempt to hang onto it as long as possible. Likewise, retrieving (or writing) data from a hard drive is tremendously expensive. Again, once SQL Server retrieves a piece of data, the server will try to hang onto that as long as possible too.

Data Cache

The data cache usually occupies the largest amount of memory. It's also very volatile. You can think of the page in the data cache as an in-memory, mirror image of a data page stored on disk. As a data page is read or written it must first be brought into the data cache. Once the page is in memory the operation can proceed. As you can imagine, SQL Server's data cache can fill up pretty quickly even for moderately active database applications.

In-Memory Data Pages

In order to expedite accessing the data pages in the data cache, SQL Server organizes the pages in a hash table structure. Recall from the discussion about join types that a hash structure requires a hashing function in order to define a logical way to create groups. For the data cache, SQL Server uses the page identifier as the basis for the hash function. You should also recall that a hash structure is like an on-demand index. The hash structure allows SQL Server to find a specific page in cache with just a few reads of memory. Likewise, SQL Server will just as easily determine that a specified page is not in the data cache, and therefore must be read from disk.

Freeing the Pages in a Data Cache

One obvious requirement before reading a page from disk into the data cache is that there has to be memory available in the data cache to support the read. If there aren't any free pages, the read operation will have nowhere to place the incoming data page. One option for performing this task would be to search the data cache for a "freeable" page every time an operation needed to put something into the data cache. This approach would perform very poorly. Instead, SQL Server strives to keep a supply of free pages ready for use. Thus, when an operation needs a data page, it can simply grab one from the set of free cache pages.

A data page that has been placed in the data cache also contains some housekeeping information. That information includes information about when the page was last accessed as well as some other information. The page replacement policy, whose job it is to determine which pages can be freed, will utilize that knowledge by using a technique known as LRU-K. This technique will examine both the last time and how often a page has been accessed, and determine if the page can be freed.

If the page can't be freed, it simply remains in the data cache. Likewise, if the page can be freed, it is written to disk if it's dirty (the page in memory has changed since it was read in from disk), removed from the hash table, and put on the list of free cache pages.

Using the technique will naturally keep valuable (highly referenced) pages in the data cache while returning insignificant pages to the free list.

> *Previous versions of SQL Server allowed the ability to mark a table so that its pages would never be freed. Therefore, the pages would remain in the data cache permanently. This is known as pinning the table. However, that option is no longer available in SQL Server 2005. Microsoft believes that the cache management is sophisticated enough to make pinning obsolete.*

The work of applying this technique falls to three operations. Primarily it's applied by the various user threads. It's also applied by the lazywriter and checkpoint operations as well.

❑ **Lazywriter:** The lazywriter process periodically examines the size of the free list. If the list is below a certain threshold, depending on the size of the data cache, lazywriter traverses the data cache and updates the free list. Any dirty pages are written to disk and then they're added to the free list.

❑ **User process:** A user process performs this function when it needs to read a page from disk into the data cache. It operates in a similar manner as the lazywriter process. Once the operation begins, the free list is checked to determine if it's too small. Be aware that this user process has consumed cache pages from the free list for its own read.

❑ **Checkpoint:** The checkpoint process also periodically examines the data cache searching for "freeable" data pages. However, unlike the lazywriter and user processes, the checkpoint process will never put data pages back on the free list.

Monitoring the Data Cache

A useful indicator concerning the performance of the data cache is the Buffer Cache Hit Ratio performance counter. It indicates the percentage of data pages found in the data cache as opposed to reading them from disk. A value of 90 percent or greater is considered ideal. A value of 90 percent means that pages were found in the data cache 90 percent of the time, whereas 10 percent of the pages had to be read from disk first. A value consistently below 90 percent indicates a need to add more physical memory.

Best Practice: Managing the Data Cache

Managing the data cache is not trivial. Therefore, one of your goals for tuning queries is making sure the queries are making optimal use of the data cache. Since you can't directly control the data cache, you'll have to take indirect steps in order to influence the data cache. This means using 64-bit architecture over 32-bit. Also, as stated in the previous chapter, designing pages with the highest row density possible will also affect the data cache. Also consider that you have a huge advantage over SQL Server's ability to optimize. SQL Server only controls bringing the data pages in and out of the data cache. It doesn't have the ability to infer future behavior of the cache, but you do. You have the ability to understand the use of the database over a period of time. Thus, coaxing the data cache to operate desirably can only be done using a human perspective.

Procedure Cache

By now you should be familiar with query plans. Not surprisingly, those plans are kept in memory. This memory component is the procedure, or plan, cache. Like the data cache, understanding how the procedure cache is managed will help you tune and troubleshoot queries.

Internally, SQL Server divides a plan into two parts. The first part is the query plan itself. The query plan is a read-only data structure used by any number of users. No user context, such as SET options or variable values, is stored here. The second part is the execution context. Here is where the user's specific data is kept.

Internal Storage

Procedure cache is known as a *cache store*. Cache stores use hash tables to manage their content. A single cache store can have more than one hash table structure. This is handy for supporting different lookup types. The procedure cache uses this aspect to look up plans by ID name.

In-Memory Plans

When any statement is executed in SQL Server, the procedure cache is searched to find an existing plan for the same statement. If an existing plan is found, SQL Server will reuse it, thus saving the work of recompiling the statement. If no existing plan is found then SQL Server will generate one.

Note that in order for this approach to be useful, the cost of searching for an existing plan has to be less than the cost of generating a plan. Fortunately, the search technique SQL Server employs is extremely efficient and inexpensive.

Zero Cost Plans

If the cost of generating a plan is very low, it will not be cached at all. These are known as *zero cost plans*. The cost of storing and searching for these plans is greater than simply generating the plan every time.

Freeing the Procedure Cache

After a query plan is generated, it stays in the procedure cache. However, just as with data pages in the data cache, query plans have to be freed up as well. For this task SQL Server uses a different technique than the one employed for cleaning up the data cache. For the procedure cache SQL Server uses an LRU technique. Each query plan and execution context has a cost and age factor. Every time a query plan or execution context is referenced the age field is incremented by the cost factor. Thus, if a query plan had a cost factor of 5 and was referenced 2 times the age factor would be 10.

The work of applying this technique falls only to the lazywriter process for the procedure cache. The process is much like the one for the data cache operation. The lazywriter process periodically scans the list of plans and execution contexts in the procedure cache. The process then decrements the age by 1 for each object scanned. Thus, once an object's age reaches 0 it is removed from the procedure cache. Note that a plan may be removed from the cache before its age reaches 0 if there is sufficient pressure on memory or if the plan isn't referenced by any connections.

Recompiling Query Plans

One aspect about query plans is that they can become ineffective through no fault of their own. Changes to the underlying tables used in a query can cause an existing query plan to become inefficient or invalid. For example, suppose a query plan uses a table scan operator to fulfill a SQL statement. A DBA then adds an index to the table. The optimal operator now might be an index seek, not a table scan. When these changes occur SQL Server attempts to determine if the changes will invalidate an existing plan. If so, it marks the plan as invalid. This, in turn, causes a new plan to be generated for the query. The conditions that cause a plan to be invalidated include the following:

❑   Structural (DDL) changes made to a table or view referenced by the query (for example, adding a column).

❑   Changing or dropping any indexes used by the query plan.

❑   Updated statistics. If statistics are updated either explicitly or automatically, then that may invalidate existing query plans.

❑   Explicitly recompiling a query.

❑   Significantly changing the key values in the tables.

❑   A table with triggers that experience a significant growth in the number of rows in the inserted or deleted tables.

In previous versions of SQL Server, whenever a SQL statement in a group of statements caused recompiling, all the statements in the group get recompiled. Stored procedures, for instance, commonly include a group of SQL statements rather than just one. Since SQL Server 2005, only the SQL statements in the group that caused recompiling is actually recompiled. The other SQL statements in the group are unaffected.

This type of statement-level recompiling enhances performance because only the changed queries cause SQL Server to generate a new plan. Yet, in previous versions all the statements in the group got recompiled whether they needed it or not.

Best Practices: Monitoring the Procedure Cache

An important indicator of the performance of the procedure cache is the Procedure Cache Hit Ratio performance counter. It indicates the percentage of execution plan pages found in memory as opposed to disk.

Just as with the data cache, SQL Server can expend a great amount of resources managing the procedure cache. Fortunately, more direct control over this is available than with the data cache. Following are a few techniques you can employ to get the most out of the procedure cache.

Parameterize queries in applications: If an application repeatedly executes the same queries and only literal values change from one execution to the next, then rewrite the code to use parameters with the query. For example, suppose an application executed the following statements:

```
Select * from Person.Contact where ModifiedDate = '2007-05-25' and LastName =
'Jones'

Select * from Person.Contact where ModifiedDate = '2007-04-01' and LastName =
'Smith'
```

This technique can lead to multiple query plans generated for what is essentially the same query. However, if you parameterize the query:

```
Select * from Person.Contact where ModifiedDate = @ChangeDate and LastName =
@Lname
```

You can now simply create parameters in the application code. Be sure to include all pertinent information about the parameters, such as datatype and length. Once that's done the code can repeatedly bind new values into the parameters and execute the command. The result will be only one query plan is generated. One thing to note here is that this applies to all queries in a group, or batch. If the example included multiple queries in a batch, then all the queries would need to be parameterized. See the section "Plan Caching Issues" for more information concerning parameterized queries.

Use fully qualified names: This is helpful because it negates the need to look up the default schema for the current user. It also means that a plan can be used by multiple users. So, a query such as:

```
Select * from ErrorLog
```

Should be rewritten as:

```
Select * from dbo.ErrorLog
```

Use remote procedure calls (RPC) events over language events: The easiest way to explain this is by giving a description of what these are, using ADO.NET. An ADO.NET command object whose CommandType is table or text will generate a language event call to the database. However, if the CommandType is procedure then the call is generated as an RPC call to the database.

An RPC call promotes more plan reuse by explicitly parameterizing a query. Also, calling a stored procedure using RPC can save execution time and CPU resource

(Continued)

(Continued)
utilization required for plan generation by causing the generation to occur only once, when the stored procedure is first run.

Carefully naming your database objects: Name your tables, functions, and procedures with the following rules in mind. Procedures should not be named with the prefix `"sp_`. Functions should not be named with the prefix `fn_`. Tables should not be named with the prefix sys. The reason is that objects beginning with these names are assumed to be in the master database. Thus, suppose you have a table named sysevent in a local database. Further assume you have a query that references that table. Without a fully qualified reference in the query, SQL Server is going to unnecessarily look in the master database before it searches the local one.

Ad hoc query text must match exactly: For ad hoc queries, the text needs to be identical from one invocation to the next. Any difference in the text, including comments, will cause SQL Server to generate different query plans, and therefore won't re-use cached plans.

Now that you've learned to gather the facts about queries, it's time to learn how to apply that knowledge. This application will result in queries better optimized than SQL Server was able to produce.

End Game: Performance Tuning T-SQL

This tuning business can be a slippery slope for analytical types. You can get so distracted by analyzing the data and the thrill of reducing costs that you spend hours optimizing things that have minimal user impact. Focus on the things that have the greatest impact to the end user. Ultimately, that means make it faster. Do you want to make things faster? Reduce the I/O in the query. Focus particularly on I/O that is caused when disk heads are moving around. Assuming that the hardware guys have optimized disk placement, we are left with making changes to our T-SQL requests that make use of good indexing schemes and as few passes as possible on these indexes. Measure results, measure results again, give up some minor gains in efficiency for maintainability, add some common sense, and you've got it.

The methodology that we are using involves reading the query execution plan, measuring actual results or key performance indicators (KPIs), and examining index and schema designs for performance enhancements. When performance tuning T-SQL this is our general process flow:

1. Continue to educate yourself on fundamentals of database design, indexes, and optimizer logic. This is really a prerequisite and an iterative task that through familiarity will enable you to see patterns well before you can back it up with analytical data.

2. Run the query and study the execution plan. Study is the operative word. The more you study, the easier the patterns will be to see.

3. Attack the high cost operators in the Execution plan, but evaluate whether there could even be another way. Know when enough is enough. Go to the next highest operator. Look for patterns.

4. Examine the Profiler results. Look for clues where estimated plans don't match real results. You may need to force the optimizer to see the light.

5. Rework the T-SQL to take advantage of different methods of doing the same thing until you find a faster way. Trial and Error with persistence supplements knowledge in a real way.

Essential Tools

Before you can start applying some performance tuning techniques and problem solving, there are prerequisite skills and knowledge that can be categorized as essential tools. The next few sections will enumerate these skills so that you can add these to your daily performance tuning toolkit.

Minimizing Caching Effects for Best KPIs

To get good performance tuning KPIs, you have to be aware of caching effects, both from a data page and a query plan perspective. One way to do this is to run a query and then cycle the server, but this is not practical. Fortunately, if you are not tuning a production environment and have ALTER SERVER STATE permissions on the server, you can run the commands found in Table 9-9 to free up cache:

Table 9-9: Methods of Eliminating Caching Effects

Command	Description
DBCC FREEPROCCACHE	Frees all cached query execution plans.
DBCC FREESYSTEMCACHE	Frees unused cached query execution plans (and any cached entries from all caches).
CHECKPOINT	Writes any dirty pages to disk.

Note that you should *not* use these commands if you are performance tuning in a production environment. Even if you are running these types of commands in a shared test environment, you should warn users of that environment that you are doing performance tuning.

Setting Up Profiler to Capture Actual Results

Gathering empirical data from the profiler is a long-standing method of gathering KPIs for performance tuning. However, note that running the profiler is expensive and it only needs to run for short evaluation periods. There are technical arguments for spooling the trace file out to a file or to the Profiler user interface (UI). In the grand scheme of things, it is more convenient to read the trace in the Profiler UI tool while you tinker until you have all the EventClasses and columns with the right filters. If you need to query the results, just save the file and use the sys.fn_trace_GetTable function to load the file into a table. When you are targeting specific data to profile and have the trace like you want it, it may make sense to create a trace using T-SQL code and have this running in the background straight to a file. To create the T-SQL code just navigate the Profiler menu options File ⇨Export ⇨Script Trace Definition⇨For SQL Server 2005. You can find the exact Trace Template used in this for both profiler and T-SQL versions ready for download at www.wrox.com.

Querying the profiler trace file is handy when you are looking for specific problems either by event class or even within the plans themselves. When you query the file, you'll notice that the rowset is not exactly what you are used to seeing in the profiler window. Namely, the EventClass is an Integer, not the descriptive field in the UI. You can find the translation to the EventClass Ids in the Books On Line under topic sp_trace_setevent, or you can download a function we wrote at www.wrox.com called ufn_GetEventClassDescription that will translate the EventClass Ids back into labels. You can then write queries like this where you refer directly to the EventClass label.

```
Select   EventClass = dbo.ufn_GetEventClassDescription(EventClass),
         [T-SQL] = CAST(TextData as NVARCHAR(MAX)),
         Duration, Reads, Writes, CPU,
         StartTime, EndTime
FROM sys.fn_trace_GetTable('c:\mytrace.trc', null) as t
WHERE dbo.ufn_GetEventClassDescription(eventclass) = 'SQL:BatchCompleted'
```

Note that the event class that we are extracting here is the one named SQL:BatchCompleted. Look for this same event class if you are using the UI. It contains the summarized actual duration, I/O, and CPU KPIs that you'll be interested in for rudimentary comparison purposes.

Prerequisite Indexes for Examples

The rest of this chapter includes examples that require the addition of some new indexes to the Adventure Works (AW) database that you can add by running this script.

```
CREATE NONCLUSTERED INDEX [IX_SalesOrderHeader_AccountNumber] ON [Sales]
.[SalesOrderHeader] ([AccountNumber] ASC ) ON [PRIMARY]
GO
CREATE NONCLUSTERED INDEX [IX_SalesOrderHeader_CreditCardApprovalCode] ON [Sales]
.[SalesOrderHeader] ([CreditCardApprovalCode] ASC) ON [PRIMARY]
GO
CREATE NONCLUSTERED INDEX [IX_SalesOrderHeader_OrderDate] ON [Sales]
.[SalesOrderHeader] ([OrderDate] ASC ) ON [PRIMARY]
```

Tuning T-SQL with a New Approach

In the database world, DBAs approach performance issues by naturally assuming that the query is the limiting constraint. Then you start tinkering with the SQL statement to achieve an excellent low-cost result only to only have it crash and burn under different conditions in the production environment. It is an art to know when to yield to the declarative nature of SQL and when to tinker. The optimizer can interpolate many alternative ways to execute even poorly written queries, but there are times when correcting an inefficiently written query can often produce dramatic gains in performance and time.

NOT IN and NOT EXISTS Rewrites are in the Past

The conventional wisdom in the past was to rewrite NOT IN statements to use NOT EXISTS statements if the subquery scanned all the rows in a subtable. Mainly this was because the subquery would perform a full scan of the clustered index. Because of the advances in the optimizer, this is no longer necessary. The optimizer allows you to be more declarative, code using either method, and still get the most efficient implementation. Looking at a proof of this is instructive. An example in the AdventureWorks database would be a query that needs to return the departments that have never had an employee. The queries using NOT IN and NOT EXISTS structures would look like this:

```
SELECT Name, DepartmentId
FROM HumanResources.Department
WHERE DepartmentId NOT IN
(SELECT DepartmentId FROM HumanResources.EmployeeDepartmentHistory)

SELECT dpt.Name, dpt.DepartmentId
FROM HumanResources.Department dpt
WHERE NOT EXISTS
(SELECT * FROM HumanResources.EmployeeDepartmentHistory hist
 WHERE hist.DepartmentId = Dpt.DepartmentId)
```

If you run these two queries side by side, you'll see that they are both 50 percent of the batch, meaning that they are the same costs from a predictive standpoint. Both the XML query plans show the exact same graphical cost components. More detailed information can be found by setting the SHOWPLAN_ALL option to ON and rerunning the query. For both you'll also get the same detailed results. Here we've abbreviated some of the contents to focus on the important aspects.

```
SELECT ... WHERE DepartmentId NOT IN   (SELECT DepartmentId FROM...
   |--Nested Loops(Left Anti Semi Join,
                  OUTER REFERENCES:([Department].[DepartmentID]))
     |--Clustered Index Scan(OBJECT:([Department].[PK_Department_DepartmentID]))
       |--Top(TOP EXPRESSION:((1)))
         |--Index Seek(OBJECT:([IX_EmployeeDepartmentHistory_DepartmentID]),
       SEEK:([EmployeeDepartmentHistory].[DepartmentID]=[Department].[DepartmentID])
        ORDERED FORWARD)
```

The results of the SHOWPLAN_ALL are read from the inner sections represented with the nested lines out to the left to the outer sections. In this plan it is not nested, so you can simply read from the bottom to the top. In this level of detail, you can see that the optimizer has chosen the best implementation for these query requests. First a SEEK is performed into the EmployeeDepartmentHistory table using the non-clustered index, which is the most narrow and contains the DepartmentId that is needed to join back to the Department Table. The only clustered index scan is against the Department table and this is because the table is so small it completely fits in a page. This is an example of how spending time to rewrite statements doesn't provide any tangible improvement. Along similar lines, the optimizer can also determine the best implementation between the IN and EXISTS styles of writing queries. We'll leave that proof to you to perform.

Rewriting by Pushing Predicates Deeper into Plans

Although the optimizer is getting better, it still has some blind spots if you aren't specific enough. We'll be going over other predicate-level changes in this chapter, and pushing predicates deeper is one of the things that require your specific communication help through a T-SQL rewrite. The principle is that predicates should be able to be applied as early as possible in a T-SQL statement. During the query processing phases the WHERE statements are processed before the HAVING statements. You should take any opportunity to reduce the row count at an earlier opportunity to save on some costs of effort. A metaphor to this is getting all the different boxes of cereal in a grocery aisle and then putting all of them back at the checkout lane except the one you want instead of just getting the one box of cereal that you want in the first place. Getting the cereal you want in the first place is analogous to pushing the conditions (or predicate) deeper into the plan (your shopping list). A real example would be looking for the average list prices of products that have product numbers starting with "VE%." Queries that perform this task with the HAVING clause can be rewritten more efficiently using WHERE clauses.

```
SELECT prod.ProductNumber, AVG(hist.ListPrice)
FROM Production.Product prod
INNER JOIN Production.ProductListPriceHistory hist
on prod.productId = hist.productId
GROUP BY prod.ProductNumber
HAVING prod.ProductNumber like 'VE%'
```

This query applies the filter as the last step. You can see this by reading the plan details (abbreviated for brevity).

```
HAVING QUERY PLAN
8|--Filter(WHERE:([Product].[ProductNumber] as [prod].[ProductNumber] like N'VE%'))
7  |--Compute Scalar
6    |--Stream Aggregate(GROUP BY:([prod].[ProductNumber])
5      |--Sort(ORDER BY:([prod].[ProductNumber] ASC))
4        |--Merge Join(Inner Join,
3            MERGE:([prod].[ProductID])=([hist].[ProductID])
2          |--Clustered Index Scan [PK_Product_ProductID]
1          |--Clustered Index Scan [PK_ProductListPriceHistory_ProductID_StartDate]
```

(The steps in the plan are numbered for reference. These numbers don't normally appear in a plan). Note that no filter is applied and the rows that are still in memory at the seventh step are the total number of summarized rows scanned in the Clustered Index Scan operation at Step 1. The following query rewrites the statement to be more efficient:

```
SELECT prod.ProductNumber, AVG(hist.ListPrice)
FROM Production.Product prod
INNER JOIN Production.ProductListPriceHistory hist
on prod.productId = hist.productId
WHERE prod.ProductNumber like 'VE%'
GROUP BY prod.ProductNumber
```

```
WHERE QUERY PLAN
5|--Compute Scalar (
4  |--Stream Aggregate(GROUP BY:([ProductNumber])
3    |--Nested Loops(Inner Join, OUTER REFERENCES:([prod].[ProductID]))
2      |--Index Seek(OBJECT:([AK_Product_ProductNumber]),
          SEEK:([prod].[ProductNumber] >= N'VE' AND [prod].[ProductNumber] < N'VF'),
          WHERE:([prod].[ProductNumber] like N'VE%') ORDERED FORWARD)
1      |--Clustered Index Seek(
          OBJECT:( [PK_ProductListPriceHistory_ProductID_StartDate]),
          SEEK:([hist].[ProductID]= [ProductID]) ORDERED FORWARD)
```

Applying the predicate in the WHERE clause reduces the number of pages read from 20 down to 8. Where did that information about paging come from? If you use the profiler to trace events while you are running the queries, you can see a metric for page reads in the output. You can also get this information from one of the new DMVs, sys.dm_exec_query_stats. These new DMVs may even be more preferred if you are troubleshooting a production environment since the overhead is much lower. Download the SQL profiler trace template that we've created for you at www.wrox.com to see the metrics that we review in this chapter, or create your own. Notice in the query plan for the WHERE query that there are several efficiencies that have been gained. First, the predicate is being realized at Step 22 instead of later in the plan. In real terms this means that the number of rows of concern have been reduced to three rows almost immediately. This means that only these three rows are read from disk into memory instead of all 395 rows that result from the JOIN of the Product and ProductListPriceHistory tables. The second efficiency is that the access methods for reading the indexes have been turned into SEEK operations instead of SCAN operations. Lastly, the sort operation in the HAVING plan has been eliminated. Sort operations typically use CPU and memory. Eliminating this step by using the ORDERED FORWARD SEEK cursors and Nested-Loop join operators reduce the CPU and memory demand as well in this plan.

The optimizer assumes that you know what you are doing and there are valid uses of the application of HAVING filters, so there are definitely times when you can tweak your T-SQL statements and get better plans. The issue here is making sure your queries match your intentions, because the optimizer can't read minds.

Using Temp Tables for Intermediary Results

If you write any reporting procedures, you undoubtedly have come upon situations where it just makes sense to store an intermediary result. If you are dealing with a highly relational OLTP structure that requires multiple traversal paths, it is almost a necessity. Creating a temp table incurs four separate cost components: the creation of the structure, the initial reading of the data, the writing of the data into the structure, and the reading of the data back out again. However, even though there is redundancy here, there are times that this is the highest-performing method. Here are some of the reasons that you want to rewrite your queries to use temp tables.

❑ You are retrieving results of a stored procedure call. In SQL Server, you have no other choice but to store the results in a temporary structure.

❑ You can reuse scenarios for complicated or involved traversals or aggregations. In this case, the temp tables are more efficient because you only have to travel the index structures once. If you are aggregating data, you are eliminating multiple CPU and Memory usages to perform redundant calculations.

❑ You are reducing the number of JOINs. In very large databases, the process of joining two large tables can be an expensive operation. Pulling the results from each table independently into temp tables and joining these results can be more efficient if the results are small.

❑ You are decreasing the complexity for maintenance purposes. Sometimes you have to give a little on the performance side to be able to maintain the query. In our shop, some of the report queries are involved. It is nice to be able to look at intermediate results to get an early indication of where a problem exists in the data when troubleshooting or code reviewing the query.

With the introduction of table variables in SQL Server 2000, there has been some debate on when to use table variables versus #temp tables. One common misconception is that table variables are created in memory and only #temp tables are created in the tempDB database. This is not true. Both are backed by pages in tempdb, but may not incur any I/O depending upon how much memory is available. If enough memory is available, then the structure is created in the data cache. If the data storage requirement exceeds memory capacity, then I/O incurs in tempDB. Table 9-10 contains a list of the differences from a performance perspective.

Table 9-10: Comparison of Table Variables and Temp Tables

Temp Table Type	Advantages
Table Variables	Use less logging and locking resources. Not affected by transaction rollbacks (less work to do). Not subject to recompilation because you can't accidently use a DDL statement to define table variables. Better for smaller intermediary results.
#Temp Tables	Can create non-clustered indexes on them for performance. Can use statistics. Can use in sp_ExecuteSql statements. Better for large intermediary results.

Generally, the rule is to use #temp tables for larger results because of the capability to apply indexing to the results for performance purposes. In terms of usability, a best practice is to define your temp table structure at the top of your query regardless of whether you use the table variables or #temp tables. One reason is that if you are not defining your structure, you are probably creating the #temp table using a SELECT INTO statement. The SELECT INTO method of creating #temp tables causes some system-table level locking that you should avoid. (This happens because any time a database object is created, like a table, it has to temporarily lock some system resources.) The other reason is that it makes troubleshooting the query much easier to be able to convert the use of a table variable to a #temp table. The decision of which temp table to use now or later in the life cycle of the query is then trivial to change.

```
--EXAMPLE OF HOW TO CODE TO BE ABLE TO USE EITHER TABLE VARIABLES OR TEMP TABLES
DECLARE @prodId TABLE (ProductId INT)  -->> CREATE TABLE #prodId(productId Int)

INSERT INTO @ProdId                    -->> INSERT INTO #ProdId
SELECT ProductId                       -->> SELECT ProductId
FROM Production.Product                -->> FROM Production.Product
```

User-Defined Functions in SELECT Statements

Scalar user-defined functions (UDF) are great for encapsulating scalar calculations, but must be examined carefully for how they are used in production queries. If you are not using UDFs in select statements, but have a procedure or UDF that is called to perform computationally complex calculations or that utilizes hierarchical or traversal-type logic, you will find that these pieces of code can be more efficiently performed by rewriting them using SQL CLR. This topic and performance issues related to using SQL CLR are covered in better detail in *Professional SQL Server 2005 CLR Programming with Stored Procedures, Functions, Triggers, Aggregates, and Types* from Wrox.

The two biggest performance bottlenecks you may encounter are using the results of a UDF as a filter and returning the results of a UDF in a column within a large result set. Performance issues are particularly exacerbated when any significant querying work is being done within the UDF. For an example look at the UDF ufnGetProductStandardCost in AW that joins the Production.Product and Production.ProductCostHistory tables and filters the ProductCostHistory table using a date range. What can happen in the life cycle of UDFs is that someone creates them with the expectation that they will be used in SELECT statements for singleton or highly selective WHERE predicates. However, the appeal of the encapsulation aspect of the UDF leads them to sooner or later being used in larger, reporting-type result sets. When this happens, there is a hidden performance impact. To examine this follow this example of this UDF being used in an indiscriminate select statement:

```
SELECT *, dbo.ufnGetProductStandardCost(ProductId, @ORDERDATE)
FROM Production.Product
```

For each row in the Production.Product table, the UDF is evaluated. If we extracted the contents of the UDF, it would be the equivalent of applying a forced correlated subquery like this:

```
SELECT *,
    (SELECT pch.[StandardCost]
    FROM [Production].[Product] p
        INNER JOIN [Production].[ProductCostHistory] pch
        ON p.[ProductID] = pch.[ProductID]
            AND p.[ProductID] = o.[ProductId]
            AND @OrderDate BETWEEN pch.[StartDate]
            AND COALESCE(pch.[EndDate], CONVERT(datetime, '99991231', 112))
        )
FROM Production.Product o
```

Both the UDF version and the Correlated subquery versions are simple to understand, but this example can also be written in a simple Join or a set-based way like this.

```
SELECT p.*, pch.[StandardCost]
FROM [Production].[Product] p
    LEFT OUTER JOIN [Production].[ProductCostHistory] pch
    ON p.[ProductID] = pch.[ProductID]
        AND @OrderDate BETWEEN pch.[StartDate]
                AND COALESCE(pch.[EndDate], CONVERT(datetime, '99991231', 112))
```

When running and comparing the examples, there are two things to point out. The first is that the cost component numbers here should not pass your sniff test. The UDF performs the same action as the correlated subquery so logically should perform the same or worse. The reason it should perform worse is that the optimizer will not be able to fold or refactor this statement into a join. Therefore, we expect that the cost would be higher for the UDF over all other methods. Table 9-11 shows the results.

Table 9-11: Comparison of Join, UDF, and Correlated Subquery

Method	% Cost	CPU	Reads	Duration
Join	9	30	20	366ms
UDF	5	4526	171097	12542ms
Correlated Subquery	86	60	2035	348ms

Comparatively against the other methods and antithetical to our expectations, the % Cost numbers clearly call the UDF method the winner. The second thing to notice is that the Compute Scalar Operator has a cost of 0 percent but the CPU and Page reads are off the chart. What is going on? To make sense of this you need to examine the query plan in Figure 9-8.

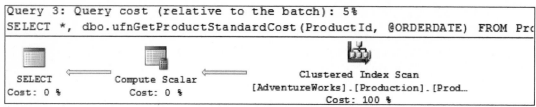

```
Query 3: Query cost (relative to the batch): 5%
SELECT *, dbo.ufnGetProductStandardCost(ProductId, @ORDERDATE) FROM Pro

    SELECT           Compute Scalar          Clustered Index Scan
   Cost: 0 %          Cost: 0 %       [AdventureWorks].[Production].[Prod...
                                                Cost: 100 %
```

Figure 9-8

Hovering over the Operator does not tell you what is going on at this step. The best way to peer into this step is looking at the Showplan Statistics Profile Event Class in the profiler. Here you'll find an explanation:

```
Compute Scalar(DEFINE:([Expr1002]=[AdventureWorks].[dbo]
  .[ufnGetProductStandardCost]...
```

Since we are sure that this computation is performed by calling the user-defined function and this function is being called per row, surely this must cost something. You can see this by again looking into the Profiler at each time the statement within the UDF is executed. Typically, after the first time the statement is run and cached, you'll see performance numbers similar to the following:

- ❑ **CPU:** 10
- ❑ **Reads:** 411
- ❑ **Duration:** 8ms

What's happening here is that the optimizer doesn't do a very good job at estimating the cost of executing user defined functions. In fact, the optimizer is essentially punting instead of providing cost information. If you just base your decisions upon the execution plans, you'd be missing a big I/O requirement of the UDF-based query. Understand that a UDF must be executed like a correlated subquery per row, but can not be optimized in combination with the SQL statement that calls them. If you are calling these separate, atomic queries for each row, you'll find that this gets more expensive the larger the result set. This doesn't mean that UDFs should never be used. The encapsulation benefits many times outweigh the performance or code complexity caused by removing them. Just make sure that the WHERE predicates are limiting results to small result sets; they just don't scale well into large result sets.

Reworking SELECT *

You can't always tune what you are being required to select, but doing so can surprisingly improve performance. It comes down to the number of pages that have to be read to produce the result. If a non-clustered index exists where all the columns you are selecting are available, then the index can be read directly instead of reading the clustered index and subsequent pages. This type of index is called a covered index. If the rows are wide or contain large data types that you don't need in your results, the punishment for the * character will be the number of pages that must be read to contain the data. Here's a simple example that demonstrates the performance costs.

```
SELECT H.SalesOrderId, D.SalesOrderDetailId
FROM Sales.SalesOrderHeader H
INNER JOIN Sales.SalesOrderDetail D ON H.SalesOrderId = D.SalesOrderId
WHERE h.SalesOrderId = 43659

SELECT *
FROM Sales.SalesOrderHeader H
INNER JOIN Sales.SalesOrderDetail D
ON H.SalesOrderId = D.SalesOrderId
WHERE h.SalesOrderId = 43659
```

The first query selects the most efficient columns that can be made for these two tables. The output of this select is not very useful, but provides a comparison for the best case, least amount of columns you can select. The second statement grabs all the columns out of both tables and represents the most data you can pull from these two tables. Table 9-12 compares the two select statements.

Table 9-12: Comparison of Specific and All-Column Selects

Method	% Cost	CPU	Reads	Duration
With WHERE Clause...				
Specific SELECT	50	0	28	198ms
SELECT *	50	80	30	345ms
Without WHERE Clause				
Specific SELECT	50	271	295	3960ms
SELECT *	50	2263	2510	19582ms

It is easy to see that the number of reads and the Merge Join Operation that occurs in the SELECT * method creates the most expensive plan. In fact, the expense increases for each additional column, as can be seen in Figure 9-9.

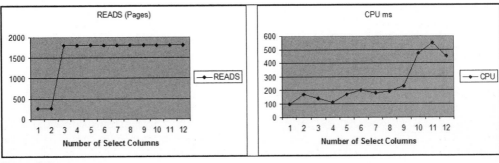

Figure 9-9

There is a point where adding additional columns has no effect on the number of reads since the pages have to be loaded anyway. The cost is paid by the merge operation that is putting the Join together between the SalesOrderHeader and SalesOrderDetail tables. This is seen in the steady increase in CPU costs for each additional column added to the Select.

Simple Select Views

If there is a performance penalty for each additional column in a select statement, how is performance affected by using views? What happens when you join to a view? To consider views from a performance perspective, separate views into two types: Simple select and Complex. A view by definition is a virtual table that should be treated as if the results were fully materialized. From a performance tuning perspective, using a simple select view is the same as selecting from a derived table. The T-SQL contents of the view does not get reorganized to make a better plan when simply selected from or joined to additional tables. You can test this by running the T-SQL contents of a view against a straight SELECT on a view. Normally, the only performance penalties from joining to views come from the overhead of loading pages of unneeded columns or from additional JOINS made to either existing view tables or new tables when additional columns are retrieved.

Performance problems can appear later in the life cycle of a view when it is being used for another purpose and an additional field is needed from an existing table in the view. What typically happens is a join is made directly to the view to retrieve the additional column. Unfortunately, the optimizer doesn't realize that this table is already part of the view and reads the table twice, once for the view, and the second time for the additional join. To see this in action, compare a select from the vEmployee view with a join back to the HumanResources.Employee Table to retrieve the NationalIdNumber, with a straight select to the underlying tables to pick up the additional column in the Employee table.

```
--SELECT FROM VIEW
SELECT v.*, Emp.NationalIdNumber
FROM [HumanResources].[vEmployee] v
INNER JOIN [HumanResources].[Employee] emp
ON V.EmployeeId = emp.EmployeeId
```

Copy the contents of the HumanResources.vEmployee view in the query window and add the additional select column for NationalIdNumber to the select list:

```
--SELECT USING BASE TABLES
SELECT
    e.[EmployeeID],c.[Title],c.[FirstName],c.[MiddleName],c.[LastName],c.[Suffix]
    ,e.[Title] AS [JobTitle],c.[Phone],c.[EmailAddress],c.[EmailPromotion]
    ,a.[AddressLine1],a.[AddressLine2],a.[City],sp.[Name] AS [StateProvinceName]
    ,a.[PostalCode],cr.[Name] AS [CountryRegionName],c.[AdditionalContactInfo]
  ,e.[NationalIdNumber]
FROM [HumanResources].[Employee] e
INNER JOIN [Person].[Contact] c
ON c.[ContactID] = e.[ContactID]
INNER JOIN [HumanResources].[EmployeeAddress] ea
ON e.[EmployeeID] = ea.[EmployeeID]
INNER JOIN [Person].[Address] a
ON ea.[AddressID] = a.[AddressID]
INNER JOIN [Person].[StateProvince] sp
ON sp.[StateProvinceID] = a.[StateProvinceID]
```

```
INNER JOIN [Person].[CountryRegion] cr
ON cr.[CountryRegionCode] = sp.[CountryRegionCode];
```

When you run these two statements, examine the two plans. You'll see that adding the Join to the view increases the number of reads from 1600 page reads to 2179 pages. The plan shows that the Employee table is indeed examined twice when the view is joined back to the Employee table.

```
|--Clustered Index Scan(OBJECT:([Employee].[PK_Employee_EmployeeID] AS [e]))
|--Clustered Index Seek(OBJECT:([Employee].[PK_Employee_EmployeeID] AS [emp]))
```

This shows that while using Views is conceptually no different from coding the statement fully, this is an instance where the optimizer can't figure out our intentions. The Optimizer doesn't parse the view SQL and our additional SQL to combine for further optimization. A good rule of thumb is that if you need a significantly narrower result set or to add columns from an additional relationship, seriously consider creating a new view for this purpose. If you are just adding a new Join table not already in the view definition as a filter, using the view adds no significant performance penalty.

Complex Views

Complex views that include aggregates, common table expressions, or even TOP statements can present an unexpected challenge. The performance issue here is that certain predicates can't be applied early enough in the planning process. Aggregates that include grouping operations use equivalency operations, so applying predicates that use different comparison rules must be delayed as filter operations later in the planning process. Applying the predicate too early could change the base view results, which violates the definition of views being resolved as if they were a virtual table. Take, for example, an aggregate query as a view.

```
--First, Create this view
CREATE VIEW vSalesOrderHeaderByAccountNumber
AS
SELECT AccountNumber, count(*) As OrderCnt
FROM Sales.SalesOrderHeader
GROUP BY AccountNumber
```

Then run a comparison using an account number predicate against the view and against the statement outside of the view.

```
--Against the view
SELECT *
FROM vSalesOrderHeaderByAccountNumber
WHERE AccountNumber LIKE '10-4020-000210'

--Statement separated from the view
SELECT AccountNumber, count(*) As OrderCnt
FROM Sales.SalesOrderHeader
WHERE AccountNumber LIKE '10-4020-000210'
GROUP BY AccountNumber
```

When you run these two comparisons, you'll notice that the estimated costs for the query against the complex view is 98 percent of the batch cost compared to 2 percent of the straight statement. This is an example of how a view can impact performance negatively. The plans tell the whole picture. The plan for the select against the view is performing an aggregation after scanning the AccountNumber index and then filtering out the results later in the plan.

```
|--Filter(WHERE:([AccountNumber] like N'10-4020-000210'))
  |--Compute Scalar(DEFINE:([Expr1003]=CONVERT_IMPLICIT(int,[Expr1006],0)))
    |--Stream Aggregate(GROUP BY:([AccountNumber]) DEFINE:([Expr1006]=Count(*)))
      |--Index Scan(OBJECT:([IX_SalesOrderHeader_AccountNumber]), ORDERED FORWARD)
```

The straight SELECT is able to build a plan to seek the AccountNumber index on the predicate and then aggregate the results. If you look at the results in SHOWPLAN_ALL, you'll see that the row count for the straight SELECT is down to 20 estimated rows after the SEEK operation while the View SELECT is still working with 32,465 estimated rows.

```
|--Compute Scalar(DEFINE:([Expr1003]=CONVERT_IMPLICIT(int,[Expr1006],0)))
  |--Stream Aggregate(DEFINE:([Expr1006]=Count(*),
          [AccountNumber]=ANY([AccountNumber])))
    |--Index Seek(OBJECT:([IX_SalesOrderHeader_AccountNumber]),
          SEEK:([AccountNumber] >= N'10-4020-000210'
          AND [AccountNumber] <= N'10-4020-000210'),
          WHERE:([AccountNumber] like N'10-4020-000210') ORDERED FORWARD)
```

The issue here is not with complex views, but with the difference between the way the LIKE operator (and others) match the arguments and how GROUP BY statements summarize groups. If you change the LIKE operator to an equal (=) operator, you'll notice that the optimizer recommends the same plan for both. This is because the predicate can be pushed deeper into the plan because equivalency operators are the same for the predicate matching and the grouping operations.

Tuning the T-SQL Predicate

Tuning the T-SQL predicate is usually the heart of the performance problem, if there is such a thing as a quick fix. The next few sections will go over some common performance problems and provide details on how to troubleshoot and remove them.

Removing Certain Implicit Conversions

If your databases aren't internationalized then you may not be aware of the implicit conversion issue that degrades performance when non-Unicode and Unicode indexes and filters are mixed in predicates. Implicit conversions aren't limited to just Unicode fields, and could occur with any compatible data type. (Non-compatible data type conversions throw compiler errors). Implicit conversions occur when parameters are provided to searchable arguments against columns, which have compatible, but not exact data types. It can happen by accident if coders are used to using the Unicode data types and a database schema has an occasional VARCHAR data type. The result is an extra operation to convert the values for comparison.

The CreditCardApprovalCode column is a regular VARCHAR data type column in the Sales.SalesOrder-Header table. Run the following query comparison, which uses NVARCHAR (Unicode) and VARCHAR data type parameters to compare the effects of the parameter types:

```
DECLARE @CreditCardApprovalCode_UNICODE NVARCHAR(30)
SET @CreditCardApprovalCode_UNICODE = N'539435Vi62867'
```

```
SELECT CreditCardApprovalCode FROM Sales.SalesOrderHeader
WHERE CreditCardApprovalCode = @CreditCardApprovalCode_UNICODE
GO
DECLARE @CreditCardApprovalCode VARCHAR(30)
SET @CreditCardApprovalCode = '539435Vi62867'

SELECT CreditCardApprovalCode FROM Sales.SalesOrderHeader
WHERE CreditCardApprovalCode = @CreditCardApprovalCode
```

Running this query generates the following query plans, seen in Figure 9-10.

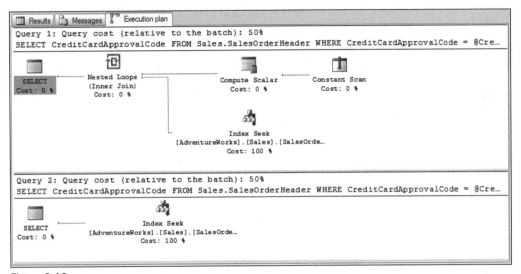

Figure 9-10

Note that when the query has a Unicode parameter there are two extra operations in the query plan. The Constant Scan and Compute Scalar Operators calculate the upper and lower range of the statistics histogram where the converted value of the Unicode parameter falls. You can see this in the plan details:

```
Nested Loops(Inner Join, OUTER REFERENCES:([Expr1005], [Expr1006], [Expr1004]))
|--Compute Scalar(DEFINE:(([Expr1005],[Expr1006],[Expr1004])=
               GetRangeThroughConvert([@CreditCardApprovalCode_UNICODE],
               [@CreditCardApprovalCode_UNICODE],(62))))
|     |--Constant Scan
|--Index Seek(OBJECT:([IX_SalesOrderHeader_CreditCardApprovalCode]), SEEK:( [Credit-
CardApprovalCode] > [Expr1005] AND [CreditCardApprovalCode] < [Expr1006]),
  WHERE:(CONVERT_IMPLICIT(nvarchar(15), [CreditCardApprovalCode],0)
=[@CreditCardApprovalCode_UNICODE]) ORDERED FORWARD)
```

The GetRangeThroughConvert definition uses the statistics histogram to calculate the upper and lower range values. The Seek then can occur against the index using the converted lower and upper range values and then the implicit conversion is applied to each value within the range. This still takes three times as long as using a parameter that doesn't require conversion. However, as you can see in Table 9-13, this is much more efficient than scanning the entire index.

Table 9-13: Comparison of Explicit Conversion Costs

Method	SubTree Cost	CPU	Reads	Duration
Conversion	0.00328314	0	2	37ms
No Conversion	0.00328314	0	2	10ms

The same type of behavior occurs if you reverse the situation and search a Unicode column with a non-Unicode parameter, except that SQL Server handles this a little differently. To experiment, run this query against the Sales.SalesOrderHeader table that has an AccountNumber column that is of type NVARCHAR.

```
DECLARE @ACCOUNTNUMBER_UNICODE NVARCHAR(30)
SET @ACCOUNTNUMBER_UNICODE = N'10-4020-000002'

SELECT AccountNumber FROM Sales.SalesOrderHeader
WHERE AccountNumber = @ACCOUNTNUMBER_UNICODE
go
DECLARE @ACCOUNTNUMBER VARCHAR(30)
SET @ACCOUNTNUMBER = '10-4020-000002'

SELECT AccountNumber FROM Sales.SalesOrderHeader
WHERE AccountNumber = @ACCOUNTNUMBER
```

When you examine these query plans you'll notice that they both look the same. If you look at the plan details, you'll see there is an implementation difference, but not as dramatic as the first example.

```
Index Seek(OBJECT:([IX_SalesOrderHeader_AccountNumber]), SEEK:([AccountNumber]=
CONVERT_IMPLICIT(nvarchar(30),[@ACCOUNTNUMBER],0)) ORDERED FORWARD)
```

After you study this for a minute, you may wonder why the optimizer didn't choose a plan like this when converting a NVARCHAR parameter to search a VARCHAR column. The answer is because of data type precedence. When comparing two compatible data types, the once with lower precedence will be converted. When comparing a VARCHAR and NVARCHAR data type, VARCHAR has the lower precedence. In the first example, the contents of the rows (of type VARCHAR) have to be converted to compare to the NVARCHAR parameter. In the second example, only the parameter (of type VARCHAR) needs to be converted for comparison to a NVARCHAR column.

This issue is not limited to just NVARCHAR and VARCHAR data types. You can see this type of behavior on any other compatible data types under similar search argument or join conditions. Just look for the CONVERT_IMPLICIT operation occurring in your query plans to see if you have this sort of issue. Performance can be easily improved by rewriting the SQL statement to match parameters to the column data types.

Using Searchable Arguments

Similar to the Implicit Conversion issues and probably the next easiest issues to fix for performance tuning are incorrectly coded WHERE predicates and search arguments. The optimizer can't save you here. You will have to be able to identify these issues and rewrite them to conform to a search argument that breaks down into an evaluation of a column by a constant. Typically, these problems result in Index Scan operations against an index. If coded correctly they will become index seek operations instead. Most examples you'll find here are beginner mistakes, but still are worth examining.

Table 9-14 lists some typical T-SQL predicates that cause the optimizer to choose suboptimal index scanning along with rewritten versions that can seek into the indexes.

Table 9-14: Searchable Predicate Performance Issues

Index Scan	Index Seek
WHERE Year(OrderDate) = 2001 AND Month(OrderDate) = 7	WHERE OrderDate BETWEEN 07/01/2001'AND '07/31/2001'
WHERE DateDiff(d, OrderDate, Getdate()) = 1034	WHERE OrderDate >=CONVERT(varchar(10), DateAdd(d, -1034, GetDate()), 101)
WHERE LEFT([AccountNumber], 11)='10-4030-014'	WHERE AccountNumber like '10-4030-014%'
WHERE CHARINDEX('10-402', AccountNumber) = 0	WHERE AccountNumber like '10-40[2]%'

One of the signs of this easily correctable bottleneck is when you see what looks like a simple WHERE predicate on an existing index but the execution plan shows an Index Scan Operator. The plan in Figure 9-11 shows two execution plans for the first example in the table above.

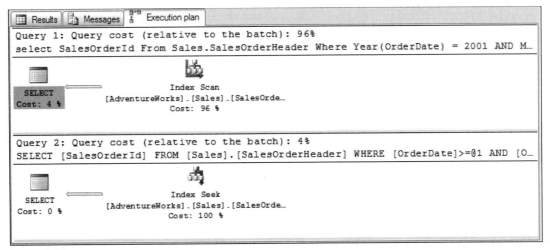

Figure 9-11

You can see that the first plan results in an Index Scan operation when the WHERE predicate is "WHERE Year(OrderDate)=2001 AND Month(OrderDate)=7". Anytime you perform a function against a column, every row must first be evaluated by the function into a scalar result before it can be retested for the comparison. Naturally, examining every row creates the scanning activity. By rearranging the predicate to "WHERE OrderDate BETWEEN '07/01/2001' AND '07/31/2001'" an intermediate result does not have to be calculated to be tested for a comparison. Instead, the index can be examined directly. You can see the difference that a simple rearrangement makes in Table 9-15. The subtree cost difference is huge, most of which is eaten up with reading 61 pages compared to the 2-page reads of the index seek. A query like this is I/O intensive and if it is causing I/O problems on your server, consider this a gift. You can easily rearrange the predicate and reap the performance benefits, but don't get too excited. This is the low-hanging fruit in the performance tuning world and you won't see these often.

Table 9-15: Costs of Scan versus Seek Operations

Method	SubTree Cost	CPU	Reads	Duration
Scan	0.0808565	30	61	250ms
Seek	0.00347912	10	2	95ms

Although rewriting predicates into searchable arguments is the best policy, you won't always achieve the stellar results you see in this example. If the column being searched does not have an index or if the evaluation is too complex, functionally the table scan may be the most efficient way to resolve the query. An example can be seen by evaluating the methods of examining an account number with a scanning LEFT() function to a LIKE operator using the pattern matching string '10-40[^2]%'. Evaluate these two queries:

```
SELECT SalesOrderId FROM Sales.SalesOrderHeader
WHERE CHARINDEX('10-403', AccountNumber) = 0

SELECT SalesOrderId FROM Sales.SalesOrderHeader
    WHERE AccountNumber like '10-40[^3]%'
```

In the query plan in Figure 9-12, the first thing you'll notice is that even though the Index Seek is being achieved, the total cost margin between the two methods, 88 percent and 12 percent, is not as dramatic as the first rewrite example.

String manipulation is not the strength of SQL Server, so even without the benefit of query plan estimations you'd expect to see more time taken in the CPU for these operations. What you might not expect is that under these conditions, you'll still incur an evaluation against every column value in the table. You can see the increased CPU usage time in Table 9-16 for the Seek method, and the suprising fact that both methods incur the exact same number of page read operations.

The duration numbers also underscore that in some circumstances, the evaluation is faster against all the column values instead of against a range of values. This is an important point to remember. The execution plan numbers reflect expected costs not speed. So if it is speed you are after, you always need to compare the duration numbers in the profiler.

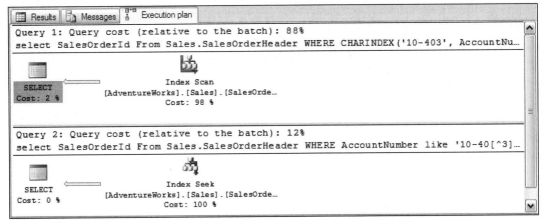

Figure 9-12

Table 9-16: Example of Smaller SubTree Cost but Higher CPU and Duration

Method	SubTree Cost	CPU	Reads	Duration
Scan	0.158634	100	166	315ms
Seek	0.0215541	181	166	463ms

After examining some of the obvious issues that may existing in the predicates of your T-SQL statements, the next obvious place to look for performance problems is in your index structures. These techniques are covered in the next section.

Tuning T-SQL to Use Indexes

The following sections cover techniques to get the most out of the indexing that is available in SQL Server. A skillful use of indexing will bolster the performance of many poor-performing queries with minimal impact to SQL Server's resources.

Minimizing Bookmark Lookups

Bookmark lookups occur when a WHERE predicate uses a non-clustered index to access the data in the table, but the index doesn't have all the columns logically to evaluate nor those necessary to return the selection. In the best-case scenarios, you either search against the clustered index, because this contains the data pages themselves, or use the smaller non-clustered indexes if everything you need to search and retrieve is there. Even if not everything you need is in the non-clustered index, it might still be used for seeking operations, although a subsequent lookup must occur to resolve the data page to retrieve the additional columns selected. This resolution can be faster if the non-clustered index includes a reference to a clustered index or slower if seeking on a heap with a row identifier. The need to make the additional I/O read is the main reason that bookmarks should be avoided if possible, but this needs to be kept in perspective. The alternative to a non-clustered index bookmark lookup is a clustered index scan, which is a table scan with help. Even SQL Server will give up and revert to a clustered index scan if the optimizer deems the bookmark lookup operation to be too expensive.

SQL Server 2005 has made some changes relative to bookmarks. One of the most obvious is a change in SP2 to add two new operators: RID Lookup and Key Lookup Operators. You'll also notice that the old SQL Server 2000 bookmark operator has been depreciated. If you haven't installed this service pack, you'll only see a Clustered Index Scan operator and you'll have to dig to find the LOOKUP keyword on the SEEK operation. Overall, you'll notice that SQL Server 2005 has less tolerance for the bookmark lookup operation and will use the clustered index scan more frequently. You can play around with this, but it appears that the break-even mark occurs when the selectivity indicates that the select density includes around 20 percent of the table rows. Until that point, you'll see these bookmark operations. To see an example, run this query:

```
SELECT PurchaseOrderNumber
FROM Sales.SalesOrderHeader
WHERE CustomerId = 75
```

In the query execution plan, the operation is Clustered Index Seek with the LOOKUP keyword to indicate a bookmark operation.

```
Nested Loops(Inner Join, OUTER REFERENCES:([SalesOrderID]))
    |--Index Seek(OBJECT:([IX_SalesOrderHeader_CustomerID]),
                SEEK:([CustomerID]=(75)) ORDERED FORWARD)
    |--Clustered Index Seek(OBJECT:([PK_SalesOrderHeader_SalesOrderID]),
                SEEK:([SalesOrderID]=[SalesOrderID] LOOKUP ORDERED FORWARD)
```

Note in the plan that the optimizer performs a SEEK operation into the SalesOrderHeader table using the SalesOrderId. Sometimes you can help the plan by giving the optimizer this information up front. Change the Query to include an additional predicate like this:

```
SELECT PurchaseOrderNumber
FROM Sales.SalesOrderHeader SOH
WHERE SOH.SalesOrderID = SOH.SalesOrderID
AND SOH.CustomerId = 75
```

Table 9-17 shows the improvement in the plan numbers accordingly.

Table 9-17: Boosting Performance with an Additional Predicate

Method	% Cost	%Key Lookup	Reads	Duration
With Supplied Seek	15	51	52	406ms
Without	85	92	50	420ms

The reason that the optimizer is giving this plan such low costing information is because the extra predicate tricks it into thinking that only one row will be resolved. You can see the difference in the number of estimated rows in the execution plan. This plan estimates that 1 row should be returned for each estimated time executed (1.2). The original plan estimates 12 rows with 12 executions for the clustered index scan. Note that in reality, the number of reads is slightly higher and there is not much duration difference.

The better way to solve this problem is to provide a covered index that contains the PurchaseOrder-Number data so that a SEEK can be formed directly on the non-clustered index. Create such an index by running this SQL in the AW database.

```
CREATE NONCLUSTERED INDEX [IX_SalesOrderHeader_CustomerID] ON [Sales]
.[SalesOrderHeader]
(
 [CustomerID] ASC
)
INCLUDE ( [PurchaseOrderNumber]) WITH (PAD_INDEX  = OFF, STATISTICS_NORECOMPUTE
= OFF, SORT_IN_TEMPDB = OFF, IGNORE_DUP_KEY = OFF, DROP_EXISTING = ON, ONLINE
= OFF, ALLOW_ROW_LOCKS  = ON, ALLOW_PAGE_LOCKS  = ON) ON [PRIMARY]
```

Running the query again shows a dramatic difference in I/O, as illustrated by Table 9-18. Page reads are down to 16 pages. These pages are essentially the difference between reading the non-clustered index (including the extra space for adding the PurchaseOrderNumber data) and the cost of loading the clustered index pages via the bookmark lookup process. The plan is also much simpler now.

```
Index Seek(OBJECT:([IX_SalesOrderHeader_CustomerID] AS [SOH]),
       SEEK:([SOH].[CustomerID]=CONVERT_IMPLICIT(int,[@1],0)),
       WHERE:([SOH].[SalesOrderID]=[SalesOrderID]) ORDERED FORWARD)
```

Table 9-18: Comparison of Covered and Non-Covered Index on Retrieval

Method	Tot Cost	CPU	Reads	Duration
Without Covered Index	0.0393727	10	52	406ms
With Covered Index	0.0032952	10	16	114ms

This new covered index includes the PurchaseOrderNumber column in the index, but it is *not* part of the indexed data. It essentially rides along for storage costs only. If the PurchaseOrderNumber column would never be used as a searchable argument, then this is a good decision. If not, then consider creating a composite index instead. The idea here is if you have a performance problem due to a highly repeated query, structure your indexes to support that retrieval to reduce the I/O on the clustered index. However, there is a point of marginal return and it doesn't make sense to go the opposite direction and have non-clustered indexes that include all the columns in the table. Follow these general guidelines when creating covering indexes to remove bookmark style lookups:

❑   If the query is not a high-volume count query, then leave it alone. Don't index it. Take the hit.

❑   If adding the included or indexed columns significantly increases the index, then weigh size of index vs. the size of the table itself. If relatively low ratio then add index.

❑   If you decide to add included columns, don't skimp. Add other highly requested, low-size columns that are needed. Don't tune one set of queries to have another incur the newly added I/O costs for no benefit.

Ordering Results

You should view ORDER BY statements with the same level of concern as DISTINCT statements. An ORDER BY statement can create a Sort operation in the query plan if the data is not already in that order. This can be a trivial thing if those columns are part of an ordered, clustered, or covering index, but can also increase the level of I/O for the query. You especially don't want Sort operations occurring that don't get used. Sort operations without indexes use a lot of CPU and memory, so remove gratuitous order by statements.

Take a simple example of sorting the results of the Sales Reason table by the ModifiedDate field. Then add a non-clustered index on the field and look at the differences.

```
--WITHOUT THE INDEX
Select * from Sales.SalesOrderHEaderSalesReason Order BY ModifiedDate
  |--Sort(ORDER BY:([ModifiedDate] ASC))
       |--Clustered Index Scan(
        OBJECT:([PK_SalesOrderHeaderSalesReason_SalesOrderID_SalesReasonID]))

--WITH THE INDEX
Select * from Sales.SalesOrderHEaderSalesReason Order BY ModifiedDate
|--Index Scan(OBJECT:([IX_SOHSR_ModifiedDate]), ORDERED FORWARD)
```

The presence of an index allows the optimizer to take a shortcut and read from the index to line up the results. Then the ORDERED FORWARD indicates that bookmark lookups are made to resolve the primary key stored in the leaf of the non-clustered index and pull the remaining columns for the table. Without an index, the clustered leaf is scanned and then the results are ordered. This is an increase in subtree cost of .08 for the indexed sort to 1.98 for the non-indexed sort. Where is the cost difference? Look in the EstimateCPU column to find the cost jump from .03 to 1.87 for the sort operation. Suffice it to say that sorting by just any column on a table should be examined for validity if you are having CPU or memory issues.

Handling Indexed Nullable Columns

Living with nullable columns always creates a logic overhead that must be considered when using the column in a filter or join. You'll encounter two common methods of either testing specifically for the null value or converting null values with either an ISNULL() or ANSI COALESCE() function. In this section, you'll see why one-size-fits-all performance recommendations can sometimes give unusual or at least unexpected results. In the AW database Production.Product table, the color column is nullable. If writing a query to select all the products that are either black or without color you'll typically see something like these two:

```
SELECT ProductId
FROM Production.Product
WHERE Coalesce(Color, N'Black') = N'Black'

SELECT productid
FROM Production.Product
```

```
WHERE color = N'Black'
         or color is null
```

Usually the action of wrapping the function around the column would produce a performance issue and the conventional wisdom would be to replace the function with searchable arguments and apply a non-clustered index. The Production.Product table is perfect for our test since it doesn't have an index on the color column. No index means that a clustered index scan (really a table scan) must be performed to read every row in the product table. Table 9-19 displays the results from the first run.

Table 9-19: Duration Comparison of Is Null and Coalesce Statements

Method	% Cost	CPU	Reads	Duration
Coalesce()	50	0	15	97ms
Is Null	50	0	15	173ms

What this tells us is that both methods require the same number of page reads. There is no performance punishment for using a function around the column. All else being equal, the results also show that the function evaluates faster than the two separate test conditions. Because of the clustered index scan and fact that this step takes up 100 percent of the cost of each individual plan, a lock-step action would be to apply a non-clustered index. However, just adding a non-clustered index doesn't always solve the problem. This is a 504 row table with 248 null values. This means there is a 49 percent selectivity calculation for a NULL value, which is just under the selectivity criteria for the optimizer to abandon the index if provided. Add one anyway. The results should look similar to those in Table 9-20.

Table 9-20: Comparison of Is Null and Coalese Statements

Method	% Cost	CPU	Reads	Duration
Coalesce()	51	10	4	126ms
Is Null	49	0	4	270ms

The results are better from an I/O perspective, but worse from a speed perspective. The reads have dropped from 15 to 4 pages. This decreased the overall costs seen in the increase of separation in subtree costs from 0.0033172 for the IsNull() method vs. 0.00457714 for the Coalesce() method. The issue remains that with the addition of the index, the Coalesce method is still faster and is even using a full Index Scan operation. The reason is because of the size of the Production.Product table. With only 504 rows, it is more efficient to employ a sequential disk read and incur the actual table scan cost than to perform an index seek. To see what happens when the table size starts to come into play, run these queries once without the index and then again after adding a non-clustered index on the CarrierTrackingNumber.

```
SELECT SalesOrderDetailId
FROM Sales.SalesOrderDetail
```

```
WHERE Coalesce(CarrierTrackingNumber, N'9429-430D-89') = N'9429-430D-89'

SELECT SalesOrderDetailId
FROM Sales.SalesOrderDetail
WHERE CarrierTrackingNumber = N'9429-430D-89'
or CarrierTrackingNumber is null
```

Table 9-21 compares the results of both queries.

Table 9-21: High Volume Comparison of Is Null and Coalese Statements

Method	Index?	% Cost	CPU	Reads	Duration
Coalesce()	N	50	90	1783	1420ms
Is Null	N	50	50	1783	1205ms
Coalesce()	Y	99	40	526	653ms
Is Null	Y	1	10	6	373ms

In the SalesOrderDetail table there are over 120K rows. Without an index, both methods pull massive pages (all of them) to perform clustered index scanning. Once the index is added to the CarrierTrackingNumber column, you can see the number of reads dropping dramatically. Along with the reducing number of rows to consider, we can now see reductions in the total time required to evaluate each row for inclusion in the results.

The point here is that you have to look at more than just whether a table or index scanning operation is occurring in the execution plan. Sometimes a scan is providing a great benefit in time and costs.

Eliminating Duplicates

DISTINCT statements are used to eliminate duplicates in data. Preferably, a non-clustered or clustered index will be scanned to retrieve the data that optionally will pass through an aggregation or sort operator. Even in the worst case scenario where the column under the DISTINCT is a non-indexed column, the clustered index will be scanned. This is a common task, but one that can be easily misused. A common misuse is to apply a DISTINCT indiscriminately against an entire set of returned columns. Fortunately, the optimizer looks into the select statement and doesn't perform any aggregation if at least one column in the SELECT is unique.

One finer point about the DISTINCT statement is instructive for digging into and understanding query planning. The point is that Non-Clustered indexes are far more favorable from an I/O perspective when performing DISTINCT Operations. Keep this in mind and limit the columns under consideration to those covered by a non-clustered index when tuning DISTINCT statements. Take this simple example of selecting DISTINCT SalesOrderIds from the Sales.SalesOrderDetail table.

```
SELECT DISTINCT SalesOrderID
FROM Sales.SalesOrderDetail
```

The Sales.SalesOrderDetail table has the indexes listed in Table 9-22. The index starting with PK% is clustered; the IX% index is not.

Table 9-22: Indexes on SalesOrderDetail Table

Index Name	Columns
IX_SalesOrderDetail_ProductID	ProductID
PK_SalesOrderDetail_SalesOrderID_SalesOrderDetailID	SalesOrderID, SalesOrderDetailID

You might expect that the scan for the SalesOrderID should occur on the clustered index field. This is, of course, one of the mantras of performance tuning — make sure you are using clustered indexes whenever possible. If you look at the query plan in Figure 9-13, you'll see that the non-clustered index by ProductId is being used. If you tinker with the plan by adding an ORDER BY statement, you can force the optimizer to use a clustered index scan instead. This equivalent action would be taken if the non-clustered index by ProductId did not exist.

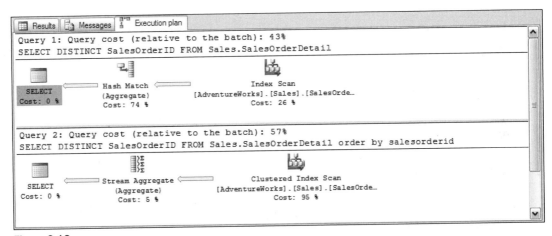

Figure 9-13

Although the costs of the two plans are close, the I/O numbers are far apart. Query 1 using the non-clustered index produces 228 logical page reads, compared to the clustered index 1,783 page reads of Query 2. What is happening here is that the non-clustered index is functioning as a covering index, since it contains both the ProductId and the SalesOrderId for each row in the table. More rows of this index can fit into an 8K page than from the clustered index. Remember that the clustered index leaf contains the page itself and in this case requires 7.5 times more pages to be loaded into memory to perform the DISTINCT operation. It is clear that you would *not* want to add the extra ORDER BY clause into this T-SQL statement to achieve a Clustered Index Scan operation to incur this extra cost. Look for non-clustered indexes on tables where you may be performing consistent DISTINCT operations to ensure that you aren't creating this performance issue.

Tuning T-SQL Common Patterns or Idioms

If you've ever felt like you've seen that performance problem before, you've probably tapped into your mental storage of the pattern and the resulting solution. Some T-SQL performance issues are recurring issues, and identifying them quickly can greatly reduce your troubleshooting work load. This section examines performance issues with some common patterns that are used in T-SQL to solve development problems.

Singleton SELECT Statements

This pattern involves selecting one and only one row from a table. The term *singleton* refers to a set with only one element — in the database world this is one row. Typically, there are two approaches to generating a singleton-type result. One option is to use the TOP statement to lift the top one (1) row based on a predicate and sort order. A second option is use a derived table to find the one clustered index value matching the applied predicate using an aggregate function. To tune these types of queries, look at the results you need from the operation. If you are returning a set of columns that can't be covered by indexes, then the column values must be looked up from the base pages. It is more efficient to look up only those rows that meet one condition rather than look up all the rows to determine the top row. Conversely, if all you need is one row with the column that is in an index, either way will perform about the same.

The TOP approach is most commonly used, because it is the most idiomatic way to grab one or more rows. T-SQL provides the language extension and simply adding the TOP statement to an existing query converts it into a singleton select. In the real world, there are more WHERE conditions than there are indexes, so this example uses several columns: TransactionDate, Quantity, and ActualCost columns that aren't indexed. The other columns are indexed.

```
SELECT TOP 1 transactionId
FROM production.transactionhistoryarchive
WHERE ProductId = 399
AND referenceOrderId = 5633
AND transactionDate = '2001-11-18 00:00:00.000'
AND quantity > 2
AND actualcost >= 0
ORDER BY transactionId DESC
```

It is important to show a query like this in some examples instead of only using the transactionId in the predicate to show the actions that SQL Server 2005 performs to filter on the additional non-indexed fields. The optimizer will determine that one of the indexed fields is selective enough to resolve to a small number of rows and then uses the clustered indexes stored on matching leaves to look up the remaining key fields. These two actions are seen in the first two operational steps of Figure 9-14, where the plan shows seeking the index on referenceOrderId and then performing the Key Lookup.

The reason for pointing this out is to show how intelligent the optimizer is at selecting the best index for the job and how that ultimately results in faster queries. Note that the remaining tasks of applying the filters to the lookup fields and grabbing the top row almost comes free. The selectivity of using the referenceOrderId field reduced the first inquiry to one row. If the ProductId index had been used, the results would have been narrowed to 786 rows. This choice by the optimizer results in a reduction of 785 additional lookup operations whether they occurred via an additional index seek or not.

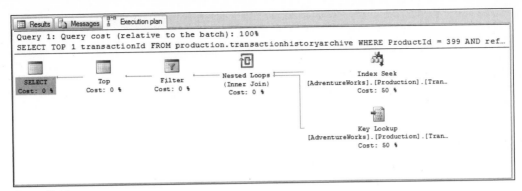

Figure 9-14

Another way to perform the same action is to use an aggregate function. An example of the same query written with an aggregate MAX function would look like this:

```
SELECT max(transactionId)
FROM production.transactionhistoryarchive
WHERE ProductId = 399
AND referenceOrderId = 5633
AND transactiondate = '2001-11-18 00:00:00.000'
AND quantity > 2
AND actualcost >= 0
```

If you looked at the execution plan for this query, you'd notice that the optimizer applied the same access methodology of using the referenceOrderId field index, but added a Stream Aggregate operator instead of a Top operator. Statistically, the sub costs are insignificant. This is partly because the index produces only one row to work with. The costing formulas used by the optimizer estimate the Stream Aggregate operator to be slightly more expensive (.0000011% compared to .0000001%) , but if you view the queries using the profiler, you'll see that the CPU and I/O page reads are exactly the same.

Now look at what happens if you change the query to return the whole row. Change the first query from "SELECT TOP 1 transactionId" to "SELECT TOP 1 *". For the second query, a typical rewrite would use a derived table to first get the maximum transactionId and then retrieve the row like this:

```
SELECT *
FROM production.transactionhistoryarchive
WHERE transactionid = (
 SELECT max(transactionId)
 FROM production.transactionhistoryarchive
 WHERE ProductId = 399
 AND referenceOrderId = 5633
 AND transactiondate = '2001-11-18 00:00:00.000'
 AND quantity > 2
 AND actualcost >= 0
 )
```

When you run the two side by side, you'll notice that the estimated costs will display query costs of 6 percent for the TOP query and 35 percent for the MAX query. However, when you look into the profiler, you see that this can't be the case. The number of I/O pages accessed by the MAX query is 33 percent more than the TOP query. If you look at the deltas in the subtree costs, you'll see the reason for the disparity is because the optimizer is overestimating the amount of sort I/O involved in executing the ORDER BY statement. The MAX query doesn't have to perform a sort to get the max transactionId, but the additional cost is borne by the second seek into the clustered index. This increases the I/O activity and the overall cost and duration. This is a case where you have to look further into the actual results to determine which method is best. It is clear so far that the TOP query is working best.

However, using the knowledge of the highly selective index, a rewrite of the MAX query can provide very detailed information to the optimizer:

```
SELECT *
FROM production.transactionhistoryarchive
WHERE transactionid = (
 SELECT max(transactionId)
 FROM production.transactionhistoryarchive
 WHERE referenceOrderId = 5633
 )
AND ProductId = 399
AND referenceOrderId = 5633
AND transactiondate = '2001-11-18 00:00:00.000'
AND quantity > 2
AND actualcost >= 0
```

The rewrite change seems insignificant on the surface, but if you examine the information in the SHOWPLAN_ALL option below, you can see that the second method is able to use the clustered index and the non-clustered index to reduce the I/O. The results of this second MAX query and a comparison against the other methods is provided in Table 9-23. Note that the number of I/O pages in the second MAX query has been reduced. Also note that the optimizer is wrong when estimating the results of pure costs.

```
SHOWPLAN_ALL INFO FOR MAX1-
|--Index Seek(OBJECT:([IX_ReferenceOrderLineID]),
        SEEK:([ReferenceOrderID]=(5633)) ORDERED FORWARD)
|--Clustered Index Seek(OBJECT:([PK_TransactionHistoryArchive_TransactionID]),
        SEEK:([TransactionID]=[TransactionID]) LOOKUP ORDERED FORWARD)
|--Clustered Index Seek(OBJECT:([PK_TransactionHistoryArchive_TransactionID]),
        SEEK:([TransactionID]=[Expr1006]) ORDERED FORWARD)
SHOWPLAN_ALL INFO FOR MAX2-
|--Index Seek(OBJECT:([IX_ReferenceOrderLineID]),
        SEEK:([ReferenceOrderID]=(5633))     ORDERED FORWARD)
|--Clustered Index Seek(OBJECT:([PK_TransactionHistoryArchive_TransactionID]),
        SEEK:([TransactionID]=[Expr1006]),
        WHERE:([ProductID]=(399) AND [ReferenceOrderID]=(5633))
```

From these results, it is easy to see that the extra work of fabricating the derived table didn't really buy much in terms of performance. To build this performance query, you needed to know information about the selectivity of an index that could change if the parameter was less selective. However, with the simple inclusion of a TOP statement and an ORDER by, you'd be able to keep up with the fanciest T-SQL programming. This is why the TOP method is preferred over other methods of generating singleton results. It is easy to use and provides decent performance.

Table 9-23: Performance Comparison of Singleton Pattern Selects

Method	% Cost	CPU	Reads	Duration
TOP	52	10	4	119ms
MAX1	29	0	6	280ms
MAX2	19	10	4	110ms

Aggregates and CTEs

Frequently requested aggregates from tables should be evaluated for potential covering indexes. Typically, in an aggregate pattern, you should be able see patterns of aggregation around an already existing index structure. Take for an example the need to summarize the cost components of a sales order in the columns: TaxAmt, Freight, and SubTotal by an order date range. If the order date is already a non-clustered index, then including these columns in the leaf level of the index will allow the optimizer to seek directly into the non-clustered index. This avoids scanning the much larger clustered index for these extra columns. Let's look at the problem from the beginning.

You are presented with the requirements to provide a summary by customer of the orders and cost components in `Sales.SalesOrderHeader` and provide percentage relationships of these figures across a period. One brute force way to write the query is like this:

```
Select CustomerId, Count(*) AS CustOrderCount, Sum(h.TaxAmt) As CustTaxAmt,
        Sum(h.SubTotal) As CustSubTotal, Sum(h.Freight) as CustFreight,
        Sum(h.TaxAmt)/(Select sum(TaxAmt) From Sales.SalesOrderHeader
                    where OrderDate >= '07/01/2001'
                    and orderDate < '12/31/2001') * 100
                    as PctCustTaxToTotalTax,
        Sum(h.Freight)/(Select sum(Freight) From Sales.SalesOrderHeader
                    Where OrderDate >= '07/01/2001'
                    and orderDate < '12/31/2001') * 100
                    as PctFreightToTotalFreight,
        CONVERT(DECIMAL(5,2),(Count(*)/
                (Select 1.*Count(*) From Sales.SalesOrderHeader
                    Where OrderDate >= '07/01/2001'
                    and orderDate < '12/31/2001') * 100))
                    as PctCustOrderCntToTotalCnt
from Sales.SalesOrderHeader h
Where OrderDate >= '07/01/2001' And OrderDate < '12/31/2001'
Group By CustomerId
```

Note that the predicate is using `OrderDate` for a filter and is grouping by `customerid`. There is a non-clustered index on customer, but no index on `OrderDate`. You'll see this evidenced by the four table scan operations for each of the times `Sales.SalesOrderHeader` is filtered by the order date range. The scan operations on `OrderDate` are labeled in Figure 9-15 as 1-4. All the other operations don't involve the use of any indexes, so you know that the non-clustered index on customer is not even used.

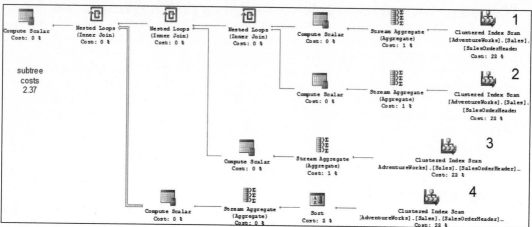

Figure 9-15

If you are forced to write this query without having any input on adding indexing structures, one thing you could do is reduce the I/O. The key to this is removing redundancy. Noticing some basic patterns, you may realize that you could make the summary operations once and then cross apply the results to each row to cut the I/O immediately in half. One nice way to do this is with the new common-table expressions. First, you describe the inner results like a derived table, but better, and you'll explore this in a second. Then cross-apply these results against the outer summary by customer Id. The plan for this query, shown in Figure 9-16, is much simpler and shows that the index (marked by labels 1 and 2) is only being read twice.

```
With Totals As (
Select    Count(*) AS OrderCount, Sum(TaxAmt) As TaxAmt,
          Sum(SubTotal) As SubTotal, Sum(Freight) as Freight
from Sales.SalesOrderHeader h
Where OrderDate >= '07/01/2001' And OrderDate < '12/31/2001'
)
Select CustomerId, Count(*) AS CustOrderCount, Sum(h.TaxAmt) As CustTaxAmt,
          Sum(h.SubTotal) As CustSubTotal, Sum(h.Freight) as CustFreight,
          Sum(h.TaxAmt)/(Totals.TaxAmt) * 100 as PctCustTaxToTotalTax,
          Sum(h.Freight)/(Totals.Freight) * 100 as PctFreightToTotalFreight,
          CONVERT(DECIMAL(5,2),(Count(*)/(1.*Totals.OrderCount)) * 100)
                  as PctCustOrderCntToTotalCnt
from Sales.SalesOrderHeader h, Totals
Where OrderDate >= '07/01/2001' And OrderDate < '12/31/2001'
Group By CustomerId, Totals.TaxAmt, Totals.Freight, Totals.OrderCount
```

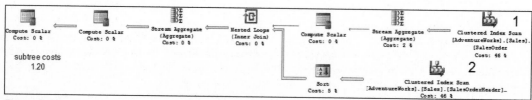

Figure 9-16

The plan could be really improved upon if an index could be added. Just adding an index on Order-Date doesn't really help the CTE, but does allow the optimizer to adjust for the brute force method. Regardless, the leaf level of the clustered index must be read to retrieve the cost components. If adding these cost components to the non-clustered index doesn't add too much storage to the index and increase significantly the number of pages that have to be read on the index, there is a significant advantage in adding these columns to the index. Since these cost components are unlikely to be search predicates, they can be added to the leaf level of the index as information only. The index doesn't consider these columns as keys so this reduces the overhead of including the column in the index statistics. Create a covering index for the order date like this:

```
CREATE NONCLUSTERED INDEX [IX_SalesOrderHeader_OrderDate] ON
[Sales].[SalesOrderHeader]  ([OrderDate] ASC)
INCLUDE ( [CustomerID],[SubTotal],[TaxAmt],[Freight])
```

You can see in Table 9-24 that the page reads have dropped significantly. This can be attributed to reading the non-clustered index leaf instead of the clustered index leaf. Clearly, this is an example of how you can reduce I/O demands on your SQL Server database.

Table 9-24: Comparison of Aggregate Methods

Method	Cost	CPU	Reads	Duration
(Without Index)				
Brute Force	2.37388	120	2827	453
CTE	1.2071	101	1410	409
(With Index - No Covering - Still uses clustered index)				
Brute Force	1.48929	150	1498	485
CTE	1.2071	110	1422	425
(With Index - Covering)				
Brute Force	0.083310	110	46	407
CTE	0.061812	60	92	394

A CTE is not necessary to achieve this I/O reduction. A solution could be coded using a derived table instead. Simply convert the CTE to a derived table in the FROM statement. However, the execution plan will remain the same. An advantage to the CTE solution is it may be easier to read, but the best part about these CTEs is that you can refer to them more than once in a batch. Multi-referencing is not something you can do with a derived table. This has the fascinating appearance that you can create a derived table that can be re-summarized while creating the results.

```
--CTE queried twice
With CustTotals As (
```

```
Select    CustomerId, Count(*) AS CustOrderCount, Sum(TaxAmt) As CustTaxAmt,
          Sum(SubTotal) As CustSubTotal, Sum(Freight) as CustFreight
from Sales.SalesOrderHeader h
Where OrderDate >= '07/01/2001' And OrderDate < '12/31/2001'
Group By CustomerId
)
Select    CustTotals.*,
          CustTotals.CustTaxAmt/Totals.TaxAmt as PctCustTaxToTotalTax,
          CustTotals.CustFreight/Totals.Freight as PctFreightToTotalFreight,
          CONVERT(DECIMAL(5,2),(CustTotals.CustOrderCount/(1.*Totals.OrderCount))
          * 100) as PctCustOrderCntToTotalCnt
From CustTotals,
   (Select Sum(CustOrderCount) as OrderCount,
           Sum(CustTaxAmt) As TaxAmt,
           Sum(CustSubTotal) As SubTotal,
           Sum(CustFreight) as Freight
            from CustTotals) Totals
```

You can query the base table once to build the CustTotals derivation. Then later, without calling the base table again, you can query the CustTotals derivation again and aggregate at a totals level. It looks as if you could really get the I/O operations down to one pass of the index. Unfortunately, although this capability is high on the cool factor and may be easy to read, the optimizer is not fooled. It still seeks into the non-clustered index on OrderDate twice. You can see this by reviewing the Showplan Statistics Profile (abbreviated here to show part of statement text and output list):

```
Index Seek(OBJECT:([IX_SalesOrderHeader_OrderDate] AS [h]), SEEK:([h].[OrderDate]
>= '2001-07-01' AND [h].[OrderDate] < '2001-12-31') ORDERED FORWARD)
[h].[CustomerID], [h].[TaxAmt], [h].[Freight]
Index Seek(OBJECT:([IX_SalesOrderHeader_OrderDate] AS [h]), SEEK:([h].[OrderDate]
>= '2001-07-01' AND [h].[OrderDate] < '2001-12-31') ORDERED FORWARD)
[h].[CustomerID], [h].[SubTotal], [h].[TaxAmt], [h].[Freight]
```

You can see the first seek on the bottom being done to output the four columns needed by the CTE; the second seek is being done for the three columns needed by the summary of the CTE. The subtree costs are also a bit higher at .0968517, making this solution not as good as the first CTE, but interesting.

Derived Tables and Correlated Subqueries

This is a common idiom where a DISTINCT clause or other aggregate operation is used to summarize parent-level data after applying WHERE predicates at the child-relationship level. In the best possible case, the filter and the columns under summation would be within clustered or covered indexes. However, a more typical example would be a query in the AW database that returns unique corresponding Purchase Order Numbers when provided a Carrier Tracking Number, even though a Carrier Tracking Number may be duplicated in the child-level, and neither item has an index whatsoever. In this instance, the query to perform this task could be written like this:

```
SELECT DISTINCT PurchaseOrderNumber
FROM Sales.SalesOrderHeader h
INNER JOIN sales.SalesOrderDetail d
ON h.SalesOrderId = d.SalesOrderId
WHERE d.CarrierTrackingNumber = N'E257-40A1-A3'
```

However, you could also use a derived table like this:

```
SELECT PurchaseOrderNumber
FROM Sales.SalesOrderHeader h
INNER JOIN (SELECT DISTINCT d.SalesOrderId
                FROM Sales.SalesOrderDetail d
                WHERE d.CarrierTrackingNumber = N'E257-40A1-A3'
                ) d
ON h.SalesOrderId = d.SalesOrderId
```

You could build a correlated subquery like this:

```
SELECT PurchaseOrderNumber
FROM Sales.SalesOrderHeader h
WHERE EXISTS (SELECT *
                FROM Sales.SalesOrderDetail d
                WHERE d.CarrierTrackingNumber = N'E257-40A1-A3'
                AND h.SalesOrderId = d.SalesOrderId
                )
```

So which of these methods provides the best performance? How do you go about evaluating this? Note first that each is using a highly selective WHERE predicate. The value E257-40A1-A3 occurs in only one row in 121,317 in the Sales.SalesOrderDetail table. This high selectivity should produce a plan where the first step can resolve to one row and will enable you to focus on the subsequent responses of the optimizer to each query method. By executing all three SQL commands in a batch, you can get an idea of the relative costs of the statements to each other. In this case these plans all resolve to the same cost. The plan in Figure 9-17 for 34 percent is the result of a rounding to the full 100 percent.

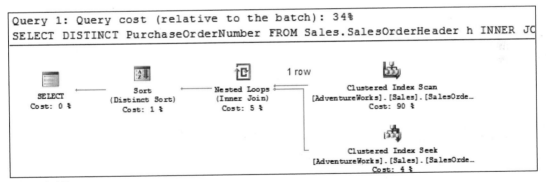

Figure 9-17

This first execution plan corresponds to the JOIN and you can see that result of the Index Scan on Sales.SalesOrderDetail results in Figure 9-18, by the one row that is used in a nested loop to seek into the matching Sales.SalesOrderHeader table. The problem is that by joining these two result sets in a nested loop the sort order can't be guaranteed, so the Sort step is added to the plan to produce the sorted result.

In the subquery method, the rows are filtered at the Sales.SalesOrderDetail level before loading one at a time into a Stream Aggregate operator. Because the subquery has to be resolved first before the

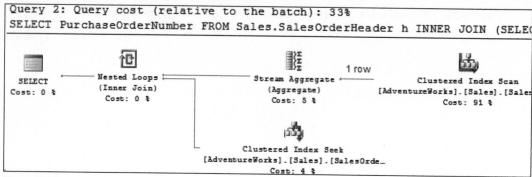

Figure 9-18

Join can occur, the optimizer chooses to use this grouping structure to maintain the order by the groups. This removes the need for the Sort step that was required for the first query method. Maintaining a sort is more efficient than writing the results and then resorting.

Many people think that correlated subqueries are the most efficient. When you examine this last method it may seem like the best combination of the two previous methods. In fact, the first three steps are the same. The difference is that a GROUP BY operation is used by the Stream Aggregate to build the sorted output for each SalesOrderId to avoid an additional sort. You can see this in the plan in Figure 9-19.

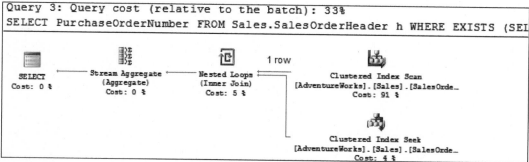

Figure 9-19

Here's where you have to start digging. Relative to all three techniques, the derived and correlated subqueries with query costs of 33 percent look equivalent. Remember that we are talking about costs, not speed, so before a final choice is made, you should look at the details provided by the profiler and reevaluate with a less selective WHERE predicate to see how each solution scales.

In the profiler under the Showplan Statistics Profile Event class, both methods display essentially the same estimates for subtree costs of 1.15691. The actual results can be determined by looking into the CPU, Reads, Writes, and Duration columns. The results, presented in Table 9-25, show that the overall duration of the derived table is statistically the same as correlated subquery and almost 40 percent faster than the full join summarization.

Table 9-25: Selective Correlated Subquery Performance Comparison

Method	% Cost	CPU	Reads	Duration
Join and DISTINCT	34	50	1241	71ms
Derived Table	33	40	1241	40ms
Correlated Subquery	33	40	1241	39ms

Remember that this example uses a very selective WHERE predicate. Decrease the selectivity removing the WHERE predicate. This run without the WHERE predicate will require more sort operations then the previous runs and can demonstrate the scaling capabilities of each method. Table 9-26 shows how the results change.

Table 9-26: Non Selective Correlated Subquery Comparison

Method	% Cost	CPU	Reads	Duration
Join and DISTINCT	34	270	1941	1690ms
Derived Table	33	91	1941	2073ms
Correlated Subquery	33	150	1941	2056ms

You'll notice a more drastic and maybe even surprising change in the total duration, even though the relative execution plan costs have remained essentially the same percentages. The slowest method is now the fastest and the two fastest are now the slowest.

If you look at the query execution plans, you'll notice that the query plan in Figure 9-20 for the Join method has changed to use a Merge Join Operator instead of a Nested Loop Operator.

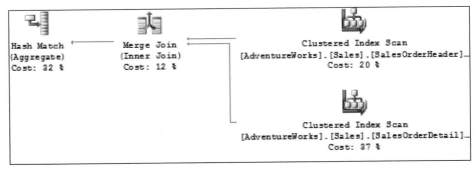

Figure 9-20

The Sort has also been exchanged for a Hash Match. These new additional operators may be more costly, but use almost no I/O, hence the decrease in duration. More importantly, the optimizer actually had the chance to alter the implementation of how the query would be executed. When we code specific implementations using derived tables and correlated subqueries, we leave the optimizer no alternatives to evaluate and we denigrate the declarative nature of T-SQL. As SQL Server advances, you are going to see more instances of where the old-school methods of rearranging SQL statements become irrelevant outside of very narrow edge-case circumstances. In this case, it appears that the Join method is easy to code and provides rather consistent performance of speed under increasing scale.

Paging and Sorting

Most applications have a need to page through a sorted resultset to display page N of M. There are several methods of meeting this requirement and evaluating them all is a dense enough topic to warrant its own chapter. Considerations for the perfect solution depend upon the selectivity options in the WHERE predicate, the number of results that the predicate yields, the number and nature of the ORDER BY scenarios allowed, whether total predicate realization as a total count is required, and finally the ease of maintainability. Since you are reading this chapter, you're probably most interested in this topic from a perspective of page-read-based performance.

The core of the problem is to apply a predicate to a set of tables and retrieve only a subset of the entire resultset ordered in a specified sort. For server-based solutions, the key is having some way to pull out the rows that constitute a viewable page by enumerating the resultset in the way it is ordered. There are two approaches to uniquely identifying the rows returned and breaking the ties: applying a numbering function to the resultset or using a unique identifying index from the results. For the results to be consistent between incremental page calls, having the primary identity key as the tiebreaker is convenient because it is intimately tied to each row. You can do the same thing with an applied function, but pay attention to how the resultset is ordered by sorting finally by the identity key. If you don't have a unique identifying key, then the only option is to use the ranking functions and deal with the results. This is equivalent to searching for T-SQL in an instantaneously indexed search engine and getting slightly different results each time. The variant results depend on how many new articles on T-SQL were added since your last search.

To follow along with the explanations for paging and sorting, you'll need to run this bit of T-SQL to create the TRANS_DATA table (which will contain 1 million row entries):

```
CREATE TABLE TRANS_TABLE(
        MYID    INT IDENTITY(1,1) NOT NULL PRIMARY KEY,
        MYDESC VARCHAR(10),
        MYDATE DATETIME,
        MYGROUPID INT)

DECLARE @I INT
SET @I = 0
WHILE @I < 1000000
BEGIN
 INSERT INTO TRANS_TABLE
 SELECT CHAR(ASCII('A') - 2 + (2 * (1 + ABS(CHECKSUM(NEWID())) % 26))),
                   DATEADD(day, ABS(CHECKSUM(NEWID())) % 365, '01/01/2007'),
                   (ABS(CHECKSUM(NEWID())) % 10)
 SET @I = @I + 1
END
```

```
CREATE NONCLUSTERED INDEX IX_TRANS_TABLE_MYDATE
ON TRANS_TABLE(MYDATE)
CREATE NONCLUSTERED INDEX IX_TRANS_TABLE_MYGROUPID
ON TRANS_TABLE(MYGROUPID)
```

CTE-Based Paging

New to SQL Server 2005 is the ranking ROW_NUMBER function, providing functionality available to ORACLE users for years. The old way to page and sort in ORACLE was to apply the ROWNUM() function to a resultset and get all the results less than the page you were interested in, then filter out the rows starting with the first row on the page. In SQL Server 2005, you can write something similar to page through the TRANS_TABLE data that would look like this:

```
DECLARE @START_ID int, @START_ROW int, @MAX_ROWS int
SELECT @START_ROW = 1, @MAX_ROWS = 25

select *
  from ( select p.*, rownum rnum
          FROM (
                SELECT ROW_NUMBER() OVER(ORDER BY MyDate, MYID) AS rowNum, *
                FROM TRANS_TABLE (NOLOCK)
                ) p
          where rownum <= @START_ROW + @MAX_ROWS - 1
        ) z
  where rnum >= @START_ROW
```

SQL Server 2005 also introduced the idea of Common Table functions, allowing for an easier way of coding the same thing. The CTE simply takes the place of the two derived tables, leaving a syntactically easier query to code.

```
DECLARE @START_ROW int, @MAX_ROWS int, @TOT_ROW_CNT int
SELECT @START_ROW = 1, @MAX_ROWS = 25;
WITH PAGED AS (
                SELECT ROW_NUMBER() OVER(ORDER BY MyDate, MYID) AS rowNum, *
                FROM TRANS_TABLE (NOLOCK)
                )
SELECT *
FROM PAGED
WHERE ROWNUM BETWEEN @START_ROW AND @START_ROW + @MAX_ROWS - 1
```

Not only is this more easily implemented, the performance and execution plans are the same (except for derived table definition). A sample of the two plans is not shown here for brevity, but can be downloaded at www.wrox.com in the code for this chapter.

You'll also find that this CTE method is the most commonly found recommendation for paging and sorting. There are other options to perform the same task, but before we examine them, there are some performance gains to add to the typical paging CTE. Note in the CTE example that all columns are being returned in the CTE. The more scalable way to arrange this is to return only the RowNum value and a lookup key to the TRANS_TABLE like this:

```
DECLARE @START_ROW int, @MAX_ROWS int, @TOT_ROW_CNT int
SELECT @START_ROW = 1, @MAX_ROWS = 25;
```

```
WITH PAGED AS (
                SELECT ROW_NUMBER() OVER(ORDER BY MyDate, MYID) AS rowNum, MYID
                FROM TRANS_TABLE (NOLOCK)
                )
SELECT TT.*
FROM PAGED PGD
INNER JOIN TRANS_TABLE TT
ON PGD.MYID = TT.MYID
WHERE ROWNUM BETWEEN @START_ROW AND @START_ROW + @MAX_ROWS - 1
ORDER BY MyDate, MYID
```

Since there is a single column identity field as a lookup on TRANS_TABLE, adding only the MYID column will be the most efficient, but this technique can work also for multi-column primary keys. You just need a way to join the CTE results back to the base table to retrieve the other values on the page of the clustered index. Because you can't access the value of the ROW_NUMBER function in the CTE, you can't reduce the realization of the rows within the CTE when you are asking for potentially everything to be returned — imagine if @START_ROW=1 and @MAX_ROWS=1,000,000. The optimizer decides it is more efficient to return all the results just in case. You can see this in the optimized plan for the CTE with all columns with a SEEK operation against each row.

```
Rows        Executes        Statement Text
1000000     1000000         |--Clustered Index Seek(OBJECT:([PK_TRANS_TABLE]),
                                     SEEK:([MYID]=[MYID]) LOOKUP ORDERED FORWARD)
```

After moving the T-SQL around, this SEEK activity drops to match our intentions:

```
Rows        Executes        Statement Text
    25          25          |--Clustered Index Seek(OBJECT:([PK__TRANS_TABLE] AS [TT]),
                                     SEEK:([TT].[MYID]=[MYID]) ORDERED FORWARD)
```

Not only are the number of rows reduced, but you'll also notice that the seek operation is no longer a bookmark lookup operation. You learned about reducing these operators earlier in this chapter, and now you can see again the savings with this T-SQL rewrite. Table 9-27 shows costs for retrieving first and last pages in.

Table 9-27: CTE Paging Performance Metrics

Method	% Cost	CPU	Reads	Duration
First Page				
ALL COLS IN CTE	87	0	105	138ms
USE JOIN FOR COLS	13	10	78	95ms
Last Page				
ALL COLS IN CTE	87	6580	3189758	6942ms
USE JOIN FOR COLS	13	1031	2312	1179ms

The conclusion is that the higher the number of rows you need to page through, the worse performance is going to get with the CTE. This is undeniably the case when all the columns are in the CTE, but the CTE that brings back just the key columns is still hovering around the 1-second mark for a million paged rows, so this may still be considered acceptable. This leads to the first and second rules of paging and sorting: keep the resultset as small as possible by controlling the WHERE predicate, and keep the columns as narrow as possible. The cost should be incurred seeking the correct page, not in retrieving, especially since you are retrieving only a page worth, typically 25 to 100 rows. In terms of optimization, this is an acceptable trade-off. Typically, a user will page through 1 to 5 pages and then change the search criteria, so having the code scale into the 39,000th and 40,000th page is not critical.

ROW_COUNT-Based Paging

Another historical option for paging is using the ROW_COUNT function to throttle the number of rows that can be returned by any statement. The goal in this method (which has been around since the SQL Server 7.0 days) is to retrieve the last identifying key into variables in one step for the starting point. Then the ROW_COUNT function is used again to restrict the resultset after querying from the starting point. An example of this method looks like this:

```
DECLARE  @START_ID int, @START_ROW int, @MAX_ROWS int,
         @START_DATETIME DATETIME, @TOT_ROW_CNT INT
SELECT @START_ROW = 1, @MAX_ROWS = 25

-- Get the first row for the page
SET ROWCOUNT @START_ROW

SELECT @START_ID = MYID, @START_DATETIME = MYDATE FROM TRANS_TABLE (NOLOCK)
        ORDER BY MYDATE, MYID

-- Now, set the row count to MaximumRows and get
-- all records >= @first_id
SET ROWCOUNT @MAX_ROWS

SELECT *
FROM TRANS_TABLE (NOLOCK)
WHERE MYID >= @START_ROW
AND MYDATE >= @START_DATETIME
ORDER BY MYDATE, MYID

SET ROWCOUNT 0
```

Logically, this option looks good. One quick seek for an entity key, and then pull only the rows that you need. Outside of making sure nothing goes wrong between the SET ROWCOUNT statements to return the ROWCOUNT state to the default, the main issue with this method is that it only excels when the sort is against the clustered index. Typically, sort and paging procedures don't just sort against the non-clustered index, but almost any column in the resultset. Table 9-28 compares this method to the tuned CTE.

You may have noticed that the CTE and ROW_COUNT examples use a non-clustered index for the sort (MYDATE). This is on purpose, to give the ROW_COUNT not too good of a show. The results presented in Table 9-29 show a dramatic difference in the page reads and speed of the CTE against the ROW_COUNT method. However, the ROW_COUNT method is a bit faster if the sort on MYDATE is removed.

Table 9-28: Non-Clustered Sort Paging Metrics

Method	% Cost	CPU	Reads	Duration
First Page				
ROW_COUNT	99	4136	6365	7221ms
CTE	1	30	82	121ms
Last Page				
ROW_COUNT	99	801	2245	992ms
CTE	1	781	2237	899ms

Table 9-29: Clustered Sort Paging Metrics

Method	% Cost	CPU	Reads	Duration
First Page				
ROW_COUNT	99	0	12	12ms
CTE	1	40	80	119ms
Last Page				
ROW_COUNT	99	641	2241	658ms
CTE	1	971	3810	1033ms

On the clustered sorts, you can see a bit of an improvement that can be made, so there may be some special scenarios where this technique can result in a lower page read requirement.

TOP @X Paging

SQL Server 2005 added the new TOP statement that can accept a row number parameter. This allows for a similar methodology as the ROW_COUNT method without the dangers of leaving the orphaned ROW_COUNT state on the connection. The performance of this method is very similar to the ROW_-COUNT method except for sorting on heaps or no indexes deep into the paging schemes. Since this is an edge-case benefit, we'll just show the query here and post the results on www.wrox.com.

```
DECLARE @START_ID int, @START_ROW int, @MAX_ROWS int, @TOT_ROW_CNT INT,
@START_DESC VARCHAR(10)
SELECT @START_ROW = 1, @MAX_ROWS = 25
```

```
-- Get the first row for the page
SELECT TOP(@START_ROW) @START_ID = MYID, @START_DESC = MYDESC
FROM TRANS_TABLE (NOLOCK)
 ORDER BY MYDESC, MYID

SELECT TOP(@MAX_ROWS) *
FROM TRANS_TABLE (NOLOCK)
WHERE MYID >= @START_ROW
AND MYDESC >= @START_DESC
ORDER BY MYDESC, MYID
```

Temp Table Paging

There are a lot of Temp table paging procedures in use, and until recently, it was not clear to us why they were being used. The performance issue is that even when used to lay down a copy of the clustered index key and the results of a ranking function, you can't get away from having to write the same results that you'll later have to reread. This is not a huge impact when the resultsets are small, but as the result row count grows this becomes the wrong method to use. The temptation to use a temp table is understandable — especially if the UI requires a return of the total number of fully realized predicate rows. If you noticed, the other method examples in this section never fully realized the predicate. Either the optimizer took a shortcut or the ROW_COUNT/TOP operations resulted in only partially realizing all the rows of the predicate. This is the secret as to why these optimizations work so well. However, if you have to return the total row count of the predicate, then pulling all the clustered IDs that match the predicate into a temp table allows you to use @@ROWCOUNT to instantly interrogate the number of a rows added, and then still have the table around to use in a JOIN.

This sounds good, and works well on small tables. However, using the one-million-row TRANS_DATA table, even a simple paging operation will eat up some I/O in tempdb. Here's a sample of the temp table paging using TRANS_DATA.

```
DECLARE @START_ROW int, @MAX_ROWS int, @TOT_ROW_CNT int
SELECT @START_ROW = 1, @MAX_ROWS = 25;

SELECT ROW_NUMBER() OVER(ORDER BY MyDate, MYID) AS rowNum,
       MYID
into #TEMP
FROM TRANS_TABLE (NOLOCK)

SELECT TT.*
FROM TRANS_TABLE (NOLOCK) TT
INNER JOIN #TEMP T
ON TT.MYID = T.MYID
WHERE ROWNUM BETWEEN @START_ROW AND @START_ROW + @MAX_ROWS - 1

DROP TABLE #TEMP
```

Again, notice that, like the CTE example, only the most important fields are in the ranking number function, that is written to the temp table #TEMP. The remainder is pulled in from the base table. This is at least a better option than dumping all column and row contents into the temp table. Table 9-30 shows the results of comparing to the CTE example.

Table 9-30: CTE Sort Paging Metrics

Method	% Cost	CPU	Reads	Duration
First Page				
TEMP	99	7300	19208*	9799ms
CTE	1	30	82	121ms
Last Page				
TEMP	99	7090	19197*	12903ms
CTE	1	781	2237	899ms

*not including writes

When you look at the comparison results, it is clear that this solution really beats up on your tempdb database and the response time is unacceptable in today's terms for a one-million row resultset. However, if the WHERE clause produces consistent multi-hundred row resultsets, the impact is not quite so pronounced and you may be able to use this method for these use cases.

Returning Total Page Numbers

One of the advantages of using the TEMP table paging method is that returning the total realized rows is easy and cheap, but does this outweigh the cost of the I/O? Capture the total realized rows from the predicate using @@ROWCOUNT after inserting the rows into the temp table like this:

```
SET @TOT_ROW_CNT = @@ROWCOUNT
```

Using ⇨ROWCOUNT is almost free. All other methods have to run a separate count operation, since the resultsets in the examples aren't fully realized. The operation to retrieve total row counts for page calculations requires a re-querying of the base table, including the WHERE predicate:

```
SELECT @TOT_ROW_CNT = COUNT(*) FROM TRANS_TABLE (NOLOCK)
--++WHERE CONDITION
```

This is not a cheap operation. You should use the * in the COUNT(*) operation to allow the optimizer to use the best index to perform the count on, but every leaf on an index will be read to perform this count. You can see the work performed by looking at the plan.

```
Rows       Statement Text
1000000    |--Index Scan(OBJECT:([IX_TRANS_TABLE_MYGROUPID]))
```

For the TRANS_TABLE all 100000 rows in the index are read, resulting in about 1740 page reads on the smallest index IX_TRANS_TABLE_MYGROUPID. If the clustered index was the only index that can be read, this would be much more expensive. The expense of this summation may even lead you to believe that using the temp table method is cheaper for paging and sorting.

Table 9-31 shows the comparison of the two methods.

Table 9-31: Paging with Temp Tables and CTE Comparison

Method	% Cost	CPU	Reads	Duration
First Page				
TEMP	99	7300	19208	9799ms
CTE	1	30+300	82+1743	121ms+2200ms

Compare the numbers between the CTE and the temp table method after adding in the additional count operation to see that the cost saved with the @@ROWCOUNT is not offset by the amount of I/O that is consumed.

Tuning the T-SQL Statement with Hints

Sometimes you might run into some issues that can't be resolved. Your data or situation just runs counter to how the optimizer approaches the solution, and you can only get the performance you need by tuning the T-SQL statement to get the plans that you've been able to simulate. This section will cover a common issue of plan caching, how to identify the issue, and how to resolve it.

Query Plan Caching Issues

Query plan caching is a wonderful thing. The idea is that a parameterized statement can be processed by SQL Server and only incur the costs of planning the best way to execute it once. This works wonderfully as long as the parameters represent evenly distributed data or you don't get too fancy and write multi-use, multi-parameter stored procedures. Performance issues occur when the first plan encountered by the optimizer isn't representative of the high-percentage usage of the procedure. The issue is that the low-percentage usage of the procedure is now cached and the high-percentage usage will have to use whatever plan was cached first. This is not optimal when the cached version is optimized for only a few rows of retrieval and the high-percentage usage is for a large row set. Rows will then be retrieved with nested loop operators that could more efficiently be retrieved with merge join operators. The opposite could also occur, but may be more difficult to detect.

To see an example of this in action, you need to produce a really low and high-selectivity predicate on a large row set. You'll use the SalesOrderHeader table for a large row set and change one of the customer's addresses to Khorixas, Namibia, for a low selectivity address. Run this query to doctor up the data in the address schema.

```
INSERT INTO person.StateProvince
SELECT 'KX', 'NA', 0, 'Khorixas', 1, newid(), getdate()
UPDATE pa
SET StateProvinceId = scope_identity()
FROM Sales.customerAddress ca
INNER JOIN person.address pa
ON ca.addressid = pa.addressid
WHERE customerid = 22103
```

To keep the noise down this procedure will just return the customerId. This is not an extremely useful procedure, but it will illustrate the plan caching issue.

```
CREATE PROC usp_OptimizeFor_Test
        (
        @COUNTRYREGIONCODE NVARCHAR(3)
        )
AS
Select h.CustomerId from Sales.SalesOrderHeader h
inner join Sales.SalesOrderDetail d
on h.SalesOrderId = d.SalesOrderId
inner join sales.CustomerAddress ca
on h.customerid = ca.customerid
inner join person.address pa
on ca.AddressId = pa.AddressId
inner join person.StateProvince pr
on pa.StateProvinceId = pr.StateProvinceId
inner join person.CountryRegion r
on pr.CountryRegionCode = r.CountryRegionCode
Where r.CountryRegionCode = @COUNTRYREGIONCODE
```

If you run the procedure using NA as the country region code parameter, you'll get three rows returned and the plan uses a nested loop to Join the inner results of the personal address to the customer address results because the statistics predict that this is a low number of rows.

```
Hash Match(Inner Join, HASH:([h].[SalesOrderID])=([d].[SalesOrderID]))
|--Hash Match(Inner Join, HASH:([ca].[CustomerID])=([h].[CustomerID]))
|   |--Hash Match(Inner Join, HASH:([pa].[AddressID])=([ca].[AddressID]))
|   |   |--Nested Loops(Inner Join, OUTER REFERENCES:([pr].[StateProvinceID]))
|   |   |   |--Nested Loops(Inner Join)
|   |   |   |   |--Clustered Index
|   |   |   |   |   Seek(OBJECT:([PK_CountryRegion_CountryRegionCode] AS [r]),
|   |   |   |   |   SEEK:([r].[CountryRegionCode]=N'NA') ORDERED FORWARD)
|   |   |   |   |--Index Scan
|   |   (OBJECT:([AK_StateProvince_StateProvinceCode_CountryRegionCode] AS [pr]),
|   |   |   |   |   WHERE:([CountryRegionCode]=N'NA'))
|   |   |   |   |--Index Seek(OBJECT:([IX_Address_StateProvinceID] AS [pa]),
|   |   |   |   |   SEEK:([pa].[StateProvinceID]=[StateProvinceID])
|   |   |   |--Index Scan(OBJECT:([AK_CustomerAddress_rowguid] AS [ca]))
|   |--Index Scan(OBJECT:([IX_SalesOrderHeader_CustomerID] AS [h]))
|--Index Scan(OBJECT:([IX_SalesOrderDetail_ProductID] AS [d]))
```

Now if you run the stored procedure again using US for the country code parameter, the stored procedure is cached, so the same plan is used — even when the row set is much higher. You can see that this call is using the cached plan by noting the events in the profiler. To see for yourself look for the SP:CacheHit event in the profiler results. Free the proc cache by running this statement:

```
DBCC FREEPROCCACHE  --DON'T RUN IN PRODUCTION ENVIRONMENTS!!
```

Now run the stored procedure again using the parameter value of US. Now look at the execution plan. We've removed the details on steps that are identical.

```
Hash Match [IDENTICAL]
|--Hash Match [IDENTICAL]
|      |--Hash Match [IDENTICAL]
|  (1)|      |--Merge Join(Inner Join,
|      |      |   MERGE:([pr].[StateProvinceID])=([pa].[StateProvinceID]),
|      |      |   RESIDUAL:([Person].[Address].
|      |      |      |--Nested Loops [IDENTICAL]
|      |      |      |      |--Clustered Index Seek [IDENTICAL]
|      |      |      |      |--Clustered Index Scan [IDENTICAL] (EXCEPT WITH 'US')
|  (2)|      |      |--Index Scan(OBJECT:([IX_Address_StateProvinceID] AS [pa]),
|      |      |      |   ORDERED FORWARD)
|      |      |--Index Scan [IDENTICAL]
|      |--Index Scan [IDENTICAL]
|--Index Scan [IDENTICAL]
```

This plan is optimized for a much larger row set. In fact, there are 61,395 rows being returned with the US parameter. You can see that the plan is optimized for this type of volume with the use of the Merge Join operator instead of the Nested Loop in the difference labeled (1). The other difference labeled (2) is a minor one, but is a bookmark lookup. This plan should have been run the first time the procedure was run, but was not because the procedure was run and cached the first time with the Namibian NA parameter. Table 9-32 shows the differences in performance.

Table 9-32: Demonstration of Plan Caching Issues

Parameter	Cached as 'NA'			Cached as 'US'		
	CPU	I/O	Duration	CPU	I/O	Duration
'NA'	111	379	204	180	408	210
'US'	280	605	2807	290	406	2222

This is why you have to jump in for the optimizer. Since you've established that the US parameterized version of this procedure is the heavy percentage use case, you'll need to ensure that the plan for this parameter is the one that is optimized. To do this, just add the following hint to the bottom of the procedure and rerun the DDL statement to create the procedure.

```
OPTION ( OPTIMIZE FOR (@COUNTRYREGIONCODE = 'US') );
```

Now if you flush the procedure cache and rerun the procedure with the NA parameter you'll get the plan for the US parameter. This OPTIMIZE FOR statement communicates directly to the optimizer that it should create a plan with the expectation that the parameter will be US. This plan will not be optimized for the NA or any other parameter, but here you are making the choice to apply your knowledge of the usage of this procedure to give the optimizer better information about how this statement should be executed.

If you are not having problems with plan caching, you may at some point experience issues with deadlocking or blocking by other processes or bad queries. We'll dig into these issues in the next section.

Tuning for Deadlocking and Blocking

Chapter 4 covers the topics of blocking and deadlocking, including techniques for capturing and recognizing blocks and deadlocks are described. This section discusses techniques and practices for handling these events.

Blocking

Before proceeding a brief review of blocking is needed. Blocking isn't necessarily a problem. It occurs regularly during the normal operation of a database. A typical scenario for blocking occurs when one user who's updating a data page prevents another user from accessing that page at the same time. When this happens the second user is blocked for a few moments until the first user completes the change and releases the page. This isn't the issue that causes performance degradation. The performance-robbing blocks are the ones that last for more than a few moments — a lot more. Imagine standing in line at a grocery store checkout. The line is moving well. The customers are steadily progressing through the line when the cashier has to stop the process and get a price check on an item. At this point everyone in the line is stopped or blocked until the price check is completed. This is the type of blocking that needs to be minimized.

In order to aid your investigation of blocking, SQL Server has provided some DMVs that are useful. Specifically, the sys.dm_os_wait_stats and sys.dm_os_waiting_tasks are particularly handy. See Chapter 4 for a more thorough description of these DMVs as well as other blocking tools.

Deadlocks

Deadlock is a variation of a block. The issue with a deadlock is that two users are trying to access an object, such as a data page or row, which the other user has locked. Each user needs to access the other user's object before completing their respective transactions, but they can't.

The June 1971 issue of *Computing Surveys* has an article by E.G. Coffman, Jr.; M. J. Elphick; and A. Shoshani entitled "System Deadlocks." In this article the authors describe four conditions that are necessary in order for a deadlock to occur. The wording of the original conditions has been changed slightly in order to understand how they apply to database objects.

❑ Database connections acquire exclusive control of the database object(s) (data page, row, index, etc.) they need. This is known as the *mutual exclusion* condition.

❑ Database connections hold database object(s) already allocated to them while waiting for additional database object(s). This is known as the *wait for* condition.

❑ Database object(s) cannot be removed from the connections holding them until the object(s) are used to completion. This is known as the *preemption* condition.

❑ A circular chain of database connections exists in which each connection holds one or more database object(s) that are requested by the next connection in the chain. This is known as the *circular wait* condition:

Note that all four conditions must occur.

You may be wondering if deadlock can be prevented, and if so, why doesn't SQL Server prevent them instead of letting them occur. In fact, it is possible to prevent or avoid deadlock states. However, it isn't practical. In order to prevent deadlock SQL Server would have to disallow any one of the four conditions required which would be a sufficient measure. For example, one technique for preventing deadlocks is to force a database process to acquire all required database objects. Furthermore, the process would not be able to continue until all objects were acquired. This would certainly work, but the impact to the users would be unacceptable.

Because prevention and avoidance aren't practical options, SQL Server implements a technique of detection and recovery. Periodically SQL Server checks to see if any connections are blocking each other — deadlock. When it finds two deadlocked connections SQL Server will choose one of the connections as the *deadlock victim* and the processing done by that connection will be rolled back. SQL Server chooses the victim based upon which one will require the least amount of work to roll back.

So, like the SQL Server engineers who strive to minimize deadlock states, you can take steps to minimize deadlock states with design and development. Also, just like SQL Server, you can design and implement a recovery scheme. The remainder of the section will be targeted toward achieving this goal.

Preventative Measures

Because deadlocks and blocking are variations on the same problem the techniques for addressing them work for both. The following steps will work toward reducing these problems.

Keeping Transactions as Short as Possible

Ideally, transactions (denoted with a BEGIN TRANS) contain only one DML statement. However, this is not always possible. It's commonplace that multiple DML statements occur within the context of a single transaction. For example, updating an employee's name and address information typically involves updating multiple tables. This is an example where you may want all statements to succeed before committing the changes, otherwise you want to roll back the changes. The goal here is to make sure that the minimum number of DML statements occur within a transaction definition, thereby making the transaction as short as possible. In addition to that you should make sure that once the transaction begins, additional tasks, such as assigning variables, verifying data, and conditional statements, have been executed.

Don't Ask for User Input During a Transaction

This seems like an obvious practice, but it's worth stating. If a transaction has a user input requirement before the transaction can finish this could definitely cause problems. Try coding the transaction without the user input requirement. If that's not practical, then at least configure the application to time out and abort a suspended transaction. This is essentially a part of the first rule. Even though you may code a transaction with only one DML statement as advised above, adding a pause for the user will effectively lengthen the transaction, which goes against the first rule.

Programming the Lowest-Possible Isolation Level

Chapter 8 describes isolation levels. The higher the isolation level, is the more likely blocking will occur. However, the multi-user nature of the system is diminished. The lower the isolation level, the less likely blocking will occur. However, the lower isolation level can increase the potential for dirty reads or lost updates. Thus, choose the lowest level that is practical in your application. Remember that SQL Server's default isolation level is Read Committed.

Locking Only When Needed

Again, this seems obvious, but you shouldn't allow your application to generate locks that aren't necessary. Doing so forces the lock manager to work unnecessarily. Resources are used unnecessarily. This could lead to blocking, which is totally unnecessary. Use an isolation level that would help this. Also when possible, using NOLOCK, table hints can help as well.

In SQL Server 2005 Microsoft added some very powerful features concerning lock management. Those are the READ_COMMITTED_SNAPSHOT database option and the SNAPSHOT isolation level. The READ_COMMITTED_SNAPSHOT database option controls the behavior of the READ_COMMITTED isolation level. When the option is off, which is the default, SQL Server will use shared locks. If the option is on, SQL Server will use row versioning to maintain the data consistency of a statement. With the SNAPSHOT isolation level, data that's read by any statement in a transaction will be consistent within that transaction since the start of the transaction.

Avoiding Lock Escalation

Recall that lock escalation occurs automatically, and it's characterized by SQL Server's process of converting fine-grain locks to coarse-grain locks. Moving a lock from page level to table level is an example of escalation. The coarser the lock the more likely blocking can occur. When SQL Server locks an entire table, all users are blocked from the table until the table lock is released. Note that when SQL Server escalates locks, it does so by promoting both row- and page-level locks to the table level. It does not promote row-level locks to page level.

One way to avoid lock escalation is to break up a few large batch operations into more numerous smaller batch operations. For example, suppose you needed to run an update statement that was going to affect half the rows in a table. Instead of running one update statement, try running multiple statements over smaller row sets.

Another option for controlling lock escalation is by using the table hints ROWLOCK or PAGLOCK. These directives won't allow SQL Server to escalate locks on the tables for which the hints are given.

Yet another option involves using SQL Server's trace flags. Trace flags are used to control some server characteristics. For disabling lock escalation, you can use trace flags 1211 or 1224. See BOL for complete details.

Considering an OLAP /DSS Solution

Many times, significant reporting is done from existing OLTP systems. If this reporting results in too much blocking you should consider creating a more report-friendly data design than OLTP. OLTP data structures place a high importance on preserving what is written into a database. This means that a high degree of normalization is usually present. Also, indexes are usually sparse. Transactions must flow into these database structures as quickly and efficiently as possible. Unfortunately this means that reporting on that data cannot be done as quickly as desired. Therefore, in those cases, creating another data store that does support reporting is an option. These structures tend to be less normalized. They also contain a high number of indexes. In short, these structures are much less likely to generate blocks.

Also, for those sites running SQL Server 2005 Enterprise edition, database snapshots are an option. A database snapshot is a read-only, static view of a source database. The snapshot is consistent with the source database at the time the snapshot was created.

Finally, another option is to use the READ_COMMITTED_SNAPSHOT database option or the SNAPSHOT isolation level. These two options can limit the amount of blocking that occurs as well.

The following techniques apply only to deadlocks, not blocking.

Setting a Deadlock Priority

As stated earlier, SQL Server will choose a deadlock victim based automatically. However, you have some control over this by specifying a deadlock priority for a given user connection. This is accomplished by using the SET DEADLOCK_PRIORITY T-SQL statement. Using this statement you can set the deadlock priority to one of three values. Those are: LOW, NORMAL, and HIGH. Within each of those settings you can further set a priority, which ranges from –10 to 10.

Trapping for Deadlock

A new technique available in SQL Server 2005 is to trap a deadlock error and retry the process. This is accomplished by using the TRY /CATCH feature of SQL Server 2005. Below is a T-SQL template example that demonstrates the structure and syntax of this approach. Using this technique, the SQL statements defined in the DML section will be attempted three times before giving up. In the CATCH block is a check to see if the error generated is a deadlock error. If it is, the DeadlockCounter variable is updated.

```
-- Declare and set variable
-- to track number of retries
-- to attempt before exiting.
DECLARE @DeadlockCount TINYINT
SET @DeadlockCount = 1

WHILE (@DeadlockCount <= 3)
BEGIN
    BEGIN TRY
        BEGIN TRANSACTION
         --DML statement(s)...

         --Note that if the statements above succeed
         --without error then this script will execute
         --the following statements. Otherwise, control
         --will jump into the CATCH section, and these
         --statements will not execute.
         SET @DeadlockCount = 99
         COMMIT TRANSACTION
    END TRY
    BEGIN CATCH
         -- Deadlock error number is 1205.
         IF (ERROR_NUMBER() = 1205)
         BEGIN
                 SET @DeadlockCount = @DeadlockCount + 1
         END
         ROLLBACK TRANSACTION
    END CATCH
END -- end while loop
```

Locking and blocking can be avoided with careful coding and adequate testing procedures, but sometimes you want to know what would happen if your database size doubled and only certain aspects of your data structures grew exponentially. We'll discuss a simulation technique to examine this issue in the next section.

Simulated Stress Testing for Query Plans

When the T-SQL has been tuned to perfection, you should start looking at what happens to the query plan as your data starts to scale out. The best way to do this is to generate data into the table, update the statistics, and start running the query. This method gives you a chance to look at not only the effect on the query plan, but you can also measure actual results. The downside is that many of your tables contain RI that creates sub-loading tasks before you can get to the table you want to test. Not only does this become another chore, but you also have to consider loading the data in a proper distribution pattern to get an accurate stress test.

If you want to get a quick simulation of the effects more rows will have on your perfect query plan, and you are in a testing environment, use the ROWCOUNT and PAGECOUNT options in the UPDATE STATISTICS command to change the metadata for a table or index. Note that these are undocumented options meant *only* for testing environments. Only use this technique when you can drop and add the table after you test. The optimizer uses the metadata that these options alter to figure out that the table is large instead of small or vice versa. This is beneficial to you for stress testing because it is difficult to get the optimizer to waste time evaluating more complicated query plans if it determines that it only has a few rows to return. By increasing the metadata row and page counts, the optimizer determines that there is value in digging deeper into the optimization layers and builds plans as if the table had those actual counts. Experiment with this by running the following script to build an Order and Detail table:

```
CREATE TABLE ORDER_HEADER(ORDER_HEADER_ID int, ORDER_NUMBER NVARCHAR(30))
CREATE TABLE ORDER_DETAIL
(ORDER_DETAIL_ID int, ORDER_HEADER_ID int, ORDER_LINE_AMOUNT MONEY)
GO
CREATE CLUSTERED INDEX [PK_ORDER_HEADER_ORDER_HEADER_ID]
ON [dbo].[ORDER_HEADER] ( [ORDER_HEADER_ID] ASC)
GO
CREATE CLUSTERED INDEX [PK_ORDER_DETAIL_ORDER_DETAIL_ID]
ON [dbo].[ORDER_DETAIL] ( [ORDER_DETAIL_ID] ASC )
```

Now run this query to get a benchmark plan using the current indexes. Note that although you did not add any rows to either of these tables, you'll still be able to get costing estimates based on the default optimizer costing models. The STATISTICS PROFILE option will allow you to review these plan estimates.

```
SET STATISTICS PROFILE ON
GO
--Summation Query
SELECT H.ORDER_HEADER_ID, SUM(ORDER_LINE_AMOUNT) AS TOTAL_ORDER_AMOUNT
FROM ORDER_HEADER H
INNER JOIN ORDER_DETAIL D
ON H.ORDER_HEADER_ID = D.ORDER_HEADER_ID
GROUP BY H.ORDER_HEADER_ID OPTION (RECOMPILE)
```

The plan estimates look good for this query. The subtree costs are low although you can see some significant I/O estimates on the Sort step. The .01126126 estimate doesn't look too outrageous, so you may feel like the indexing schemes are ready for prime time (see Figure 9-21).

Normal Statistical Distribution
Indexes: Clustered on Order_Header.Order_Header_ID, Order_Detail.Order_Detail_ID

EstimateRows	EstimateIO	EstimateCPU	TotalSubtreeCost	StmtText
1	0	0	0.01793276	SELECT H.ORDER_NUMBER, SUM(ORDER
1	0	0.0000011	0.01793276	|--Compute Scalar(DEFINE:([Expr1006]=CAS
1	0	0.0000011	0.01793276	|--Stream Aggregate(GROUP BY:([H].[OR
1	0.01126126	0.00010002	0.01793166	|--Sort(ORDER BY:([H].[ORDER_NUM
1	0	0.00000418	0.00657038	|--Nested Loops(Inner Join, OUTER
1	0.003125	0.0001581	0.0032831	|--Clustered Index Scan(OBJEC
1	0.003125	0.0001581	0.0032831	|--Clustered Index Seek(OBJEC

Figure 9-21

Before you test this theory, take other benchmark snapshots of the perfmon counters and key metrics from the core DMVs. Save this data for comparison later. Test your indexing structures and T-SQL code by tricking SQL Server into thinking that your tables have now grown exponentially larger. How do you do this? By running the undocumented options on the UPDATE STATISTICS command to set the row and page counts to 100K. This command tricks the optimizer into thinking that the table is now bigger than it is during optimization. Use these queries to increase the statistics for the order header and detail tables:

```
update statistics ORDER_HEADER with rowcount = 100000, pagecount = 100000
update statistics ORDER_DETAIL with rowcount = 100000, pagecount = 100000
```

Now rerun the summation query again and compare the results; see Figure 9-22. The difference is in the row count estimates and subtree costs. The optimizer is behaving as if we actually had a large number of rows in these tables. Note that the Sort step is now supplemented with an additional Merge Join Operation and is showing an increase in I/O costs when joining on the ORDER_HEADER_ID in the ORDER_DETAIL ([D]) table.

Simulated 100K Page Distribution
Indexes: Clustered on Order_Header.Order_Header_ID, Order_Detail.Order_Detail_ID

EstimateRows	EstimateIO	EstimateCPU	TotalSubtreeCost	StmtText
31622.78	0	0	149.4041	SELECT H.ORDER_HEADER_ID, SUM(ORD
31622.78	0	0.003162278	149.4041	|--Compute Scalar(DEFINE:([Expr1006]=CAS
31622.78	0	0.07581139	149.4009	|--Stream Aggregate(GROUP BY:([H].[OR
100000	0	0.2269282	149.3251	|--**Merge Join**(Inner Join, MERGE:([D].
632.4555	0.01126126	0.009280448	74.91154	|--Sort(ORDER BY:([D].[ORDER_H
632.4555	0	0.7043872	74.891	| |--Hash Match(Aggregate, HASH:
100000	74.07646	0.110157	74.18661	| |--Clustered Index Scan(OBJE
100000	74.07646	0.110157	74.18661	|--Clustered Index Scan(OBJECT:([t

Figure 9-22

The issue here is that there is no index on the ORDER_HEADER_ID in the ORDER_DETAIL table. If you added the ORDER_HEADER_ID to the clustered index on the ORDER_DETAIL table, you could eliminate this cost as well as the first Clustered Index Scan operator. Run this query to drop and add this new index on ORDER_DETAIL:

```
DROP INDEX [PK_ORDER_DETAIL_ORDER_DETAIL_ID] ON [dbo].[ORDER_DETAIL]
GO
```

```
CREATE CLUSTERED INDEX [PK_ORDER_DETAIL_ORDER_HEADER_ID] ON [dbo]
.[ORDER_DETAIL] ([ORDER_DETAIL_ID] ASC, [ORDER_HEADER_ID] ASC)
GO
```

Now when you run the summation query again (see Figure 9-23), you'll see that the estimates go back to a plan with low estimated row counts, I/O, and CPU costs, and the extra Merge Join Operator has been eliminated.

Simulated 100K Page Distribution
Indexes: Clustered on Order_Header.Order_Header_ID, Order_Header.Order_Number
Order_Detail.Order_Detail_ID, Order_Header_ID

EstimateRows	EstimateIO	EstimateCPU	TotalSubtreeCost	StmtText
1	0	0	0.00657148	SELECT H.ORDER_HEADER_ID, SUM(ORI
1	0	0.0000011	0.00657148	|--Compute Scalar(DEFINE:([Expr1006]=CA
1	0	0.0000011	0.00657148	|--Stream Aggregate(GROUP BY:([H].[O)
1	0	0.00000418	0.00657038	|--Nested Loops(Inner Join, OUTER R
1	0.003125	0.0001581	0.0032831	|--Clustered Index Scan(OBJECT:(
1	0.003125	0.0001581	0.0032831	|--Clustered Index Seek(OBJECT:(

Figure 9-23

Using the ROWCOUNT and PAGECOUNT options in the UPDATE STATISTICS command doesn't compete with having real data with real statistics, but it does give you a quick way to evaluate how well your SQL query is written and how well the index schemes will perform under increasing conditions. Once you feel that your plan is well formed and the index schemes hold up well under stress testing you can drop the table and re-script it to remove these false row and page counts.

Summary

This chapter has covered a lot of ground. You may not be at checkmate with the optimizer, but you should be able to hold your own with the information that we've covered. You started with an in-depth dive into the details of the optimizer and the operators that it uses to execute T-SQL statements. This enabled you to read the execution plans and use this information to troubleshoot what may be going wrong with the way the optimizer is handling your T-SQL requests.

In the second half of this chapter, you looked at what you could do tactically to performance-tune T-SQL statements by examining the data provided to you in the execution plans and the profiler. You looked at approaches of rewriting and reorganizing T-SQL to get the most performance gains. You developed a troubleshooting protocol that looked at tuning T-SQL predicates and the effect of indexing on common query tasks. For the problems that you'll see daily, you examined some common T-SQL pattern and programming idioms to see best practices examples from a performance perspective. For the odd scenario, you followed an example of how to use statement-level hints to improve a bad plan-caching issue. There are no easy ways to succeed at chess; you have to simply play the game and learn from experience. The same rules apply when performance tuning T-SQL statement in SQL Server 2005. The best decisions are made with the most accurate data.

Part III

Preventative Measures and Baselining Performance with Tools

10

Capturing, Measuring, and Replaying a Workload Using SQL Profiler

A system's performance can be measured at any time with any workload. A workload contains rich data for a specific scenario and time period. In this chapter, a workload refers to SQL trace output data that can be replayed by SQL 2005 Profiler. Analyzing trace events in a workload helps with troubleshooting, performance tuning, and measuring database usage data for capacity planning. Using SQL Profiler to capture, measure, and replay a workload provides an inexpensive approach to establish and compare SQL Server performance baselines.

This chapter covers the necessary building blocks for using SQL Profiler to replay a workload. After learning how to capture, measure, and replay a workload, you will walk through three usage scenarios. The first scenario demonstrates a process using the Profiler's replay feature to measure the overall performance gain for a workload. The second scenario compares the result of using workload replays on different SQL server configurations. The last scenario demonstrates using Profiler to send multiple workloads to a single server.

Capturing Workloads for Replay

Workload data contains what really happened in a SQL Server instance. With captured data, you can analyze usage patterns of database objects and system resource consumptions for database objects.

The scope of the workload should be specific. For example, a workload is configured for collecting a specific database application daily load. The workload contents should be reasonably easy to analyze by a person or by a computer program. The workload's file size should be easy to transport through networks.

Characterizing a Workload for Replay

Characterizing a SQL Server database workload is a way to abstract or take small samples from massive SQL Server events. A workload should have a specific purpose, a list of measurable contents, and a pre-defined timeframe.

Baseline (Daily Peak, Seasonal Peak)

Some businesses require the collection of performance data on a regular basis to ensure the integrity of the service level agreement (SLA). Many answers to performance questions need transactional data for support. To establish a baseline for an SLA, identifying measurable items in the SLA is an example of workload characterization. Most servers in production experience daily peak hours and seasonal peaks. In SQL Server 2005, there is no built-in feature to report daily (weekly, monthly) user transactions by category or response time on certain user transactions. For capacity planning, to predict business growth scenarios, it is a common practice to establish a baseline first.

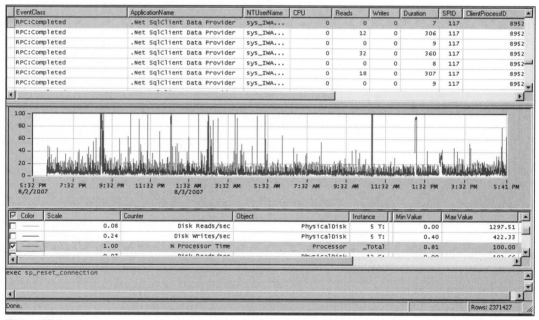

Figure 10-1

Then, there are several options. For simple scenarios, trending analysis may be sufficient. Large organizations might find that specialized commercial tools for analytical or simulation modeling are desirable. You might need to rely on other business information to find seasonal peak loads. For accounting systems, monthly closing; for Internet banking, pay days or monthly payment due days; for retail stores, holiday shopping seasons.

Using Profiler to replay workloads on a reference server provides a quick way to compare a new workload with a baseline workload. For example, you may want to replay a 24-hour workload on a reference server for benchmark purposes. Later, you can replay another set of workloads and compare overall timings for the replays.

SQL Profiler TSQL_Replay template is specifically designed for collecting all necessary trace events so that it guarantees trace output data will be able to replay from SQL Profiler. You can use all trace events in the TSQL_Replay template as a starting point for the baseline workload configuration. In addition to all the columns defined in the replay template, the following columns are useful for performance analysis:

❑ **RPC:Completed event:** Add TextData, CPU, Duration, Reads, and Writes columns.

❑ **SQL:BatchCompleted event:** Add CPU, Duration, Reads, and Writes columns.

SQL Profiler provides a quick way to visualize overall database transaction distributions over a 24-hour time period when combining a full day's workload with the system performance data. Refer to the example in Figure 10-1.

Specific Performance Tuning

Most often, you collect SQL database trace events when troubleshooting a specific issue or making improvements to a specific database object. For troubleshooting and performance tuning, samples might be taken from a specific database object, a database, a user, or a connecting server.

Some database administrators like to collect a single full workload for a long period so as not to miss any critical events; others like to collect very specific trace events for a narrower period. The best practice is to minimize system resource impact and catch trace events at the right time. Some best practices were covered in Chapter 5.

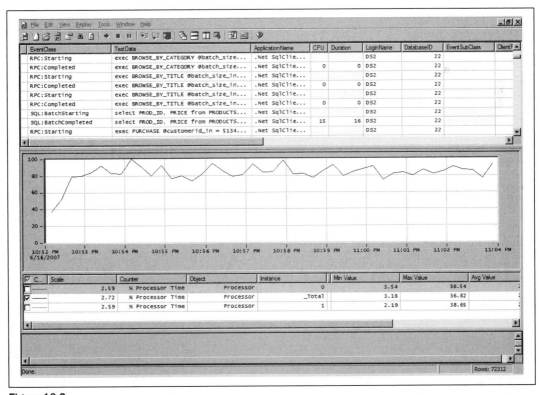

Figure 10-2

For a specific performance tuning task, only relevant trace data is needed. In case you have to deal with a large workload, you can use the Profiler post-filter to create a subset of workload trace data from a large set of workload trace files. First, open the workload into Profiler, filter the events of interest, and then save the data to another trace file. More details will be covered later in the chapter.

Figure 10-2 is a sample for a single database containing 10 minutes of workload from an online e-business created using the aforementioned method.

Meeting Requirements for Workload Replays

SQL 2005 Profiler Replay will check for the presence of required events and columns. To replay a workload file or trace database table, the following event classes and data columns must be specified in the trace.

These are the event classes:

- ❏ CursorClose (only required when replaying server-side cursors)
- ❏ CursorExecute (only required when replaying server-side cursors)
- ❏ CursorOpen (only required when replaying server-side cursors)
- ❏ CursorPrepare (only required when replaying server-side cursors)
- ❏ CursorUnprepare (only required when replaying server-side cursors)
- ❏ Audit Login
- ❏ Audit Logout
- ❏ ExistingConnection
- ❏ RPC Output Parameter
- ❏ RPC:Completed
- ❏ RPC:Starting
- ❏ Exec Prepared SQL (only required when replaying server-side prepared SQL statements)
- ❏ Prepare SQL (only required when replaying server-side prepared SQL statements)
- ❏ SQL:BatchCompleted
- ❏ SQL:BatchStarting

These are the data columns:

- ❏ EventClass
- ❏ EventSequence
- ❏ TextData
- ❏ ApplicationName
- ❏ LoginName

- ❑ DatabaseName
- ❑ DatabaseID
- ❑ ClientProcessID
- ❑ HostName
- ❑ ServerName
- ❑ BinaryData
- ❑ SPID
- ❑ StartTime
- ❑ EndTime
- ❑ IsSystem
- ❑ NTDomainName
- ❑ NTUserName
- ❑ Error

If the workload file does not contain the above events and columns, the replay will return an error and stop replaying the file. For example, if you use the SQL Profiler Standard trace template to collect data, you will see the error message in Figure 10-3 from SQL Profiler when you replay the trace.

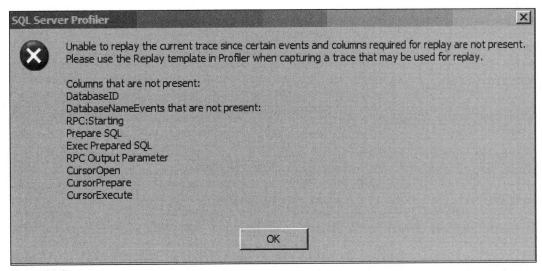

Figure 10-3

The easiest way to meet the minimum requirements for event classes and data columns is to use the SQL Profiler TSQL_Replay trace template directly or to add more event classes in addition to the TSQL_Replay trace template.

To replay a workload on the target server, the following requirements must be met:

❑ All logins (both SQL and Windows) and database users contained in the workload must exist already on the target and in the same database as the source server where the workload data was collected. Otherwise, you need to create them in the target SQL server instance and database.

❑ All logins and users in the target must have the same permissions they had in the source.

❑ All login passwords must be the same as those of the user who executes the replay.

❑ The database IDs on the target ideally should be the same as those on the source. However, if they are not the same, matching can be performed based on DatabaseName if it is present in the trace.

❑ The default database for each login contained in the trace must be set to the respective target database of the login. To set the default database of the login, use the sp_defaultdb system stored procedure.

If you are new to performing the SQL Server administration tasks listed above, you should capture a small workload (with one or two logins in the workload data), practice the Profiler replay, and become comfortable with each requirement listed above.

For a large set of trace files with many different logins, it might be time-consuming to go through all the logins in the workload files and recreate them in the target server. To transfer logins and passwords between different versions of SQL Server, refer to the Microsoft article, "How to Transfer Logins and Passwords Between Instances of SQL Server," at http://support.microsoft.com/kb/246133.

To replay all database query events correctly, the database must be reset to its original state. This means that if a workload contains multiple databases, you will need to create a backup for each database in the workload.

Capturing a Workload

The steps for defining and capturing a workload are the same as the ones used in creating a SQL trace. Be sure your workload definitions have met the minimum replay requirements. Save the workload output to a file or a set of rollover files. Define a time to stop the trace. To schedule a job to capture the workload, it is advisable to save these definitions to a T-SQL script file. With minimum modifications for output file specification and the stop time, you can use SQL agent job to facilitate the workload data collection. Using server-side traces is considered to be the best practice. Chapter 5 contains a description of how to create server-side traces.

Figure 10-4 is an example of using SQL Profiler to create a workload using the following settings:

❑ **Trace provide type:** Microsoft SQL Server 2005

❑ **Use the template:** TSQL_Replay

❑ **Save to File:** x\temp\myWorkload004.trc with max file size 200 MB, file rollover has been enabled.

❑ **Enable trace stop time:** 6/17/07, 1:54:58PM

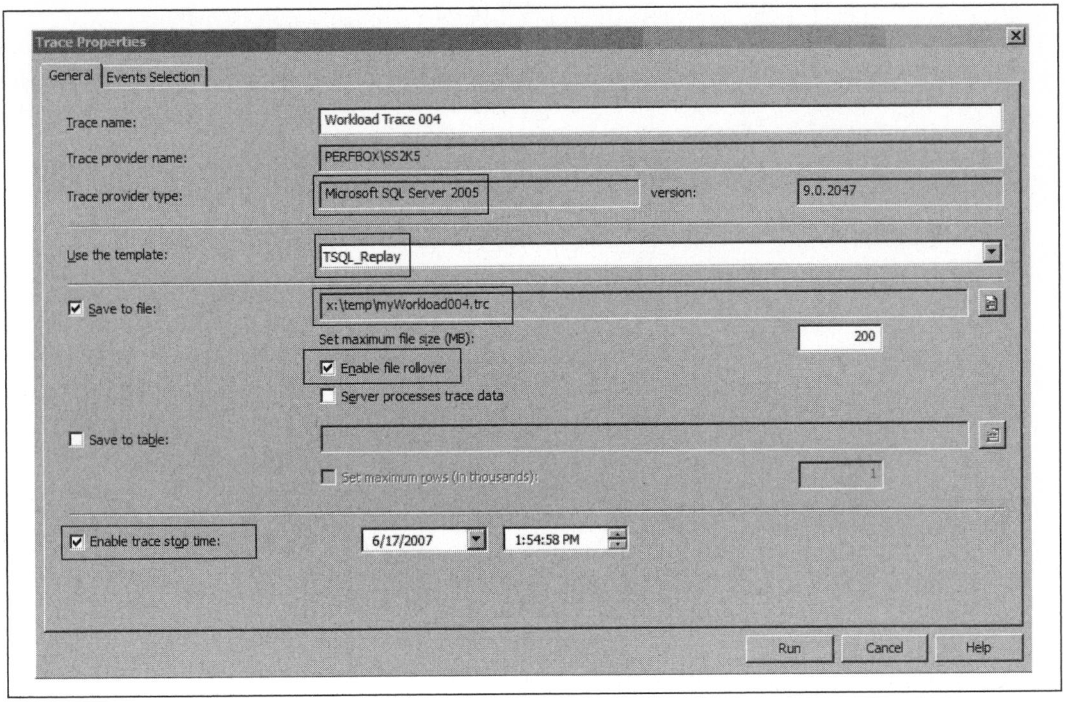

Figure 10-4

If you use SQL 2005 Profiler to create and capture a workload on a SQL Server 2000 instance, be aware that the trace provider uses Microsoft SQL Server 2000 (see Figure 10-5). This means that if you use the TSQL_Replay template, it uses the event class definitions in SQL Server 2000. If you want to replay this workload in SQL 2005 Profiler, it is a good idea to define a new user template to correlate with the SQL 2005 TSQL_Replay template definition.

Modifying a Workload in a Trace Table for Special Needs

SQL Server 2005 Profiler offers a limited filtering capability when replaying a workload. You can filter to replay trace events for a specific system server process ID (SPID) or a specific time-range, but you cannot replay based on an application, a database, or a user login. When it is necessary to focus on a smaller scope, you may want to make a subset workload from the original workload.

Making a Subset of a Workload

There are two main approaches to making a subset of a workload. The first option is to open the workload file in Profiler. From the Events Selection tab, use the column filters to bring up the Edit Filter dialog box, and then configure the filter as shown in Figure 10-6. Save the trace data to a new workload file.

If the workload data is already in a database table, the second option is to use T-SQL statements to create a subset of the workload. Alternatively, workload data can be saved as an XML file, thereby allowing you to modify the contents manually or programmatically.

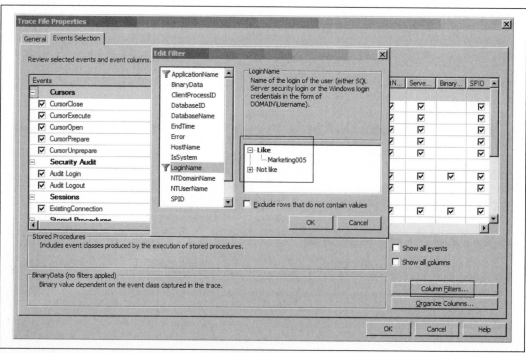

Figure 10-5

Figure 10-6

The following example shows how to remove events associated with login IDs SQLUser1 and NT AUTHORITY from the Tracedata_from_SQL2005_Profiler_001 trace table:

```
DELETE myTraceData.dbo.Tracedata_from_SQL2005_Profiler_001
WHERE LoginName in ('SQLUser1', 'NT AUTHORITY\SYSTEM')
```

Another example is to remove some events that might not be relevant to your application:

```
DELETE myTraceData.dbo.Tracedata_from_SQL2005_Profiler_001
WHERE ApplicationName = 'SQLAgent - Alert Engine'
```

To replay a trace that was collected on a SQL 2000 server, if the user ID in a database is different from the login ID, you may want to refer to the Microsoft article at http://support.microsoft.com/kb/286239/en-us?spid=2852&sid=1207 to resolve the issue. To get around this issue, you may find that it is easier to import trace data into a database table and modify the database name or login name in the trace table to match up with the target environment.

Re-calculating the Delay Interval between Events

You may have a specific need to replay a set of events at the same speed at which the events were originally generated. SQL 2005 Profiler replays events at the fastest server speed capacity. Profiler ignores time intervals between events. If you are interested in replaying events on a target server with a time delay to simulate original event timing, you need to calculate the timing between events programmatically and add corresponding time delay events in a new workload database table.

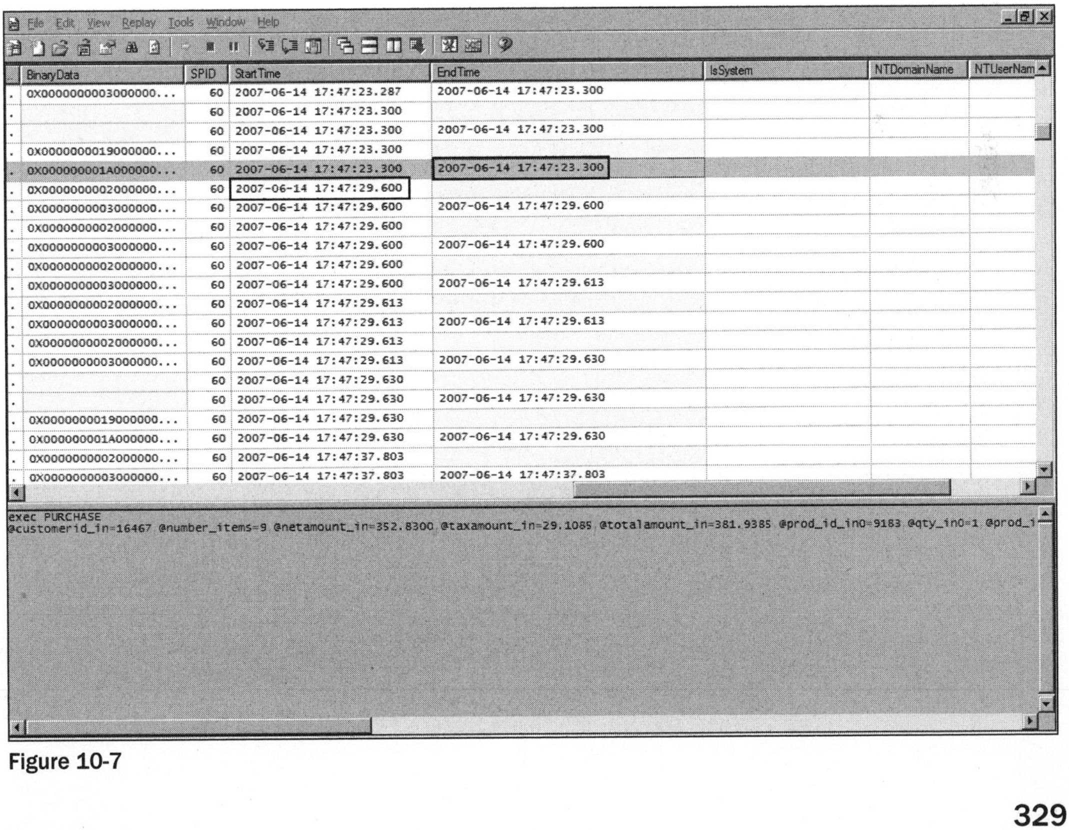

Figure 10-7

329

In Figure 10-7, as highlighted, the stored procedure Purchase was completed at timestamp 2007-06-14 17:47:23.300, and the next event started at 2007-06-14 17:47:29.600. There is about a six-second time gap between the two events.

To simulate the time delay, you can add a WAITFOR DELAY statement between events in the workload data table as in Figure 10-8. This will force the Profiler to delay the time interval between events. The source code is a T-SQL script that will be available from the publisher's web site. This script loops through the events, looks for time delays between events, and creates a new workload database table with time delays. This technique enables Profiler to deal with specific needs.

EventClass	TextData	LoginN...	Da...	D...	StartTime	EndTime
SQL:BatchCompleted	select PROD_ID, PRICE from ...	sa	DS2	17	2007-06-14 17:47:23.300	2007-06-14 17:47:23.300
RPC:Starting	exec PURCHASE @customerid_i...	sa	DS2	17	2007-06-14 17:47:23.300	
RPC:Completed	exec PURCHASE @customerid_i...	sa	DS2	17	2007-06-14 17:47:23.300	2007-06-14 17:47:23.300
SQL:BatchStarting	WAITFOR DELAY '00:00:06:300'	ds2000	DS2			
RPC:Starting	exec LOGIN @username_in='us...	sa	DS2	17	2007-06-14 17:47:29.600	
RPC:Completed	exec LOGIN @username_in='us...	sa	DS2	17	2007-06-14 17:47:29.600	2007-06-14 17:47:29.600
RPC:Starting	exec BROWSE_BY_CATEGORY @ba...	sa	DS2	17	2007-06-14 17:47:29.600	
RPC:Completed	exec BROWSE_BY_CATEGORY @ba...	sa	DS2	17	2007-06-14 17:47:29.600	2007-06-14 17:47:29.600
RPC:Starting	exec BROWSE_BY_TITLE @batch...	sa	DS2	17	2007-06-14 17:47:29.600	
RPC:Completed	exec BROWSE_BY_TITLE @batch...	sa	DS2	17	2007-06-14 17:47:29.600	2007-06-14 17:47:29.613
RPC:Starting	exec BROWSE_BY_TITLE @batch...	sa	DS2	17	2007-06-14 17:47:29.613	
RPC:Completed	exec BROWSE_BY_TITLE @batch...	sa	DS2	17	2007-06-14 17:47:29.613	2007-06-14 17:47:29.613
RPC:Starting	exec BROWSE_BY_CATEGORY @ba...	sa	DS2	17	2007-06-14 17:47:29.613	
RPC:Completed	exec BROWSE_BY_CATEGORY @ba...	sa	DS2	17	2007-06-14 17:47:29.613	2007-06-14 17:47:29.630
SQL:BatchStarting	select PROD_ID, PRICE from ...	sa	DS2	17	2007-06-14 17:47:29.630	
SQL:BatchCompleted	select PROD_ID, PRICE from ...	sa	DS2	17	2007-06-14 17:47:29.630	2007-06-14 17:47:29.630
RPC:Starting	exec PURCHASE @customerid_i...	sa	DS2	17	2007-06-14 17:47:29.630	
RPC:Completed	exec PURCHASE @customerid_i...	sa	DS2	17	2007-06-14 17:47:29.630	2007-06-14 17:47:29.630
SQL:BatchStarting	WAITFOR DELAY '00:00:08:173'	ds2000	DS2			
RPC:Starting	exec LOGIN @username_in='us...	sa	DS2	17	2007-06-14 17:47:37.803	
RPC:Completed	exec LOGIN @username_in='us...	sa	DS2	17	2007-06-14 17:47:37.803	2007-06-14 17:47:37.803

WAITFOR DELAY '00:00:06:300'

Figure 10-8

Measuring Workload Performance

A workload collected from a real environment contains time series data with raw performance measurements. The following sections provide examples for measuring overall system resource usage in a workload. A workload replay-time provides a measurement that allows you to compare performance.

Preliminary Analysis of the Workload

When you collect workload data from a SQL Server instance, it is best to collect Windows performance counters at the same time. Please refer to Chapter 2 for applicable and useful counters.

This section provides T-SQL sample scripts to summarize overall users' activities and corresponding system resource consumptions in a workload. All queries retrieve data from the original workload file named DS2_40Threads_20Min_3SecThink.trc through the T-SQL fn_trace_gettable built-in function.

The source script (176399 Ch10_SourceTSQL_Scripts.sql) is available at www.wrox.com. At the end of this section, summary information is listed in a table.

Most of the user database requests come from two trace events: RPC:Completed and SQL:Batch-Completed. The following query aggregates CPU and I/O usages from these two events. Figure 10-9 shows the results.

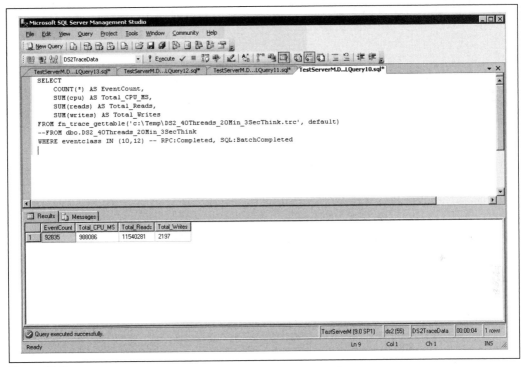

Figure 10-9

```
SELECT
       COUNT(*) AS EventCount,
       SUM(cpu) AS Total_CPU_MS,
       SUM(reads) AS Total_Reads,
       SUM(writes) AS Total_Writes
FROM fn_trace_gettable('c:\Temp\DS2_40Threads_20Min_3SecThink.trc', default)
--FROM dbo.DS2_40Threads_20Min_3SecThink
WHERE eventclass IN (10,12) -- RPC:Completed, SQL:BatchCompleted
```

The following query is similar to the above, but it is designed to group usage information by user transactions. It is useful to help understand which user queries use the most system resources in a workload. Figure 10-10 shows the results.

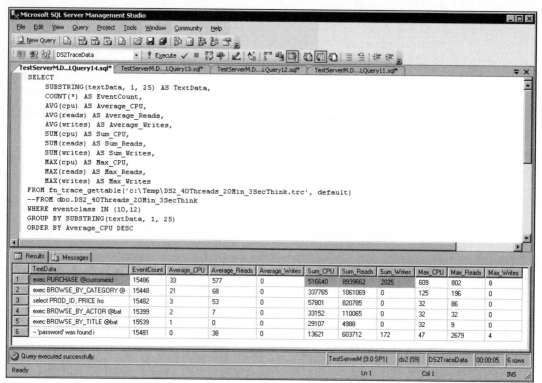

Figure 10-10

The technique used in the query to truncate the textData column to an arbitrary length (25, in the query below) may not be perfect for complex user transactions. It will require sophisticated logic to identify and group user transactions accurately; the Read80Trace utility is an example. See the article "Description of the SQL Server Performance Analysis Utilities Read80Trace" at http://support.microsoft.com/kb/887057.

```
SELECT
    SUBSTRING(textData, 1, 25) AS TextData,
    COUNT(*) AS EventCount,
    AVG(cpu) AS Average_CPU,
    AVG(reads) AS Average_Reads,
    AVG(writes) AS Average_Writes,
    SUM(cpu) AS Sum_CPU,
    SUM(reads) AS Sum_Reads,
    SUM(writes) AS Sum_Writes,
    MAX(cpu) AS Max_CPU,
    MAX(reads) AS Max_Reads,
    MAX(writes) AS Max_Writes
FROM fn_trace_gettable('c:\Temp\DS2_40Threads_20Min_3SecThink.trc', default)
--FROM dbo.DS2_40Threads_20Min_3SecThink
WHERE eventclass IN (10,12)
GROUP BY SUBSTRING(textData, 1, 25)
ORDER BY Average_CPU DESC
```

As Figure 10-10 shows, highlighted in the result window, the user transaction named PURCHASE used more system resources than any other transaction. The total PURCHASE transaction count 15,486 was about 17% (15486 ÷ 92835) of the total user transactions in the workload. This PURCHASE transaction used about 52% (516,640 ÷ 988,086) of total CPU, and 77% ((8,939,662+2025) ÷ (11,540,281+2197)) of disk I/O resources.

The next query reports average resource utilization by transaction, and Figure 10-11 shows the results. Note that the workload was collected from the SQL 2000 trace provider, and the duration is in milliseconds. As a reminder, in SQL 2005 trace provider, the duration measurement is in microseconds (one millisecond equals 1,000 microseconds). Since most DBAs are used to millisecond measurements in the duration column, it is a good idea to make your analysis script consistent across SQL 2000 and 2005. In other words, when you analyze SQL 2005 duration data in a trace file, divide the value by 1,000 to convert it to milliseconds.

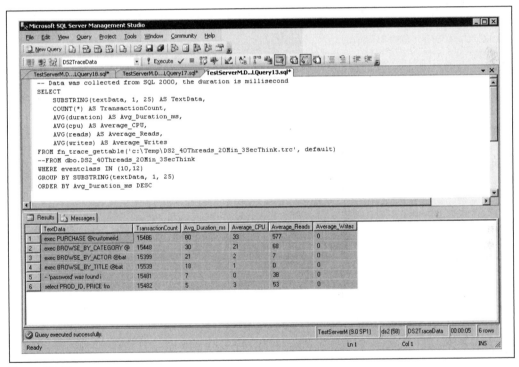

Figure 10-11

```
-- Data was collected from SQL 2000, the duration is millisecond
SELECT
       SUBSTRING(textData, 1, 25) AS TextData,
       COUNT(*) AS TransactionCount,
       AVG(duration) AS Ave_Duration_ms,
       AVG(cpu) AS Average_CPU,
       AVG(reads) AS Average_Reads,
       AVG(writes) AS Average_Writes
FROM fn_trace_gettable('c:\Temp\DS2_40Threads_20Min_3SecThink.trc', default)
```

```
--FROM dbo.DS2_40Threads_20Min_3SecThink
WHERE eventclass IN (10,12)
GROUP BY SUBSTRING(textData, 1, 25)
ORDER BY Ave_Duration_ms DESC
```

As shown in Figure 10-11, the Avg_Duration_ms column can be used to gauge average response time for each user database transaction. For example, the response time for the BROWSE_BY_CATEGORY is about 30 milliseconds.

Here is the workload's overall system resource utilization:

- ❑ Total CPU (Millisecond): 988,086
- ❑ Reads: 11,540,281
- ❑ Writes: 2,197

Table 10-1 shows the user transactions from the original workload.

Table 10-1: User Transactions in the Original Workload

RPC and SQL Batch Events	Counts	Avg. Duration (ms)	Avg. CPU (ms)	Avg. Reads	Avg. Writes
exec PURCHASE @customerid	15,486	80	33	577	0
Exec BROWSE_BY_ CATEGORY @	15,448	30	21	68	0
exec BROWSE_BY_ACTOR @bat	15,399	21	2	7	0
exec BROWSE_BY_TITLE @bat	15,539	18	1	0	0
--'password' was found i	15,481	7	0	38	0
select PROD_ID, PRICE fro	15,482	5	3	53	0

New Performance Reference for a Workload Replay

SQL 2000/2005 Profiler does not replay trace events at the same speed that they originally occurred. To compare the same workload in different testing environments (hardware, software) you need to re-establish the workload performance reference.

The replay time from a Profiler replay provides you with a new performance reference. In addition to measuring the performance as listed in Table 10-1, you can compare different replay-times in different server configurations.

In the following example, the workload represents 10 minutes of evenly distributed trace events. As Figure 10-12 indicates, the Profiler reported that it replayed the entire workload in 8 minutes, 29 seconds, and 114 milliseconds.

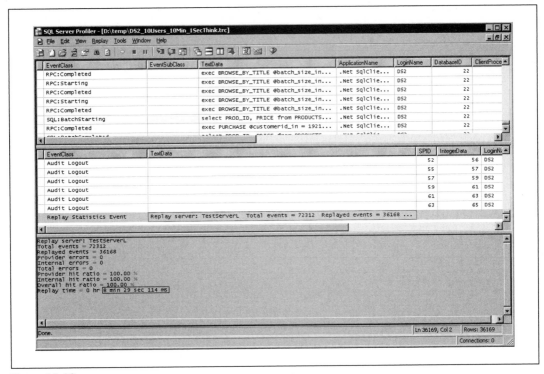

Figure 10-12

Sometimes it is beneficial to capture both system performance metrics and SQL events during the workload replay. Note that the default Profiler setting excludes the events from SQL Profiler. When you trace a workload during the workload replay, be sure to configure the ApplicationName column filter to include the SQL Server Profiler application as shown in Figure 10-13.

Each time the workload is replayed on a stable target server with a constant load under the same database conditions, the results should be consistent. If the results vary by a large percentage, check to see if the replay has encountered any errors. You need to restore the database between each run.

The total workload replay time provides an overall measurement for the total response time of the workload. For performance tuning, after making any improvement on the target server and replaying the workload, simply compare the new replay time with the reference replay time established earlier. This will provide evidence of any overall performance gain.

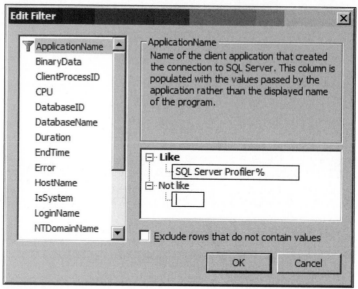

Figure 10-13

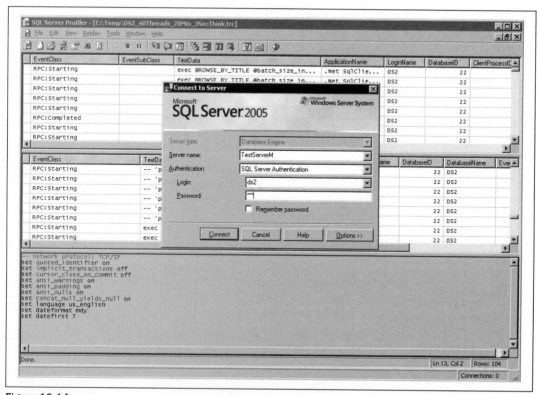

Figure 10-14

Replaying a Workload

If the workload has met the Profiler replay requirements and the target server has been fully prepared for processing the workload, replaying a workload is very simple. From SQL Profiler, select File → Open → Trace File → and select a workload file to load into Profiler. From the Profiler menu, select Replay and then choose Start to start replaying. Profiler will bring up a connection screen. Fill in all required information for connecting to a target server, as shown in Figure 10-14.

After the connection is made, you will see a screen similar to Figure 10-15. Click OK, and the replay starts.

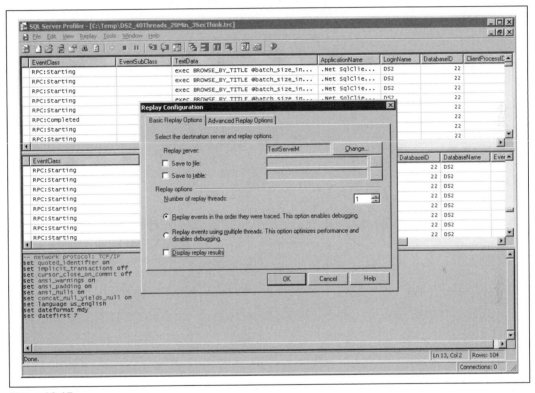

Figure 10-15

Replaying the same workload on different servers provides a quick way to benchmark server performances for the workload. When you are looking for possible database consolidation opportunities, replaying multiple workloads on a target server may provide valuable information.

This chapter has discussed how to characterize and measure a workload. The rest of the chapter will present three workload-replaying scenarios.

- ❏ **Scenario 1:** This scenario demonstrates the simple use of the replay feature. Using replay time helps analyze the total impact of performance tuning on a workload.

- ❏ **Scenario 2:** In this scenario, we use Profiler to send the workload to different servers. During workload replays, we will observe and compare performances.

- ❏ **Scenario 3:** We replay multiple workloads on a single server.

337

The remainder of the chapter covers the workload collection used in the three scenarios above. You do not have to reproduce the same workload to follow through the three scenarios. It is best to focus on how the Profiler replay feature is applied in different scenarios. The sample workload data file (Ch10_Sample_Workload_DS2_40Threads_20Min_3SecThink.trc) and the sample database (DS2) used in the chapter are available for download at www.wrox.com.

Best Practice

Regardless of whether trace data is stored in trace files or a database trace table, using Profiler to replay a trace is CPU-intensive. It is considered the best practice to use a separate and dedicated server to replay trace data, not your target server that receives the workload.

It is also important to configure these two servers (the server replays the trace and the target server receives the workload) on the same network subnet with minimum network hops and maximum throughputs.

Workload Generation for Case Scenarios

Workload data for the three scenarios was prepared in the following manner. An open source tool, DVD Store Version 2 (DS2), was used to simulate database transactions from a dedicated server. SQL Profiler was used to define and collect a workload.

DS2 is a complete online e-commerce test application with a backend database component, a web application layer, and driver programs. You can find details about this application and download DS2 from the web site http://linux.dell.com/dvdstore/readme.txt. DS2 simulates an online transaction processing (OLTP) workload for an order entry system. The multi-threaded driver program included in the DS2 package supports SQL Server 2000. Each thread of the OLTP driver connects to the database and makes a series of T-SQL stored procedure calls that simulate customers logging in, browsing online items, and making purchases. Each completed sequence of actions (logging-in, browsing, and purchasing) is counted as a single customer order.

The DS2 package comes with a DS2 database. It has the following tables: Customers, Orders, OrderLines, Cust_Hist, Productss, Inventory, Reorder, and Categories. DS2 comes in three standard sizes listed in Table 10-2. We used the medium size for generating workloads in the scenarios. Since the multi-threaded driver program has not been updated for SQL Server 2005, we installed the DS2 database in a SQL Server 2000 instance.

Table 10-2: DS2 Database Sizes

Database	Size	Customers	Orders	Products
Small	10 MB	20,000	1,000/month	10,000
Medium	1 GB	2,000,000	100,000/month	100,000
Large	100 GB	200,000,000	10,000,000/month	1,000,000

Since DS2 supports multiple operating systems, the installation and configuration of DS2 requires recompiling source codes on your Windows platform. It also requires modifying the connection string of the DS2 database in the source code.

In the following scenarios, we used the DS2 benchmark tool and simulated 40 concurrent users for 20 minutes. Each user logged into a DVD online store, browsed one to five individual items, and then made one subsequent purchase.

Here are the source server and workload characteristics:

❑ **Hardware Profile:** Intel Pentium III 662 Mhz; two processors; 1 GB of RAM;

❑ **SQL Server Edition:** SQL Server 2000 SP4

❑ **Customer Order:** An average customer order consists of one login, three production searches, and one purchase.

❑ **Percentage of New Customers:** 20%

❑ **Measurement Interval:** 20 minutes

❑ **Warm-Up Time:** 1 minute

❑ **Number of concurrent threads:** 40

❑ **Think-Time** (This delay simulates a customer's think-time from product search to final purchase.): 3 seconds

After DS2 completed the simulation, it provided the following statistical measurements (see Figure 10-16):

❑ Customer Orders per minute: 732

❑ Total number of logins during run: 12,180

❑ Total number of browses during run: 45,329

❑ Total number of purchases during run: 15,151

❑ Average login time in milliseconds: 11

❑ Average new customer registration time in milliseconds: 27

❑ Average browse time in milliseconds: 28

❑ Total data collection run time: 1,241 seconds (20.68 minutes)

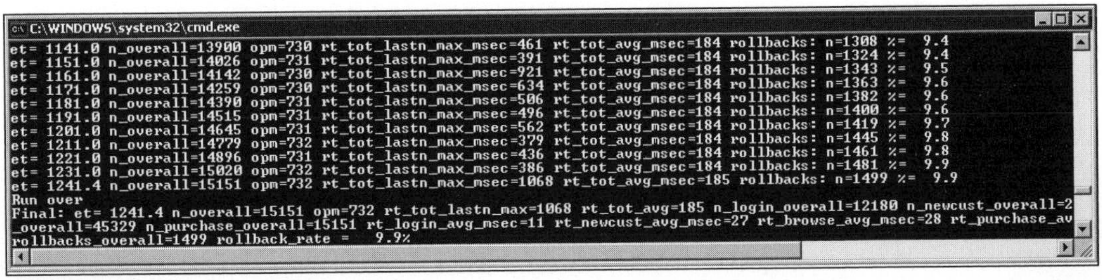

Figure 10-16

During the DS2 simulation, we captured all the database events in a workload. The DS2 database resided on a SQL Server 2000 instance. We started a SQL 2005 Profiler trace on a remote server to connect to the DS2 database. There were 185,768 trace events collected.

In addition to the SQL Profiler's TSQL_Replay template definition, we added the following columns: CPU, Reads, Writes, and Duration. We configured the workload definition to capture the user login named DS2, and then saved the trace output data into the file `DS2_40Threads_20Min_3SecThink.trc`.

SQL Profiler provides options to replay a trace in either a single thread or multiple threads. In the following scenarios, for simplicity and clarity, we used a single-threaded execution.

Scenario 1: Validating Performance Improvement

After establishing a workload that represents a specific scenario for the current environment, the point is then to reuse this workload for specific performance tuning in a different environment. Performance gains can be measured based on the whole workload.

In this scenario, we will use index tuning with the workload we have collected. First, we will replay the workload and record the total time it takes in the testing environment. Then, we will try to find opportunities that will enhance performance through index tuning. At the end, we will replay the workload again to compare and confirm any gain.

Having generated the workload, we use the following steps to complete this scenario:

1. Replay the workload on a developer's desktop PC and record this replay time to use as a benchmark reference.

2. Perform index tuning exercises by using SQL DTA, to make a tuning change.

3. Replay the workload again on the same developer's desktop PC to confirm performance gain.

Figure 10-17 shows the results of Step 1. The replay time was 26 minutes, 29 seconds, and 650 ms (1,589 seconds). This replay time will be used as a base reference.

> *It is important to repeat each step at least three times to confirm you are getting reproducible results and are not seeing the results of a cold versus warn cache. It is wise to let SQL Server automatically update statistics. (Example: exec sp_dboption 'ds2', ' auto update statistics', 'true')*

In Step 2, we used Database Tuning Adviser (DTA) to validate indexes in the DS2 database by feeding each of the DS2 stored procedures into the tool. Figure 10-18 shows that the DTA recommended a new index for the PRODUCTS table. DTA estimated a 98 percent improvement from which the stored procedure BROWSE_BY_CATEGORY will benefit. The question is how this improvement will affect the overall workload.

In this scenario, we used Profiler replay as a validation tool to confirm the performance improvement.

After adding the new index recommended by DTA to the PRODUCTS table, we replayed the workload again (see Figure 10-19).

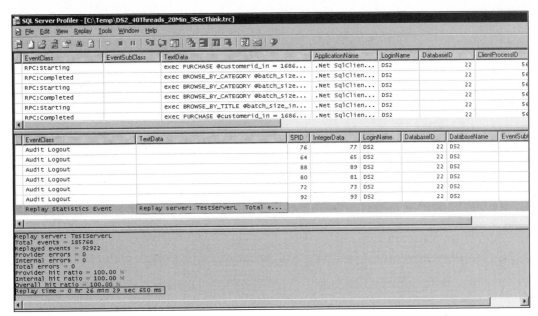

Figure 10-17

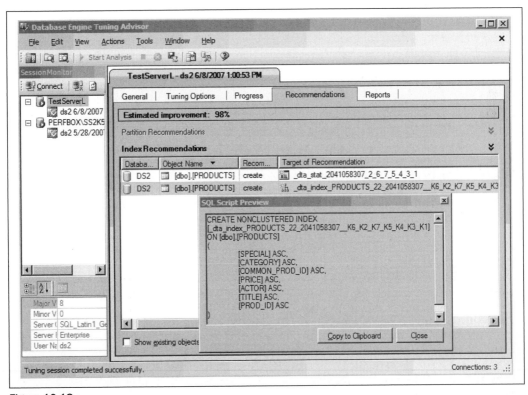

Figure 10-18

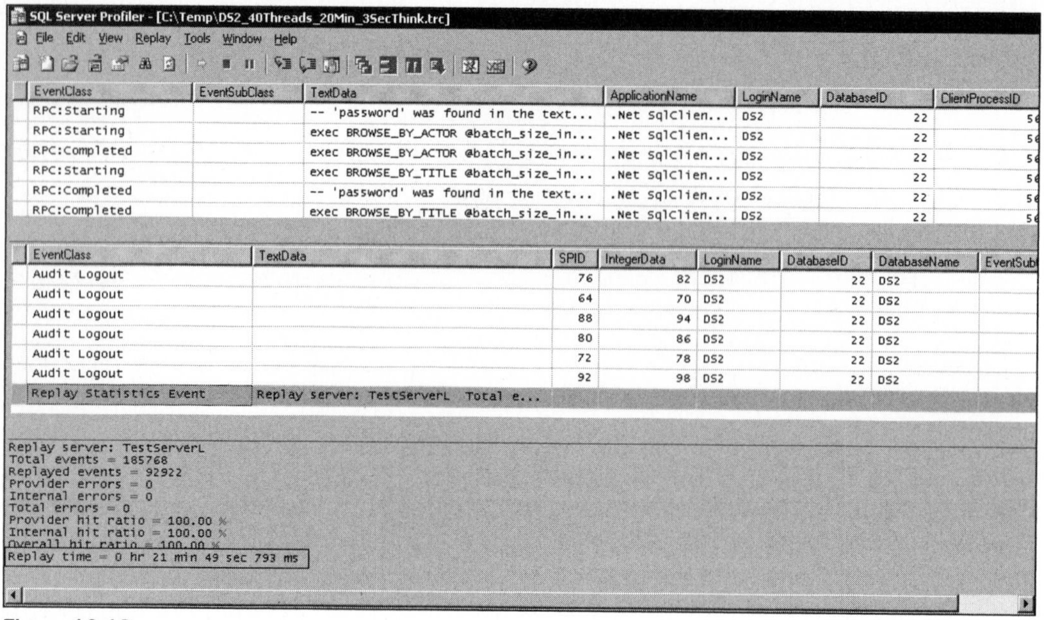

Figure 10-19

Figure 10-19 shows that the time from the new replay is 21 minutes, 49 seconds, and 793 ms (1,309 seconds). Comparing this replay time with the base reference replay time (1,589 seconds, see Figure 10-17), it is a 17.6 percent improvement for the whole workload. The percentage improvement is calculated as follows: $(1 - 1309/1589) \times 100 = 17.6\%$.

Now, let's calculate what the improvement was for the BROWSE_BY_CATEGORY stored procedure after adding the new index suggested by DTA.

Before adding the index, from Figure 10-17 we see that the replay time for the whole workload is 26 minutes, 29 seconds, and 650 ms (1,589 seconds). From Table 10-1 we see that the stored procedure BROWSE_BY_CATEGORY is executed 15,448 times; and the average duration to execute the procedure is 30 milliseconds. The total cumulative time spent for the procedure is 463 seconds (15,448 occurrences multiplied by 30 milliseconds equals to 463 seconds). The overhead of the rest of the procedure executions is 1,126 seconds (1,589 seconds minus 463 seconds equals to 1,126 seconds).

After adding the index, from Figure 10-19 we see that the total replay time is 1,309 seconds. Assuming the overhead of all other procedure executions remain the same (1,126 seconds), the new overhead of the procedure BROWSE_BY_CATEGORY is 183 seconds (1,309 minus 1,126 equals to 183). Now we can calculate the average execution time for the stored procedure call after adding the new index. This average execution time is 11.8 seconds (183 seconds divided by 15,448 occurrences equals to 11.8 milliseconds). Finally, the percentage improvement in the execution time for the stored procedure is about 61 percent: $(1 - 11.8/30) \times 100 = 61\%$.

In this scenario, we demonstrated how to use Profiler replay to validate a performance estimate from DTA. Based on a single stored procedure execution of BROWSE_BY_CATEGORY, DTA estimated a 98 percent improvement with the suggested index. Using Profiler replay you saw this new index improved

17.6 percent for the whole workload. By replaying the original workload, the duration time of the stored procedure actually improved 61 percent.

Scenario 2: Replaying a Workload in Different Environments and Measuring Overall Response Time

In this scenario, we are simulating a situation in which we need to upgrade SQL Server 2000 to a newer version on better hardware configurations. We want to have a quick estimate of the workload improvement on different server configurations.

We will use the workload collected from the DS2 application mentioned earlier. We will replay the workload on different servers. The following four servers with different hardware and software configurations will be used:

❑   **TestServerL:** This server is equipped with the same hardware and software as the server on which the workload data was collected: Intel Pentium III 662 MHz; 2 processors; 1 GB of RAM; 80 GB RAID 5 locally attached; SQL Server 2000 Enterprise SP4.

❑   **TestServerM:** This server has a faster processor speed and 4 processors; Intel Pentium III Xeon 700 MHz; 4 processors; 3.5 GB of RAM; 120 GB RAID 5 locally attached; SQL Server 2005 Enterprise SP1.

❑   **TestServerH:** This server has more power compared to the other testing servers. A 64-bit (*x*64) SQL Server was installed: Intel Pentium Xeon 3.6 GHz; 4 processors; 6 GB of RAM; 450 GB RAID 10 locally attached; SQL Server 2005 *x*64 Enterprise SP1.

❑   **TestServerG:** This server has the same configuration as TestServerH but is solely dedicated for replaying workloads. Since SQL 2005 Profiler replays trace events at the highest speed possible, it uses high CPU during the trace replay. For this reason, we will isolate the Profiler load on this dedicated server.

In SQL 2005 Profiler, there are two main options for replaying trace data (or workload data). The first option is to play the events in the sequence they were collected. The second option is to play the workload concurrently using multiple threads.

For this scenario, to get consistent results, the best option is to use a single-threaded sequential replay. For certain workloads and applications, a multiple-threaded replay can be used if the workload has been fully analyzed for event arrival rates and event synchronizations. Figure 10-20 shows the Replay Configuration options.

Figure 10-21 shows the workload replay on the server TestServerL. This server has an almost identical hardware and software configuration as the source server from which we collected the workload performance data.

To summarize the results from TestServerL in Figure 10-21, the SQL Profiler replayed 92,922 events in 17 minutes 10 seconds. The workload file contained 20 minutes of event executions from the DS2 application. During the replay, even though a single threaded execution was selected, the replay finished in less than 20 minutes. This demonstrated that the SQL 2005 Profiler replay does not replay events at the same speed at which the events were collected. We will use this replay time (17 minutes 10 seconds) as a reference measurement.

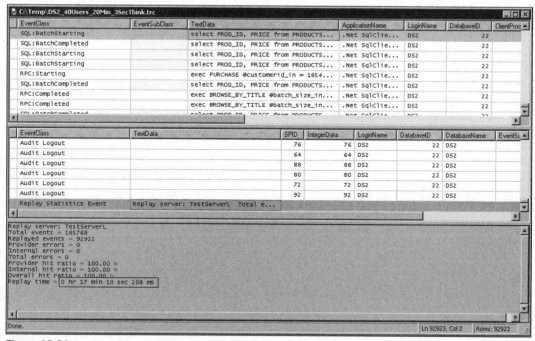

Figure 10-20

Figure 10-21

Figure 10-22 shows the workload replay on the server TestServerM.

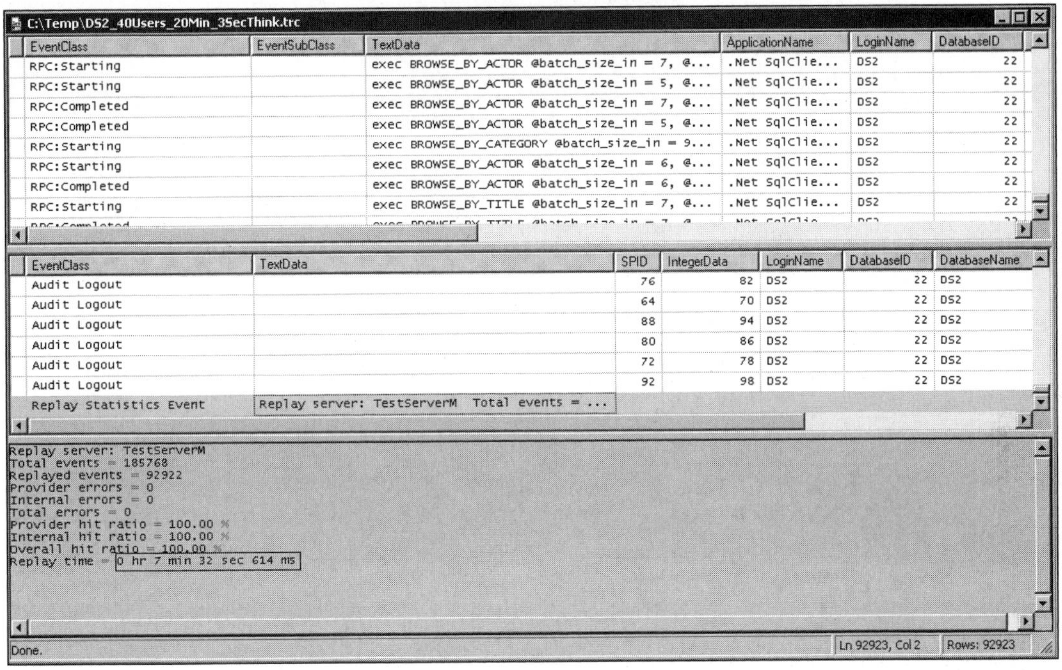

Figure 10-22

To summarize the result from TestServerM in Figure 10-22, the SQL Profiler replayed the same 92,922 events in 7 minutes 32 seconds. It finished in less than half the time of the replay from the server Test-ServerL. This result is expected since this server has four processors and three times more physical memory, and it has SQL Server 2005 installed. For detailed analysis on hardware improvement, you can measure performance on hardware devices during the replay. In this scenario, we are more interested in overall SQL query response time in terms of the whole workload.

Figure 10-23 shows the workload replay on the server TestServerH.

To summarize the result from TestServerH in Figure 10-23, the replay finished in 3 minutes and 52 seconds. It was more than four times faster than the reference measurement (17 minutes and 10 seconds) from the server TestServerL. This impressive result was achieved by the combination of better hardware and SQL Server 2005 (x64).

To summarize this scenario, we collected a workload from a SQL Server 2000 instance and replayed the workload on three servers with different hardware and software configurations. During each workload replay, no additional user applications were running on the server. Table 10-3 shows the results. With a well-defined workload, SQL Profiler Replay provides sufficiently accurate estimates of how the workload performs on a target server.

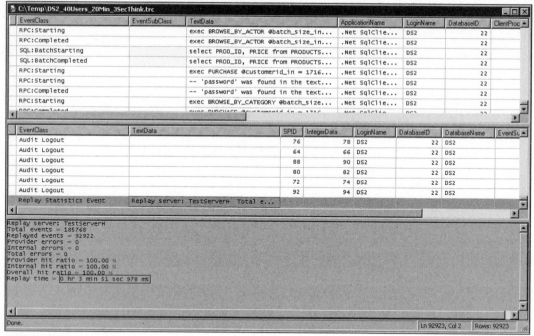

Figure 10-23

Table 10-3: Scenario 2 — Results

Testing Server	Replay Time	Replay Time in Seconds	Performance Comparison
TestServerL	17 min 10 sec	1030	1 (reference)
TestServerM	7 min 32 sec	452	2.2 times faster
TestServerH	3 min 52 sec	231	4.4 times faster

Scenario 3: Replaying Multiple Workloads on a Target Server

Wouldn't it be nice if we could replay multiple workloads on a target server to see if the target server could deliver the expected performance? In this scenario, we will use the SQL Profiler as a client load driver with multiple replay sessions connecting to a target SQL Server 2005 instance.

There are many ways to set up this testing environment; however, two factors need to be considered. The first factor is that SQL profiler is not a specialized tool for load testing; replaying a large workload consumes high CPU. For this reason, we will use a dedicated multi-processor server for SQL Profiler. The second factor to consider is the network overhead between the two servers. In this scenario, we will put all servers in the same network segment.

We will use the workload collected from the DS2 application mentioned earlier and three servers for this study:

❑ **TestServerH:** This is the target server where we have the DS2 database installed. Multiple Profiler replay sessions will be connected to this server. The server capacity is planned for consolidating workloads from other SQL servers. A full database backup of DS2 has been prepared to reset the database to a proper state. It uses Intel Pentium Xeon 3.6 GHz 4-Proc, 6 GB RAM with SQL Server 2005 (x64-bit).

❑ **TestServerG:** This server is dedicated for SQL Profiler (profiler90.exe) to drive the workloads. It has the same server configuration as TestServerH. It uses: Intel Pentium Xeon 3.6 GHz 4-Proc, 6 GB RAM with SQL Server 2005 (x64-bit).

❑ **TestServerM:** This server is mainly used for collecting performance data from the TestServerH. It has a 32-bit SQL Server 2005 installed as an optional server to drive the workload in addition to the TestServerG. We will use Windows 2003 System Performance (Perfmon) and SQL 2005 Profiler tools to collect performance data. It uses: Intel Pentium III Xeon 700 MHz; 4 processors; 3.5 GB of RAM; SQL Server 2005 Enterprise SP1.

We replayed the same workload (DS2_40Threads_20 Min_3SecThink.trc) from each of the SQL Profiler connections (from both TestServerG and TestServerM) to the target server TestServerH with five-second separations. All workload replay sessions were finished within 17 minutes.

Table 10-4 shows individual workload replay performance:

Table 10-4: Workload Replay Performance Measurement

Workload Replayed from	Profiler Instance	Replay Time
TestServerG	1	12 min 17 sec 700 ms
TestServerG	2	12 min 6 sec 637 ms
TestServerG	3	12 min 27 sec 231 ms
TestServerG	4	16 min 55 sec 739 ms
TestServerM	1	15 min 46 sec 11 ms

We will look at the target server TestServerH performance from a system resource point of view and a SQL query performance point of view, and then summarize results.

The following figures show the system resource point of view:

❑ **CPU Utilization:** We collected the system counter, % Processor Time, for the total instance (_Total) from the target server. Figure 10-24 indicates that during the workload replay, the processor time persisted between 60 and 80 percent.

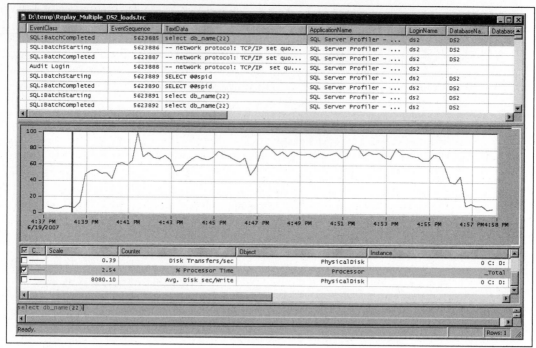

Figure 10-24

❏ ***Disk I/O:** We measured the disk throughput in terms of average disk seconds per read (write). The Avg. Disk sec/Read (Write) is the average time, in seconds, it takes a computer to read (write) from the disk. As shown in Figure 10-25, the average time for a read is about four milliseconds (for a write, it is two milliseconds). The threshold for the disk on the server is 25 milliseconds.

❏ **Database Batch Requests per Second:** Figure 10-26 shows the number of batch requests sent to SQL Server, which averaged about 361 requests per second.

❏ **SQL Server Memory:** The buffer cache hit ratio indicates the percentage of requested data found in the memory buffer. Figure 10-27 indicates the average was 99.85 percent.

The following figures show the SQL query performance point of view:

❏ ***User-Transaction Response Time:** As shown in Figure 10-28, on average, all user transactions responded in milliseconds. Source scripts can be downloaded from the publisher's web site.

❏ **Number of RPC and Batch Completed per Minute Distributions:** Figure 10-29 shows that the first result column represents timestamps and the second column represents the number of database events (RPC:Completed and SQL:BatchCompleted) completed by SQL Server per minute.

Copy and paste the above results to Excel. Graphing the information provides a minute-by-minute view of total RPC and SQL Batch Completed events, as shown in Figure 10-30.

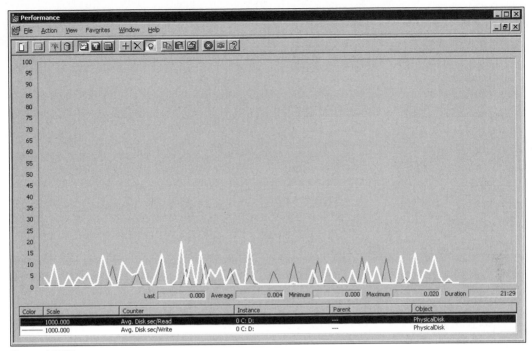

Figure 10-25

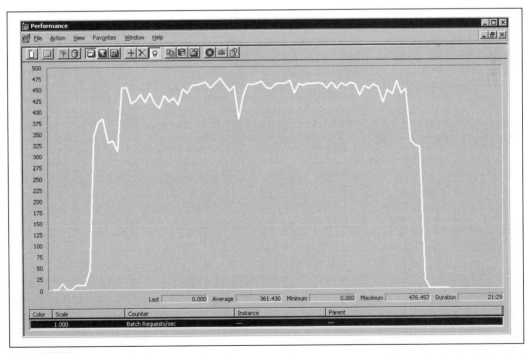

Figure 10-26

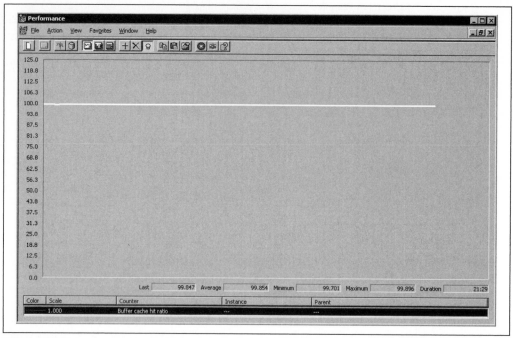

Figure 10-27

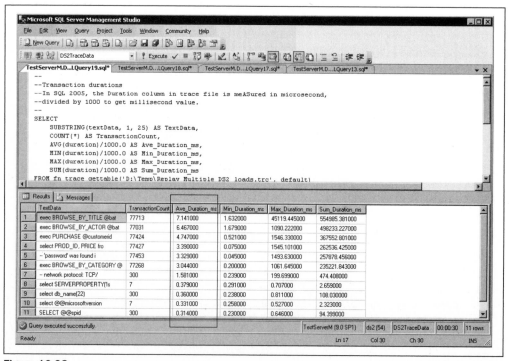

Figure 10-28

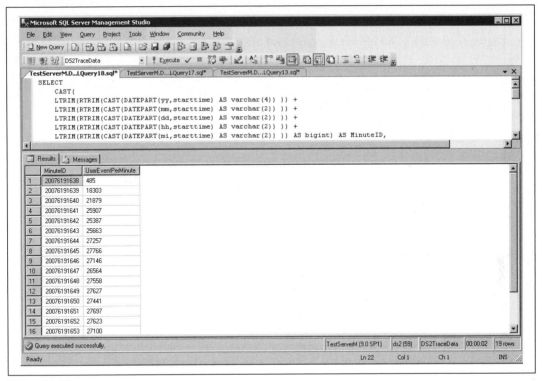

Figure 10-29

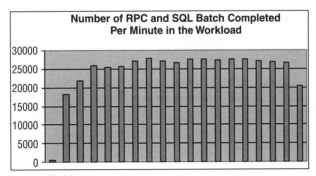

Figure 10-30

To summarize results in this scenario, the target server TestServerH received five workloads from different Profiler replay sessions. All database user transactions were completed within milliseconds. Disk I/O and memory are within their thresholds. Even though CPU consumptions are on the high side, the target server TestServerH handled workloads well. With well-defined workload definitions and a target server preparation, SQL Profiler replay can be used to analyze an overall performance for workload consolidations.

Summary

Capturing, measuring, and replaying a workload are techniques for using SQL Profiler to benchmark performance improvements and establish a performance baseline. In this chapter, you have learned the requirements and setup for each of these techniques. Three scenarios were used to demonstrate the practical use of these techniques. The scenarios covered using the Profiler's replay feature to measure overall performance gain for a workload, using workload replays on different server configurations to benchmark performance differences, and using Profiler to send multiple workloads to a single server.

Even though the Profiler's Replay feature has limitations, such as high CPU consumption for replaying large workloads, it is still a valuable, versatile, and powerful tool for many performance tuning and baseline scenarios.

11

Tuning Indexes

Indexes are the solution to many performance problems but as in most parts of life, too much of a good thing can be bad for you. A thorough understanding of indexes is essential for a DBA to make the right choices and SQL Server 2005 brings new features and options to help even the most hardened indexing expert. We've broken this chapter into four sections to make it easy to dip into:

❑ **"Section 1: Indexing Review"** discusses indexing terminology and introduces some new features and tips. This should be regarded as a refresher rather than an introduction.

❑ **"Section 2: Tuning"** focuses on using Database Tuning Advisor and the built-in tuning tool. It also covers tuning indexes with no server impact using the built-in Dynamic Management Views.

❑ **"Section 3: Maintenance"** is predominantly the domain of the operational DBA and will show you how and why you need to maintain your indexes.

❑ **"Section 4: Table and Index Partitioning"** is an advanced topic but is made much more accessible with the built-in features of SQL Server 2005. This section covers how, why, and where you should implement it.

Sample Database

This chapter uses a very simple database called People to demonstrate the concepts. The database contains only four tables:

```
CREATE TABLE people
(
personId UNIQUEIDENTIFIER DEFAULT newsequentialid(),
firstname VARCHAR(80) not null,
lastname VARCHAR(80) not null,
dob DATETIME not null,
dod DATETIME null,
```

```
    sex CHAR(1) not null
)
go
CREATE TABLE boysnames
 (
 ID INT IDENTITY(0,1) not null,
 [name] VARCHAR(80) not null
 )
go
CREATE TABLE girlsnames
 (
 ID INT IDENTITY(0,1) not null,
 [name] VARCHAR(80) not null
 )
go
CREATE TABLE lastnames
 (
 ID INT IDENTITY(0,1) not null,
 [name] VARCHAR(80) not null
 )
go
```

The scripts to create the database, tables, and stored procedures can be found at www.wrox.com. If you want to follow the examples you should run createDatabase.sql, createTables.sql, createStored-Procedures.sql, and loadNames.sql before continuing.

The key table is people and you want to insert into it as fast as you can. Each insert into this table has to do lookups in three reference tables and then some calculations to determine the rest of the data to be inserted. The three reference tables are a list of male names, a list of female names, and a list of last names.

For reference, here is a description of the stored procedures that are used:

❑ usp_namesInsert: Randomly generates names for the three reference tables. Used by the load-Names.sql script, which should be run before starting.

❑ usp_generateDOB: Generates random birth dates within the last 110 years. Used by usp_peopleInsert.

❑ usp_peopleInsert: Inserts a boy and a girl to the people table.

❑ usp_loopPeopleInsert: Runs usp_peopleInsert 10000 times. This default can be overriden by passing a value to the @people parameter.

❑ usp_birthInsert: Inserts a new boy and girl record with today's date as the date of birth.

❑ usp_loopBirthInsert: Runs usp_birthInsert 10000 times. This default can be overriden by passing a value to the @people parameter.

❑ usp_marriageUpdate: Matches a boy and girl together and updates the girl's surname to be the same as the boy's surname.

❑ usp_loopMarriageUpdate: Runs usp_marriageUpdate 10000 times. This default can be overriden by passing a value to the @people parameter.

❑ usp_deathDelete: Deletes a boy and a girl record from the people table.

❑ usp_loopDeathDelete: Runs usp_deathDelete 1000 times. This default can be overriden by passing a value to the @people parameter.

Section 1: Indexing Review

Indexes are used to provide fast access to data and are very often the first area to look at when tuning a system. This is because the performance gains for well-designed and maintained indexes can be considerable and they can be implemented relatively quickly. Adding, removing, or rebuilding an index can be a quick win for you in terms of performance so it is definitely worth your time to learn more about what they are and what indexing strategies SQL Server professionals employ.

There are two basic types of indexes: clustered and nonclustered. A *clustered index* defines the physical order that the data in a table is stored. You can only have one per table and it can be compared to the contents page at the beginning of this book. For example, to get to this chapter you might have read the contents page to get the page number and come straight here, or you might just have flicked through all the pages until you got here. In SQL Server terms these relate to a clustered-index seek and a clustered-index scan, respectively.

A *non-clustered index* does not affect the physical ordering of the data and can be compared to the index at the back of this book. If you wanted to know which page discussed "Fill Factor," for example, you could look at the index, get the exact page number, and go straight there. You can have up to 249 non-clustered indexes on single table but it's difficult to imagine a scenario where that would be a better choice than normalizing the table. See Chapter 8 for details on normalization.

B-Trees

SQL Server implements indexes as balanced trees, or b-trees for short. The idea behind a balanced tree is to ensure that it costs the same to read any data page in the tree. It consists of a single root page, multiple intermediate-level pages, and leaf-level pages. The intermediate-level (or non-leaf) pages are split and new levels created when new data is added to ensure that every page requires the same number of reads to find. Figure 11-1 shows an example of a b-tree with three levels.

Each level grows in width as large as the pages at the next level up can keep track of and a new level is created when the existing tree can't track any more pages. The size of each index record is affected by the size of the indexed column, so the narrower the indexed column the more you can fit on a page and the fewer levels you'll have in your index. Each level takes 1 logical read (index trees will usually be cached) so the shallower your index tree the better. You can use the following code to view the depth of all the user-created indexes in the current database:

```
SELECT object_name(i.object_id) AS 'table name',
       i.[name] AS 'index name',
       indexproperty(i.object_id, i.[name], 'indexdepth') as 'indexdepth'
FROM  sys.objects o (nolock),
 sys.indexes i (nolock)
WHERE o.object_id = i.object_id
 AND index_id between 1 and 250
AND o.type = 'u'
```

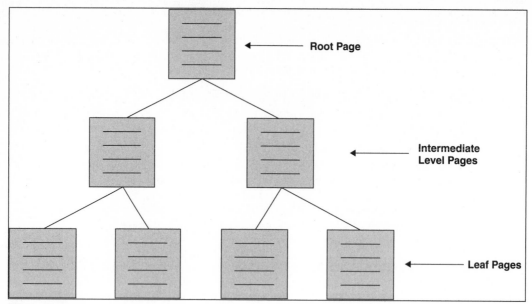

Figure 11-1

Leaf-level pages are connected by what is called a doubly-linked list so that SQL Server can move forward or backward at the leaf-level without having to traverse the non-leaf levels. This benefits range scans in particular where SQL Server seeks to the first leaf page and can then scan forward or backward from there.

The Fill Factor

Fill factor allows you to configure how much free space to leave on each leaf-level page to allow for more inserts without causing a page split. A page split occurs when an index record needs to be inserted into a leaf page that's already full so the single page is split into two pages to allow the insert to happen. This operation isn't bad on its own but if there are lots of inserts causing page splits it can affect performance.

Fill factor is specified as a percentage to fill each page when you create or rebuild an index and the free space isn't maintained, so you need to specify it again with each index rebuild. The default is 0, which means fill the page entirely and has the same effect as specifying 100. A fill factor of 70 would leave 30 percent free space on each page.

You should specify a fill factor (70 is a common rule of thumb) when the underlying table has a high number of inserts and your index isn't on a sequential column. For example, in the People database there is an index on the name column in the lastnames table. New inserts into the table will trigger an index update which might be anywhere in the index tree because the name inserted is unlikely to be sequential to the previous value. If the leaf page it inserts to is full, a page split occurs. If the index were on the id column the row would be inserted to the right of the index tree (because it's sequential) where you're far less likely to have a full-page so you wouldn't need to use a non-default fill factor.

Clustered Indexes

The leaf level of a clustered index contains all the data, which is why we refer to it as defining the physical ordering of the rows. A common question is, "What should I put my clustered index on?" Here are some sensible guidelines that you can follow to make that decision a bit easier:

❑ **Unique data:** A clustered index key (the column(s) you choose to create a clustered index on) has to be unique. If the data itself isn't unique then SQL Server will add a 4-byte UniqueIdentifier to every duplicate value to allow you to use that key. You can avoid this unnecessary overhead (as small as it might be) by creating your index on a column that already has unique values.

❑ **Narrow data:** A narrow column will help to keep your clustered index b-tree short and will help to keep your other indexes smaller. The clustered index key is duplicated at the leaf-level of every non-clustered index you create so it affects all your other indexes.

❑ **Static data:** Changes to the key can be costly, as the change needs to be cascaded to the non-clustered indexes and the foreign keys if your cluster key is also the primary key. Your cluster key should be static to avoid cascading updates. See Chapter 8 for details on primary/foreign keys and referential integrity.

Clustering on an Identity Column

An identity column in SQL Server is an automatically generated incremental integer that makes an ideal clustered index key.

❑ It's naturally unique within the table.

❑ It's narrow because an integer is only 4 bytes in size.

❑ It's static because it has no relevance to the business data.

❑ It's incremental.

This creates a natural "hot spot" because the pages needed for INSERT will already be in cache and it helps to reduce fragmentation caused by page-splits. The caveat is that this isn't appropriate for a very high number of inserts because the hot spot will become the bottleneck. If you're going to have more than 400 inserts a second to a table, you should look at alternatives.

UniqueIdentifier/GUID

UniqueIdentifier is a SQL Server data type for GUIDs (Globally Unique IDentifiers) which are 16-byte computer generated values created based on your hardware (to an extent) to try and guarantee uniqueness. It's not actually unique but getting a duplicate is comparable in probability to winning the lottery.

They would seem to be ideal for merging data from different sources, because they'll be unique from any source, but GUIDs tend to be avoided as a clustering key because of their large size, complexity in debugging, and their random nature, causing slow inserts. They are created by the newID() function and you can test it yourself by running select newID(). On one of our laptops this was the GUID it produced:

```
D29F244C-541C-4542-9CEF-BEF305FDA3D4
```

SQL Server 2005 has a new function for creating GUIDs that ensures that each one is greater than the previous one created on the same machine. The function is newsequentialID(), and it can only be used as the DEFAULT value for a column with datatype UNIQUEIDENTIFIER. There is such a column in the sample database and selecting the top 5 personID values from the people table on this laptop shows 5 sequential GUIDs:

```
311A5A22-743F-DC11-9145-000E7B82B6DD
321A5A22-743F-DC11-9145-000E7B82B6DD
331A5A22-743F-DC11-9145-000E7B82B6DD
341A5A22-743F-DC11-9145-000E7B82B6DD
351A5A22-743F-DC11-9145-000E7B82B6DD
```

The people table was populated by running usp_loopPeopleInsert, if you want to try it yourself.

NewsequentialID() helps to avoid the slowdown associated with inserting random values, which might make it appealing, but the size of the key and the complexity it introduces when debugging (complex because it's long and not human, readable) still exists. Because of this, identity remains the most popular clustered index key.

Natural versus Surrogate Keys

There is much debate about this topic within the database community, with good arguments for either side and compelling justification for a middle ground. The debate is about choosing a primary key, and your primary key doesn't have to be your clustered index key. It's a schema tuning decision and is covered in detail in Chapter 8.

Let's review the details here as it's relevant to the discussion. The index keys that you've seen so far are known as *surrogate keys* because they have no meaning to the business data; they were generated automatically by the system. You've already seen the advantages of clustering on a surrogate identity key above.

A natural key has meaning to the business, but the same best practice rules for a clustered index key should be applied when evaluating it as a choice for primary key. It is much harder to find an ideal natural key than it is to just use surrogate keys. Natural keys tend to have the risk of change because they're known to the business. A stock code might be the first choice as a natural primary key but it's still feasible that the business might want to change it, which will have a cascading effect.

A Bad Clustered Index Choice

A good example of a bad clustered index key would be lastname, because:

- ❑ It's wide, so inserts could take longer and non-clustered indexes will also be larger.
- ❑ It's not unique, so SQL Server has to apply a unique identifier, which wastes time.
- ❑ It's volatile, which will cause cascading updates, and relocation, which introduces fragmentation.

The Right Clustered Index

Generally the best table structure is the right clustered index. The *right* clustered index key is always going to be debatable. In this chapter we use surrogate keys for most scenarios and will create one to cluster on if it doesn't exist. However, there are always exceptions.

I tend to treat a clustered index as being for the benefit of SQL Server internally to give me the most consistently good insert/update performance and rely on non-clustered indexes for improving query response times.

Heaps

A table without a clustered index is known as a *heap* because there is no enforced order to the data; all inserts go to the end of the table. This makes inserts very fast, and heaps are often used in data loading scenarios where the indexes are re-applied afterwards. They are also good for forward-only scenarios like auditing, where you're always writing to the end of the table and not deleting anything.

Small tables can often benefit from being a heap where the data is so small that the optimizer always chooses a table scan rather than an index. In most heap scenarios, however, you should apply a non-clustered index to the heap or every access to the table would need to be a table scan.

Nonclustered Indexes

The non-leaf levels of a nonclustered index are exactly the same as those of a clustered index. Where the b-trees differ is in what they contain at the leaf level. When you traverse a b-tree in a clustered index, the leaf level is the data itself. When you traverse a non-clustered tree, the leaf level contains a pointer to the data. This pointer can take two forms depending on the underlying table structure. If the table is a heap, the pointer will be a Row IDentifier (RID), which is an 8-byte value representing the file id, page, and slot number.

If the table has a clustered index, then the pointer is actually the clustered index key. When you traverse the b-tree the leaf level will contain the non-clustered key and the clustered key. When SQL Server has the clustered index key, it can then traverse the clustered index to get the rest of the data. This extra b-tree traversal means that non-clustered indexes are better when your data has high selectivity.

Covering Indexes

A covering index means that all the columns required to provide the result set of a query are found at the leaf-level of a non-clustered index. This means all the columns in the SELECT statement *and* the WHERE clause (if there is one). For example, if I had a clustered index on `dbo.people.personID` and a non-clustered index on `dbo.people.lastname`, a query like `select personID, lastname from people` would be covered by the non-clustered index. All the data is available at the leaf level of the index without having to go to the underlying clustered table.

If you added `firstname` to the SELECT statement or to a WHERE clause, the query wouldn't be covered, and a trip to the clustered index would be required. You could drop the non-clustered index and recreate it on `lastname, firstname` to get a covering index, but you have to balance the overall system requirements with the need to tune specific important queries. Trying to cover every query would be detrimental to the performance of most systems and shouldn't even be necessary.

Include Columns

This is a great feature introduced with SQL Server 2005 that allows you to include columns at the leaf-level of an index without them being part of the index tree. The sole purpose of this is to have more covered queries and it provides a number of additional benefits as well:

❑ Index keys have a limitation of 900 bytes and 16 columns. Included columns don't count toward this limitation so they provide an easy workaround to get more data into an index.

❑ All data types except text, ntext, and image can be used as included columns. Varchar(max), nvarchar(max), varbinary(max), and XML data types are not allowed to be index keys, but you can include the data from these types in an index by using the include feature.

❑ It reduces the size of the index tree. By only having lookup columns in your index key and covering index columns as included columns, you reduce the size of the non-leaf levels, which makes maintaining the index more efficient.

❑ In the previous example you could create the non-clustered index like this:

```
CREATE NONCLUSTERED INDEX idx_lastname
ON people (lastname)
INCLUDE (firstname)
```

to include the firstname at the leaf level of the index without making it an indexed column. Any query using this index would find peopleID, lastname, firstname at the leaf level of the index.

Disabling Indexes

The ability to disable an index was introduced in SQL Server 2005 to meet the needs of customers who required indexes to be created periodically for short-term needs. For example, a report may gain huge benefits from a particular index, but the business only needs it once per year. You don't want the overhead of managing an index that's used once per year, so you can disable it for most the year and just enable it when you need to.

Disabling an index effectively drops it and just keeps the definition, so you don't need to remember the details of the indexes that need to be re-created when it comes to run the report; just enable the ones already there. Enabling an index is the same as creating it from scratch; you just don't need to specify the structure.

We've also seen customers using this in data load scenarios where they disable the indexes beforehand and enable them again after the load to save time dropping and recreating. It's only really useful for non-clustered indexes, though, as disabling a clustered index prevents access to the underlying data.

You disable and enable indexes using the ALTER INDEX command:

```
ALTER INDEX idx_lastname
ON dbo.people
DISABLE
ALTER INDEX idx_lastname
ON dbo.people
REBUILD
```

Statistics

Statistics are used by the optimizer to help it decide on the most efficient way to execute a query. They are created for every index. Internally, SQL Server builds a histogram using up to 200 values from your index and calculates the number of rows that fall between each value (the gap between each value is called an interval) and the density of values within an interval. Density is a measure of the number of duplicate values. Armed with this information the optimizer can choose whether or not to use particular indexes without having to read the data. Basic information on all the statistics on a table can be viewed with `sp_helpstats` and detailed information on a particular set of statistics can be viewed using DBCC SHOW_STATISTICS. For example, if you create this index:

```
CREATE NONCLUSTERED INDEX idx_name
ON lastnames(name)
```

And run `sp_helpstats` on the lastnames table:

```
sp_helpstats 'lastnames', 'ALL'
go

statistics_name     statistics_keys
------------------  ---------------
idx_name        name
```

If you've been running all the code examples so far in this chapter you'll also see some statistics on the ID column, which are prefixed with _WA_Sys_. These are auto-generated statistics from running the `usp_looppeopleinsert` stored procedure. The different ways statistics are created are discussed in the next section.

You can see that there are statistics on the name column, which you can then have a look at in more detail using DBCC SHOW_STATISTICS:

```
DBCC SHOW_STATISTICS ('lastnames','idx_name')
go
Name                 Updated                Rows    Rows Sampled
---------------      --------------------   ------  -------------
idx_lastname     Jul 31 2007 12:05AM  2000    2000

Steps  Density  Average key length String Index
------ --------  ------------------ ------------
192    1        44.231                  YES
All density    Average Length Columns
-------------  -------------- --------
0.0005         44.231          name

RANGE_HI_KEY
-------------------------------------------------------
ABQPXHSRBWEOXYQSNBBJESAXRUXFDCIXKICFVXKXPYVJXLTVMLHD
AFRQGVFFXBOGXGYVUCGCJDETEQWTEAWLY
AKFVETQFWEGANVGMAIJQJIKEBCFHSFMFANVFMBAGJUCLSADQQWQEBE
ASYBJUDGKJJUBUBXWYMLPBAJOEWVDPWLKHBRHRJABAWVLVECTPH
AWGEMFCXBSINYRUUSTUSITXMWNTWURALDNALYYKWF
BAGCHFEOOVJTTJMSMOSOEAIAC
BCEIDGWQSCVWVTVCLJBIK

RANGE_ROWS     EQ_ROWS        DISTINCT_RANGE_ROWS  AVG_RANGE_ROWS
-------------  -------------  --------------------- ---------------
6              1              6                    1
7              1              7                    1
11             1              11                   1
11             1              11                   1
7              1              7                    1
14             1              14                   1
7              1              7                    1
```

You can see that these statistics were updated July 31 2007 and there are 2000 rows of which 2000 were sampled, so you know that these statistics were taken will a FULL/100% sample size. The statistics consist of a histogram of 192 values (I've only printed the top 7) with a density of 1, which means that each value is unique. The names column in the lastnames table was populated with random characters, so these results are consistent with the table usage.

Drop the index now so it doesn't interfere with the tuning later on:

```
DROP INDEX lastnames.idx_name
```

Creating Statistics

Statistics can be created in a number of different ways. You can create them automatically, manually, or by creating an index.

CREATE INDEX

As you've already seen, when you create an index, statistics of the same name are automatically created for the columns within the index to help the optimizer choose whether or not that index is useful. Thus, the idx_name index has a set of statistics called idx_name.

AUTO_CREATE_STATISTICS

By default, SQL Server 2005 will automatically create statistics on columns where they can be of use to the optimizer. This occurs when a column without an index is used in a WHERE clause and statistics created as a result of this are prefixed by _WA_Sys_. For example, if you look at the people table:

```
sp_helpstats 'people', 'ALL'
go
This object does not have any statistics or indexes.
```

You can see that there are no statistics currently. If you then run a SELECT statement with the lastname column in the where clause:

```
SELECT firstname,lastname FROM people WHERE lastname = 'Bolton'
```

And then look for statistics again:

```
sp_helpstats 'people', 'ALL'
go
statistics_name               statistics_keys
---------------------------- ---------------
_WA_Sys_00000003_0C85DE4D  lastname
```

You can see that statistics have been automatically generated. Looking at the automatically generated statistics in a database can give you an idea of where you might have missing indexes, because it indicates where an index could have been used by the optimizer. You can use this code to check for all statistics in your database that are not associated with an index:

```
sp_msforeachtable "print 'Table Name:?' EXEC sp_helpstats '?', STATS"
```

Automatic statistics creation is controlled by the AUTO_CREATE_STATISTICS database option and can be disabled if necessary.

CREATE STATISTICS

If you are confident that you know all the potential queries against your database, you can disable AUTO_CREATE_STATISTICS and CREATE STATISTICS manually on one or more columns that don't already have an index. You just have to specify a name for the statistics, the columns you want them on, and the sample size you require. Databases that have frequent data loads can have AUTO_CRE-ATE_STATISTICS disabled to prevent automatically created statistics from having to be maintained. It's an unusual scenario though, so for most systems you work on having AUTO_CREATE_STATISTICS enabled is by far the best option.

Updating Statistics

As you change the data in your table, the statistics that were originally created may not accurately represent the distribution of your data, leading to the optimizer making poor choices. There are three ways to keep your statistics up-to-date:

AUTO_UPDATE_STATISTICS

This is a database option that, when enabled, triggers the optimizer to automatically update statistics when a test for current statistics fails. The effect of this in most cases is that statistics are automatically updated after 20 percent of the rows have been changed unless it's a small table (< 500 rows) where auto update won't be triggered unless nearly all the rows change. Most of the time you don't need to worry about updating your statistics because this option is enabled by default.

AUTO_UPDATE_STATISTICS_ASYNC

When a test for current statistics fails, the query that prompted the check has to wait for the statistics to be updated. This can cause unpredictable response times in environments with frequently changing data, which is a problem for companies that favor predictability over efficiency. One of the authors of this book worked with an investment bank a few years ago on their trading platform, which ran on SQL Server 2000. They experienced this exact problem and had to disable automatic updating entirely because the implication of a query waiting for a statistics update meant that the stock trade price it provided was too old.

This database option is new to SQL Server 2005 and is more commonly referred as Asynchronous Statistics Update. It allows queries that cause a statistics update to continue compiling using the old statistics while the update is queued in a background process, thus providing more predictable performance. The risk of course is that the optimizer might choose a less efficient execution plan.

Disabling Automatic Update Statistics

There are a number of ways to disable automatic updating of statistics that provide more granularity than disabling it entirely at the database level:

- ❏ sp_autostats can be used to disable or enable it for individual indexes or tables.
- ❏ You can specify STATISTICS_NORECOMPUTE when you create an index with CREATE INDEX.
- ❏ You can specify NORECOMPUTE when creating or updating statistics with CREATE or UPDATE STATISTICS.

UPDATE STATISTICS

You can manually update a set of statistics or all the statistics for a specified index using this statement. There are a couple of options that are worth commenting on:

❑ **FULLSCAN:** Calculates statistics based on all the data. This gives the most accurate results but takes the most time to create. Without this option SQL Server does a quick scan on the object to determine the minimum sample size required to get good results and uses that.

❑ **RESAMPLE:** Inherits the sample size that was used the last time the statistics were updated.

You can use `sp_updatestats` as a wrapper for UPDATE STATISTICS. This allows you to update all the statistics in an entire database using this one statement.

ALTER INDEX REBUILD

When you rebuild an index, SQL Server takes advantage of the fact that you're "touching" every page by using it as an opportunity to update the statistics with the equivalent of FULLSCAN as described in the previous section. One customer had a nightly maintenance job that updated statistics with the default sample size straight after they rebuilt their indexes! Not only was their maintenance period longer but the result was less accurate statistics!

The following code will show you the creation date of the statistics for all the user-created indexes in the current database:

```
SELECT object_name(o.id) AS 'Table Name',
       i.name AS 'Index Name',
       stats_date(i.id, i.indid) AS 'Statistics Date'
  FROM sys.sysobjects o (NOLOCK),
       sys.sysindexes i (NOLOCK)
 WHERE o.id = i.id
   AND o.type = 'u'
   AND i.indid BETWEEN 1 AND 250
   AND i.name NOT LIKE '_wa_sys%'
ORDER BY object_name(o.id), i.name
GO
```

Indexed Views

SQL Server allows you to create a clustered index on a view, which has the effect of persisting the view to disk making it more like an actual table. You can even create non-clustered indexes on top of an indexed view. The benefit of this is that aggregates in your view will be pre-calculated and you can pre-join tables storing the results on disk.

The optimizer in the Developer and Enterprise Editions of SQL Server will even evaluate if an indexed view would be useful without the view being referenced. In other editions you have to reference the view manually and specify the NOEXPAND hint so SQL Server treats it like a normal table.

Indexed views are most useful in scenarios where there are lots of joins and aggregations. Fortunately, you don't need to analyze that yourself; SQL Server comes with a tuning tool to help you decide.

Section 2: Tuning with DTA

The Database Tuning Advisor is a physical database design tool that replaces and builds on the technology in the Index Tuning Wizard in SQL Server 2000. It accepts as input a workload in the form of a T-SQL script containing a set of SELECT, DELETE, and UPDATE statements or a SQL Profiler trace, and will output a T-SQL script consisting of recommendations for the creation, dropping and partitioning of indexes, indexed views, and statistics. It will also give you an estimated performance improvement if you implement the recommendations. Figure 11-2 shows a high-level architecture of DTA.

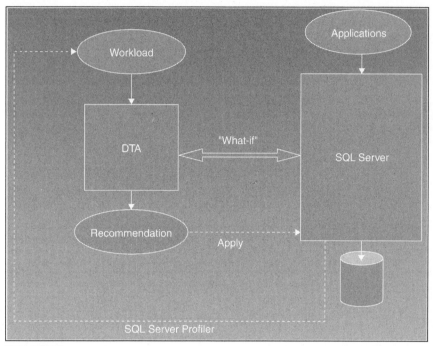

Figure 11-2

It used to be that the DBA had to spend a lot of time reviewing the database design, learning about data distribution, then finding and examining in detail the main queries, and then manually tuning indexes to try and find the best set of indexes to suit individual queries. With DTA this slow and laborious process is no longer needed. You can use DTA to tune individual queries as they are being developed and to tune whole workloads as they become available.

DTA does this either by analyzing individual queries from SQL Management Studio or a SQL Server Profiler Trace file. The workload should contain at least one example of each query called, but it doesn't need to contain repeated calls to the same procedure as you would expect to see in a trace from a production system. This is because DTA will only tune each unique query. It isn't going to look at the interaction of all the queries in the result set and provide a balanced set of indexes to suit a mix of INSERT, UPDATE, and DELETE statements. It will instead simply look at each query and provide recommendations to improve that query. So the DBA still has some work to do in deciding which indexes to implement to get the best compromise between insert, update, and delete performance.

Now you'll jump straight into using DTA to create some indexes.

Using DTA to Tune Individual Queries

Imagine a scenario where a developer DBA is writing queries for a new database and wants to create an initial set of indexes. You have to have a database with data in it and that data has to be representative of the final data distribution. In the sample workload, you'll examine the index recommendations with three levels of data in the target tables. Table 11-1 lists the numbers of rows in each table where you'll run DTA for the DTApeopleInsert.sql query.

Table 11-1: Number of Rows for Each Tuning Stage

Table	Insert	Update
People	0	1,000,000
BoysNames	100	100
GirlsNames	100	100
LastNames	2,000	2,000

Before starting to run DTA, you need to figure out how to determine the effectiveness of each of the DTA recommendations. DTA will give you its expectation of performance improvement, but you should check its effectiveness for yourself, so you need to have some way to measure before and after performance.

You'll use three metrics for this. The first is the insert time for each row. To get this you can use a simple stored procedure that calls the insert stored procedure multiple times and reports how many rows it has inserted and the insert rate at pre-determined intervals. The second metric is the output of the statistics IO. You can gather this data using SQL Server management Studio, by turning on the Query option for statistics IO. The third metric is the statistics time.

Before you start tuning, you need to capture your starting metrics. To make sure you get consistent results, you also need to capture a cold time and several warm times and then average the warm times. A cold time is the time it takes to run a query against SQL Server for the first time. The execution plan and data aren't in cache, so everything has to be created from scratch. Subsequent runs of the query will be much quicker (warmed up) because of caching and will be more representative of a live system. Measuring performance gains against average warm times will give you the best idea of what gains to expect on a busy system.

One other thing you'll look at in this example is the wait time during the query execution. You can only do this if you run the procedure in a tight loop because unless the query is very slow-running, you won't be able to capture the instantaneous results you need to see any waits. By running in a tight loop, you can sample the wait stats repeatedly and stand a good chance of seeing what the query is waiting on.

Start off by capturing stats for the `usp_peopleInsert` stored procedure with an empty people table. To make sure the server is in a cold state, use the following commands before each cold run to flush memory to disk, and make sure you get a full stored procedure compile cycle on the first run. This is much faster than restarting SQL Server every time and gives good repeatable results.

```
dbcc dropcleanbuffers
dbcc freeproccache
```

Now run the stored procedure and see how fast it goes by using this script:

```
use People
go

truncate table people
go

dbcc dropcleanbuffers
dbcc freeproccache
go

set statistics time on
set statistics io on
go

-- Cold run
exec usp_peopleInsert
go

-- first warm run
exec usp_peopleInsert
go

-- second warm run
exec usp_peopleInsert
go

-- third warm run
exec usp_peopleInsert
go

set statistics time off
set statistics io off
go

-- we ran the SP to insert 2 people 4 times, so we should have 8 people in the DB
select count (*) from people
go
```

The following are the results of executing the procedure several times:

```
Cold Run

SQL Server parse and compile time:
```

```
            CPU time = 0 ms, elapsed time = 89 ms.

 SQL Server Execution Times:
            CPU time = 0 ms,  elapsed time = 1 ms.
 Table 'BoysNames'. Scan count 1, logical reads 1, physical reads 1, read-ahead
 reads 0, lob logical reads 0, lob physical reads 0, lob read-ahead reads 0.

 SQL Server Execution Times:
            CPU time = 0 ms,  elapsed time = 1 ms.
 Table 'GirlsNames'. Scan count 1, logical reads 1, physical reads 1, read-ahead
 reads 0, lob logical reads 0, lob physical reads 0, lob read-ahead reads 0.

 SQL Server Execution Times:
            CPU time = 0 ms,  elapsed time = 1 ms.
 Table 'lastNames'. Scan count 1, logical reads 8, physical reads 8, read-ahead
 reads 0, lob logical reads 0, lob physical reads 0, lob read-ahead reads 0.

 SQL Server Execution Times:
            CPU time = 0 ms,  elapsed time = 5 ms.

 SQL Server Execution Times:
            CPU time = 0 ms,  elapsed time = 1 ms.
 Table 'BoysNames'. Scan count 1, logical reads 1, physical reads 0, read-ahead
 reads 0, lob logical reads 0, lob physical reads 0, lob read-ahead reads 0.

 SQL Server Execution Times:
            CPU time = 0 ms,  elapsed time = 1 ms.
 Table 'GirlsNames'. Scan count 1, logical reads 1, physical reads 0, read-ahead
 reads 0, lob logical reads 0, lob physical reads 0, lob read-ahead reads 0.

 SQL Server Execution Times:
            CPU time = 0 ms,  elapsed time = 1 ms.
 Table 'lastNames'. Scan count 1, logical reads 8, physical reads 0, read-ahead
 reads 0, lob logical reads 0, lob physical reads 0, lob read-ahead reads 0.

 SQL Server Execution Times:
            CPU time = 0 ms,  elapsed time = 29 ms.

 SQL Server Execution Times:
            CPU time = 0 ms,  elapsed time = 2 ms.
 SQL Server Execution Times:
            CPU time = 0 ms,  elapsed time = 1 ms.
 Table 'people'. Scan count 0, logical reads 1, physical reads 0, read-ahead reads
 0, lob logical reads 0, lob physical reads 0, lob read-ahead reads 0.

 SQL Server Execution Times:
            CPU time = 0 ms,  elapsed time = 91 ms.
 Table 'people'. Scan count 0, logical reads 1, physical reads 0, read-ahead reads
 0, lob logical reads 0, lob physical reads 0, lob read-ahead reads 0.

 SQL Server Execution Times:
            CPU time = 0 ms,  elapsed time = 217 ms.


 -- Warm Run times
```

```
SQL Server parse and compile time:
   CPU time = 0 ms, elapsed time = 1 ms.

SQL Server Execution Times:
   CPU time = 0 ms,  elapsed time = 1 ms.
Table 'BoysNames'. Scan count 1, logical reads 1, physical reads 0, read-ahead
reads 0, lob logical reads 0, lob physical reads 0, lob read-ahead reads 0.

SQL Server Execution Times:
   CPU time = 0 ms,  elapsed time = 1 ms.
Table 'GirlsNames'. Scan count 1, logical reads 1, physical reads 0, read-ahead
reads 0, lob logical reads 0, lob physical reads 0, lob read-ahead reads 0.

SQL Server Execution Times:
   CPU time = 0 ms,  elapsed time = 1 ms.
Table 'lastNames'. Scan count 1, logical reads 8, physical reads 0, read-ahead
reads 0, lob logical reads 0, lob physical reads 0, lob read-ahead reads 0.

SQL Server Execution Times:
   CPU time = 16 ms,  elapsed time = 1 ms.

SQL Server Execution Times:
   CPU time = 0 ms,  elapsed time = 1 ms.
Table 'BoysNames'. Scan count 1, logical reads 1, physical reads 0, read-ahead
reads 0, lob logical reads 0, lob physical reads 0, lob read-ahead reads 0.

SQL Server Execution Times:
   CPU time = 0 ms,  elapsed time = 1 ms.
Table 'GirlsNames'. Scan count 1, logical reads 1, physical reads 0, read-ahead
reads 0, lob logical reads 0, lob physical reads 0, lob read-ahead reads 0.

SQL Server Execution Times:
   CPU time = 0 ms,  elapsed time = 1 ms.
Table 'lastNames'. Scan count 1, logical reads 8, physical reads 0, read-ahead
reads 0, lob logical reads 0, lob physical reads 0, lob read-ahead reads 0.

SQL Server Execution Times:
   CPU time = 0 ms,  elapsed time = 31 ms.

SQL Server Execution Times:
   CPU time = 0 ms,  elapsed time = 1 ms.
Table 'people'. Scan count 0, logical reads 1, physical reads 0, read-ahead reads
0, lob logical reads 0, lob physical reads 0, lob read-ahead reads 0.

SQL Server Execution Times:
   CPU time = 0 ms,  elapsed time = 1 ms.
Table 'people'. Scan count 0, logical reads 1, physical reads 0, read-ahead reads
0, lob logical reads 0, lob physical reads 0, lob read-ahead reads 0.

SQL Server Execution Times:
   CPU time = 0 ms,  elapsed time = 2 ms.
```

```
SQL Server Execution Times:
   CPU time = 16 ms,  elapsed time = 36 ms.
```

There is some very useful information in this output. Looking at both the cold and warm run outputs, you can see that they are both pretty fast, with a cold run elapsed time of 217 milliseconds (ms) and a warm run elapsed time of 36 ms.

Looking at the cold run stats and focusing on the number of physical reads, you can see that there were a total of 10 physical reads, 1 to read the boysnames table, 1 to read the girlsnames table, and 8 to read the lastnames table into memory.

The warm run stats show that there were no physical reads, only logical reads. The parse and compile time was also greatly reduced. This tells you that the query didn't need recompiling, which is good, as it will save you a lot of time each time it's called.

The warm run stats also show that it's taking about 30 to 40 ms for each insert.

Given that you are only issuing 10 reads to execute the query, and that repeated calls don't invoke additional physical reads, it's going to be hard to improve performance by further reducing these already low numbers. It's also going to be hard to see any small time-based improvements when the time taken is already so small at just 30 to 40 ms.

To make it easier to observe small changes in performance, you are going to need to execute the queries hundreds or thousands of times and then look at the overall stats for a very large number of executions. This will help highlight any small changes.

To do this you need to put the script into a loop and run it thousands of times to see if that gives a better measurement. Use the following command line statement:

```
sqlcmd -E -d people -Q"exec usp_loopPeopleInsert 3000, 500"
```

These are the results of the usp_loopPeopleInsert stored procedure:

```
Inserted 1000 people in 670mS at a rate of 1492.54 per Second
Inserted 1000 people in 720mS at a rate of 1388.89 per Second
Inserted 1000 people in 656mS at a rate of 1524.39 per Second
Inserted 1000 people in 686mS at a rate of 1457.73 per Second
Inserted 1000 people in 720mS at a rate of 1388.89 per Second
```

The inserts are going fast enough that you are getting between 1400 and 1500 inserts per second.

Now you should look to see what you are waiting on. To do that, you modify the sqlcmd line as follows so it would run for considerably longer. Then you can query the sys.processes table to see what the wait types are for your query. Here is the modified cmd line:

```
sqlcmd -E -d people -Q"exec usp_loopPeopleInsert 20000, 1000"
```

This is the query that will let you monitor what you are waiting on:

```
set nocount on
while 1 > 0
```

```
begin
  select spid, kpid, blocked, waittime, lastwaittype, waitresource
  from master..sysprocesses
  where program_name = 'SQLCMD'
  waitfor delay '00:00:00.05'
end
```

These are the results of the query (cleaned up to save space):

spid	kpid	blocked	waittime	lastwaittype
55	3336	0	0	WRITELOG
55	3336	0	0	WRITELOG
55	3336	0	0	WRITELOG
55	3336	0	0	WRITELOG

Not surprisingly, on such a simple insert on a very basic slow disk, most of the time is spent waiting on the log write. What the information here has told you is that most of the stats are meaningless except for the raw write rate that comes out of the usp_peopleInsert stored procedure.

One final check before going on to DTA is to take a look at the output of SHOWPLAN_TEXT to see what the query plan looks like. You can then compare this with the query plan after applying any recommendations from DTA and see how it changes.

```
SET SHOWPLAN_TEXT ON;
GO
exec usp_peopleInsert
go
SET SHOWPLAN_TEXT OFF;
GO
```

I find it easier to read the output for SHOWPLAN_TEXT in text mode rather than the default grid mode. To do this go to the Query menu in Management Studio select Results To ⇨ Results to text. The output is too verbose to include here in full. The key elements of interest of the plan are shown here:

```
|--Table Scan(OBJECT:([People].[dbo].[BoysNames]))
|--Table Scan(OBJECT:([People].[dbo].[GirlsNames]))
|--Table Scan(OBJECT:([People].[dbo].[lastNames]))
```

This shows that you are using a table scan to get the names from the lookup tables. In most cases this works just fine as the tables are so small (boysNames and girlsNames), but this isn't so optimal on last-Names, where the table has 2000 rows and occupies 7 or 8 database pages.

Now see what DTA recommends for you. Running DTA against the sample query is very simple. Go to the tools menu and select Database Engine Tuning Advisor. This brings up the Database Engine Tuning Advisor, shown in Figure 11-3.

First you have to load the DTApeopleInsert.sql script as the workload. Next change the database for workload analysis from master to people. Last of all, select which database you want to tune by selecting the people database. Now you are ready to start the analysis session by clicking the Start Analysis button at the left end of the toolbar. When you start the analysis session, DTA adds a new Progress tab and updates its analysis progress as shown in Figure 11-4.

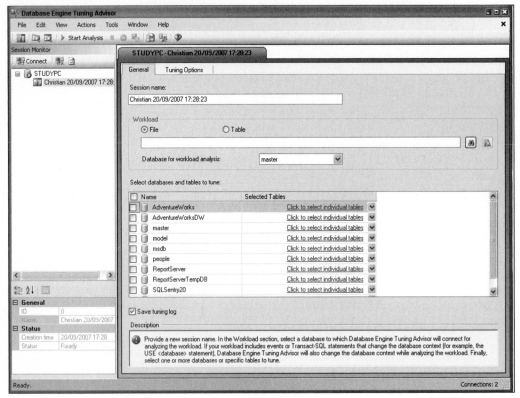

Figure 11-3

When the analysis is complete DTA adds two more tabs: Recommendations and Reports.

For the Insert query, DTA has recommended that you create a clustered index on the lastNames table. This will reduce the number of reads of the lastNames table from right down to one or two on each query. Percentage-wise, this is a large reduction.

Now you should implement the recommendation and see what the performance difference is. Start by looking at the stats time and I/O after adding the clustered index on lastNames. The following is an abbreviated stats output showing just the key areas that have changed:

```
-- COLD Run

Table 'lastNames'. Scan count 1, logical reads 9, physical reads 1, read-ahead
reads 7, lob logical reads 0, lob physical reads 0, lob read-ahead reads 0.


Table 'lastNames'. Scan count 0, logical reads 2, physical reads 0, read-ahead
reads 0, lob logical reads 0, lob physical reads 0, lob read-ahead reads 0.


SQL Server Execution Times:
```

```
    CPU time = 15 ms,  elapsed time = 590 ms.
-- Warm Run

Table 'lastNames'. Scan count 1, logical reads 9, physical reads 0, read-ahead
reads 0, lob logical reads 0, lob physical reads 0, lob read-ahead reads 0.

Table 'lastNames'. Scan count 0, logical reads 2, physical reads 0, read-ahead
reads 0, lob logical reads 0, lob physical reads 0, lob read-ahead reads 0.


SQL Server Execution Times:
   CPU time = 0 ms,  elapsed time = 4 ms.
```

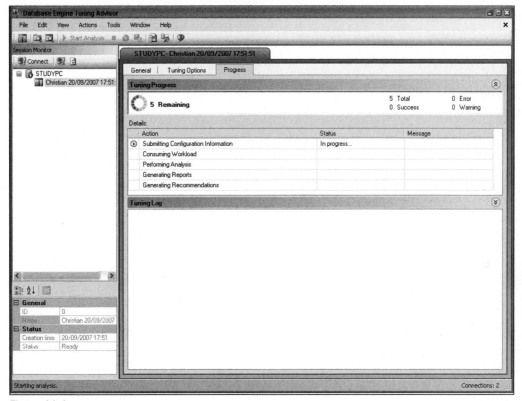

Figure 11-4

There are two differences between these stats and the earlier pre-indexed stats. Now that you are using the clustered index on lastnames, the number of logical reads is reduced dramatically from eight down to two. In addition, when the table is read on the cold run, now it's getting read in using a Read Ahead, which brings the whole table into memory much more quickly than if you use a regular table scan as you did before indexing.

Now take a look at the SHOWPLAN_TEXT output and confirm what you are observing in the I/O stats. Here is the relevant section from the plan output:

```
|--Clustered Index Scan(OBJECT:([People].[dbo].[lastNames].[cix_LastNames_ID]))
```

This shows that you are in fact using the newly added clustered index. Now see how much this affects the execution of the query. Remember that before you were able to achieve 1300–1400 inserts per second.

```
Inserted 1000 people in 530mS at a rate of 1886.79 per Second
Inserted 1000 people in 606mS at a rate of 1650.17 per Second
Inserted 1000 people in 610mS at a rate of 1639.34 per Second
Inserted 1000 people in 533mS at a rate of 1876.17 per Second
```

This shows that the rate of insertion has increased to 1600–1900 per second. That's quite an improvement for adding a clustered index.

Run the monitor script again to check what you're waiting on.

```
set nocount on
while 1 > 0
begin
    select spid, kpid, blocked, waittime, lastwaittype, waitresource
    from master..sysprocesses
    where program_name = 'SQLCMD'
    waitfor delay '00:00:00.05'
end
```

spid	kpid	blocked	waittime	lastwaittype
54	5804	0	0	WRITELOG
54	5804	0	0	WRITELOG
54	5804	0	0	WRITELOG
54	5804	0	0	WRITELOG

No surprises there, it remains the log that's limiting the insert performance.

Indexes for Updates

Next you want to tune the update query usp_marriageUpdate. Start that by capturing some metrics around the query's performance. Before you do that, fill the table up a bit by writing a million rows to the people table. You need that many to be able to get a full set of results for the usp_marriageUpdate query, which pulls out the top 1000 rows for a given date range.

Truncate the people table, and run usp_loopPeopleInsert to fill it with 1,000,000 rows. After that you can start capturing metrics around the raw performance again by running the script DTAmarriage Update.sql. Here is the code to do this if you want to follow along:

```
USE people
GO
TRUNCATE TABLE people
GO
EXEC usp_loopPeopleInsert 500000
GO
```

Here are the results of the cold run and three warm runs, edited to remove the many extra rows and with some additional formatting for clarity:

```
Table '#boys'.
Scan count 0, logical reads 1003, physical reads 0, read-ahead reads 0, lob logi-
cal reads 0, lob physical reads 0, lob read-ahead reads 0.

Table 'people'.
Scan count 1, logical reads 1824, physical reads 0, read-ahead reads 1904, lob logi-
cal reads 0, lob physical reads 0, lob read-ahead reads 0.

SQL Server Execution Times:
   CPU time = 63 ms,  elapsed time = 1197 ms.

(1000 row(s) affected)
Table '#girls'.
Scan count 0, logical reads 1003, physical reads 0, read-ahead reads 0, lob logi-
cal reads 0, lob physical reads 0, lob read-ahead reads 0.

Table 'people'.
Scan count 1, logical reads 1897, physical reads 0, read-ahead reads 64, lob logi-
cal reads 0, lob physical reads 0, lob read-ahead reads 0.

SQL Server Execution Times:
   CPU time = 46 ms,  elapsed time = 866 ms.

(1000 row(s) affected)

SQL Server Execution Times:
   CPU time = 0 ms,  elapsed time = 1 ms.
Table '#boys'.
Scan count 1, logical reads 4, physical reads 0, read-ahead reads 0, lob logi-
cal reads 0, lob physical reads 0, lob read-ahead reads 0.

SQL Server Execution Times:
   CPU time = 0 ms,  elapsed time = 1 ms.
Table
'#girls_____
_____0000000000A0'.  Scan   count   1,   logical
reads 4, physical reads 0, read-ahead reads 0, lob logical reads 0, lob physi-
cal reads 0, lob read-ahead reads 0.

SQL Server Execution Times:
   CPU time = 0 ms,  elapsed time = 1 ms.

Table 'people'.
Scan count 2, logical reads 32281, physical reads 0, read-ahead reads 14172, lob log-
ical reads 0, lob physical reads 0, lob read-ahead reads 0.

Table 'Worktable'.
Scan count 1, logical reads 5, physical reads 0, read-ahead reads 0, lob logi-
cal reads 0, lob physical reads 0, lob read-ahead reads 0.

SQL Server Execution Times:
   CPU time = 813 ms,  elapsed time = 8350 ms.
(1 row(s) affected)
```

```
SQL Server Execution Times:
   CPU time = 0 ms,  elapsed time = 1 ms.

SQL Server Execution Times:
   CPU time = 0 ms,  elapsed time = 1 ms.

SQL Server Execution Times:
   CPU time = 922 ms,  elapsed time = 10464 ms.
```

This shows that the cold run took almost 10 seconds to complete.

The warm run looks like this:

```
SQL Server parse and compile time:
   CPU time = 0 ms, elapsed time = 1 ms.
SQL Server parse and compile time:
   CPU time = 0 ms, elapsed time = 1 ms.

Table '#boys'.
Scan count 0, logical reads 1003, physical reads 0, read-ahead reads 0, lob logi-
cal reads 0, lob physical reads 0, lob read-ahead reads 0.

Table 'people'.
Scan count 1, logical reads 1895, physical reads 0, read-ahead reads 0, lob logi-
cal reads 0, lob physical reads 0, lob read-ahead reads 0.

SQL Server Execution Times:
   CPU time = 47 ms,  elapsed time = 216 ms.

(1000 row(s) affected)
Table '#girls'.
Scan count 0, logical reads 1003, physical reads 0, read-ahead reads 0, lob logi-
cal reads 0, lob physical reads 0, lob read-ahead reads 0.

Table 'people'.
Scan count 1, logical reads 1765, physical reads 0, read-ahead reads 0, lob logi-
cal reads 0, lob physical reads 0, lob read-ahead reads 0.

SQL Server Execution Times:
   CPU time = 47 ms,  elapsed time = 46 ms.

(1000 row(s) affected)

SQL Server Execution Times:
   CPU time = 0 ms,  elapsed time = 1 ms.
Table '#boys'.
Scan count 1, logical reads 4, physical reads 0, read-ahead reads 0, lob logi-
cal reads 0, lob physical reads 0, lob read-ahead reads 0.

SQL Server Execution Times:
   CPU time = 0 ms,  elapsed time = 3 ms.
Table '#girls'.
Scan count 1, logical reads 4, physical reads 0, read-ahead reads 0, lob logi-
cal reads 0, lob physical reads 0, lob read-ahead reads 0.
```

```
SQL Server Execution Times:
   CPU time = 0 ms,  elapsed time = 1 ms.
Table 'people'.
Scan count 2, logical reads 32281, physical reads 0, read-ahead reads 0, lob logi-
cal reads 0, lob physical reads 0, lob read-ahead reads 0.

Table 'Worktable'.
Scan count 1, logical reads 4, physical reads 0, read-ahead reads 0, lob logi-
cal reads 0, lob physical reads 0, lob read-ahead reads 0.

SQL Server Execution Times:
   CPU time = 703 ms,  elapsed time = 713 ms.

(1 row(s) affected)
SQL Server Execution Times:
   CPU time = 15 ms,  elapsed time = 1 ms.

SQL Server Execution Times:
   CPU time = 812 ms,  elapsed time = 980 ms.
```

There was a significant improvement between the cold and warm run, down to a reduction in the compilation time and faster access as the tables are now mostly loaded into memory. This is seen in the reduction in read ahead reads between the cold and warm runs.

This procedure is taking between 10 seconds for a cold run and 1 second for a warm run so it should be much easier to see any improvement that DTA can make. However, you'll still run it in a loop and see what the average update rate is over a longer period of executions.

This is the command to run:

```
sqlcmd -E -d people -Q"exec usp_loopMarriageUpdate 100, 10"
```

These are the results:

```
Married 20 people in 15326mS at a rate of 1.30497 per Second
Married 20 people in 18610mS at a rate of 1.07469 per Second
Married 20 people in 15470mS at a rate of 1.29282 per Second
Married 20 people in 14610mS at a rate of 1.36893 per Second
Married 20 people in 14890mS at a rate of 1.34318 per Second
Married 20 people in 17076mS at a rate of 1.17123 per Second
```

The results show that the query is taking between 1 and 1.36 seconds to execute so it should be relatively easy to see any performance improvement.

Before going on to run DTA, take a quick look at the wait types. Run the command again and also run the monitoring code and capture the waits from sysprocesses. The output should look something like this:

```
set nocount on
while 1 > 0
begin
   select spid, kpid, blocked, waittime, lastwaittype, waitresource
```

```
    from master..sysprocesses
    where program_name = 'SQLCMD'
    waitfor delay '00:00:00.05'
end

spid  kpid   blocked waittime                 lastwaittype
52    4212   0       546                      LOGMGR_RESERVE_APPEND
52    4212   0       0                        SOS_SCHEDULER_YIELD
```

There was a pretty even split between these two wait types. SQL Server Books Online (SQL BOL) explains what each of the wait types mean. Look these up either by searching for the wait type or by searching for `sys.dm_os_wait_stats`.

The `LOGMGR_RESERVE_APPEND` occurs when you are waiting to see if truncating the log will give you enough space to write the current log record. In this case, the database was configured with the simple recovery model, and the log file is on a very slow disk, so you should expect to see a lot of log-related waits.

`SOS_SCHEDULER_YIELD` occurs when a task voluntarily yields the scheduler and has to wait for a new quantum. These are quite different from the wait types in the insert query, which is expected because the update has a very different characteristic than the insert.

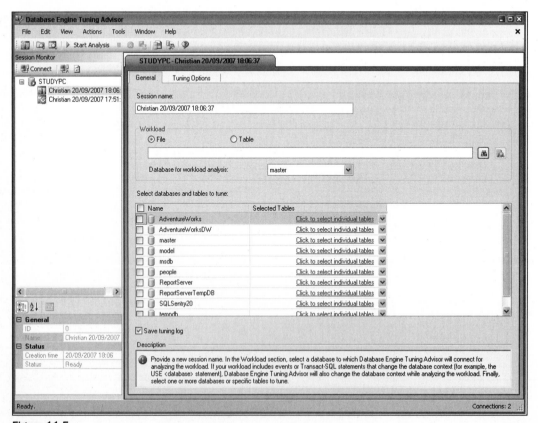

Figure 11-5

Now see what DTA has to say about this workload. This time you'll see how to run DTA against a workload. The next step is to set up SQL Server Profiler to capture a trace file, which is covered in Chapter 5. The key things you need to remember when setting up SQL Server Profiler for this trace are twofold: use the tuning template and ensure that the files are set to rollover, although the overall file size will be trivial.

Once Profiler is set up and the trace is running, execute the usp_marriageUpdate stored procedure once and then stop the trace, which saves the file. Now you have a workload trace file on disk, and you can start DTA and use it to tune the workload. Launch DTA and connect to your SQL Server. If you have been following the earlier sections, you will see the earlier trace sessions in the left hand pane of DTA, as shown in Figure 11-5.

This is another part of DTA that is worth briefly mentioning. Each of your tuning sessions is saved, so you can go back and review what you asked DTA to tune and the recommendations DTA came up with. However, if you just use the default session names, as you have been doing, then the tuning session names don't really have a lot of meaning and pretty soon it's difficult to know what each session was for. Therefore, you should come up with a naming scheme that makes sense to you. This will help you find the session you're looking for in the future.

After setting the database to People in both the drop-down selection and the list of databases to tune, you need to tell DTA that you want to tune a file and where the file is. Either type in the file name and full path or use the browse button to select the trace file you just created, as shown in Figure 11-6.

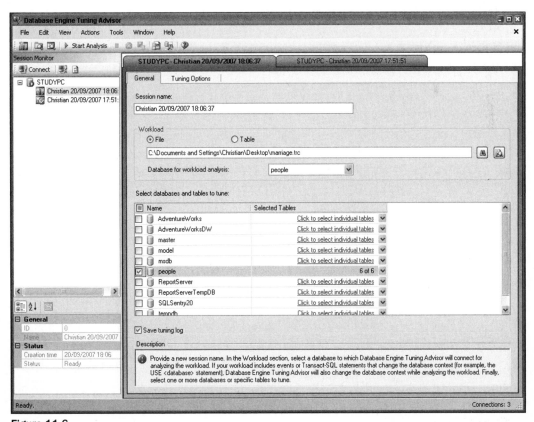

Figure 11-6

Now you can start the Analysis session again and see what results DTA has for you this time. You can see those results in Figure 11-7.

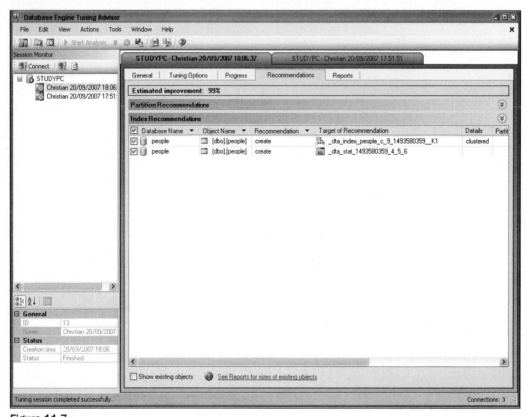

Figure 11-7

This time DTA has two recommendations and reckons it can improve things by 99 percent. Take a closer look at what you can do with these recommendations. To do this, just scroll the recommendations window way over to the right to find the `Definition` column. If you hover over this, a tooltip pops up telling you to click on the link to get a T-SQL script of the recommendations. Doing so will reveal a script like that shown in Figure 11-8.

You can now either copy this script to the clipboard and from there into a file or directly into SQL Server Management Studio to be executed. Alternatively, after taking a look at the recommendations, you can have DTA run them for you by selecting Apply Recommendations from the Actions Menu.

Before doing that, take a look at some of the other information in the Reports tab. This area of DTA holds a lot of useful information about what DTA did and why. In the simple case you have been working with here, most of the interesting information is on the Statement cost reports. Start with the first report in the list, shown in Figure 11-9.

This shows the various statements in the workload and the estimated improvement that DTA expects to come from the recommendation. In this case, the improvement all comes from the `update` statement, which the tuning report believes will be improved by 99.90 percent.

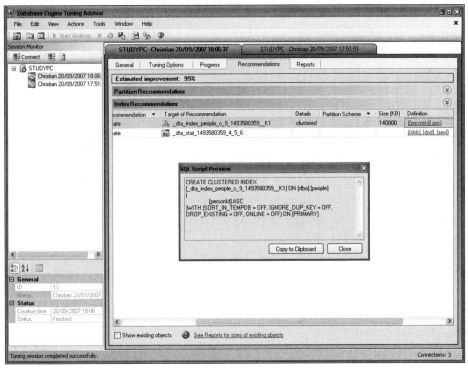

Figure 11-8

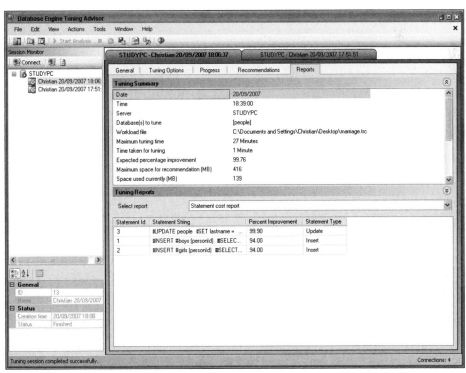

Figure 11-9

To apply the changes, simply let DTA make them. When you select Apply Recommendations, DTA asks if you want to run the script now or schedule it for some time in the future. Choose to make the changes right away so you can see the immediate impact. While it's executing, DTA shows the status of the changes, as you can see in Figure 11-10.

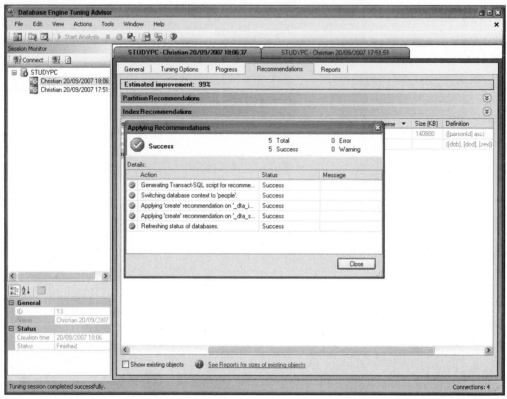

Figure 11-10

Next, go back and see how fast your queries are running. Start with the output of stats I/O and stats time. Running the same script again now gives you the following results.

This is the cold run:

```
SQL Server parse and compile time:
   CPU time = 0 ms, elapsed time = 1 ms.
SQL Server parse and compile time:
   CPU time = 0 ms, elapsed time = 63 ms.

Table '#boys'.
Scan count 0, logical reads 1003, physical reads 0, read-ahead reads 0, lob logi-
cal reads 0, lob physical reads 0, lob read-ahead reads 0.

Table 'people'.
```

```
Scan count 1, logical reads 1759, physical reads 3, read-ahead reads 1974, lob logi-
cal reads 0, lob physical reads 0, lob read-ahead reads 0.

SQL Server Execution Times:
   CPU time = 32 ms,   elapsed time = 851 ms.

(1000 row(s) affected)
Table '#girls'.
Scan count 0, logical reads 1003, physical reads 0, read-ahead reads 0, lob logi-
cal reads 0, lob physical reads 0, lob read-ahead reads 0.

Table 'people'.
Scan count 1, logical reads 1794, physical reads 0, read-ahead reads 0, lob logi-
cal reads 0, lob physical reads 0, lob read-ahead reads 0.

SQL Server Execution Times:
   CPU time = 46 ms,   elapsed time = 49 ms.

(1000 row(s) affected)

SQL Server Execution Times:
   CPU time = 0 ms,   elapsed time = 1 ms.
Table '#boys'.
Scan count 1, logical reads 4, physical reads 0, read-ahead reads 0, lob logi-
cal reads 0, lob physical reads 0, lob read-ahead reads 0.

SQL Server Execution Times:
   CPU time = 0 ms,   elapsed time = 1 ms.
Table '#girls'.
Scan count 1, logical reads 4, physical reads 0, read-ahead reads 0, lob logi-
cal reads 0, lob physical reads 0, lob read-ahead reads 0.

SQL Server Execution Times:
   CPU time = 0 ms,   elapsed time = 1 ms.
Table 'people'.
Scan count 2, logical reads 9, physical reads 0, read-ahead reads 0, lob logi-
cal reads 0, lob physical reads 0, lob read-ahead reads 0.

Table 'Worktable'.
Scan count 1, logical reads 5, physical reads 0, read-ahead reads 0, lob logi-
cal reads 0, lob physical reads 0, lob read-ahead reads 0.

SQL Server Execution Times:
   CPU time = 94 ms,   elapsed time = 1012 ms.
```

This is the result for the warm run:

```
SQL Server parse and compile time:
   CPU time = 0 ms, elapsed time = 1 ms.
SQL Server parse and compile time:
   CPU time = 0 ms, elapsed time = 1 ms.

Table '#boys'.
```

```
Scan count 0, logical reads 1003, physical reads 0, read-ahead reads 0, lob logi-
cal reads 0, lob physical reads 0, lob read-ahead reads 0.

Table 'people'.
Scan count 1, logical reads 1793, physical reads 0, read-ahead reads 0, lob logi-
cal reads 0, lob physical reads 0, lob read-ahead reads 0.

SQL Server Execution Times:
   CPU time = 32 ms,  elapsed time = 44 ms.

(1000 row(s) affected)
Table '#girls'.
Scan count 0, logical reads 1003, physical reads 0, read-ahead reads 0, lob logi-
cal reads 0, lob physical reads 0, lob read-ahead reads 0.

Table 'people'.
Scan count 1, logical reads 1736, physical reads 0, read-ahead reads 0, lob logi-
cal reads 0, lob physical reads 0, lob read-ahead reads 0.

SQL Server Execution Times:
   CPU time = 46 ms,  elapsed time = 447 ms.

(1000 row(s) affected)

SQL Server Execution Times:
   CPU time = 0 ms,  elapsed time = 1 ms.
Table '#boys'.
Scan count 1, logical reads 4, physical reads 0, read-ahead reads 0, lob logi-
cal reads 0, lob physical reads 0, lob read-ahead reads 0.

SQL Server Execution Times:
   CPU time = 0 ms,  elapsed time = 1 ms.
Table '#girls'.
Scan count 1, logical reads 4, physical reads 0, read-ahead reads 0, lob logi-
cal reads 0, lob physical reads 0, lob read-ahead reads 0.

SQL Server Execution Times:
   CPU time = 0 ms,  elapsed time = 1 ms.
Table 'people'.
Scan count 2, logical reads 9, physical reads 0, read-ahead reads 0, lob logi-
cal reads 0, lob physical reads 0, lob read-ahead reads 0.

Table 'Worktable'.
Scan count 1, logical reads 4, physical reads 0, read-ahead reads 0, lob logi-
cal reads 0, lob physical reads 0, lob read-ahead reads 0.

   CPU time = 78 ms,  elapsed time = 494 ms.
```

That's reduced the CPU time for the warm run from 812 mSec to 78 mSec, although the elapsed time only came down from around 1 sec to 500 mSec. Now see how fast it runs in a tight loop:

```
Married 20 people in 9860mS at a rate of 2.0284 per Second
Married 20 people in 8890mS at a rate of 2.24972 per Second
```

```
Married 20 people in 9110mS at a rate of 2.19539 per Second
Married 20 people in 6936mS at a rate of 2.88351 per Second
Married 20 people in 5280mS at a rate of 3.78788 per Second
Married 20 people in 5376mS at a rate of 3.72024 per Second
```

That's pretty remarkable; you have gone from just over 1 update per second to 2–4 updates per second.

Now check the waits again:

```
spid   kpid   blocked  waittime          lastwaittype
58     4688   0        859               LOGMGR_RESERVE_APPEND
```

This time the waits are predominantly this one wait type.

Finally, take a quick look at the `showplan_text` output to see how the DTA recommendations are changing the query plan.

This is the showplan output for the update before applying the DTA recommendations:

```
            |--Table  Update(OBJECT:([People].[dbo].[people]),  SET:([People].[dbo].
[people].[lastName] = RaiseIfNull([Expr1016])))
               |--Table Spool
                   |--Compute Scalar(DEFINE:([Expr1016]=[Expr1016]))
                       |--Nested Loops(Left Outer Join)
                           |--Top(ROWCOUNT est 0)
                           |    |--Table
Scan(OBJECT:([People].[dbo].[people]), WHERE:([People].[dbo].[people].
[personID]=[@girlID]) ORDERED)
                           |--Assert(WHERE:(CASE WHEN [Expr1015]>(1) THEN (0) ELSE
NULL END))
                               |--Stream
Aggregate(DEFINE:([Expr1015]=Count(*), [Expr1016]=ANY([People].[dbo].[people].
[lastName])))
                                   |--Table
Scan(OBJECT:([People].[dbo].[people]), WHERE:([People].[dbo].[people].
[personID]=[@BoyID]))
```

You can clearly see that you are using a table scan to apply the update to People.

This is the showplan output after applying the DTA recommendations:

```
         |--Clustered Index
Update(OBJECT:([People].[dbo].[people].[_dta_index_people_c_6_2089058478__K1]),
SET:([People].[dbo].[people].[lastName] = RaiseIfNull([Expr1016])))
               |--Table Spool
                   |--Compute Scalar(DEFINE:([Expr1016]=[Expr1016]))
                       |--Nested Loops(Left Outer Join)
                           |--Top(ROWCOUNT est 0)
                           |    |--Clustered Index
Seek(OBJECT:([People].[dbo].[people].[_dta_index_people_c_6_2089058478__K1]),
SEEK:([People].[dbo].[people].[personID]=[@girlID]) ORDERED FORWARD)
                           |--Assert(WHERE:(CASE WHEN [Expr1015]>(1)
```

```
THEN (0) ELSE NULL END))
                                    |--Stream
Aggregate(DEFINE:([Expr1015]=Count(*),       [Expr1016]=ANY([People].[dbo].[people].
[lastName])))
                                    |--Clustered Index
Seek(OBJECT:([People].[dbo].[people].[_dta_index_people_c_6_2089058478__K1]),
SEEK:([People].[dbo].[people].[personID]=[@BoyID]) ORDERED FORWARD)
```

This starts with the clustered Index tag, showing that you are now using the newly created clustered index to apply the update, and this is what's giving you the big benefit.

Reassessing Inserts after Adding Update Indexes

Now go back and measure the impact the update indexes have had on the insert procedure. You haven't done anything else to the insert procedure, but the update procedure added a clustered index to People. Now the insert procedure will have to contend with the additional overhead of index maintenance, inserting new records and splitting index pages. It's going to be interesting to see how much slower this makes the inserts and how it changes what you are waiting on.

Start by looking at the stats time and I/O output.

```
-- COLD RUN
SQL Server parse and compile time:
   CPU time = 0 ms, elapsed time = 51 ms.

SQL Server Execution Times:
   CPU time = 0 ms,  elapsed time = 1 ms.
Table 'BoysNames'. Scan count 1, logical reads 1, physical reads 1, read-ahead
reads 0, lob logical reads 0, lob physical reads 0, lob read-ahead reads 0.

SQL Server Execution Times:
   CPU time = 0 ms,  elapsed time = 21 ms.
Table 'GirlsNames'. Scan count 1, logical reads 1, physical reads 1, read-ahead
reads 0, lob logical reads 0, lob physical reads 0, lob read-ahead reads 0.

SQL Server Execution Times:
   CPU time = 0 ms,  elapsed time = 1 ms.
Table 'lastNames'. Scan count 1, logical reads 9, physical reads 1, read-ahead
reads 7, lob logical reads 0, lob physical reads 0, lob read-ahead reads 0.

SQL Server Execution Times:
   CPU time = 0 ms,  elapsed time = 2 ms.

SQL Server Execution Times:
   CPU time = 0 ms,  elapsed time = 1 ms.
Table 'BoysNames'. Scan count 1, logical reads 1, physical reads 0, read-ahead
reads 0, lob logical reads 0, lob physical reads 0, lob read-ahead reads 0.

SQL Server Execution Times:
   CPU time = 0 ms,  elapsed time = 1 ms.
Table 'GirlsNames'. Scan count 1, logical reads 1, physical reads 0, read-ahead
reads 0, lob logical reads 0, lob physical reads 0, lob read-ahead reads 0.
```

```
SQL Server Execution Times:
   CPU time = 0 ms,  elapsed time = 1 ms.
Table 'lastNames'. Scan count 0, logical reads 2, physical reads 0, read-ahead
reads 0, lob logical reads 0, lob physical reads 0, lob read-ahead reads 0.

SQL Server Execution Times:
   CPU time = 0 ms,  elapsed time = 29 ms.
SQL Server parse and compile time:
   CPU time = 0 ms, elapsed time = 1 ms.


SQL Server Execution Times:
   CPU time = 0 ms,  elapsed time = 1 ms.
Table 'people'. Scan count 0, logical reads 3, physical reads 1, read-ahead
reads 0, lob logical reads 0, lob physical reads 0, lob read-ahead reads 0.

SQL Server Execution Times:
   CPU time = 0 ms,  elapsed time = 63 ms.
Table 'people'. Scan count 0, logical reads 3, physical reads 0, read-ahead
reads 0, lob logical reads 0, lob physical reads 0, lob read-ahead reads 0.

SQL Server Execution Times:
   CPU time = 0 ms,  elapsed time = 1 ms.

SQL Server Execution Times:
   CPU time = 0 ms,  elapsed time = 168 ms.

-- WARM RUN

SQL Server parse and compile time:
   CPU time = 0 ms, elapsed time = 1 ms.
SQL Server parse and compile time:
   CPU time = 0 ms, elapsed time = 1 ms.


SQL Server Execution Times:
   CPU time = 0 ms,  elapsed time = 1 ms.
Table 'BoysNames'. Scan count 1, logical reads 1, physical reads 0, read-ahead
reads 0, lob logical reads 0, lob physical reads 0, lob read-ahead reads 0.

SQL Server Execution Times:
   CPU time = 0 ms,  elapsed time = 1 ms.
Table 'GirlsNames'. Scan count 1, logical reads 1, physical reads 0, read-ahead
reads 0, lob logical reads 0, lob physical reads 0, lob read-ahead reads 0.

SQL Server Execution Times:
   CPU time = 0 ms,  elapsed time = 1 ms.
Table 'lastNames'. Scan count 1, logical reads 9, physical reads 0, read-ahead
reads 0, lob logical reads 0, lob physical reads 0, lob read-ahead reads 0.

SQL Server Execution Times:
   CPU time = 0 ms,  elapsed time = 1 ms.

SQL Server Execution Times:
```

```
      CPU time = 0 ms,  elapsed time = 1 ms.
Table 'BoysNames'. Scan count 1, logical reads 1, physical reads 0, read-ahead
reads 0, lob logical reads 0, lob physical reads 0, lob read-ahead reads 0.

SQL Server Execution Times:
      CPU time = 0 ms,  elapsed time = 1 ms.
Table 'GirlsNames'. Scan count 1, logical reads 1, physical reads 0, read-ahead
reads 0, lob logical reads 0, lob physical reads 0, lob read-ahead reads 0.

SQL Server Execution Times:
      CPU time = 0 ms,  elapsed time = 1 ms.
Table 'lastNames'. Scan count 0, logical reads 2, physical reads 0, read-ahead
reads 0, lob logical reads 0, lob physical reads 0, lob read-ahead reads 0.


SQL Server Execution Times:
      CPU time = 0 ms,  elapsed time = 1 ms.
Table 'people'. Scan count 0, logical reads 3, physical reads 0, read-ahead
reads 0, lob logical reads 0, lob physical reads 0, lob read-ahead reads 0.

SQL Server Execution Times:
      CPU time = 0 ms,  elapsed time = 1 ms.
Table 'people'. Scan count 0, logical reads 3, physical reads 0, read-ahead
reads 0, lob logical reads 0, lob physical reads 0, lob read-ahead reads 0.

SQL Server Execution Times:
      CPU time = 0 ms,  elapsed time = 3 ms.

SQL Server Execution Times:
      CPU time = 0 ms,  elapsed time = 33 ms.
```

On the cold run, you increased the number of logical reads from 1 to 3. Physical reads didn't change because the whole database is pretty well cached by now. This change is too small to see on a single run, so you'll need to run the query a few thousand times. Before you do that, take a look at the showplan_text output.

The only obvious change here is that you can see that you are now doing an insert into a clustered index table versus the heap you were inserting into before:

```
|--Clustered Index
Insert(OBJECT:([People].[dbo].[people].[_dta_index_people_c_6_2089058478__K1]),
SET:([People].[dbo].[people].[firstName] = RaiseIfNull([@BoysName]),[People].
[dbo].[people].[lastName] = RaiseIfNull([@lastName]),[People].[dbo].[peop
```

Now look to see how this has changed the insert rate when you run usp_loopPeopleInsert. This is now reporting the following:

```
Inserted 10000 people in 5250mS at a rate of 1904.76 per Second
Inserted 10000 people in 5296mS at a rate of 1888.22 per Second
Inserted 10000 people in 5233mS at a rate of 1910.95 per Second
Inserted 10000 people in 5300mS at a rate of 1886.79 per Second
Inserted 10000 people in 5233mS at a rate of 1910.95 per Second
```

This shows that you haven't caused any impact on the insert rate, which remains at around 1800 to 1900 per second. This is more evidence that the limiting factor for this insert is the speed with which you can write to the log (not surprisingly, on a laptop system this is pretty slow). This can also be the case on a large enterprise server where the amount of log activity could be much higher but the log files are on a slow disk or poorly configured disk array, which yet again ultimately limits insert performance.

The wait stats for the query show that you are still waiting on `WriteLog`, so you haven't seen a change to the point where the new index started to be the bottleneck.

Too Many Indexes?

One final scenario you are going to look at is how DTA tells you when you have too many indexes. To make this obvious, you'll add a whole stack of other indexes to the four tables in this scenario, run DTA against the insert and update procedures, and see what it tells you about indexes you aren't using.

Here is the script to create some bad indexes to see what DTA will recommend:

```
-- Create Bad indexes
use people
go

create clustered index cix_boysnames on BoysNames ( ID, Name)
go
create index ix_boysnames_id on BoysNames (id)
go
create index ix_boysnames_name on BoysNames (name)
go

create clustered index cix_girlsnames on GirlsNames ( ID, Name)
go
create index ix_Girlsnames_id on GirlsNames (id)
go
create index ix_Girlsnames_name on GirlsNames (name)
go

create clustered index cix_LastNames on LastNames ( ID, Name)
go
create index ix_Lastnames_id on LastNames (id)
go
create index ix_Lastnames_name on LastNames (name)
go
create clustered index cix_people on people(firstname)
go
create index ix_people_id on people(personid)
go
create index ix_people_dob on people(dob)
go
create index ix_people_lastname on people(lastname)
go
create index ix_people_dod on people(dod)
go
create index ix_people_sex on people(sex)
go
```

Here are the results of running the query usp_loopPeopleInsert:

```
Inserted 1000 people in 1203mS at a rate of 831.255 per Second
Inserted 1000 people in 750mS at a rate of 1333.33 per Second
Inserted 1000 people in 640mS at a rate of 1562.5 per Second
Inserted 1000 people in 673mS at a rate of 1485.88 per Second
Inserted 1000 people in 656mS at a rate of 1524.39 per Second
```

These results show that insert performance has dropped dramatically. The worst batch is at only 831 inserts per second. This is about half the best rate achieved, which was nearly 2000 inserts per second. The wait stats show that you are still waiting on the log write, although you are clearly spending a lot more time in maintaining the indexes and in reading extra pages. The stats I/O time shows that you are incurring a few extra reads on the boysnames and girlsnames tables, but otherwise there isn't a great difference in the stats. The showplan indicates that there is an index scan on both boysnames and girlsnames, rather than the single-page table scan that was there before. This is what is accounting for the extra page reads:

```
|--Index Scan(OBJECT:([People].[dbo].[BoysNames].[ix_boysnames_name]))
|--Index Scan(OBJECT:([People].[dbo].[GirlsNames].[ix_Girlsnames_name]))
|--Index Scan(OBJECT:([People].[dbo].[lastNames].[ix_Lastnames_name]))
```

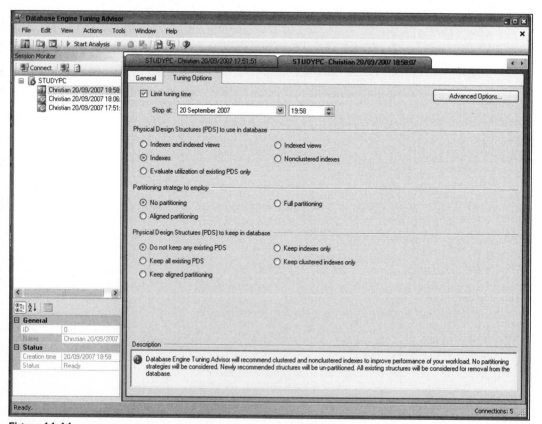

Figure 11-11

In addition, you are no longer using a useful clustered index on lastNames, but you have to use the non-clustered index, which results in an extra page read required on every lastNames access. Overall the performance degradation isn't that great. On a system with a faster disk, performance might be considerably higher.

Now see what DTA has to say about all these extra indexes. You can use the trace file you captured earlier from the `usp_loopMarriageUpdate` trace but you'll have to change the DTA options. Open DTA and select the trace file you used earlier. Select the Tuning Options tab and in the group titled Physical Design Structures (PDS) to keep in database, change the default selection from Keep all existing PDS to Do not keep any existing PDS. You can have DTA advise you about additional indexes as well by keeping the same options selected under the PDS section or you can choose for DTA to just show you which indexes to remove. For now, ask DTA to examine the existing indexes and to recommend additional indexes if it finds any, as shown in Figure 11-11.

Now you can start the Analysis Session and see what results DTA provides you with. The results are shown in Figure 11-12.

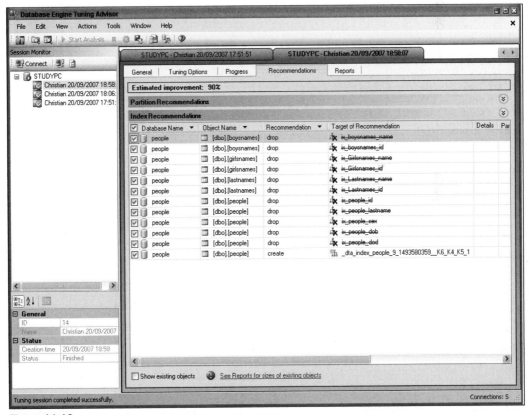

Figure 11-12

DTA has easily found the bad indexes. It's recommending that you drop 12 of them and then in their place create two new indexes and two new statistics.

Tuning a Workload

Tuning a whole workload is just as easy. The biggest problem with tuning a workload is creating the trace file of the workload in the first place, as you need to determine what to put into the trace file. In the sample scenario, there are only five different queries. Even if they are called in very different patterns, DTA doesn't really care about how frequently the statement is called; it's just looking for queries that it can tune. To create a workload file to tune, all you need to do is gather one example of each of your queries and pass that to DTA, and it will provide recommendations for the whole workload.

To see how this works, start from the point where you have a workload trace file — in this case named workload.trc. Open DTA and change the name of the session to represent what you are doing. Call this trace session **Mixed Workload with No indexes**, indicating that you are starting out with no indexes in the database.

Select the file that contains the trace file you previously created and then select the tuning options you want. In this case, you are only interested in new indexes. After selecting the database to tune, start the analysis. In this sample scenario, DTA came back with the recommendations shown in Figure 11-13.

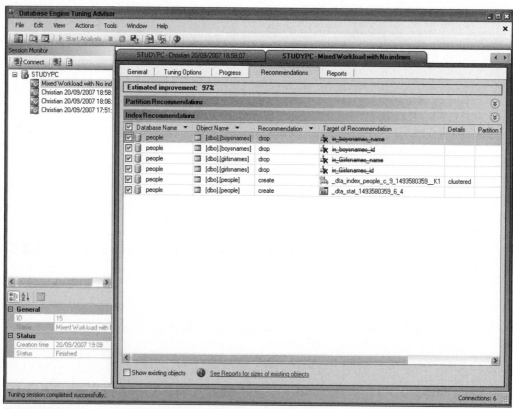

Figure 11-13

A note of caution when tuning a workload: DTA will make recommendations based upon the cost estimates for each part of the workload. In a workload with a variety of queries, DTA will focus on the big gains and so may miss out on recommendations for some of the smaller queries. Because of this, it's still worthwhile to tune individual queries after applying recommendations for the whole workload.

A good example of this can be seen when DTA didn't recommend indexes on the lastnames table when tuning the workload. When you tuned just the usp_peopleInsert procedure, DTA was able to see enough of an improvement to recommend indexes. Figure 11-14 shows the recommendations DTA comes up with for the lastnames table when tuning the usp_peopleInsert procedure.

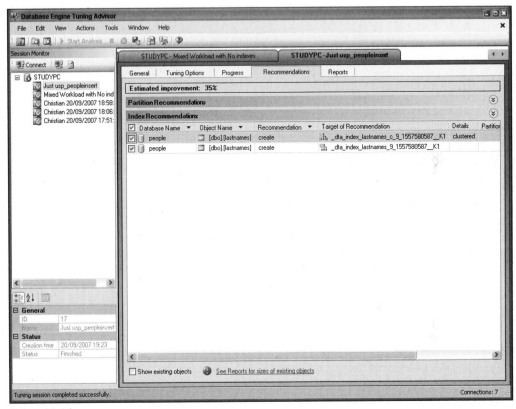

Figure 11-14

Section 3: Index Maintenance

There are a number of problems that can occur with indexes over time as data changes in the underlying table. As rows are inserted, deleted, and updated, the distribution of data through the index can become unbalanced, with some pages becoming fully packed. This results in additional inserts causing immediate page splits. Other pages can become very sparsely packed, causing many pages to have to be read to access a few rows of data. These problems can be easily overcome with some simple index maintenance.

The first thing you need to do is implement some monitoring to figure out when the indexes are getting to the stage where they need attention. The second step is figuring out which of the various options for index maintenance you should use to clean up the index.

Monitoring Index Fragmentation

In SQL Server 2000, you used DBCC showcontig to monitor index fragmentation. With SQL Server 2005, you now have a new function, sys.dm_db_index_physical_stats. The syntax for this function is detailed in full in BOL, so here's a look at running it the People sample database:

```
use People
go

SELECT *
FROM sys.dm_db_index_physical_stats
  (
  DB_ID('People'),
  OBJECT_ID('People'),
  NULL,
  NULL ,
  'DETAILED'
  )
go
```

The results provide a lot of information, but there are just a few things you really want to focus on. In fact, to get the information you need on the level of fragmentation, you can just use look at these columns:

```
SELECT index_id, index_level, avg_fragmentation_in_percent
FROM sys.dm_db_index_physical_stats
  (
  DB_ID('People'),
  OBJECT_ID('People'),
  NULL,
  NULL ,
  'DETAILED'
  )
go
```

What you are looking for is any level of index where the avg_fragmentation_in_percent is higher than 0, although low single digits are also acceptable. In the case of the People table, I dropped and recreated the table, then created the indexes, and then loaded 200,000 rows. After executing these steps the results don't look so good and show a high level of index fragmentation:

index_id	index_level	avg_fragmentation_in_percent
1	0	98.6089375760737
1	1	96.4285714285714
1	2	0
6	0	1.38666666666667
6	1	57.1428571428571
6	2	0
7	0	98.3564458140729
7	1	100
7	2	0
8	0	99.1496598639456
8	1	98.4375
8	2	0
9	0	98.4857309260338

9	1	88.8888888888889
9	2	0
10	0	98.772504091653
10	1	40
10	2	0

You should definitely try to resolve the fragmentation problem on these indexes. The following section shows you how to handle this fragmentation.

Removing Fragmentation

Now that you know you have fragmented indexes, there are three options for cleaning them up. The first is to drop and recreate each index. This is the most intrusive option. When an index is dropped, it is not available for use. Moreover, the drop and create operations are atomic, so the table is locked while this is happening and not available for use. The second option is to use the statement ALTER INDEX REORGANIZE, which became available with SQL Server 2005. This statement replaces DBCC INDEXDEFRAG. The third option is to use the other new statement, ALTER INDEX REBUILD. This replaces DBCC DBREINDEX.

If you have the luxury and time to take the table offline, you should use the first option, dropping and recreating the indexes. If you need to keep the table online, you should use either of the ALTER INDEX options. REORGANIZE is always an online operation and is interruptible without losing any progress, but it isn't as effective as REBUILD. Index rebuilds default to an offline operation where the index is taken offline for the duration of the operation. However, SQL Server 2005 introduced the ability to rebuild online. It achieves this by duplicating the index and rebuilding the second copy before switching the index requests to the newly rebuilt index and dropping the old one. This all happens transparently and utilizes the row versioning feature in SQL Server 2005 to manage index updates during the rebuild, so expect extra activity in TempDB.

You can run each option on the badly fragmented indexes to see how each one does.

You'll start with ALTER INDEX REORGANIZE. After running this command:

```
ALTER INDEX all ON people REORGANIZE
```

The index fragmentation now looks like this:

index_id	index_level	avg_fragmentation_in_percent
1	0	0.960960960960961
1	1	96.4285714285714
1	2	0
6	0	1.38740661686233
6	1	57.1428571428571
6	2	0
7	0	2.53968253968254
7	1	100
7	2	0
8	0	1.9639407598197
8	1	98.4375
8	2	0

9	0	2.031144211239
9	1	88.8888888888889
9	2	0
10	0	2.45464247598719
10	1	40
10	2	0

It's made an improvement. It's not the best it could be, but it was fast.

Now try the next option, ALTER INDEX REBUILD:

```
ALTER INDEX all ON people REBUILD
```

After running this command, the indexes look like this:

index_id	index_level	avg_fragmentation_in_percent
1	0	0
1	1	11.7647058823529
1	2	0
6	0	0
6	1	0
6	2	0
7	0	0
7	1	0
7	2	0
8	0	0
8	1	12.5
8	2	0
9	0	0
9	1	0
9	2	0
10	0	0
10	1	0
10	2	0

It's pretty easy to see the large improvement in this over the results from REORGANIZE, and don't forget that you now have statistics updated with a 100 percent sample size.

Finally, drop and recreate the indexes. After doing this the indexes look like this:

index_id	index_level	avg_fragmentation_in_percent
1	0	0
1	1	0
1	2	0
6	0	0
6	1	0
6	2	0
7	0	0
7	1	0
7	2	0
8	0	0

8	1	12.5
8	2	0
9	0	0
9	1	0
9	2	0
10	0	0
10	1	0
10	2	0

You've all but eliminated the fragmentation and certainly all the fragmentation that matters. An index rebuild will remove all the fragmentation problems and this demonstration is just to show that a drop and recreate of an index can remove more fragmentation than a rebuild.

Section 4: Partitioned Tables and Indexes

Now you'll get started with digging into the details of some of these awesome new features, starting with one that you should be particularly excited about: the new partitioned tables and indexes. You'll start with why you would need to use this new feature, and then how you should use it. You'll also discover more about what partition tables and indexes are and find out more about how you use them.

Reasons for Using Partitioned Tables and Indexes

Partitioned tables are a way to spread a single table over multiple partitions, and while doing so each partition can be on a separate file group. There are several reasons for doing this, which are covered here.

Faster and Easier Data Loading

If your database has a very large amount of data to load, you might want to consider using a partition table. *A very large amount of data* doesn't mean a specific amount of data, but any time the load operation takes longer than is acceptable in the production cycle.

A partition table lets you load the data to an empty table that's not in use by the live data and so has less impact on concurrent live operations. Clearly there will be an impact to the I/O subsystem, but if you also have separate file groups on different physical disks, even this has a minimal impact on overall system performance.

Once the data is loaded to the new table, you can perform a switch to add the new table to the live data. This switch is a simple metadata change that executes very quickly. So partition tables are a great way to load large amounts of data, with limited impact on users touching the rest of the data in a table.

Faster and Easier Data Deletion or Archiving

For the very same reasons, partition tables also help you to delete or archive data. If your data is partitioned on boundaries that are also the natural boundaries on which you add or remove data, then the data is considered to be aligned. When your data is aligned, deleting or archiving data is as simple as switching a table out of the current partition and then unloading or archiving it at your leisure.

There is a bit of a catch to this part, in that with archiving, you often want to move the old data to cheaper or different storage. The switch operation is so fast because all it does is change metadata; it doesn't move any data around. To get the data from the file group where it lived to the archiving file group on cheaper storage, you can't just switch; you actually have to move the data. However, you are moving it when the partition isn't attached to the existing partition table, so although this may take quite some time, it will have minimal impact on any queries executing against the live data.

Faster Queries

Surely the chance to get faster queries has you very interested. One thing that the Query Optimizer can do when querying a partitioned table is to eliminate searching through partitions that it knows won't hold any results. This is referred to as *partition elimination*. This only works if the data in the partitioned table or index is aligned with the query. By *aligned*, we mean that the data has to be distributed through the partitions in a way that matches the search clause on the query. You can see more about the specifics of this as you get into the details of how to create a partitioned table.

Sliding Windows

A sliding window is basically the same as the data deletion/archiving scenario described previously, whereby you add new data and then delete or archive old data. It's kind of like sliding a window of new data into the current partition table, and then sliding an old window of data out of the partition table.

Prerequisites for Partitioning

Before you get all excited about partitioned tables, you should remember that partitioning is only available with SQL Server 2005 Enterprise edition. There are also some expectations about the hardware in use, in particular the storage system, although these are implicit expectations, and you can store the data anywhere you want to. You just won't get the same performance benefits as if you had a larger enterprise storage system with multiple disk groups dedicated to different partitions.

Creating Partitioned Tables

When you decide to create a partitioned table for the first time, you can get pretty well lost in the documentation for partition functions, range left versus range right, partition schemes, and how to actually create something that would work. The following sections will run through the way to think about this process. If you've been reading through the whole chapter and want to continue following the examples, you should drop and recreate the tables by running `createtables.sql` and `loadnames.sql`. Now load the people table with 200,000 rows:

```
EXEC usp_loopPeopleInsert 100000, 10000
-- inserts 100,000 couples and prints progress every 10,000 rows.
GO

EXEC sp_spacedused people
GO
```

name	rows	reserved	data	index_size	unused
people	**199998**	28936 KB	28880 KB	8 KB	48 KB

Creating a Partition Table from an Existing Table

You're going to start with an existing table and turn it into a partitioned table, but you're going to keep it all within the same file group to avoid having to physically move the data around.

The partition function determines how your data is split between partitions. The first step is to create the partition function. Here is the code for a partition function that splits the table called People into multiple partitions based on the DOB field:

```
-- Range partition function for the People table,
-- every 10 years from 2006 - 110 = 1896,
-- start the first partition at everything before 1 Jan 1900

-- 1890-1900, 1900-1910, 1910 - 1920, 1920-1930, 1930-1940, 1940-1950, 1950-1960,
-- 1960-1970, 1970-1980, 1980-1990, 1990-2000, 2000 onwards
CREATE PARTITION FUNCTION [peopleRangePF1] (datetime)
AS RANGE RIGHT FOR VALUES ('01/01/1900', '01/01/1910', '01/01/1920', '01/01/1930',
    '01/01/1940', '01/01/1950','01/01/1960', '01/01/1970', '01/01/1980',
    '01/01/1990', '01/01/2000', '01/01/2005', '01/01/2006'
    );
GO
```

This example is based on the sample database, tables, and procedures mentioned at the beginning of the chapter in the "Sample Database" section. Files to create this can be found on the book's web site at www.wrox.com.

Most of this looks straightforward, but there is one new bit of syntax that's needs explaining; `range right for values`. It's there to determine how the boundary condition is applied at the actual range value. It does this by telling the function what to do with data that exactly matches the range boundary. In this case, the first range boundary is 01/01/1900. What should the function do with data that matches that value? Does it go above or below? Range Right tells the function to put the matching data into the right side (higher values, or above the range boundary) of the data, whereas range left tells the function to put the data into the left side (lower values, or below the range boundary) of the data.

> Something else to watch for here when using `datetime` fields is the precise date and time you're matching. In this example, you have the luxury of not worrying about the exact placement of a few values close to the boundary that may get into the next partition. In a production system, you will be concerned that the partition holds exactly the values you want. In that case, you need to pay particular attention to the exact date and time constant you specify for the range boundary.

The second step is to create the partition scheme, as follows:

```
CREATE PARTITION SCHEME [peoplePS1]
AS PARTITION [peopleRangePF1]
TO ([PRIMARY], [PRIMARY], [PRIMARY]
, [PRIMARY], [PRIMARY], [PRIMARY]
, [PRIMARY], [PRIMARY], [PRIMARY]
, [PRIMARY], [PRIMARY], [PRIMARY]
, [PRIMARY], [PRIMARY]);
GO
```

This is pretty simple syntax. The main thing you need to look out for is the exact number of partitions to be created. The partition function created 13 boundaries, so you need to have 13 + 1 = 14 partitions for the data to go into.

Because you are partitioning an existing table and I don't want you to have to move the data, you're keeping it all on the existing file group.

Now you're going to create a clustered index partitioned using the partition scheme to "rebuild" the data into the correct partitions:

```
CREATE CLUSTERED INDEX cix_People ON people(dob,personID)
ON peoplePS1(dob)
```

The clustered index key is on dob *and* personID because dob is the partition key and personID will make each index record unique (see Section1: Clustered Indexes). An index created with the same partition scheme as the underlying table is referred to as an *aligned index*. This isn't a requirement but will be the default when creating an index on an already partitioned table.

Finally, you can check the system metadata to confirm that you have partitioned correctly. To do this there is some new syntax you can use to determine the partition that data lives on: $partition. Here is an example of using this to see how many rows are on each partition:

```
-   this will tell us how many entries there are in each partition
SELECT $partition.PeopleRangePF1(dob) [Partition Number], count(*) AS total
FROM people
GROUP BY $partition.PeopleRangePF1(dob)
ORDER BY $partition.PeopleRangePF1(dob)

Partition Number total
---------------- -----------
1                5379
2                18240
3                18206
4                18259
5                18147
6                18075
7                18295
8                18131
9                18313
10               18242
11               18091
12               8987
13               1810
14               1823
```

Using this syntax, you can see the number of rows on each partition to confirm the data is distributed as you planned for.

Switching in New Data to the Partitioned Table

Now that your table is partitioned, you need a way to add new data offline and switch that new data into the partitioned table. The first step is to create a table to hold all the new data to be loaded. This needs to have an identical layout to the partitioned table:

```
-- Create a new People table to hold any births after 09/20/2007
-- MUST BE IDENTICAL to People
CREATE TABLE newPeople (
  [personID] [uniqueidentifier] NULL DEFAULT (newsequentialid()),
  [firstName] [varchar](80) NOT NULL,
  [lastName] [varchar](80) NOT NULL,
  [DOB] [datetime] NOT NULL,
  [DOD] [datetime] NULL,
  [sex] [char](1) NOT NULL
) on [PRIMARY]     -- Must be on the same filegroup as the target partition!
```

After doing this, you need to create modified versions of the usp_birthInsert and usp_loopBirth-Insert stored procedures to insert rows to the newPeople table rather than inserting to the People table. For this example, call the new procedures usp_newbirthInsert and usp_loopNewBirthInsert.

Inserting to the new table will be fast because it's empty and there are no indexes to slow down the insert rate. Insert some data into the table — a hundred thousand rows should do it. Do this by running usp_loopNewBirthInsert. Changing the arguments will determine how many rows it inserts.

```
EXEC usp_loopNewBirthInsert 50000, 10000
GO
```

Next, create a clustered index to match the partitioned index:

```
-- create the index on the new table.
CREATE CLUSTERED INDEX cix_newPeople ON newPeople(dob,personID)
```

One more thing you need to do is create a check constraint on the new table to ensure that the data matches the partition function boundary you are about to set up:

```
-- Before we do the switch,
-- create a check constraint on the source table
-- to enforce the integrity of the data in the partition
ALTER TABLE newPeople
ADD CONSTRAINT [CK_DOB_DateRange]
CHECK ([DOB] >= '09/20/2007');
GO
```

Now you can start making changes to the live partition to prepare it for the new set of data you want to load. The first step is to alter the partition scheme to specify where the new partition is going to live. This has to be on the same file group as the new table. In this case, it's easy as everything is on the Primary file group anyway. In a production system with multiple file groups this would be one of the empty file groups available. For more details on using multiple file groups, see the ''Partitioning a Production System'' section coming up shortly.

```
-- alter the partition scheme to ready a new empty partition
ALTER PARTITION SCHEME PeoplePS1
NEXT USED [PRIMARY];
GO
```

The next step is to create the new partition boundary in the partition function. This is done by using an ALTER PARTITION FUNCTION statement. In this case, you have a range right function, your new data is for Sept. 20, 2007, and you want all the new data to be in the new partition, so using RANGE RIGHT, you specify the boundary as Sept. 20, 2007.

```
-- Split the newest partition at Sept 20, 2007
-- This is a RANGE RIGHT function,
-- so anything on 09/20 goes into the NEW partition,
-- anything BEFORE 09/20 goes into the OLD partition
-- The new partition this creates goes to the new partition
-- we prepared in the alter scheme above
ALTER PARTITION FUNCTION PeopleRangePF1()
SPLIT RANGE ('09/20/2007');
GO
```

The next step is going to switch the new data into the partition, but before doing that, check to see how many people you have in the newPeople table.

```
EXEC sp_spaceused newPeople
GO

name          rows       reserved        data            index_size       unused
-------------------------------------------------------------------------------------
newPeople     99998      14472 KB        14416 KB        8 KB             48 KB
```

Now you can apply the switch and move all those people into the new partition.

```
-- Now switch in the data from the new table
ALTER TABLE newPeople
SWITCH      -- No partition here as we are switching in a NON partitioned table
TO People PARTITION 15;  -- but need to add the partition here !
GO
```

The switch ran very quickly. Now check how many people are in which table. First, look at how many people are in the newPeople table:

```
EXEC sp_spaceused newPeople
GO

name          rows       reserved        data            index_size       unused
-------------------------------------------------------------------------------------
newPeople     0          0 KB            0 KB            0 KB             0 KB
```

As expected, the table is empty. And hopefully all 99,998 people are in the partitions table in the new partition:

```
--  this will tell us how many entries there are in each partition
SELECT $partition.PeopleRangePF1(dob) [Partition Number], count(*) AS total
FROM people
GROUP BY $partition.PeopleRangePF1(dob)
ORDER BY $partition.PeopleRangePF1(dob)

Partition Number total
---------------- -----------
1                5571
```

```
2                 18381
3                 18245
4                 18139
5                 17970
6                 18106
7                 17934
8                 18360
9                 18153
10                18297
11                18168
12                9051
13                1852
14                1771
15                99998
-- We now have a 15th partition with all the new people in it
```

Querying the partition table, you now have a 15th partition with 99998 people in it.

Deleting Data from the Partitioned Table

After a new set of data that that represents a new day, week, or month of data has been added to your table, you also need to move out the old data by either deleting or archiving it somewhere. The first step in this process is to create a new table to put the data into. This needs to be an empty table that has the exact same structure as the partition table and it needs to be on the same file group as the partition you are going to remove. You'll also need to create the same index structure as before.

```
-- Step one, we need a table to put the data into
CREATE TABLE oldPeople (
  [personID] [uniqueidentifier] NULL DEFAULT (newsequentialid()),
  [firstName] [varchar](80) NOT NULL,
  [lastName] [varchar](80) NOT NULL,
  [DOB] [datetime] NOT NULL,
  [DOD] [datetime] NULL,
  [sex] [char](1) NOT NULL
) ON [PRIMARY]
-- Must be on the same filegroup as the source partition!

-- we need a clustered index on DOB to match the partition
CREATE CLUSTERED INDEX cix_oldPeople ON oldPeople(dob, personID)
GO
```

Note that you don't need a check constraint on this table as it's moving out of the partition, not into it.

Now that you have the table and clustered index to match the partitioned table and index, you can execute the switch to move out a set of data. This is done using the ALTER TABLE SWITCH statement again, but note that now the syntax has changed a little and you have to specify partition numbers.

```
-- now go switch out the partition
ALTER TABLE People
SWITCH partition 1     -- which partition are we removing
TO OldPeople
-- No partition here as we are switching to a NON partitioned table
GO
```

Now check and see how many rows are in each partition again.

```
--  this will tell us how many entries there are in each partition
SELECT $partition.PeopleRangePF1(dob) [Partition Number], count(*) AS total
FROM people
GROUP BY $partition.PeopleRangePF1(dob)
ORDER BY $partition.PeopleRangePF1(dob)


Partition Number total
---------------- -----------
2                18381
3                18245
4                18139
5                17970
6                18106
7                17934
8                18360
9                18153
10               18297
11               18168
12               9051
13               1852
14               1771
15               99998
-- Notice that partition 1 has gone!

-- lets see how many people are now in the oldPeople table
EXEC sp_spaceused oldPeople
GO


name        rows    reserved    data        index_size    unused
-------------------------------------------------------------------------------
oldPeople   5571    904 KB      784 KB      16 KB         104 KB
```

You can see that partition 1 is no longer part of the partition table, and that the rows from that partition are now in the oldPeople table.

There is one more bit of tidying up to perform and that's to alter the partition function to merge the old range that you no longer need. This is done using another ALTER PARTITION function statement, where you specify the old boundary that you no longer need.

```
-- next we can merge the first partition
ALTER PARTITION FUNCTION PeopleRangePF1()
MERGE RANGE ('01/01/1900');
GO
-- now check the partition layout after the merge

--  this will tell us how many entries there are in each partition?
select $partition.PeopleRangePF1(dob) [Partition Number], count(*) as total
from people
group by $partition.PeopleRangePF1(dob)
order by $partition.PeopleRangePF1(dob)
```

```
/*
Partition Number total
---------------- -----------
Partition Number total
---------------- -----------
1               18381
2               18245
3               18139
4               17970
5               18106
6               17934
7               18360
8               18153
9               18297
10              18168
11              9051
12              1852
13              1771
14              99998
*/
-- Now we only have partitions 1-14 again
```

That was all quite straightforward but you aren't quite done yet. You have moved the old partition data out of the partition table but it's still on the same file group, consuming your most expensive storage. You want the data to be on the cheaper storage for archiving or in some location ready to be backed up and deleted.

To do this, you need to physically move the data from one file group to another. There are several ways you can do this but the fastest and most efficient is to use a select into. There are three steps you need to complete here.

1. Alter the default file group to be the archiving file group.

2. Select into a new table.

3. Alter the default file group back.

Here is the code you can use to do this:

```
-- Once its slid out, we have to physically move the data
-- to a different filegroup for archiving storage
-- Change the default filegroup to be cheapDisks
-- This is so that the SELECT INTO creates the new table on cheapDisks
ALTER DATABASE people ADD FILEGROUP cheapDisks
GO
ALTER DATABASE people ADD FILE (NAME = cheapdisk1, FILENAME = 'D:\cheapdisk.ndf')
TO FILEGROUP cheapDisks
GO
ALTER DATABASE people MODIFY FILEGROUP cheapDisks DEFAULT
GO

-- Move the data!
```

```
SELECT * INTO archivePeople
FROM oldPeople

-- alter the default filegroup back again!
ALTER DATABASE People MODIFY FILEGROUP [primary] DEFAULT
GO

-- you can now drop the oldPeople table
DROP TABLE oldPeople
```

Finally, look at the system metadata to see where your new table is living. The following is the query that can be used for this, with abreviated results showing just the objects of interest:

```
-- Lets check which filegroup all our objects are on
SELECT  OBJECT_NAME(i.object_id) AS  ObjectName,  i.name AS  IndexName,  f.name as
filegroupName
FROM sys.indexes AS i INNER JOIN sys.filegroups AS f ON i.data_space_id = f.data_
space_id
WHERE i.object_id > 100

-- Returns
ObjectName        IndexName         filegroupName
----------        ----------        -------------
boysnames         NULL              PRIMARY
girlsnames        NULL              PRIMARY
lastnames         NULL              PRIMARY
newPeople         cix_newPeople     PRIMARY
archivePeople     NULL              cheapDisks
```

You can see that archivePeople is now in the cheapDisks file group.

Partitioning a Production System

The scenarios covered so far help to show how you can implement a sliding window scenario but they gloss over some of the finer details that are going to be the key points on a production system. One of the main issues on a production system is going to be that you will have multiple file groups matched to different physical storage.

The only place this really changes any of what you've seen so far is when you're creating and altering the partition scheme. So rather than the example you saw earlier, you would create a partition scheme using something like this:

```
CREATE PARTITION SCHEME [PeoplePS1]
AS PARTITION [PeopleRangePF1]
TO ([FileGroup1], [FileGroup2], [FileGroup3] );
GO
```

Each of your partitions go to a different file group.

When you create file groups, you need to make sure you have enough not just for the live table, but also for new data and for the old data before it's moved to archiving storage or deleted, so you need file groups for at least the number of live partitions, plus two more; one for the new data and one for the old data.

An alternate physical layout might have multiple partitions sharing the same file group. The exact detail of laying out physical disks is beyond the scope of this chapter but is touched on in Chapter 6.

Partitioning and DTA

DTA will provide partitioning recommendations if you ask it to. To do this you need to change the tuning options on the Tuning Options tab. In the group titled Partitioning strategy to employ, change the default setting of No Partitioning to full partitioning. You also need to determine what kind of queries to tune. It's no good using your INSERT, DELETE, or SWITCH queries as DTA isn't really interested in them. You have to tune the SELECT statements that go against the non-partitioned table. The reason DTA isn't interested in INSERT, DELETE, or SWITCH statements is that it can't improve their performance by adding indexes so it ignores them and looks only at the statements it can tune: SELECT.

If the table is big enough and the queries would benefit from partitioning, DTA will provide scripts to create the partition function, the partition scheme, and the clustered index. Here is an example of a DTA partitioning recommendation received from a different database. The underlying table has 57,000,000 rows, uses 1.8 GB of data space, and 3.6 GB of index space.

```
CREATE PARTITION FUNCTION [_dta_pf__2533](int) AS RANGE LEFT FOR VALUES (103863552,
196930103, 203421423, 246065168, 269171113, 269702979, 270375078, 273695583,
276447808, 280951053, 298459732, 298855583, 299375843, 299810346, 301474640)

CREATE PARTITION SCHEME [_dta_ps__8258] AS PARTITION [_dta_pf__2533] TO ([PRIMARY],
[PRIMARY], [PRIMARY], [PRIMARY], [PRIMARY], [PRIMARY], [PRIMARY], [PRIMARY],
[PRIMARY], [PRIMARY], [PRIMARY], [PRIMARY], [PRIMARY], [PRIMARY], [PRIMARY],
[PRIMARY])

CREATE NONCLUSTERED INDEX [_dta_index_myTable_6_741577680_23810504_K1_K2_K3] ON
[dbo].[myTable]
(
  [Col1] ASC,
  [Col2] ASC,
  [Col3] ASC
)WITH (SORT_IN_TEMPDB = OFF, DROP_EXISTING = OFF, IGNORE_DUP_KEY = OFF, ONLINE =
OFF) ON [_dta_ps__8258]([Colx])
```

Summary

This chapter covered four key areas, starting off with a solid overview of SQL Server 2005 indexing before moving on to tuning indexes with the Database Tuning Advisor and comprehensively covering the various options available and how implement the recommendations. Then you looked at how to check and remove fragmentation from your database followed by an examination of the details of partitioning. You looked at how to set up partitioning and covered three main scenarios: creating a partition from an existing table, adding a new partition, and deleting an old partition.

12

How Fast and Robust
Is Your Storage?

The storage subsystem is the foundation for all the data that lives in SQL Server. The performance, robustness, and reliability of the storage subsystem affect everything you build on it in SQL. For this reason it is essential that you have a solid understanding of what your storage subsystem can deliver and have confidence in its robustness and reliability.

The best way to build that solid understanding of the storage subsystem's performance potential is to measure it using a performance test. There are several ways to do this, and this chapter discusses several options before diving into using one in more detail. The tool of choice for this chapter is SQLIO.

The best way to build confidence in the robustness and reliability of the storage subsystem is to run a stress test on it. There are multiple ways you can do this, and this chapter discusses several ways you might do this before digging into the details of using the latest tool from Microsoft: SQLIOSIM.

Obviously, everyone's system is different. You will have your system configured according to your various needs. Depending on your system, you will have a certain amount of disk space. You will have assorted programs running on different schedules. As you follow along with this chapter, it is likely that you will have different measurements and readings than some of the ones I will provide. That is fine. Don't get too caught up comparing those specific numbers. The important thing to take away from this chapter is an understanding of the core principles involved here.

Performance Testing, Stress Testing, and Real-Life Performance

A lot of people I speak to about storage performance are confused about the difference between these three completely different aspects of testing storage and how the results of one type of test might relate to a different aspect of performance.

Performance Testing

In performance testing, your objective is to measure how fast you can get something done, and not how many of something you can do, which is subtly different. What does this mean? In a performance test you need to give the test subject (your disks) one thing to do (one I/O request), and then see how quickly it gets done. Then you give it another thing to do and see how quickly it does that. Basically you throw sequential requests at the test subject, and observe how long each one takes.

You have to be a little careful that your performance test doesn't turn into a stress test, and in some cases your performance test might start to look a bit like a stress test, but your focus is always on how quickly you got the job done, and not in how many you could get done.

Stress Testing

In stress testing the objective is to apply stress to the system and see how it holds up. In a stress test you throw many concurrent requests at the test subject and see how it responds. In comparison with the performance test, which was a sequential test, the stress test is a parallel test. And your focus here is on how many requests you manage to process in the allotted period. Another part of the stress test is usually concerned with correctness. It's no good getting a great number if half the results are wrong.

Real-Life Performance

In attempting to assess real-life performance, the objective is to assess both how quickly a single response may be served (a performance test) and also how many you can do at the same time (a stress test). Real-life performance is also concerned with more complex operations than you would have looked at in either the performance or stress tests. In the performance and stress tests, you were interested in much smaller units of work, such as a single disk's I/O or a few disks' I/O together. In a real-life test you are interested in the actual units of work a user might do. In this case you must then have some concept of the way that a real user interacts with the system and exactly what database and I/O operations each user might cause.

A common way of looking at this is to use the use-case methodology to model the system's users and the interactions those users have with the system (the cases).

A simple example of this comes from a system I worked on long ago. It was a telecom company's billing system. In this instance, a user would be the telephone company's users, the billing system, or a customer service rep. Take for example the customer service rep (CSR). One task the CSR has to perform is to answer billing queries from the customer. To do this he or she has to perform many queries to get the data they want. A typical case might be for the CSR to start by issuing a search query to find the customer's account based upon any one of the acceptable account identifiers: the customer's address, phone number, account number, address, and so on. From there the CSR can query for all the call records for a given time period, and from there pull up the details of a specific call record. This may then result in an update, or a write of a new record to indicate a customer query on the bill that needs further investigation by some other part of the company.

So in this use case, you have the following DB operations:

❑ Customer search query
❑ Customer account details query

- ❑ Customer billing records summary query
- ❑ Customer billing record detail query
- ❑ Billing record exception insert

Depending on exactly how the system has been designed and written, these queries could result in many different I/O patterns at the disk level, but let's take a fairly optimal scenario. In that case, the storage level I/O for this could be something like:

- ❑ Customer search query
  - ❑ Random/Sequential read
- ❑ Customer account details query
  - ❑ Random/Sequential Read
- ❑ Customer billing records summary query
  - ❑ Random/Sequential read
- ❑ Customer billing record detail query
  - ❑ Random/Sequential Read
- ❑ Billing record exception insert
  - ❑ Random Write

From this you can see that the overall use case is a mix of random and sequential read activity, as well as a small amount of random write activity (in this case, probably just a single write activity as you are only writing a single record). However, if you had to update an index because of that one write, there could follow a number of random/sequential write activities as the index is updated.

Putting It All Together

How do the results from a performance test relate to the real-life performance you can expect to see from your SQL Server application? The answer depends on the I/O characteristics of your application.

Some applications have a simple and highly predictable I/O pattern. An example of one of these might be an OLTP system where you will expect to see a very high volume of random reads and writes. This is easy to predict, and the relation to the performance test results is pretty clear. The user should expect to see I/O performance very closely related to the results of random read and random write activity in the performance tests.

On the other hand, someone with a complex DSS system where the I/O characteristics of the application will consist of a mix of large overnight batch updates and then large query activity throughout the day will be much more difficult, but you could start by estimating that the overnight loads will consist of a mix of random and sequential write activity with some read activity thrown in. The challenge for the creators of the overnight batch load is to minimize the random read activity and the random write activity and to try to maximize the sequential write activity. In this case you can expect the system to experience performance of maybe 50–75 percent of the sequential I/O rate from the performance test. The daytime performance will then be a mix of random and sequential read activity. The challenge for the creators of this system is to maximize the sequential read activity and to work to increase the size of each read to again maximize I/O performance. This can be achieved by tuning the T-SQL and indexes to maximize the use of ReadAhead. The performance can be approximately predicted for each different I/O type, but coming up with an overall approximation isn't really possible. This is where a real-life test is necessary to see what will really happen.

Storage Performance

The Performance of the Storage Subsystem is the foundation stone for the performance of the applications you build in SQL Server. Having a good baseline of the performance your storage subsystem can deliver is an essential step in the journey to a SQL Server system with good performance. In this section you will learn about tools to use for running a performance test, and then you will learn about the various metrics available to measure performance.

Storage Performance Measuring Tools

There are quite a few tools available that measure different aspects of storage performance. Many of them are specialized to a single application, some for Exchange (LoadSim and JetStress), and others for file system benchmarking (IOZone) The two most frequently used for pure storage performance measurement are IOMeter and SQLIO.

IOMeter

This tool is perhaps the most referenced tool for storage subsystem performance measurement. It is both a performance tool and a stress tool. Originally developed by Intel, it was given to the open source community. Versions are available from the open source community for Windows, Linux, Netware, and many variations of Unix. IOMeter's default configuration is to operate as a stress test, and it takes quite some reconfiguration to get it to operate as a performance tool, but it can be done.

SQLIO

This is a very simple but powerful tool available from Microsoft. No one is really sure why this tool is called SQLIO as it really doesn't really have anything to do with SQL other than that it was originally written by a developer in the SQL Server team. SQLIO is a highly configurable I/O performance test tool. SQLIO requires a good understanding of its various parameters to get any kind of test going, but once a batch file is written, it's reusable. It does a great job of allowing you to write repeatable performance tests. It's not designed to act as a stress test tool, and if you try to use it as such you will quickly discover its limitations.

SQLIOStress/SQLIOSim

SQLIOSim is the new replacement to SQLIOStress. SQLIOStress was originally written by CSS (Customer Service and Support) to help them troubleshoot troublesome storage reliability issues. SQLIOSim is the new version of this tool and was written by the SQL Server development team. It's a complete rewrite and is based upon the I/O code within SQL server, but it doesn't require SQL to be installed to run. People often mention these tools in the context of performance testing. However, although its possible to get a performance measure from these tools, their primary purpose is to stress test and to check a storage subsystem for reliability.

What Do You Want to Measure?

Now that you have established that you want to measure performance, what do you actually want to measure? This section covers a number of different metrics relevant to storage performance.

IOPS

Input/Output operations per second (IOPS) is a measure of how many input or output requests you serviced per second. This is a good starting point, but the number you get is a function of the subsystem's actual throughput and the size of the I/O request.

Here is an example that helps illustrate this is a simple single disk test. The disk is capable of delivering 5 MB/Sec for Random read activity. Test that throughput by issuing 4 KB I/Os. You get an IOPS of 5 MB / 4 KB = 1250. That sounds great, but now test with a 64 KB block size, and you get only 78 IOPS, That doesn't sound so great when you compare it with 1250, yet you are still getting the same 5 MB/Sec throughput.

So although IOPS is an interesting metric, you really need to know more about what kind of I/O was being used for the test.

Best Practice

Consider what kind of I/O was being issued when reading IOPS.

Block Size

Block size is very important to your test results, but it's a parameter you want to drive into the tests, rather than being something you need to measure. When attempting to measure I/O performance of a real-life storage subsystem, block size is something you will want to measure. In this case block size gives you an indication of what size I/Os SQL is issuing.

MB/Sec

This is one of the key metrics for any storage subsystems performance. This tells you how many MB of data you got on or of off the storage subsystem in one second. Watch carefully for the differences between MB (Mega Bytes) and Mb (Mega bits) as one MB is 8 times larger than one Mb, or 8 Mb = 1 MB, and the disk manufacturers and other storage vendors love those big numbers (Mb) to make their particular product look better than the rest.

Another example of the difference between MB and Mb is relevant to I/O throughput. A disk capable of delivering a throughput of 5 MB/Sec is the same as a disk delivering a throughput of 40 Mb/Sec.

When looking at MB/Sec numbers, you must also consider the latency at which that throughput was achieved. MB/Sec and Latency are both a function of the overall disk throughput. Be careful of very high throughput (MB/Sec) figures that are achieved at the cost of excessively high latencies.

Latency

This is another key metric, and is tells you how long you had to wait for each I/O to complete. It needs to be considered along with the throughput in MB/Sec. Latencies of less than 5 milliseconds (mSec) are great, latencies from 5–10 mSec are acceptable, and 10–20 mSec may be acceptable. Generally, however, 20 mSec is considered to be the outer limit of acceptability. Latencies of greater than 20mSec are a warning sign that the storage is being over stressed. The SQL Server Best Practices team has written a number of papers related to storage performance that all recommend latencies around these numbers. Just to recap on those numbers as they are so important, here they are again:

- ❑ Less than 5 mSec — Excellent
- ❑ 5–10 mSec — Good
- ❑ 10–20 mSec — Poor
- ❑ Greater than 20 mSec — Bad

As mentioned previously, always look at the MB/Sec and latency together. When you're looking at disk throughput, discount any throughput that's achieved at latencies of over 10 mSec.

Best Practice

When reading throughput, always consider the MB/Sec and latency together

---

Disk Queue Length

This is another indicator you need to consider when looking at the throughput. It often will go hand in hand with latency. Disk Queue Length is the length of the disk queue, or the number of I/O requests the disk has queued up while it has been busy working on the current I/O request. You will find any number of different recommendations for what this should be, and it's very difficult to figure out exactly what number is good as there are many places this value can be observed from the Perfmon logical disk counters, through the physical disk counters, and down further into the storage stack if an array controller or intelligent storage subsystem exposes additional counters.

Best Practice

Disk Queue Length should be 0 or 1 at the disk. Consider the storage structure and where in the storage stack this counter is being measured.

Measuring I/O Performance

In this section you will learn about the tools you can use to measure I/O performance. There are two primary sets of tools you can for this: Perfmon counters and SQL Server DMVs.

Perfmon Counters

There are just a handful of Perfmon counters you are interested in when looking at storage performance. What is a little confusing about them is that the same counters appear under two different counter objects: physical disk and logical disk.

Let's first go through the basic counters; then you'll see a little more about the difference between the physical and logical disk counters.

% Disk Read Time, % Disk Time, and % Disk Write Time, % Disk Idle Time

These counters indicate the percentage of time in the sample period that the disk was reading, writing, in use (reads and writes), or idle. It's an interesting set of counters to watch and can be useful for high level monitoring of storage performance. However, as soon as you need to look at the performance in more detail, these counters are at too high a level to provide more direction.

Avg. Disk Bytes/Read, Avg. Disk Bytes/Transfer, and Avg. Disk Bytes/Write

This counter indicates the average number of bytes per read, write, or transfer (read and write). The average is across all I/Os issued in the sample period. This counter is very useful to help tell you what size I/Os are being issued. However, if there are a lot of differently sized I/Os issued within the sample period, the results aren't that useful. If you can isolate the activity generating each I/O type and execute that activity over a few sample periods, the counter will give you a much more useful reading.

Avg. Disk Queue Length, Avg. Disk Read Queue Length, and Avg. Disk Write Queue Length

This counter indicates the average disk queue length. The disk queue length is the number of requests that are waiting to be sent to the disk. Again the average is over the sample period. This counter is very useful, but its results can be misleading and will vary based upon different I/O subsystems. High values for the disk queue length can indicate that you are over stressing the disk subsystem, and this is especially so if they are combined with a rise in the latency of the I/Os. However when working with a large storage array with many disks, you will not see the real value at the disk, as the counter only operates on queue lengths within the software stack.

Avg. Disk Sec/Read, Avg. Disk Sec/Transfer, and Avg. Disk Sec/Write

This counter is telling you the latency of each I/O. That is how long each read or write took. It's an average over the sample period, so if the sample period contains many different types of I/O, the results are less useful than if the sample contains a set of one type of I/O. When converted to mSec, it's directly comparable to the results from the SQLIO test described below.

Disk Bytes/Sec, Disk Read Bytes/Sec, and Disk Write Bytes/Sec

This counter tells you the throughput in Bytes/Sec. It's a very useful counter for determining how close you are to maxing out the I/O capacity of the storage subsystem, or in showing you how much throughput the storage subsystem has during a perf test. When converted to MB/Sec, it's directly comparable to the results of the SQLIO tests described later in this chapter.

Disk Reads/Sec, Disk Transfers/Sec, and Disk Writes/Sec

This counter tells you how many I/O Operations Per Second (IOPS) you are getting. This is another really useful counter. You can compare the numbers here directly with the results of the SQLIO tests.

Physical Disk vs. Logical Disk

The difference between the physical and logical disk counters can be confusing. I have a fairly simple model that I use to help explain the difference. The logical disk counters are counters of the I/O at the top of the OS, right next to the Application layer. The physical disk counters are measuring I/O performance at the bottom of the OS, right before the I/Os head across to the driver and leave the processor for the many layers of the software and hardware stack between the OS and the surface of the disk.

Another way to think about this is to consider a few examples.

In the first example in Figure 12-1, you will consider a single disk system where the disk has four partitions, and each of these is mounted as a separate disk C, D, E, F. Initially you might think that the physical disk counters would show just the one physical disk, but because the disk is partitioned before it's presented to the OS, the physical disk counters will still show four disk instances. The logical disk counters will also show four disk instances.

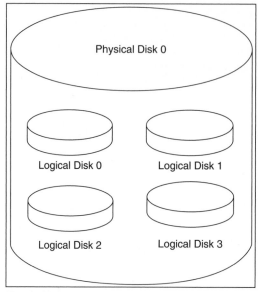

Figure 12-1

In the second example in Figure 12-2, consider the other extreme of a small RAID array of four disks configured into a simple stripe set. The array controller presents this to the OS as a single disk which is mounted as D. You might think that the physical disk counters would show the four disks in the drive array, but the OS doesn't know anything about four disks, it only knows about the D disk presented to it by the Array controller card. The logical disk counters will again show just a single instance for the D drive.

In the third example in Figure 12-3, look at the four disks attached to a four channel SATA card and mounted as four separate disks. These disks are then combined into a software RAID set inside the OS, and mounted as D. In this case the logical disk counters will show a single instance D whereas the physical disk counters will show four instances, one for each of the disks.

Unfortunately there isn't a Best Practice that covers which set of counters to monitor. In some cases you will want to use the Physical Disk counters. In other cases such as when using mount points, you will want to monitor the Logical Disk counters. Having an understanding of where each set of counters is monitoring will help you make the decision about which set is right for your case.

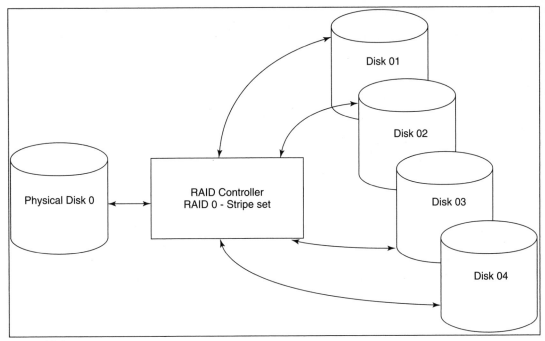

Figure 12-2

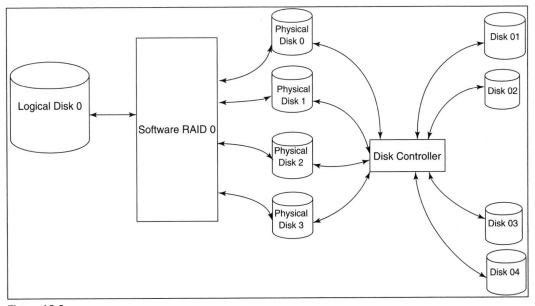

Figure 12-3

Looking at I/O Performance from within SQL Server

There are a number of very useful DMVs in SQL Server 2005 that show you information about the I/Os being generated by SQL Server.

The four I/O-related DMVs are:

- ❏ sys.dm_io_backup_tapes
- ❏ sys.dm_io_pending_io_requests
- ❏ sys.dm_io_cluster_shared_drives
- ❏ sys.dm_io_virtual_file_stats

Only two of these are of any interest here, and these are discussed below.

sys.dm_io_pending_io_requests

This DMV shows any pending I/O requests. This is actually a view, so you can select directly from it using the following T-SQL:

```
select * from sys.dm_io_pending_io_requests
```

This will give you a result set that looks similar to the output in Table 12-1, but will reflect any outstanding I/O requests on your system at the time it was run.

However if you have no pending I/O requests, you get nothing.

Table 12-1 is a very long table that won't fit on the printed page. It has been broken into three segments for easier viewing.

sys.dm_io_virtual_file_stats

This DMV shows you the cumulative I/O counters for each file configured in SQL Server and is the replacement of the SQL Server 2000 function `fn_virtual_file_stats`. This DMV is a function rather than a view, so it needs to be given arguments for the database id and file. These values can be null, but don't default to null, so you have to use the following T-SQL to get all the file stats:

```
Select * from sys.dm_io_virtual_file_stats (null,null)
```

The parameters for this function are the database id and the file id.

Table 12-2 shows an example of the first few lines of the result set when we ran this on one of our SQL Servers.

Table 12-2 is a very long table that won't fit on the printed page. It has been broken into three segments for easier viewing.

What's more useful is to target the function at either a specific database, or preferably a specific file. To do that you can use something like the following T-SQL.

First, find out what DBs you have available:

```
Select * from sys.databases
```

Table 12-1: Output from sys.dm_io_pending_io_requests

io_completion_request_address	io_type	io_pending_ms_ticks	io_pending
0x161D0C08	disk	328	1
0x161ECB78	disk	328	1
0x161CBEF0	disk	328	1
0x164C3FD0	disk	312	1
0x161AEC00	disk	203	1
0x161C9C68	disk	203	1

io_completion_routine_address	io_user_data_address	scheduler_address
0x01042572	0x071B3168	0x006DC040
0x01042572	0x071819A4	0x006DC040
0x01042572	0x071C4404	0x006DC040
0x01042572	0x0717CCC0	0x006DC040
0x01042572	0x073AAB7C	0x006DC040
0x01042572	0x0740AFF8	0x006DC040

io_handle	io_offset
0x00000AC4	3948134400
0x00000AC4	4011196416
0x00000AC4	4011524096
0x00000ACC	8559542272
0x00000AC0	547766272
0x00000AC0	547946496

Then, find what files you have for a given database:

```
Select * from sys.database_files
```

Now run the query for the database and file you are interested in:

```
Select * from sys.dm_io_virtual_file_stats (DB_ID('tempdb'),2)
```

Table 12-2: Output from sys.dm_io_virtual_file_stats

database_id	file_id	sample_ms	num_of_reads	num_of_bytes_read
1	1	-1568777343	32041	555245568
1	2	-1568777343	165	1388544
2	1	-1568777343	21265151	9.18027E+11
2	2	-1568777343	1164	70148096
2	4	-1568777343	21144937	9.17142E+11

io_stall_read_ms	num_of_writes	num_of_bytes_written	io_stall_write_ms
141224	825	6799360	3467
897	4873	3683840	3721
1596900444	23121253	1.32498E+12	2342759655
62562	3698286	2.27204E+11	39249458
1680433554	23142095	1.32683E+12	2351237062

io_stall	size_on_disk_bytes	file_handle
144691	30605312	0x00000688
4618	23592960	0x0000068C
3939660099	31457280000	0x000007D0
39312020	31457280000	0x00000704
4031670616	20971520000	0x000007D4

Table 12-3 shows the results we obtained when we ran this on one of our SQL Servers. Your results will differ based on how much I/O you are pushing to temdb and how your tempdb is configured.

Table 12-3 is a very long table that won't fit on the printed page. It has been broken into three segments for easier viewing.

Another challenge with this DMV is that these are the cumulative numbers since SQL Server was last started. On a system that's been running for some time, they will be very large and may reflect a workload that was run once a long time ago.

To get results that reflect recent activity, you will need to write some T-SQL to sample this function and write the results into a table, and then some additional SQL that queries that table to show you the changes over a given period.

Table 12-3: More Output from sys.dm_io_virtual_file_stats

database_id	file_id	sample_ms	num_of_reads	num_of_bytes_read
2	1	−1568482343	21266054	9.18039E+11
2	2	−1568482343	1164	70148096
2	4	−1568482343	21145932	9.17155E+11

Io_stall_read_ms	num_of_writes	num_of_bytes_written	io_stall_write_ms
1596933746	23124688	1.32502E+12	2342777357
62562	3698286	2.27204E+11	39249458
1680479682	23145483	1.32687E+12	2351254446

Io_stall	size_on_disk_bytes	file_handle
3939711103	31457280000	0x000007D0
39312020	31457280000	0x00000704
4031734128	20971520000	0x000007D4

Here is a simple example that shows the use of a temporary table and WAITFOR to show the change in the values for a given file over a 10 second period:

```
-- Capture sample 1
Select *, 1 as sample, getdate() as sample_time
into #dmv_samples
from sys.dm_io_virtual_file_stats (DB_ID('tempdb'),null)

-- Wait for some interval, im using 10 seconds, or just run manually
whenever you want to see whats changed?
waitfor delay '00:00:10'

-- Capture sample 2
insert #dmv_samples
Select *, 2 , getdate()
from sys.dm_io_virtual_file_stats (DB_ID('tempdb'),null)

-- Find the difference between sample 1 and 2
-- Not all columns change, so we only want deltas for
-- num_of_reads
-- num_of_bytes_read
-- io_stall_read_ms
-- num_of_writes
-- num_of_bytes_written
-- io_stall_write_ms
-- io_stall
```

```
select w2.database_id
, w2.file_id
, w2.sample_ms - w1.sample_ms as sample_ms_delta
, w2.num_of_reads - w1.num_of_reads as num_of_reads_delta
, w2.num_of_bytes_read - w1.num_of_bytes_read as num_of_bytes_read_delta
, w2.io_stall_read_ms - w1.io_stall_read_ms as io_stall_read_ms_delta
, w2.num_of_writes - w1.num_of_writes as num_of_writes_delta
, w2.num_of_bytes_written - w1.num_of_bytes_written as num_of_bytes_written_delta
, w2.io_stall_write_ms - w1.io_stall_write_ms as io_stall_write_ms_delta
, w2.io_stall - w1.io_stall as io_stall_delta
, datediff(ms, w1.sample_time, w2.sample_time) as interval_ms
from #dmv_samples as w1 inner join #dmv_samples as w2 on w1.database_id = w2
.database_id and w1.file_id = w2.file_id
where w1.sample = 1
and w2.sample = 2
order by 1,2

drop table #dmv_samples
```

Table 12-4 shows the resultset for this example. Your results will vary depending on how much work is going on in the database you're looking at when you run the query.

Table 12-4 is a very long table that won't fit on the printed page. It has been broken into three segments for easier viewing.

Table 12-4: Recent Activity Output from sys.dm_io_virtual_file_stats

database_id	file_id	sample_ms_delta	num_of_reads_delta
2	1	10016	181
2	2	10016	0
2	4	10016	190

num_of_bytes_read_delta	io_stall_read_ms_delta	num_of_writes_delta
1482752	4536	353
0	0	0
1556480	5478	347

num_of_bytes_written_delta	io_stall_write_ms_delta	io_stall_delta	interval_ms
16146432	1545	6081	10016
0	0	0	10016
16416768	1487	6965	10016

Using SQLIO

SQLIO is a highly configurable tool for measuring storage performance. One of the biggest challenges facing anyone trying to use SQLIO for the first time is the overwhelming number of options. Without clear guidance it becomes a daunting task to get the tool to give you anything meaningful.

Along with the download comes some sample scripts that Mike Ruthruff, a PM on the SQL Server Customer Advisory team, wrote. These are a great place to start, but you really need to spend quite some time playing with the tool and trying to figure out really what you want to see before you can modify the samples in a way to give you the results you want.

What I am going to share with you here is the methodical process I developed to help assess storage performance. Then I am going to show you how to process the results and end up with a visual representation of the performance of your storage system. Along the way you will look at a couple of performance bottlenecks that I found while setting up a real life SQL Server storage system.

Getting Started with SQLIO

Okay, so much for all the talk. Let's get started with running SQLIO!

The first thing you need to do is download SQLIO from the Microsoft download center. This currently exists at www.microsoft.com/downloads/details.aspx?FamilyID=9a8b005b-84e4-4f24-8d65-cb5344 2d9e19&DisplayLang=en.

The download center occasionally gets reorganized, so the link may get broken. If that's the case then a quick internet search for SQLIO should locate its new home.

After you have downloaded and installed it to your favorite tools folder (I put mine in c:\tools\sqlio as it's short and easy to find), you will see that you received a number of files along with sqlio.exe:

- ❑ **EULA.txt:** This contains all the usual legal stuff.
- ❑ **Param.txt:** This is a sample param file, more on what you use this for later.
- ❑ **Readme.txt:** This is an expanded version of the built in help. This is actually the help file that originally came with SQLIO, so it has lots of really useful details on all the arguments. However, it's worth noting that not all of them work with this version of SQLIO.
- ❑ **Sqlio.exe:** This is the one you want!
- ❑ **Using SQLIO.rtf:** This is a good place to get started on using SQLIO and includes some basic scripts to get you going.

Running SQLIO

Now that you have SQLIO installed, try using it.

The first thing you need to do is to open a command prompt. Because SQLIO is a console app, you can just double click it in Explorer, and it will run. However, because the output goes to the console if you start it by double clicking it, when it's finished the console closes and your results all disappear.

So it's better to run it by opening a command prompt and navigating to the folder where you installed SQLIO. This is one place where the benefit of a short simple path pays dividends.

Now just type SQLIO and you will see results as shown in Figure 12-4.

```
C:\Tools\SQLIO\RTW>Intermediate.bat > intermediate_results.txt
C:\Tools\SQLIO\RTW>
```

Figure 12-4

Without asking, SQLIO ran a test for you. It used a default set of parameters. It used these parameters to create an 8 MB file in the local directory and ran a single threaded read test using a 2 KB block size for 30 seconds on that file.

It is displaying the results from that test, and you can see at the bottom of the display two of the results SQLIO can give you: the IOPS which was 115.03, and the MB/Sec which was 0.22.

Both of these numbers are pretty poor, but then this is on a desktop machine on the system disk while I am writing this in Word, and listening to Windows Media Player stream music, and the OS is doing all kinds of other things that consume disk I/O, so the numbers aren't really a good representation of the potential performance possible from this particular disk.

On a dedicated disk that's not being used for anything other than SQL Server, the results you get may still vary greatly. This is because the results you get on your disk will depend on the following factors:

- ❑ The disks rotational speed, (5400, 7200, 10 K, 15 K rpm)
- ❑ How fast the heads can move from track to track
- ❑ How smart the on disk electronics are at getting the head from one location to the next
- ❑ How big a cache the disk has
- ❑ What interface is being used to connect the disk to the interface card (SCSI, SAS, SATA, ATA)
- ❑ The cache of your interface card
- ❑ Whether the disk is part of a RAID array
- ❑ How the RAID array is configured
- ❑ How efficient the driver is
- ❑ How many other disks are on that interface card
- ❑ What kind of system bus the computer has (PCI, PCI-X, PCI-Express)
- ❑ How many other cards are on the system bus
- ❑ What interface chipset the motherboard has

There are a lot of factors, all of which play a part in determining the performance of the disk subsystem and which will alter the results you get.

Well, that was a good start, but now you really want to get SQLIO working for you. Have a look at some of the arguments you can supply to SQLIO. Go back to the folder where you installed SQLIO, and take some time to read the readme.txt file and the Using sqlio.rtf file.

Running a Basic I/O test

What you want to do now is use SQLIO to run a basic performance test on a disk. You can start doing this with just a single command line, but that only gives you a single data point. What you really need is a series of connected data points so that you can see how the disk actually performs.

There are four basic types of I/O you want to consider: Read, Write, Sequential access, and Random access. You want to know how your disk performs under each of these different I/O types.

However there are also a lot of other ways that I/O can be driven that alter the results you get, so now you have to take a look at some of the other parameters to SQLIO. The key ones you want to manipulate through your performance tests are going to be the block size, the number of threads SQLIO is going to use, and the number of outstanding I/Os it will issue. You also have to determine how big a file you want to use for testing and how long you want to run the test for. Finally you need to tell SQLIO where you want it to create its test file.

Before you get caught up in all the details, let's just do a basic test and see what happens. Following is a basic set of test arguments that will run a 2-minute test and create a 2 GB test file in the root of the D drive.

```
sqlio.exe -kW -s120 -f64 -i512 -b64 -LS D:\TestFileA.dat
```

Figure 12-5 shows the result of this run. Your results will vary depending on your system.

Now you can see the full output that SQLIO will give you. This includes the IOPS and MB/Sec that you saw before, and Min, Avg, and Max latency stats, as well as a great latency histogram.

From this you can see that this disk is currently performing at 10.91 MB/sec and 174.60 IOPS, but you have to qualify this with the I/O type, which was Sequential Write, and the block size, which was 64 KB.

Changing any of the other parameters may well deliver different results, and that's what you really want to see: how the disk delivers different results as you alter one parameter at a time.

Using Parameter Files

One thing you will notice about the preceding example is that it differs from those in the sqlio.rtf file, in that the previous example doesn't use a parameter file to specify the target. I used to use parameter files, but when you get to the Advanced SQLIO examples below, you will see why they are limited, so I switched to not using them.

The basic format of a parameter file is:

```
<Filename> <Number of Threads> <Optional Mask> <Optional File size in MB>
```

A simple example would be to put the following into a file called param.txt:

```
D:\TestFileB.dat 1 0x0 2048
```

Then you would use this in the SQLIO command line:

```
sqlio -kW -s10 -frandom -o8 -b8 -LS -Fparam.txt
```

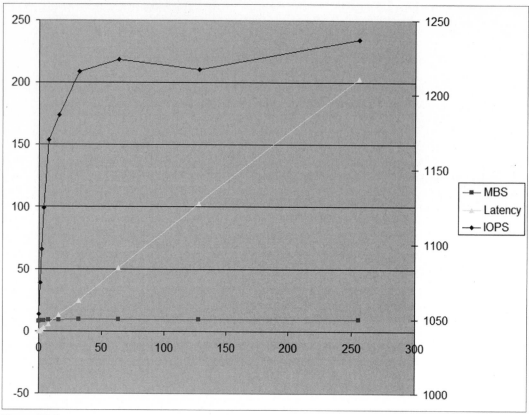

Figure 12-5

This will then run a test with the following parameters:

```
-kW = Write
-s10 = run the test for 10 seconds
-frandom = make the I/Os random
-o8 = use 8 outstanding I/Os
-b8 = Use an 8KB block
-LS = display latencies measured using the system timers
-Fparam.txt = use the param file param.txt
```

Figure 12-6 shows the result of this test.

These results gave you different results, with about the same IOPS but much lower MB/Sec and much higher latency.

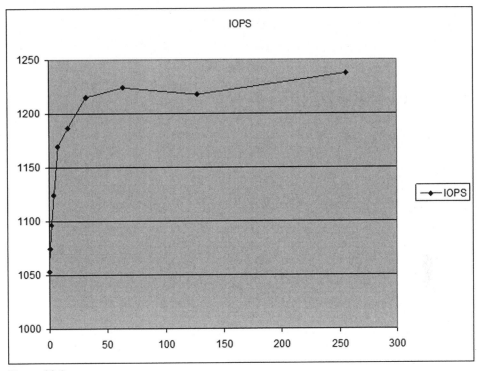

Figure 12-6

Intermediate SQLIO

Now that you have covered the basics of running SQLIO, you need to start putting together some more comprehensive tests that give you more data points so that you can see the I/O characteristics of the disk.

The first set of the tests you are going to run is going to look at the random write performance of the D drive. To do this you will put together a simple batch file that will call SQLIO a number of times, each time with one of the parameters changed. In this test you will keep the duration of each test fixed at 10 seconds, the block size will be fixed at 8 KB, the number of threads will be fixed at one thread, the number of files will be fixed at just one file, and the file size will be fixed at 2 GB. The one parameter you are going to vary is the number of outstanding I/Os, and this parameter will be varied from 0 through 1, 2, 4, 8, 16, and right on up to 256.

The batch file to do this looks like this:

```
call sqlio -kW -s10 -frandom -o0 -b8 -t1 -LS D:\TestFileA.dat
call sqlio -kW -s10 -frandom -o1 -b8 -t1 -LS D:\TestFileA.dat
call sqlio -kW -s10 -frandom -o2 -b8 -t1 -LS D:\TestFileA.dat
call sqlio -kW -s10 -frandom -o4 -b8 -t1 -LS D:\TestFileA.dat
call sqlio -kW -s10 -frandom -o8 -b8 -t1 -LS D:\TestFileA.dat
```

```
call sqlio -kW -s10 -frandom -o16 -b8 -t1 -LS D:\TestFileA.dat
call sqlio -kW -s10 -frandom -o32 -b8 -t1 -LS D:\TestFileA.dat
call sqlio -kW -s10 -frandom -o64 -b8 -t1 -LS D:\TestFileA.dat
call sqlio -kW -s10 -frandom -o128 -b8 -t1 -LS D:\TestFileA.dat
call sqlio -kW -s10 -frandom -o256 -b8 -t1 -LS D:\TestFileA.dat
```

Note that you are relying on the fact that the file `TestFileA.dat` was created in the earlier test. In the advanced section you will see a more comprehensive batch that takes care of the file creation as well. Alternatively you could alter the batch file to use the file `TestFileB.dat` that you created in the earlier example.

If you run this batch file, you are going to end up with results that scroll out of the console's display buffer, so you will lose them unless you do something to redirect the results to file. To facilitate that, the above code was written into `Intermediate.bat`, and run using the following:

```
Intermediate.bat > intermediate_results.txt
```

Now when it runs all you see are the results shown in Figure 12-7.

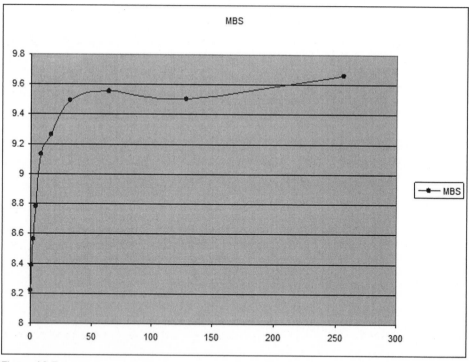

Figure 12-7

Take a look at the results, which should look similar to the following:

```
C:\Tools\SQLIO\RTW>call sqlio -kW -s10 -frandom -o0 -b8 -t1 -LS D:\TestFileA.dat
sqlio v1.5.SG
using system counter for latency timings, 3579545 counts per second
```

```
1 thread writing for 10 secs to file D:\TestFileA.dat
    using 8KB random I/Os
using current size: 2048 MB for file: D:\TestFileA.dat
initialization done
CUMULATIVE DATA:
throughput metrics:
IOs/sec:    125.71
MBs/sec:      0.98
latency metrics:
Min_Latency(ms):  0
Avg_Latency(ms):  7
Max_Latency(ms):  23
histogram:
ms: 0  1  2  3  4  5  6  7  8  9 10 11 12 13 14 15 16 17 18 19 20 21 22 23 24+
%:  3  2  9 18 14  6  0  0  0  0  1 10 19 14  2  0  0  0  0  0  0  0  0  0  0
```

So you have lots of results, but they aren't in a very useful format. What you really want is the results of all the tests in a more compact format that helps you more easily visualize what the numbers all mean.

One way to do this is to use some scripting to parse the results file and extract the relevant information into a CSV-formatted file.

When this is done the results look like the following (note that the results that follow come from a different disk subsystem that the advanced section will cover in more detail):

```
1053.30,8.22,0
1074.40,8.39,0
1096.90,8.56,1
1124.40,8.78,3
1169.64,9.13,6
1186.52,9.26,13
1215.38,9.49,25
1223.54,9.55,51
1217.18,9.50,103
1237.02,9.66,203
```

This list of numbers isn't very interesting as you don't know what each column is. The first column is the number of IOPS, the second column is the throughput in MB/Sec, and the final column is the average latency in mSec.

Now you can put this into either Excel or a SQL database and create either an Excel chart or an SSRS report to help visualize what the data is telling you.

For simplicity you can use Excel, so the results of this test when dropped into Excel and charted are shown in Figure 12-8.

On the chart shown in Figure 12-8, the X axis is the number of outstanding I/Os, the left Y axis is for MB/Sec and Latency, while the right Y axis is for IOPS.

Its always a little challenging getting three very different sets of numbers onto one chart. Excel makes this a little easier by allowing a secondary axis, but in the case of this data, you really need to plot each data series on a separate chart (see Figure 12-9).

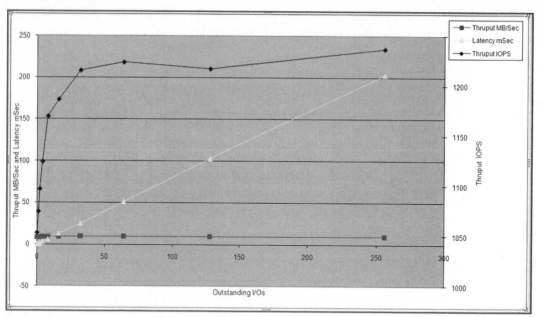

Figure 12-8

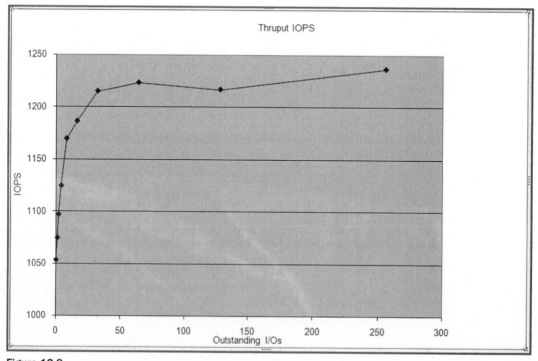

Figure 12-9

430

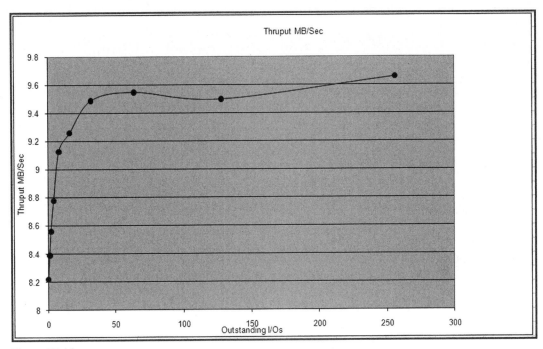

Figure 12-10

The chart shown in Figure 12-10 shows that the number of IOPS very quickly flattens out. The point you are looking for on this chart is the knee in the plot (just before the plot starts to go horizontal, somewhere about mid way between vertical and horizontal). In this case, that's about 1,180 IOPS, and from the X axis that occurred at 16 Outstanding I/Os. It's a little hard to see exactly what the number of outstanding I/Os was when you hit the knee as the scale is so small there. This is where you can go back to the raw data, and once you know what you're looking for, it's easier to find the point in the data that you are looking for.

The chart in Figure 12-11 shows the throughput in MB/Sec. The point you are looking for again is the knee point (where the plot turns from vertical over to horizontal). Somewhere in here is where you hit the maximum realistic throughput, which coincides with the Peak IOPS and is the point at which latency starts to exceed acceptable limits (10 mSec) In this case, the knee is around 9.3–9.5 MB/Sec, and is actually a little higher than the point at which the latency exceeded your limit of 10 mSec. In this case the peak throughput occurred at about 9.5 MB/Sec, although throughput continued to increase slowly, but only as you experienced a completely unacceptable increase in latency up to 200 mSec.

The chart shown in Figure 12-11 shows that you very quickly exceeded the acceptable limits of latency which is 10 mSec. In fact going back to the data you can see that latency was 6 mSec at just 8 outstanding I/Os. Given this, the maximum acceptable throughput for this disk array for this I/O type is 1,169 IOPS and 9 MB/Sec which occurred at 8 outstanding I/Os.

You can use the same technique to test the Random Read and Sequential Read and Write for the storage subsystem.

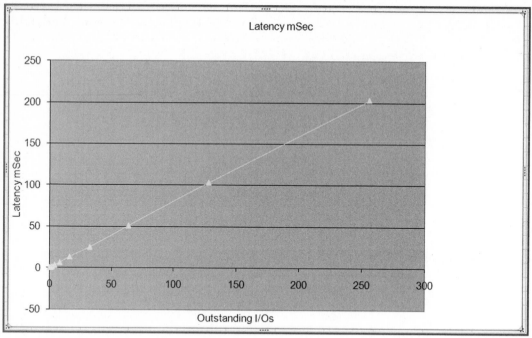

Figure 12-11

Table 12-5: Intermediate SQLIO Results

Outstanding I/Os	Throughput IOPS	Throughput MB/Sec	Latency mSec
0	1053.3	8.22	0
1	1074.4	8.39	0
2	1096.9	8.56	1
4	1124.4	8.78	3
8	**1169.64**	**9.13**	**6**
16	1186.52	9.26	13
32	1215.38	9.49	25
64	1223.54	9.55	51
128	1217.18	9.5	103
256	1237.02	9.66	203

After running all four sets of tests, you can plot all 4 different I/O types on a single chart for that metric, so the results will look similar to Figures 12-12 through 12-14. Figure 12-12 shows the throughput in IOPS. Figure 12-13 shows the throughput in MB/Sec. Figure 12-14 shows the latency in mSec.

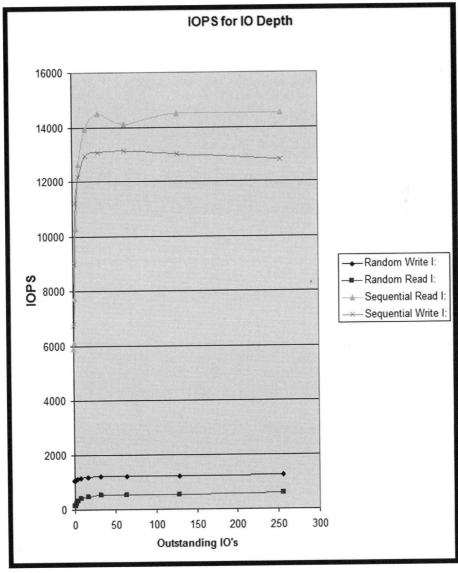

Figure 12-12

Now you have a much more complete picture of the overall performance of this particular disk subsystem as you vary the number of outstanding I/Os.

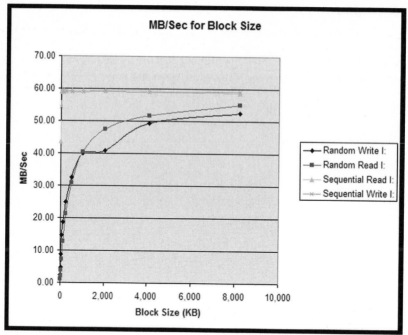

Figure 12-13

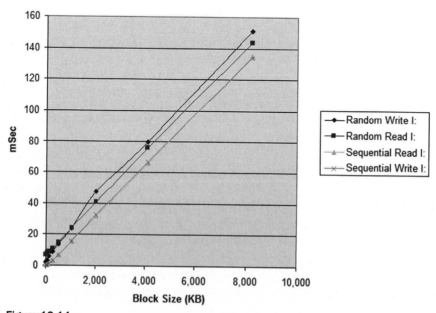

Figure 12-14

Advanced SQLIO

In the intermediate SQLIO section, you saw how to use multiple batch files to test the performance of a storage subsystem as you changed a single I/O characteristic, the number of outstanding I/Os. This only gives you part of the picture of the overall storage subsystem's performance, and you can see that there are a number of other parameters you need to vary to get a full picture of the performance.

The other parameters you have yet to vary are:

- ❑ B - Number of threads
- ❑ C - Number of Files
- ❑ D - Duration
- ❑ E - Block Size

Then there are a number of other factors you might want to test for as well, including:

- ❑ The file size
- ❑ Where the file is on the disk
- ❑ Whether the file was just created

The file size affects the ability of any cache to contain the whole file. A file that's smaller than the available cache can be completely contained in cache. The other factor with file size is how much data you are reading and writing in the test. With a small file size and a high-speed disk system, you stand a good chance of completely reading and writing the whole file, which will guarantee the entire file is in cache by the end of the test. With a much larger file and a slower disk, you stand a good chance that most of the file will not be cached by the end of the test. Depending on what you want to test, you can alter your file size accordingly.

Accessing files located on the outside sectors of a disk is faster than accessing files on the inside of a disk. This is due to the geometry of the disk and the fact that the head, which is fixed, has a higher speed over the surface of the disk on the outside of the disk compared to when it's over the inside. The impact of this is that files created on the outside of the disk will have higher performance than files created on the inside of the disk. One way to observe this is to start with an empty disk and then create 8 test files that completely fill the disk. Test the performance of I/O to the first and last files and compare the results to see this effect.

If the file was created immediately before you run the test, then it will remain cached at the start of the test. A file that's in the cache will show much faster access times than a file that's not in the cache. It's important to test both cached and uncached performance as there will be a large difference between the two sets of results. To test a cached file (warm cache), create a small file ($< 1.0 \times$ the size of the cache) and run the test immediately after creating the file. To test an uncached file (cold cache), create multiple large files (> 2–$4 \times$ size of the cache) and run the test on the first file created. Make sure the test duration and I/O rates are such that the whole file will not be read or written during the test.

Just because these variables are there, that doesn't mean that it's a valuable test to perform. Some of these variables produce useful data; others don't deliver real performance data but can be used to confirm the validity of other results.

Examples of parameters that don't provide good test results are Number of threads, Number of files, and duration of the test (once the test duration is above 3–5 seconds). If you run a series of tests while varying these parameters, the results will be pretty uninteresting. However, you will do this later in the chapter for the sake of completeness, and see just what the results look like.

Next you are going to see a more complex set of batch files that will exercise all of these options.

Best Practice

For each set of tests you run, create a new folder and copy all the test files into that folder.

Give the folder a meaningful name so that when you come back in 2–3 years time, you can still figure out what the test was for. For example:

```
C:\sqlio\tools\test 1 single disk sata raid controller
```

Then run the test from that folder, and all the result files will get put there.

Process all the test results into this folder, and use it to store any notes or additional documentation about the particular I/O configuration you tested.

The following is the complete batch file used to run a single set of tests. In this case this is the set of tests to vary the block size while keeping all other variables constant.

```
@echo off
rem SQLIO test E
rem CONSTANTS
rem Duration = 10s
rem Outstanding I/Os = 0 <DEFAULT>
rem Files = 1
rem File Size = 2GB
rem Threads = 1

rem VARIABLES
rem Block Size= 8,16,32,64,128,256,512,1024,2048,4096,8192

echo #Block Size 8,16,32,64,128,256,512,1024,2048,4096,8192 - 2GB file run for
10 seconds each.

if %1x == x goto Error
echo Test Drive %1:

if exist %1:\TestFileE.dat del %1:\TestFileE.dat

echo Create a 2GB file for testing
call sqlio.exe -kW -s120 -f64 -i512 -b64 -LS %1:\TestFileE.dat

echo Test for RANDOM WRITE
call sqlio -kW -s10 -frandom -t1 -b8 -LS %1:\TestFileE.dat
call sqlio -kW -s10 -frandom -t1 -b16 -LS %1:\TestFileE.dat
call sqlio -kW -s10 -frandom -t1 -b32 -LS %1:\TestFileE.dat
call sqlio -kW -s10 -frandom -t1 -b64 -LS %1:\TestFileE.dat
call sqlio -kW -s10 -frandom -t1 -b128 -LS %1:\TestFileE.dat
call sqlio -kW -s10 -frandom -t1 -b256 -LS %1:\TestFileE.dat
call sqlio -kW -s10 -frandom -t1 -b512 -LS %1:\TestFileE.dat
call sqlio -kW -s10 -frandom -t1 -b1024 -LS %1:\TestFileE.dat
```

```
call sqlio -kW -s10 -frandom -t1 -b2048 -LS %1:\TestFileE.dat
call sqlio -kW -s10 -frandom -t1 -b4096 -LS %1:\TestFileE.dat
call sqlio -kW -s10 -frandom -t1 -b8192 -LS %1:\TestFileE.dat

echo repeat for RANDOM READ
call sqlio -kR -s10 -frandom -t1 -b8 -LS %1:\TestFileE.dat
call sqlio -kR -s10 -frandom -t1 -b16 -LS %1:\TestFileE.dat
call sqlio -kR -s10 -frandom -t1 -b32 -LS %1:\TestFileE.dat
call sqlio -kR -s10 -frandom -t1 -b64 -LS %1:\TestFileE.dat
call sqlio -kR -s10 -frandom -t1 -b128 -LS %1:\TestFileE.dat
call sqlio -kR -s10 -frandom -t1 -b256 -LS %1:\TestFileE.dat
call sqlio -kR -s10 -frandom -t1 -b512 -LS %1:\TestFileE.dat
call sqlio -kR -s10 -frandom -t1 -b1024 -LS %1:\TestFileE.dat
call sqlio -kR -s10 -frandom -t1 -b2048 -LS %1:\TestFileE.dat
call sqlio -kR -s10 -frandom -t1 -b4096 -LS %1:\TestFileE.dat
call sqlio -kR -s10 -frandom -t1 -b8192 -LS %1:\TestFileE.dat

echo repeat for Sequential READ
call sqlio -kR -s10 -fsequential -t1 -b8 -LS %1:\TestFileE.dat
call sqlio -kR -s10 -fsequential -t1 -b16 -LS %1:\TestFileE.dat
call sqlio -kR -s10 -fsequential -t1 -b32 -LS %1:\TestFileE.dat
call sqlio -kR -s10 -fsequential -t1 -b64 -LS %1:\TestFileE.dat
call sqlio -kR -s10 -fsequential -t1 -b128 -LS %1:\TestFileE.dat
call sqlio -kR -s10 -fsequential -t1 -b256 -LS %1:\TestFileE.dat
call sqlio -kR -s10 -fsequential -t1 -b512 -LS %1:\TestFileE.dat
call sqlio -kR -s10 -fsequential -t1 -b1024 -LS %1:\TestFileE.dat
call sqlio -kR -s10 -fsequential -t1 -b2048 -LS %1:\TestFileE.dat
call sqlio -kR -s10 -fsequential -t1 -b4096 -LS %1:\TestFileE.dat
call sqlio -kR -s10 -fsequential -t1 -b8192 -LS %1:\TestFileE.dat

echo repeat for Sequential Write
call sqlio -kW -s10 -fsequential -t1 -b8 -LS %1:\TestFileE.dat
call sqlio -kW -s10 -fsequential -t1 -b16 -LS %1:\TestFileE.dat
call sqlio -kW -s10 -fsequential -t1 -b32 -LS %1:\TestFileE.dat
call sqlio -kW -s10 -fsequential -t1 -b64 -LS %1:\TestFileE.dat
call sqlio -kW -s10 -fsequential -t1 -b128 -LS %1:\TestFileE.dat
call sqlio -kW -s10 -fsequential -t1 -b256 -LS %1:\TestFileE.dat
call sqlio -kW -s10 -fsequential -t1 -b512 -LS %1:\TestFileE.dat
call sqlio -kW -s10 -fsequential -t1 -b1024 -LS %1:\TestFileE.dat
call sqlio -kW -s10 -fsequential -t1 -b2048 -LS %1:\TestFileE.dat
call sqlio -kW -s10 -fsequential -t1 -b4096 -LS %1:\TestFileE.dat
call sqlio -kW -s10 -fsequential -t1 -b8192 -LS %1:\TestFileE.dat

goto Done

:Error
echo Bad args p1 = %1

:Done
echo Test E Complete

echo Deleting Test File
if exist %1:\TestFileE.dat del %1:\TestFileE.dat
rem Test E COMPLETE
```

You can then run this from another batch file like the following. This file runs all the tests from A through E:

```
@echo off
Rem
Rem      RUN_A_E.BAT
Rem
Rem Batch file to execute sqlio tests A,B,C,D,E
Rem will also attempt to start Perfmon counter log called SQLIO
Rem Create this by running the batch file "Logman sqlio.bat"
Rem Will also do a dir of the target disk before and after the test run.
Rem This helps diagnose problems when we run out of disk space.
rem
rem Check we have a drive specified as the first argument
if %1x==x goto Help
if %1x==? goto Help
if %1x==-? goto Help
if %1x==/? goto Help


rem Check disk space first
dir %1: > PreTestDir.txt

echo Start Perfmon
logman start "SQLIO"
echo start all tests

echo start test A
call run_sqlio_testA.bat %1 > run_sqlio_testA.txt

logman stop "SQLIO"
timeout /t 5
logman start "SQLIO"

echo start test B
call run_sqlio_testB.bat %1 > run_sqlio_testB.txt

logman stop "SQLIO"
timeout /t 5
logman start "SQLIO"

echo start test C
call run_sqlio_testC.bat %1 > run_sqlio_testC.txt

logman stop "SQLIO"
timeout /t 5
logman start "SQLIO"

echo start test D
call run_sqlio_testD.bat %1 > run_sqlio_testD.txt

logman stop "SQLIO"
timeout /t 5
logman start "SQLIO"

echo start test E
call run_sqlio_testE.bat %1 > run_sqlio_testE.txt
```

```
logman stop "SQLIO"

rem Post test disk check
dir %1: > PostTestDir.txt
@echo DONE !!!
Goto Done

:Help
@echo ****************************************
@echo *
@echo * Run-A-E.Bat [Drive letter]
@echo *
@echo * You entered :
@echo *  Run-A-E.Bat p1=%1
@echo *
@echo ****************************************

:Done
```

After running this batch file, you end up with test result files for tests A, B, C, D, and E. These all need processing, which you will see in more detail after first learning about setting up a Perfmon counter log using Logman.

Capturing Perfmon Data while Running SQLIO Tests

Logman is a command line utility that ships with the Windows 2000 resource kit and can be used to automate Perfmon from a batch file.

It's very simple and very useful when writing batch files to drive testing.

This is the batch file that uses Logman to create the counter log.

```
@echo off
@echo Create a counter log called SQLIO

call Logman create counter "SQLIO" -si 01 -v nnnnnn -o "c:\perflogs\sqlio"
-c "\LogicalDisk(*)\*" "\PhysicalDisk(*)\*" "\Processor(*)\*" "\System\*"

call logman query "SQLIO"

@echo Done
```

Batch Processing SQLIO Results

Now you have a folder full of test results, and you need to do some processing on them to turn them into data where you can visualize what's happening with your I/O performance, and have the raw data available for easier examination and comparison.

To do this you can use a simple VBScript file, a batch file, and Excel with a macro to load the results into a workbook already setup with charts to show the results. The first step is to convert the raw output from SQLIO into a CSV file. Do this by using the batch file Process-All-Results.bat. After running this batch file, you will have a folder full of CSV files, one for each of the tests you ran.

Next you need to get the results into Excel.

439

Displaying SQLIO Results

There are at least two ways to display the results. You can import the results CSV files into a SQL database, and write your own SQL Server Reporting Services reports to display the results, or you can use Excel. The Excel option is easy to transport to different systems and allows you to keep all the results data in the same place.

On the web site for the book in the folder for this chapter, there is a file called SQLIO_RESULTS.XLS. To load the results into Excel, start by opening the Excel spreadsheet SQLIO_RESULTS.XLS. You may need to alter your security settings as the spreadsheet contains macros, and Office security disables these by default.

Once you have the spreadsheet open and macros enabled, you can import all the results by running the macro LoadAtoE. This requires that the results be in the same folder as the spreadsheet, which is the best place to keep everything so that multiple test runs each live in their own folder.

After running the macro, you will now have all the test results loaded and have charts showing all the I/O results.

Best Practice

After processing the results into sqlio_results.xls, rename the file to include something that helps distinguish this copy of the results spreadsheet. Excel doesn't like opening multiple copies of a workbook with the same name. And by using a unique name for each copy of the results file, it's easier to navigate between multiple results for comparison.

Interpreting I/O Results

Now that you have all the test results in a visual format, you can take a look at some of the results. The results you are looking at here come from a 4 disk SATA RAID 0 array I threw together for the purpose of showing some real life test results for this book. I am using RAID 0 for this array as its for a read only database system that's completely reloaded from a source database every night. The users are also able to deal with a loss of the system for a day if any failure occurs and the database needs to be rebuilt and reloaded from scratch.

In a production system you should ideally be using RAID 1 + 0 (striping and mirroring) or a variation of one of the RAID types that uses mirroring and not PARITY for its redundancy. A discussion on the merits of different RAID types is beyond the scope of this chapter, but there are many excellent resources online if you need to read up on the different RAID types.

For example, if you wanted to look for any possible bottlenecks in the storage subsystem and see how well the subsystem scaled from 1 to 4 disks, you could do the following: When putting the array together, first configure the four disks as four separate disks, and then run the full set of tests on one of the disks. Then reconfigure the array as 2 × 2 disk stripe sets and again rerun the full set of tests. Finally, configure the array as a four-disk stripe set (RAID 0) and rerun the full set of tests.

1 Disk Tests

Let's take a look at the results of the 1 disk test for Test E, Altering Block Size (see Figures 12-15 through 12-17).

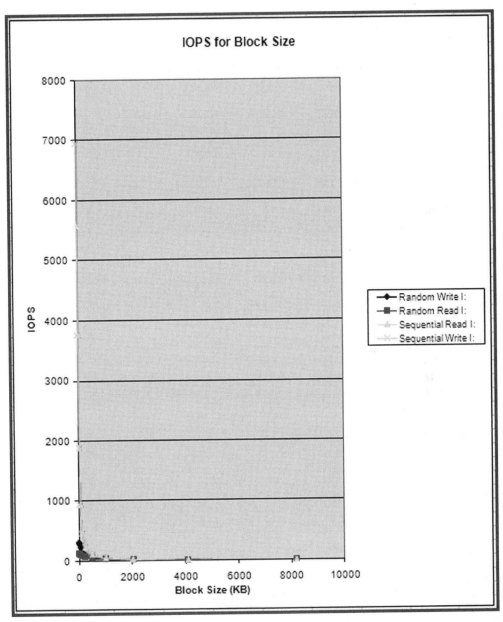

Figure 12-15

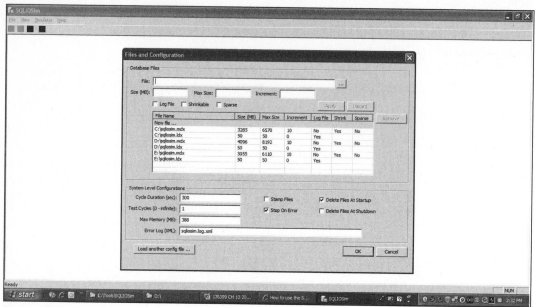

Figure 12-16

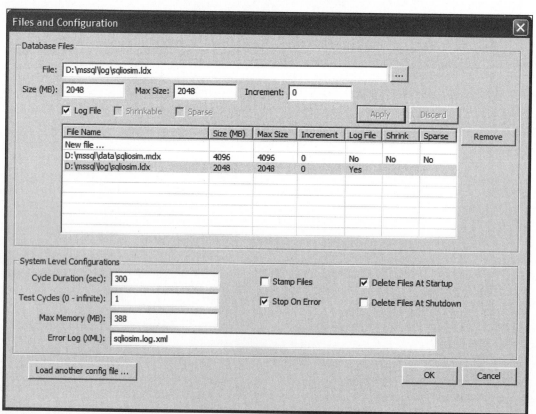

Figure 12-17

The raw data for this test is shown in Table 12-6.

Table 12-6: Single-Disk Test Results

Read/Write	Sequential/Random	Block Size	IOPS	MB/Sec	Avg Latency
W	random	8	310.10	2.42	2
W	random	16	298.30	4.66	2
W	random	32	278.50	8.70	3
W	random	64	234.80	14.67	3
W	random	128	149.69	18.71	6
W	random	256	99.40	24.85	9
W	random	512	65.00	32.50	14
W	random	1,024	40.03	40.03	24
W	random	2,048	20.46	40.93	48
W	random	4,096	12.32	49.28	80
W	random	8,192	6.57	52.63	151
R	random	8	130.69	1.02	7
R	random	16	130.00	2.03	7
R	random	32	123.60	3.86	7
R	random	64	117.40	7.33	8
R	random	128	102.50	12.81	9
R	random	256	85.50	21.37	11
R	random	512	61.50	30.75	15
R	random	1,024	40.40	40.40	24
R	random	2,048	23.72	47.45	41
R	random	4,096	12.93	51.75	76
R	random	8,192	6.87	55.02	144
R	sequential	8	5,586.80	43.64	0

Continued

Table 12-6: Single-Disk Test Results (continued)

Read/Write	Sequential/Random	Block Size	IOPS	MB/Sec	Avg Latency
R	sequential	16	3,767.30	58.86	0
R	sequential	32	1,892.50	59.14	0
R	sequential	64	948.30	59.26	0
R	sequential	128	474.10	59.26	1
R	sequential	256	237.00	59.25	3
R	sequential	512	118.60	59.30	7
R	sequential	1,024	59.30	59.30	16
R	sequential	2,048	29.65	59.31	32
R	sequential	4,096	14.83	59.32	66
R	sequential	8,192	7.34	58.74	135
W	sequential	8	6,958.20	54.36	0
W	sequential	16	3,765.30	58.83	0
W	sequential	32	1,884.40	58.88	0
W	sequential	64	947.40	59.21	0
W	sequential	128	470.40	58.80	1
W	sequential	256	236.40	59.10	3
W	sequential	512	118.00	59.00	7
W	sequential	1,024	59.00	59.00	16
W	sequential	2,048	29.55	59.10	33
W	sequential	4,096	14.75	59.01	67
W	sequential	8,192	7.38	59.11	134

Now let's see what you can determine as the I/O characteristics of this single disk.

To start off with, you want to know what is the max throughput you can possibly get from this disk at an acceptable latency (max of 10mSec). That's a fairly easy one; you need to find the highest MB/Sec figure (and the corresponding IOPS) where latency is < 10 msec. From just looking through the data, you can see that this occurs at about 59 MB/Sec, and this is for Sequential access, and you are getting similar numbers of both Read and Write. Now the IOPS is a little more difficult, as you are getting about the same MB/Sec, but with different block sizes you get very different IOPS numbers. However this is what you should expect. The disk is capable of transferring a maximum of 59 MB/Sec, and it can either do that as a lot of small accesses or fewer larger accesses. The limits to this seem to be that you can go down to 16–32K blocks before throughput drops below 58.86 MB/Sec, and you can go up to 1024–2048 KB before seeing latency go above 10 mSec.

So, you could reasonably characterize this disk as being capable of 60 MB/Sec for 16 KB to 2048 KB Sequential Reads and Writes.

Its Random access capabilities are lower. You only got 24.85 MB/Sec and 99.40 IOPS at 256 KB block size for Random Write, and 12.81 MB/Sec and 102.50 IOPS at 128 KB block size for Random Read. (However, the next result for Random read at 21.37 MB/Sec and 85.50 IOPS is only at 11 mSec latency, so you might rerun this test two to three more times and see if you can get that latency to drop, or alternatively use the higher figure with a caveat that it's just above the acceptable latency limit.)

2 Disk Tests 32 KB Stripe

The next step was to configure two of the disks into a stripe set and rerun the tests. Following is the table of results for that set of tests. There were a number of options for setting the stripe size for the array, and the smallest at 32K was chosen for this test.

Stripe Size

The Stripe Size is the amount of data written to each disk in the stripe set before a write moves on to the next disk in the set. For writes smaller than the stripe size, the write will only go to one disk, provided the write is aligned. For more on disk alignment, see Chapter 6.

For writes larger than the stripe size, the write will go to (write size/stripe size) disks. The benefit of this is that you can now write to more than one disk at the same time, thus increasing the throughput to the disk.

Table 12-7: Two-Disk Test E Results

Read/Write	Sequential/Random	Block Size	IOPS	MB/Sec	Avg Latency
W	random	8	495.9	3.87	1
W	random	16	412.2	6.44	1
W	random	32	311.7	9.74	2
W	random	64	285	17.81	2
W	random	128	198.4	24.8	4

Continued

Table 12-7: Two-Disk Test E Results (continued)

Read/Write	Sequential/Random	Block Size	IOPS	MB/Sec	Avg Latency
W	random	256	150.6	37.65	6
W	random	512	102.7	51.35	9
W	random	1024	73.4	73.4	13
W	random	2048	33.84	67.69	29
W	random	4096	20.23	80.94	48
W	random	8192	11.36	90.91	87
R	random	8	133.9	1.04	6
R	random	16	124.6	1.94	7
R	random	32	114.7	3.58	8
R	random	64	110.5	6.9	8
R	random	128	100.8	12.6	9
R	random	256	90.3	22.57	10
R	random	512	66.2	33.1	14
R	random	1024	39	39	25
R	random	4096	16.14	64.59	61
R	random	8192	10.1	80.8	98
R	sequential	8	5552.8	43.38	0
R	sequential	16	4082.5	63.78	0
R	sequential	32	2593.4	81.04	0
R	sequential	64	1555.6	97.22	0
R	sequential	128	789.7	98.71	1
R	sequential	256	411.2	102.8	2
R	sequential	512	205	102.5	4
R	sequential	1024	102.3	102.3	9

Continued

Table 12-7: Two-Disk Test E Results (continued)

Read/Write	Sequential/Random	Block Size	IOPS	MB/Sec	Avg Latency
R	sequential	2048	51.6	103.2	18
R	sequential	4096	26	104	37
R	sequential	8192	13.05	104.46	76
W	sequential	8	6898.2	53.89	0
W	sequential	16	4398.6	68.72	0
W	sequential	32	2722.7	85.08	0
W	sequential	64	1494.1	93.38	0
W	sequential	128	771.9	96.48	1
W	sequential	256	394.4	98.6	2
W	sequential	512	202.1	101.05	4
W	sequential	1024	99.6	99.6	9
W	sequential	2048	50.61	101.23	19
W	sequential	4096	25.45	101.83	38
W	sequential	8192	12.76	102.08	77

Let's do the same process of finding the max throughput for each I/O type again. First off let's look for the maximum throughput. This time you got 102.3 MB/Sec and 102.3 IOPS for 1024 KB Sequential Reads at 9mSec latency. In comparison Sequential Write managed 99.6 MB/Sec and 99.6 IOPS again at 1024 KB and 9mSec latency.

Random access performance was proportionally similar to the 1 disk results in that the best random write results were at 51.35 MB/Sec and 102.7 IOPS for 512 KB blocks and 9 mSec latency. Random Read performance peaked at 12.6 MB/Sec and 100.8 IOPS for 128 KB blocks and 9 mSec latency.

4 Disk Tests 32 KB Stripe

The next step was to reconfigure the array into a 4-disk stripe set. The smallest stripe size of 32 KB was chosen again.

Before you look at the results, let's take a quick guess at what you might think you should see this time. Let's go back and summarize the changes between the 1 disk and 2 disk results, and from there extrapolate what you should get for the 4 disk tests.

Table 12-8 lists the MB/Sec results.

Table 12-8: Summary of 1 and 2 Disk Test Results

Test	1 Disk	2 Disk
Random Read	12.81	12.6
Random Write	24.85	51.35
Sequential Read	59	102.3
Sequential Write	59	99.6

So it looks like Random Read will stay at around 12 MB/Sec, Random Write should almost double to close to 100 MB/Sec, and sequential access should double to around 200 MB/Sec.

Let's take a look at the results and see what you actually got (see Table 12-9).

Table 12-9: Four-Disk Test E Results

Read/Write	Sequential/Random	Block Size	IOPS	MB/Sec	Avg Latency
W	random	8	1037.4	8.1	0
W	random	16	857	13.39	0
W	random	32	625.29	19.54	1
W	random	64	344.5	21.53	2
W	random	128	255.9	31.98	3
W	random	256	171.8	42.95	5
W	random	512	130.4	65.2	7
W	random	1024	95.9	95.9	9
W	random	8192	11.82	94.6	83
R	random	8	140.4	1.09	6
R	random	16	136.4	2.13	6
R	random	32	123.9	3.87	7

Continued

Table 12-9: Four-Disk Test E Results (continued)

Read/Write	Sequential/Random	Block Size	IOPS	MB/Sec	Avg Latency
R	random	64	112.5	7.03	8
R	random	128	101.7	12.71	9
R	random	256	93	23.25	10
R	random	512	54.71	27.35	17
R	random	1024	36.6	36.6	26
R	random	2048	29.8	59.6	33
R	random	4096	18.2	72.8	54
R	random	8192	10.84	86.79	91
R	sequential	8	6102.1	47.67	0
R	sequential	16	4025.4	62.89	0
R	sequential	32	2649.8	82.8	0
R	sequential	64	1553	97.06	0
R	sequential	128	820.3	102.53	1
R	sequential	256	424	106	2
R	sequential	512	218.1	109.05	4
R	sequential	1024	110.8	110.8	8
R	sequential	2048	55.9	111.8	17
R	sequential	4096	28.15	112.61	35
R	sequential	8192	14.15	113.24	70
W	sequential	8	6636	51.84	0
W	sequential	16	4635	72.42	0
W	sequential	32	2549.3	79.66	0
W	sequential	64	1462	91.37	0

Continued

Table 12-9: Four-Disk Test E Results (continued)

Read/Write	Sequential/Random	Block Size	IOPS	MB/Sec	Avg Latency
W	sequential	128	754.4	94.3	1
W	sequential	256	392.2	98.05	2
W	sequential	512	194.2	97.1	4
W	sequential	1024	100.6	100.6	9
W	sequential	2048	50.51	101.03	19
W	sequential	4096	25.4	101.6	38
W	sequential	8192	12.8	102.4	77
W	random	2048	39.5	79	24
W	random	4096	22.23	88.92	44

Starting from the top, you got a best result for Random Write of the 95.9 MB/Sec with 95.9 IOPS for 1024 KB blocks at 9 mSec latency. That's pretty close to the predicted results.

For Random Read you got 12.71 MB/Sec with 101.7 IOPS at 128 KB block size and 9 mSec latency. Again this is exactly what you predicted.

For Sequential Read you got 110.8 MB/Sec and 110.8 IOPS for 1024 KB blocks at 8 mSec latency. That's nowhere near the 200 MB/Sec that was predicted.

For Sequential Write you got 100.6 MB/Sec and 100.6 IOPS for 1024 KB blocks at 9 mSec latency. Again this is nowhere near the numbers you predicted, so now you need to go figure out why you aren't getting what you expected.

Before looking for the bottleneck, do one final test run using a different stripe size to see if this has any impact.

Testing Multiple Configurations

There are a lot of other configurations you could run tests against. For best results, test as many different configurations as possible. Process the results, write them up, and store the results somewhere safe so that you can refer back to them in the future when you are investigating a possible storage performance issue or when you are considering a storage configuration change and need to compare the results for the new configuration against the results from this set of tests.

Investigating Storage Bottlenecks

It's beyond the scope of this book to go into the details of how to troubleshoot storage bottlenecks. However, it can show you how you may want to approach this particular problem. Read Chapter 6 for more details on storage configuration, and also look for the latest Best Practices from the SQL Server best practices team on storage configuration.

Mapping Out the Storage Subsystem

The first thing that was done in this case was to draw out each part of the storage stack from the CPU through to the disk surface and attempt to put the theoretical bandwidth for each piece of the stack. Figure 12-18 shows the storage stack.

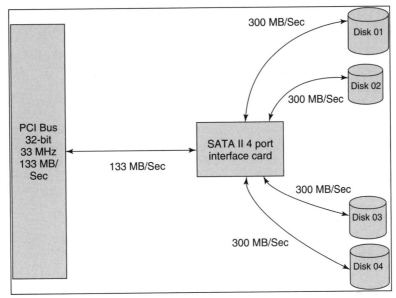

Figure 12-18

I had to go digging into the motherboards spec to get the details for the I/O chipset, and the PCI bus, and as soon as I drew the diagram with these details, the bottleneck became obvious. It's the PCI bus. As an older machine, this machine only has a 32-bit, 33 MHz PCI bus, and the maximum theoretical throughput on this bus is 133 MB/Sec. I normally expect to see about 70–80 percent of the theoretical throughput as the real life achievable throughput, and 80 percent of 133 MB/Sec is 106 MB/Sec, which is pretty close to the maximum results you saw.

Although at first this might seem to be a big problem, you are still getting 100 MB/Sec from this four-disk array, and the random write throughput is now at almost 100 MB/Sec.

Random Read Performance

You might be questioning why Random Read performance didn't increase as you added more disks to the array. This is because adding more disks doesn't help Random Read performance. A Random Read requires that the controller find a new location on the disk, and it requires a full seek to get the heads to the new location. Adding disks won't increase the speed with which a single disk can rotate to the correct location and the disk's head can move to the correct track.

The only way to increase random read throughput is to buy faster disks or add more memory to the controller for its read cache and hope that you get a lot of cache hits, although even with a massive read cache, you still want to know what the cost of a cold (cache miss) random read is versus the cost of a hot read (reading from the cache).

Another way you might see an increase in random read performance that is really cheating is when you increase the block size to the extent that you do a single random read to the head of a massive block and then get sequential access to the rest of the block. I don't really count this as meaningful random read performance, but some folks selling disks might try this on you to sell their disks/disk array by trying to persuade you that their system has better random read performance.

Random Write Performance

Given this information about Random Read performance, why then do random writes increase as you add disks? The reason for this is because as you add more disks there is a greater chance that you can spread your writes across multiple disks, so the controller can parallelize writes to all disks in the array when there are enough writes. The other way that writes benefit is that random writes will benefit greatly from even a small cache on the controller. This allows the controller to turn a seemingly random stream of writes into blocks of sequential writes to each disk.

WARNING!

This can be seriously dangerous to the health of your SQL data if you allow write caching when the controller doesn't have battery backup to ensure the writes are written in the event of a power failure.

If in doubt turn off write caching and suffer slower performance, but have the benefit of knowing your data is secure.

Comparing I/O Results

In the previous pages you have looked at the performance characteristics of several different test configurations using just one of many tests that are available in the suite of tests provided with the code for this book.

One question you should ask yourself as you read this is how you can use these tests to compare different storage configurations. Table 12-8 showed how you can compare thruput from two different disk subsystems. In this case, the results from Test E were used (the test where block size was varied). If your target system has very specific I/O characteristics, then you should consider creating a customized test to exercise the I/O characteristics of your target system.

If you're not really sure what your target system's I/O characteristics will be, then a set of general purpose tests like those provided here is a great place to start.

Run the tests on each configuration, then examine the test results looking for the best throughput for each I/O type: Random Read (R-R), Random Write (R-W), Sequential Read (S-R), and Sequential Write (S-W).

Extract the throughput in MB/Sec, and note the latency and IOPS (and relevant block size) at which the maximum values were obtained. Now that you have a set of four values (MB/Sec for R-R. R-W, S-R, S-W) that represent the maximum throughput of each test configuration, you can much more easily compare different systems than when you are looking at either a lot of lines plotted on charts or large tables of numbers.

Here is a table of real-life test results from a number of different storage subsystems. Using this approach it is easy to identify the storage with the best throughput.

Table 12-10: SQLIO Summary Results from Different Storage Subsystems

System	Random Write	Random Read	Sequential Read	Sequential Write
A	96 MB/s at 1 MB	23 MB/s at 256 KB	110 MB/s at 1 MB	100 MB/s at 1 MB
B	101 MB/s at 1 MB	24 MB/s at 256 KB	114 MB/s at 1 MB	104 MB/s at 1 MB
C	38 MB/s at 256 KB	12 MB/s at 128 KB	126 MB/s at 1 MB	35 MB/s at 256 KB
D	14 MB/s at 128 KB	3 MB/s at 32 KB	96 MB/s at 512 KB	16 MB/s at 128 KB
E	26 MB/s at 256 KB	17 MB/s at 128 KB	118 MB/s at 1 MB	31 MB/s at 256 KB
F	96 MB/s at 1 MB	193 MB/s at 2 MB	195 MB/s at 2 MB	159 MB/s at 1 MB

All the results in the table are MB/Sec at max latency of 10 mSec. These results are from running test E, which varies the block size. The block size is given for each result. Here is a further breakdown:

❑ System A is a desktop system with a four-port SATA adapter on a PCI bus. The four disks are configured as a single RAID 0 stripe set using a 32 K stripe size. This adapter has a 64 MB cache that is not configurable.

❑ System B is the same as system A with the exception that this time the array is configured using a 128 KB stripe size.

❑ System C is a rack mounted server system with 4 × 73 GB SCSI disks, using a caching RAID controller. The cache on the controller is believed to be 128 MB. The four disks are configured into a RAID 0 array with an 8 KB stripe size.

❑ System D, same as system C but using RAID 5 with 8 KB stripe.

❑ System E, same as system C but using RAID 10 and an 8 KB stripe.

❑ System F is another rack mounted server, this time connected to an Enterprise class SAN system with 120 × 10 K rpm SCSI disks. The SAN has 64 GB cache, and is connected to the server via 4 × 2 Gb fibers onto 2 × dual port HBAs. The limiting factor in these tests is that any single path to the SAN has a maximum capacity of around 200 MB/Sec, which is the approximate max throughput of a single 2 Gb fiber.

Note that the random read and write times are very high. This is because when reading and writing large blocks, you pay the price of just one costly seek, and then the remainder of the block is transferred by sequential I/O. This maximizes the performance of the storage. It doesn't necessarily give you the best set of results to see what real-life performance will be like.

To see the storage at its worst, see the results from a test where there is a small block size and little ability for the storage to use its cache such as in Test A or Test B.

Don't forget that it's not always going to be the system with the highest throughput that is the best system for any given solution. You have to ensure that the I/O characteristics of the system tested match the I/O requirements of the target system. It's no good choosing a configuration that delivers excellent results for large block size sequential reads and writes if you are building a system that will be issuing very high numbers of small block size random reads and writes.

SQLIO Best Practices

Make sure the size of the file is 2–4 times larger than your disk cache.

Run the test for long enough to ensure you're getting the results you want.

Share your results with the rest of the team, including the hardware vendor, to validate the results and investigate unexpected outcomes.

Run a full set of tests every time you change anything in the storage configuration.

Compare I/O perf results with observations from Perfmon captured daily, weekly, and monthly.

Look for changes in I/O performance over time to indicate a potential performance-to-reliability issue.

Test failure scenarios. Pull a disk from your raid array and see what happens to performance with the disk missing, *and* when the array is rebuilding when you replace it!

Storage Reliability

To help build your confidence in the robustness and reliability of your storage subsystem you need to run a stress test. There are a number of tools you can use for this. LoadSim and JetStress are I/O stress tools optimized for Exchange I/O patterns. IOMeter is another highly configurable open source I/O stress tool. This chapter focuses on the latest I/O stress test tool from Microsoft: SQLIOSim.

SQLIOStress is a tool written by the SQL Server support team. It was the preferred tool for stress testing SQL Server I/O, but has since been replaced by SQLIOSim.

SQLIOSim

SQLIOSim is a new I/O stress tool that simulates SQL Server 2005 I/O patterns. It was written by the SQL Server engine team and is based upon the same code that SQL Server uses for its I/O. Like SQLIOStress, SQLIOSim doesn't require SQL Server to be installed to run and is a standalone stress test tool.

SQLIOSim is the I/O stress test tool of preference for stress testing an I/O subsystem that's going to be used with SQL Server.

Using SQLIOSim

The first step is to download the tool from the Microsoft download center. The starting point for this is to find the related KB article. Currently this is 231619 and is located at http://support.microsoft.com/kb/231619.

After downloading the appropriate msi and installing it to your favorite location (here: c:\tools\sqliosim) the next step is to figure out how to run it, and how to get it to test the disks you want tested.

There are actually two executables in the download: sqliosim.exe which is the GUI version and sqliosim.com, which is the console app version. You are going to start out using the GUI version so you can get started quickly, but will then switch to using the console app as this is the version you will run from command files in automated testing.

If you are running this on a machine running Windows Vista, then you will find that the GUI throws up an error when you first start it. This is because SQLIOSim is trying to be helpful by scanning your PC for local disks and attempting to create default test files in the root of each disk on first startup. Unfortunately Vista doesn't like anyone creating files in the root of the C drive, so you will get two error messages about creating c:\sqliosim.mdx and sqliosim.ldx. You can either turn off UAC in Vista and restart your PC or just ignore the errors and add additional files elsewhere on the C drive later.

After starting the GUI application for the first time, you are presented with the default configuration screen which on my Vista laptop with C and D drives (and after UAC prevented SQLIOSim from creating files on C) looks like Figure 12-19. The screen you see will vary from this depending on the OS you are running and how many disks your system has.

The first thing you want to do is change the configuration to point to the disk you want to test. In this example, this is the D drive, at a location called d:\mssql\data and d:\mssql\log.

To do that the additional default files specified on C and E had to be deleted, and the name and settings of the default data and log file on the D drive had to be changed. The max size of the data file was changed to 4096 and the increment was set to 0. Futhermore, the following was changed: The size of the log file was set to 2048 MB and autogrow was turned off by setting the max size to be the same as the size. The increment for the Log was already 0. On your system, there might be some minor differences, but the process will be similar.

One thing to note is that SQLIOSim uses the default file extensions mdx and ldx rather than the SQL Server defaults of mdf and ldf. If you don't like these extensions, you can change them to anything you like. One reason for leaving them as is would be that you can't then confuse files created by SQL Server with files created by SQLIOSim, and if you're running SQLIOSim on a system with SQL Server already installed, you won't be able to destroy the data in any database files by running SQLIOSim on the same files.

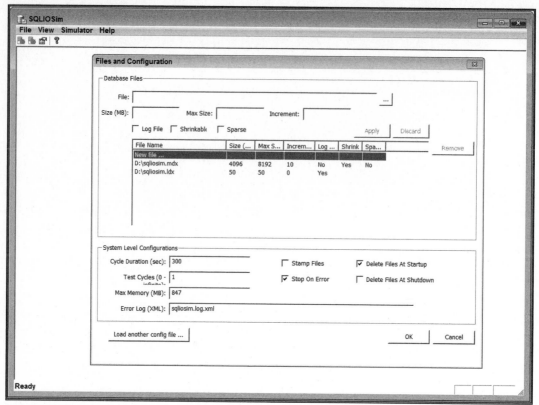

Figure 12-19

Figure 12-20 shows the configuration dialog after making these changes.

After making these changes and accepting the new configuration, it's time to start the test run. You can do this either by clicking the run test button on the toolbar or by selecting the menu item Simulator ⇨ Start (or press F12).

After starting the test, SQLIOSim immediately springs into life, with the main display now split into test status at the top and Log information at the bottom (see Figure 12-21).

If you are running on Vista and you didn't disable UAC, then you will immediately see a couple of errors reported as SQLIOSim attempts to read attributes from the root of the D drive. A workaround for these is to use Run As and run SQLIOSim as an Administrator.

The default test time is 300 seconds and the default number of iterations is 1, so after 5 minutes you have some results to go look at.

After the test completes, the status section of the display will disappear. What remains is the log of results. I'm not going to reproduce it here as it's particularly verbose, but what you are looking for in the test results is any indication of errors.

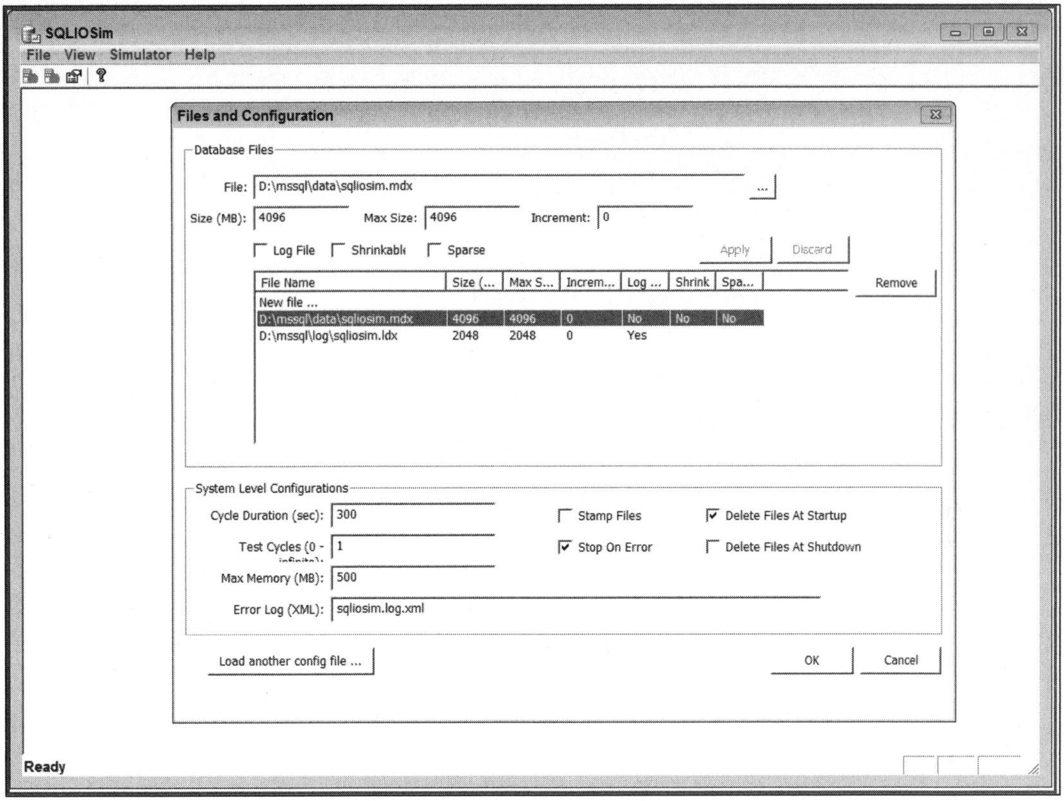

Figure 12-20

On most of my other systems, you can see a set of results comparable to Figure 12-21.

Running SQLIOSim on a Windows XP machine resulted in two errors. Errors are highlighted in red in the Log viewer. You can see them both in Figure 12-22.

Take a look at the details and see what the errors are all about.

First off the User is CreateFileStream. The description of the error is "Unable to get disk cache info for D:\" and scrolling over to the right a bit reveals that the function is CLogicalFile::GetDiskGeom. The results also show that the source file is `fileio.cpp`, and that this function lives at line 382. Unless you have source access, this really isn't much use, but it is kind of interesting.

With this information, you can deduce that the error was caused because SQLIOSim had trouble reading my disk's geometry information. As this is a local IDE disk, there's nothing to worry about.

According to blog entries for SQLIOSim, this error is in fact a known bug in SQLIOSim that will be fixed in a future release. These entries are a great place to get started with finding out more about using SQLIOSim. You can find these blogs by doing a web search for *SQLIOSim*. One of the best is the PSS SQL Server Engineers blog.

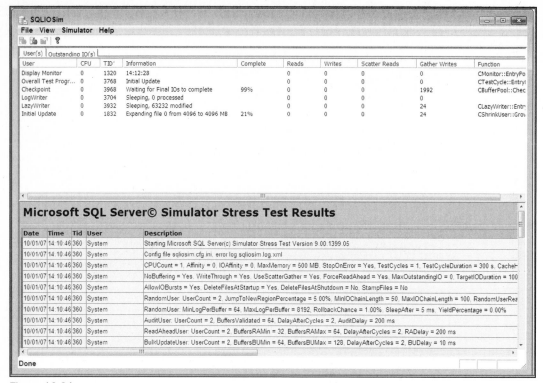

Figure 12-21

Figure 12-22

This event is just a warning, and not an error, so it can be discarded as a potential reliability issue. Other errors should be investigated fully.

Later in the chapter you will look into the results in more detail.

Best Practice for SQLIOSim Test Duration

The default configuration for SQLIOSim is to run only for 5 minutes. In most cases that isn't long enough to uncover deep problems, and the best practice is that you configure SQLIOSim to run for at least two hours, and preferably longer to uncover any potential storage reliability issues. To configure this, change the test configuration so that it now uses a test duration of 600 seconds, or 10 minutes, and change the number of cycles to 12 to get a 2-hour test, or 18 for a 3-hour test (see Figure 12-23).

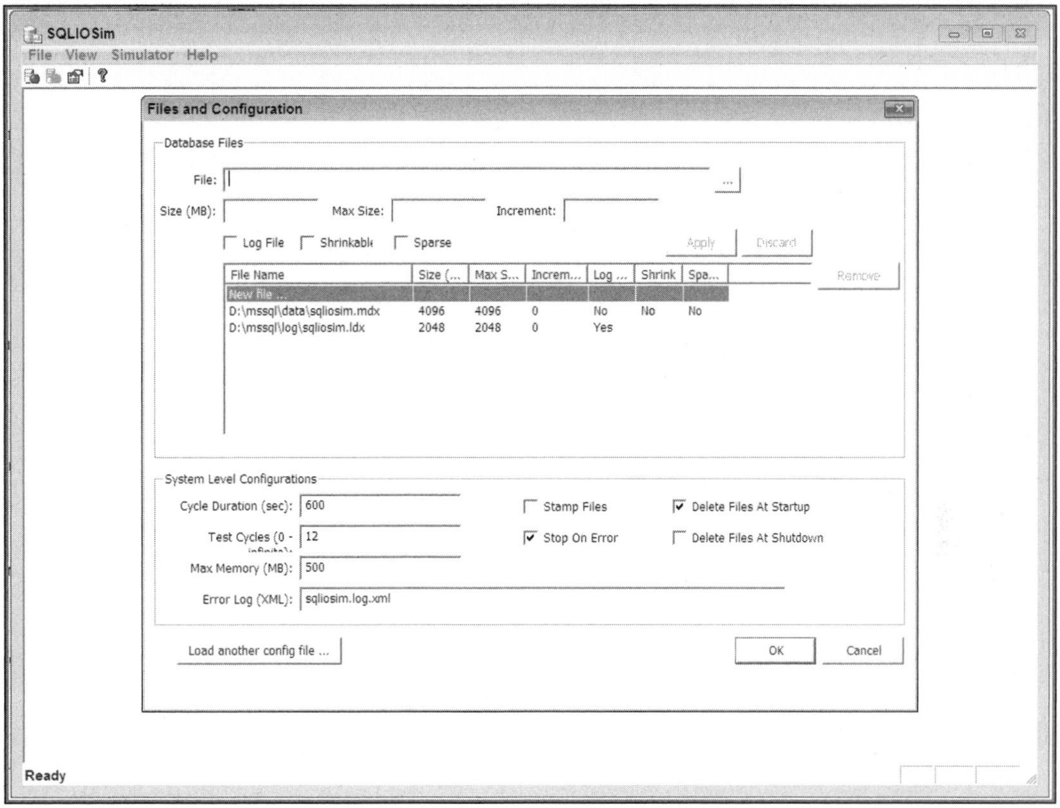

Figure 12-23

Running Other Tests

In the download for SQLIOSim, there are several additional configuration files you can use as the basis for tests, and there is a wealth of information about all the different parameters that you can configure in your configuration files.

For now let's run through each of the different config files supplied and see what they give you.

The first problem is that all the config files have files specified on an F drive. Assuming that, like me, you don't have an F drive, when you try to open the config file, SQLIOSim throws an error and clears any config settings it seems to have read from the file.

To overcome this requires a little bit of XML hacking through Notepad. All you need to do is edit the XML file and change the `FileName=` lines from this:

```
[File1]
FileName=f:\sqliosim.mdx
InitialSize=100
MaxSize=100
```

```
Increment=10
Shrinkable=FALSE
LogFile=FALSE
Sparse=FALSE

[File2]
FileName=f:\sqliosim.ldx
InitialSize=50
MaxSize=50
Increment=0
Shrinkable=FALSE
LogFile=TRUE
Sparse=FALSE
```

To this:

```
[File1]
FileName=D:\mssql\data\sqliosim.mdx
InitialSize=100
MaxSize=100
Increment=10
Shrinkable=FALSE
LogFile=FALSE
Sparse=FALSE

[File2]
FileName=D:\mssql\log\sqliosim.ldx
InitialSize=50
MaxSize=50
Increment=0
Shrinkable=FALSE
LogFile=TRUE
Sparse=FALSE
```

Your values might differ from this, and will reflect the disks available on your system.

Now that's done, and you can save the file. SQLIOSim will open the CFG file and let you run the test.

Take a look at each of the pre-configured INI files and see what they give you.

- ❑ Sqliosim.hwcache.cfg.ini
    - ❑ Minimizes reads
    - ❑ Makes files small to keep them fully in memory
    - ❑ No sequential reads
- ❑ Sqliosim.nothrottle.cfg.ini
    - ❑ Removes I/O throttling
    - ❑ Minimizes the time to wait to increase I/O volume
- ❑ Sqliosim.seqwrites.cfg.ini
    - ❑ Minimizes reads
    - ❑ Makes files small to keep them fully in memory

❑ Makes files non-shrinkable

❑ No sequential reads

❑ No random access

❑ Bulk updates in big chunks without delays

❑ Sqliosim.sparse.cfg.ini

  ❑ Uses only 32 MB of memory

  ❑ Makes target I/O duration large enough to enable many outstanding I/O requests

  ❑ Disables scatter/gather APIs to issue separate I/O requests for every 8 KB page

  ❑ Creates a 1 GB non-shrinkable file

  ❑ Creates a 1 GB non-shrinkable secondary sparse stream in the file

Although these are a good set of options, what you are looking for is something that simulates the I/O activity on your OLTP, or DSS system, and then you might also look at a range of other operations such as bulk-loading data or running DBCC. To do this you are going to have to create your own config file. To create your own config file, you have to dig into the details of the different ini file sections.

Configuring SQLIOSim

Although it looks like you can adjust all the configuration settings through the user interface, in reality all you can do through the user interface is choose a different config file and specify the settings for the test files (the FileX section of the config file), and some of the system level configuration settings (which aren't specified in the config file). You can't even see what the settings are for the other key configuration sections, which are discussed here:

❑ **Filex:** This section allows you to set the attributes of the files to be tested.

❑ **Config:** The config section allows you to set the same settings as are available through the configuration dialog box. These are settings that control the execution of the test such as run duration, number of runs, and so on. There are a number of other settings available in this section that can't be set through the user interface, and these are:

  ❑ CPUCount

  ❑ CacheHitRatio

  ❑ MaxOutstandingIO

  ❑ TargetIODuration

  ❑ AllowIOBursts

  ❑ NoBuffering

  ❑ WriteThrough

  ❑ ScatterGather

  ❑ ForceReadAhead

  ❑ StampFiles

For more details on these settings please refer to KB article 231619 on configuring SQLIOSim.

- ❑ **RandomUser:** The RandomUser section controls the operation of a SQL Server workload requesting random I/O, such as a user of an OLTP system. Enable these tests by setting the User-Count to a value > 0.

- ❑ **AuditUser:** This section controls simulation of DBCC operations. Use this to simulate operations/administration activity on SQL Server. Enable these tests by setting the UserCount to a value > 0.

- ❑ **ReadAheadUser:** This section controls simulation of Read Ahead activity. This is I/O activity that simulates DSS style workloads with large parallel queries. Enable these tests by setting the UserCount to a value > 0.

- ❑ **BulkUpdateUser:** This section controls simulation of Bulk operations such as Select Into, Bulk Insert, or any other non-logged operations. Enable these tests by setting the UserCount to a value > 0.

- ❑ **ShrinkUser:** This section controls the simulation of DBCC Shrink operations. It also controls growing operations. Enable these tests by setting one of the files to have an increment value > 0 and setting shrinkable to be true. If increment=0 and shrinkable is false, these tests will be disabled.

Configuration for OLTP Simulation

Here is a sample config file that simulates an OLTP workload. For an OLTP workload, you need to increase the amount of random user activity and decrease the non OLTP type activity such as Read Ahead, AuditUser, and Bulk update as these are not typical OLTP type activities. This is achieved by altering the default config.ini file in the following way. The UserCount for the RandomUser section is set to 256 and the UserCount for AuditUser, ReadAheadUser, and BulkUpdateUser are all set to 0. ShrinkUser activity is disabled by setting shrinkable=false on all the files to be tested.

```
[CONFIG]
ErrorFile=sqliosim.oltp.log.xml
CPUCount=1
Affinity=0
IOAffinity=0
MaxMemoryMB=388
StopOnError=TRUE
TestCycles=12
TestCycleDuration=600
CacheHitRatio=1000
NoBuffering=TRUE
WriteThrough=TRUE
MaxOutstandingIO=0
TargetIODuration=100
AllowIOBursts=TRUE
UseScatterGather=TRUE
ForceReadAhead=TRUE
DeleteFilesAtStartup=TRUE
DeleteFilesAtShutdown=FALSE
StampFiles=FALSE
[RandomUser]
UserCount=256
JumpToNewRegionPercentage=500
```

```
MinIOChainLength=50
MaxIOChainLength=100
RandomUserReadWriteRatio=9000
MinLogPerBuffer=64
MaxLogPerBuffer=8192
RollbackChance=100
SleepAfter=5
YieldPercentage=0
CPUSimulation=FALSE
CPUCyclesMin=0
CPUCyclesMax=0
[AuditUser]
UserCount=0
BuffersValidated=64
DelayAfterCycles=2
AuditDelay=200
[ReadAheadUser]
UserCount=0
BuffersRAMin=32
BuffersRAMax=64
DelayAfterCycles=2
RADelay=200
[BulkUpdateUser]
UserCount=0
BuffersBUMin=64
BuffersBUMax=128
DelayAfterCycles=2
BUDelay=10
[ShrinkUser]
MinShrinkInterval=120
MaxShrinkInterval=600
MinExtends=1
MaxExtends=20
[File1]
FileName=D:\mssql\data\sqliosim.mdx
InitialSize=4096
MaxSize=4096
Increment=0
Shrinkable=FALSE
LogFile=FALSE
Sparse=FALSE
[File2]
FileName=D:\mssql\log\sqliosim.ldx
InitialSize=2048
MaxSize=2048
Increment=0
Shrinkable=FALSE
LogFile=TRUE
Sparse=FALSE

[File3]
FileName=
```

Configuration for DSS Simulation

This is a sample INI file to simulate a DSS workload. For a DSS workload you want a lot of ReadAhead activity and some BulkUpdate activity. If your environment is predominantly Bulk Update, then you can set the BulkUpdateUser higher. If your workload is predominantly ReadAhead, then set the ReadAheadUser higher (256) and set the BulkUpdateUser lower (0). This configuration differs from the default in that UserCount for ReadAheadUser is set to 256, and UserCount for BulkUpdateUser is set to 5. UserCount for RandomUser and AuditUser is set to 0. ShrinkUser simulation is disabled by setting `shrinkable=false` on all the files to be tested.

```
[CONFIG]
ErrorFile=sqliosim.dss.log.xml
CPUCount=1
Affinity=0
IOAffinity=0
MaxMemoryMB=388
StopOnError=TRUE
TestCycles=12
TestCycleDuration=600
CacheHitRatio=1000
NoBuffering=TRUE
WriteThrough=TRUE
MaxOutstandingIO=0
TargetIODuration=100
AllowIOBursts=TRUE
UseScatterGather=TRUE
ForceReadAhead=TRUE
DeleteFilesAtStartup=FALSE
DeleteFilesAtShutdown=FALSE
StampFiles=FALSE
[RandomUser]
UserCount=0
JumpToNewRegionPercentage=500
MinIOChainLength=50
MaxIOChainLength=100
RandomUserReadWriteRatio=9000
MinLogPerBuffer=64
MaxLogPerBuffer=8192
RollbackChance=100
SleepAfter=5
YieldPercentage=0
CPUSimulation=FALSE
CPUCyclesMin=0
CPUCyclesMax=0
[AuditUser]
UserCount=0
BuffersValidated=64
DelayAfterCycles=2
AuditDelay=200
[ReadAheadUser]
UserCount=256
BuffersRAMin=32
BuffersRAMax=512
DelayAfterCycles=200
RADelay=200
```

```
[BulkUpdateUser]
UserCount=5
BuffersBUMin=256
BuffersBUMax=1024
DelayAfterCycles=15
BUDelay=1000
[ShrinkUser]
MinShrinkInterval=120
MaxShrinkInterval=600
MinExtends=1
MaxExtends=20
[File1]
FileName=D:\mssql\data\sqliosim.mdx
InitialSize=4096
MaxSize=4096
Increment=0
Shrinkable=FALSE
LogFile=FALSE
Sparse=FALSE
[File2]
FileName=D:\mssql\log\sqliosim.ldx
InitialSize=2048
MaxSize=2048
Increment=0
Shrinkable=FALSE
LogFile=TRUE
Sparse=FALSE

[File3]
FileName=
```

Configuration for DBCC Simulation

This is a sample INI file to simulate a DBCC workload. A DBCC workload is simulated by the AuditUser, so you want to set this high, and the other user types low. This configuration differs from the default in that UserCount for AuditUser is set to 256, and UserCount for BulkUpdateUser, RandomUser and ReadAheadUser is set to 0. ShrinkUser simulation is disabled by setting `shrinkable=false` on all the files to be tested.

```
[CONFIG]
ErrorFile=sqliosim.dbcc.log.xml
CPUCount=1
Affinity=0
IOAffinity=0
MaxMemoryMB=388
StopOnError=TRUE
TestCycles=12
TestCycleDuration=600
CacheHitRatio=1000
NoBuffering=TRUE
WriteThrough=TRUE
MaxOutstandingIO=0
TargetIODuration=100
```

```
AllowIOBursts=TRUE
UseScatterGather=TRUE
ForceReadAhead=TRUE
DeleteFilesAtStartup=FALSE
DeleteFilesAtShutdown=FALSE
StampFiles=FALSE
[RandomUser]
UserCount=0
JumpToNewRegionPercentage=500
MinIOChainLength=50
MaxIOChainLength=100
RandomUserReadWriteRatio=9000
MinLogPerBuffer=64
MaxLogPerBuffer=8192
RollbackChance=100
SleepAfter=5
YieldPercentage=0
CPUSimulation=FALSE
CPUCyclesMin=0
CPUCyclesMax=0
[AuditUser]
UserCount=256
BuffersValidated=64
DelayAfterCycles=2
AuditDelay=200
[ReadAheadUser]
UserCount=0
BuffersRAMin=32
BuffersRAMax=512
DelayAfterCycles=200
RADelay=200
[BulkUpdateUser]
UserCount=0
BuffersBUMin=256
BuffersBUMax=1024
DelayAfterCycles=15
BUDelay=1000
[ShrinkUser]
MinShrinkInterval=120
MaxShrinkInterval=600
MinExtends=1
MaxExtends=20
[File1]
FileName=D:\mssql\data\sqliosim.mdx
InitialSize=4096
MaxSize=4096
Increment=0
Shrinkable=FALSE
LogFile=FALSE
Sparse=FALSE
[File2]
FileName=D:\mssql\log\sqliosim.ldx
InitialSize=2048
MaxSize=2048
```

```
Increment=0
Shrinkable=FALSE
LogFile=TRUE
Sparse=FALSE

[File3]
FileName=
```

Running SQLIOSim from the Command Line

The command line arguments you can use when running SQLIOSim.com are the same as those on the config dialog box of the GUI, and are:

- ❑ **-cfg:** Specify the config file.
- ❑ **-save:** Save the resulting config file to this file. Use this as a way to create a new config file.
- ❑ **-log:** Specify the log file location. This is where the results are written.
- ❑ **-dir:** Specify the directory where the test files are created.
- ❑ **-d:** Set the duration of the main test pass.
- ❑ **-size:** Specify the initial size of the data file.

Using this information it's pretty easy to automate SQLIOSim from a batch file. Here is a simple example of calling SQLISim from a batch file.

```
@echo off
Rem Example Batch file calling SQLIOSim
Rem minimum we need to do is pass the config file we want to use
Rem

Call sqliosim.com -cfg sqliosim.oltp.cfg.ini
```

Interpreting Results from SQLIOSim

The results from the test run are displayed in the user interface when running the GUI version and are also saved into the log file specified in the test configuration. What you want to see is just a lot of informational messages. Warnings are OK as well. These are usually telling you that you waited longer than expected for an I/O to complete.

What you don't want to see are any errors. These are highlighted in red in the GUI version. Any errors need to be investigated as these are potential reliability problems that have been discovered somewhere within the storage subsystem.

The log file is an XML formatted file, and there is an `ErrorLog.xslt` provided in the download.

When there is an error the log file will contain a section like the following:

```
<ENTRY TYPE='ERROR' TIME='15:49:13' DATE='07/29/07' TID='3696'
User='CreateFileStream' File='e:\yukon\sosbranch\sql\ntdbms\storeng\util\
```

```
sqliosim\fileio.cpp' Line='382' Func='CLogicalFile::GetDiskGeom'
HRESULT='0x80070057' SYSTEXT='The parameter is incorrect.'>

<EXTENDED_DESCRIPTION>Unable to get disk cache info for D:\</EXTENDED_DESCRIPTION>

</ENTRY>
```

In the case of this particular error, this is actually a known bug in SQLIOSim, and this isn't actually an error condition, but just a warning.

For most errors SQLIOSim will write a dump file called SQLSimErrorDump00000.txt. The dump file contains the expected data, the received data, and the difference. This is the information that's going to help diagnose what the problem is. The pattern of the failure, or the difference between expected and received data, is the key to diagnosing the problem. Here is an example of some of the contents of a dump file for a single bit error. These single bit errors are often caused by memory, and not by the storage subsystem. They still need to be thoroughly investigated.

```
Data mismatch between the expected disk data and the read buffer:
File: e:\sqliosim.mdx
Expected FileId: 0x0
Received FileId: 0x0
Expected PageId: 0x1C5E8
Received PageId: 0x1C5E8
Expected CheckSum: 0x60EFEBEC
Received CheckSum: 0x60EFEBEC
Calculated CheckSum: 0x8430E184 (does not match expected)
Expected Buffer Length: 0x2000
Received Buffer Length: 0x2000


++++++Difference data available at the end of dump+++++++


 Data buffer received:
<data buffer omitted>

0x000280  E5 6C 28 FA 33 40 EF 22 D9 F5 6D 09 52 8F 63 6A D7 49 22 BD 9C 15
A1 9E EA CC 59 4C 2B 76 BD 2E    .1(.3@."..m.R.cj.I".......YL+v..

 Data buffer expected:
<data buffer omitted>

0x000280  E5 6C 28 FA 33 40 EF 22 D9 F5 6D 01 52 8F 63 6A D7 49 22 BD 9C 15
A1 9E EA CC 59 4C 2B 76 BD 2E    .1(.3@."..m.R.cj.I".......YL+v..

Data buffer difference:
<Most of data buffer omitted>
0x000220
0x000240
0x000260
0x000280                                   08
0x0002A0
0x0002C0
```

```
0x0002E0
0x000300


First not matching position: 0x28B
Bytes different: 0x1


File I/O calls history dump

Function            Handle       Offset       Bytes   Ret bytes      Start
End Rslt      Error    TID
WriteFileGather       0x5fc     0x38b80000    262144     262144   163493843
163493843    1        0   3236
WriteFileGather       0x5fc     0x38b40000    262144     262144   163493843
163493843    1        0   3236
WriteFileGather       0x5fc     0x38b00000    262144     262144   163493843
163493843    1        0   3236
WriteFileGather       0x5fc     0x38ac0000    262144     262144   163493843
163493843    1        0   3236

<Data omitted>
```

Interpreting the results from SQLIOSim is a very complex and technical process. You can attempt this using the knowledge provided in Bob Dorr's white papers on SQL Server I/O. If this proves inconclusive, then you are going to have to contact some expert assistance. This means contacting Microsoft or your hardware vendor for support.

Diagnosing errors any further is beyond the scope of this book due to the complexity of the failures and the constant evolution of hardware and firmware.

Background Reading on SQL Server I/O

Bob Dorr has written two excellent articles on the internals of SQL Server I/O. These should be required reading for anyone investigating I/O issues.

These two articles are titled: "SQL Server 2000 I/O Basics" (www.microsoft.com/technet/prodtechnol/sql/2000/maintain/sqlIObasics.mspx) and "SQL Server I/O Basics Chapter 2" (www.microsoft.com/technet/prodtechnol/sql/2005/iobasics.mspx).

Another great article on I/O is "Storage Top 10 Best Practices" (www.microsoft.com/technet/prodtechnol/sql/bestpractice/storage-top-10.mspx).

Best Practice for Dealing with SQLIOSim Errors

Find the failure pattern in the dump file.

Open a support incident with Microsoft, or your hardware vendor for assistance with identifying the root cause of the problem.

> **Best Practice for Storage Configuration**
>
> BEFORE starting any performance or stress testing, you should always ensure you have the very latest firmware and drivers for every component in your storage stack.

Summary

This chapter started by discussing the importance of measuring storage performance. You looked at the different metrics you might want to monitor, looked at different tools available to measure I/O performance, then looked in detail at measuring performance using SQLIO. Then you looked at SQLIOSim and how you can use this tool to measure storage robustness and reliability. Finally, you recapped the best practices introduced through the chapter.

In the next chapter, you will look at the SQL Performance Dashboard, and see how to use this exciting new tool to capture key performance information.

13

SQL Server 2005 Performance Dashboard Reports

There are millions of deployments of SQL Server across the world ranging from the free SKU of SQL Server Express Edition to SQL Server Enterprise Edition. Each SQL Server environment is configured differently, has different business requirements, and serves different purposes. If you're a good DBA in a perfect world, you'll have a handle on many of these. You know your required up-time, integrated systems, dependencies, and so on. If something goes down, you are probably aware of it and can resolve it quickly. If you are an IT Professional who manages multiple server types or if you work in an enterprise that runs dozens of applications on top of hundreds of SQL Servers, it's impossible to know all of your systems inside and out. You rely on monitoring tools to alert you when there's a problem.

Now imagine that you work for Microsoft in SQL Server customer support. Each year you engage with hundreds of different businesses with thousands of SQL Servers. You have no prior knowledge of the environment or the business requirements. It's your job to get up to speed immediately. You need to sift through symptoms, identify the underlying problems, and minimize the impact of the resolution to bring the business back online as soon as possible. Oh, and one more thing: You have to do this remotely and your only connection with the business is through the telephone.

The challenges you face as a DBA diagnosing problems in your environment are amplified when you need to bring in a third party to help you remotely. Thus, it is critical that you can quickly discover at a high level what could potentially be wrong with your environment and subsequently dive deeper into that area to identify the underlying problem.

From a support perspective, performance troubleshooting and tuning is an area that frequently starts with a lack of appropriate high-level information. A customer will call support and say something like, "my SQL Server is slow" or "my web app is slow and we think it is because of SQL." This is not actionable high-level information. This requires the support specialist to spend a significant amount of time to understand the environment and collect sets of metrics that will eventually narrow it down to a few specific items.

Supportability

To improve supportability in SQL Server 2005, a set of features was introduced to help you understand what is going on inside your instance:

❑ Catalog views

❑ Dynamic management views (DMVs) and functions

❑ Default trace

Catalog Views

Catalog views are a set of views that return SQL Server catalog information. The catalog views are essentially read-only versions of the system tables that were available in SQL Server 2000.

For more information on catalog views, visit `http://msdn2.microsoft.com/en-us/library/ms174365.aspx`.

Dynamic Management Views and Functions

Many DBAs complained that when a problem would arise with SQL Server 2000, they were unable to see what was going on inside their instance. With SQL Server 2005, dynamic management views and functions were introduced to expose the data experts' need to identify problems.

In order for SQL Server to run, it needs to keep track of a massive amount of information. It manages connections, sessions, requests, memory allocations, index usage statistics, and so on. Much of this information could be potentially useful in tracking down a performance problem. Dynamic management views (DMVs) expose these internal data structures as virtualized tables. You can use T-SQL to query the DMVs. Here are a few examples:

To get a list of user sessions on your system, run this:

```
SELECT * FROM sys.dm_exec_sessions
WHERE is_user_process = 1
```

To get a list of current requests on your system, run this:

```
SELECT * FROM sys.dm_exec_requests
```

To get a list of the top 25 most impactful SQL statements by total physical reads recently run on your instance, run this:

```
SELECT TOP(25) qs.*,
(SELECT TOP 1
    SUBSTRING(st.text,statement_start_offset / 2+1,
        ( (CASE WHEN statement_end_offset = -1
```

```
            THEN (LEN(CONVERT(nvarchar(max),st.text)) * 2)
            ELSE statement_end_offset END) - statement_start_offset) /
2+1)) AS sql_statement
FROM sys.dm_exec_query_stats qs
CROSS APPLY sys.dm_exec_sql_text(sql_handle) st
ORDER BY total_physical_reads DESC
```

sys.dm_exec_sql_text is a dynamic management function. It is a table-valued function that accepts one parameter, sql_handle. By using the CROSS APPLY operator, you can call this TVF with the sql_handle from each row of sys.dm_exec_query_stats.

These are just a few quick examples of how you can use three DMVs. As of SQL Server 2005 Service Pack 2, there are over 80 dynamic management views and functions. All of the DMVs follow this naming convention: sys.dm_ + <short group identifier> + _ + <descriptive name>. Thus, if you want to find all DMVs, you can query the catalog view sys.all_objects and filter on this information.

To obtain a comprehensive list of all of the dynamic management views and functions, run this:

```
SELECT * FROM sys.all_objects
WHERE
[schema_id] = schema_id('sys') AND
[name] LIKE N'dm_%' AND
[is_ms_shipped] = 1
ORDER BY name ASC
```

For more information on dynamic management views and functions, visit http://msdn2.microsoft .com/en-us/library/ms188754.aspx.

The Default Trace

Many performance problems can be associated with improper configuration, poor schema design, and bad application architecture. It is common to have a solution that is working perfectly fine and then out of nowhere performance problems arise. These seemingly spontaneous performance problems are not random — there are underlying reasons for them. Many times they are caused by human error. For example, a DBA might change an sp_configure value or drop an index and not fully understand the ramifications of that action. Another possible reason could be that a scheduled script could fail part way through, and without proper error handling, it will leave your server in an inconsistent state. The unfortunate part is that you probably will not realize there is a problem until one of your customers complains about a business application days later. At this point, the symptoms may be far removed from the underlying problem with no easy-to-follow paper trail. Unless you have a proactive monitoring solution, you will have little idea what changed or where to begin your investigation.

Time and time again, SQL Server customer support services helps customers who have not instrumented any type of proactive monitoring. SQL Server customer support services has developed best practices and know what data would be useful. So to help future customers, the SQL Server product team has leveraged customer support services's expertise and created a lightweight proactive monitoring solution: the default trace. You can think of the default trace as a *flight recorder*. It is a mechanism to record potentially important events so that you can reference them should there be a problem in the future. Unlike the DMVs, the data found in the default trace is persistent across server restarts. This means that if your SQL Server instance is restarted or stopped, all of the useful event information is retained and still available.

The default trace is a server-side trace that is on by default for all SQL Server 2005 instances. Microsoft has predefined over 30 events to be traced, including `Object:Created`, `Object:Deleted`, `Data File Auto Grow`, and `Data File Auto Shrink`. Although 30 events may seem like a lot for a trace, these events are very lightweight and should not seriously impact the performance of your instance. In almost all cases, the benefits of the default trace outweigh the minimal overhead imposed.

The default trace contains the following trace events shown in Table 13-1:

Table 13-1: The Default Trace Events

Event ID	Event Name
18	Audit Server Starts And Stops
20	Audit Login Failed
22	ErrorLog
46	Object:Created
47	Object:Deleted
55	Hash Warning
69	Sort Warnings
79	Missing Column Statistics
80	Missing Join Predicate
81	Server Memory Change
92	Data File Auto Grow
93	Log File Auto Grow
94	Data File Auto Shrink
95	Log File Auto Shrink
102	Audit Database Scope GDR Event
103	Audit Schema Object GDR Event
104	Audit Addlogin Event
105	Audit Login GDR Event
106	Audit Login Change Property Event
108	Audit Add Login to Server Role Event

Continued

474

Table 13-1: The Default Trace Events (continued)

Event ID	Event Name
109	Audit Add DB User Event
110	Audit Add Member to DB Role Event
111	Audit Add Role Event
115	Audit Backup/Restore Event
116	Audit DBCC Event
117	Audit Change Audit Event
152	Audit Change Database Owner
153	Audit Schema Object Take Ownership Event
155	FT:Crawl Started
156	FT:Crawl Stopped
157	FT:Crawl Aborted
164	Object:Altered
167	Database Mirroring State Change
175	Audit Server Alter Trace Event

For a description of all of the trace events available in SQL Server 2005, go to
http://msdn2.microsoft.com/en-us/library/ms186265.aspx.

If you would like to see what trace events are running for the default trace, you can load the Active Traces report or run the following code:

```
SELECT t.EventID, t.ColumnID, e.name as Event_Description, c.name as
Column_Description
  FROM ::fn_trace_geteventinfo(1) t
    JOIN sys.trace_events e ON t.eventID = e.trace_event_id
    JOIN sys.trace_columns c ON t.columnid = c.trace_column_id
```

If you believe that the overhead from the default trace is too much for your environment, you can disable it with the following sp_configure command:

```
EXEC sys.sp_configure N'show advanced options', N'1'
RECONFIGURE WITH OVERRIDE
GO
EXEC sys.sp_configure N'default trace enabled', N'0'
GO
```

```
RECONFIGURE WITH OVERRIDE
GO
EXEC sys.sp_configure N'show advanced options', N'0'
RECONFIGURE WITH OVERRIDE
GO
```

The contents of the default trace can be displayed like any other trace with the `fn_trace_gettable` function. It stores the data in up to five trace files with a 20 MB rollover threshold. If you want to see all of the events that have been persisted into the trace files, perform the following steps:

1. Query the `sys.traces` catalog view to get the file name of the default trace.

2. Parse out the folder path and append `log.trc` to it.

3. Pass in the name of the base log file to `fn_trace_gettable`.

Here is a sample script:

```
--Variables
DECLARE @default_trace_current_filename NVARCHAR(520);
DECLARE @default_trace_filename NVARCHAR(520);
DECLARE @index int;
DECLARE @max_files int;

--Get the current filename for the default trace
SELECT @default_trace_current_filename = [path]
FROM sys.traces
WHERE is_default = 1;

--Reverse the string
SET @default_trace_current_filename =
REVERSE(@default_trace_current_filename)

--Find the last '\'
SELECT @index  = PATINDEX('%\%', @default_trace_current_filename)

--Revert the string back to normal
SET @default_trace_current_filename =
REVERSE(@default_trace_current_filename)

--Parse out the directory name and append 'log.trc'
SET @default_trace_filename = LEFT(@default_trace_current_filename ,
LEN(@default_trace_current_filename) - @index) + '\log.trc';

--Display metadata for the default trace
SELECT *
FROM sys.traces
WHERE is_default = 1;
```

```
--Display the current filename
SELECT @default_trace_current_filename

--Display the base filename
SELECT @default_trace_filename

--Show the contents of the current default trace file
SELECT * FROM fn_trace_gettable(@default_trace_current_filename, 1)

--Get the maximum file count for the default trace
SELECT @max_files = [max_files]
FROM sys.traces
WHERE is_default = 1

--Show the contents of all default trace files
SELECT * FROM fn_trace_gettable(@default_trace_filename, @max_files)
```

Difficulties

Each of these catalog views, DMVs, and the default trace exposes an enormous amount of useful information. There is no longer a problem of the data not being available. The toughest part now is to sift through the mountains of data and combine them into something meaningful and actionable. Educational resources such as books, tutorials, and other miscellaneous training will help you find your way through the management data available. After a short while of hands-on experience, you will probably amass dozens of scripts in a personal script library that take advantage of a few of the 80+ dynamic management views and functions. Your scripts give you easier access to the data, but there is still a steep learning curve in making you more effective. Microsoft has taken another step in making you more effective and addressed precisely this pain point by releasing the SQL Server 2005 Performance Dashboard Reports.

Performance Dashboard Reports

The Performance Dashboard Reports give you an interactive way to diagnose performance-related problems on a SQL Server instance. The reports take data from the dynamic management and catalog views and give you a graphical overview of the current state of your SQL Server instance.

Prerequisites

The Performance Dashboard Reports leverage new features introduced in SQL Server 2005 Service Pack 2. Thus, your SQL Server components must be from at least SQL Server 2005 Service Pack 2 or later.

Service Pack 2 needs to be applied to the Management Tools as well as each SQL Server relational database engine instance that you want to monitor using the Performance Dashboard Reports.

Installing the Performance Dashboard Reports

To install the Performance Dashboard Reports, follow these steps:

1. Download SQLServer2005_PerformanceDashboard.msi from the Microsoft Download Center (`www.microsoft.com/downloads/details.aspx?familyid=1D3A4A0D-7E0C-4730-8204-E419218C1EFC&displaylang=en`), shown in Figure 13-1.

Figure 13-1

2. Save SQLServer2005_PerformanceDashboard.msi (see Figure 13-2).

3. Run SQLServer2005_PerformanceDashboard.msi (see Figure 13-3).

4. Take note of the installation path on the Feature Selection page of the installation wizard (see Figure 13-4).

> *The default directory is* `Program Files\Microsoft SQL Server\90\Tools\PerformanceDashboard\`.

5. Continue until you complete the setup wizard (see Figure 13-5).

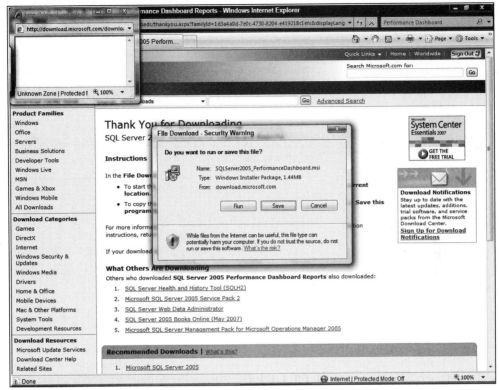

Figure 13-2

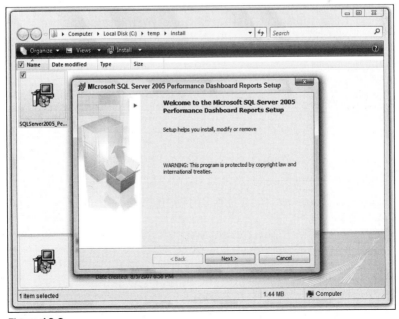

Figure 13-3

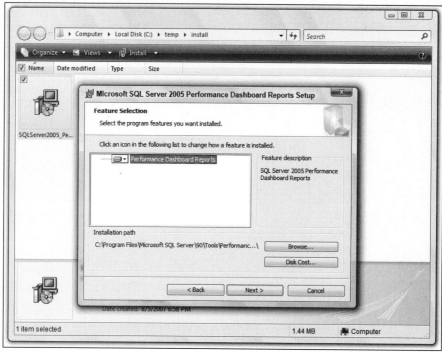

Figure 13-4

Figure 13-5

6. Locate your installation directory (see Figure 13-6).

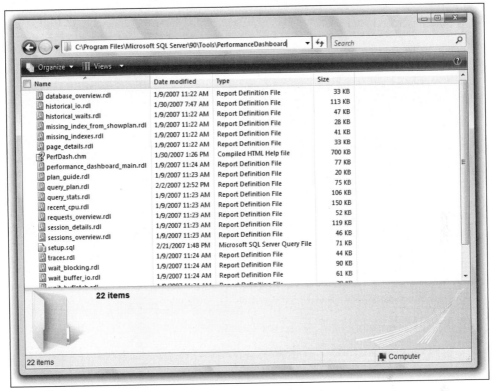

Figure 13-6

7. Run setup.sql on every SQL Server engine instance you would like to monitor with the Performance Dashboard Reports (see Figures 13-7 through 13-9).

Running the Performance Dashboard Reports

Using the Performance Dashboard Reports is as simple as running a custom report from within Management Studio.

Follow these instructions:

1. Connect Object Explorer to a SQL Server 2005 Relational Engine instance (see Figure 13-10).

2. Right-click the server instance node (see Figure 13-11).

3. Navigate to Reports ⇨ Custom Reports (see Figure 13-12).

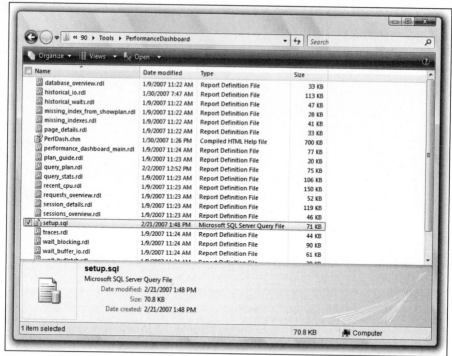

Figure 13-7

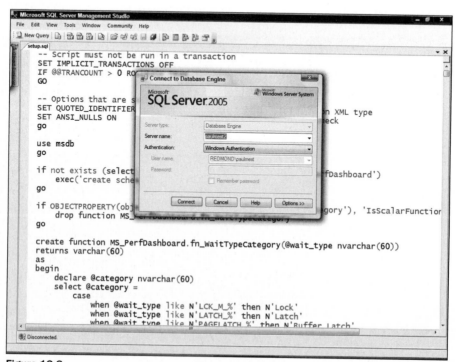

Figure 13-8

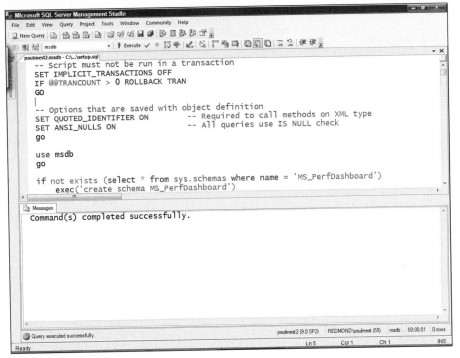

Figure 13-9

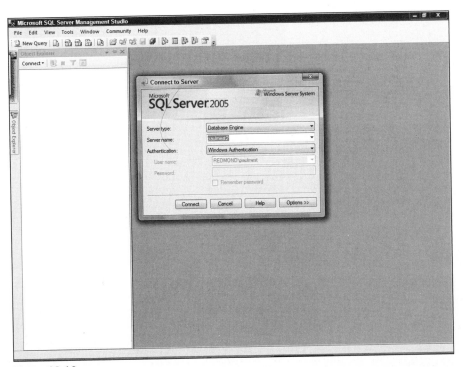

Figure 13-10

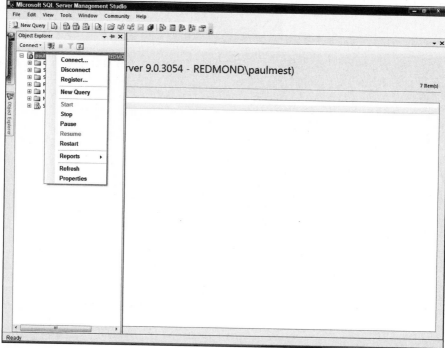

Figure 13-11

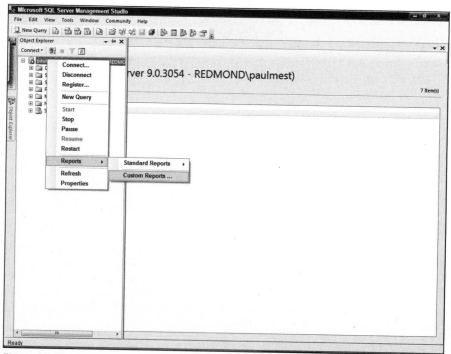

Figure 13-12

4. Open the performance_dashboard_main.rdl file from your Performance Dashboard Reports installation directory (see Figure 13-13).

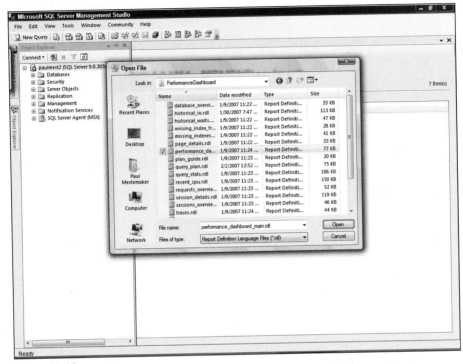

Figure 13-13

5. Choose Run (see Figure 13-14).

Custom reports execute queries under the context of your user connection in Management Studio. Refer to the section on security later in this chapter.

6. The custom report loads in a new tab. You will now see an overview of your system with the Performance Dashboard Report (see Figure 13-15).

Architecture

If you are experiencing a performance problem, you may be wary of adding additional overhead to your instance. The Performance Dashboard Reports have very low overhead and very few dependencies. By understanding how they work and their architecture, you should feel more secure in using them in your production environments.

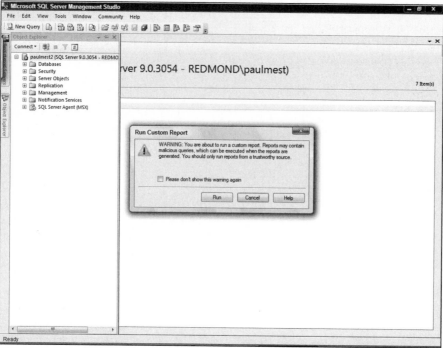

Figure 13-14

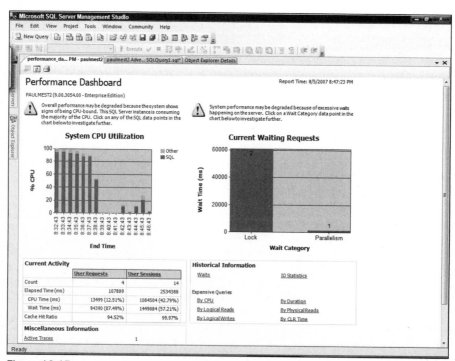

Figure 13-15

Overhead

Since these reports are intended to troubleshoot performance problems, they were carefully designed to minimize the potential impact on your system. The Performance Dashboard Reports do not store data over time, they do not require reporting services, they do not create a new database, and there will be absolutely no overhead when you are not interacting with them. By having an interactive drill-through experience, data can be loaded gradually. This means that a small amount of high-level information can be retrieved with the dashboard report. Then, based on what you see, you can click a link to see more information about requests or a graph to inspect locks. This will load a new report targeted to that specific scenario, consequently minimizing the footprint by only loading the data you are potentially interested in.

MSDB

The Performance Dashboard Reports `setup.sql` file creates functions and stored procedures in MSDB. These objects are commonly used by the reports. If you want to learn how the DMVs are used by the Performance Dashboard Reports, browse through the `setup.sql` source or browse the objects in MSDB after installation.

Management Data

Almost all information is obtained through the DMVs and catalog views. There is also one report that allows you to drill into active traces. Even though many Windows administrators are familiar with performance counters, performance counters are not used for these reports. Since the Performance Dashboard Reports rely solely on SQL Server technologies and do not capture information over time, they do not leverage any system performance counters.

Reporting Services

When you diagnose a performance problem, you want to minimize the set of moving parts. So while the Performance Dashboard Reports use standard SQL Server Reporting Services technology, they do not require a SQL Server 2005 Reporting Services server. They use client-side Reporting Services technology. Management Studio parses the T-SQL queries out of the RDL files, gathers the data from the instance, and passes it to the ReportViewer control to render the report.

You can launch multiple reports or multiple instances of the same report on separate tabs. This is a quick way to compare information across servers or to compare information on the same server over time. If you want to save this information, you can export the reports to Excel or PDF.

Security

The Performance Dashboard Reports are executed like any other custom report. Custom reports are run in the same security context as your connection to Object Explorer. This means that if you are connected as a sysadmin, all of the report queries will be executed in that context. This is fine if you trust the reports you are running. If you download a report from the Internet and run it as a system administrator, be aware that that report can run not only SELECT, but also INSERT, UPDATE, and DELETE statements.

If you do not connect as sysadmin and want to connect as a low-privileged user, you will be able to run the Performance Dashboard Reports, but you will not see any useful or sensitive data. To view data from the DMVs, you will need VIEW_SERVER_STATE and VIEW_DATABASE_STATE privileges.

Common Usage Scenarios

Now that you know how to open a custom report and you have the basic idea of how the Performance Dashboard Reports work, look at the first report: the Performance Dashboard.

Performance Dashboard

This report is designed to give a quick overview of the performance of a SQL Server 2005 instance. There are two main graphs: System CPU Utilization and Current Waiting Requests.

The System CPU Utilization graph shows the last 15 minutes of CPU usage. It breaks down CPU usage by the SQL Server instance processor usage compared to other processes. The data in this graph is not obtained through performance counters. Instead, it is obtained through the DMV sys.dm_os_ring_buffers. If you would like to see how this is calculated without using performance counters, run the following:

```
USE [MSDB]
GO
sp_helptext 'MS_PerfDashboard.usp_Main_GetCPUHistory'
GO
```

The Current Waiting Requests graph in the upper right hand corner groups similar waits together in predefined wait categories such as Lock, Network IO, Buffer IO, and Sleep. If you would like to see how these are grouped, run the following:

```
USE [MSDB]
GO
sp_helptext 'MS_PerfDashboard.fn_WaitTypeCategory'
GO
sp_helptext 'MS_PerfDashboard.usp_Main_GetRequestWaits'
GO
```

An alert with a yellow triangle and black exclamation point will be displayed above each of these graphs if certain common bottlenecking conditions are met. For example, if the CPU Utilization is greater than 80 percent, it is likely that your instance is CPU bound, and you will be given recommended next steps based on whether the CPU is used by SQL or another process.

Locking/Blocking

The Performance Dashboard makes it easier to identify resource waits. On the Current Waiting Requests graph in the upper right hand corner of the Performance Dashboard, you can see both the total length of process wait time as well as the total number of processes waiting on a specific wait type (see Figure 13-16).

You can see in this example that there are six waiting sessions: Five are waiting on Lock and one is waiting on Sleep. The total wait time for Sleep is almost 100 seconds and the total wait time for Lock is over 200 seconds. If you click the blue bar representing Lock, you will be prompted to open another report tailored to blocked sessions (see Figure 13-17).

Choose Run to bring up the Blocking Report (see Figure 13-18).

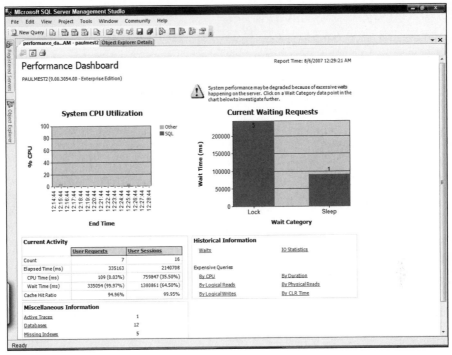

Figure 13-16

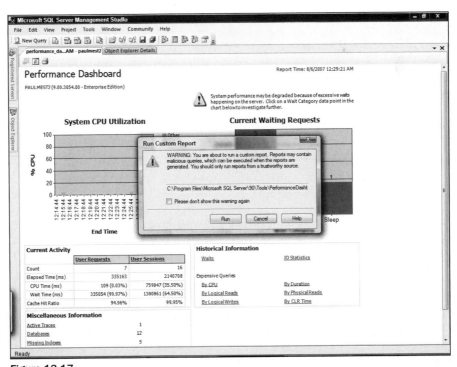

Figure 13-17

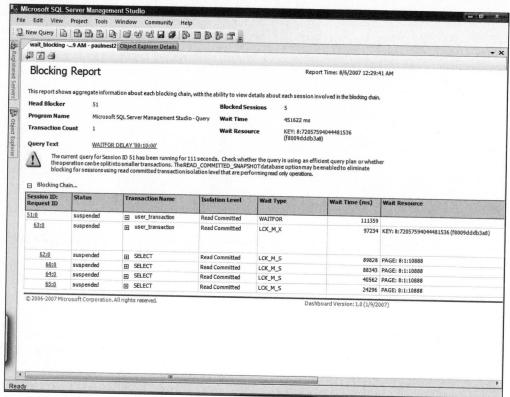

Figure 13-18

In the Blocking Report, you will see that session 51 is the *head blocker*. This is the session on which all other sessions in this blocking tree are waiting. If you look at the Query Text you can see what the head blocker is waiting on: WAITFOR DELAY '00:10:00'.

By expanding the blocking chain, you can see all of the sessions:

❑   Session 63 is waiting on 51.

❑   Session 62 is waiting on 63.

❑   Sessions 60, 64, 65 are waiting on 62.

To find out what statements are waiting, you can drill-through on one of the sessions to open the Session Details report. Not only will this show you what statement is currently executing, it will show other miscellaneous information about the session as well. The Session Details report lists all of the settings for a specific session. It gives you the session ID, login name, login time, hostname, and program name to help you identify what spawned the session. It also gives you aggregated information over the session's lifetime. You can see the aggregate CPU time, reads, and writes. You can also see what requests are executing in this session or what the last request was. If a request is currently executing, you can see the query text as well as up-to-date statistics on the request. Finally, you can expand the View SET options table to see useful settings like your ANSI settings and your Transaction Isolation Level.

Missing Indexes

In SQL Server 2005, when the query optimizer performs an operation like a table scan and detects that an index that is not present would be useful for that statement, it forms an index recommendation. This recommendation can be accessed from two places:

❑　Missing index DMVs

❑　Showplan XML

The Missing Indexes report combines data from three of the missing index DMVs (Sys.dm_db_missing_index_details, sys.dm_db_missing_index_groups, and sys.dm_db_missing_index_group_stats) to show you what statements could have benefited from an index. In addition to the statement, it also shows the percentage estimate cost for maintaining the index and estimated benefit for using the index (see Figure 13-19).

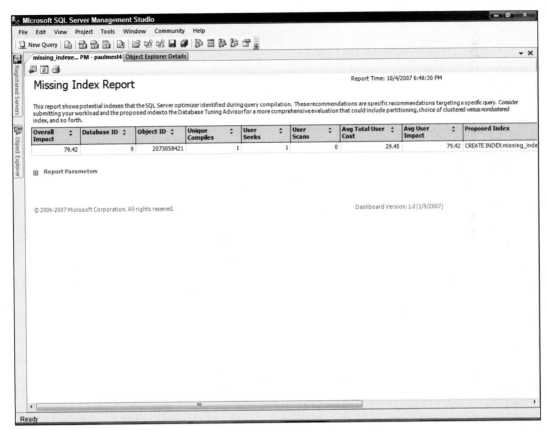

Figure 13-19

Unlike the Database Engine Tuning Advisor, these index recommendations from the Performance Dashboard Reports only take in the statement being executed in its current context. This does not account for the amount of work to maintain the index.

Other Reports

In addition to the reports already shown, there are a number of other reports available in the Performance Dashboard Reports, including the following:

- ❏ Blocking
- ❏ Buffer IO
- ❏ Buffer Latch
- ❏ Database Overview
- ❏ Expensive Queries
- ❏ Generic Waits
- ❏ Historical IO
- ❏ Historical Waits
- ❏ Latch Waits
- ❏ Missing Indexes — XML Showplan
- ❏ Page Details
- ❏ Performance Dashboard
- ❏ Plan Guide
- ❏ Query Plan
- ❏ Recent CPU Utilization
- ❏ Requests Overview
- ❏ Session Details
- ❏ Session Overview
- ❏ Traces

For use cases and more information about each of these reports, read the Performance Dashboard Reports Help file. The `PerfDash.chm` file can be found in your installation directory. The default path is `\%ProgramFiles\%\Microsoft SQL Server\90\tools\PerformanceDashboard\PerfDash.chm`.

Limitations

The SQL Server 2005 Performance Dashboard Reports brings performance troubleshooting to the masses. It's no longer a secret art to combine a few DMVs and then try to make sense of tables of data. This is a big step in the right direction of packaging common uses into these reports. Before you get too excited, keep the following in mind:

- ❏ They only work with Service Pack 2 and later.
- ❏ They only present a snapshot data.
- ❏ They do not compare data to a baseline.

- ❏ They focus on a single instance.
- ❏ They cannot be copied and pasted.

They Require Service Pack 2

The Performance Dashboard Reports require SQL Server 2005 Service Pack 2 or later. The service pack must be applied to each instance you wish to monitor. With Service Pack 2 there were a few bug fixes to a couple of key DMVs as well as the introduction of new T-SQL functionality.

Service Pack 2 must also be applied to the workstation from which you're using Management Studio. The entire custom reporting infrastructure was added with SP2.

This requirement will become less of an issue over time.

They Only Present a Snapshot of Data

The reports will only show information from one moment in time. They do not automatically refresh like System Monitor or the Activity Monitor.

Also, the reports do not store any history. This means that you must diagnose a problem as it's occurring. This can be difficult for transient waits such as Buffer IO or locks that last for a few seconds or less.

They Do Not Compare to Baseline

If your instance has 74 open sessions and 45 requests and is experiencing 10 blocking sessions for 30 seconds each, do you know if this is normal behavior? This could be how your applications behave, or this could be terrible. If you personally aren't familiar with what is expected, the Performance Dashboard Reports become a little less useful.

In an ideal world, you will capture a number of metrics over similar time intervals or during similar workloads to create what is known as a baseline. You can then compare an interval or workload to the acceptable baseline and determine whether something is out of ordinary. Unfortunately, you aren't always working in an ideal world, and Performance Dashboard Reports don't provide the built-in functionality to create a baseline for you.

Another tool was recently released from Microsoft: DMVStats (`www.codeplex.com/sqldmvstats`). It complements the Performance Dashboard by providing a basic snapshot and baseline mechanism. It is a shared source project available on CodePlex.

They Are Instance-Centric

The Performance Dashboard Reports can only show data for one instance at a time. This is an improvement over looking at raw data from T-SQL queries on an instance-by-instance basis. However, the reports are not a tool to monitor an enterprise. They do not have automated data gathering sessions or a centralized reporting infrastructure like System Center Operations Manager.

Many SQL Server customers who have multiple instances of SQL Server will not have the time to run the Performance Dashboard Reports on each instance. Those customers may resort to using the reports only when SCOM alerts them that a performance problem may be happening on one of their instances.

They Cannot Be Copied and Pasted

Due to limitations in the ReportViewer control, it is not possible to select, copy, and paste the contents from the reports into another application like a Word document or an e-mail. The reports can be exported to PDF or Excel files with mixed success. The best results are obtained by exporting to Excel and then formatting to your liking or copying the text from Excel and pasting into an e-mail.

Related Links

There are several links that can be of great assistance:

- ❏ **Performance Dashboard Reports:**
  www.microsoft.com/downloads/details.aspx?FamilyId=1D3A4A0D-7E0C-4730-8204-E419218C1EFC&displaylang=en

- ❏ **DMVStats:**
  www.codeplex.com/sqldmvstats

- ❏ **SQL Server 2005 Service Pack 2:**
  http://support.microsoft.com/kb/913089/

- ❏ **SQL Server 2005 Waits and Queues:**
  www.microsoft.com/technet/prodtechnol/sql/bestpractice/performance_tuning_waits_queues.mspx

- ❏ **PerfDash.chm:**
  C:\Program Files\Microsoft SQL Server\90\Tools\PerformanceDashboard

Summary

These Performance Dashboard Reports really put a great user interface on what used to be a pain to visualize. You do not have to run any T-SQL queries yourself. You do not have to join data from multiple locations with complex SQL. You do not have to understand a dozen different DMVs. All of this information is presented to you in an efficient and intuitive tool that you can use to quickly get up to speed on the performance of your instance.

Part IV

Roadmap to Server Performance

14

Best Practices for Designing for Performance from the Start

Not many architects start software projects to create applications to sit on shelves unused, but that can be the reality if the product doesn't meet user expectations. If performance is required in an application, you should approach the project with performance in mind from the start. Too often, the DBA resources are brought in at the end of the design, or worse, at the end of the development process to figure out how to speed things up. To prepare for database-level performance issues, you absolutely have to understand how the application works and how the database resources are going to be used. In new agile development processes, we see database designers and developers being added to development teams. This is a good thing. If you are a developer, add SQL Server performance skills to your toolset. It takes these two skill sets together to implement successful, high-performance projects.

Performance problems are usually caused by contention for common resources. Disk heads can only move to so many places at one time. Only so many pages and procedures can be cached in one moment. The more information you have about the system, the better performance tuning decisions you'll be able to make. This chapter is designed for the DBA who is pulled into a development project before or perhaps after the physical model has already been formalized. Yet it's still early enough for the DBA to have a hand in troubleshooting the design and capturing some important predicative metrics prior to going to production. You'll be provided guidance on how to capture performance requirements and then use this information to evaluate existing design decisions. You'll also be provided with detailed TSQL queries and a benchmark data model that you can use to tie performance requirements to actual metrics. As you break down the main performance concerns you'll enter this information into the benchmark data model to use in future communication. Creating high performance databases starts with understanding these performance requirements and applying common sense, but it is even more important to communicate these issues to developers, project managers, and users in a language that everyone can understand.

Understanding Your Performance Requirements

If you didn't ask what your performance requirements were to start with, ask now! If you are interested in following best practices, understand the application and the performance requirements of the database. Are you dealing with more OLTP or OLAP requirements? All performance decisions are tradeoffs. You can't make any performance decisions without understanding these requirements. The next few sections will guide you through a set of questions that will give you a good grounding for the situation that you are in. Most of these recommendations are focused on OLTP requirements that support the concepts of normalization discussed in Chapter 8.

How Many Users Will the Database Support?

The number of users that a software product is designed to support is a critical design data point for software development and is just as important for database modeling and support. The number of users and the nature of how they will use this database will provide valuable clues about how resources will be consumed in the database. Resource contention is typically the biggest issue that you are trying to minimize when performance tuning any database after the fact. Spending time up front to understand the user scale will provide some of this insight.

User Scale

A user scale describes a category of users that perform certain use cases in a system. A simple count of the estimated users is not what you are interested in. You need to know which one of these three typical user scale groupings you should anticipate as you approach designing from the start.

❏ **Mom and pop single user scale:** This user scale describes a single user performing sequential actions dictated by use cases. The user need not be a human being. Automated services that perform database activities should also be counted as a single user. If this is your only user scale, you don't have too many distinct users, and you are not going to have to worry too much about inter-user resource conflicts. This category is the most forgiving for bad design decisions.

❏ **Corporate user scale:** This user scale describes multiple users performing parallel actions. Here's where you need to dig into what the users in this pool are doing. This can be done easily if you are provided with the use cases defined by the software development processes. Understanding the use cases helps determine how the data will proliferate into the system and provides insight about what data flows occur in parallel, in serial, or in batch modes. The advantage to this group is that the number of users is predictable. You should be able to plan and stress test existing designs when users are increased.

❏ **Infinite user scale:** In this user scale, you have the same concerns as with the corporate user, but the difference is that the number of users can't be predicted. You'll find this user scale around web apps that are exposed on the Internet. This user scale requires extra thought and planning to deal with the performance challenges of not being able to predict the loads on design patterns. You'll find that programming to this user-scale is challenging and not many shops do this well.

User Roles or Personas

A user role provides a model for the way a user will interact with the database. Alan Cooper in *The Inmates Are Running the Asylum* introduces a similar concept of the persona for interface development.

These personas or user roles are critical for understanding the different types of users who are going to be interacting in the database. If you can put a face on the type of user who will use the software and then let those faces represent the user groups, you'll be able to ask better questions during the design and evaluation processes. Knowing that 30 users are going to be added to a database means one thing if 29 of the 30 users are going to be performing minor set-up tasks and quite another if 29 of the users are to be performing transactional tasks. Separate and understand how many users are going to be performing each of these known persona roles.

❑   **Set-up:** This role performs sequential, create, update, and delete activity on minimal transaction volumes. The key is that this activity occurs infrequently. Examples are setting up new entity records or adding new types to type tables.

❑   **Transactional:** This role represents the workhorse of the software or system. The use cases performed by this role create user transactional volume in the database both from a transaction count and frequency perspective. It is the count of the users in this user group that you are interested in when you ask, "How many users?" There can be many slices of this role, some performing more transactional activity than others. An example could be an accounts payable role and an accounts receivable role. Both perform transactional activity in similar volumes, but may touch different parts of the model.

❑   **Gatekeeper:** This role performs the role of a Gatekeeper. Generally, this role performs state change activities in a database. The transaction volumes can be high or not. Actions include manually approving transactions or automatically running integration activities on schedules.

❑   **Report:** This role requests read-only information from the system. If data is in your OLTP environment, it is a performance killer to read highly relational data from it. Here's where you may need to double-count users to get an accurate idea of who is performing this role. Find out when these reports are run. Are they run every day at a certain time or on demand? This information can help you design windows for maintenance and provide a heads up when numbers change.

After you have a good idea of how many users you have for each of these general role types, find out what level of concurrency is required for each role on a typical processing day. Preferably have this information in time slices by hour. This will give you an idea of the types of read-only or write-intensive loads that you'll have in the database during a typical day. This can also help you determine the uptime requirement discussed later in this section. Take the time now to record the personas and the roles that they will perform like the table below. These entries can be entered directly into the benchmark_persona table in the benchmark model that you can download from www.wrox.com.

Table 14-1: Persona Roles for a Sample Database Project

Persona Label	Role	Persona Description
Sue Order Taker	Transactional	Employee that takes orders over the phone
B2B Order Taker	Transactional	Web B2B Service that accepts new sales orders
Matt Supervisor	Gatekeeper	Employee that approves sales orders
John Report	Reporting	Employee that runs reports

User Segmentation

Are users segmented by customer, division, or company? If your database has to support different segments of users that play all the user roles, then you'll want to look for opportunities of partitioning tables by a segmented identifier. An identifier can optimally be a foreign key to another table or can simply be a code value. Adding the identifier into all the transactional tables allows for scalability in the future of using logical or physical partitioning strategies.

User Location

Where are the users located? Do you have requirements to deal with data delivery through low-speed means like modems or cell phone networks? These requirements force you to be interested in where those Transactional Role users are located regardless of whether they are real humans or services. The performance requirements are different when you need to cope with network latencies or just simple application latency from users walking away from machines in the middle of transactions. You'll need this information to formulate a strategy of maintaining transactional integrity across this latency and to develop a locking strategy.

What Is the Nature of the User-Role Access Requirements?

Within each user role, you need to dig into what the users are actually going to be doing. Entering in the results of a phone call has a different data throughput then handling a programmable logic control streaming in data through a service. Find out the percentage each user role performs for insert, update, read, and delete operations. You are looking for use-case based activities such as frequent update and select activities occurring in a single table with high transaction volume. These operations can cause contention for a common resource.

What Is the User Response Time Requirement?

Consideration of the user response requirements is important. Understanding user-role access requirements leads into determining whether user response time cannot be compromised or whether a high level of performance is even required. In the case of capturing PLC (programmable logic control) output, an architectural decision to add a messaging protocol like MSMQ (Microsoft Messaging Queue) to provide the failsafe capabilities can release the real-time performance requirements from the database. The queue messages can then be processed in an offline manner providing the same functionality without the failure points. Other activities like user-based data entry may not need high performance. Does the row entered need to be immediately available for another process?

Design efforts should focus on determining whether the main activities of a user role are read only or transactional. Performance tuning is about tradeoffs. Optimizing tables for reporting operations renders insert and update operations suboptimal. If most of the activities performed by a role are read only, then you can develop strategies to replicate and distribute data to other servers to reduce the workload on a core transactional server.

What Is the Uptime Requirement?

In today's world, uptime is becoming a 24-hour-a-day, 7-days-a-week requirement. Intra-Corporate, single-time zone systems may sometimes be more forgiving. Knowing your downtime windows provides the opportunity to increase performance by performing statistics updates, stored procedure recompilation, index rebuilding, and other maintenance activities. You can also choose to run the batch-based use cases during this time.

Another component of uptime requirements is asking how much data is required to be stored. How long does it need to be online, near-online and offline? You'll notice that highly transactional systems used by banks to provide checking and savings transactions typically restrict certain expensive transactions to a date and time limits. Retrieval of online check copies or statements is an example of this type of restriction. This is optimal from a performance standpoint, but can be frustrating for a user if they are running behind balancing the family checkbook and can't easily get to older data. American Express handles this by showing only the last few months of statements online. However, you can get archived copies moved online, by using a request process that takes only a few hours or a day at most. This is an example of a smart compromise. The uptime requirement is met without incurring all the storage or transactional costs. Look at this type of solution for your uptime requirements while asking the question of how much is really needed to be online.

What Is the Required Throughput of Business Transactions?

One of the key responsibilities of a DBA or architect managing a database is to understand the throughput of the core business transaction performed on a routine basis. With this understanding, you'll be able to zero in on a large physical model and focus on the high-impact areas for performance improvement. To get the full picture, you need to identify the core tables in the database by usage type and then apply some benchmark numbers through a data-flow analysis.

Identifying Core Tables by Usage Type

If you are lucky to be involved in the design decisions early enough, get a handle on the logical model and provide input. If not, get caught up. It is easier to see normalization issues at this altitude, and this should be the starting point for any performance analysis. What you are looking for here is a rate of growth. After gaining some experience with different project logic models, you'll start to notice that tables in the logical model can be separated and viewed in these categories.

- ❑ **Type tables:** Type tables are simple representation of enumerations. These tables contain an ID and a description field. Although these tables are small, they will be folded into many queries for UI and reporting purposes to translate the ID that is typically stored in an entity or transactional table type. If you are tempted to create one monolithic type table, see the section later in this chapter on single-use schemas.

- ❑ **Master data tables:** These tables are the structures that usually represent master data concepts. Examples from AdventureWorks database are the Department, Employee, and Shift. Master data tables have many attributes that are physically represented by a few common models. Although it is possible to have applications that have large numbers of these structures, entry requirements are typically low volume and reflect a slow rate of growth.

- ❑ **Association tables:** Association tables are structures that glue entities together. These tables hold identifying keys from each entity and little else. The ProductDocument and StoreContact tables are examples of this type in the AdventureWorks database.

- ❑ **Transactional header tables:** These table types contain root-level information about transactions. These are the parent tables to high-volume transactional detail tables and can contain state information as well as summary information for the child detail transactions. These tables are generally your hotspots because they experience updates as well as steady retrieval since these are the topmost node in a hierarchy.

❑ **Transactional detail tables:** These tables are the child-level transaction information for the parent transactional header tables. A best practice design for these tables is to design them for insert-only operations as much as possible. Provide state types to mark them as inert instead of deleting rows during high availability periods. Rows marked in inert states can be more easily removed in offline periods with little impact prior to reindexing operations. If updates are allowed to these tables, you'll need to look here for performance tuning as well.

❑ **Workflow tables:** These tables represent event-based operations that are required during the workflow of a business process. Different flavors of these types of tables include stateful workflow queues where the rows stay indefinitely and only a state is changed as an entity moves through a business process. Another option is a net-zero workflow queue where the entity ID is moved into the structure and once the action is taken by the process and verified then the entity ID is removed from the queue structure. This is an enterprise development concept that isn't represented in the AdventureWorks database.

❑ **Historical tables:** These tables are INSERT mode only and contain audit or historical information. Typically, these tables are populated by insert triggers from entity or transactional tables.

❑ **System tables:** These tables are seldom issues for performance tuning. They contain administrator-level information like database version or settings to define processes. These tables are very seldom altered.

Once you have iterated through your logical or physical model and have categorized your tables, it is a good practice to create a set of administration tables to store this metadata either directly in your database or in a separate administration-only database. Later in this chapter, you'll use this type of information to create benchmarks that enable you to evaluate the growth of the design structures as the database moves through a full-development life cycle. You can use this format as an example of applying this categorization to some of the tables in AdventureWorks.

Table 14-2: Separating Tables by Usage Type

AdventureWorks Table	Type
SalesOrderHeader	TRANSACTIONAL HEADER TABLE
SalesOrderHeaderSalesReason	ASSOCIATION TABLE
SalesPerson	MASTER DATA TABLE
SalesPersonQuotaHistory	HISTORICAL TABLE

If you periodically store row counts for each of these tables, you'll be able to be proactive in performance design and tuning. The results from the AdventureWorks analysis show only four tables that qualify as high transactional tables: SalesOrderHeader, SalesOrderDetail, PurchaseOrderHeader, and PurchaseOrderDetail. You should pay special attention to these tables for insert and update performance issues. Other tables such as the TransactionHistoryArchive table contain high row counts, but are INSERT-based only. You probably won't have write issues with this table but will probably need to watch the table for read optimizations. However, before you can make that determination, there is one more analysis that you need to make regarding use-case throughput.

Identifying Core Use-Case Throughput

Throughput is the measurement of the number of rows input into each entity as the result of a defined use-case. If you have the metrics for this type of information, you can monitor the performance of the database in terms that management understands. How many times are you asked what will happen if two new customers are added to the system? If you know the use cases that the customers will be performing and an instance count, you should be able to provide immediate sizing and performance impact information. If something performance-based is affecting the system, you should be able to identify proactively the use cases that are going to be the most affected. You can do these things if you have core use cases and associate them to the tables in the schema.

If you are involved in the beginning with the database design, keep track of the core use cases. First, understand what the system is supposed to do. Then identify the core tasks that are architecturally significant from a database perspective. If you are examining a rating engine, the tasks of creating rate structures and using rate structures in calculations are the most architecturally significant tasks for the system. These core use cases are the reason that the system was created in the first case. Creating the master data entities is important, but this activity is not the essence of a rating system. Once you examine the core use cases and enumerate them, store this metadata in your database as well. To have this data available for later benchmarking processes, gather this type of information for core use cases. Table 14-3 shows an example of mapping use cases to database operations. In the table, each use case may be represented by multiple database operations, for example, the use case entering a sales order requires the insertion of 1 SalesorderHeader, and many sales order detail records. In the table, the number of inserts is shown as 3, which in the case of the example is the average number of detail records inserted for each header.

Table 14-3: Identifying Use Cases and Table Usage

Use Case	Database Object	Update	Insert	Select	Delete
Entering a sales order	Sales.SalesOrderHeader	0	1	0	0
	Sales.SalesOrderDetail	0	3	0	0
Approving a sales order	Sales.SalesOrderHeader	1	0	0	0
Running a sales report	vSalesPersonSalesByFiscalYears	0	0	2000	0

The first use case is entering a sales order. When this activity occurs, you may expect one row to be inserted into the SalesOrderHeader table and an average of three rows to be inserted into the SalesOrderDetail table. The second use case of approving a sales order only involves a single update to the SalesOrderHeader. If the stored procedures and views that are involved in these use cases were known, then they would be entered here as well. The last use case is running a report that should result in selecting an average of 2,000 rows from the vSalesPersonSalesByFiscalYears view. You could also add the component tables to the use case that make up the view for even better tracking of resource usage.

If we were to enter the use case of adding a product, we would be looking at many more inserts and updates, but the point is to know your core use cases. This information is useful if stored as metadata in the database. You'll use this metadata later in the chapter to examine data flow growth, and having it provides the answers to most of the common questions that you'll get later on from a planning and performance tuning perspective. These data are stored in the Benchmark_UseCase_Object_Assn table in the benchmark data model. To provide use case information at the persona level, take the time to map the personas to each use case as shown in Table 14-4.

Table 14-4: Mapping Personas to Use Cases

Persona	Use Case
Sue Order Taker	Entering a sales order
B2B Order Taker	Entering a sales order
Matt Supervisor	Approving a sales order
John Report	Running a sales report

What Is the Software Application's Core Architecture?

It's not enough to have all your ducks in a row from the database perspective. Many highly tuned databases have been brought to their knees over a poorly designed application or an overly permissive WHERE predicate in a report. If you are not involved with the application design, have a discussion with the architect of the software to get this type of understanding before you start making performance tuning plans. Here are some of the big performance killers that you would be interested in:

❑ **Large result sets:** Many apps take the stance of delivering all the rows to the client and allow the client to perform paging and sorting. Although there are use cases where this is legitimate, evaluate whether the users are just paging two or three pages into the results and changing the search criteria. Allowing the client to manage this activity in this case (like most cases) is wasteful.

❑ **Disconnected composite activities:** Apps that have composite-type operations should send those operations to the server in a composite action. Activities that perform multiple network round trips to validate and then look up the next action in a process stack should move that decision step into a business tier or into a parent stored procedure.

❑ **Long-running transactions:** Apps that open transactions over long periods create blocking and resource contention issues. There are applications that calculate invoice detail while holding transactions open for hours. Applications of that type could be improved by using a state type on the header table that is updated upon completion of building the detail and only hold transactions at the detail level.

❑ **Incorrect cursor usage:** There are two types of design issues to monitor. The first refers to apps that open keyset cursors on database tables and then update through the recordset. If this is occurring at any great frequency and your app is not designed for a single-user, then have this reworked to send update and insert transactions through a stored procedure. This could also refer to iterative solutions performed in TSQL instead of using set-based approaches. To uncover cursor use, run this extraction query, which examines syscomments to look for cursor declarations, and use `sp_helptext` to examine each procedure or function body:

```
SELECT object_name(id) FROM syscomments
WHERE text LIKE '%DECLARE%CURSOR%'
```

Understanding the basics of how a software solution or system is using the database will provide a high level of insight for the work that you will need to perform for performance purposes. Don't forget that there may be multiple systems accessing a common data platform, so consider these as well when gathering information about application architecture. You should be interested in whether the application is architected for heavy user-entry or process-oriented entry. User-entry apps are generally granular in the transaction style. Process-oriented application can also be granular, but can be capable of sending granular transactions at a much higher throughput.

Evaluating Schemas for Performance Unknowns

It would be ideal if you can be involved early on in an application design process to gather the performance requirements prior to an implementation. This is not always possible, and sometimes you are handed logical models and are expected to implement them. Without this inside knowledge, designing for performance is a challenge for sure, but surprisingly you can get close if you follow a few basic common-sense guidelines.

- ❑ **Design for simplicity:** Anything you can think of that is considered well-designed is reliable, easy-to-use, easy-to-maintain, and amazingly simple. When you experience a well-designed thing, you think to yourself, "Why didn't I think of that?" This same idea should be applied when building applications. If a table design is too complicated to explain and is clearly not aligned to the business model, then no matter how "neat" it is, it is poorly designed and is bound to create performance issues.

- ❑ **Design with third normal form in mind:** Research shows that third normal form is generally the place where performance maximums are met. Go back to Chapter 8 if you are unsure how to determine whether a database is in this form.

- ❑ **Design using the single-responsibility principle:** This is an object-oriented concept that is extremely relevant to database design. Each data structure should have a single responsibility. Each data column should have a single purpose. Violating this principle is asking for trouble. Not only is the data model ambiguous, but the logic needed to interpret multi-use structures and columns is involved. Some logic may be removed from the database and only be interpreted by reviewing the software.

- ❑ **Design with enterprise scope in mind:** But don't overdo it. Not everything needs to be designed with enterprise-grade rigor. If you can think ahead about increasing input or output and start with input entry points like stored procedures, the development process already starts on the right foot.

These basic design guidelines are useful, but they make more sense if you can see them applied with some real context. The next sections will expand these principles and provide some concrete examples of how you can use them to meet your performance requirements.

Simple Schemas

Keep it simple. We have a rule in our shop that if looking at a model requires you to slow down and study it the model probably needs to be rethought. This is not to say that you can always simplify every business problem into a handful of patterns, but it does mean that you can go overboard trying to come up with something original. Put new models to a sniff test with your team or user group and see how much you have to defend the model. If everyone understands it and it meets the business requirements, then you're probably okay.

Run the profiler to capture TSQL statements that are being submitted during the heavy usage periods. If you see TSQL statements that use too many case statements or look overly complicated, then the statement may be bad, or it may be an indication that the underlying structure or design is just not right. Developers are problem solvers who will rise to a challenge to find a solution — even though the solution may be detrimental to database performance. If the statement starts to create blocking or long-running situations, you should be picking this up during your benchmarking processes. We'll go over how to start some of these metrics later in the benchmarking section.

Single-Use Tables

Design tables that have single uses. This comes from an object-oriented concept called the *single-responsibility principle*. The idea is that each table in the system should have a single responsibility and that's it. You can see violations of this in places like the type tables. Instead of creating a unique type table for each type, you'll see a logical design for one type table that has a type within itself. Undoubtedly, someone looked at the type table structure (that is typically an identifier and a description) and thought how convenient it would be from a software perspective to create only one object capable of performing maintenance on one structure instead of a proliferation of type tables. An example of the two methods is shown in Figure 14-1.

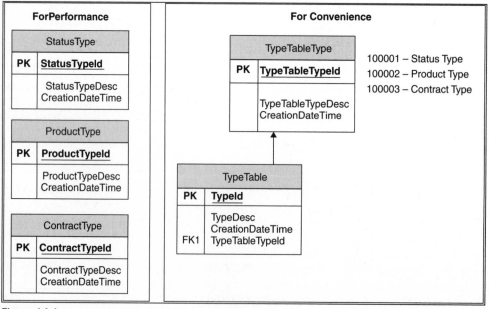

Figure 14-1

The reason that this design is not a good idea from a performance perspective is that the combined "For Convenience" model tables are going to be hotspots in the database. Every need to translate a type table will need to go through these tables. This design is also not optimal when you need to scale out. In the performance design, only the status type table is used for translation lookups of status types. This table is not affected by requests for a different type table like the contract type. If you find later that you are getting too many requests for the status type, we can scale out by moving this type table onto another file resource. The "For Convenience" design will become the bottleneck for requests for type description translations. If you are convinced that your user scale will only be single user based, this may never be a problem. However, if your user scale is known to be corporate or infinite, starting with a known bottleneck pattern like this is asking for trouble.

Single-Use Columns

Design columns with the same single-responsibility principle. Reject designs that attempt to reuse a column in a model design. These designs result in complicated queries that can't be easily optimized. Take for example a simple invoice model where two entity types can be invoiced. Figure 14-2 shows two different approaches to resolving this modeling problem.

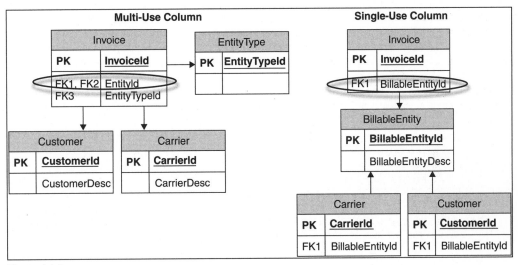

Figure 14-2

The approach that violates the single-use column rule uses a general EntityId attribute in the invoice model to represent either the Carrier or the Customer entity identifier. In order to be able to interpret the EntityId field, an entity type table has to be added with two entries: Customer and Carrier. To provide a listing of all the invoices with a description of the entity, the query would look like this:

```
SELECT INV.*, CAR.CARRIERDESC AS BILLABLEENTITYDESC
FROM INVOICE INV
INNER JOIN CARRIER CAR
ON CAR.CARRIERID = INV.ENTITYID
AND INV.ENTITYTYPEID = 100000
UNION
```

```
SELECT INV.*, CUST.CUSTOMERDESC as BILLABLEENTITYDESC
FROM INVOICE INV
INNER JOIN CUSTOMER CUST
ON CUST.CUSTOMERID = INV.ENTITYID
AND INV.ENTITYTYPEID = 100001
```

In contrast, the second example models a super type entity called a BillableEntity. Each subentity associates itself with the billable entity. This attribute is common to both subentities, namely the description is moved up into the super type. This enables the Invoice entity to have a single relationship to a billable entity. The query is also easier and more efficient from an optimizer perspective.

```
SELECT INV.*, BI.BILLABLEENTITYDESC
FROM INVOICE INV
INNER JOIN BILLABLEENTITY BI
ON INV.BILLABLEENTITYID = BI.BILLABLEENTITYID
```

The query plans will show you what you already know. The first query has to pass the clustered index twice to examine the invoice table under each of the subtype conditions. Look for the Clustered Index Scan operations in this plan for the first UNION-based query.

```
Merge Join(Union)
|--Nested Loops(Inner Join, OUTER REFERENCES:([INV].[EntityId]))
|    |--Clustered Index Scan(OBJECT:([Invoice1].[PK_Invoice1] AS [INV]),
|        WHERE:([Invoice1].[EntityTypeId] as [INV].[EntityTypeId]=(100000))
|                         ORDERED FORWARD)
|    |--Clustered Index Seek(OBJECT:([Carrier1].[PK_Carrier1] AS [CAR]),
|        SEEK:([CAR].[CarrierId]=[Invoice1].[EntityId] as [INV].[EntityId])
|                         ORDERED FORWARD)
|--Nested Loops(Inner Join, OUTER REFERENCES:([INV].[EntityId]))
|--Clustered Index Scan(OBJECT:([Invoice1].[PK_Invoice1] AS [INV]),
|    WHERE:([Invoice1].[EntityTypeId] as [INV].[EntityTypeId]=(100001))
|        ORDERED FORWARD)
|--Clustered Index Seek(OBJECT:([Customer1].[PK_Customer1] AS [CUST]),
|    SEEK:([CUST].[CustomerId]=[Invoice1].[EntityId] as [INV].[EntityId])
|    ORDERED FORWARD)
```

By abstracting the carrier and customer entities into a billable entity, only one pass is needed on the invoice index. This can be seen in the difference in the total subquery costs of .018 for the multi–use column option and .006 for the single-use — a 66 percent difference.

```
Nested Loops(Inner Join, OUTER REFERENCES:([INV].[BillableEntityId]))
|--Index Scan(OBJECT:( [Invoice2].[IX_INVOICE2_BILLABLE_ENTITY_ID] AS [INV]))
|--Clustered Index Seek(OBJECT:( [BillableEntity].[PK_BillableEntity] AS [BI]),
|    SEEK:([BI].[BillableEntityId]= [BillableEntityId] as [INV].[BillableEntityId])
|        ORDERED FORWARD)
```

You may think that you haven't really done anything by pushing the abstraction down one layer, but there is a difference. If you needed attributes from the subtypes, you don't need any information about the types of the subtypes to create a query to do this. It would simply use a LEFT OUTER JOIN for each potential subtype like this.

```
SELECT INV.*, BI.BILLABLEENTITYDESC, CAR.*, CUST.*
FROM INVOICE2 INV
```

```
INNER JOIN BILLABLEENTITY BI
ON INV.BILLABLEENTITYID = BI.BILLABLEENTITYID
LEFT OUTER JOIN CARRIER2 CAR
ON BI.BILLABLEENTITYID = CAR.BILLABLEENTITYID
LEFT OUTER JOIN CUSTOMER2 CUST
ON BI.BILLABLEENTITYID = CUST.BILLABLEENTITYID
```

Performance should not be the only driving factor for eliminating multi-use column designs. These designs also make the model ambiguous. You can't glance at the invoice table and readily understand that the EntityId represents both the primary key for the carrier and the customer entities. This breaks the first principle of keeping things simple. In the next section, we'll look at how having too many nullable columns is another way models get ambiguous.

Eliminating Ambiguous Null Fields

Excessive use of nullable fields may be a dead giveaway for performance problems in an OLTP database. You'll see designs like this when developers get too lazy to implement a relational design or too greedy and want the database design to map back to an architecture that is easier for them to implement. One example of this would be a table designed with many fields to record dates and times for an entity that goes through many states. Update operations are the most expensive in an OLTP database structure. With this type of design you are guaranteeing that this table will be updated for each stage encountered that requires a new date. A relational approach would incur an INSERT operation instead. Figure 14-3 shows the two implementations.

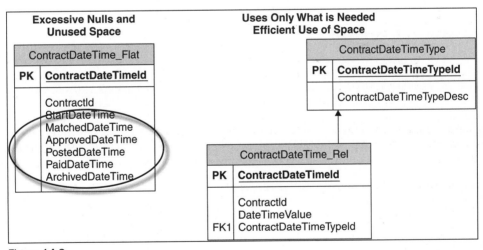

Figure 14-3

Here's where you get into some clear tradeoffs by using these two implementations. For read operations, the flat structure will make your job much easier. For write operations, you have to search the table to find the row, and then lock the page to update the dates. Here is where you need the information from the performance requirements of the application that uses this database to help you decide the best implementation. Table 14-5 lists some of the advantages and disadvantages.

Table 14-5: Tradeoff Matrix for Relational and Non-Relational Structures

Flat	Relational	Comparison
Y	N	Single SQL Statement for read, updates, and deletes
N	Y	JOIN Required
N	Y	Physical model looks like logical model
N	Y	Page scan requires minimal I/O
N	Y	Only applicable columns are stored
Y	N	Optimized for reads
N	Y	Optimized for writes

If you looked at your performance requirements and you have heavy emphasis on report roles and little emphasis on transactional roles, the flat implementation would be the better choice. However, if you have heavy transactional requirements, opt for the relational solution. Remember that you can still get to this type of structure by processing the data in an offline period to build cubes as long as your user response time requirements can still be met. It is generally easier to go from data that are more granular and work back to summarized data than to work the other way around.

ID-Based Partitioning

If during your analysis of user performance requirements you discover that you have quite a bit of user segmentation, make sure that you design the capabilities into the tables to enable separation directly to these user segments. User segmentation is indicative of product-based software development. If your application is provided as a service, each user segment probably uses the software in a separate environment. User segments limit data to specific customer-based information, not as representative of security levels, but more on a customer level. One easy way to segment an application is to create a copy of the database and create a new environment, whether it is a website or a file share that the program can use to connect to the database. Another way to segment can be as simple as adding an identifier for the user segment into each table in the database. For performance, don't just think that you can provide this separation via a relationship. It is not good enough to have the segment information through a relationship with the user login; you need the attribute of segmentation directly on the transactional entities themselves.

Denormalization for Performance

As you develop in both OLTP and OLAP database environments, you really start to get the fact that OLTP is all about maintaining the integrity and speed of the write operation. Therefore, as you model out the physical structure of the database, the write operation becomes the main concern from a performance perspective. The problem is that everything can be done at a cost. The offsetting cost of the write optimization is the creation of performance problems for the read operations. It is difficult to keep a balance when you have heavy reporting requirements from your OLTP database. One of the compromises is to denormalize selective data by moving it up into higher levels of domain hierarchy so you can reduce the need to traverse multiple JOIN levels for the information. You should have a good reason before you go down the denormalization road. It should be something that you do selectively.

If you see some abnormal I/O usage during the development process, dig into those procedures to see what manipulations are being performed to find specific instances for denormalization. An example is a model where there are trips that have many stops. Each stop is given an order sequence so that it can be determined in which order the stops are encountered. Trip entities are inserted first and then all the stops are added at once and related to the trips. During your benchmarking process, you may notice some queries that have logic to determine the ultimate origination and destination of a trip from the stop records. Figure 14-4 shows an example of a normalized and denormalized approach to modeling this trip and stop relationship.

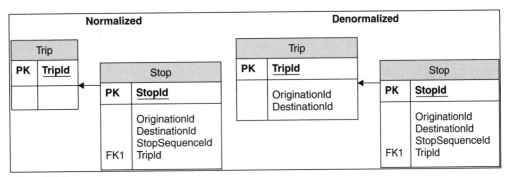

Figure 14-4

If you are using the normalized model version, your query logic first aggregates the join between the trip and stop to find the last StopSequenceId for each trip. This stop should be the Ultimate Destination. The Ultimate Origin of a trip is the stop with the StopSequenceId of one (1). With both StopSequenceIds, you just need to join both back to the trip and summarize to get the two rows into one result. The query is messy and looks something like this:

```
--Summarize to One Row Per Trip
SELECT TripID, MAX(UltOrigId) As UltOrigId, MAX(UltDestId) as UltDestId
FROM (
        --Gets One row by Trip For Origin / One row by Trip for Destination
        SELECT TRP.TripId, UltOrigId = Case when STP1.StopSequence = 1
                                    then STP1.OriginId else null end,
                UltDestId = case when STP1.StopSequence = DEST.StopSequence
                                    then STP1.DestinationId else null end
        FROM TRIP TRP
        INNER JOIN (
                --Get the Last Sequence
                SELECT T.TripId, MAX(StopSequence) as StopSequence
                FROM STOP STP
                INNER JOIN TRIP T
                ON STP.TripId = T.TripId
                Group By T.TripId
                ) DEST
        ON TRP.TripId = DEST.TripId
        INNER JOIN STOP STP1
        ON DEST.TripId = STP1.TripId
```

```
      WHERE DEST.StopSequence = STP1.StopSequence
      OR STP1.StopSequence = 1
) OUTERQRY
GROUP BY TripID
```

By moving the destination and origination fields up to the TRIP entity as well as the STOP, the query will get much easier, reduce the need for three joins, and decreases I/O requirements. This change is equivalent to using the denormalized version of the relationships in Figure 14-4. The query is now simple.

```
SELECT TripId, OriginationId, DestinationId FROM TRIP
```

This change will also not be a big deal for the software since the logic was already inserting all the stops at one time. The Trip will now additionally need to be updated when the stops are inserted. The big consideration here is what this extra update costs and how that compares with the decrease in the cost of traversing through those relationships. These types of determinations need to be made before too much denormalization occurs.

Performance Effect of Functions in Views

Views provide great abstractions for development activity. The same convenience they provide can become a performance nightmare when developers don't look behind the view and begin to do things like building views on top of views or embedding user-defined functions in views. If you have a standard to name views with a preceding *v* or similar marking, you can find the instances where views are stacked by searching with wildcards in the sysComments table like this:

```
Select * from sysComments where text like '%from v%' and type = 'V'
```

When views have embedded user-defined functions, you may not realize that you are incurring heavy costs for running them. If you are just looking at the XML query execution plan, the optimizer minimizes the cost by showing low percentage scalar operators. Don't neglect to look at the full query execution plan to see the detailed and broken out costs. You can see an example using the AdventureWorks user-defined function `ufnGetProductListPrice` in a view to calculate the current product list price across all the products with today's date like this.

```
CREATE VIEW vGetProductListPriceForToday
AS
Select ProductId, dbo.ufnGetProductListPrice(ProductId, getdate()) as CurrentPrice
FROM Production.Product
```

When you simply select from the new view, the query plan looks like Figure 14-5.

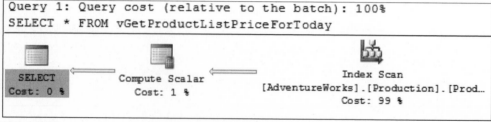

Figure 14-5

512

With SHOWPLAN_ALL set to on, you can see that more is going on with this scalar computation than was shown visually. Look at the profiler or run the query with SET STATISTICS IO to ON, and you'll see that a large amount of I/O (170,000 reads) is taking place somewhere other than an index scan on the production.product table. It makes sense that a function querying other tables should incur that cost on each row materialized in the view. What isn't so clear is why the optimizer hides the ultimate impact of those details from you. The result is that programmers relying upon optimizer feedback in the query plan may create situations where the queries become performance issues as the result sets grow. To counter this, continue to educate your developers. Outside of that, you can look for function calls in syscomments, assuming they are named with the dbo.fn prefix by using this query:

```
SELECT * FROM syscomments
WHERE Text like '%dbo.fn%'
```

Evaluating Indexes for Performance

There is just not enough index design activity occurring in today's data modeling activities. It seems like all the time is spent in the table modeling, but indexes can really change the performance of a database negatively or positively depending upon how they are implemented. If you are working on improving performance for an application that has some transactional history, you're in luck. You can evaluate index performance by using the new Dynamic Management View (DMV) that provides index usage statistics named sys.dm_db_index_usage_stats. In this view you can determine which indexes have never been used and which indexes are consistently being used. If you follow the recommendations in the benchmarking section of this chapter, you'll be able to observe usage patterns on your index schemes of time and make meaningful adjustments.

If there are indexes on a table that aren't being used, then performance is being affected because indexes are being built that are never used. These statistics will help back up explanations to others who insist on doing things like placing an index on a column that has low selectivity (that is, a small number of distinct values relative to the number of rows). This creates useless indexes that can reduce performance. The database server has to not only search the entire set of rows that match the key value, but it must also lock all the affected data and index pages. This process can slow down or even block the performance of incoming update requests.

No-Thought/Default Indexing

If you are in the beginning of a database project and are unsure about how to model indexes, start with the no-thought or default indexing schemes. Adjust your indexing once you are able to re-evaluate the database with actual transaction information. Consider following these suggestions for starters:

❑ Create indexes on all primary keys. (This should be a given.)

❑ Create indexes on all foreign keys. Assuming you are going into a development phase on a new database, this won't hurt. There are some situations where foreign key indexes may not be needed, but go with the 80/20 rule and evaluate later.

❑ Don't create additional indexes for columns that are already in an index. This is unnecessary and may result in the index not being used.

❑ Order columns in your composite indexes by selectivity. The columns with the most selectivity should go first. You may also combine two not very selective columns in a composite index, resulting in a more selective index. Columns that have high-cardinality or distinct values are highly selective and should be up front in a composite index.

Simple Access Pattern Indexing

After you have the basics all set up, go over and ask software developers for any of their software class or UML modeling diagrams. DBAs should get these or at least ask for them when they get the logical data models. Class-modeling diagrams have some good information about how the software is designed to interact with the database. If you look for the methods on the classes, you might see methods called `GetEmployeeByName()` or `SelEmployeesByBirthDate()`. These method calls provide excellent information about how you should be indexing other attributes in the database model that are not part of key structures but are providing a level of access.

In the two Employee selection method examples above, you would want to examine the model around the employee to determine where the attributes of Employee Name and Birth Date are stored. Then add non-clustered indexes around these attributes. If you don't have access to the modeling instructions, you'll have to have similar information stored on a regular basis from the DMV for indexes.

Complex Access Pattern Indexing

Look at adding covering indexes to eliminate bookmark lookups. One of the easiest ways to find these index candidates is by looking for high values in the User_Lookups column in the Index DMV `sys.dm_db_index_usage_stats`. It may be possible to speed up some queries by adding columns as included columns into non-clustered indexes for performance reasons. If a high volume (repetitive) TSLQ query can use a few columns stuffed into the nonclusted index to avoid scanning a clustered index, this is a significant reduction in I/O activity. The trick is figuring out which columns are referenced by the query. These columns are the select list columns and any required join or sort columns. This technique of covering a query with an index is particularly useful and not only reduces I/O, it speeds up response time. However, it takes more time to carefully evaluate and tune.

Benchmarking for Evaluation

Earlier in the chapter, we encouraged the creation of a set of benchmark tables to store some metadata about the nature of the database objects. You categorized tables in a database according to their functional purposes and stitched them together with high impact use-cases to be able to talk back to business owners about database issues in their terms. In SQL Server 2000, you could not get object-level usage statistics. In this section, you'll use the DMVs exposed in SQL Server 2005 to add to this metadata the statistical information that you'll need to be able to refer to when deciding whether the database is meeting the performance requirement expectations.

Creating the Benchmark Schema

Earlier we discussed capturing information in a meta-data format for expected performance requirements like persona and use cases. These data are useful when you can connect these user-concepts to real metrics from the database objects themselves. As part of this chapter, we've created a model to allow the capturing of database statistics. To create these tables download the script from www.wrox.com. The scripts will create the tables and populate the type table information to match the discussions earlier in the performance requirements section of this chapter.

Extracting Object_Id-Level Information from DMVs

After working with the new DMVs in SQL Server 2005, we were blown away by the amount of information that was available. This awe stopped cold for a minute when we realized that the Object_Id wasn't embedded into many of the DMV outputs. Where's the Object_Id? The DMV information is wonderful, but you have to have the database object without trying to guess by looking at the plan or examining the SQL text. After scrambling around a bit, we realized that the Object_Id is available in any of the functions that take either a sql_handler or a plan_handle. The system-level table-value functions all return the database identifier and the object identifier when you pass in either handle.

Table 14-6: Functions to Return Plans or SQL Statements from DMVs

System TVF	Input Required to Retrieve Object_Id
Sys.dm_exec_sql_text	SQL_Handle
sys.dm_exec_text_query_plan	Plan_Handle
sys.dm_exec_query_plan	Plan_Handle

We'll use these system TVFs to data-mine DMV information by object_Id for our benchmarking metrics evaluation.

Capturing Table Throughput

Often when a new member is added to our development team, they want to know how the data flows through the model as time and processes progress. If you are responsible for designing with performance in mind from the start, you are going to want to be able to pull out this type of information from your development and testing environments. A start is to record row counts by table on an hourly, daily, or weekly basis during the testing phases of your project.

There are several ways to get the row count information from the database. One way is to iterate through a cursor and count the rows in each table, but the more elegant way is to use the stored procedure sp_msforeachtable. This undocumented stored procedure will perform an action on each table based on the input command and is simple to use. The TSQL looks like this:

```
CREATE PROC usp_StoreBenchMarkTableDataVolumeHistory
AS
/*STORE TABLE ROW COUNTS FOR BENCHMARK TABLES
  ======================================================*/
DECLARE @MYSQL NVARCHAR(2000)
SET @MYSQL = N'INSERT INTO Benchmark_Table_DataVolumeHistory select Object_Id(''?''),
getdate(), count(*) from ?';
EXEC sp_msforeachtable @MYSQL
```

The date uses the current date so that you can put this TSQL snippet into any scheduled process under any schedule. The result is that the process can control how frequently it needs to run.

515

Monitoring Index Usage

After recording table throughput, the next thing that you'll want to monitor and benchmark is the index usage history. This will give you the data you need to evaluate your index choices. If you see more user scans than user seeks, then you need to examine the database object to see if it can be tuned for performance in any way. If you have already created the benchmark table for this data, you can use this procedure to store index usage periodically.

```
CREATE PROC usp_StoreBenchMarkObjectIndexUsage
AS
/*STORE INDEX USAGE HISTORY COUNTS FOR BENCHMARK TABLES
   ========================================================*/
INSERT into Benchmark_Object_IndexUsageHistory
Select    dmv.object_id
          ,sampledatetime=Getdate()
          ,index_id
          , user_seeks
          , user_scans
          , user_lookups
from sys.dm_db_index_usage_stats dmv
inner join Benchmark_Table bt
on dmv.object_id = bt.object_id
```

TempDB Usage

Some applications really look good in their native databases but are not hospitable to the Temp database. You don't want to be monitoring a database through the development stage only to be blindsided when you go to production and find that the temp database requirement that you had in testing can't be met in the production environment. You'll also find if the temp database is being overly used that something may not be right with the modeling and you may need to denormalize a few select things. However, you can't make those judgments without something to look at. Run this query on a regular basis to capture the TempDB usage history for the database:

```
CREATE PROC usp_StoreTempDBHistory
AS
/*STORE TEMPDB USAGE HISTORY AS SERVER LEVEL
   ========================================================*/
INSERT INTO Benchmark_TempDBHistory
SELECT getdate(),
 SUM(user_object_reserved_page_count) * 8 as user_objects_kb,
 SUM(internal_object_reserved_page_count) * 8 as internal_objects_kb,
 SUM(version_store_reserved_page_count) * 8 as version_store_kb,
 SUM(unallocated_extent_page_count) * 8 as freespace_kb
FROM sys.dm_db_file_Space_Usage
where database_id = 2
```

Notice that this information is stored at the server level. This won't be much help to you if you have more than one database on a server. To dig into tempDB and see what database objects are using these resources, you need to look at the DMV sys.dm_db_task_space_usage. This new DMV shows the allocation and de-allocation of pages per task in tempDB for your database. Page counts are stored in snapshots at user and internal object levels. Internal objects are structures like work tables, spools, work files for hash joins, or sort operations. User objects are structures like user-defined tables and indexes, system tables, global temp tables, local temp tables, and table-valued functions. Capture this object-level temp db usage by using this procedure:

```
CREATE PROC usp_StoreObjectTempDBHistory
AS
/*STORE TEMPDB USAGE HISTORY AT OBJECT LEVEL
   ======================================================*/
INSERT INTO Benchmark_Object_TempDBHistory
SELECT
    obj.objectid as [Object_Id],
    getdate() as SampleDateTime,
    sum(tmp.user_objects_alloc_page_count) AS user_objects_alloc_page_count,
    sum(tmp.user_objects_dealloc_page_count) AS user_objects_dealloc_page_count,
    sum(tmp.internal_objects_alloc_page_count)
            AS   internal_objects_alloc_page_count,
    sum(tmp.internal_objects_dealloc_page_count)
            AS internal_objects_dealloc_page_count
  FROM sys.dm_db_task_space_usage AS tmp
    LEFT OUTER JOIN sys.dm_exec_requests AS req
    ON tmp.session_id = req.session_id
      OUTER APPLY sys.dm_exec_sql_text(req.sql_handle) AS obj
   WHERE tmp.session_id > 50
 AND obj.objectid is not null
Group BY obj.ObjectId
```

Capturing Blocking Information

Applications that have long-running or slow-running queries may be affected by blocking. Blocking can occur when two processes are competing for the same resources or during simple system locking. For a guide to eliminating these bottlenecks, go back to Chapter 4. If you can identify issues with blocking, you may have problems with the data model or the application design. It may indicate that transactions are hierarchically at too high a level or that the level of transaction isolation is too broad. There are many places to look for blocking information in SQL Server 2005. For our purposes of recording this information periodically, store blocking information from the DMV sys.dm_db_index_operational_stats in terms of wait metrics by object identifier.

What you need to be able to do prior to rolling out a database is go back through these metrics and examine what objects are incurring any level of blocking. Blocking can occur at the table or the index level and since this is how the information is provided in the DMV, you'll just keep that same level of granularity. You can roll up to object-level summaries when you need to and be able to drill down into the index level for tuning:

```
CREATE PROC usp_StoreObjectBlockingHistory
AS
/*STORE OBJECT BLOCKING HISTORY
   ======================================================*/
BEGIN
  INSERT INTO Benchmark_Table_BlockingHistory
  SELECT s.object_id
    , SampleDateTime = getdate()
    , indexname=i.name, i.index_id
    , [block_pct]=cast (100.0 * row_lock_wait_count / (1 + row_lock_count) as
      numeric(15,2))
```

```
      , row_lock_wait_ms = row_lock_wait_in_ms
      , [avg_row_lock_waits_ms]=cast (1.0 * row_lock_wait_in_ms / (1 + row_lock_
        wait_count) as numeric(15,2))
    from sys.dm_db_index_operational_stats (db_id(), NULL, NULL, NULL) s
      ,sys.indexes i
    where objectproperty(s.object_id,'IsUserTable') = 1
    and i.object_id = s.object_id
    and i.index_id = s.index_id
    And row_lock_wait_count <> 0
    END
```

Monitoring High CPU Usage

To tune a system for CPU usage, you need to have an idea of which database objects are creating the most contention for CPU resources. You can find the total amount of CPU time and the number of executions of any database object in the DMV sys.dm_exec_query_stats. To make this data useful, you'll need to aggregate the statistics by object and store them historically. Here is the TSQL that can be run to store this information periodically.

```
CREATE PROC usp_StoreObjectCPUHistory
/*STORE CPU USAGE HISTORY
   =======================================================*/
AS
BEGIN
  INSERT INTO Benchmark_Object_CPUHistory
  SELECT
        objectid
        , getdate() As SampleDateTime
        , total_cpu_time
        , total_execution_count
        , number_of_statements
  FROM (
  SELECT
        qs.sql_handle
        , sum(qs.total_worker_time) as total_cpu_time
        , sum(qs.execution_count) as total_execution_count
        , count(*) as  number_of_statements
  FROM
        sys.dm_exec_query_stats qs
  GROUP BY qs.sql_handle ) dt
  Cross Apply sys.dm_exec_sql_text(dt.sql_handle) eqp
  WHERE ObjectId is not null
END
```

High CPU usage can be caused by many different design decisions as well as external influences like hardware configurations. Some of the things to look for to reduce CPU usage are:

❑ **Aggregate operations:** Look for high-cost Stream Aggregate operators in query execution plans.

❑ **Intensive calculations:** Look for TSQL operations that have intermediate calculations that use Stream Aggregate operators or string parsing activity

❑ **Table variables:** Look for instances where too many rows are being inserted into table variables. Use #temp tables instead.

❑   **Parallelism:** Heavy use of parallelism can create CPU usage issues and should appear in your batch processes and not in transactional contexts.

Monitoring High I/O Offenders

I/O is the lifeblood of a relational database system. You use I/O to read and write pages from the disk and swap old pages for new. Because this requires a mechanical disk head movement in today's current technology, I/O bottlenecks are typical in terms of performance. What's important is being able to monitor issues related to I/O usage prior to releasing a new database to a production environment.

To monitor I/O, use the DMV sys.dm_exec_query_stats to capture logical and physical read and write statistics. The logical stats give you information about how optimally the execution plans are being chosen. Typically you want the logical stats to be as low as possible. This may be achieved by tuning TSQL for performance by rewriting the statement. See Chapter 9 for some of these techniques. Other things to look for are high physical read stats and combinations of logical read and writes. Use this query to store these stats periodically.

```
CREATE PROC usp_StoreObjectIOHistory
/*STORE IO USAGE HISTORY
  ======================================================*/
AS
BEGIN
 INSERT INTO Benchmark_Object_IO_History
 Select ObjectId , GetDate() as SampleDateTime
         , (total_logical_reads/Cast(execution_count as Decimal(38,16)))
             as avg_logical_reads
         , (total_logical_writes/Cast(execution_count as Decimal(38,16)))
             as avg_logical_writes
         , (total_physical_reads/Cast(execution_count as Decimal(38,16)))
             as avg_physical_reads
         , Execution_Count
 from (
 select
           Sum(total_logical_reads) as total_logical_reads
         , Sum(total_logical_writes) as total_logical_writes
         , Sum(total_physical_reads) as total_physical_reads
         , Sum(execution_count) as execution_count
         , sh.objectid
 from sys.dm_exec_query_stats
 Cross Apply sys.dm_exec_sql_text(sql_Handle) sh
 Where objectId is not null
 Group By objectid
 ) SubQry
END
```

Communicating Performance Issues

Users and managers want to know why you can't be more proactive with communication performance issues. It is one thing to communicate that you have some blocking issues or some expensive I/O queries in the database. It is another thing to be able to describe who and what is being impacted. If you use these benchmark tables and insert the information, you can make the connection between the database objects and the use cases, roles, or personas that use those objects. This is the difference between reporting that you've got an abnormal blocking issue with the tables Sales.SalesOrderHeader and Sales.SalesOrderDetail and reporting that the two use cases for "Entering a Sales Order" and "Approving a Sales Order" are going to be affected.

If you were following along with the sample tables and created your lists of use cases, classified your tables by types, and associated your use case to your tables, then you are in great shape to put this information into a data structure. A data structure like the one shown in Figure 14-6 can be used to build some meaningful queries. This information becomes even more meaningful when combined with real data extracted and stored periodically from the DMVs.

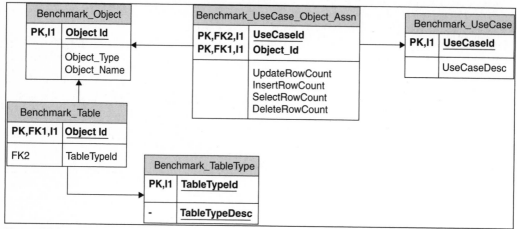

Figure 14-6

Figure 14-6 shows the traversal path to get from the database objects that are being benchmarked back to the use cases that are affected.

By enumerating the use cases in the Benchmark_UseCase table and having the stored number of update, insert, select, or delete operations for a typical use case such as approving a sales order, you can generate easy projections when the use case of sales order approval increases or decreases.

You can also use this model to report growth issues in use case terms. Figure 14-7 shows the difference between reporting the results only in database terms, and folding the use case description into the data to help provide meaning to the report for external communication.

	object_id	Object_Name	Starting_Row_Count	Ending_Row_Count	pct_Growth
1	722101613	SalesOrderHeader	31465	31465	0.000000000000
2	610101214	SalesOrderDetail	121317	121317	0.000000000000

	UseCaseDesc	object_id	Object_Name	Starting_Row_Count	Ending_Row_Count	pct_Growth
1	Approving a sales order	722101613	SalesOrderHeader	31465	31465	0.000000000000
2	Entering a sales order	610101214	SalesOrderDetail	121317	121317	0.000000000000
3	Entering a sales order	722101613	SalesOrderHeader	31465	31465	0.000000000000

Figure 14-7

You can see that the first set of results in Figure 14-7 show row growth from a table-based perspective. This is sometimes difficult to communicate when you are lobbying for more disk space from predictive increases in use-case activity. The second set of results relates these growth rates to individual use cases and provides a picture that is much more understandable to a non-technical person.

You can also traverse the model to provide performance metrics in terms of the different personas that will be using the system. The use cases connect the personas to database objects and allow you to get an idea of what the impact would be for adding new numbers of these personas to a database, as you can see in Figure 14-8.

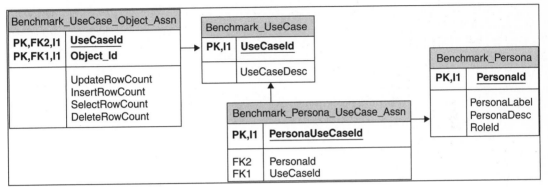

Figure 14-8

There are many ways you can use this information if you store the statistics at various intervals during the testing and quality assurance processes. Check out the scripts that are available at www.wrox.com for more examples and some sample growth and analysis queries.

Summary

In this chapter, you looked at how to integrate issues of performance early into the design process by asking questions about the performance requirements of the application and database environment. By understanding the nature of the user roles and use cases that will be performed, you can make some general design decisions based on solid, best practices. Recording metrics to benchmark performance metrics throughout the testing and quality assurance processes allows you to be proactive and see issues before you are in production. Some adjustments can be made after systems are in production, but they are usually minor. The major changes that can be made occur in the design phases of project. If you can implement a proactive benchmarking methodology, you'll be able to bring these items up before you'll have to deal with them in production environments. Remember that performance problems can be real database-level resource issues, or they can simply be perceptions of speed. Combine your knowledge of database performance problems to communicate back to user groups both in technical terms and in the language that they understand. Before you turn on the switch to production, follow along in Chapter 17 for more guidance in communicating your performance tuning and more political issues.

15

Successful Deployment Strategies

The application life cycle goes through a series of very important steps before the actual deployment. Just like any other application, the database platform is also expected to be reliable and agile. A lot of deployments fail due to a lack of sufficient planning and performance testing during the earlier stages. This chapter aims to provide some guidelines and best practices to follow for a successful deployment of your application databases.

Your production system can be compared to a supply chain process. The world of supply chains consists of incoming orders that are fulfilled by servers (machines, humans, and so on). The servers source various components that are then assembled together to make the final product. These products are then stored in inventory to be shipped out to customers. The capacity of a supply chain environment is determined by the capacity of the slowest process within the supply chain. A process that restricts a supply chain from achieving maximum throughput is known as a bottleneck. A bottleneck may arise due to multiple factors such as machine breakdowns, lack of resources, or simply poor planning.

Similarly, a typical production scenario consists of users that request information from the application or database through the use of queries or transactions. These transactions are then processed by the various servers (computers) after having assimilated the information from various sources such as cache, memory, disk, and so on. Once the information has been gathered, the replies are then sent back to the users.

As it is in a supply chain environment, a production scenario consists of bottlenecks that could cause slowdowns at various stages of the process. Bottlenecks could arise due to slower memory, slow processing power, I/O queues due to a slow storage subsystem, and so on. The important point to remember is that no matter what the bottleneck may be, the actual capacity of the production system is constrained by the bottleneck areas. No matter how fast your processors are, if the disk I/O is causing the slowness, the processors will remain idle as they wait for replies from the storage subsystem.

Our goal is to identify these bottlenecks and hopefully mitigate them during the pre deployment stages. We talk about various aspects of the application life cycle starting from sizing your architecture to partitioning large tables without delving into the actual details, as they have been covered elsewhere in this book. However, as luck would have it, even though a lot can be done during the pre-deployment stages, every DBA faces issues post production. The latter part of the chapter talks about certain limitations faced when tuning production systems.

Best Practice

Find the bottlenecks before your production deployment.

Sizing

One of the most important steps in the database deployment life cycle is sizing. In order to accurately size a production environment it is important to take into consideration a variety of factors such as database size, number of transactions, number of users, and so on. Incorrectly sized production architecture often becomes the main reason for poor performance.

The SQL Server database world has become increasingly complex over the years. Today, multi-terabyte databases run alongside small to medium-size implementations. The variability in deployments is enormous and this leads to numerous hardware combinations possible. Thus, every deployment is different and there is no one-size-fits-all policy. Nevertheless, there are some common guidelines followed by most companies around the world when it comes to sizing their database architecture.

The process begins with the choice of a hardware vendor which for medium to large companies seldom differs from project to project. The next step involves answering a series of questions to determine the specific hardware requirements for the deployment. This process differs from application to application and is based on the criticality of the applications. However, below are some more common questions that every DBA needs to answer when correctly sizing a SQL Server database deployment:

- ❑ What editions of SQL Server will be deployed?
- ❑ How many SQL Server instances will be deployed?
- ❑ How many databases per instance?
- ❑ How many users per database?
- ❑ Average size of a database?
- ❑ Average estimated size of tempdb?
- ❑ High availability requirements?

These questions are meant to provide the DBA with valuable insight into the SQL Server deployment. Answering some of the questions may require the help of the development team or business analyst team. This process is generally easier for packaged applications such as Siebel, PeopleSoft, or SAP, as the application vendor typically provides a list of recommended hardware configurations for the database backend. A sizing review may also be provided by these vendors as a paid option. If your application is specific to your organization and has been developed internally, then prior to deploying your production application you should ensure that your hardware has been certified by Microsoft and is a part of the hardware compatibility list found at www.windowsservercatalog.com.

Best Practice

Ask the right questions.

One other important part of the sizing process involves choosing the correct SQL Server Edition for the production deployment. SQL Server 2005 is available as five different editions and each of these editions has different sets of features and licensing costs. The different editions are listed below. For a complete list of features, please refer to SQL Server 2005 Books Online.

- ❑ SQL Server 2005 Enterprise Edition (32-bit and 64-bit)
- ❑ SQL Server 2005 Standard Edition (32-bit and 64-bit)
- ❑ SQL Server 2005 Workgroup Edition (32-bit only)
- ❑ SQL Server 2005 Developer Edition (32-bit and 64-bit) — Not for production server deployment
- ❑ SQL Server 2005 Express Edition — Not for production server deployment

Although the correct SQL Server edition is important, equally important is the correct Windows operating system version/edition. SQL Server 2005 deployments can also be run side by side with older versions. For a complete listing of side-by-side support, refer to SQL Server 2005 Books Online. It is also important to note that the amount of memory that can be addressed by SQL Server is determined by the edition of SQL Server being deployed.

Best Practice

Choose the correct edition of SQL Server.

Additional Features

Most companies deploy one or more of the other features available while installing SQL Server 2005. These features are listed below:

- ❑ SQL Server 2005 Management Tools
- ❑ SQL Server 2005 Reporting Services
- ❑ SQL Server 2005 Notification Services
- ❑ SQL Server 2005 Analysis Services
- ❑ SQL Server 2005 Integration Services
- ❑ SQL Server 2005 Replication

Each of the features comes with a unique set of installation requirements. SQL Server Management Tools require Windows client machines to be installed and are essential to managing and maintaining a SQL 2005 Server environment. Similarly, SQL Server 2005 Reporting Services — a powerful reporting tool — requires IIS to be installed. Thus, additional features add to the complexity of the design process and may require understanding of components beyond the core database engine.

Best Practice

Beware of complexities when deploying additional features.

High Availability and Disaster Recovery

Along with sizing the database infrastructure, it is also important to incorporate high availability and disaster recovery into the overall architecture design. A high availability SQL Server solution will mask the effects of a hardware or software failure while ensuring that applications remain available and minimizing downtime. However, before you select a high-availability solution, it is important to understand the goals of this solution. SQL Server 2005 comes with several features that increase the availability of production databases, but these features are different in terms of what they can achieve and typically require additional infrastructure that will add to your cost of implementation. Before you start to design your highly available SQL Server solution, you should answer some of the following questions to get a sense of what features that you should deploy:

- ❑ Is failover going to be automatic or manual?
- ❑ Is a failure going to be detected automatically and appropriate action taken?
- ❑ Is Transparent Client Redirect important?
- ❑ How much downtime can you afford?
- ❑ What is the typical size of your transaction logs?
- ❑ Where are the failover servers located? In the same datacenter, a different datacenter in the same building, a different building, and so on.

After you have answered some of these questions, it is much easier to pick the correct feature that will help you achieve your high-availability goals.

Best Practice

Don't deploy high-availability features until you know what you want, to avoid duplicating efforts.

Backup and Restore

Any good high-availability strategy must include detailed plans on backing up and restoring SQL Server databases. SQL Server 2005 provides numerous ways to back up a database such as full, differential, log, and file group backups. Log backups are critical for production deployments, as they are essential for point-in-time recovery during database failures. A large number of third-party vendors exist that provide backup solutions for SQL Server. If you have the budget or the need for extra features, you should take a look at some of these vendors. Part of a sound backup strategy is a plan to restore databases in case of failures. This plan should include regular testing of backups to ensure that backups are good and will not fail to restore. SQL Server 2005 introduced the concept of online restores, which is applicable to databases with multiple file groups. Provided the primary file group is online and active, the other secondary file groups can be restored while users continue to access the date in the rest of the database, minimizing downtime in case only a part of the database is affected and needs to be restored.

Best Practice

Always have a sound backup and restore strategy. If this is a production system you *must* have log backups.

Clustering

SQL 2005 failover clustering provides high availability support for SQL Server 2005 instances. This setup usually consists of two or more nodes that share a set of disks. One of the nodes is the primary node and has control over all shared services and drives. The front end application connects to the database using a "virtual" name as opposed to the actual host name. This provides for seamless failover between the primary and secondary nodes without the need for any reconfiguration on the front-end application. However, the clustering solution does not protect against disk failure. If the shared disk drives fail, there could be potential damage to the SQL Server databases. However, most storage arrays today provide some sort of fault tolerance to minimize the loss of data due to disk failures.

Clustering is a great choice when there is a need for automatic failover in case of hardware or software failures and minimal downtime. However, it is important to note that even though SQL Server may fail over automatically in case of a failure, the front end application may detect a lost connection to the database, causing users to re-login in such a scenario.

Best Practice — Clustering

Be aware of the limitations of SQL Server clustering.

Database Mirroring

Database Mirroring, a new feature introduced in SQL Server 2005, helps overcome some limitations posed by clustering. The process of database mirroring involves setting up a hot standby mirror database and can be configured for automatic failover. There are three different configurations that provide varying levels of fault tolerance. Database Mirroring provides seamless failover capabilities for the database as well as the applications, provided the application supports database mirroring. This feature can also be used to avoid downtime incurred when doing hardware or software upgrades to the primary server, provided all updates have propagated over to the secondary or standby node. This might seem like a costlier solution because in addition to extra servers, additional storage is also required. It is important to note, however, that a standby server can participate in multiple mirroring sessions and can also be used for reporting purposes through the use of database snapshots since the mirrored database cannot be directly accessed or queried against using Management Studio or any other tools.

> ### Best Practice — Mirroring
> Ensure your application supports database mirroring.

Log Shipping

One of the more basic yet quite powerful high availability features available with SQL Server involves the process of shipping transaction logs from a primary database to a standby server and then restoring the logs onto a standby database. Depending on how often logs are restored on the standby server, the standby database may technically be minutes or even hours behind the primary database and so does not provide a no-data-loss failover scenario.

Replication

SQL Server Replication is a feature that allows a SQL Server database acting as a publisher to publish data to one or more subscribers. There are three different types of replication: Snapshot, merge, and transactional. Typically, one of these three types of replication fit the needs of most organizations. Replication also allows filtering of data from the publisher to the subscriber, allowing the subscriber to receive a subset of the data.

SQL Server 2005 offers a host of high-availability features and depending on the needs of the organization, one or more of these features can be implemented fairly easily. The disaster recovery planning stage is the correct time to make the choice, keeping in mind that hardware requirements differ between features.

Load Testing

Load testing an application or database is the process of exercising your would-be production system by subjecting it to the largest loads that it can handle. This can also be referred to as endurance testing as the goal of the exercise is to determine whether the production system will sustain itself under maximum load, such as the number of transactions that will be seen during peak working hours. Load testing is also used to detect any bugs that would not normally surface during cursory testing such as memory management issues, buffer issues, and I/O bottlenecks. The most important goal, however, is to determine the maximum number of transactions per second that the entire production system can handle without causing visible slowness to the users. Stress testing on the other hand is used to determine the maximum capacity of the production system. This is usually accomplished by subjecting the system to larger than usual workloads to determine the breaking point for the system. Stress testing is important because there will always be that one unthinkable day when there is complete chaos in the system and everyone seems to be entering thousands of transactions or pulling massive reports (such as at the end of the quarter).

There are many ways to load test the hardware. Some involve the use of enterprise-class load-testing applications such as Mercury Interactive, and others use simpler methods such as the SQL Server Profiler playback feature. Whatever may be the method, what is important is to replicate a true production scenario so that any bottlenecks or performance limitations are clearly visible and can be rectified prior to deployment.

Load testing an enterprise application involves many tiers such as web servers, application servers, and database servers. Prior to beginning load testing, it is essential that all software is installed using the configuration intended to be used in a production scenario. Often enterprise load-testing software requires that specific load-testing scripts be created to replicate actual user interactions. Take, for example, a call center application that is going to use SQL Server 2005 as a database and is going to be used daily by 10,000 users on average. What might be some of the load-testing scripts that need to be created? Typically, call center users constantly query the database for information pertaining to customers, orders, or products. They would also perform operations that update customer information such as addresses, names, and telephone numbers as well as enter new orders and activities. All these operations can be recorded as scripts and then replayed while simulating thousands of users. What is important here is to get the correct mix of transactions. This information is usually gathered by either monitoring user interaction or through business analysts who have a sound understanding of the different ways the application is used.

SQL Server 2005 also provides some limited ways of performing load testing, but these are usually limited to the database servers. One such method involves the use of the query playback feature. This is especially useful when an application that has already been deployed is being moved to a new set of servers, including new database servers. You can capture queries using SQL Server Profiler on the existing hardware and then replay them back in the same order on the new hardware. This would give a sense of how well the new hardware manages to withstand the load as well as show any performance gains that were achieved.

Best Practice

Load testing is essential to knowing the limits of your production system.

Managing Change

Change management is one aspect of deployment that most people tend to forget. A production environment is usually a finely tuned environment that is very sensitive to change. In most real-life scenarios database administrators are reluctant to make changes to production environments unless those changes have been thoroughly tested. The reality, however, is that changes do happen and sometimes these changes go unnoticed until problems start creeping up on some parts of the application. This is the reason why changes have to be managed and duly recorded. Changes in a database environment can be of various sorts: Database schema changes, stored procedure code changes, database hardware changes and so on. What is important here is to ensure that whatever the change may be, there is always a plan in place to back out of the changes if things don't go as expected. For code-related changes, it is important to ensure that version control is in place. This can easily be accomplished through the use of software such as Microsoft Visual Source Safe. Visual Source Safe allows users to maintain multiple versions of the same code and also promotes collaboration and sharing through the process of checking out and checking in changes. Another great tool to use is the Visual Studio Team Edition for Database Professionals. This tool, in addition to allowing version control, also allows for rules to be set to ensure standardization of check-in code. Schema changes can be disruptive, and it is always a good idea to have the current objects scripted out and stored in a versioning repository such as VSS before applying any changes. This also helps in quick reversal as opposed to completely restoring the database. However, it is always important to have a full backup of your database before making any changes, irrespective of the size and impact of the changes.

Best Practice

Always track changes so that it is much easier to retrace your steps in case something goes wrong.

Dealing with Large Tables

It is quite normal these days for database tables to contain tens of millions of rows. Although they certainly help store large amounts of data, they can be quite a maintenance nightmare. SQL Server 2005 introduced the concept of partitioning tables and indexes to facilitate easier management as well as better performance when dealing with tables with a high number of rows. If you anticipate that your production database is going to have very large tables and if you want to take advantage of the new partitioning functionality, it is best to make such plans during the database design stage.

When a table is partitioned, the data in the table is split horizontally into buckets that can then be placed in different file groups and over different set of drives if need be. The partitions of a table or indexes are treated as a single logical entity when querying or updating the data. It is important to keep in mind while partitioning the data the manner in which the data is going to be queried. If most queries against a table involve selection based on last name, then it is useless to partition the data by date.

Partitioning is also a great choice when only parts of a table are used for updates, inserts, and deletes while the rest is used primarily for selects. For example, consider a very large table that contains order-related information dating back to 2001. If the current month's data is used for updates or deletes and the rest of the older data is used for selects, then it would be ideal to partition the data by month. This would also be useful when performing maintenance operations as defragmentation and index rebuilds can happen on the current month's partition while the older read only data continues to be available for querying. Had partitioning not been used in this case, performing maintenance operations would involve tying up the entire table.

Partitions are also used when performing data archiving and provide a very quick mechanism of transferring data from a transactional table to an archive table for reporting purposes. This is achieved through the process of partition switching, wherein the actual data is not moved; instead metadata is changed to the new location where the data is being stored.

The following sections discuss some code related to partitioning tables.

Partition Functions

Creation of a partition function is the first step to partitioning tables. A partition function tells SQL Server how to partition the data.

```
CREATE PARTITION FUNCTION PF_SQLROCKS AS RANGE LEFT FOR VALUES (1, 100, 1000)
```

This will create four partitions, as indicated in Table 15-1.

Table 15-1: Partition functions

Partition Number	Data Values
1	< = 1
2	> 1 and < = 100
3	> 100 and < = 1000
4	> 1000

Partition Schemes

The partition scheme defines the file groups that are used to hold the data for various partitions that have been created in the table. If you can plan ahead, a good idea is to have more file groups available to assign partitions later in case the table grows. However, you cannot assign a smaller number of file groups than partitions.

```
CREATE PARTITION SCHEME PS_SQLROCKS
AS PARTITION PF_SQLROCKS
TO (DB_FG1, DB_FG2, DB_FG3, DB_FG4)
```

This will assign file groups to the partitions as indicated in Table 15-2.

Table 15-2: Partition schemes

Partition Number	Data Values	File Group
1	< = 1	DB_FG1
2	> 1 and < = 100	DB_FG2
3	> 100 and < = 1000	DB_FG3
4	> 1000	DB_FG4

Partition Tables or Indexes

Once the partition function and partition scheme have been created, you can create a partitioned table or index.

```
CREATE TABLE SQLROCKS (COL1 int, COL2 nvarchar(100))
ON PS_SQLROCKS (COL1)
CREATE CLUSTERED INDEX IX_SQLROCKS
ON SQLROCKS (COL1)
ON PS_SQLROCKS (COL1)
```

Tuning Using SQL Server Profiler

SQL Server 2005 Profiler is a great resource to use during preproduction to tune long-running queries, fix locking and deadlocking issues, and identify potential bottlenecks related to I/O, memory, and processors. Installed as part of the SQL Server2005 management tools, the profiler comes with a variety of options and selections that can provide the user with highly detailed data as to what is actually happening on the database. SQL Server Profiler also provides the ability to replay server workloads. Although this is a feature that may not be of much use when deploying an application for the first time, it is especially useful when changing hardware.

Tuning Using the Database Engine Tuning Advisor

Another great tool to assist you in your tuning needs is the Database Engine Tuning Advisor. This tool can be used as both a graphical interface as well as a command line application and can be used to tune SQL Server databases by analyzing the performance of workloads executed against the databases. The reports generated by the advisor help augment the information required to successfully tune a SQL Server database.

Consequences of Incorrectly Sizing the Production Environment

A couple of years ago we undertook a massive multi-million dollar project to deploy Siebel Enterprise applications companywide. The implementation consisted of databases deployed on SQL Server. Our planning was immaculate, all the necessary precautions had been taken, and we were sure that nothing would go wrong on D-Day. We went live over a weekend, and on Monday morning all users started accessing the new application. Everything was fine until about 10 a.m., and then some unfortunate events started to unfold. The machine that served as the database server was under severe load, processor usage was consistently over the danger mark, processor queues were very high, and we started to see memory pressure as well. By 12 p.m. the server was offline and so was the newly deployed Siebel application. So what was the problem? After careful analysis, it was determined that the database servers had not been sized correctly and that we were facing what we called *memory pressure*. The servers needed more memory and as luck would have it, we would have to order it from the vendor who had a two-day turnaround time. The consequences of incorrect sizing can be severe and could lead to hours or even days of downtime for some of your most critical applications. Hence, the importance of load testing or stress testing as discussed earlier.

So what can you do post production? Options are limited. If memory is the problem and if there are free DIMM slots, it could be easy to add capacity. If I/O is the problem, then the issue could be as complex as reconfiguring the underlying storage subsystem or as simple as splitting up the indexes and data and placing them in separate data files. However, if the problem lies with the actual number of processors, then it could lead to a replacement of the existing hardware. Subsequent actions to an incorrect sizing problem entirely depend on the actual problem; however, whatever the case may be, the problem could cripple your production environment and cause unneeded stress during a go live deployment.

Schema Issues in Production

Database schemas for enterprise applications such as SAP, Oracle, Siebel, and so on cannot typically be altered using straight database commands, and most vendors don't recommend altering the database schema without the help of application experts (which entails additional fees). But experience has shown that there are often instances of poor performance that arise due to issues caused by the schema.

For example, a typical SQL Server database for a Siebel application contains more than 2000 tables and some of the larger, more heavily used tables contain as many as 60 indexes. Why so many indexes? This is because Siebel tests every possible customer scenario that they can think of and then designs the database schema accordingly. However, what most customers get is a heavily indexed database consisting of hundreds of indexes that are probably never going to be used. Prior to SQL Server 2005, it was nearly impossible to report on index usage. Even if you could ascertain that 50 percent of the indexes in your database were not being used, there was no method to disable them; you could only drop those indexes. Dropping indexes was strictly prohibited by Siebel. Although this case is specific to Siebel, I am sure you have seen or heard of such scenarios before.

So what can you do in such cases? Well, SQL 2005 comes with a new set of catalog views that provide a fair bit of information that greatly enhances the DBA's understanding of database indexes. One view that focuses on index usage is called sys.dm_db_index_usage_stats. This view provides information about user seeks, scans, and lookups, as well as updates. It also tells you the last time the index was accessed. It is very easy to now determine if an index is being used or not.

This brings us to the second question: Why is it important to track this information? This is because excess indexes created on a table tend to slow down insert, update, and delete operations. Indexes also take up precious storage space and therefore keeping the number of indexes down to the most needed ones will help you reduce storage costs. SQL 2005 introduced the concept of disabling indexes instead of dropping them. As stated, this is especially important in the case of packaged applications. When you disable an index, the index definition still remains in the system catalog; however, the index is not used by the database engine and contains no underlying data. So, as far as the application is concerned, the index is still present in the database. If you need to recreate this index at a later stage, you could do so by rebuilding the index.

A few months ago, I received information about a slow running query. On investigating further I discovered that the query had parameter values prefixed with N, indicating that the values were of the Unicode datatype. However, the actual table columns were non Unicode. This was causing an index scan versus an index seek, resulting in some degree of slowness. This is a typical situation in which there is very little that can be done without changing the table schema. Since changing the schema was not an option, we could only tweak the query so much to improve performance, and hence there were limitations to tuning the production system.

However, there are a few things that can be done on a regular basis to ensure that a production system is healthy. First is the process of defragmentation. Fragmentation in a database can cause performance problems and a database can be defragmented either online or offline. Online defragmentation is one of the new features introduced in SQL Server 2005, but care should be taken while carrying out this operation, especially during peak production hours. I have also noticed that if the database is in full recovery model, online defragmentation can cause the log to grow very quickly. A suggestion here would be to change the recovery model to bulk-logged before defragmenting tables. Online defragmentation can easily be accomplished by using the following code:

```
ALTER INDEX IX_SQLROCKS REBUILD
WITH ONLINE = ON
```

Of course, the offline option is always available for the less adventurous. There have been some changes with respect to the syntax, but for the most part the underlying fundamentals are still the same.

Indexes can also be added online now — another new feature with SQL Server 2005. However, as always, care should be taken when adding indexes to tables in a production environment. From personal experience, I still see some blocking behavior when trying to add indexes to heavily used tables, though it is much reduced from earlier versions. You can create indexes online with the following code:

```
CREATE INDEX IX2_SQLROCKS ON SQLROCKS (COL2)
WITH ONLINE = ON
```

Best Practice

Keep your database defragmented. Don't add indexes without testing and unless absolutely essential. Adding unnecessary indexes can have a negative impact on performance.

Avoiding Changing Code to Fix Issues

One of my other favorite new features of SQL 2005 is the ability to use plan guides. Plan guides give DBAs the ability to add hints to queries without changing the physical query. Plan guides can be used to force query plans, supply join hints, or restrict the use of parallel processing to a specific number of processors. Plan guides are perfect for a production scenario where queries that are performing poorly cannot be changed due to restrictions posed by the application vendor.

The Query

Here is a query that could benefit from the use of Plan Guides. The following query returns 604,000 rows, and you want that query to return the first 40 rows as soon as possible so that the user can start seeing the data before having to wait for all 604,000 rows to be returned.

```
SELECT A.RevisionNumber,A.OrderDate,A.DueDate,A.ShipDate,A.Status,
B.OrderQty,B.ProductId,
C.AccountNumber,C.CustomerType,
D.FirstName,D.MiddleName,D.LastName,D.EmailAddress,
E.AddressLine1,E.AddressLine2,E.StateProvinceId,E.PostalCode
FROM
SALES.SALESORDERHEADER A
```

```
INNER JOIN SALES.SALESORDERDETAIL B ON A.SALESORDERID=B.SALESORDERID
INNER JOIN SALES.CUSTOMER C ON A.CUSTOMERID = C.CUSTOMERID
INNER JOIN SALES.INDIVIDUAL F ON C.CUSTOMERID = F.CUSTOMERID
INNER JOIN PERSON.CONTACT D  ON F.CONTACTID = D.CONTACTID
INNER JOIN SALES.CUSTOMERADDRESS G ON A.CUSTOMERID = G.CUSTOMERID
INNER JOIN PERSON.ADDRESS E ON G.ADDRESSID = E.ADDRESSID
```

The Query Plan

The following query plan is generated from the query in the previous section. The plan is doing a large number of scans as it retrieves all the rows from the joined tables. However, the goal is to return the first 40 rows as soon as possible but without changing the code. This is where plan guides come in to the picture.

```
|--Hash Match(Inner Join, HASH:([C].[CustomerID])=([G].[CustomerID]))
     |--Compute
Scalar(DEFINE:([C].[AccountNumber]=[AdventureWorks].[Sales].[Customer].
[AccountNumber] as [C].[AccountNumber]))
|     |--Compute
Scalar(DEFINE:([C].[AccountNumber]=isnull('AW'+[AdventureWorks].[dbo].
[ufnLeadingZeros]([AdventureWorks].[Sales].[Customer].[CustomerID] as [C].
[CustomerID]),"")))
|          |--Clustered Index
Scan(OBJECT:([AdventureWorks].[Sales].[Customer].[PK_Customer_CustomerID] AS [C]))
     |--Hash Match(Inner Join,
HASH:([E].[AddressID])=([G].[AddressID]))
          |--Index
Scan(OBJECT:([AdventureWorks].[Person].[Address].[IX_Address_AddressLine1_Address
Line2_City_StateProvinceID_PostalCode] AS [E]))
          |--Hash Match(Inner Join,
HASH:([G].[CustomerID])=([F].[CustomerID]))
               |--Index
Scan(OBJECT:([AdventureWorks].[Sales].[CustomerAddress].[AK_CustomerAddress_rowguid]
AS [G]))
               |--Hash Match(Inner Join,
HASH:([D].[ContactID])=([F].[ContactID]))
                    |--Clustered Index
Scan(OBJECT:([AdventureWorks].[Person].[Contact].[PK_Contact_ContactID] AS [D]))
                    |--Hash Match(Inner Join,
HASH:([F].[CustomerID])=([A].[CustomerID]))
                         |--Clustered Index
Scan(OBJECT:([AdventureWorks].[Sales].[Individual].[PK_Individual_CustomerID]
AS [F]))
                         |--Merge Join(Inner Join,
MERGE:([A].[SalesOrderID])=([B].[SalesOrderID]), RESIDUAL:([AdventureWorks].[Sales].
[SalesOrderHeader].[SalesOrderID] as [A].[SalesOrderID]=[AdventureWorks].[Sales].
[SalesOrderDetail].[SalesOrderID] as [
                              |--Clustered Index
Scan(OBJECT:([AdventureWorks].[Sales].[SalesOrderHeader].[PK_SalesOrderHeader_Sales
OrderID] AS [A]), ORDERED FORWARD)
                              |--Clustered Index
Scan(OBJECT:([AdventureWorks].[Sales].[SalesOrderDetail].[PK_SalesOrderDetail_Sales
OrderID_SalesOrderDetailID] AS [B]), ORDERED FORWARD)
```

The Plan Guide

Let's create a plan guide such that SQL Server will always return the first 40 rows as soon as possible so that the user can start accessing the data while the rest of the rows are being processed. An important point to note here is that SQL Server matches the statements of the query submitted with the query statement stored in the plan guide, so the statement stored in the plan guide needs to be exactly the same for it to be effective.

```
sp_create_plan_guide
@name = N'OrderDetails_Guide',
@stmt = N'SELECT A.RevisionNumber,A.OrderDate,A.DueDate,A.ShipDate,A.Status,
B.OrderQty,B.ProductId,
C.AccountNumber,C.CustomerType,
D.FirstName,D.MiddleName,D.LastName,D.EmailAddress,
E.AddressLine1,E.AddressLine2,E.StateProvinceId,E.PostalCode
FROM
SALES.SALESORDERHEADER A
INNER JOIN SALES.SALESORDERDETAIL B ON A.SALESORDERID = B.SALESORDERID
INNER JOIN SALES.CUSTOMER C ON A.CUSTOMERID = C.CUSTOMERID
INNER JOIN SALES.INDIVIDUAL F ON C.CUSTOMERID = F.CUSTOMERID
INNER JOIN PERSON.CONTACT D  ON F.CONTACTID = D.CONTACTID
INNER JOIN SALES.CUSTOMERADDRESS G ON A.CUSTOMERID = G.CUSTOMERID
INNER JOIN PERSON.ADDRESS E ON G.ADDRESSID = E.ADDRESSID',
@type = N'SQL',
@module_or_batch = NULL,
@params = NULL,
@hints = N'OPTION (FAST 40)'
```

The Query Plan after Creation of the Plan Guide

Here is the query plan after the plan guide has been created.

```
|--Nested Loops(Inner Join, OUTER REFERENCES:([A].[SalesOrderID], [Expr1020]) WITH
UNORDERED PREFETCH)
        |--Nested Loops(Inner Join, OUTER
REFERENCES:([A].[SalesOrderID], [Expr1019]) WITH UNORDERED PREFETCH)
    |    |--Nested Loops(Inner Join, OUTER
REFERENCES:([G].[CustomerID], [Expr1018]) WITH UNORDERED PREFETCH)
    |    |    |--Nested Loops(Inner Join, OUTER
REFERENCES:([F].[ContactID], [Expr1017]) WITH UNORDERED PREFETCH)
    |    |    |    |--Nested Loops(Inner Join, OUTER
REFERENCES:([G].[AddressID], [Expr1016]) WITH UNORDERED PREFETCH)
    |    |    |    |    |--Nested Loops(Inner Join, OUTER
REFERENCES:([F].[CustomerID], [Expr1015]) WITH UNORDERED PREFETCH)
    |    |    |    |    |    |--Compute
Scalar(DEFINE:([C].[AccountNumber]=[AdventureWorks].[Sales].[Customer].[Account
Number] as [C].[AccountNumber]))
    |    |    |    |    |    |    |--Nested Loops(Inner Join, OUTER
REFERENCES:([F].[CustomerID], [Expr1014]) WITH UNORDERED PREFETCH)
    |    |    |    |    |    |                   |--Clustered Index
Scan(OBJECT:([AdventureWorks].[Sales].[Individual].[PK_Individual_CustomerID]
AS [F]))
```

```
    |   |   |   |   |   |              |--Compute
Scalar(DEFINE:([C].[AccountNumber]=isnull('AW'+[AdventureWorks].[dbo].[ufnLeading
Zeros]([AdventureWorks].[Sales].[Customer].[CustomerID] as [C].[CustomerID]),"")))
    |   |   |   |   |   |              |--Clustered Index
Seek(OBJECT:([AdventureWorks].[Sales].[Customer].[PK_Customer_CustomerID] AS [C]),
SEEK:([C].[CustomerID]=[AdventureWorks].[Sales].[Individual].[CustomerID] as [F].
[CustomerID]) ORDERED FORW
    |   |   |   |   |        |--Clustered Index
Seek(OBJECT:([AdventureWorks].[Sales].[CustomerAddress].[PK_CustomerAddress_Customer
ID_AddressID] AS [G]), SEEK:([G].[CustomerID]=[AdventureWorks].[Sales].[Individual].
[CustomerID] as [F].[CustomerID]) ORD
    |   |   |   |        |--Clustered Index
Seek(OBJECT:([AdventureWorks].[Person].[Address].[PK_Address_AddressID] AS [E]),
SEEK:([E].[AddressID]=[AdventureWorks].[Sales].[CustomerAddress].[AddressID] as [G].
[AddressID]) ORDERED FORWARD)
    |   |   |        |--Clustered Index
Seek(OBJECT:([AdventureWorks].[Person].[Contact].[PK_Contact_ContactID] AS [D]),
SEEK:([D].[ContactID]=[AdventureWorks].[Sales].[Individual].[ContactID] as [F].
[ContactID]) ORDERED FORWARD)
    |   |        |--Index
Seek(OBJECT:([AdventureWorks].[Sales].[SalesOrderHeader].[IX_SalesOrderHeader_
CustomerID] AS [A]), SEEK:([A].[CustomerID]=[AdventureWorks].[Sales].[Customer
Address].[CustomerID] as [G].[CustomerID]) ORDERED FORWARD)
    |        |--Clustered Index
Seek(OBJECT:([AdventureWorks].[Sales].[SalesOrderHeader].[PK_SalesOrderHeader_
SalesOrderID] AS [A]), SEEK:([A].[SalesOrderID]=[AdventureWorks].[Sales].[Sales
OrderHeader].[SalesOrderID] as [A].[SalesOrderID]) LOOKUP ORDERED FO
        |--Clustered Index
Seek(OBJECT:([AdventureWorks].[Sales].[SalesOrderDetail].[PK_SalesOrderDetail_
SalesOrderID_SalesOrderDetailID] AS [B]), SEEK:([B].[SalesOrderID]=[Adventure
Works].[Sales].[SalesOrderHeader].[SalesOrderID] as [A].[SalesOrderID]) ORD
```

Notice the remarkable difference between the query plans. There are a lot more index seeks than scans as the query is attempting to return the first 40 rows as quickly possible. This is great as the user is not kept waiting for the data to be returned. This has been accomplished without making any changes to the original query.

Best Practice

Plan guides are a fantastic way to avoid changing code, but they have limitations.

Summary

Size your environment correctly, understand the implications of incorrect sizing, and always remember to leave room for growth. Manage your changes effectively; a good set of change management procedures along with an enterprise change management tool will always help diagnose problems and help revert back to normalcy quicker. Always ensure that your backups are good and test them on an ongoing basis; don't assume anything. Use some of the cool new features available in SQL 2005 such as partitioning, plan guides, and online index creation. Keep your database healthy — defragment on a regular basis and rebuild indexes as necessary. Take the correct steps to a successful and trouble-free deployment.

Index

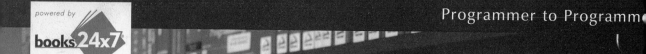